Irish Taxation –
Law and Practice

7th edition   **Volume I**

Edited by Dr. Gerardine Doyle

Authors:
Caitriona Gaynor
Pat Kennedy
Paul Murphy
Margaret Sheridan
Raymond Holly

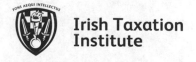

Irish Taxation
Institute

Irish Taxation Institute
South Block
Longboat Quay
Grand Canal Harbour
Dublin 2

Telephone: +353 1 6631700
Fax: +353 1 6688367
E-mail: info@taxireland.ie
Web: www.taxireland.ie

First Edition 2003
Fourth Edition 2006
Fifth Edition 2007
Sixth Edition 2008
Seventh Edition 2009

A catalogue reference for this book is available from the British Library.

The object of this book is to explain in broad detail the principles and practice of taxation in the Republic
of Ireland. The book is not intended as a detailed exposition of the extensive volume of statute and case
law relating to taxation.

While every effort has been made to ensure the accuracy of the material in this book, neither the
Institute nor the authors accept any responsibility for loss or damage occasioned by any person acting,
or refraining from acting, as a result of this material. Any views or opinions expressed are not necessarily
subscribed to by the Institute. Professional advice should always be sought before acting on any
interpretation of the legislation in this book.

ISBN 978-1-84260-186-0
10 9 8 7 6 5 4 3 2 1

Printed in Ireland by

ColourBooks Ltd., Baldoyle, Dublin 13

FOREWORD

I am delighted to welcome readers to this, the seventh edition of *Irish Taxation – Law and Practice*, one of the Irish Taxation Institute's most popular titles and the text of choice for lecturers and students of taxation throughout Ireland.

Following from previous years, the text is divided into two separate volumes, each with a distinct set of features. Volume 1 is the authoritative text on taxation policy, law and practice in Ireland and covers a range of areas including the theory of taxation, VAT, income tax, capital gains tax, corporation tax and capital acquisitions tax. New to this edition, the introductory chapter of Volume 1 also includes an informative summary of the structures and roles of key stakeholders in Irish taxation including the Department of Finance, the Revenue Commissioners, the Irish Taxation Institute (ITI) and the profession. Volume 2 contains comprehensive assignments and solutions together with an updated set of revision questions.

ITI is committed to promoting an awareness of taxation and careers therein. Our initiatives at third level include the **Fantasy Budget Competition**, the **Third Level Essay Competition** at both undergraduate and postgraduate levels and various special taxation awards. For further information, please contact Grace McRandal, Senior Manager of Professional Education at +353 1 6631713 or e-mail gmcrandal@taxireland.ie.

I would like to extend my sincere thanks to Dr Gerardine Doyle, Dr Emer Mulligan, Pat Kennedy, Paul Murphy, Margaret Sheridan, Caitriona Gaynor, Martina Whyte, Laurence May and finally Raymond Holly in this his first year as a co-author for their excellent work on this year's update, which enhances the already impressive standard of the publication and affirms its status as the essential introduction to Irish taxation for students and general readers alike.

JIM RYAN
President
Irish Taxation Institute

Note on the Text

This book is based on legislation in force for 2009, which includes:

- Finance Acts 1967 to 2009 (inclusive); *inclu*

- Taxes Consolidation Act 1997, as amended;

- Capital Acquisitions Tax Consolidation Act 2003, as amended;

- Social Welfare (Consolidation) Act 1993, as amended;

- Stamp Duties Consolidation Act 1999, as amended;

- Value-Added Tax Act 1972, as amended;

Throughout the text, "Ireland" and "Irish" should be read as referring solely to the Republic of Ireland.

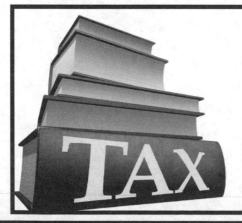

Contents

Volume I

Section I   Introduction

Section II   Value-Added Tax

5   ACCOUNTING FOR VAT: INVOICING, DEDUCTIONS
     AND SPECIAL PROCEDURES/CATEGORIES

Section III   Income Tax

11 TAX CREDITS, TAX BANDS AND INCOME LEVY

Section IV Capital Gains Tax

Section V   Corporation Tax

Section VI   Capital Acquisitions Tax

TABLE OF CASES

TABLE OF STATUTES AND LEGISLATION

LIST OF ABBREVIATIONS

AER .... *All England Law Reports*

ATC .... Annotated Tax Cases

FA .... Finance Act

HC .... High Court (Ireland)

ICTA 1988.. Income and Corporation Taxes Act 1988 (UK)

ILRM .... *Irish Law Reports Monthly*

ITA 1967 .... Income Tax Act 1967

ITC .... Official Reports of Irish Tax Cases

ITR .... *Irish Tax Reports*

JFL .... *Irish Journal of Family Law*

KB .... Law Reports, King's Bench Division (UK)

Para .... Paragraph

Pt .... Part

QB .... Law Reports, Queen's Bench Division (UK)

s .... Section

SC .... Supreme Court (Ireland)

Sch .... Schedule

SDCA .... Stamp Duties Consolidation Act 1999

STC .... *Simon's Tax Cases*

SW(Con)A... Social Welfare Consolidation Act 1993

TC .... Official Reports of United Kingdom Tax Cases

TLR .... *The Times Law Reports*

TCA .... Taxes Consolidation Act 1997

VA .... Value-Added Tax Act 1972

Section I

Introduction

FONS AEQUI INTELLECTUS

1

IRISH TAXATION – PRINCIPLES AND POLICY

In this chapter, you will deal with the following:

- Historical aspects of Irish taxation

- Sources of tax law and information

- The objectives of taxation

- The tax base and methods of classifying taxes

- The characteristics of an ideal tax system

- Stakeholders in Irish taxation policy and administration

The editor, Gerardine Doyle, wishes to thank the former editor, Moira O'Halloran for her contribution to the initial development of this publication. In particular, the editor wishes to acknowledge that some material in section 1.2 of Chapter 1 draws upon Moira's book *From Boroimhe to Bit – the Art of Taxation*.

1.1   Introduction

"To tax and to please, no more than to love and to be wise, is not given to men."

This quotation, attributed to Edmund Burke in a parliamentary address in 1774, sums up the difficulty associated with designing an ideal tax system. The purpose of this chapter is to explain why taxation is necessary and to discuss some of the general principles of taxation and their application in the Irish context. The commentary is presented as follows:

- section 1.2 is concerned with the historical development of taxation, with particular reference to the Irish story,

- section 1.3 outlines the criteria that provide a framework within which specific tax measures and proposed reforms can be evaluated,

- section 1.4 explains the role of taxation in the economy,

- section 1.5 addresses the methods of classifying taxes, and

- section 1.6 is concerned with defining the tax base, and

- section 1.7 summarizes the structure and roles of the key stakeholders in Irish tax policy and administration

1.2   Historical Aspects of Taxation

1.2.1   General

Earliest forms of taxation consisted of the outright acquisition of men and goods when needed. For example, Réamonn (1981) refers to *prisage* or *prizage*, a duty which dates from 1177 in Ireland. It was levied on ships importing wine and involved the requisitioning of one-ninth of the wine for the king's use. In general, more formal taxes involving the collection of cash were initially introduced as "war taxes". In ancient Rome, indirect taxes in the form of expenditure taxes on important goods such as slaves were a vital source of revenue for the expanding empire. In addition, the ancient Roman administration kept records of the property of each citizen, and a wealth tax known as the *tributum* was levied on citizens in respect of their recorded property. This was abolished in 167 BC when "the spoils of war made it no longer necessary to raise large sums of money from Roman citizens" (James and Nobes, 2005 p. 212). In Britain, income tax was first introduced in 1799 to fund the Napoleonic wars.

The introduction of a formal system of taxation in Ireland to a large extent mirrors the British experience, as for much of its recent history, even prior to the Act of Union of 1800, Ireland was under British rule. In the Middle Ages, taxation generally took the form of feudal dues imposed on estates in territories under the English Crown and customs duties imposed on imports and exports. The administration and collection of customs and excise in Ireland was greatly formalised in 1662 with the enactment of two Acts, which provided for the establishment of an Office of Revenue Commissioners in Ireland and a system of accounting for revenues collected to the king.

Other taxes were introduced in Ireland on an *ad hoc* basis during the seventeenth and eighteenth centuries. A hearth tax was introduced by an Act of 1662 to compensate the Crown for the imminent abolition of the feudal dues referred to above. This was payable at a rate of 2s. per annum on every fire hearth or stove, with certain exceptions. Stamp duties were introduced by the Stamp Act of 1774 and have remained an important source of tax revenues in Ireland to the present day. In 2006, they represented almost 6% of tax receipts – more than the total revenues from capital acquisitions tax and capital gains tax combined. For the tax year 2007, stamp duties collected fell to 5% of total taxes collected, equivalent to the aggregate of capital gains tax and capital acquisition tax. Window taxes were introduced in Ireland in 1799 and probably explain why windows in many of the country's large 18th century houses were bricked up in the early part of the nineteenth century – an early example of tax planning. Window taxes were abolished in 1851.

1.2.2   The introduction of income tax

While William Pitt introduced income tax in England in 1799, it was not extended to Ireland until Gladstone was Chancellor of the Exchequer in 1853. The interim period saw much debate on whether or not the same taxes should apply in both Ireland and England. Sir Robert Peel, on introducing his system of income tax in England in 1842, argued that the unique nature of Irish society meant that the efficient collection of income tax in Ireland would be "a matter of grave consideration" (Réamonn, p. 37). In dealing with a nation beset by famine, he felt that it was more appropriate to increase stamp duties and to introduce a special duty on spirits manufactured in Ireland.[1]

Gladstone argued that Peel's measures failed to yield an amount equivalent to that which an income tax would generate. As a firm advocate of the harmonisation of taxes in the UK and Ireland, he was adamant that exempting one country from taxation would lead to the "over-taxation" of another. In 1853, notwithstanding the social and economic problems that were the legacy of the Great Famine of 1845 – 49, Gladstone extended Peel's system of income tax to Ireland in the first of his 13 Budgets as Chancellor of the Exchequer. It should be noted that this tax had quite a high entry level: the first £150 of income was exempt from tax, and this effectively excluded a large portion of the population from the scope of income tax. Income above this level was taxed at 3%.

Ironically, Gladstone had originally intended income tax to be a temporary measure and had hoped to abolish it by 1860. However, rapid increases in public expenditure meant that this was not feasible. Thus, in 1923 – some 70 years later – Peel's system of income

---

[1]   The onerous levy on whiskey contributed to the growth of illegal distilling in Ireland in the 19th century, an activity which required the Revenue Commissioners to provide their own dedicated police corps (*na ribhínigh*) for the period from 1824–1857 (Réamonn, 1981).

tax, subject to some amendments, was still broadly the basis for the income tax code. Following the formation of the Irish Free State in 1922, this code was taken over by the Irish Government in 1923. Together with the various adaptations necessitated by the establishment of the Irish Free State, by the Constitution of 1937 and by Irish Finance Acts from 1923 onwards, it formed the basis of the income tax legislation consolidated in the Income Tax Act 1967. This legislation was later incorporated into the Taxes Consolidation Act 1997 ("TCA 1997").

1.2.3 The introduction of value-added tax (VAT)

As well as inheriting an income tax code from our historical link with Britain, the Government of the Free State also adopted the system of indirect taxation that had applied prior to 1922. In fact, in the early years of the new State, the bulk of net receipts were derived from indirect taxation. Réamonn (1981) observes that, in 1924, direct taxes on the income of individuals and companies amounted to less than 24% of total receipts, estate and stamp duties accounted for approximately 6% of total receipts and more than 70% of revenues were collected from customs and excise duties and levies.

By the early 1960s, receipts from indirect taxation were derived mainly from duties imposed on a limited number of goods such as beer, spirits, tobacco and hydrocarbon oils. In 1962–63, tax receipts from this narrow base accounted for more than 40% of total government revenue. The dominance of this source of revenue meant that the public finances would be highly sensitive to a fall in the yield from any of these goods. In order to reduce the dependency of the Exchequer on these commodities, and also with a view to potentially reducing rates of income tax, the then Minister for Finance, Dr James Ryan, elected to introduce a turnover tax. This was a form of indirect taxation common in many Western European countries at that time. In Ireland, it involved a charge of 2.5% on all retail turnover and on receipts from the provision of services. To complement the turnover tax, a wholesale tax was introduced in 1966 at a rate of 5%. By 1969, the wholesale tax rate was increased to 10%, but certain "luxury" goods became chargeable at 15% in June of that year.

To facilitate Ireland's accession to the European Economic Community (EEC) in 1973, both of these taxes were replaced by value-added tax (VAT). VAT is an indirect tax applied at each stage in the production and distribution of goods and services. Although collected at each stage in the chain of supply on the basis of the value added by the trader, the cost is ultimately borne by the final consumer.[2] Two EEC Council Directives provided a loose framework for the new VAT legislation, which came into effect on 1 November 1972. However, with a view to increased harmonisation and integration across Member States, another Council Directive was agreed in 1977. This, the Sixth Council Directive, came into force on 1 January 1978 and forms the cornerstone of our current VAT legislation, the VAT Acts 1972–2009.

---

2   It is not always possible, however, to attribute the burden of taxation to the final consumer. A supplier may alter his pricing mechanism so as to ensure his goods remain attractive to the final consumer, thereby absorbing the VAT cost and effectively enduring the burden of taxation.

1.2.4 The introduction of capital taxes

Stamp duties have been a feature of taxation in Ireland since 1774. Estate duties, or death duties, were first introduced in Ireland by Sir William Harcourt, Chancellor of the Exchequer, in 1894. However, it was not until 1974 that the introduction of other, more contemporary "capital taxes" in Ireland was proposed. In February of that year, the then Minister for Finance, Mr Richie Ryan, presented a White Paper to both Houses of the Oireachtas outlining the Government's proposals in relation to capital gains tax (CGT), capital acquisitions tax (CAT) and wealth tax. All three taxes were introduced over the following three years. However, the wealth tax was very short-lived and was abolished with effect from 5 April 1978– within three years of its original introduction.

CGT had been introduced in the UK in 1965 and the Irish Capital Gains Tax Act 1975 was, in most areas, essentially taken word for word from the existing UK legislation. The new legislation applied to both individuals and companies, and provided for the first time for the taxation of gains arising on the disposal of capital assets. Prior to this, capital receipts were, by and large, free of tax; generating increases in wealth via capital value growth as opposed to via income was much more tax efficient and presented considerable scope for tax planning. The 1975 Act and amendments provided for by subsequent Finance Acts and enactments were later incorporated into the TCA 1997.

The CAT provisions were legislated for in the Capital Acquisitions Tax Act 1976. This provided for both gift and inheritance tax on property passing from one individual to another. Ironically, the impetus for the gift tax, which survives today, was the short-lived annual wealth tax of 1975–78. In the absence of a gift tax to complement an annual wealth tax, wealth tax could be avoided or reduced where a donor made sufficient gifts to reach a lower wealth tax bracket. The introduction of inheritance tax coincided with the termination of estate duties arising on legacies and under succession law.

Drafting of the CAT Act 1976 was a somewhat more onerous task than that of drafting the CGT Act 1975. A capital transfer tax on the lifetime transfer of assets had been introduced in the UK in the previous year but, at the time, there was no example of a country with a common law legal system that had an inheritance tax in operation. Inheritance tax in its current form was not introduced in the UK until 1986.

The provisions of the CAT Act 1976 and subsequent Finance Acts were consolidated in 2003 and can now be found in the CAT Consolidation Act 2003.

Probate tax, which involved an additional levy of 2% on estates of the deceased, was introduced by Finance Act 1993 but was later abolished in respect of deaths occurring on or after 6 December 2000.

1.2.5 The introduction of corporation tax

Prior to 1976, companies were subject to income tax and corporation profits tax on their income and CGT on their gains. In 1976, a single tax on companies' profits (which included both income and chargeable gains) was introduced. The new provisions were provided for in the Corporation Tax Act 1976 and the necessary amendments were made to the income tax and CGT legislation. The 1976 Act and amendments provided for by subsequent Finance Acts were later incorporated into the TCA 1997.

1.2.6   Sources of law

The Acts referred to above and currently in force are the main statutory sources of law considered by tax practitioners. For the purposes of this text, readers will be most concerned with the provisions of the TCA 1997 and the VAT Acts 1972–2006. These Acts are revised and updated on an annual basis in response to legislative amendments introduced by Finance Acts. The annual Finance Acts generally implement changes and new tax measures announced by the Minister for Finance in his Budget statement in December of each year. This statement outlines the Government's Budget plans for the year and how it proposes to finance these plans.

In addition to understanding the statutory framework, given that our legal system is based on common law, knowledge of case law precedent is also essential. Decisions in cases heard in Irish courts form binding precedents, which must be followed in subsequent cases in the absence of distinguishing facts. Accordingly, an Irish taxpayer has a right to rely on such precedents and they constitute a vital source of law. Case law precedent is generally relied on in the absence of statutory legislation on specific issues and also in interpreting legislation where components may not be clearly defined. Because of the similarities (which have evolved for historic and other reasons, as outlined above) between our tax codes, there is a wealth of UK case law pertinent to Irish tax law.

Decisions from other common law jurisdictions do not form binding precedents that Irish courts are obliged to follow. They are, however, very persuasive and, accordingly, in most instances where a tax issue has already been the subject of judicial consideration in a UK court, it is not challenged again in the Irish courts. Nonetheless, there are exceptions (most notably in the area of tax avoidance), and caution should be exercised in relying on UK precedent.

The European Union (EU) also represents an important source of tax law. In recent times, decisions of the European Court of Justice (ECJ) have become increasingly influential. In fact, the Finance Acts of 1999 and 2001 both enacted legislative changes in response to ECJ decisions.[3] More recently (December 2005), the ECJ issued its ruling on the *Marks & Spencer* case (C–466/03). The Finance Act 2007 legislated for the ECJ decision. Readers are referred to Chapter 32, section 32.2.2.2 and Appendix I of that chapter for a detailed discussion of the case and of the Finance Act 2007 amendment.

EU Directives also have a significant influence on Irish legislation. This is most notable in the area of VAT, where the provisions of EU Directives form the basis of domestic legislation in Member States. However, a number of Directives relating to direct taxation are also relevant. The "Parent/Subsidiary Directive" is concerned with implementing a

---

3   Readers are referred to the decisions in *Imperial Chemical Industries plc. (ICI) v Colmer (HMIT)* (Case C-264/96) ECJ [1998] BTC 304 and in "the St Gobain case" (ECJ judgment of 21 September 1999: *Compagnie de Saint-Gobain, Zweigniederlassung Deutschland v Finanzamt Aachen-Innenstadt* (Case C 307/97)).

common system of taxation where parent companies and their subsidiaries operate in different Member States. The "Mergers Directive" is concerned with facilitating cross-border mergers and transfers of assets between companies located in different Member States. The provisions of these Directives were introduced by legislative amendments contained in the Finance Acts of 1991 and 1992.

Two further Directives have been incorporated into Irish legislation by the provisions of Finance Act 2004. A Directive on the taxation of income and savings (the "Savings Directive") provides for information exchange between Member States. The "Withholding Tax Exemption Directive" aims to eliminate withholding taxes on interest and royalty payments between associated companies in different Member States. Not all EU countries are covered by the Withholding Tax Exemption Directive: Greece and Portugal may continue to apply withholding taxes to interest and royalties, while Spain reserves the right to withhold taxes on royalty payments.

Finally, although not legally binding, documented details of Revenue practice in specific areas can throw light on the practical treatment of many technical statutory issues that require further explanation. Such information can be found in official *Statements of Practice*, in information leaflets issued by Revenue and in *Tax Briefing*, a bimonthly Revenue publication on technical issues. In addition, details of past rulings and concessions granted by Revenue can be obtained under the Freedom of Information Act 1997 and Freedom of Information Amendment Act 2003. To a lesser extent, details of UK Inland Revenue practice are also helpful.

1.3 Desirable Characteristics of Taxation

It is possible to evaluate systems of taxation and individual tax measures on the basis of clearly defined criteria. For example, in his landmark publication *The Wealth of Nations* (1776), Adam Smith proposed four canons of taxation:

- **Equity:** The tax should be fair.

- **Certainty**: It should be possible to determine the tax liability with reasonable exactitude and minimal subjectivity.

- **Convenience**: It should be possible to collect the tax with minimal effort on the part of the administrator and with minimal disruption to the taxpayer.

- **Efficiency**: The tax should minimise distortionary effects on consumer behaviour and the revenue collected from the tax should justify the costs of collection.

The Irish Commission on Taxation, established in the 1980s, used a variation of this framework when it focused on issues of equity, efficiency and simplicity in assessing various aspects of the Irish regime. Effectively, this involved consideration of Smith's canons of "certainty" and "convenience" under the single heading "simplicity".

It should be borne in mind that Smith (1776) wrote at a time when the main function of taxation was to generate funds for public finance. While this is still the case, in more recent times taxation has also been used as an instrument of social and economic policy (see 1.4 below). Accordingly, the criterion of efficiency presented by Smith (1776) has been extended somewhat to also encompass the issue of incentives, i.e., a tax incentive may be perceived as efficient insofar as it encourages desirable social behaviour and economic activity.

Clearly, not all criteria will be relevant in all cases, and certain other matters may need to be addressed in considering specific taxation proposals. In addition, it should be noted that there may be trade-offs between individual criteria, and policy-makers will invariably be forced to sacrifice certain objectives at the expense of others. For example, in the Irish context, a number of tax reliefs have been introduced in recent years for expenditure on property development in certain clearly defined geographical areas. These measures may be viewed as efficient where they encourage investment in those areas most in need of economic development. On the other hand, the measures may be perceived as inequitable on the basis that those most likely to benefit from the tax reliefs are the wealthy members of society. The less well-off do not have the resources to make such investments.

Indeed, the then Minister for Finance Charlie McCreevy specifically referred to this trade-off in the context of the property schemes in his Budget speech of 1 December 2004:

> *"For the successful operation of such schemes and to achieve the common good, we need to ensure the right balance is achieved between the benefit to the investor and the good of the community."*

Realistically, given the conflicts between individual canons of taxation, it may not be possible to design an ideal tax system. Nonetheless, the criteria are useful, as they provide a framework within which tax proposals may be considered. They also help to identify and highlight criticisms that might otherwise be overlooked.

1.4 The Role of Taxation in the Economy

As described at 1.2.1 above, many taxes were historically introduced to finance war. More recently, with the advent of the Welfare State, and the provision by most modern governments of certain services and public goods for the benefit of citizens, taxation has become a tool used by governments to generate public finance, to redistribute resources to the less well-off and to encourage certain desirable behaviour.

1.4.1 Tax as a source of public finance

The Government needs revenue to fund our infrastructure, our education system, our healthcare service, our public transport system, etc. There are a number of options available to it. It can simply charge for the goods or services provided. This is the method by which the Government funds our public transport system. It is also the method that some local authorities controversially implemented to fund the cost of refuse collection.

However, this method is not appropriate to the provision of certain public goods, where the beneficiaries are not clearly identifiable. For example, who should be charged for services provided by the Department of the Environment aimed at ensuring we have clean air? Who should be charged for the services of An Garda Síochána in policing our streets? It would be very difficult to charge for these services and even more difficult to prevent those who do not pay from benefiting. In addition, where additional individuals can benefit from the provision of a service at no extra cost to the provider, it would be inefficient to exclude them on the basis that they have not paid. For example, there are unlikely to be additional costs associated with allowing an extra child to sit in a classroom so, if there was not a system of free primary education in this country, it would be inefficient to exclude a child who could not afford to pay. In fact, there would undoubtedly be a benefit to society in granting that child a free education.

Thus, as an alternative to charging for certain goods and services that it provides, the Government must generate finance from some other source. A second option available to the Government is to create more money and use it to finance these goods and services. This tried and tested method invariably leads to devaluation of the currency and inflation. Another option is to simply borrow more money. However, there are limits on the amount that can be raised in this way.

Taxation has proved to be the favoured method of raising public finance in most modern economies and usually represents the greater part of government revenue. Such reliance on taxation to raise public finance creates a phenomenon known as "the burden of taxation". At a household or individual level, this can be measured as the total tax paid expressed as a percentage of household or personal income. At a macro level, the burden of taxation is usually measured by expressing government tax receipts as a percentage of gross domestic product (GDP). The first table below shows the national tax burden, i.e., total tax revenues expressed as a percentage of GDP, for all OECD countries for a selection of years from 1975 to 2007.

Table 1: Total tax revenue as percentage of GDP

	1975	1985	1990	1995	2000	2005	2006	2007 Provisional
Canada	32.0	32.5	35.9	35.6	35.6	33.4	33.3	33.3
Mexico		17.0	17.3	16.7	18.5	19.9	20.6	20.5[3]
United States	25.6	25.6	27.3	27.9	29.9	27.3	28.0	28.3
Australia	25.8	28.3	28.5	28.8	31.1	30.8	30.6	30.8
Japan	20.9	27.4	29.1	26.8	27.0	27.4	27.9	n.a
Korea	15.1	16.4	18.9	19.4	23.6	25.5	26.8	28.7
New Zealand	28.5	31.1	37.4	36.6	33.6	37.5	36.7	36.0
Austria	36.7	40.9	39.6	41.2	42.6	42.1	41.7	41.9
Belgium	39.5	44.4	42.0	43.6	44.9	44.8	44.5	44.4
Czech Republic				37.5	35.3	37.5	36.9	36.4
Denmark[1]	38.4	46.1	46.5	48.8	49.4	50.7	49.1	48.9
Finland	36.5	39.7	43.5	45.7	47.2	43.9	43.5	43.0
France[1]	35.4	42.8	42.0	42.9	44.4	43.9	44.2	43.6
Germany[2]	34.3	36.1	34.8	37.2	37.2	34.8	35.6	36.2
Greece	19.4	25.5	26.2	28.9	34.1	31.3	31.3	n.a
Hungary				41.3	38.0	37.2	37.1	39.3
Iceland	30.0	28.2	30.9	31.2	37.2	40.7	41.5	41.4
Ireland	28.7	34.6	33.1	32.5	31.7	30.6	31.9	32.2
Italy	25.4	33.6	37.8	40.1	42.3	40.9	42.1	43.3
Luxembourg	32.8	39.5	35.7	37.1	39.1	37.8	35.9	36.9
Netherlands[4]	40.7	42.4	42.9	41.5	39.7	38.8	39.3	38.0
Norway	39.2	42.6	41.0	40.9	42.6	43.5	43.9	43.4
Poland				36.2	31.6	32.9	33.5	n.a
Portugal	19.7	25.2	27.7	31.7	34.1	34.7	35.7	36.6
Slovak Republic					33.8	31.8	29.8	29.8
Spain[1]	18.4	27.6	32.5	32.1	34.2	35.8	36.6	37.2
Sweden	41.2	47.3	52.2	47.5	51.8	49.5	49.1	48.2
Switzerland	23.9	25.5	25.8	27.7	30.0	29.2	29.6	29.7
Turkey	11.9	11.5	14.9	16.8	24.2	24.3	24.5	23.7
United Kingdom	35.2	37.6	36.1	34.5	37.1	36.3	37.1	36.6
Unweighted average:								
OECD Total	29.4	32.7	33.8	34.8	36.1	35.8	35.9	n.a
OECD America	28.8	25.0	26.8	26.7	28.0	26.9	27.3	27.4
OECD Pacific	22.6	25.8	28.5	27.9	28.8	30.3	30.5	n.a
OECD Europe	30.9	35.3	36.1	37.1	38.4	38.0	38.0	n.a
EU 19	32.2	37.6	38.2	38.9	39.4	38.7	38.7	n.a
EU 15	32.2	37.6	38.2	39.0	40.6	39.7	39.8	n.a

n.a indicates not available.

Note: EU 15 area countries are: Austria, Belgium, Denmark, Finland, France, Germany, Greece, Ireland, Italy, Luxembourg, Netherlands, Portugal, Spain, Sweden and United Kingdom.

EU 19 area countries are: EU 15 countries plus Czech Republic, Hungary, Poland and Slovak Republic.

1. The total tax revenue has been reduced by the amount of the capital transfer that represents uncollected taxes.
2. Unified Germany beginning in 1991. Starting 2001, Germany has revised its treatment of non-wastable tax credits in the reporting of revenues to bring it into line with the OECD guidelines. The impact of this change is shown in Table D in Part I of this report.
3. Secretariat estimate, including expected revenues collected by state and local governments.
4. Secretariat estimates for the years 2006 and 2007. The heading 6000 has been estimated for the both years and the amount of the custom duties for the year 2006.

Source: OECD (2008) Revenue Statistics 1965–2007. © OECD Publishing. Reproduced by permission of OECD Publishing.

Table 2: Taxes on income, profits and capital gains as percentage of GDP[2]

	1965	1970	1975	1980	1985	1990	1995	2000	2005	2006
Canada	9.9	13.8	15.1	14.4	14.4	17.4	16.5	17.8	15.9	16.2
Mexico				4.8	3.8	4.7	4.1	5.0	4.8	5.2
United States	11.9	13.4	11.8	13.2	11.6	12.6	12.8	15.1	12.7	13.5
Australia	10.7	11.7	14.5	15.0	15.4	16.3	15.9	18.1	18.2	18.1
Japan	8.0	9.4	9.3	11.7	12.5	14.6	10.3	9.4	9.3	9.9
Korea			3.7	4.4	4.3	6.5	6.2	6.8	7.5	7.9
New Zealand	14.5	16.2	19.0	21.4	21.6	22.3	22.4	20.2	23.6	22.8
Austria	8.6	8.5	9.6	10.4	10.8	10.1	10.8	12.1	11.9	12.0
Belgium	8.6	10.7	15.6	16.9	17.9	15.5	16.6	17.3	17.2	16.8
Czech Republic							9.4	8.0	9.1	9.0
Denmark[1]	14.0	20.0	22.6	23.8	26.6	28.0	30.1	29.8	31.1	29.5
Finland	12.6	14.0	15.8	14.0	16.2	17.1	16.5	20.3	16.8	16.6
France[1]	5.4	5.8	5.6	6.7	6.8	6.7	7.0	11.1	10.3	10.7
Germany	10.7	10.2	11.8	12.8	12.5	11.3	11.3	11.2	9.8	10.8
Greece	1.6	2.4	2.6	4.2	4.5	5.2	6.4	9.3	7.9	7.5
Hungary							8.6	9.2	8.8	9.1
Iceland	5.6	5.9	6.8	7.6	6.4	9.2	10.6	14.8	17.6	18.3
Ireland	6.4	7.7	8.6	11.3	12.0	12.2	12.7	13.2	11.7	12.7
Italy	4.6	4.5	5.4	9.3	12.4	13.8	14.2	14.0	12.9	14.0
Luxembourg	9.9	10.1	14.1	15.4	17.0	14.0	14.6	14.1	13.0	12.5
Netherlands	11.7	11.9	14.2	14.1	11.2	13.8	10.9	10.0	10.8	10.7
Norway	12.9	13.3	13.5	17.7	16.9	14.4	14.3	19.2	21.4	22.0
Poland							11.1	9.7	6.4	7.0
Portugal	3.9	4.4	3.4	4.5	6.5	7.1	7.9	9.6	8.2	8.5
Slovak Republic								7.0	5.7	5.8
Spain[1]	3.6	3.2	4.1	5.9	6.8	10.0	9.4	9.8	10.6	11.4
Sweden	19.2	20.5	20.8	20.2	20.0	21.7	18.6	21.2	19.4	19.4
Switzerland	7.2	8.5	11.4	11.2	11.7	12.0	11.9	13.2	13.0	13.5
Turkey	3.1	3.1	5.0	6.9	4.3	5.0	4.8	7.1	5.3	5.3
United Kingdom	11.3	14.9	15.8	13.3	14.5	14.2	12.7	14.5	13.9	14.7
Unweighted average:										
OECD Total	9.0	10.2	11.2	12.0	12.3	12.9	12.4	13.3	12.8	13.0
OECD America	10.9	13.6	13.4	10.8	9.9	11.6	11.2	12.7	11.1	11.6
OECD Pacific	11.1	12.4	11.6	13.1	13.5	14.9	13.7	13.6	14.6	14.7
OECD Europe	8.5	9.5	10.9	11.9	12.4	12.7	12.3	13.3	12.7	12.9
EU 19	8.8	9.9	11.3	12.2	13.1	13.4	12.7	13.2	12.4	12.6
EU 15	8.8	9.9	11.3	12.2	13.1	13.4	13.3	14.5	13.7	13.8

Note: EU 15 area countries are: Austria, Belgium, Denmark, Finland, France, Germany, Greece, Ireland, Italy, Luxembourg, Netherlands, Portugal, Spain, Sweden and United Kingdom.

EU 19 area countries are: EU 15 countries plus Czech Republic, Hungary, Poland and Slovak Republic.

1. The total tax revenues have been reduced by the amount of capital transfer. The capital transfer has been allocated between tax headings in proportion to the reported tax revenue.

2. Category 1000 in Revenue Statistics.

Source: OECD (2008) Revenue Statistics 1965–2007. © OECD Publishing. Reproduced by permission of OECD Publishing.

The second table illustrates that the tax burden in Ireland is quite low, in fact lower than that of most other OECD countries. This is surprising in view of our relatively high marginal rate of income tax: 47% until the Suppplementary Budget 2009. The marginal rate comprises income tax of 41%, PRSI (Pay-Related Social Insurance) of 4% (for employees) and a health contribution levy of 2%. The Supplementary Budget 2009 increased this marginal rate to 51% for individuals with income up to €75,036 (41% income tax, 4% PRSI, 4% health levy and 2% income levy. For individuals with income exceeding €75,036, the marginal rate of income tax has been increased to 54% (41% income tax, 4% PRSI, 5% health levy and 4% income levy). Where income exceeds €174,980, the income levy increases to 6%, thereby bringing the marginal rate of income tax to 56%). Social security contributions (PRSI) and the health contribution are included in the definition of tax on the basis that they are mandatory payments. The relatively low burden of taxation in Ireland is not, it would appear, attributable to our rates of income tax, but rather to our narrow tax base. Property and wealth taxes have not been a dominant feature of taxation in Ireland and the income tax base has been narrowed by numerous special incentive regimes.

1.4.2 Tax as a mechanism for redistributing income and wealth

In addition to being used to generate public finance, governments also endeavour to use the tax system to transfer resources from wealthy members of society to the less well- off in an equitable manner.

Effecting a redistribution of income can be accomplished to some degree by having a progressive income tax. A progressive tax system seeks to collect proportionately more tax from those on higher incomes. A very progressive income tax system will reduce disparity in after-tax income. A proportional income tax is one that is levied at the same rate on all income. Progressivity in the Irish tax system is attempted by taxing the first band of income at a standard rate of 20% and the balance of income in excess of this band at a higher rate of 41%. The income tax system was made more progressive in the Supplementary Budget 2009, as illustrated in the previous paragraph whereby the marginal rate of income tax increase from 51% to 56% as income increases.

For most of the 1980s and early 1990s, there were three rates of income tax in Ireland. 1992 saw the removal of one of the bands and, since then, we have had just two rates of income tax. However, this does not necessarily infer that inequality in the distribution of after-tax income in Ireland has increased. Other tax measures, such as the replacement of the system of personal allowances with a tax credits system[4] and efforts to exclude those on the minimum wage from the tax net, may have compensated for the reduced number of bands. The Supplementary Budget 2009 has had the effect of reintroducing three rates of income tax due to three rates of the income levy, 2%, 4% and 6%.

---

4   Readers are referred to Chapter 11 of Section II of this book, regarding the system of tax credits and personal allowances.

The concept of progressivity is not confined to income tax. For example, our VAT system endeavours to be progressive by taxing luxury goods consumed more heavily than every day goods. Accordingly, a rate of VAT of 21% applies to "luxury" items such as jewellery, DVD players, etc., while essential goods such as basic foodstuffs, children's clothing and oral medicines are zero-rated. However, there is a view that, despite such efforts to differentiate between luxury goods and essentials, VAT is a regressive tax. A regressive tax is a tax that takes a decreasing proportion of income. To the extent that the less well-off in society consume a greater proportion of their incomes on goods/ services, VAT may be regressive. For an analysis of the composition of net tax receipts for 2007 and 2008, readers are referred to 1.6 below. In this analysis it can be seen that Ireland relies heavily on transaction taxes (30.7% of tax receipts from VAT, 12.9% from Customs and Excise duties and 6.8% from stamp duty); a total of 50.4% of the total tax receipts.

The application of a more favourable system for the taxation of capital gains suggests that the interaction between income tax and capital gains tax is important in considering progressivity in the Irish tax system. Until 2009 capital gains were subject to tax at a rate of 20% (25% for disposals made after 8 April 2009), whereas income can be taxed at effective rates of up to 47% (51-56% from 2009 (including PRSI, health levy and income levy). As investment in capital assets is generally confined to more affluent individuals, this discrepancy in rates may be perceived as inequitable and regressive. In addition, capital taxes and, in particular, wealth taxes, can be an important tool in the redistribution of wealth.

While increased taxes on the wealthy and other progressive tax measures can reduce disparity in after-tax income and wealth, they only truly have a redistributive effect where the revenues from such measures are used efficiently. Efforts to effect a redistribution of income cannot be considered without looking also at social welfare reforms and legal initiatives, such as the introduction of a minimum wage. Certainly, tackling poverty is not something that can be accomplished by reforming the tax system in isolation, since many of those who may be classified as poor in accordance with the generally accepted measures and benchmarks are outside the tax net.

Some of the more radical proposals for tax and welfare reform suggest that the two systems should be totally integrated. In Ireland, a working group led by the Department of the Taoiseach considered the implications of the introduction of a "Basic Income" scheme. In its purest form, this would involve the replacement of the existing system of welfare payments and personal tax credits with a single basic income payment paid unconditionally to everyone. While social welfare reforms and such radical schemes are outside the scope of this analysis, the reader should be aware of their importance as redistribution tools.

An international comparison of income tax paid by families across the G-7 countries including Ireland and Sweden, was performed in by the Library of Parliament in Canada (2006) which carried out a survey of double and single income families with two children. This analysis revealed that at the lower levels of income (€25,000), Irish families paid little or no income tax, compared to 20% in Sweden and the mid-teens percentages in France, Germany and Italy. At income levels of approximately €50,000, Irish families paid less tax than those in any other country surveyed and paid half of the tax paid by families of similar income levels in Germany and Sweden. However, as family income levels increased to €75,000, Ireland moved to the middle of the league table where Irish families were paying similar income tax to families in Canada, France, the UK and the US, while families in Germany, Sweden and Italy paid approximately 10% more income tax (KPMG, 2009).

1.4.3   Tax as an instrument of economic and social policy

Tax is also used to encourage certain behaviour that might benefit society and the economy as a whole. For example, a number of tax reliefs have been introduced in recent years for expenditure on property development in certain clearly defined geographical areas. These measures are targeted at encouraging investment in those areas most in need of economic development. Areas such as Temple Bar, which has been transformed in the last 20 years from a state of fatigue to a hub of economic and social activity, appear to be tangible evidence of the success of these measures in accomplishing their stated objectives.[5]

All incentives require careful consideration from a cost/benefit perspective as there is clearly a cost to the Exchequer in terms of the tax foregone to incentivise certain behaviour or sectoral activity. Encouraging desirable behaviour through the tax system does not necessarily have to cost the Government money in terms of revenues foregone. Heavy taxes on petrol and tobacco are targeted partly at discouraging their consumption, thereby improving the environment, but have the added benefit of generating substantial revenue. Another example of such an effective measure is the 15-cent plastic bag levy. The objective of this measure was "to educate the shopping public towards moving away from plastic packaging towards biodegradable and recyclable alternatives" (Revenue's Annual Report, 2002, p. 57).

Anecdotal evidence from a trip to the supermarket would suggest that the measure has been very successful in encouraging more environmentally-friendly shopping habits; it has simultaneously yielded more than €50 million for the Exchequer from the date of its introduction on 4 March 2002 to 31 December 2006. The amount collected during 2006 was in excess of €18.7 million.[6] This amount increased to €22.49 million during 2007. The levy was increased from 13c to 22c per bag, with effect from 1 July 2007.

Not all tax measures accomplish their stated objectives and, very often, unforeseen results can arise. In 1997, in an effort to dampen booming property prices, the Government prohibited relief for interest expenses (on loans to purchase residential

---

5   Some research suggests that the success of Temple Bar is not specifically attributable to tax incentives. See the findings of a survey carried out by Indecon on behalf of Temple Bar properties in KPMG's *Study on the Urban Renewal Schemes* (Dublin: The Stationery Office, 1996). In addition, the 2005 Government studies into the incentive schemes highlighted some shortcomings. For example, Goodbody (2005) observed that the Rural Renewal Scheme had little direct impact on economic activity and resulted in an excess supply of housing in the scheme area.

6   Revenue's Annual Report, 2006, page 55.

properties) in calculating taxable rental income. The objective of this measure was to dissuade investors from purchasing residential property, thereby making the market more "first-time buyer friendly". While the impact of this measure is difficult to gauge, it does not appear to have achieved its goal. Property prices continued to rise and a new problem emerged – a shortage of affordable rental properties in the private sector. Within two years of its introduction, the restriction was withdrawn and, in calculating taxable rental income, a deduction is again available for landlords in respect of interest expenses incurred on loans to purchase rental properties.

1.5 Classification of Taxes

Taxes can be classified in many different ways. The analysis here is concerned with the distinction between direct and indirect taxes, and with the classification of taxes by tax base. As highlighted in Section 1.4.2 above, taxes may also be classified by their rate structure, i.e., progressive, regressive or proportional.

1.5.1 Direct versus indirect

Direct taxes are those that are assessed directly on the individual or entity at whom or at which they are targeted. Examples include income tax, corporation tax, capital gains tax and capital acquisitions tax, all of which are levied directly on the taxpayer intended to bear the final tax burden. Indirect taxes, on the other hand, are taxes that are collected from persons other than those that are intended to bear the final burden of tax. VAT and customs and excise duties are examples of indirect taxes.

It is important to note that the final burden of taxation does not necessarily rest with the person that was intended to bear it. For example, in the case of VAT, the burden of taxation is targeted at the final consumer and collected from traders involved in the chain of supply. To the extent that the final price for the goods charged to the ultimate consumer is set by market forces and not by suppliers on a cost-plus-VAT basis, it may be necessary for suppliers to tolerate the VAT cost through reduced prices for customers.

1.5.2 Taxes on corporations

Taxes on corporations are generally levied on the corporate entity as direct taxes calculated as a percentage of taxable profits. Such taxes are often classified in accordance with the type of corporation tax system, i.e., in accordance with the treatment of shareholders with respect to underlying corporation tax paid by the company. Broadly speaking, there are two models – the classical system and the imputation system. However, many countries operate hybrids of these of systems, i.e., partial imputation systems.

Under the classical system, no credit is given to shareholders for the underlying corporation tax paid on profits. Corporate profits are taxed in full without deduction for appropriations of profits by way of distributions. Distributions are taxed in the hands of individual shareholders and no credit is given for the corporation tax already paid by the company on the profits out of which such distributions are paid. Accordingly, there is double taxation of the same profits – the profits are taxed in the hands of the company and again as dividends in the hands of the shareholder. This is the system that has applied in Ireland since April 1999. While we have a system of dividend withholding tax in Ireland, this is simply a system for the advance payment of the shareholder's income tax liability. Credit is given to the shareholder for this advance payment of income tax, but no credit is given for the corporation tax paid on the corporate profits out of which dividends are paid.

Under an imputation system, corporation tax is "imputed" to the shareholders who receive dividends, and credit is given for this corporation tax in calculating the final income tax liability.

Assuming a company has taxable income of €100,000 and pays corporation tax at a rate of 12.5%, it will be in a position to pay a dividend of €87,500 to shareholders.

Under the classical system, assuming just one shareholder who pays tax at the marginal rate and ignoring PRSI and the health contribution levy, the shareholder will be taxed under Schedule F at 41% on the amount of the cash dividend received. Thus, additional tax of €35,875 will be payable at shareholder level and no credit is granted for the underlying corporation tax already suffered in the amount of €12,500. Thus, the total tax suffered on the taxable profit of €100,000 is €48,375 (€35,875 + €12,500) and this represents an effective rate of 48.375% (12.5% + (87.5% × 41%)).

Under a system of full imputation, the shareholder is deemed to have received a gross dividend of €100,000 (albeit that a net cash amount of only €87,500 is received). The gross amount of €100,000 is taxed at the marginal rate of 41% and full credit is granted for the underlying corporation tax already suffered in the amount of €12,500. Thus, the shareholder's liability is calculated as follows:

	€
Schedule F: Gross dividend	100,000
Income tax at 41%	41,000
Credit for underlying corporation tax	(12,500)
	28,500

Thus, the total tax suffered on taxable profit of €100,000 is €41,000 (€12,500 + €28,500) and this represents a total effective rate of 41%.

In Ireland, prior to April 1999, credit was given to shareholders for a portion of the underlying corporation tax suffered by companies and, accordingly, Ireland operated a partial imputation system until 1999. This imputation system has been replaced with a classical system. See Chapter 19 (section 19.5) for the taxation treatment of distributions from an Irish resident company received by an Irish resident individual and Chapter 28 (section 28.2).

1.5.3   Classification by tax base

The tax base is some quantifiable collection of like items upon which tax is levied. The main tax bases upon which taxes are levied in Ireland are income and expenditure and, to a much lesser extent, wealth.

Income tax and corporation tax are both examples of taxes based on income. Value-added tax and excise duties are examples of taxes based on expenditure. Wealth taxes may be defined as taxes on the accumulated resources or wealth of an individual. Traditionally, they take the form of annual taxes on the taxpayer's net assets. Capital acquisitions tax is regularly referred to as a wealth tax. However, it can be argued that capital acquisitions tax is not a true tax on wealth but rather a form of income tax levied on movements in wealth or on capital transfers. On this basis, the only real forms of wealth tax that we have experience of in Ireland are the 1975 wealth tax, abolished within three years of its introduction, and a short-lived residential property tax, which was abolished in 1997. Similarly, many would argue that capital gains tax is, in effect, an income tax and, more specifically, a tax on realised capital income.

Choosing the most appropriate tax base is a controversial matter and, in practice, most administrations favour some balance of all three. A brief commentary on the problems associated with each of the alternative tax bases is worthwhile at this stage, in advance of considering the Irish tax base.

1.5.3.1   Income

Problems arise in defining income because the everyday meaning precludes certain factors that clearly constitute an increase in the value of economic resources. Arguments have been advanced in favour of a more comprehensive definition of income that would include capital gains, gifts and inheritances, lottery and gambling winnings, and various types of non-cash income. This is on the basis that capital appreciation is akin to interest or rent – i.e., it is a form of return for investors on certain types of capital asset. To preserve equity and neutrality, returns on non-income-bearing assets should be taxed on the same basis as income-bearing assets. This can be accomplished by widening the definition of income and applying the same tax system and rates to all forms of income. However, this is not the case in Ireland, where current income such as interest and dividends are taxed at rates of up to 41%, while capital income in the form of realised gains on assets is generally only taxed at a rate of 25%. Furthermore, unrealised capital gains are not taxed at all.

The other major problem with income as a basis for taxation is one of measurement. Even if we unanimously agree on a definition of income, measuring the factors to be included in that tax base can pose certain problems. How to account for inflation and adjusting nominal income such that taxpayers are taxable on their real purchasing power is one such problem. Indexing personal tax credits and rate bands in line with the consumer price index is one method by which the Government may give relief to taxpayers in times of high inflation.

Furthermore, even if we can accurately measure the real purchasing power of an individual's income, differing personal circumstances of taxpayers may create a drain on this income in varying degrees. The Irish system attempts to deal with this matter by providing for a system of tax credits granted to taxpayers on the basis of their personal circumstances. In measuring income, the choice of unit of taxation is also very relevant. Moves towards "individualisation" of our tax system have caused considerable controversy in Ireland in recent times.[7]

1.5.3.2 Expenditure

Proponents of expenditure as the tax base argue that it eliminates the problems of a narrowing of the tax base on the basis of definitions. All expenditure would be taxed irrespective of whether the expenditure is out of salary, lottery winnings or capital transfers in the form of gifts or inheritances. Theoretically, expenditure should equate to income less savings. If we take the view that saving and investing constitute desirable social behaviour, expenditure tax is preferable to income tax on the basis that it encourages saving at the expense of spending. In addition, it would eliminate the need for wealth taxes, as all accumulated wealth would eventually be consumed.

On the downside, using expenditure as the tax base fails to take account of life-cycle patterns. Very often those who spend most are young people who have more active social lives and who are in the process of establishing homes. Such individuals are less likely to save and more likely to borrow than middle-aged individuals and senior citizens. Thus, there is a mismatch between income and expenditure, and the tax burden may be highest in years when surplus cash-flow is weakest.

In addition, the exclusion of savings from the tax base may mean that onerously high levels of taxation on consumption are necessary.

1.5.3.3 Wealth

Despite its potential as a tool for redistributing resources to the less well-off, wealth taxes have never proved popular in Ireland, due to problems associated with valuation of the tax base and difficulties associated with collection.

Is it fair to tax an individual with substantial low return investments and little or no earnings potential more onerously than someone with few investments but with sought-after professional qualifications and substantial earnings potential? A comprehensive wealth tax would endeavour to establish the present value of earnings potential. Accordingly, measurement problems arise. Even more traditional tangible assets can be difficult to value. Very often a professional valuation is necessary to preserve objectivity. This can be very costly for a taxpayer.

---

7   See O'Halloran, M., *From Bóraimhe to Bit – The Art of Taxation* (Dublin: Irish Taxation Institute, 2005).

The burden of collection of income taxes on items such as salary and interest can easily be transferred to employers and lending institutions. However, wealth taxes must be administered directly by the Government and, accordingly, can be expensive to collect.

Finally, wealth does not equate to cash-flow. It is feasible that a taxpayer may be forced to sell a capital asset in order to fund his wealth tax liability. This may be perceived as inequitable by the individual taxpayer and may not constitute desirable behaviour from the perspective of society as a whole.

1.6   The Tax Base in Ireland

In 1982, the Irish Commission on Taxation considered suitable alternative tax bases for the purposes of direct taxation in Ireland. It concluded that "the tax base should be defined on a comprehensive basis to include all real increases in the command over economic resources" (Commission on Taxation, 1982, page 115). It argued in favour of a comprehensive definition of income, which would reflect the taxpayer's control over society's resources. Accordingly, the definition should include "capital gains, bequests and gifts received, lottery and casual gambling winnings, compensation payments for loss of office and non-money income" (Commission on Taxation, 1982, page 117). Thus, all forms of increase in economic resources would be taxed in the same way, and this would preserve equity and eliminate behaviour targeted at channelling income to activities or items taxable on a more favourable basis. In addition, the inclusion of all types of receipt in the income tax base would eliminate the need for separate taxes on wealth, capital gains, and gifts and inheritance.

While it acknowledged the theoretical advantages of expenditure as the tax base, it argued that the complete replacement of income tax with a direct expenditure tax was not a feasible proposition for the foreseeable future. It did, however, suggest that a comprehensive income tax could be complemented by a progressive direct expenditure tax at higher rates. The application of a progressive system of rates to a comprehensive definition of income would lead to heavy taxation of windfall capital receipts that accrue irregularly over time and this could lead to certain inequities. To eliminate this problem, it proposed that a single rate of income tax should be applied to the comprehensive income tax base, and progressivity should be preserved by the introduction of a direct expenditure tax at higher progressive rates.

Despite the strong theoretical arguments put forward by the Commission in favour of a comprehensive definition of income, income tax in Ireland is currently applied to the more conventional narrow base, and separate taxes apply to realised capital gains and capital transfers in the form of gifts and inheritances. This system of direct taxation is supplemented by indirect taxes on expenditure in the form of VAT and duties. Thus, the proposals of the Commission have been largely ignored in this regard, and the result is that we currently have 10 separate taxes applying in Ireland, each with its own unique set of rules and rates, etc. An analysis of the revenues from these different taxes in 2007 and 2008 is set out below and in the accompanying pie charts. The major changes are in the

% of gross receipts from stamp duties (due to the downturn in the property sector) and capital gains tax (due to material losses in the stock market), both of which reduced significantly in 2008 compared to 2007.

Total Amount Collected/Gross Receipts				
	2007		2008	
	€m	%	€m	%
Duties, Taxes and Levies				
Value Added Tax	19,248	29.10	17,992	29.95
Income Tax	16,788	25.38	16,593	27.63
Corporation Tax	7,329	11.08	6,046	10.06
Excise	6,127	9.27	5,703	9.49
Stamp Duties	3,309	5.00	1,813	3.01
Capital Gains Tax	3,161	4.78	1,494	2.48
Capital Acquisitions Tax	397	0.60	351	0.58
Customs	280	0.42	260	0.43
Collection on behalf of other Departments/Agencies (PRSI, health, income and environmental levies	9,503	14.4	9,810	16.37
Total	**66,143**	**100**	**60,061**	**100**

Source: Annual Report Revenue Commissioners 2008, www.revenue.ie

The comparison across Ireland and the UK illustrates the extent to which Ireland has relied on transaction taxes (50.4% for Ireland compared to 32.4% for the UK). Transaction taxes are sensitive to changes in the economic climate. As a consequence, the changing economic environment of 2008 and 2009 has had a significant impact on the tax receipts for those years. This led to the Supplementary Budget 2009 where the government has sought to collect additional tax revenue of 1.8 billion during 2009. In his budget speech, the Minister for Finance acknowledged that the revenue base is too low and announced his intention to broaden the Irish tax base in future years. This could include new forms of taxation such as carbon taxes and tax on property. The measures introduced in the Supplementary Budget 2009 have doubled the income and health levies and have lowered the income levels at which the progressive levy rates begin to apply thus increasing the tax burden progressively for all taxpayers. PRSI, capital gains tax, capital acquisitions tax, Deposit Interest Retention Tax and insurance levies were also increased. The tax base may be further altered in 2010 as the Government is awaiting the report of the Commission on Taxation, which is due to publish its findings no later than 30 September 2009.

The Commission on Taxation

The Commission on Taxation was established on 14 February 2008 to review the structure, efficiency and appropriateness of the Irish taxation system.

Its terms of reference are as follows: (www.taxcommission.ie)

'The Commission is invited, in the context of maintaining an equitable incidence of taxation and a strong economy, to consider the structure of the taxation system and specifically to

■ consider how best the tax system can support economic activity and promote increased employment and prosperity while providing the resources necessary to meet the cost of public services and other Government outlays in the medium and longer term;

■ consider how best the tax system can encourage long term savings to meet the needs of retirement;

■ examine the balance achieved between taxes collected on income, capital and spending;

■ review all tax expenditures with a view to assessing the economic and social benefits they deliver and to recommend the discontinuation of those that are unjustifiable on cost/benefit grounds;

■ consider options for the future financing of local government, and

■ investigate fiscal measures to protect and enhance the environment including the introduction of a carbon tax.'

The Commission is required to perform this review in the context of the commitments contained in the Programme for Government which include keeping the overall tax burden low and implement further changes to enhance the rewards of work while increasing the fairness of the tax system, introducing measures to lower carbon emissions and Ireland's commitment to retaining the 12.5% rate of corporation tax as a key aspect of Ireland's inward investment strategy.

Total Amount Collected/Gross Receipts - 2008

(PRSI) 16.37
(CAT) 0.58 (C) 0.43
(CGT) 2.48
(SD) 3.01
(E) 9.49
(CT) 10.06
(IT) 27.63
(VAT) 29.95

- ■ Value Added Tax-€17,992m (29.95)
- ■ Income Tax-€16,593m (27.63)
- □ Corporation Tax-€6,046m (10.06)
- □ Excise-€5,703m (9.49)
- ■ Stamp Duties-€1,813m (3.01)
- ■ Capital Gains Tax-€1,494m (2.48)
- ■ Capital Acquisitions Tax-€351m (0.58)
- □ Customs-€260m (0.43)
- ■ Collection on behalf of other Departments/Agencies (PRSI, health, income and environmental levies-€9,810m (16.37)

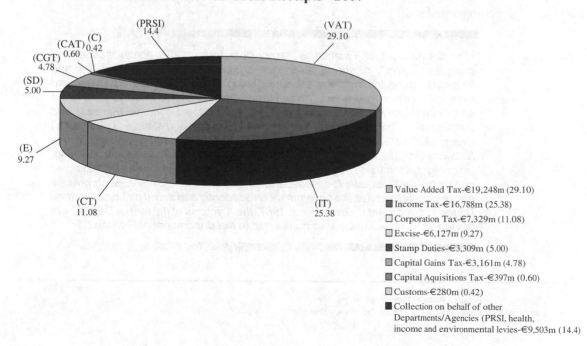

Total Amount Collected/Gross Receipts - 2007

(PRSI) 14.4
(CAT) 0.60 (C) 0.42
(CGT) 4.78
(SD) 5.00
(E) 9.27
(CT) 11.08
(IT) 25.38
(VAT) 29.10

- ■ Value Added Tax-€19,248m (29.10)
- ■ Income Tax-€16,788m (25.38)
- □ Corporation Tax-€7,329m (11.08)
- □ Excise-€6,127m (9.27)
- ■ Stamp Duties-€3,309m (5.00)
- ■ Capital Gains Tax-€3,161m (4.78)
- ■ Capital Aquisitions Tax-€397m (0.60)
- □ Customs-€280m (0.42)
- ■ Collection on behalf of other Departments/Agencies (PRSI, health, income and environmental levies-€9,503m (14.4)

1.7   Stakeholders in Irish Taxation Policy and Administration

An understanding of the key "players" in Irish taxation policy and administration brings a sense of context to the study of any aspect of taxation. The key stakeholders in Irish taxation include Government, the Oireachtas, the Department of Finance, the Office of the Revenue Commissioners (Revenue), the tax profession and, of course, the taxpayer community. The following is a summary of the structure and function of the Department of Finance, Revenue and the tax profession.

Department of Finance

The Department of Finance plays a key role in the economic, fiscal and financial management of Ireland's economy by advising and supporting the Minister for Finance and the members of the Houses of the Oireachtas. The Department also engages in the implementation of government policy, as laid down by each Programme for Government, and the management of the public sector. In carrying out its work the Department is guided by the following mission:

'To support the achievement of the Government's economic and social objectives by promoting a sound, sustainable economic and budgetary environment, continuing improvements in the efficiency of public services, and an effective framework for financial services.[8]'

The work of the Department is governed by a number of important pieces of legislation. The following is an extract from the Department's website information relation to governing legislation:

"The Department of Finance is responsible for "…. the administration and business generally of the public finance of Ireland and all powers, duties and functions connected with the same, including in particular, the collection and expenditure of the revenues of Ireland from whatever source arising…." Ministers and Secretaries Act, 1924. A government order - the Economic Planning and Development (Transfer of Departmental Administration and Ministerial Functions) Order, 1980 - allocated additional functions to the Department of Finance. These functions are principally to promote and coordinate economic and social planning, including sectoral and regional planning, to identify development policies, to review the methods adopted by departments of state to implement such policies and generally to advise the government on economic and social planning matters. Under a government order of March 1987, the functions of the former Department of the Public Service were also transferred to the Department of Finance.[9]"

---

8   Department of Finance Website Homepage, July 2009
9   Department of Finance Website – "How the Department Works", July 2009

The work of the Department is divided into the following six divisions:

1. Taxation and Financial Services Division (TFSD)

2. Budget, Economic and Pensions Division (BEPD)

3. Sectoral Policy Division (SPD)

4. Personnel and Remuneration Division (PRD)

5. Organisation, Management and Training Division (OMTD), and

6. Corporate Services Division (CSD)

From a taxation perspective, one of the key functions of the Minister for Finance and his/her Department is to prepare the annual Budget for the Irish economy and to initiate the Finance Bills that will bring those changes from Budget to legislation. A bill is a draft statute. Bills are not drafted by the Oireachtas but by legislative drafters who are officials in the Office of the Parliamentary Council to the Government.

The Finance Bill is unique in that it begins with the Budget, which is usually held in December. The Constitution requires that each Government department prepare estimates of their receipts and expenditure for the coming financial year. Abridged versions of these estimates are usually published in advance of the Budget.

On Budget day, the Minister for Finance presents the following to the Dáil:

- Budget Measures – these are the changes to be introduced in the Budget and the cost to the exchequer of each of these measures

- Financial Resolutions – these allow for immediate budgetary changes to come into effect, for example, changes in excise duty on alcohol;

- Budget Statistics & Tables – these provide budgetary projections for the next three years

- White Paper on Receipts & Expenditure – this is the opening position for the Budget and is published the Saturday before the Budget.

At the end of the Budget debate, the Minister seeks permission to circulate the Finance Bill, and this is generally granted. The Finance Bill is then drafted by the Parliamentary Draftsmen, with the Attorney General reviewing if necessary. Once drafted, the Finance Bill progresses onto the first stage, accompanied by its Explanatory Memorandum.[10]

---

10   AITI Research Module FA 2008 by Gráinne Duggan

The following diagram demonstrates how the Finance Bill becomes the Finance Act[11]

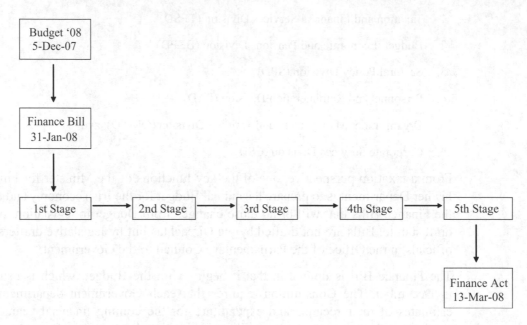

The Office of the Revenue Commissioners

The Office of the Revenue Commissioners was established by Government Order in 1923 and is responsible for the assessment, collection and management of taxes and duties. Its role also encompasses the implementation of proper import and export controls. Revenue is not responsible for determining taxation policy; setting taxation policy is the role of the Department of Finance. However, Revenue regularly provides policy advice on taxation issues to the Government and, to this end, has established four Revenue Legislation Services Divisions which have policy, legislation and interpretation functions for the various taxes. In fact, Revenue comprises 16 divisions as follows:

- Investigations and Prosecutions Division;

- Human Resources Division;

- Revenue Solicitor's Office;

- Information, Communications and e-Business Division;

- Collector General's Division;

- four Revenue Legislation Service Divisions (as described above);

- four Regional Divisions;

- Large Cases Division; and

■ two National Office Divisions, which are concerned with supporting the Board in setting corporate strategy and in developing operational policy.

The four Regional Divisions are concerned with customer service and are responsible for the compliance and audit functions in four geographically defined regions. The Large Cases Division is responsible for customer service, compliance and audit functions relating to the largest businesses and wealthiest individuals in the State.

It is important to bear in mind that the Appeal Commissioners operate independently of the Revenue Commissioners. They are appointed by the Minister for Finance under Section 850 of the Taxes Consolidation Act, 1997 and are responsible for the hearing of appeals by taxpayers against decisions of the Revenue Commissioners concerning direct and indirect taxes and duties.

Further information on the role, structure and powers of the Revenue Commissioners is provided in Chapter 7 of this book, within Section II on Value Added Tax.

The Tax Profession

Ireland has a very strong and highly skilled body of tax professionals. A properly trained cadre of tax professionals is essential to ensuring that Ireland is at the forefront of international tax professionalism; both in terms of the high standards set for professional qualification as a tax adviser and in continuing professional development.

The role of the tax adviser is to assist individual and corporate taxpayer clients in the efficient management of their tax obligations. Tax considerations are at the fore in any commercial or personal transaction. As a result the tax adviser works directly with the top-level decision makers in executing any deal. Broadly speaking, the work of a tax adviser can be split into two areas: tax compliance and tax consultancy.

Tax compliance involves ensuring that a taxpayer client meets their tax return and tax payment obligations on a periodic basis as well as for any once-off transactions that may take place. Tax consultancy is a core business advisory service and involves providing tax advice on transactions ranging from the incorporation of a small sole trader to advising a large multinational corporation on how to relocate their business headquarters to Ireland.

By fulfilling the above roles tax advisers assist in the more efficient running of the tax administration system. This is particularly relevant in terms of the self assessment system which operates in Ireland. A more onerous workload would be placed on the tax administration system in the absence of tax advisers.

The Irish Taxation Institute (ITI) is the leading professional body for taxation affairs in Ireland. Its 6,000 strong membership comprises Registered Tax Consultants, accountants, barristers, solicitors and other business professionals. The ITI's mission is to support an efficient, fair and competitive tax system that encourages economic and social progress. Founded in 1967, the ITI works with corporate leaders, Government, Revenue, other professional and representative groups, and the general public to help in the administration and development of the Irish and EU tax systems.

ITI has been Ireland's foremost provider of taxation professionals through the three-year Associateship of the ITI (AITI) and one-year Technician Member of ITI (TMITI) tax qualification courses for over 40 years. ITI provides a number of services to the profession including lifelong learning and professional development, representation of the profession to Government, the Revenue Commissioners and international stakeholders and a information services including tax commentary and legislation publications, daily, weekly and monthly bulletins and the leading tax journal in Ireland, *Irish Tax Review.*

Registered Tax Consultants and other professionals interact with the Revenue Commissioners on matters of tax administration via the Taxes Administration Liaison Committee (TALC). The Taxes Administration Liaison Committee (TALC) was established in 1989 and is a liaison committee between the Revenue Commissioners, the Irish Taxation Institute (ITI), the Consultative Committee of Accountancy Bodies of Ireland (CCABI) and the Law Society of Ireland.

TALC is a forum for the making of representations between Revenue and practitioners on the administration of tax in Ireland. It is not a forum for legislation or policy formation. TALC comprises Main TALC and six sub-committees as follows:

- TALC Direct Taxes Technical Sub-committee

- TALC Indirect Taxes Sub-committee

- TALC Sub-committee on Collection Issues

- TALC Simplification Sub-committee

- TALC Capital Taxes Sub-committee

- TALC Audit Sub-committee

The ITI is represented at all of the TALC committees by members and ITI executive staff.

When TALC was set up 1989, the terms of reference were set down as follows:

1. The function of the Committee is to review and make recommendations to achieve more effective and efficient administration of the direct taxes, stamp duties and value added tax. These may relate to either administrative practices of the Office of the Revenue Commissioners or of tax practitioners.

2. In the formulation of any recommendations, the Committee shall have due regard to the views and responsibilities of the Office of the Revenue Commissioners and the interests of taxpayers and tax practitioners and its recommendations shall be consistent with the objective of achieving an efficiency and consistency of administration which has due regard to statute, minimises compliance costs, promotes the highest possible level of voluntary compliance by taxpayers and the expeditious treatment of taxpayers by the Office of the Revenue Commissioners.

3. The Committee shall not accept representations on behalf of, or consider matters relating to, individual cases.

4. Membership will be at senior level from the Office of the Revenue Commissioners and appropriate bodies representing tax practitioners. The Committee will itself keep under consideration its current membership and any requests for amendment or extension.

WHAT YOU SHOULD NOW KNOW

On completion of this chapter, you should be able to:

✓ Describe some historical aspects of Irish taxation.

✓ Explain the impact of the UK tax system and the EU on the current Irish tax system.

✓ Describe the relevant sources of tax law and tax information.

✓ Describe the desirable characteristics of an ideal tax system and illustrate the nature of the trade-off between these characteristics.

✓ Describe the roles and structures of the key stakeholders in Irish taxation.

✓ Outline the objectives of taxation.

✓ Describe three methods for classifying taxes and describe the tax base in Ireland.

✓ Criticise various aspects of the Irish tax system in the context of the criteria of equity, efficiency and simplicity.

✓ Complete the Assignments and the Questions in Irish Taxation Law and Practice, Volume 2.

References and Recommended Further Reading

APPLEBY, T., and F. O'HANLON (2008), *The Taxation of Capital Gains*, Irish Taxation Institute.

BARRET, A., J. LAWLOR, S. SCOTT (1997), *The Fiscal System and the Polluter Pays Principle: A Case Study of Ireland*, Ashgate Publishing.

BLACKWELL, J. and F. CONVERY (1991), 'The impact of the Urban Incentives in Ireland in *Proceedings of the Sixth Annual Conference of the Foundation of Fiscal Studies.*

BRENNAN, F., P. MOORE, H. O'SULLIVAN (2008), *Corporation Tax,* Irish Taxation Institute.

CALLAN, T and B. NOLAN (1999), *Tax and Welfare Changes, Poverty and Work Incentives in Ireland 1987–1994,* Policy Research Series Paper No. 34, Dublin: The Economic and Social Research Institute.

CALLAN, T., B. NOLAN, J. WALSH, J., MCBRIDE, R. NESTOR (2000), "Basic Income in Ireland: A Study for the Working Group on Basic Income." *Final Report*, Department of the Taoiseach,
http://www.taoiseach.gov.ie

CALLAN, T., M. KEENEY, B. NOLAN, J. WALSH (2001), *Reforming Tax and Welfare*, Policy Research Series Paper No. 42, Dublin: The Economic and Social Research Institute.

CALLAN, T., R. LAYTE, A. VAN SOEST, J. WALSH, J. (2003) *Taxes Benefits and Labour Market Responses: New Evidence for Ireland*, Policy Research Series Paper No. 48, Dublin: The Economic and Social Research Institute.

COMMISSION ON TAXATION (1982), *First Report: Direct Taxation*, Dublin: Stationery Office.

DÁIL ÉIREANN, Dáil Debates,
http://historical-debates.oireachtas.ie

DEPARTMENT OF FINANCE (2002), *Budget Speech 2003,*
http://www.finance.gov.ie

DEPARTMENT OF FINANCE (2004), *Budget Speech 2005,*
http://www.finance.gov.ie

DEPARTMENT OF FINANCE (2005), *Budget Speech 2006,*
http://www.finance.gov.ie

DEPARTMENT OF FINANCE (2006), *Budget Speech 2007,*
http://www.finance.gov.ie

DEPARTMENT OF THE TAOISEACH (2002), *Basic Income – A Green Paper*, http://www.taoiseach.gov.ie

DOWLING, B. and O. KEEGAN (1992), 'Fiscal Policies and the Built Environment', *Environment and Development in Ireland*, Environmental Institute, UCD.

GOODBODY ECONOMIC CONSULTANTS (2005), *Review of Area-Based Tax Incentive Renewal Schemes,* Dublin: Department of Finance, http://finance.irlgov.ie

HEDERMAN O'BRIEN, M. (ed.) (2002), *One Size Fits All? EU Taxation Policy,* The Institute of European Affairs and The Institute of Taxation in Ireland.

HENEHAN, P.J. and A. WALSH (2003), "The Rule of Law or the Rule of Caprice", *Irish Tax Review*, 16(5): 447 - 456.

HONOHAN, P. (2001), "European and International Constraints on Irish Fiscal Policy" in Budget Perspectives Proceedings of ESRI / FFS Conference, 9/10/2001.

INDECON (2005), *Review of Property-Based Tax Incentive Schemes,* Dublin: Department of Finance, http://finance.irlgov.ie

JAMES, S. and C. NOBES (2005), *The Economics of Taxation – Principles, Policy and Practice,* Prentice Hall.

KPMG (1996), *Study on the Urban Renewal Schemes,* Dublin: Department of the Environment.

KPMG (2009), *Taxing Times - Supplementary Budget 2009 and Current Tax Developments*.

LYMER, A., L. OATS, D. HANCOCK (2004), *Taxation – Policy and Practice*, AccountingEducation.com Publishing.

MADDEN, D. (2000), "Taxation, Debt and the Public Finances", in O'Hagan (ed.), *The Economy of Ireland – Policy and Performance of a European Region*, eighth edition, Gill and McMillian.

MAGUIRE, T. (2008), *Direct Tax Acts, Irish Taxation Institute.*

MARTYN, J. and P. RECK (2008), *Taxation Summary,* Irish Taxation Institute.

McATEER, W., G. REDDIN, G. DEEGAN (2008), *Income Tax,* Irish Taxation Institute.

OECD (2004), Analytical Databank, http://www.oecd.org

OECD (2006), *Revenue Statistics, 1965 - 2006*, 2007 Edition, http://www.oecd.org

OECD (2004), *Taxing Wages 2003/2004,* http://www.oecd.org

O'HALLORAN, M. (2005), *From Bóraimhe to Bit – the Art of Taxation,* Irish Taxation Institute.

RÉAMONN, S. (1981), *History of the Revenue Commissioners*, Institute of Public Administration.

SMITH, A. (1776), *The Wealth of Nations Books IV–V*, London: Penguin (1999 reprint).

THE REVENUE COMMISSIONERS (2002), *Effective Tax Rates for High Earning Individuals,* http://www.finance.gov.ie

THE REVENUE COMMISSIONERS (2004), *Effective Tax Rates of Top 400 Earners: Report for the Tax Year 2001,* http://www.finance.gov.ie

THE REVENUE COMMISSIONERS (2003), *Annual Report – 2002,* http://www.revenue.ie

THE REVENUE COMMISSIONERS (2003), *Statistical Report – 2002,* http://www.revenue.ie

THE REVENUE COMMISSIONERS (2004), *Annual Report – 2003,* http://www.revenue.ie

THE REVENUE COMMISSIONERS (2004), *Statistical Report – 2003,* http://www.revenue.ie

THE REVENUE COMMISSIONERS (2005), *Annual Report – 2004,* http://www.revenue.ie

THE REVENUE COMMISSIONERS (2005), *Statistical Report – 2004,* http://www.revenue.ie

THE REVENUE COMMISSIONERS (2006), *Annual Report – 2005,* http://www.revenue.ie

THE REVENUE COMMISSIONERS (2006), *Statistical Report – 2005,* http://www.revenue.ie

THE REVENUE COMMISSIONERS (2007), *Annual Report – 2006,* http://www.revenue.ie

THE REVENUE COMMISSIONERS (2007), *Statistical Report – 2006,* http://www.revenue.ie

Section II

Value-Added Tax

2

INTRODUCTION TO
THE EUROPEAN DIMENSION

In this chapter, you will deal with the following:

- The European dimension to VAT

- The evolution of a common VAT system

- Council Directive 2006/112/EC

- Derogation

- The interplay between EU and domestic VAT legislation

- The role of the European Court of Justice

- The role of the European Commission

- The role of the Council of the European Union

- The role of the European Parliament

- The VAT Committee

- Mutual assistance

- The Fiscalis programme

2.1   Introduction

Any study of value-added tax (VAT) would be incomplete without reference to the international dimension of VAT and, more importantly for Ireland, the European dimension. All developed countries (with the notable exception of the USA) and an increasing number of developing countries have value-added tax, or a slight variant, often referred to as general sales tax (GST).

The VAT system in operation throughout the European Union is currently provided for in Council Directive 2006/112/EC, which directive came into force on 1 January 2007. Prior to that date, the Sixth Directive (Council Directive 77/388/EEC) provided the basis for the VAT system throughout the EU.

Council Directive 2006/112/EC forms the basis for national VAT legislation in the 27 EU member states. Furthermore, many developing countries have modelled their VAT system on that of the EU and, hence, have modelled their national VAT legislation on the Sixth Directive.

It has always been a condition of entry for each applicant Member State to have in place a VAT system which accords with the VAT Directive. Any derogation sought and received by an applicant will form part of its Treaty of Accession. Currently, the countries making application for admission to the EU are Turkey and a number of the former Yugoslav states, Bulgaria and Romania having joined with effect from 1 January 2007.

A very important element of the European dimension to VAT, and one which is often overlooked, is the fact that each Member State contributes a proportion of its VAT yield to the European Commission in order to fund, in conjunction with customs duties and GNP resources, the Commission itself, the Common Agricultural Policy, and various structural, regional and cohesion funds. The contributions are collectively known as Community Own Resources (COR).

2.2   The Evolution of a Common System of VAT

VAT was not the first indirect tax the public was obliged to pay in Ireland. While VAT was introduced on 1 November 1972 as one of the prerequisites for Ireland to join the then European Economic Community (EEC) on 1 January 1973, it replaced two indirect taxes that operated in Ireland from the 1960s until our accession to the EEC, namely turnover tax @ a rate of 2.5% (introduced in 1963) and wholesale tax @ a rate of 5% (introduced in 1966).

Apart from replacing these taxes with VAT, the EEC prohibited, and continues to prohibit, the use by any Member State of a tax similar in nature to VAT. Hence the abolition of both wholesale and turnover taxes in Ireland and taxes in other Member States considered similar in nature to VAT.

In 1972, the then six Member States of the EEC – Belgium, France, Germany, Italy, Luxembourg and the Netherlands – had in place a broadly similar VAT system, which was based on the First Council Directive (67/227/EEC) and the Second Council Directive (67/228/EEC) of 11 April 1967.

While the First and Second Council Directives provided a very loose framework for the then six EEC Member States and the three new members Denmark, Ireland and the UK, it was felt that a more integrated framework was necessary to harmonise national VAT legislation. With this increased harmonisation and integration in mind, the European Commission drafted the Sixth Council Directive of 17 May 1977 (77/388/EEC).

In 1977 the Sixth Directive (Council Directive 77/388/EEC) was implemented and took effect from 1 January 1978. The Sixth Directive was a major step toward integrating and unifying the VAT systems throughout the expanded EU. At the time of its implementation the EU consisted of nine member states with the then expectation of expansion to include 12 countries. The Sixth Directive consisted, eventually, of 61 Articles and 12 Annexes. For 18 of the current EU member states who were not members at the time of its introduction in 1977 – Greece (joined in 1981), Spain and Portugal (1986), Sweden, Finland and Austria (1995) and Cyprus, Czech Republic, Estonia, Hungary, Latvia, Lithuania, Malta, Poland, Slovakia and Slovenia (May 2004), Bulgaria and Romania (2007) part of each State's negotiations contained an undertaking to have a VAT system conforming with the provisions of the Sixth Directive in operation on accession. Throughout its 29 year existence the Sixth Directive was amended no less than 32 times.

A sign of just how complex VAT was becoming was the introduction of Council Regulation (EC) No 1777/2005, effective from 1 July 2006. The regulation gave legal effect to certain very specific guidelines (interpretations) in relation to a number of Articles of the Sixth Directive. These guidelines have been unanimously agreed by the VAT Committee (see 2.10 below).

The Sixth Directive and certain provisions of the First Council Directive remained in force until their repeal by Council Directive 2006/112/EC of 28 November 2006. The repeal was effective from 1 January 2007. (The Second Council Directive was previously repealed by the Sixth Directive).

A full understanding of VAT would not be possible without reference to Council Directive 77/338/EEC, commonly called the Sixth Directive, which came into force on 1 January 1978 and continued in force for 29 years until it was replaced by the Council Directive 2006/112/EC on 1 January 2007.

2.3 Council Directive 2006/112/EC – The VAT Directive

2.3.1 Introduction

With effect from 1 January 2007 a new directive, Council Directive 2006/112/EC of 28 November 2006, came into force. As taxation is one of the areas where unanimous voting is required, the adoption of this directive was by unanimous vote of the Council of the European Union (the Council). (The Council of Ministers of Finance of the Member States).

From the First Directive, through the Second Directive and the Sixth Directive to Council Directive 2006/112/EC we can see the ever-increasing complexity of VAT and the ever-increasing pursuit of conformity to a common VAT system throughout the 27 member states that currently form the European Union.

2.3.2   The VAT directive

Unlike its predecessor the Sixth Directive, Council Directive 2006/112/EC does not have a 'name'. Therefore throughout this book, from time to time, the current EU legislation in force governing the operation of VAT will be referred to as 'the VAT directive' or Council Directive 2006/112/EC.

As with any Directive, the VAT directive has the dual purpose of securing the necessary uniformity of Community law and, at the same time, respecting the diversity of national traditions and structures. The aim of the VAT directive is the harmonisation of the law while, at the same time, respecting the principle of subsidiarity.

The VAT directive is published in all the official languages of the European Union. It consists of a preamble, 15 Titles, broken down into a series of 413 Articles. It also contains a series of 12 Annexes.

The VAT directive was introduced on 1 January 2007 and replaced the Sixth Directive and that part of the Second Directive which was still in force at that time. At the time of its replacement the Sixth Directive had been amended several times and it was felt necessary to 'recast' it for reasons of clarity and rationalisation.

The VAT directive consists of a series of 'building blocks' through which the VAT system unfolds in a logical and rational manner. Thus Title I outlines the subject matter and scope of VAT, Title II defines the territorial scope of VAT, Title III defines an accountable person, i.e. a person who carries out transactions subject to VAT, Title IV defines taxable transactions, i.e. transactions which are subject to VAT, Title V defines the place where such transactions occur, and so on. It defines when VAT is chargeable, the amount on which VAT is chargeable, rates of VAT, exemptions from VAT, the right to deduct VAT and obligations. It also defines certain special schemes for traders and provides for derogation of its provisions.

2.3.3   Conformity and primacy

National VAT legislation, throughout the 27 EU member states, must conform with Council Directive 2006/112/EC. Where national legislation does not accord with the VAT directive, it being Community-based legislation, then the VAT Directive takes primacy and the offending national legislation must be amended. Established case law of the European Court of Justice (ECJ) determines that an appellant may rely on the VAT directive in challenging national legislation. For further information on the primacy of the VAT directive, readers should consult the ECJ case of *Ursula Becker und Finanzamt Münster-Innenstadt* (Case 8/81).

The ECJ has, over time, established the principle of 'direct effect' in relation to the provisions of the VAT directive. Thus, a person aggrieved by certain provisions of national VAT legislation may rely upon the provisions of the VAT directive before their national tax authorities.

2.3.4 Amendments

An amendment to the VAT directive, Council Directive 2006/112/EC, may be made only by means of an amending Council Directive. The European Commission initiates all amendments, which may come about for a variety of reasons.

An amendment must have the unanimous approval of the Council. A varying period of time is always granted to Member States to transpose any change brought about through an amendment to the Directive into national VAT legislation.

2.4 Derogation from Council Directive 2006/112/EC

Derogation occurs where a Member State is allowed to either retain or introduce a measure to national VAT legislation that derogates from the VAT directive. It is very important to be aware of this concept as the VAT directive cannot be relied upon to challenge the particular derogation which, by its very nature, will not accord with the VAT directive. Derogation from the VAT directive is always given by means of a Council Decision addressed to the Member State(s) concerned. To obtain derogation from a particular provision, the applicant Member State must obtain the unanimous approval of the Council. A prime consideration in deciding whether or not to grant derogation is certainty that it will not lead to distortion of competition in the EU.

In the case of Ireland, there are a number of derogations, some of which were retained on commencement of the then Sixth Directive in 1978 and some of which were since granted. Council Directive 2006/112/EC deals with derogation at Title XIII (Articles 370–396). Derogation is a complex matter. Some of the more important Irish derogations include those relating to property (2.4.1), catering (2.4.2) and admission to sporting events (2.4.3).

2.4.1 Property

Derogation in relation to property (derogation from Article 135 Council Directive 2006/112/EC) has existed since the introduction of the Sixth Directive in 1977. The creation of long leases (equal to or in excess of 10 years) in Ireland is deemed to be a supply of goods, which is liable to VAT when certain conditions are fulfilled (s4, VAT Acts 1972–2009).

A further derogation (from Article 21.1(a), Sixth Directive) was granted in 1997 which provided that the person to whom the supply is made is the person liable to pay the VAT where a surrender or assignment of a leasehold interest is made (s4(8), VAT Acts 1972–2009). In the case of a surrender, the accountable person is the landlord, and in the case of an assignment, the accountable person is the assignee. Article 199,

Council Directive 2006/112/EC now enables member states to make the recipient of certain supplies the person liable for the payment of VAT, thus negating the need for the derogation received by Ireland.

(Students are referred to Chapter 6, Property Transactions and Building Services, for a more detailed discussion of the VAT treatment of property transactions).

2.4.2 Catering

Derogation in relation to catering (derogation from Article 14, Council Directive 2006/112/EC) has also existed since the introduction of the Sixth Directive in 1977. The provision of food by means of a vending machine or, in the operation of a hotel, restaurant, canteen, bar, etc. is a supply of a service rather than a supply of goods (s5(2), VAT Acts 1972–2009). This derogation has been rendered somewhat superfluous by a subsequent decision of the European Court of Justice, which decided that the provision of a meal was the provision of a service rather than the supply of goods.

(Students are referred to Chapter 3 – The General Principles, for a more comprehensive discussion of what constitutes supplies of goods and services).

2.4.3 Admission to sporting events

Ireland is unique among EU member states in exempting from VAT the promotion of and admission charges to all sporting events. This derogation resulted from the permitted continuation of the VAT treatment that existed prior to the introduction of the Sixth Council Directive on 1 January 1978.

2.5 Community Legislation and Domestic Legislation – The Interaction

At the outset the interplay between legislation enacted at EU level (i.e. Directives, Regulations and Decisions) and domestic legislation (i.e. Acts, Regulations and Orders) may be difficult to understand. However, a basic understanding is necessary for a full appreciation of the operation of the VAT system.

EU Directives do not have 'direct application' in member states. By this we mean that a directive itself is not considered to be legislation in force in any member state. Therefore domestic legislation must be enacted to give effect to the provisions of an EU Directive. However, EU Directives do have 'direct effect', i.e. a person is entitled to rely on a Directive if it's provisions have not been given effect through the implementation of obligatory domestic legislation giving effect to the provisions of the directive (see 2.3.3 above).

In the case of VAT, the provisions of Council Directive 2006/112/EC are given effect in Ireland by way of the Value Added Tax Acts, 1972–2007.

Under Article 249 of the EC Treaty EC Regulations have 'direct application', i.e. EC Regulations do not require transposition into Irish law and are themselves considered to be legislation in force in each EU member state.

EC decisions (Council Decision) addressed to particular member states (e.g. in the case of derogation from the provisions of the VAT directive) have 'direct effect' and must be given force through the enactment of domestic legislation.

It is important to remember therefore that Community legislation will always take priority over domestic legislation in so far as the operation of VAT is concerned.

2.6 Role of the European Court of Justice

2.6.1 Introduction

Given the primacy of Community law and the development of legislation through the precedent of case law, the European Court of Justice (ECJ) plays a very important role as far as VAT is concerned.

The core mission of the ECJ is to strengthen the judicial protection of citizens of the EU and to ensure that EU law is interpreted uniformly throughout the EU.

To date, approximately 330 cases have been dealt with by the ECJ in relation to VAT. All judgments of the Court must be published in the *Official Journal of the European Communities* ("OJ").

Similar to our own Supreme Court, the ECJ is playing an increasing part in the development and interpretation of VAT legislation throughout the EU. Whilst the VAT directive lays out the groundwork it is increasingly left to the judiciary to interpret and therefore define rules relating to VAT.

2.6.2 Referrals for interpretation (preliminary rulings)

A VAT case may be referred, on a point of law/interpretation, to the ECJ for "preliminary ruling" by any of the courts in a Member State. Such a referral can be made by the Appeals Commissioner or by the District, Circuit, High or Supreme Courts in Ireland. Where interpretation is in doubt, the Supreme Court must refer the matter to the ECJ.

Generally, a referral is made to the ECJ to interpret a point of law or to interpret the meaning or intention of a particular part of the VAT directive. In such cases, the ECJ will issue a judgment in relation to the question(s) put to it – and only the question(s) put to it – and will then refer the matter back to the referring court in the Member State concerned to deal with the case. However, the referring national court dealing with the matter is bound by the interpretation of the ECJ and must accord with such interpretation in reaching its decision. Indeed, each and every decision/interpretation of the ECJ in relation to VAT must be given effect in the drafting and implementation of the national VAT legislation, in each Member State.

2.6.3 Infraction proceedings (failure to fulfil obligations)

Where the Commission is satisfied that a Member State has not transposed the VAT directive, or any amending Directive, into national VAT legislation, or where the

Member State is incorrectly interpreting or implementing Community law or has failed to implement a judgment of the ECJ, it may commence infraction proceedings against the Member State concerned at the ECJ.

Again, the decision of the ECJ is binding. It will also make a decision with regard to costs.

Prior to commencing infraction proceedings the Commission will issue a 'Reasoned Opinion' to the member state concerned indicting its concern in relation to a particular matter. The Reasoned Opinion may seek an explanation of the matter, and will generally make a recommendation as to how the Commission wishes to see the matter resolved.

In the past, the Commission has successfully taken infraction proceedings against Ireland on the matter of the application of VAT to toll charges. The ECJ held that toll charges were liable to VAT and were not VAT exempt, as had been the treatment in Ireland. As a result of the decision of the ECJ, the VAT Acts 1972–2009, were changed so that commercially operated toll charges became liable to VAT at the standard rate (currently 21.5%) from 1 September 2001.

(Students are referred to the case study at the end of this chapter.)

On 25 July 2006 the Commission issued a Reasoned Opinion to Ireland in relation to its treatment of local authorities when the Commission indicated that such bodies should be accountable persons in certain circumstances, and accordingly requested Ireland to amend its VAT legislation. As Ireland failed to amend its VAT legislation as requested the Commission, on 15 December 2006, commenced infraction proceedings against Ireland. A ruling by the ECJ is awaited at the time of publication.

2.6.4   Composition of the European Court of Justice

Since 1 January 2007, the ECJ has 27 judges, one from each Member State. Each is appointed for a term of six years. The judges come from a variety of legal backgrounds and few, if any, are judges in their own Member State. They are assisted by a number of attorneys (Advocates-General).

While dealing with cases, the ECJ sits in chambers. The court sits in chambers of three or five judges. Finally, there is the Grand Chamber consisting of 13 judges. The Grand Chamber deals with the most serious problems, such as a challenge to Community law, the need to depart from earlier jurisprudence, etc.

Generally, five judges sit together to hear a VAT case.

2.6.5   The Advocate-General's opinion

As indicated above, eight Advocates-General assist the ECJ. The Advocate-General examines relevant past case law, the legislation and the case to hand. He/she will prepare an opinion in relation to the case, which is published on the official EU website. The opinion is not binding precedent.

The Court, in issuing a subsequent ruling, may agree with the opinion of the Advocate-General or may disagree.

In a very small number of cases the matter may proceed directly to judgement without an opinion of the Advocate-General.

2.6.6 Binding precedent

As indicated above, the interpretation of the ECJ in relation to the VAT directive or its decision in any referral, appeal or infraction proceeding is final and binding. There is no higher arbiter in relation to VAT.

The Court's findings set precedent, which must be adhered to and may not be overturned, save in the most exceptional of circumstances. Indeed, some few cases referred to the ECJ have not been heard, on the basis that the Court indicated it had already opined on the matter raised.

2.7 Role of the European Commission

2.7.1 Introduction

From a VAT perspective, the European Commission has a number of very important roles. Given that VAT is a Europe-wide tax as opposed to a national tax, the requirement of the Commission's input is central to the progression and operation of the VAT system.

The Commission has a specific Directorate-General, DG XXI, which deals with taxation, including customs, the harmonised excises and VAT.

2.7.2 Initiating and drafting legislation

The Commission has a fundamental role in both initiating and drafting amendments to the Sixth Directive.

Only the Commission may initiate an amendment to Council Directive 2006/112/EC. Where the Commission determines that a particular amendment is required, or one has been requested by the Council, it drafts a proposed amendment and presents it to the Council. The Council may accept the amendment in full or reject it. In the case of partial acceptance, the Commission will be requested to redraft, taking account of the views of the Council.

As there is a requirement for unanimous approval by the Council for acceptance of an amendment, drafting can sometimes be a very long process before consensus is reached.

2.7.3   Monitoring transposition and implementation

Another key role of the Commission is monitoring the transposition of the VAT Directive and any subsequent amending Directives into national VAT legislation throughout the EU. The Commission continually monitors each Member State to ensure that each amending Directive has been transposed correctly into national legislation, as is obligatory.

In addition to transposition, the Commission will monitor implementation of the VAT Directive and amending Directives. It will ensure that both interpretation and administrative practice in relation to national VAT legislation is in accordance with the objectives of the VAT Directive.

2.7.4   Challenging divergence

The Commission will challenge any divergence from the objectives of the VAT Directive. Such divergence can occur as a result of incorrect transposition, incorrect interpretation or administrative practice in one or more Member States.

In the first instance, the Commission will write to the Member State(s) concerned advising it of their position, by way of a Reasoned Opinion (see 2.5.4 above), either asking for an explanation from or issue an instruction to the national tax authorities in relation to the issue. In the event of a failure to comply, the Commission will initiate a legal action at the ECJ, known as an infraction proceeding, against the Member State concerned (see 2.6.3 above).

It is worth noting that not all actions commenced by the Commission are successful. A binding decision will be made by the ECJ in all cases. The decision is binding on both the Commission and the Member State(s) concerned.

2.7.5   Lodging a complaint with the Commission

Any citizen of an EU Member State may lodge a complaint with the European Commission if they believe that a Directive, including the VAT directive, is not being implemented or if they believe national legislation is not compatible with EU legislation. The person does not have to be affected by the offending legislation or its non-implementation. There are set procedures for making a complaint. The Commission is obliged to keep the complainant fully informed in relation to the progress of the matter, the response of the Member State concerned and the actions being taken by the Commission.

Any action undertaken by the Commission will be published in official publications of the Commission indicating the issue of a Reasoned Opinion and/or the commencement of infraction proceedings.

An added incentive for the Commission is the fact that their own resources are funded from a percentage of the VAT yield in each Member State.

2.8 Role of the Council of the European Union

In adopting community laws the Council may be obliged to act by a simple majority of its members, by a qualified majority of its members or by a unanimous decision. In the policy area of taxation, the Council must act on the basis of a unanimous decision. The Council is the legislative body as far as VAT is concerned.

The Council is composed of different members (ministers from the governments of all 27 member states) depending on the policy area being dealt with. In the case of VAT, the Council consists of the Ministers for Finance/Economics from each of the 27 Member States, sometimes referred to as ECOFIN.

2.9 Role of the European Parliament

The European Parliament has a very limited role in the policy area of taxation. When the Commission proposes a Directive, it must consult the Parliament. The Parliament may approve, reject or make amendments to the Commission's proposals. The Commission is not obliged to take any account of rejections or amendments recommended by the Parliament.

2.10 The VAT Committee

Article 398, Council Directive 2006/112/EC, established an advisory committee known as the VAT Committee. It consists of representatives of the Member States and the Commission. The VAT Committee prepares guidelines for the tax authorities of the Member States, particularly in areas that are open to interpretation. Such guidelines are not binding on the Member States.

In 1997, the Commission proposed a Directive that would make the VAT Committee's opinions binding by transforming the committee into a regulatory committee. The Council has not adopted the proposed Directive.

2.11 Mutual Assistance – Cross-Border Co-operation

Given that VAT is a Europe-wide tax, a necessary element is the ability of Member States to pursue liabilities in other Member States, i.e., cross-border. Thus, there needs to be a mechanism whereby, if an accountable person resident or established in one Member State incurs a VAT liability in another Member State and fails to discharge (pay) the amount due, the Member State owed the VAT can pursue the debt. The facility is used where an accountable person fails to pay an amount of VAT due.

Two separate pieces of EU legislation deal with mutual assistance between member states Council Directive 76/308/EEC of 15 March 1976 and Council Regulation (EC)

1798/2003. The scope of both pieces of legislation is quite wide and the Council Regulation automatically forms part of Irish VAT legislation without the need for transposition. The tax authorities in one Member State may seek the assistance of the tax authorities in another Member State in relation to a wide range of matters.

The tax authorities seeking information send details of the information required to the tax authorities where the accountable person with the records which can produce the information resides or is established. Increasingly, with the growth of trans-border multinationals, the tax authorities in member states are actively seeking assistance from tax authorities in other member states through the use of these mutual assistance provisions.

The assistance sought may range from the pursuit of an assessment against an individual to the request for information to *'... help them to effect a correct assessment of VAT'*.

2.12   Fiscalis Programme

This is an EU action programme set up to reinforce the functioning of the various indirect taxation systems (VAT, harmonised excises, customs, etc.) of the internal market. The programme aims to achieve a high common standard of understanding of Community law among the tax officials of the various EU Member States and to continually improve co-operation among officials of the Member States and the Commission.

The programme generally consists of the exchange of officials between Member States for periods not exceeding six months. It also consists of the provision of training courses by the Commission in the field of indirect taxation for officials of the Member States.

In addition to the 27 EU Member States, the programme is also open to officials from applicant countries.

2.13   Case Law – Cross-Reference to Community Legislation

In reading case-law, i.e. cases referred to the ECJ, initiated prior to 31 December 2006 all reference to Community-based VAT legislation will be a reference to the relevant Article(s) in the Sixth Council Directive. With effect from 1 January 2007 all judgments on cases initiated thereafter will make reference to relevant Article(s) in Council Directive 2006/112/EC, the VAT directive.

Articles in the Sixth Council can be cross-referenced to Articles in Council Directive 2006/112/EC by referring to the Correlation Table, Annex XII, Council Directive 2006/112/EC.

2.14   Further Information

Further information on the institutes of the European Union may be found at: www.curia.europa.eu/en

Additional information on a wide range of publications about and by the various EU institutions may be accessed at www.bookshop.europa.eu

2.15   Summary

The following diagram summarises the European dimension of VAT.

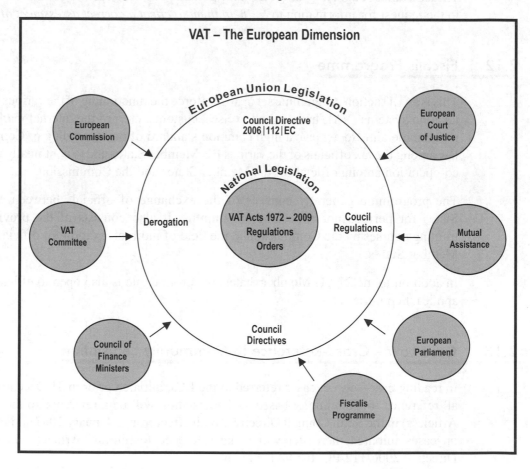

CASE STUDY

Commission of the European Communities v Ireland (Case C-358/97)

Your assignment is based on the judgment of the European Court of Justice in the case of the Commission of the European Communities v Ireland (Case C-358/97). The judgment was delivered on 12 September 2000.

Please read the judgment, which can be sourced at: www.europe.eu.int/cj/en/content/juris/index.htm.

It may take a second read to get used to the style of reporting used. The judgment is broken down into 79 numbered parts:

Part 1 outlines what the plaintiff, i.e., the European Commission, seeks.

Parts 2–9 outline the relevant Irish and European VAT legislation.

Parts 10–21 outline the procedure undertaken up to the commencement of litigation.

Part 22 outlines the substance of the case, i.e., the two areas where the Commission seeks a judgment.

Parts 23–58 deal with the first claim, i.e., the non-compliance with the Sixth Directive, being Ireland's failure to levy VAT on toll charges.

Parts 59–78 deal with the second claim, i.e., the failure by Ireland to pay to the Community's Own Resources (COR) the amount that should have been paid had VAT been levied on the toll charges.

Part 79 deals with the matter of costs. Finally, there is the decision of the Court.

WHAT YOU SHOULD NOW KNOW

On completion of this chapter, you should be able to:

- ✓ Discuss the importance of Council Directive 2006/112/EC.
- ✓ Understand the primacy of EU legislation.
- ✓ Explain the concept of derogation.
- ✓ Understand the interplay between EU VAT legislation and domestic VAT legislation.
- ✓ Discuss the role of the various institutions of the EU in relation to VAT.
- ✓ Understand cross-border co-operation in the field of VAT.
- ✓ Read and discuss an ECJ case.
- ✓ Complete the Assignments in Irish Taxation Law and Practice, Volume 2.

3

THE GENERAL PRINCIPLES

In this chapter, you will deal with the following:

- The transactional nature of VAT
- The scope of VAT
- National VAT legislation
- The charge of VAT
- The multi-stage nature of VAT
- Supply of movable goods
- Supply of services
- Place of supply of goods
- Place of supply of services
- Rates of VAT

- VAT-exempt supplies
- The "Package or Cocktail Rule"
- The "Two-Thirds Rule"
- Input VAT deduction
- Accountable persons
- VAT group registration
- Waiver of exemption
- The taxable amount (the consideration)
- "Deeming" provisions

3.1 General Principles

3.1.1 Introduction

Value-added tax (VAT) is a multi-stage, indirect tax on consumption.

The receipts from VAT in the tax year 2008, expressed as a percentage of gross tax receipts amounted to 29.95% (€17,992 million), compared with 29.10% in 2007 (see 1.6, Chapter 1). These figures indicate that the Exchequer is heavily reliant on the consumption of goods and services to generate public finance.

VAT is only levied where there is consumption. By "consumption", we mean that services or goods supplied have been consumed. There are numerous examples from ECJ case law that deal with the concept of consumption.

By "multi-stage", we mean that VAT is applied at each stage in the production and distribution of goods and services.

VAT is classified as an indirect tax because (unlike direct taxes, such as income tax and corporation tax, which are paid directly to the Exchequer by the person to whom the tax is applied) it is collected and remitted to the Exchequer at various stages by accountable persons (VAT-registered traders). The VAT remitted at each stage is based on the value added by the trader, hence the name Value-Added Tax (see 3.2.1 below).

Although collected and remitted in stages, VAT is paid entirely by the final consumer. In most cases, the final consumer is the general public.

VAT is also charged on goods imported from outside the EU (see 4.2.2, Chapter 4) and on the intra-Community acquisition of goods (see 4.2.5, Chapter 4).

3.1.2 The transactional nature of VAT

VAT is a tax that is applied to a transaction. A transaction consists of a supply (of goods or services) for which there is consideration (generally a payment). In addition, there must be a direct link between the supply and the consideration.

Sometimes a transaction is "deemed" to occur to enable a charge of VAT to be applied. (See 3.16 for further discussion on the use of "deeming provisions" in VAT legislation.)

A transaction liable to VAT is generally referred to as a "taxable transaction". A transaction not liable to VAT is referred to as either an "exempt transaction" or as a "non-taxable transaction".

3.1.3 The scope of VAT

For VAT to apply to a particular transaction, the transaction must fall within the scope of VAT. Once a transaction is within the scope of VAT, it may be liable to VAT at one of four differing VAT rates, or it may be exempt from VAT.

This is an important concept and is central to understanding VAT. Most economic transactions are within the scope of VAT, if not within Ireland, then within the territory of another EU Member State.

An employee supplying his/her services to an employer is not within the scope of VAT. Furthermore, the issue of new stocks, new shares, new debentures or new securities made to raise capital, is also outside the scope of VAT.

3.1.4 National VAT legislation

The operation of VAT in Ireland is provided for through the Value-Added Tax Acts 1972–2009 (VAT Acts), together with a number of regulations and orders. While the VAT Acts are the primary source of VAT law, many other pieces of legislation are made use of for the implementation and operation of VAT in Ireland. For example, legislation concerning the operation of the appeals procedure and many other procedural and administrative matters in relation to VAT is provided for in the Taxes Consolidation Act (TCA) 1997.

Each year, the VAT Acts are updated, generally by way of amendments contained in the Finance Act. They may also be amended by way of a European Communities Regulation, whereby a provision of Council Directive 2006/112/EC may be transposed immediately into national VAT legislation.

The VAT Acts are not yet consolidated. The primary Act is the Value-Added Tax Act 1972 and this is amended each year by certain sections of the Finance Act. The Value-Added Tax Act 1972 and the amending sections of the successive Finance Acts are collectively referred to as the Value-Added Tax Acts 1972–2009. The Revenue Commissioners have indicated that in early 2010 it is their intention to publish a new Consolidated VAT Act.

In November 2006 a large number of the then existing VAT regulations (in the form of separate Statutory Instruments) were repealed and replaced by Value-Added Tax Regulation, 2006 [SI 548 of 2006]. This new Statutory Instrument updated and consolidated existing VAT regulations; it also introduced a few new regulations. These Regulations can be viewed at *http://www.revenue.ie/publications/legisltn/si548_06.doc.*

As the VAT Directive came into force recently the various cross-references to the Directive contained in the VAT Acts, 1972–2009, were changed by provisions of Finance Act 2007. [Section 97 and Schedule 3 thereof refer].

3.2　The Charge to VAT

Section 2(1) of the VAT Act states:

s2 VA 72

"With effect on and from the specified day a tax, to be called value-added tax, shall, subject to this Act and regulations, be charged, levied and paid—

(a)　on the supply of goods and services effected within the State for consideration by a taxable person acting as such, other than in the course or furtherance of an exempt activity, and

(b)　on goods imported into the State."

This is referred to as the charging section and is the basis of the charge to VAT in Ireland. Analysing it, we see that, for VAT to apply, certain conditions must be met. These conditions define the scope of VAT in Ireland. The conditions are:

- there must be a supply of goods or services;
- the supply must be effected within the State (Ireland);
- the supply must be for consideration;
- the supply must be made by an accountable person, i.e., a person in business;
- the supply must be made in the course or furtherance of business.

A further condition has been added through the interpretation of the European Court of Justice (as exemplified in the case of Tolsma RJ (case 16/93) among others): There must be a direct link between the supply and the consideration. Thus if there is a supply and there is a consideration but the direct link between both is missing then the supply is not within the scope of VAT.

VAT is chargeable on imports from non-EU countries at the appropriate VAT rate as applies to the sale of the goods within the State.

3.3　VAT – A Worked Example of the Multi-Stage, Indirect Nature of the Tax

At this stage, a simple worked example will best illustrate the nature of VAT.

The term "input VAT" describes the VAT incurred by a VAT-registered person when he/she purchases goods or services from another VAT-registered trader.

The term "output VAT" describes the VAT charged by a VAT-registered person when he/she sells goods or services to another person (including another VAT-registered trader).

As you can see in the example below, the output VAT charged by a supplier of goods or services equals the input VAT incurred by the person acquiring the goods or services.

Example 3.1

	Input VAT (21.5%)	Output VAT (21.5%)	VAT Remitted
Manufacturer			
Produces goods	Nil		
Sale to wholesaler €10,000 + VAT		€2,150	
Receives payment of €12,150 (€10,000 + €2,150)			€2,150
Wholesaler			
Acquires goods for €10,000 + VAT	€2,150		
Sale to distributor for €14,000 + VAT		€3,010	
Receives payment of €17,010 (€14,000 + €3,010)			€860
Distributor			
Acquires goods for €14,000 + VAT	€3,010		
Sale to distributor for €21,000 + VAT		€4,515	
Receives payment of €25,515 (€21,000 + €4,515)			€1,505
Retailer			
Acquires goods for €21,000 + VAT	€4,515		
Sale to customer for €30,000		€5,308.64	€793.64
Receives payment of €30,000 (inc. VAT of €5,308.64)[1]			
Accumulated VAT remitted			€5,308.64

Customer pays €30,000 (including VAT of €5,308.64) to the retailer.

Ignoring the cost of the goods and looking only at the VAT amounts attached to the price, we see:

- the manufacturer remits €2,150 VAT but collects it from the wholesaler;

- the wholesaler remits €860 VAT but collects €3,010 VAT (€2,150 + €860) from the distributor;

- the distributor remits €1,505 VAT but collects €4,515 VAT (€2,150 + €860 + €1,505) from the retailer;

- the retailer remits €793.64 VAT but collects €5,308.64 VAT (€2,150 + €860 + €1,505 + €793.64) from the customer.

As you can see, the customer ultimately pays the entire VAT of €5,308.64 that accumulates on the series of transactions.

---

1   A Ministerial Order implemented in 1973 prohibits retailers from advertising VAT-exclusive prices to the general public. This is why the price quoted to the general public is VAT-inclusive.

Value-added

The value added by the wholesaler is the difference between sale price and cost price: €4,000 (€14,000 – €10,000). The VAT remitted is essentially based on the value added (€4,000 @ 21.5% = €860). In practice, this is calculated by deducting "input VAT" from "output VAT" (in this case, €3,010 – €2,150 = €860).

3.4   Supplies of Goods[2]

s3 VA 72   The following constitute a supply of movable goods for VAT purposes:

- the transfer of ownership of goods by agreement;

- the sale of movable goods through an undisclosed agent;

- the handing over of goods that are subject to a hire-purchase agreement;

- the compulsory purchase or legal seizure of goods;

- the transfer of goods within a business by a business person from a taxable activity to an activity exempt from VAT;

- the appropriation of movable goods by a business person for private use.

While most supplies of goods are quite straightforward, more complex supplies cause problems. The latter two supplies identified above may be complex, particularly as the business person may not realise a supply has taken place. These issues are best illustrated using the following examples.

3.4.1   Movable goods used for VAT-exempt purposes

If a business person applies movable goods previously used for making taxable supplies to an exempt use, then a supply for VAT purposes is "deemed" to have taken place (see 3.20 for further discussion of "deeming" in VAT legislation). For instance, if a bank which purchased a computer system for the purpose of its leasing business (taxable activity) starts using the computer system for transacting its lending business (VAT-exempt activity), then it is "deemed" to have made a taxable supply. The "deemed" consideration (see 3.18) in respect of the supply is the cost to the bank of acquiring the goods. The bank must account for output VAT on the supply. The bank is said to have made a "self-supply".

---

2   Special provisions relate to the supply of immovable goods (land and buildings) – see Chapter 6.

3.4.2 Movable goods appropriated for non-business use

If a business person appropriates movable goods for private use, then a supply for VAT purposes is also "deemed" to have taken place. For instance, if a car-dealer who purchased a car for the purpose of his business (taxable activity) decides to give the car to his daughter, then he is "deemed" to have made a taxable supply. The "deemed" consideration in respect of the supply is the cost to the car-dealer of acquiring the car. The car-dealer is said to have made a "self-supply" and he must account for output VAT on the supply.

3.5 Supply of Services

Section 5(1) of the VAT Act states that:

> " *'supply'*, in relation to a service, means the performance or omission of any act or the toleration of any situation other than the supply of goods …"

The definition is a broad "catch-all" one. It basically states that a supply that is not a supply of goods, is a supply of services. Apart from the more obvious services, the following are also supplies of services for VAT purposes:

- the supply of food and drink fit for consumption without further preparation:

  – by a vending machine,

  – by a hotel, canteen, restaurant, etc;

- the operation of a canteen by a business – the business is said to have made a "self-supply";

- the supply of a service through an undisclosed agent;

- leasing and hiring of goods.

3.5.1 Self-supply of a service

As a result of a decision at the ECJ in the case of Hotel Scandic Gasaback AB (case C-412/03) both the legislation and administrative practice dealing with the "self-supply" of a service has been changed with effect from 1 May 2006.

According to section 5(3), VAT Acts, 1972–2009, a self-service is deemed to occur, subject to the presence of a VAT regulation, in any of the following circumstances:

(a) Where physical movable assets of the business, upon which input VAT has been claimed (see 3.11), are used for the private purposes of the business or employees or for any purpose other than the business;

(b) Where a service is carried out free of charge by an accountable person for his/her own private use or that of employees or for any purposes other than those of such person's business;

(c) Where a business carries out a service for itself on the condition that if such a service was supplied by a third party, the input VAT incurred would not be deductible by the business.

However, before any of the above has effect in law, the specific circumstance must be provided for by way of VAT Regulations. To date, the only VAT Regulation made concerning the self-supply of a service is one which makes the supply of canteen services by a business, to its employees, a "self-supplied" service [Regulation 34, VAT Regulations 2006].

3.5.2   Canteens

Since 1 May 2006, the supply of services in a canteen provided by a business for its employees can be categorised as follows:

(a) where the canteen is operated by the business and a charge for meals is made, then VAT is accounted for on the actual receipts, or

(b) where the canteen is operated by a commercial caterer, acting as agent of the business and a charge for meals is made, then VAT is accounted for on the actual receipts by the business (which VAT is collected from the customer by the agent on behalf of the business), or

(c) where the canteen is operated by the business and no charge is made for meals, then VAT is accounted for on the cost of supplying the service (such cost may include caterer's charges, light, heat, catering equipment, canteen staff wages, canteen overheads, etc), or

(d) where the canteen is operated by a commercial caterer acting as principal (i.e. not an agent of the business), then VAT is accounted for,

   (i) by the business on the cost of supplying the service (such cost may include caterer's charges, light, heat, catering equipment, canteen staff wages and canteen overheads), and,

   (ii) by the commercial caterer on the receipts from customers and charges which he makes to the business.

You will note that in the case of (c) and (d) above a "self-supply" of a service occurs, i.e., a supply is being made because the business uses it assets to provide a catering service and does not receive any payment from the customer in relation to such supply. [Note in the case of (c) above, no payment is made at all and in the case of (d) above, no payment is made to the business concerned.] In both cases, the business must account for VAT on a "deemed" consideration, i.e., the cost to it of supplying the catering service to its employees.

Example 3.2

A manufacturing company provides a free canteen service to its employees. The canteen occupies 15% of the factory space. The monthly light and heating bill is €10,000. The company pays €15,000 per month to an independent caterer. It also pays €3,000 wages per month to canteen staff and annual rates of €120,000. Even though it does not charge for the meals, it must pay VAT each month, at 13½%, on the cost of supplying the service. The monthly VAT liability arising for the business in relation to the "self-supply" of a catering service amounts to €2,835.00 and is calculated as follows:

Cost (€)	Apportionment	VAT (@13½%)	
10,000	15%	202.50	[10,000 × 15% × 13½%]
15,000	none	2,025.00	[15,000 × 13½%]
3,000	none	405.00	[3,000 × 13½%]
120,000	/12 × 15%	202.50	[120,000 / 12 × 15% × 13½%]
		€2,835.00	

3.5.3 Private use of a business property

Where property that formed part of the assets of a business at the time of its acquisition or development is used during the 20-year period immediately following such acquisition or development for:

- the private use of the person in business or his/her staff, or

- a purpose other than those of the business,

then a supply of services is deemed to take place, i.e., a "self-supply" has occurred (see Chapter 6).

3.6 Place of Supply

Place of supply rules are very important in determining if a particular supply of goods or services is within the charge of VAT in Ireland (see 3.2). Here we will look at the general rules that determine the place of supply of movable goods and services.

Remember that a supply will only be liable to Irish VAT when the place of supply is determined to be Ireland.

3.6.1 Place of supply of goods

In the case of goods being transported across a border, the place of supply is where transportation begins. In the case of goods not requiring transport, the place of supply is where the goods are when the supply is made.

However, the following important exceptions should be noted:

Where goods are assembled or installed by or on behalf of the supplier, the place of supply is where the goods are assembled or installed, e.g., an Irish manufacturer contracts with a French supplier to supply and install machinery on his premises in

Ireland. As the machine is installed by or on behalf of the French supplier, the place of supply of the goods (the machine) is Ireland.

3.6.2 New council directives on place of supply of services

Council Directive 2008/08/EC of 12 February 2008, and Council Directive 2008/117/EC of 16 December 2008 amended the VAT Directive, substantially changing the rules in relation to the place of supply of services. The majority of the provisions come into force on 1 January 2010 (some of the provisions come into force on various dates subsequent to 1 January 2010), by which time domestic VAT legislation must be amended. The present rules relating to cross-border services, in particular those relating to the place of supply are described in Chapter 4. The next edition of this book will describe the rules as they will be after 1 January 2010.

Where goods are supplied on board vessels, aircraft or trains where the destination is in a Member State other than the state of departure, then the place of supply is where the transport begins, e.g., goods supplied on a ferry travelling from Ireland to France are deemed to be supplied in Ireland and, as such, are liable to Irish VAT. Goods supplied on a ferry from France to Ireland are deemed to be supplied in France and are liable to French VAT.

3.6.3 Place of supply of services

s5(5) VA 72 There is little difficulty in determining the place of supply of most services. The general rule in relation to the place of supply of a service is that the service is supplied where the supplier has his/her establishment. If the supplier has more than one establishment, the place of supply is where the establishment most concerned with the supply, is situated.

Thus, if you lease a car, or, have a haircut or stay in a hotel in Ireland, the place of supply is Ireland and you will be charged Irish VAT on the service.

However, there are some very important exceptions to this general rule. Among the most important exceptions to the place of supply rules are the following:

- Services connected with property (land and buildings) are deemed (see 3.16) to be supplied where the property is located. Thus, where an architect based in Dublin designs a building in Spain, the place of supply of his/her services is Spain. The supply of the service is not liable to Irish VAT.

- Transport services and services ancillary to transport (except cross-border transport of goods within the EU) are deemed to take place where the transport takes place. Thus, if an Irish-established haulage company carries goods from London to Moscow, the supply of the transport service will not be liable to Irish VAT.

The following services are deemed to be supplied where they are physically performed:

■ Cultural, artistic, entertainment, sporting, scientific and educational services;

■ Exhibitions, conferences and trade fairs;

■ Work on and valuation of movable goods. Thus, if a German-established engineering firm sends someone to repair a machine in a factory in Ireland, the place of supply is Ireland and the service is liable to Irish VAT.

■ Vehicles, ships,

■ The hiring out, by an Irish business, of means of transport (road/rail vehicles, ships, aircraft, etc.) that are used outside the EU. In this case, the place of supply is where the means of transport is "used and enjoyed". Therefore, if an aircraft leasing company established in Ireland leases a jet that will fly between Geneva and Moscow, then the place of supply is not Ireland and Irish VAT will not apply.

■ Certain services performed by "Intermediaries" are deemed to be supplied where the underlying transaction is supplied. [Note this is a new provision and will come into effect on 1 January 2008.]

■ When certain services are supplied cross-border, both the place of supply and the person liable to charge and account for the VAT changes. (This issue is considered in further detail in Chapter 4 – Cross-Border Trade.)

3.7   Rates of VAT Applied to Taxable Goods and Services

Once it has been established that a particular supply of goods or services is within the scope (charge) of VAT in Ireland (see the conditions at 3.2), then either of the following applies:

The supply of the goods or services is liable to VAT (referred to as "taxable supplies") at one of the following rates:

■ 0%   referred to as "the zero rate";

■ 4.8%   applicable to the sale of live cattle, horses, sheep, goats, pigs, deer and greyhounds and to the hire of horses and certain nominations;

■ 13.5%   the reduced rate;

■ 21.5%   the standard rate.

or

The supply of the goods or service is exempt from VAT (referred to as "exempt supplies").

Where goods or services are liable to a charge of VAT, they are referred to as "taxable goods" or "taxable services".

3.7.1 The zero rate

Goods and services liable to VAT at the zero rate are listed in the Second Schedule, Value-Added Tax Acts 1972–2009. The zero rate applies to the following:

■ goods exported to destinations outside the EU;

■ goods dispatched to VAT-registered customers in other EU Member States;

■ goods purchased by travellers for destinations outside the EU;

■ transport services associated with the export and import of goods (to/from destinations outside the EU);

■ the supply, repair and hiring of sea-going vessels of 15 tonnes or more;

■ the supply, repair and hiring of aircraft used by a transport undertaking operating chiefly for reward on international routes;

■ goods and services supplied to VAT 13B authorised businesses (see 4.8, Chapter 4);

■ most animal feeds (excluding pet foods);

■ most fertilisers (excluding packs of less than 10kg weight);

■ food and drink (with some notable exceptions, including: alcohol, soft drinks, biscuits, chocolate, ice cream, crisps, etc., meals served in a hotel, restaurant, etc., and hot take-away food);

■ oral medicines (for people and animals);

■ seeds and plants used for food production;

■ books and certain other printed matter;

■ children's clothing and footwear;

■ certain medical equipment;

■ the supply of goods or services to "International Bodies", recognised as such by the public authorities in their host Member State.

The list is not exhaustive – for a complete list, the VAT Acts should be consulted.

3.7.2   The reduced rate

Goods and services liable to VAT at the reduced rate (13.5%) are listed in the Sixth Schedule of the Value-Added Tax Acts 1972–2009. The reduced rate applies to the following:

- solid fuel, electricity, gas and oil used for domestic or industrial heating;

- the provision of food and drink

  - by a vending machine, or

  - in a hotel, restaurant, canteen, etc. (excluding alcohol and soft drinks);

- the provision of hot food, i.e., food heated to above ambient room temperature at a take-away outlet, supermarket, garage, etc;

- biscuits (non-chocolate);

- cinema admissions;

- fairground amusement admissions;

- commercial sports facility charges;

- golf clubs (membership and green fees);

- admissions to museums, galleries, exhibitions, etc., other than those operated by recognised cultural bodies;

- veterinary services;

- agricultural services;

- seeds and bulbs used for the agricultural production of bio-fuels;

- live poultry and live ostriches;

- shrubs and plants supplied by nursery and garden centres (non-food producing);

- newspapers, magazines and certain printed matter;

- hotel, guesthouse and caravan/campsite lettings;

- short-term car hire;

- works of art;

- certain antiques and manuscripts;

- repairs of goods (movable and immovable);

- personal services (health studio, hairdressing, manicure, etc.);

- non-oral contraceptives;

- most photography and development services;

- car-driving instruction;

- property (land and buildings);

- building work (see Chapter 6);

- concrete and concrete blocks;

- waste disposal.

The list is not exhaustive – for a complete list, the VAT Acts 1972–2009 should be consulted.

3.7.3 The standard rate

Once the supply of goods and/or services is within the charge of VAT, is not liable to VAT at the zero or reduced rates and is not exempt from VAT (see 3.8), then the standard rate (21.5% applies on or after 1 December 2008) applies. Thus, most goods and services not listed at 3.7.2, 3.7.3 and 3.8 are liable to VAT at the standard rate. Examples include the supply of adult clothing, cosmetics, jewellery, motor cars, computers, accountancy services, etc.

3.8 VAT-Exempt Supplies

Supplies of certain goods and services are exempt from VAT. This means that VAT is not applied to transactions involving such goods and services, even though the supply is within the scope of VAT.

It is very important to distinguish between transactions that are exempt from VAT and transactions that are liable to VAT at the zero rate. At first, they may appear the same, i.e., VAT is not applied. However, that is where the similarity ends. In the case of zero-rated goods, the trader is obliged to register for VAT, is obliged to retain records and, most importantly, can recover VAT charged to him by other VAT-registered traders and VAT charged on the importation of goods by him/her. In the case of exempt supplies, generally speaking, the trader cannot recover VAT charged to him/her by other VAT-registered traders or VAT charged on the importation of goods by him/her. He/she cannot register for VAT and is obliged, under VAT law, to retain only very limited records.

Goods and services that are exempt from VAT are listed in the First Schedule of the Value-Added Tax Acts 1972–2009. Exemption applies to the following:

- most financial services, including:
  - trading in shares;
  - banking services;
  - granting and managing credit,
  - management of certain investment undertakings;
- insurance services;
- insurance agency services;
- public postal services;
- national broadcasting services;
- the letting of property (land and buildings), including residential and student accommodation;
- educational services;
- professional medical services;
- dental services, dentures and dental prostheses;
- optical services;
- hospital services;
- care and welfare services;
- home care services supplied by persons recognised by the HSE under section 61A of the Health Act 1970;
- catering services to patients in a hospital/nursing home and to students in a school;
- promotion of and admission to circuses live musical and theatrical events (where no facilities for food or drink are available during the performance);
- passenger and accompanying baggage transport;
- travel agents and tour operators;
- betting and lotteries;
- lotteries;
- supply of investment gold (other than to the Central Bank of Ireland);
- funeral undertaking;

- supplies for the benefit of members by certain organisations (e.g., society/union membership, etc.);

- sporting facilities run by not-for-profit organisations;

- supply of movable goods where a right to deduct input VAT or acquisition did not arise (see 3.9.2).

The list is not exhaustive and for a complete list, the VAT Acts 1972–2009 should be consulted.

3.9   Multiple and Composite Supplies

Where two or more supplies (of goods and/or services) are made together, it may be difficult to determine whether there is a supply of a service, or goods, or both. Similarly there may be difficulty in determining the rate of VAT to apply to the supply or to particular parts of the supply. This is a very complex area and has been the subject of a number of Appeal hearings in Ireland and determinations by the ECJ.

With effect from 1 May 2006, the "package (or cocktail) rule" has been replaced. Since 1 May 2006, where more than one supply of goods and/or services are jointly supplied as part of a package for a single consideration, then the supply is treated for VAT purposes as either a "multiple supply" or as a "composite supply". The legislation defines both but in order to fully understand each, three other types of supplies are defined, namely an individual supply, a principal supply and an ancillary supply.

A "multiple supply" means two or more individual supplies made in conjunction with each other for a total consideration (price) covering all of the supplies and where the individual supplies do not constitute a "composite supply".

A "composite supply" means a supply comprising two or more supplies of goods and/ or services made in conjunction with each other where one of the supplies is a principal supply and the other supplies are ancillary supplies.

An "individual supply" is a supply of goods or services which forms part of a multiple supply but which is capable of being a supply of goods or a supply of a service in its own right.

A "principal supply" means the supply of goods or services which constitute the predominant part of a composite supply and to which any other supply made in conjunction with it is an ancillary supply.

An "ancillary supply" means a supply which is not physically and economically dissociable from a principal supply and can only be supplied as a means of better enjoying the principal supply.

In the case of a multiple supply (i.e. a supply consisting of more than one individual supply) the consideration will be apportioned between the various individual supplies and rates of VAT appropriate to each individual supply will be applied.

In the case of composite supply (i.e. a supply consisting of a principal and ancillary supply(ies)), the VAT rate applicable to the entire composite supply will be the VAT rate applicable to the principal supply.

Regulation 21, VAT Regulations, 2006, deals with the apportionment of consideration in the case of multiple and composite supplies.

The matter of what constitutes a multiple or composite supply has been made further complicated by the recent determination of the ECJ in the case of Talacre (case C-251/05). In its judgement the Court held that the supply of a caravan/mobile-home with fittings was in fact a single supply, liable to VAT at two different rates, one for the caravan and one for the fitted furnishings (fridge, cooker, etc.). [Many would previously have considered the supply to be either a composite or multiple supply.]

No doubt there will be further litigation in this area before the question of composite/multiple supplies is fully "bedded down".

3.10 The "Two-Thirds Rule"

The "Two-Thirds Rule" applies to both movable and immovable goods where there is a contract for the supply of a service. It is important that the contract be for the supply of a service and not for the supply of goods.

Where the VAT-exclusive cost to the supplier of the goods in a contract for the supply of a service is less than two-thirds of the contract price, the rate of VAT applicable to the entire supply is that applicable to the supply of the service.

Where the VAT-exclusive cost to the supplier of the goods in a contract for the supply of a service exceeds two-thirds of the contract price, the rate of VAT applicable to the supply of the goods is applied to the entire contract. In general, this means that the standard rate (currently 21.5%) is applied, instead of the reduced rate (currently 13.5%), to the supply.

Where the VAT-exclusive cost of goods exceeds two-thirds of the contract price, the supplier may apply the reduced rate of VAT to the service element of the contract when he/she shows separate consideration for the goods and for the service. The goods will be liable at the rate of VAT applicable to the goods – generally, the standard rate. Readers are referred to 6.11, Chapter 6, for further commentary on this issue.

3.11 Deduction of Input VAT

Central to the operation of a value-added tax system is a right, on the part of the VAT-registered person, to deduct input VAT charged to him/her by suppliers of goods and services, and a right to deduct VAT charged at the point of entry on imports. VAT should not be a cost on the trader, but rather a cost for the final consumer.

Consider a retailer who purchases goods and then applies VAT on the sale. The retailer has paid VAT to his supplier when acquiring the goods for resale. In order to ensure that the charge of VAT is a cost only to the consumer, the retailer may, in computing his/her VAT liability, deduct the input VAT charged to him/her by suppliers. This right of deduction does not apply just to input VAT incurred on goods resold but extends to all input VAT incurred on purchases made to enable the VAT-registered trader carry on his/her business.

Thus, where a retailer incurs VAT on acquiring a new premises, he/she is entitled to reclaim from Revenue the VAT incurred on the acquisition. Similarly, where a haulier incurs input VAT on a truck or on diesel, he/she may reclaim the input VAT incurred.

In computing the amount of VAT he/she must pay over to the Revenue, the VAT-registered trader may claim a deduction for input VAT incurred, before arriving at that amount. Where the output VAT payable on his/her supplies of goods and services exceeds the input VAT deductible on his/her purchases, an amount (the difference) is payable to Revenue. Where the input VAT deductible on his/her purchases exceeds the output VAT payable on his/her supplies of goods and services, the excess amount is reclaimed from Revenue.

Only a VAT-registered trader may deduct input VAT.

Sometimes a deduction of input VAT is referred to as a "recovery of input VAT" by the VAT-registered trader. You should be familiar and comfortable with the use of either deduction or recovery in relation to input VAT.

Deduction of input VAT is considered in further detail in Chapter 5 (Accounting for VAT: Invoicing, Deductions and Special Procedures/Categories).

3.12 Taxable Persons

A "taxable person" is any person who independently carries on any business in the State. Therefore, the concept of a taxable person covers persons who supply, in the course of business, goods and services which are liable to VAT and/or goods and services which are exempt from VAT. The redefinition of a taxable person has been included in the VAT Act in order to align it more fully with the VAT Directive.

A taxable person who supplies goods or services within the State, which are liable to VAT is also an "accountable person" (see 3.13).

3.13 Accountable Persons

s8 VA 72

The name "accountable person" is given to the person who is obliged to or elects to register for value-added tax, or to a person who waives exemption and registers for value-added tax. An accountable person is the only person who can legally charge VAT on a supply of goods or services.

An accountable person charges VAT on his/her supplies (output VAT) and may recover VAT incurred on the purchase of goods and services (input VAT), with some notable exceptions (see 5.3.2, Chapter 5).

The Revenue Commissioners maintain a register of accountable persons. A VAT registration number is issued to each person who so registers. The VAT registration number consists of the letter IE followed by seven numeric characters and one alpha character, e.g., IE 9907112K. (The IE identifies the VAT registration as having being issued in Ireland.)

3.13.1   Persons obliged to register and account for VAT

The following persons are obliged to register for VAT:

- established traders supplying taxable goods only, with an annual turnover in excess of €75,000 in a continuous 12-month period;

- established traders supplying taxable services only, with an annual turnover in excess of €37,500 in a continuous 12-month period;

- established traders supplying both goods and services, where the turnover from the supply of taxable goods is at least 90% of the total turnover, must register for VAT if turnover exceeds or is likely to exceed €75,000 in a continuous 12-month period;

- established traders supplying both goods and services, where the turnover from the supply of taxable services exceeds 10% of total turnover, must register when total annual turnover exceeds €37,500 in a continuous 12-month period;

- non-established traders (foreign traders) supplying goods/services in Ireland, regardless of turnover;

- With effect from 1 September 2008 principal contractors who receive supplies of services consisting of construction operations from subcontractors;

- business persons who receive certain services from abroad (see 4.3, Chapter 4);

- business persons who acquire goods (value in excess of €41,000) from other EU Member States (see 4.2.5, Chapter 4);

- foreign traders who sell goods from abroad to persons in Ireland who are not registered for VAT (distance selling – see 4.2.6, Chapter 4) and whose annual turnover exceeds €35,000 in a calendar year.

- Government departments, government agencies and local authorities that receive certain services from abroad (see 4.3, Chapter 4) or that acquire goods (value in excess of €41,000) from other EU Member States (see 4.2.5, Chapter 4);

3.13.2 Persons who exercise a "landlord's option to tax"

In certain circumstances a landlord may opt to tax rental income in respect of the letting of property, which letting would otherwise be an exempt supply of a service. (see Chapter 6 for a fuller discussion on this.)

3.13.3 Persons who exercise a "joint option for taxation"

In certain circumstances the vendor and purchaser of property, the supply of which would otherwise be exempt from VAT, may jointly exercise an option in writing to have VAT chargeable on the supply of the property. (see Chapter 6 for a fuller discussion on this.)

3.13.4 Electing to register for VAT

The following persons may voluntarily elect to register and account for VAT, although they are not obliged by law to do so:

- established traders whose turnover from the supply of taxable goods or services does not exceed the thresholds indicated above;

- farmers;

- sea fishermen who supply unprocessed fish to other accountable persons (e.g., to retailers, processors, etc.).

Given the very low thresholds for registration currently in force, the choice of electing to register for VAT will be available to only a very small minority of traders. More often than not, it will only be something that a trader who is employed and who sets up a small "after-hours" business will consider.

Where a trade is below the threshold for obligator VAT registration consideration may be made of whether or not a trader is making supplies to other VAT-registered traders or private individuals. Where supplies are being made to other VAT-registered traders, the additional charging of VAT will not increase the cost to the buyer.

Where the customer is a private individual, he/she is usually only concerned with the VAT-inclusive price. To add VAT to the sales price may either make the supply too costly or may erode the profit for the trader. In this regard, the rate of VAT applicable to the trader's goods or services is also relevant, i.e., whether it is 0%, 13.5% or 21.5%.

3.13.4.1 Advantages of electing to register for VAT

VAT incurred on most business expenses, including set-up costs, may be recovered if a trader is registered for VAT. Often, input VAT on setup costs may be at the standard rate (currently 21.5%), while output VAT may be at the reduced (currently 13.5%) or zero rates. Thus, there may be a cash-flow advantage for the business in registering for VAT.

For example, a small café will charge VAT to its customers at a rate of 13.5% but may be in a position to reclaim VAT on the cost of furniture, fittings and equipment at a rate of 21.5%. Accordingly, in a start-up situation (at which time the business is least likely to exceed the relevant turnover threshold), voluntarily registering for VAT may lead to a VAT refund.

A person who supplies zero-rated children's clothes is likely to find him/herself in receipt of VAT refunds on a regular basis. VAT on outputs will be zero, while VAT on inputs (e.g., telephone expenses, electricity, etc.) will be at various rates of up to 21.5%.

3.13.4.2 Disadvantages of electing to register for VAT

The main disadvantage of electing to register for VAT is the increased administrative burden:

- The business will be obliged to comply with the relevant VAT legislation and regulations, e.g., it will be obliged to issue VAT invoices, retain records that it otherwise would not have been obliged to retain and file returns on a regular basis. Such procedures can be expensive and time-consuming.

- The business will run the risk of being subjected to a VAT inspection and of being exposed to penalties and interest in respect of any additional amounts of VAT found to be due.

- The business may have to repay certain amounts of input VAT recovered upon cancellation of an election.

In addition, registering for VAT means that VAT will have to be charged to customers, and this could potentially lead to a loss of competitiveness.

3.14   VAT Group Registration

A number of accountable persons (including companies and individuals) may apply to the Revenue Commissioners for "group registration". The Revenue Commissioners may grant group registration status to the applicants where they are satisfied that the applicants are closely bound by:

- financial,

- organisational, and

- economic links.

In general, the applicants must be under common control, i.e., one or other of the applicants must exercise control over the others through share-ownership or otherwise. All applicants must be established in the State and an applicant may only be a member of one VAT group.

Each group member will continue to issue and receive VAT invoices in their own name in respect of transactions with non-group members.

The effect of the VAT grouping is to treat all VAT group members as a single accountable person insofar as VAT is concerned.

Once the VAT group registration has been approved, one of the applicants, the nominated group remitter, will file VAT returns on behalf of the group. VAT returns for the other individual companies are no longer necessary. The other members are designated "non-remitters" and cannot file VAT returns.

VAT is not applied to transactions between group members. Therefore, where one group member supplies goods or services to another group member, there is no requirement to issue a VAT invoice and VAT is not applied to the consideration.

While the VAT grouping provides administrative and possibly cash-flow benefits for the members, it should be noted that one of the effects of group membership is joint and several liability in relation to the VAT liability of any group member. For this reason, you generally do not find individuals or partnerships of individuals in VAT groups.

Where some of the VAT group members make VAT-exempt supplies (see 3.8) the inclusion of such business in the group may dilute the input VAT recovery (see 5.3.3, Chapter 5) of the group as a whole. The input VAT recovery of the group must reflect the input VAT recovery of each member of the VAT group.

This is an area where some companies engage in VAT planning to maximise input VAT recovery.

It should also be noted that property transactions between group members are excluded from the provisions of group membership, i.e., a supply of property from one group member to another may attract VAT.

The Revenue Commissioners may compulsorily group-register companies that have financial, economic and organisational links where it would be in the interests of efficient administration of the tax, or collection of the tax, to do so.

3.15   Waiver of Exemption

A person who supplies investment gold may waive exemption from VAT, register for VAT and recover input VAT incurred on the purchase of gold while continuing to exempt the supply of investment gold (which he/she has converted the gold into).

A formal application must be made to Revenue (local tax office) to waive exemption. A waiver is not normally backdated prior to the taxable period in which the application is made.

3.16 The Taxable Amount (Consideration)

The amount on which tax is chargeable, sometimes referred to as the "consideration", must be ascertained in order to apply the charge of VAT.

In most instances, the amount is easily identifiable. In a shop, the price displayed or the price you are quoted is the taxable amount. For us, the general public, the amount will be inclusive of the charge of VAT. For traders (e.g., buying from wholesalers/distributors), the amount will be exclusive of VAT, to which VAT will be added at the appropriate rate.

s10(1) VA 72   The legislation defines the amount on which tax is chargeable as being

> *"…the total consideration which the person supplying goods or services becomes entitled to receive in respect of or in relation to such supply of goods or services, including all taxes, commissions, costs and charges whatsoever but not including value-added tax chargeable in respect of the supply."*

Where the consideration does not consist wholly of money, the amount on which tax is chargeable is an amount equal to the open-market price of the goods or services supplied.

s10(3) VA 72   If, for any "non-business reason", the consideration is less than the open-market value, then the amount on which tax is chargeable is the open-market price.

This is a very important piece of legislation. Where Revenue believes that the amount on which the VAT charge has been calculated is below market value, anti-avoidance legislation enables it to impose market value and insist that the charge of VAT be calculated on the open-market price.

s10(3A) VA 72   Finance Act 2007 introduced additional anti-avoidance legislation which enables an officer of the Revenue Commissioners to determine the value on which VAT is chargeable on certain transactions between connected persons. This provision is for the purposes of dealing with potential VAT avoidance and evasion.

s10(4) VA 72   As outlined at 3.4 above, the use of goods for exempt purposes or the appropriation of goods for private use by an accountable person constitute taxable supplies, and the taxable amount for the purpose of charging VAT is the cost to the accountable person of acquiring the goods. Thus, where a car-dealer gives a new car from stock to his daughter, he must calculate the output VAT on the cost to him (exclusive of VAT) of acquiring the car.

3.17 "Deeming" Provisions in VAT Legislation

One of the less straightforward aspects of VAT is the use of "deeming provisions". Sometimes, a supply arises in circumstances where there is no consideration and/or where it is not in the "course or furtherance of business" – remember the conditions necessary for a charge of VAT.

Consider the case of the car-dealer who gifts a car to his daughter – there is no consideration and it is not in the course or furtherance of business. In order for a charge of VAT to arise, the supply is "deemed" to be for a consideration (the cost of acquiring the car) and it is "deemed" to be in the course or furtherance of business.

In the case of installed or assembled goods, the place of supply is "deemed" to be where the assembly or installation takes place. It could be where the supplier was located, it could be where the customer was located, but to define exactly where it is, VAT legislation uses the concept of "deeming".

In the case of a supply of food by a hotel, the legislation "deems" it to be a supply of a service and not a supply of goods.

In the case of an undisclosed agent, the VAT legislation "deems" that there is a simultaneous supply of a service to the agent and by the agent.

Where a local authority acquires goods from another EU Member State, the acquisition is "deemed" to have been made in the "course or furtherance of business" for the purpose of establishing a charge of VAT.

The VAT Acts 1972–2009 are littered with the word "deemed", and it is a concept which you should understand, as it is necessary to ensure that certain transactions come within the charge (scope) to VAT. It may be small comfort, but a UK Appeal Court Judge once said of VAT and VAT practitioners:

"Beyond the everyday world, both Counsel have explained to us, lies the world of VAT, a kind of fiscal theme park in which factual and legal realities are suspended or inverted ... in this complex parallel universe relatively uncomplicated solutions are a snare and a diversion."

– Lord Justice Sedley, Court of Appeal (E & W);
Case: Royal and Sun Alliance Insurance Group plc. (co/3494/99).

3.18   Summary

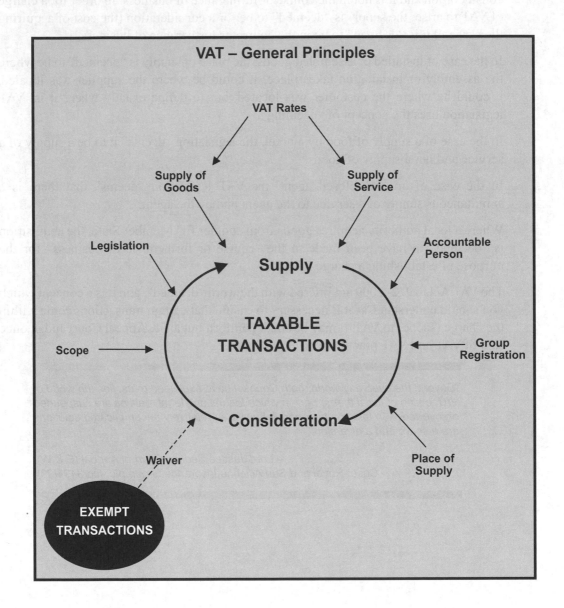

VAT – General Principles

VAT Rates

Supply of Goods

Supply of Service

Legislation

Accountable Person

Supply

TAXABLE TRANSACTIONS

Scope

Group Registration

Consideration

Waiver

Place of Supply

EXEMPT TRANSACTIONS

WHAT YOU SHOULD NOW KNOW

On completion of this chapter, you should be able to:

- ✓ Explain when the charge to VAT arises.

- ✓ Describe the transactional nature of VAT.

- ✓ Describe what constitutes a supply of goods.

- ✓ Describe what constitutes a supply of services.

- ✓ Understand and distinguish between a multiple supply and a composite supply.

- ✓ Describe the VAT treatment of the appropriation of goods for private use or for the purposes of an exempt activity.

- ✓ Understand when a "self-supply" does/does not arise in the case of canteens.

- ✓ Appreciate the importance of the place of supply.

- ✓ Identify the rates of VAT that apply in Ireland and the goods and services to which they apply.

- ✓ Identify goods and services that are exempt from VAT.

- ✓ Discuss the distinction between "exempt" and "zero-rated".

- ✓ Explain the Two-Thirds Rule.

- ✓ Identify those persons who are obliged to register for VAT.

- ✓ Identify those persons who may register for VAT.

- ✓ Discuss the advantages and disadvantages of voluntarily registering for VAT, and describe the factors that should be considered in deciding whether or not to voluntarily register for VAT.

- ✓ Identify the circumstances where an application for group registration may be granted, and discuss the advantages and disadvantages of having a VAT group registration.

- ✓ Explain what constitutes the taxable amount.

- ✓ Explain what is meant by "deeming" in VAT legislation.

- ✓ Calculate a basic VAT liability for an accountable person.

- ✓ Complete Questions and the Assignments in Irish Taxation Law and Practice, Volume 2.

4

CROSS-BORDER TRADE

In this chapter, you will deal with the following:

- Exported goods
- Imported goods
- Intra-Community dispatches
- Distance selling from Ireland
- Intra-Community acquisitions
- Self-accounting for VAT
- Distance selling into Ireland
- Goods installed and assembled
- Triangulation
- Services received

- Services supplied abroad
- Intra-Community transport services
- Use and enjoyment provisions
- Intermediary services
- VAT 13B authorisation
- Eighth and Thirteenth Directive reclaims
- VAT 60A
- Intrastat filing
- VIES filing

4.1 Introduction

With Ireland's accession to the then EEC in January 1973, the creation of the Single Market in January 1993 and the continued growth in the 'Celtic Tiger' years, trade with other EU Member States and third countries (those outside the EU) has expanded. Nowadays, almost every Irish business has some cross-border trading activity.

Whether it be a multinational exporting computers to the USA, a fruit distributor acquiring oranges from Spain, a local authority buying a fire engine in the UK, or an Irish architect designing an office block in France, a transaction has occurred and thought must be given to applying the correct VAT treatment.

From a VAT perspective, cross-border trade can first be divided into trade in goods or trade in services. A further distinction can also be made between goods and services being supplied into Ireland and goods and services being supplied out of Ireland. A distinction must be made between trade with other EU Member States and trade with third countries (non-EU countries). Finally a distinction should be made between trade with other businesses (B2B) and trade with consumers (B2C).

The Single Market refers to the economic marketplace, consisting of all 27 EU Member States. VAT presented one of the barriers to trade within the EU. With effect from 1 January 1993, measures were put in place, in so far as is possible, to ensure VAT does not act as a barrier to cross-border trade within the EU. Recently, further barriers to trade have been removed through the harmonisation of invoicing requirements (which is still ongoing) and the removal of the obligation for businesses in one Member State to appoint a fiscal representative in another Member State when trading there.

Further enhancements to the VAT system have been put in place via Council Directives 2008/8/EC, 2008/9/EC and 2008/117/EC which, commencing in January 2010, should further reduce barriers to cross-border trade within the EU.

Since 1 January 1993, VAT at the point of entry of goods into Ireland no longer applies in respect of goods acquired from other EU Member States, except where the goods concerned carry a duty of excise, i.e., alcohol, tobacco and mineral oil products. In the case of each of these, facility to defer the payment of VAT exists for traders.

> With effect from 1 January 2010 major changes already incorporated into the VAT Directive will be transposed into domestic VAT legislation. At the time of going to print the changes to domestic legislation have not yet been published. This book therefore describes the VAT treatment currently applying to cross-border trade in services, i.e. pre 1 January 2010. The next edition, 2010/2011, will describe the VAT treatment applying post 1 January 2010.

4.2 Goods

We will first look at cross-border trade in goods. Goods may be exported (to third countries) from Ireland, dispatched to another EU Member State, imported (from third countries) into Ireland, or acquired from another EU Member State. Note that the terms "import" and "export" are not used in relation to trade with other EU Member States since the inception of the Single Market in January 1993. Instead, we refer to "intra-Community supplies" or "dispatches" (supplies to other EU Member States) and "intra-Community acquisitions" (supplies received from other EU Member States).

4.2.1   Goods exported to third countries (non-EU countries)

Place of supply

s3(6) VA 72   As discussed previously (see 3.6, Chapter 3), the place of supply in relation to goods requiring transportation (as all goods to be exported require) is where transportation begins. Therefore, the place of supply is Ireland and a charge to VAT arises in Ireland. The goods must leave the country.

Rate of VAT

2nd Sch VA 72   The rate of VAT applicable to goods that are exported is 0% in all circumstances. Whether the purchaser is in business or is a private individual is irrelevant, and the rate applicable to such goods if supplied within Ireland is irrelevant. The logic behind this zero-rating is to ensure that Irish products remain competitive in an international context. If domestic rates of VAT were applied to exports, traders based in a jurisdictions with low VAT rates would have a competitive advantage over Irish traders. Furthermore, as VAT is a tax on consumption, we should recall that consumption in relation to exports will occur outside of Ireland.

Evidence of export

The legislation does not specify what constitutes evidence of export. However, an accountable person must retain sufficient evidence that the goods have been exported. Such evidence will include a cargo bill of lading, a cargo manifest, evidence of payment from abroad, contract for sale, etc.

In the absence of evidence, a Revenue official may contend that the goods have never left the country and apply the rate that would be appropriate if the goods were sold within the country.

Transportation and ancillary services

Transportation and ancillary transport services (loading, unloading, packing, etc.) supplied in respect of the export of goods are liable to VAT at 0%. Therefore, the internal leg of the transport, e.g., from the factory in Athlone to the port in Cork, is also liable to VAT at 0%.

4.2.2   Goods imported from third countries

VAT on Importation

s2 VA 72   Where goods are imported from third countries, VAT is applied at the point of importation in accordance with section 2, VAT Acts 1972–2008. VAT is applied to the total cost price (CIF), including any custom, excise, insurance and landing costs (transport costs) payable.

Rate of VAT

The rate of VAT applicable is the same as that applicable to the supply of such goods within Ireland.

Thus, where a load of concrete blocks is imported, the rate of VAT applicable is 13.5%. Where a consignment of bananas is imported from Equador, the rate of VAT applicable is 0%. Where computer parts are imported from Japan, the rate of VAT applicable is 21.5%. The logic behind the application of VAT at the point of importation is again to ensure that Irish suppliers remain competitive relative to their foreign counterparts. If Irish VAT was not applied at the point of importation, then, all other things being equal, it would be cheaper for Irish customers to import products from abroad than it would be to purchase identical products from an Irish supplier. The charge of VAT at importation is provided for in the charging section of the VAT Acts 1972–2009 (section 2).

However, where the importer has a VAT 13B authorisation, the rate of VAT applicable to the imported goods is 0% (see 4.8 below).

Transportation and ancillary services

The supply of domestic/intra-EU goods transport services in connection with the importation of goods, where the value of those services is already included in the declared value of the goods at importation, is zero-rated (see paragraph (xvia) Second Schedule, VAT Acts 1972–2009). The haulier supplying such services will be required to retain documentary evidence to support the zero rating. This may take the form of verification from the customs clearance agent or shipping company, etc.

4.2.3   Goods dispatched to persons registered for VAT in other EU Member States

"Intra-Community dispatches" refers to supplies to VAT-registered customers in other EU Member States. "Distance selling" refers to supplies to persons in other EU Member States not registered for VAT and is considered at 4.2.4.

Dispatches to VAT-registered persons

Where goods are dispatched from Ireland to VAT-registered traders in other EU Member States, the accountable person (in Ireland) must obtain and include his/her customer's VAT registration number on the invoice issued. He/she must also retain evidence that the goods have been dispatched. If the customer fails to supply a valid VAT registration number, then the provisions at 4.2.4 apply. The VAT-registered customer in the other EU Member State makes an intra-Community acquisition of the goods (see 4.2.5 below).

Place of supply

s3(6) VA 72 As discussed previously (see 3.6.3, Chapter 3), the place of supply in relation to goods requiring transportation (as all goods to be dispatched require) is where transportation begins. Therefore, the place of supply is Ireland and a charge to VAT arises in Ireland.

Rate of VAT

2nd Sch VA 72 The rate of VAT applicable to goods that are dispatched to customers registered for VAT in other EU Member States is 0%. The goods must leave the country.

Evidence of dispatch

The legislation does not specify what constitutes evidence of dispatch. However, an accountable person must retain sufficient evidence that the goods have been dispatched. Such evidence will include the customer's VAT registration number, a cargo bill of lading, a cargo manifest, evidence of payment from abroad, contract for sale, etc. Because of the risk posed by "carousel fraud",[1] Revenue will be particularly vigilant.

4.2.4 Goods dispatched to persons not registered for VAT in other EU Member States (distance selling)

s5(6) VA 72 Where physical goods are dispatched by an accountable person established in Ireland, to persons not registered for VAT (usually members of the general public) who reside in other EU Member States, the place of supply can be Ireland. However, once a certain threshold is reached, the Irish-established trader must register for VAT in the country to which the goods have been dispatched and, accordingly, that country is the place of supply. Alternatively, the Irish trader need not wait until the threshold is reached and may elect to register for VAT in the country to which the goods are dispatched from the outset.

Where goods are dispatched and the threshold is not reached, and the Irish trader does not elect to register in the other EU Member State(s), then Irish VAT is applied to the goods.

Once the Irish trader registers for VAT in the other EU Member State(s), then the place of supply is the country of destination and local VAT is applied to the goods. The trader is not required to have a presence in the country to register for VAT.

---

1   "Carousel fraud" is the term given to a particular type of VAT fraud facilitated by the Single Market. It usually involves high-worth, low-volume goods (e.g., computer parts). The goods are invoiced from trader to trader across several EU Member States with a particular trader "dropping out" of the chain. This trader will supply the goods, most probably to a legitimate trader in the same Member State as himself/herself, and will not account for the VAT invoiced. The customer will deduct the VAT charged because he/she will have a valid VAT invoice. It is estimated that carousel fraud costs the UK exchequer c.stg£1.5billion per year.

The registration threshold for distance selling into Luxembourg, Austria, Germany, France and the Netherlands is €100,000 per calendar year. The registration threshold for distance selling into Ireland, Spain, Belgium, Finland and Greece is €35,000 per calendar year. The registration threshold for distance selling into Italy is €27,889 and €35,000 for Portugal.

The registration thresholds for non-Euro countries are currently as follows:

■ UK (including the Isle of Man): Stg£70,000 per calendar year;

■ Sweden: SEK320,000 per calendar year;

■ Denmark: DKK280,000 per calendar year;

■ The 10 new EU Member States have each set a distance-selling threshold in local currency equivalent approximately to €35,000. On joining the Euro zone, the threshold for each will be €35,000.

Generally, distance selling applies to mail-order sales and goods advertised on the Internet but physically supplied.

4.2.5 Goods acquired from other EU Member States by persons registered (or required to register) for VAT in Ireland (intra-Community acquisitions)

s2(1A)
VA 72

Since 1 January 1993, a charge to Irish VAT arises on the acquisition of goods from other EU Member States. Section 2(1A), VAT Acts 1972–2009 states:

> *"… with effect on and from the 1st day of January, 1993, value-added tax shall, subject to this Act and regulations, be charged, levied and paid—*
>
> *(a) on the intra-Community acquisition of goods, other than new means of transport, effected within the State for consideration by an accountable person, and*
>
> *(b) on the intra-Community acquisition of new means of transport effected within the State for consideration."*

This is a very important concept. We normally think of VAT applying to the supply of goods. However, in this case the legislation stipulates that the charge to VAT also applies to the acquisition of goods in certain circumstances.

s3A VA 72

An intra-Community acquisition is deemed to occur where the dispatch or transportation of the goods ends in the Member State that issued the VAT registration number of the acquirer.

The procedure is a simple transposition of the procedure outlined in 4.2.3 (the dispatch of goods to a trader registered for VAT in another EU Member State). Accordingly, where an Irish-registered trader wishes to acquire goods from a French supplier, the Irish trader will furnish the French supplier with his/her Irish VAT number, the French trader will zero rate the goods in France and the Irish trader will account for Irish VAT on the acquisition in his/her VAT return.

Where the Irish trader is not registered for VAT in Ireland, French VAT should be applied (see 4.2.6 below).

The procedure is discussed in further detail below and differs slightly where the subject matter of the intra-Community acquisition is a new means of transport.

4.2.5.1   Acquisition of new means of transport

The legislation applies to everyone in the case of new means of transport (which are defined in the legislation and include new cars, new pleasure crafts and new small aircraft). Thus, when anyone already registered for VAT in Ireland, together with someone not registered for VAT, acquires a new means of transport from another EU Member State, he/she must account for VAT in respect of the acquisition. He/she must pay Irish VAT on the value of the means of transport. The vendor will not apply local VAT when he is satisfied that the new means of transport is dispatched from the Member State where purchased (see 4.2.3). The customer in Ireland accounts for VAT in respect of the acquisition.

In the case of persons not already registered for VAT (private individuals), payment of the VAT is made at a local vehicle registration tax (VRT) office, operated by the Revenue Commissioners.

4.2.5.2   Acquisition of goods by VAT-registered persons

s3A VA 72   In the case of goods, other than new means of transport, only accountable persons (VAT-registered persons) must account ("self-account") for the charge of VAT on the value of the intra-Community acquisitions, i.e., acquisitions from other EU Member States. Two important issues arise at this point, firstly, who must register and account for the VAT and, secondly, how do such registered persons self-account for the VAT in Ireland?

4.2.5.3   Who must self-account for VAT in Ireland?

s8(1A) VA 72 Anyone in business in Ireland who acquires goods (intra-Community acquisitions) totalling in excess of €41,000 in a continuous period of 12 months must register and account for VAT in respect of the acquisitions.

By presenting his/her VAT registration to the vendor in the other EU Member State, the person who acquires the goods will avoid the charge of foreign VAT (see 4.2.5).

Most people will already be registered for VAT. However, the obligation to register and self-account for VAT also extends to certain categories of persons who may not make accountable supplies in the normal course of their activities. Thus, anyone making VAT-exempt supplies (including hospitals, schools, charities, trades unions, etc.), unregistered farmers and fishermen, local authorities, Government departments, and statutory bodies, etc., is required to register for VAT in respect of intra-Community acquisitions. Such registration only applies in respect of the intra-Community acquisition of the goods. The threshold for such registration is €41,000 in a continuous 12-month period.

4.2.5.4 How is VAT accounted for on intra-Community acquisitions?

Once registered for VAT, the person accounts for VAT on the intra-Community acquisition by showing the VAT charged on the acquisition as output VAT on his/her VAT return.

In the case of persons making accountable supplies in Ireland (i.e., persons registered for VAT in respect of supplies of goods or services which are liable to VAT at 0%, 4.8%, 13.5% or 21.5%), a simultaneous input VAT credit for the same amount may be taken on the same return. This has the effect of rendering the transaction VAT neutral, i.e., output VAT = input VAT in respect of the intra-Community acquisition.

In the case of persons not making taxable supplies, i.e., anyone making VAT-exempt supplies (hospitals, schools, charities, etc.), unregistered farmers and fishermen, local authorities, Government departments and statutory bodies who were obliged to register in respect of the acquisition, an input VAT deduction may not be made. The output VAT (the charge of VAT arising on the acquisition) must be remitted by the VAT-registered person to the Collector-General.

Example 4.1: A trader making taxable supplies in Ireland

An Irish VAT-registered trader purchases a computer in France. He quotes his VAT registration and receives the goods without a charge of VAT. The acquisition of the goods creates an obligation on the Irish trader to account for VAT.

Thus, the trader will account for output VAT on the value of the goods received. However, as he/she uses the goods for the purposes of his/her taxable supplies, he/she may deduct a similar amount of input VAT. This renders the transaction VAT neutral.

Thus, the outcome is similar to the trader buying the computer in Ireland. The Irish supplier will charge the trader VAT, but the trader will be in a position to recover the input VAT on his/her VAT return. Accordingly, the VAT will not be a cost.

Example 4.2: A trader making exempt supplies in Ireland

An Irish insurance company purchases a computer in France. As its supplies are VAT-exempt, it is not registered for VAT. Where the total value of its intra-Community acquisitions exceeds € 41,000, it must register for VAT. It quotes its VAT registration to its cross-border supplier and receives the goods without a charge of VAT. The acquisition of the goods creates an obligation on the insurance company to account for VAT.

Thus, the insurance company will account for output VAT on the value of the goods received. However, as it uses the goods for the purposes of its VAT-exempt insurance supplies, it may not deduct a similar amount in lieu of input VAT (see below).

Thus, the outcome is similar to the insurance company buying the computer in Ireland. The Irish supplier will charge the insurance company VAT, but the insurance company will not be able to recover the input VAT, as it uses the computer for VAT-exempt supplies.

4.2.6 Goods acquired from other EU Member States by persons not registered (or required to register) for VAT in Ireland

Where physical goods are dispatched to Irish-resident persons not registered for VAT (usually members of the general public) by an accountable person established in another EU Member State, the place of supply can be the Member State from which the goods are dispatched. However, once a certain threshold (€35,000 in the case of Ireland) is reached, the foreign-established trader must register for VAT in Ireland and, accordingly, the place of supply will be Ireland. Alternatively, they need not wait until the threshold is reached and may elect to register for VAT in Ireland from the outset.

Where goods are dispatched and the threshold is not reached, and the foreign trader does not elect to register in Ireland, then the rate of VAT applicable in the country of dispatch is applied to the goods.

Once the foreign trader registers for VAT in Ireland, then the place of supply is Ireland and Irish VAT is applied to the goods. The trader is not required to have a presence in Ireland to register for VAT.

The registration threshold for distance selling into Ireland is €35,000 in a calendar year.

Generally, distance selling applies to mail-order sales and goods advertised on the Internet but physically delivered.

4.2.7 Goods installed or assembled

s3(6) VA 72 Throughout the EU, where goods are installed or assembled by, or on behalf of, the supplier, the place of supply is the country where the goods are installed or assembled.

Thus, if a German engineering company supplies machinery to a business in Ireland and sends employees to Ireland to assemble and/or install the machine, the place of supply of the machine is Ireland.

4.2.7.1 Who must account for the VAT on the supply?

Once it has been established that the place of supply of the goods is Ireland, we must determine who is obliged to account for the VAT incurred.

Where the buyer of the goods is a VAT-registered person or is making VAT-exempt supplies (including hospitals, schools, charities, etc., or an unregistered farmer or fisherman, a local authority, a Government department or a statutory body), then the buyer must account for the output VAT arising on the supply. If not already registered for VAT, the purchase of the goods may require the buyer to register for VAT if he is not already registered.

Where the goods have been bought for the purpose of its business by a person making supplies of taxable goods or services, then a simultaneous input VAT credit may be deducted by the buyer, thus rendering the transaction VAT neutral. In other cases (purchasers making VAT-exempt supplies, including hospitals, schools, charities, etc., or unregistered farmers and fishermen, local authorities, Government departments, and statutory bodies), the buyer must account for and pay the output VAT arising on the goods supplied to them and no input VAT deduction is available.

4.2.8 "Triangulation"

As we have seen above, the place of supply in relation to the intra-Community cross-border supply of goods between VAT-registered persons is where the transportation begins. A separate charge to VAT also arises on the acquisition of the goods in the country of destination.

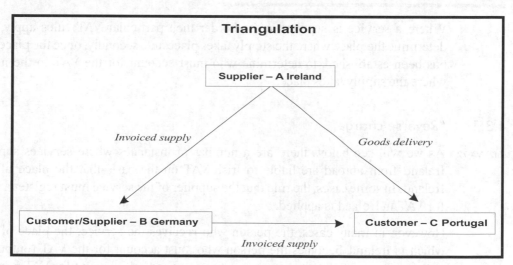

Very often, goods are supplied to an accountable person in one EU Member State and are in turn supplied by that person to an accountable person in another EU Member State. However, it is common for the goods to be shipped from the country of the first supplier directly to the country of the final customer without entering the country of the intermediate supplier (see diagram above).

In the above scenario, Supplier A sells goods to Customer B who in turn, as Supplier B, sells goods to Customer C. Under the normal rules, Customer/Supplier B would be obliged to register for VAT in either Ireland (if he took ownership of the goods there), or in Portugal, as he has made an intra-Community acquisition of the goods there if he doesn't take ownership in Ireland.

The concept of "triangulation", which applies throughout the EU, provides that Customer/Supplier B is not obliged to register for VAT in Portugal in respect of the intra-Community acquisition, rather Customer C is deemed to have made the intra-Community acquisition in Portugal.

The invoicing sequence in the case of "triangulation" is as follows:

- Supplier A quotes Customer B's VAT registration on his/her invoice and zero-rates the supply.

- Supplier B quotes Customer C's VAT registration on his/her invoice and zero-rates the supply.

- Customer C makes the intra-Community acquisition in respect of the goods and self-accounts for VAT on the acquisition.

Triangulation is another product of the Single Market, introduced in 1993. It is an attempt to reduce the bureaucratic burden associated with cross-border trade in the EU.

4.3 Services Received from Abroad

Where a service is supplied cross-border then particular VAT rules apply, firstly, to determine the place where the supply takes place and, secondly, once the place of supply has been established, to determine who must account for the VAT in the jurisdiction where the supply takes place.

4.3.1 "Reverse charge"

s8(2) VA 72 As we will see below, there are a number of instances where services supplied into Ireland from abroad are liable to Irish VAT on the basis that the place of supply is Ireland. In some cases, the rule that the supplier of the service must register and account for VAT in Ireland is applied.

However, in many cases, the person who **receives** the service, the place of supply of which is Ireland, becomes the person who must account for the VAT (output VAT). If not already registered, the person must register and self-account for VAT arising on the value of the service received. This principle is known as the "reverse charge". It is a very important principle.

Where the person in Ireland receives the service for the purpose of his/her taxable supplies, then he/she may claim a simultaneous input VAT credit, thus rendering the transaction VAT neutral.

The threshold for registration in the case of receipt of such services is nil.

4.3.2 The general rule

s5(5) VA72 The general rule in relation to the place of supply of a service is that the service is supplied where the supplier is established. However, there are many exceptions to this rule in the case of the cross-border supply of services.

4.3.3 Services connected with immoveable goods (land and buildings) located in Ireland

Place of supply

s5(6) VA 72 Throughout the EU, the place of supply of services connected with land and buildings is deemed to be where the property is located.

Among the services covered by this provision are the services of builders, estate agents, surveyors, architects, engineers, etc. Furthermore, the services of insurance providers, consultants, solicitors, accountants, etc. are also deemed to be supplied where the property is located where their service is connected with property.

Who must register and account for VAT in Ireland?

Where the services relate to construction operations and are supplied by a foreign sub-contractor to an Irish principal contractor then the principal contractor is the accountable person and must account for VAT on the services received. The foreign sub-contractor is not an accountable person and does not register for VAT in Ireland.

In all other cases, where foreign persons supply services connected with property located in Ireland, the foreign suppliers must register for and charge Irish VAT on their supplies, even though that foreign supplier has no establishment in Ireland.

4.3.4 Cultural, artistic and entertainment services supplied in Ireland

Place of supply

As we saw earlier, the place of supply of such services is where they are physically performed (see 3.6.2, Chapter 3).

Who must register and account for VAT in Ireland?

Where such a service is supplied by a person not established in Ireland to a promoter or agent established in Ireland, then the Irish-established promoter or agent is deemed to have received the service and, as recipient, must register and account for VAT in Ireland.

Where such a service is supplied by a person not established in Ireland to a promoter or agent also not established in Ireland, then the promoter or agent is deemed to have received the service and, as recipient, must register and account for VAT in Ireland.

4.3.5 Fourth Schedule services supplied cross-border to persons[2] in Ireland

Sch.4 VA 72 Fourth Schedule services are those which are listed in the Fourth Schedule, Value-Added Tax Acts 1972–2009. Among the services provided for by the Fourth Schedule are:

---

2   Persons include a VAT-registered person, anyone making VAT-exempt supplies (including hospitals, schools, charities, etc.), or an unregistered farmer or fisherman, a local authority, a Government department, or a statutory body.

- transfers and assignment of copyrights, licences, patents and similar rights;

- hiring out of movable goods;

- advertising services;

- services of consultants, engineers, consultancy bureaux, lawyers, accountants and similar services;

- data-processing and the provision of information;

- telecommunications services;

- radio and television broadcasting services;

- electronically supplied services[3];

- banking, financial and insurance services;

- provision of staff;

- services of intermediaries in procuring any of the above services for his/her principal.

- access to, and transmission through, natural gas and electrical distribution systems

(A copy of the Fourth Schedule can be found at Appendix I to this chapter.)

Place of supply

s5(6)(e) VA 72 Where any of the above services are received from a person established abroad by a VAT-registered person or anyone making VAT-exempt supplies (including hospitals, schools, charities, etc.), an unregistered farmer or fisherman, a local authority, a Government department or a statutory body, the place of supply is Ireland.

Who must account for the VAT?

s8(2) VA 72 Where any of the above services are received from a person established abroad by a VAT-registered person or anyone making VAT-exempt supplies (including hospitals, schools, charities, etc.), an unregistered farmer or fisherman, a local authority, a Government department or a statutory body, then the person liable to account for VAT in Ireland on the basis of the reverse charge (outlined at 4.3.1 above) is the recipient of the service.

If any of the above-mentioned persons receives a Fourth Schedule service, they are obliged to register for VAT, if not already registered. Each is required, though not

---

3   See 4.7.

obliged, to advise the foreign service provider (in the case of service providers from other EU Member States) of his/her Irish VAT registration.

Where the service has been received for the purposes of his/her business by a person making taxable supplies of goods or services, then a simultaneous input VAT credit may be deducted by the receiver, thus rendering the transaction VAT-neutral. In other cases (service receivers making VAT-exempt supplies (including hospitals, schools, charities, etc., unregistered farmers and fishermen, local authorities, Government departments and statutory bodies), the recipient must account for and pay the output VAT arising on the service received without a deduction of input VAT.

4.3.6   Fourth Schedule services received by private persons in Ireland

Where a private person receives a Fourth Schedule service in Ireland, the place of supply does not move to Ireland, and local VAT applicable in the country where the supplier is established will be applied by the supplier.

Where "electronic services" (see 4.7) are supplied by a non-EU based trader to private individuals in the State (a B2C supply), the non-EU-based trader is regarded as supplying services in Ireland and is obliged to register for Irish VAT, irrespective of the value of his turnover. This registration requirement may be avoided where the non-EU-based supplier avails of a special scheme, which involves registering for VAT in one EU Member State of his/her choice in respect of all supplies of electronic services to private individuals throughout the EU.

It is important to bear in mind that this regime applies only to electronically supplied services, not to other Fourth Schedule services (see 4.3.5) and only in the case of B2C supplies. The legislation ensures compliance with one of the primary OECD recommendations with regard to indirect taxation of e-commerce, i.e., that "consumption taxes should only apply in the jurisdiction of consumption."

4.4   Services Supplied Abroad from Ireland

4.4.1   Services connected with immoveable goods (land and buildings) located outside Ireland

Place of supply

The place of supply of services connected with land and buildings is deemed to be where the property is located. Examples of such services are listed at 4.3.3.

The place of supply of services by Irish-established persons is not Ireland. Irish VAT is not applicable, though local VAT in the country where the property is located may apply. This may or may not require the Irish service supplier to register for VAT in the particular country where the property is located. The rules applicable in each particular country must be observed by the Irish supplier.

4.4.2 Fourth Schedule services supplied cross-border to business persons outside Ireland and to private persons outside the EU

Where an Irish-established business person supplies a Fourth Schedule service (see 4.3.5) to a person in business abroad or to a private individual outside the EU, then the place of supply is where the service is received. A recipient established in another EU Member State must self-account for any local VAT arising. A recipient established outside the EU must observe his/her domestic VAT legislation, where appropriate. (However, please see the use and enjoyment rules outlined at 4.6.)

4.4.3 Fourth Schedule services supplied cross-border to private persons within the EU

Where an Irish-established business person supplies any Fourth Schedule service to a private person resident in the EU, the place of supply is Ireland. The Irish supplier must apply the Irish rate of VAT to his/her supply.

4.5 Intra-Community Transport of Goods

s5(6)(f)

VA 72

The place of supply of intra-Community transport services, i.e., the cross-border transport of goods from one EU Member State to another, is determined by specific rules. When goods cross borders, then the means, which transport the goods, also cross borders. The same rules apply throughout the EU. The general rule is that the place of supply is where the transport begins.

In the case of cross-border haulage, the place of supply and the person who must account for VAT depends on the VAT status of the customer (the person who receives the haulage services). (Remember, the following rules apply only where goods are transported across borders *within* the EU.)

4.5.1 Goods transported from Ireland to another EU Member State

Where the customer is registered for VAT in another EU Member State and advises the Irish haulier of his VAT registration in that State, the place of supply of the service is in the country that issued the customer with his/her VAT registration. The VAT-registered customer will self-account for the VAT on the haulage service in the country in which he/she is registered for VAT (see 4.3.1).

The haulier should always obtain a copy of the customer's VAT registration number and include it on his/her invoice to the foreign customer.

Remember, where the customer presents an Irish VAT registration, even where the goods are transported to another EU Member State, the place of supply is Ireland and the haulier charges Irish VAT.

Where the customer is a private individual in another EU Member State, the place of supply is Ireland (where transport begins) and the service is liable to Irish VAT.

4.5.2 Goods transported from another EU Member State to Ireland

Where the customer is registered for VAT in Ireland and advises the haulier in another EU Member State of his Irish VAT registration number, the place of supply of the service is Ireland (the country that issued the customer with his/her VAT registration). The VAT-registered customer will self-account for Irish VAT on the haulage service (see 4.3.1).

Where the customer is a private individual in Ireland, the place of supply is in the other EU Member State (where transport begins) and the service is liable to domestic VAT in that country. Where the haulier is not established in that country (say, an Irish haulier goes over to collect the goods), he will have an obligation to register for VAT in that country and charge domestic VAT on the haulage service provided for that customer.

4.5.3 Table detailing place of supply of intra-Community transport services

The table below details the place of supply and the person who must account for VAT.

Type/location of customer and direction of transport service	Place of est. of Haulier	Place of supply	Person who must account for VAT
Business customer in Ireland Intra-EU transport to/from Ireland	Ireland	Ireland	Haulier
Business customer in Ireland Intra-EU transport to/from Ireland	OMS[4]	Ireland	Business customer
Business customer in OMS Intra-EU transport to/from Ireland	Ireland	OMS	Business customer
Business customer in OMS Intra-EU transport to/from Ireland	OMS	OMS	Haulier if same OMS as customer, otherwise business customer
Private customer in Ireland or OMS Intra-EU transport to Ireland	Ireland/OMS	OMS of departure	Haulier
Private customer in Ireland or OMS Intra-EU transport from Ireland	Ireland/OMS	Ireland	Haulier

4.6 Cross-Border Services – Use and Enjoyment Provisions

In an attempt to eliminate certain "distortions of competition" that may arise due to the application or otherwise of VAT, "use and enjoyment" provisions, which are exceptions to the normal rules, are used. Below is a list of the current use and enjoyment provisions. The place of use and enjoyment of the service is used to determine the applicability of VAT.

---

4   (OMS = Other Member State of the EU.)

4.6.1 Hiring out of movable goods

s5(6)(d)
VA 72

When a person established outside the EU hires out movable goods, the goods are treated for VAT purposes as hired in the country in which the goods are used. For example, if a US company hires and uses computers in Ireland, the hire service is treated as taking place in Ireland and is chargeable to Irish VAT.

4.6.2 Leasing means of transport outside the EU

s5(6)(dddd)
VA 72

Notwithstanding the provisions of s5(5) VAT Acts 1972–2009, the place of supply of services, consisting of the hiring out of means of transport by a person established in the State, shall be deemed to be outside the Community where such means of transport are, or are to be, effectively used and enjoyed outside the Community.

4.6.3 Telecommunications services

s5(6)(dd) &
(ddd) VA 72

Where a telecommunications service provider established outside the EU supplies a service (including a telephone card) to a private person in Ireland, the place of supply is Ireland.

Where a telecommunications operator established in Ireland supplies a service (including a telephone card) to a private individual whose usual place of residence is outside the EU, but who uses and enjoys the service in Ireland, the place of supply is Ireland.

4.6.4 Banking, financial and insurance services

Where a banking, financial or insurance service is supplied, in the course or furtherance of business, by a person established in the State to a private person not usually resident in the State, and where the service is used and enjoyed in the State, then the place of supply is the State. (However, most such services are exempt from VAT.)

4.6.5 Electronic services

Where electronic services are supplied by a person from an establishment outside the EU to a private person in Ireland (B2C), the place of supply is Ireland. The service supplier is obliged to register for VAT in one Member State of the EU (see 4.7).

4.6.6 Money transfer services

Where money transfer services are supplied by intermediaries to non-EU principals, then the place of supply is Ireland, where the services are used and enjoyed in Ireland.

4.7   Electronic Services

s1 VA 72   Electronic services include the following:

(a) website supply, web-hosting, distance maintenance of programs and equipment;

(b) supply and updating of software;

(c) supply of images, text and information, and making databases available;

(d) supply of music, films and games, including games of chance and gambling, and of political, cultural, artistic, sporting, scientific and entertainment broadcasts and events; and

(e) supply of distance teaching.

Since 1 July 2003, electronic services have been added to the Fourth Schedule, giving effect to a European Council Directive. This affects the place of supply when they are received for business purposes (see 4.3.5). Thus, when received for business purposes in Ireland, the place of supply is Ireland and the recipient must 'self-account' for VAT on the value of the supply. Where electronic services are supplied by a non-EU-based trader to private individuals in the State, the non-EU-based trader is regarded as supplying services in Ireland and is obliged to register for Irish VAT irrespective of the value of his turnover.

This registration requirement may be avoided where the non-EU-based supplier avails of a special scheme that involves registering for VAT in one particular EU Member State of his/her choice in respect of all supplies of electronic services to private individuals throughout the EU. It is important to bear in mind that this regime applies only to electronically supplied services and not to other Fourth Schedule services (see 4.3.6) and only in the case of B2C. The new legislation ensures compliance with one of the primary OECD recommendations with regard to indirect taxation of e-commerce, i.e., that "consumption taxes should only apply in the jurisdiction of consumption".

4.8   Intermediary Services

Where an intermediary, acting in the name of and on behalf of, a principal, supplies services it can sometimes be difficult to determine the place of supply of such services.

An intermediary acting in the name of and on behalf of a principal, is often referred to as an "undisclosed agent." Such a person is deemed to simultaneous buy in and supply the service concerned.

The following general rules apply:

- the services of such intermediaries relating to intra-EU transport and ancillary services – the same rules as for the providers of such transport and ancillary services apply

- the services of such intermediaries relating to Fourth Schedule services the same rules as for the providers of the services concerned apply

- the services of such intermediaries relating to anything other than the above categories – the place of supply is where the underlying transaction takes place. However, where the customer of the such intermediary services is identified for VAT in a member state, other than where the underlying transaction takes place, then the place of supply is in the member states that issues the customer with his VAT registration.

4.9   VAT 13B Authorisation

s13A VA 72 When 75% or more of the turnover of a person who is registered for VAT in Ireland derives from the following:

- exports, and/or

- dispatches to VAT-registered persons in other EU Member States, and/or

- contract work carried out on goods imported, which will subsequently be exported, and/or

- contract work, which is deemed to be supplied in another EU Member State, i.e. where the customer (the owner of the goods) is registered for VAT in another EU member state,

then the VAT-registered person is a "qualifying person" and may apply to the Revenue Commissioners for a VAT 13B authorisation. The application is made by way of a VAT 13A form. Once granted, this authorisation will allow him/her to receive all imports at 0%, will allow him to receive and account for all intra-Community acquisitions at 0% and will enable all Irish VAT-registered persons to supply all goods and services to him/her at 0%. However, the purchase of cars, petrol, food, accommodation and entertainment services do not qualify for the 0% rate and the supplier must charge Irish VAT at the appropriate rate.

The authorisation is of enormous cash-flow benefit to the holder, is normally granted for a two-year period and is renewable. The holder is obliged to ensure that he/she continues to qualify for the authorisation, and he/she must advise Revenue and surrender the authorisation where his/her trade activity changes and he/she is no longer a qualifying person.

A copy of a VAT 13B application form can be found at Appendix II to this chapter.

4.10   Eighth and Thirteenth Directive Reclaims

Where a foreign trader not established in Ireland incurs VAT on goods or services supplied to him in Ireland and he/she uses such goods and services for the purposes of his/her taxable supplies abroad, then he/she may reclaim the VAT incurred in Ireland.

A foreign trader can incur VAT in Ireland in many ways, e.g., he/she may have to purchase diesel in Ireland, he/she may have to pay Irish VAT on services supplied in Ireland, renting space at a trade fair, etc.

In the case of a foreign trader who is registered for VAT in another EU Member State, a claim must be made under the provisions of the Eighth Council Directive. The name derives from the title of the European Council Directive implementing the right of recovery of VAT incurred in another EU Member State.

In the case of a foreign trader who is established outside the EU, but carries on an activity that would be liable to VAT if it were carried on in Ireland, a claim must be made under the provisions of the Thirteenth Council Directive. The name derives from the title of the European Council Directive implementing the right of recovery of VAT incurred in any EU Member State by a person not established in the EU.

The final date for filing the claim is 30 June of the year immediately following the year to which the claim relates. The claims must be filed with the Revenue Commissioners in Ireland, and must be supported by evidence of VAT registration/tax compliance in the country of establishment and by the original invoices issued by the Irish supplier of the taxable goods and services.

The reverse also applies, i.e., where a trader who is registered for VAT in Ireland incurs VAT in another EU Member State, then he/she may make an Eighth Directive reclaim in that country.

This is one of the many measures put in place to break down any barriers to international trade and to eliminate distortion of competition, which may arise. Of course it is not obligatory to file an Eighth or Thirteenth Directive claim.

The period that it takes to receive the refund varies enormously from country to country. In the case of Italy it can take several years to obtain an Eighth Directive refund.

Example 4.3: Eighth Directive Reclaim

A trader who is VAT registered in Ireland hires a booth at a trade-show in October 2006 in Germany to display his goods. The trade-show organiser issues him with a German VAT invoice charging €1,500 VAT.

If the Irish trader wishes to recover the German VAT charged to him then he must file a claim, supported by original invoice and evidence of his tax status in Ireland with the German tax authorities not later than 30 June 2007.

With effect from 1 January 2010 Council Directive 2008/09/EC will come into force. This will replace the Eighth Directive. Until then the provisions of the Eighth Directive remain in force.

4.11   VAT 60A/Authorisation

As we have seen, the place of supply is one of the important factors in determining whether or not a supply is within the charge of VAT. If the place of supply of the goods or service is Ireland and all other necessary conditions are fulfilled, then the supply is liable to VAT in Ireland. Where the place of supply is Spain and all other necessary conditions are fulfilled, then the supply is liable to VAT in Spain, and so on.

Where Ireland is the place of supply, generally the standard rate (21.5%) will apply to services provided to foreign-established traders. For example, an Irish company may hire out means of transport to a foreign customer or may provide administrative services. Both such supplies of services are liable to VAT in Ireland (see 4.3.2). As we have seen above, where the foreign trader uses the services for the purposes of making taxable supplies in his/her own country, he/she may reclaim the VAT charged via an Eighth or Thirteenth Directive reclaim.

A provision, known as a VAT 60A, exists to enable the service provider to charge VAT at 0% on services supplied in Ireland to foreign traders. The VAT 60A is issued to the foreign trader by the Revenue Commissioners. Once he/she presents the VAT 60A to the supplier of the services, the supplier is obliged to charge VAT at 0% on the particular service identified on the VAT 60A. This facility is of cash-flow benefit to the foreign trader who now no longer has to make a VAT Eighth/Thirteenth Directive reclaim.

Among the conditions necessary to obtain a VAT 60A[5] authorisation are:

■ the foreign trader must be carrying on an activity in his/her own country, which, if carried on in Ireland, would be a taxable supply;

■ the foreign trader must have evidence of VAT registration and/or tax compliance in his/her own country;

■ the foreign trader must not be making any taxable supplies in Ireland;

■ the service being supplied to the foreign trader must be on a regular basis (it may not be a once-off supply of a service).

The VAT 60A applies to the supply of services only and not to the supply of goods.

4.12   Intrastat Filing

Since the abolition of fiscal controls on the movement of goods within the EU from 1 January 1993, a mechanism had to be put in place to enable Member States to record data in relation to the movement of such goods. The mechanism of recording such

---

5   A copy of a VAT 60A form can be found at Appendix III to this chapter.

movement either into or out of Member States is by way of traders filing Intrastat returns.[6] The filing is only in respect of goods.

In the case of goods dispatched from Ireland to other EU Member States, the threshold for detailed filing is €635,000 annually. If the value of dispatched goods is less than this amount, then the value of the goods only must be included on the periodic VAT returns filed by the VAT-registered trader. Where the value of the goods exceeds the threshold, then detailed monthly Intrastat returns must be filed.

In the case of goods acquired in Ireland from other EU Member States, the threshold for detailed filing is €190,500 annually. If the value of acquired goods is less than this amount, then the value of the goods only must be included on the periodic VAT returns filed by the VAT-registered trader. Where the value of the goods exceeds the threshold, then the appropriate detailed Intrastat returns must be filed monthly.

As you can see, some traders may not have to file any Intrastat returns, some may have to file in respect of dispatches, some may have to file in respect of acquisitions and some may have to file in respect of both dispatches and acquisitions.

4.13   VAT Information Exchange System (VIES) Filing

The VAT Information Exchange System (VIES) is a database of information available to the tax authorities containing information in relation to dispatches of goods made by each accountable person registered for VAT in all Member States of the EU. The information is available to the VAT authorities in all EU Member States. Among other things, the database is used to combat fraud and to verify the veracity of VAT registration numbers supplied by traders in one Member State to traders in another Member State.

Any VAT-registered person who dispatches goods to VAT-registered persons in other EU Member States is obliged to file a periodic VIES return.[7] Unlike the Intrastat return, there is no *de minimus* threshold.

The return will include the name and VAT registration number of the supplier, the VAT registration number of each customer and the value of sales to each customer compiled on an quarterly basis.

Any person may input any EU VAT registration to a specific European Commission website and receive confirmation as to whether the number is a valid registration or not.

---

6   A copy of an Intrastat return can be found at Appendix IV to this chapter.
7   A copy of a VIES return can be found at Appendix V to this chapter.

4.14 Summary

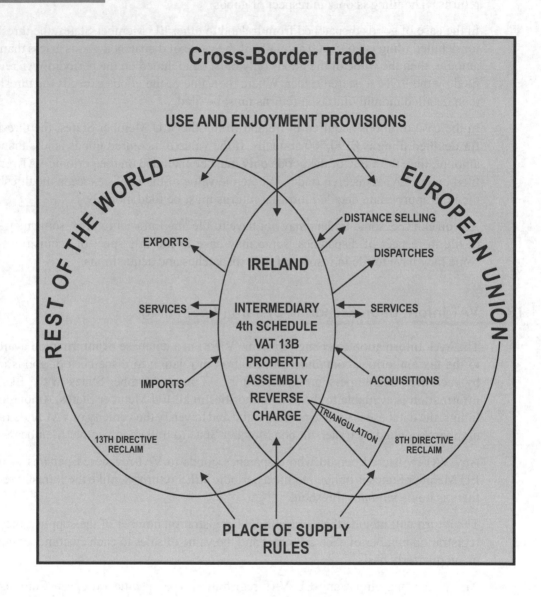

Cross-Border Trade

USE AND ENJOYMENT PROVISIONS

REST OF THE WORLD

EUROPEAN UNION

IRELAND

INTERMEDIARY
4th SCHEDULE
VAT 13B
PROPERTY
ASSEMBLY
REVERSE
CHARGE

EXPORTS

SERVICES

IMPORTS

DISTANCE SELLING

DISPATCHES

SERVICES

ACQUISITIONS

TRIANGULATION

13TH DIRECTIVE
RECLAIM

8TH DIRECTIVE
RECLAIM

PLACE OF SUPPLY
RULES

WHAT YOU SHOULD NOW KNOW

On completion of this chapter, you should be able to:

- ✓ Discuss the VAT implications of engaging in international trade with other EU Member States and with non-EU countries.

- ✓ Describe the distinction between the VAT treatment of goods and services supplied to and received from foreign traders.

- ✓ Explain the difference between exports/imports and dispatches/acquisitions, and describe the VAT treatment of each.

- ✓ List the circumstances in which VAT must be accounted for on intra-Community acquisitions.

- ✓ Explain the concept of "triangulation".

- ✓ Identify the place of supply of a variety of services supplied to or received from other countries.

- ✓ List the Fourth Schedule services.

- ✓ Explain the reverse charge principle.

- ✓ Identify the place of supply of intra-Community transport services.

- ✓ Describe the means of mitigating and/or recovering VAT on certain cross-border trade and the means for improving the cash-flow position of businesses involved in international trade.

- ✓ The place of supply of services provided by intermediaries.

- ✓ Describe the filing requirements in relation to cross-border trade.

- ✓ Be aware of intermediary service rules.

- ✓ Complete Questions and the Assignments in Irish Taxation Law and Practice, Volume 2.

Appendix I

Fourth Schedule

Services that are taxed where received:

(i)   transfers and assignments of copyright, patents, licences, trademarks and similar rights;

(i*a*)   hiring out of movable goods other than means of transport;

(ii)   advertising services;

(iii)   services of consultants, engineers, consultancy bureaux, lawyers, accountants and other similar services, data-processing and provision of information (but excluding services connected with immoveable goods);

(iii*a*) telecommunications services;

(iii*b*) radio and television broadcasting services;

(iii*c*) electronically supplied services; *see 4.7

(iii*d*) the provision of access to, and of transportation or transmission through, natural gas and electricity distribution systems, and the provision of other directly linked services (with effect from 1 January 2005);

(iv)   acceptance of any obligation to refrain from pursuing or exercising, in whole or in part, any business activity or any such rights as are referred to in paragraph (i);

(v)   banking, financial and insurance services (including re-insurance and financial fund management functions, but not including the provision of safe deposit facilities);

(vi)   the provision of staff;

(vii) the services of intermediaries who act in the name and for the account of a principal when procuring for him any services specified in paragraphs (i) to (vi).

Appendix II

Specimen of VAT 13A form

FORM VAT 13A

VALUE ADDED TAX - SECTION 13A VAT ACT 1972   (Note 1)

(BEFORE COMPLETING THIS FORM PLEASE READ THE NOTES ON THE REVERSE)

Application by a taxable person in accordance with Section 13A VAT Act 1972 for an authorisation to:

○ have certain goods and/or services supplied to him/her at the zero rate of VAT.

○ account for VAT on certain EC acquisitions at the zero rate.

○ import certain goods without payment of VAT   (Note 2)

1. Name: _____   2. Address: _____

3. Trading Name (if any): _____

4. Telephone number: _____   5. VAT Number: **IE** [ ][ ][ ][ ][ ][ ][ ][ ]

6. Exact description of Business: _____   (Note 3)

7. VAT 67 Authorisation number (if applicable)   [ ][ ][ ][ ][ ][ ]   (Note 4)

8. Group registration remitter's VAT number   IE [ ][ ][ ][ ][ ][ ][ ]   (Note 5)
   (if different to 5 above)

9. Turnover details

   (i)   Total annual turnover from supplies of goods and services IR£ _____   (Note 6)

   (ii) Annual turnover from zero rated intra EC supplies and exports included in (i) IR£ _____

DECLARATION

I/We hereby apply for an authorisation in accordance with Section 13A VAT Act 1972, and declare that the above information is correct. I undertake to supply any further information which may be requested in connection with this application.   (Note 7)

Signed: _____   Date: _____

Status: _____   (Note 8)

SPECIMEN

*ACCOUNTANT'S CERTIFICATE

(To be completed by the Accountant who normally prepares and/or audits the applicant's accounts)

I/We certify that the turnover for the year ended _____ in respect of the zero rated intra EC supplies and exports amounted to IR£ _____ and that this figure comprises at least 75% of the total annual turnover from supplies of goods and services for the same year.

Signed: _____

Date: _____

Accountant's Name & Address: _____

_____

_____

[*Not applicable in the case of a new company (see Note 7)]

**THIS APPLICATION SHOULD BE SUBMITTED TO THE APPLICANT'S LOCAL INSPECTOR OF TAXES.
FOR ADDRESSES SEE THE APPENDIX TO THE STATEMENT OF PRACTICE - *SP VAT/1/93.***

NOTES

Note 1

A Statement of Practice **SP VAT/1/93** which explains the provisions of Section 13A VAT Act 1972 in detail is available from your local tax office.

Note 2

The provisions of Section 13A VAT Act 1972 will apply in the case of all goods and services with the following exceptions:
(a)   certain motor vehicles and petrol
(b)   services consisting of the provision of food and drink, the hire of certain motor vehicles, accommodation, entertainment, and other personal services.

Note 3

Please describe the exact nature of the business.

Note 4

If you hold an Authorisation (VAT 67) which enables you to import raw materials free of VAT then, on receipt of your authorisation under Section 13A VAT Act 1972, you should immediately return the authorisation (VAT 67) to your local tax office.

Note 5

A group registration (i.e. where a number of companies are treated as a single taxable person for VAT purposes) can only be authorised under Section 13A if at least 75% of the *group's* total annual turnover is derived from exports or intra-EC supplies. Individual members of the group registration cannot obtain authorisations unless the group as a whole is authorised.

Note 6

Total annual turnover includes exempt supplies but does not include goods which have been sold and subsequently leased back.

Note 7

If the application relates to a new business it should be supported by a statement from the IDA or similar State agency that it is estimated that the zero-rated intra EC supplies and exports by the applicant will amount to at least 75% of the applicant's total turnover from supplies of goods and services in the first year of trading.

Note 8

The person who signs the application should be a person duly authorised to sign and be responsible for the accuracy of the information given e.g. company secretary, owner or partner.

Appendix III

Specimen of VAT 60A form

 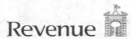

VAT 60A

Revenue

Application by a Foreign Trader who is not established in Ireland for relief from Value-Added Tax (VAT) on charges for Services supplied to it by Irish Supplier(s).

SPECIMEN

1. Details of Foreign Trader *Please complete this section in BLOCK LETTERS.* *Please read notes on page 2.*	**OFFICIAL USE ONLY** 1. Customer ID: _____

1. Details of Foreign Trader
Please complete this section in BLOCK LETTERS.
Please read notes on page 2.

Name: _____

Telephone Number: _____

Address: _____
_____
_____

Nature of Business: _____
_____

Where are you established?   ☐ Within EU
(✓Tick as appropriate)   ☐ Outside EU

Tax Reference Number: _____
If you are established in the EU please quote your VAT Registration No. If you are established outside the EU please quote your tax reference number in the country in which you are established.

Is this your first application for relief? *(✓Tick as appropriate)*   ☐ Yes   ☐ No

If no, please quote your Customer ID No. *(if available)*: _____
You will have been allocated a Customer ID No. by us when you made your first application for relief

OFFICIAL USE ONLY
1. Customer ID: _____

2. C/TS or C/Reg required? ☐ Yes ☐ No
Received on: _____

3. Date of C/TS: _____

4. Letter sent: _____
   Reply received: _____

5. Copy of lease required? ☐ Yes ☐ No
Received on: _____

6. Form 60B Issued on: _____

7. Period of validity of Approval to Zero-Rate
From: _____ To: _____

Copy to IOT _____ on _____

---

2. Details of Supplier of Services in Ireland
If there is more than one supplier, please provide the following details in respect of the other supplier(s) on a separate page.

Name: _____   Telephone Number: _____

Address: _____
_____

VAT Registration No.: _____   Local Tax Office : _____

Nature of Service(s) to be supplied to Foreign Trader detailed in section 1: _____

Will that/those Service(s) be provided on a continuous basis?: *(✓Tick as appropriate)* ☐ Yes ☐ No

Is the Irish supplier holding or will the Irish supplier hold stocks of goods in Ireland on behalf of the Foreign Trader detailed in section 1 [other than stocks of goods for onward consignment to regular customers, in accordance with Section 3(8) of the VAT Act, 1972 as amended]. *(✓Tick as appropriate)*
☐ Yes ☐ No

Page 1   *Please complete page*

3. Declaration

Anyone who knowingly makes a false statement for the purpose of obtaining relief from VAT is liable to penalties. Please delete text in <u>bold,</u> as appropriate, and then sign the declaration below if satisfied that it is accurate.

I/ _____ **(if the foreign trader is a company, insert the company name here)** wish(es) to apply for relief from VAT on charges in respect of services supplied to **me/it** within Ireland.

I declare that—
(a) **I supply/** _____ **(if the foreign trader is a company, insert the company name here) supplies** no goods or services in Ireland; *(The consigning of goods direct to Irish customers from outside Ireland does not constitute supply within Ireland.)*
(b) **I am/** _____ **(if the foreign trader is a company, insert the company name here)** is not established in Ireland;
(c) **I am/** _____ **(if the foreign trader is a company, insert the company name here)** is not registered nor **am I/is it** required to register for VAT in Ireland. *(If you need to check whether you are required to register for VAT in Ireland, please contact the Taxes Central Registration Office, Office of the Revenue Commissioners, 9/15 Upper O'Connell St., Dublin 1, Ireland. (Tel. 00 353 1 865 3000 or Fax 00 353 1 874 6078));*
(d) the services supplied to **me/** _____ **(if the foreign trader is a company, insert the company name here)** by the Irish supplier detailed in section 2 will be used only in connection with the business detailed in section 1 above; and
(e) the particulars stated on this form are true and correct to the best of my knowledge and belief.

Signature: _____   Date: _____

Position in the Company (if applicable): _____
If you are signing on behalf of a Company, you must be authorised to sign on behalf of the Company

<u>IMPORTANT</u> - *Please read the following notes <u>before</u> you submit your application*

1. Before you submit this claim form please ensure that—
   * you have completed all sections including signing the declaration in section 3;
   * you have attached all supporting documentation i.e.
     * an in-date Certificate of Taxable Status if you are established *within the EU*. This certificate is available from your own tax authorities , *or*
     * Certificate from the official authority of the country in which you are established if you are established *outside the EU*. This certificate should contain the name, address and official stamp of the official authority, your name, address and business registration number and a statement as to the nature of the economic activity carried on by you, *and*
     * a certified true copy of the lease if the business in which you are engaged involves leasing.
2. A person is established in a Member State if that person has in that State:
   * the seat of his or her economic activity, *or*
   * a fixed establishment from which business transactions are effected, *or*
   * if no such seat or fixed establishment exists, his or her domicile or normal place of residence.
3. Claim form together with supporting documentation should be returned to:
   VAT (Unregistered) Repayments Section
   Office of the Revenue Commissioners
   Kilrush Road
   Ennis
   Co. Clare, Ireland.

   Tel: 00 353 65 684 1200. FAX : 00 353 65 684 9248. E-Mail : unregvat@revenue.ie
4. Further copies of this claim form may be obtained from the above address or downloaded from our website (www.revenue.ie/publications/curntfms/curfrms.htm).

Appendix IV

Specimen of Intrastat form

Brief Note on the completion of the INTRASTAT return. (Full explanatory notes are included in the current VIES & INTRASTAT Trader's Manual which is available from the return address shown overleaf.)

Box 4 Separate forms are used for ARRIVALS (imports) and for DISPATCHES (exports). In the case of ARRIVALS "A" must be inserted in this box and for DISPATCHES "D" must be used.

Box 5 The number of lines of data entered on each return must be inserted here. If a continuation sheet is used, then the box must show the total no. of lines including those on the continuation sheet(s).

Column 8 Each line of data must be numbered for each return, starting at 1 each time i.e. if an arrivals return and a dispatches return are being submitted for the same period each return must start at 1 and the total number of lines in each return entered in boxes 5 on each form respectively.

Column 9 For Commodity Code use the Combined Nomenclature or the first 8 digits of the appropriate Customs and Excise Tariff Code.

Column 10, 11, 12, 13, 15 See Tables below. (Ireland's Country Code IE should never appear in column 10)

Column 14 INVOICE VALUE is the invoice value of the goods rounded to the nearest EURO but does not include V.A.T.

Column 16 From 1/1/98, most traders are not required to complete this column - Contact VIMA office regarding thresholds. For DISPATCHES (exports) the Statistical Value is the invoice value adjusted to an F.O.B. basis at point of exit from the State. For ARRIVALS (imports) the STATISTICAL VALUE will be the invoice value adjusted to a C.I.F. basis at the point of entry to the State. (Value to be rounded to the nearest EURO)

Column 17 Weight of the goods (exclusive of packaging) in kgs. as required.

Column 18 For certain goods as well as the weight in kgs, the secondary quantities are required e.g. no. of units or square metres. The Combined Nomenclature or the Customs and Excise Tariff of Ireland should be consulted.

N.B. Where a Trader has no Intra-Community Trade in a particular return period, a "NIL" return should be submitted for that period.

CODES FOR USE IN COMPLETION OF INTRASTAT RETURN

BOX 10/11 - E.U. COUNTRIES CODE

	Code
AUSTRIA	AT
BELGIUM	BE
CYPRUS	CY
CZECH REPUBLIC	CZ
DENMARK	DK
ESTONIA	EE
FINLAND	FI
FRANCE	FR
GERMANY	DE
GREAT BRITAIN	GB
GREECE	GR
HUNGARY	HU
ITALY	IT
IRELAND	IE
LATVIA	LV
LITHUANIA	LT
LUXEMBOURG	LU
MALTA	MT
NETHERLANDS	NL
NORTHERN IRELAND	XI
POLAND	PL
PORTUGAL	PT
SLOVAKIA	SK
SLOVENIA	SI
SPAIN	ES
SWEDEN	SE

BOX 12 MODE OF TRANSPORT

	Code
AIR	4
FIXED Transport Installations	7
Own Propulsion	9
POST	5
RAIL	2
ROAD	3
SEA	1
Transport by Inland Waterway	8

BOX 13 NATURE OF TRANSACTION

	Code
Sales/Purchases etc	1
Returned goods or replacement goods	2
Aid Goods	3
Goods for processing	4
Goods after processing	5
Goods for/after repair	6
Joint defence or intergovernmental production programmes	7
Building materials for construction contracts etc	8
Other transactions including hire and operational leasing over 2 years	9

BOX 15 DELIVERY TERMS

	Code
Carriage Paid to	CPT
Carriage Insurance Paid to	CIP
Cost and Freight (C & F)	CFR
Cost, Insurance and Freight	CIF
Delivered at Frontier	DAF
Delivered Ex Quay	DEQ
Delivered Ex Ship	DES
Delivered Duty Unpaid	DDU
Delivered Duty Paid	DDP
Ex Works	EXW
Free Alongside Ship	FAS
Free on Board	FOB
Free Carrier	FCA
Other terms not listed above	XXX

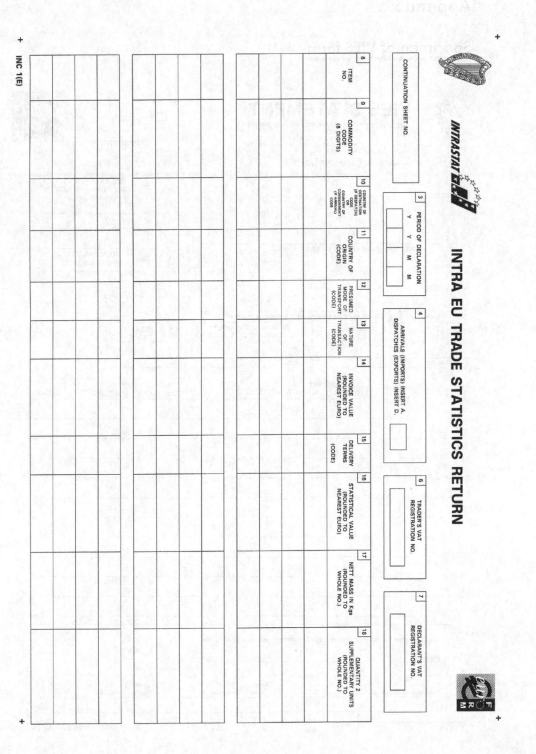

INTRASTAT

INTRA EU TRADE STATISTICS RETURN

CONTINUATION SHEET NO.

3 PERIOD OF DECLARATION
Y Y M M

4 ARRIVALS (IMPORTS) INSERT A. DISPATCHES (EXPORTS) INSERT D.

6 TRADER'S VAT REGISTRATION NO.

7 DECLARANT'S VAT REGISTRATION NO.

8 ITEM NO.	9 COMMODITY CODE (8 DIGITS)	10 COUNTRY OF DESTINATION (IF DISPATCH) OR COUNTRY OF CONSIGNMENT (IF ARRIVAL) CODE	11 COUNTRY OF ORIGIN (CODE)	12 PRESUMED MODE OF TRANSPORT (CODE)	13 NATURE OF TRANSACTION (CODE)	14 INVOICE VALUE (ROUNDED TO NEAREST EURO)	15 DELIVERY TERMS (CODE)	16 STATISTICAL VALUE (ROUNDED TO NEAREST EURO)	17 NETT MASS IN Kgs (ROUNDED TO WHOLE NO.)	18 QUANTITY 2 SUPPLEMENTARY UNITS (ROUNDED TO WHOLE NO.)

INC 1(E)

Appendix V

Specimen of VIES form

VIES STATEMENT

RETURN TO: OFFICE OF THE REVENUE COMMISSIONERS
VIMA OFFICE
P.O. BOX NO. 43 DUNDALK, CO. LOUTH
PHONE: (042) 9353300 FAX: (042) 9353388
LoCall: 1890-251010

DECLARANT'S NAME AND ADDRESS

FORM

FOR OFFICIAL USE

2	DECLARANT'S VAT REGISTRATION NO.

3	TRADER'S NAME AND ADDRESS	4	TRADER'S VAT REGISTRATION NO.

*** Please notify VIMA office of any change of address or trading circumstances ***

5	TYPE	6	PERIOD Y Y M M	7	TOTAL VALUE OF SUPPLIES OF GOODS (EXPORTS) IN EURO	8	NO. OF ITEMS
M/Q/A1/A2							

9 ITEM NO.	10 CUSTOMER VAT REGISTRATION NO. (See Table Overleaf)	11	VALUE OF SUPPLIES OF GOODS (EXPORTS) IN EURO	12 FLAG

13

I declare that the information given in this statement is true and complete.

Signature

Date

Full Name of Signatory

Area Code   Telephone No.

Area Code   Fax. No.

VS1(E)   VIEST1   [SEE NOTES OVERLEAF]

Brief notes on the completion of the VIES Statement. (Full details can be found in the current VIES and INTRASTAT Trader's Manual, which has been issued to each registered trader involved in Intra Community trade. Copies of the Manual are available from the return address overleaf.)

Box 7   This should be a total of all values entered in Column 11.

Box 8   The total number of lines of information should be entered here.

Column 9   Each line of data must be numbered in sequence starting with 1 for each return.

Column 10   You must quote your E.U. customer's VAT Registration No., not forgetting to include the national prefix. See table below.

     A Trader may contact VIMA to verify that a VAT Number quoted is valid.

Column 11   The total invoiced value of all goods supplied to the E.U. customer (whose no. you have shown in Column 10) is entered here, rounded to the nearest EURO.

Column 12   Insert "T" if the goods are involved in Triangulation (Contact VIMA for details).

Traders are advised that before inserting customers VAT Registration Number in Box 10, they should verify National Prefix and V.A.T. Number format with Table hereunder.

EU COUNTRY	NATIONAL PREFIX	V.A.T. NUMBER FORMAT	EXAMPLE
Austria	AT	One Letter and eight digits	AT U12345678
Belgium	BE	Nine digits	BE 123456789
Cyprus	CY	Eight digits and one letter	CY 12345678M
Czech Republic	CZ	Eight, nine or ten digits	CZ 12345678
			CZ 123456789
			CZ 1234567891
Denmark	DK	Eight digits	DK 12345678
Estonia	EE	Nine digits	EE 123456789
Finland	FI	Eight digits	FI 12345678
France	FR	Eleven digits	FR 12345678912
Germany	DE	Nine digits	DE 123456789
Greece	EL	Nine digits	EL 123456789
Hungary	HU	Eight digits	HU 12345678
Ireland	IE	Seven digits and one letter or six digits and two letters	IE 1234567A IE 1Z23456A
Italy	IT	Eleven digits	IT 12345678912
Latvia	LV	Eleven digits	LV 12345678912
Lithuania	LT	Nine or twelve digits	LT 123456789
			LT 123456789123
Luxembourg	LU	Eight digits	LU 12345678
Malta	MT	Eight digits	MT 12345678
Netherlands	NL	Eleven digits and one letter	NL 123456789B12
Poland	PL	Ten digits	PL 1234567891
Portugal	PT	Nine digits	PT 123456789
Slovakia	SK	Ten digits	SK 1234567891
Slovenia	SI	Eight digits	SI 12345678
Spain	ES	Eight digits and one letter or seven digits and two letters	ES A12345678 or ES X1234567W
Sweden	SE	Twelve digits	SE 123456789012
United Kingdom	GB	Nine digits or twelve digits if the number represents a sub-company within a group	GB 123456789 or GB 123456789123

N.B.   Where a Trader has no Intra-Community Supplies in a particular return period, a "NIL" Statement should be submitted for that period.

Value-Added Tax

VIES STATEMENT CONTD.

4	TRADER'S VAT REGISTRATION NO.

6	PERIOD Y Y M M

9 ITEM NO.	10 CUSTOMER VAT REGISTRATION NO.	11 VALUE OF SUPPLIES OF GOODS (EXPORTS) IN EURO	12 FLAG
B1	B2	B3	B4 E/L
B1	B2	B3	B4 E/L
B1	B2	B3	B4 E/L
B1	B2	B3	B4 E/L
B1	B2	B3	B4 E/L
B1	B2	B3	B4 E/L
B1	B2	B3	B4 E/L
B1	B2	B3	B4 E/L
B1	B2	B3	B4 E/L
B1	B2	B3	B4 E/L
B1	B2	B3	B4 E/L
B1	B2	B3	B4 E/L
B1	B2	B3	B4 E/L
B1	B2	B3	B4 E/L
B1	B2	B3	B4 E/L
B1	B2	B3	B4 E/L
B1	B2	B3	B4 E/L
B1	B2	B3	B4 E/L
B1	B2	B3	B4 E/L
B1	B2	B3	B4 E/L

VS1A(E)

5

ACCOUNTING FOR VAT: INVOICING, DEDUCTIONS AND SPECIAL PROCEDURES/CATEGORIES

In this chapter, you will deal with the following:

- Invoicing
- Deductibility of input VAT
- Accounting for VAT
- Margin Schemes & Special Schemes
- Local authorities

- Farmers
- Sea fishermen
- Agricultural contractors
- Hire Purchase transactions

5.1 Introduction

The purpose of this chapter is to illustrate how a trader arrives at his/her VAT liability. Remember, it is the VAT-registered person i.e. the accountable person, who must account for and pay the VAT, which he/she has collected, to the Collector-General.

This chapter will show how output VAT is arrived at, how deductions for input VAT incurred can be made and how a trader's VAT liability is computed. The chapter will also deal with certain categories of persons for whom accounting for VAT has its own peculiar rules.

5.2 VAT Invoices and Credit Notes

s17 VA 72   VAT invoices are central to the operation of the VAT system, not only in Ireland but also throughout the EU. For the supplier of the goods and services, the VAT invoice forms the basis for identifying output VAT. For the customer, the VAT invoice forms the basis for identifying input VAT.

Similarly, VAT credit notes form the basis for reducing the output VAT of the supplier. For the customer, the VAT credit note forms the basis for reducing input VAT.

5.2.1 Who may issue a VAT invoice/credit note?

Only a VAT-registered person may issue a VAT invoice or a VAT credit note. It is a serious offence for anyone other than a VAT-registered person to issue a VAT invoice.

5.2.2 In what circumstances must a VAT invoice be issued?

A VAT invoice must be issued by a VAT-registered person to another VAT-registered person in Ireland in respect of the taxable supply of goods or services. A VAT invoice must also be issued to a person registered for VAT in another EU Member State in respect of the taxable supply of goods or services. Furthermore, a VAT invoice must be issued to a person in another EU Member State in respect of distance selling. A VAT invoice must also be issued to State departments, local authorities, statutory bodies and persons carrying on exempt activities in respect of the supply of goods and/or services

5.2.3 When must a VAT invoice/credit note be issued?

A VAT invoice must be issued, at the latest, by the fifteenth day of the month immediately following the supply of the goods or services, or following receipt of part-payment in respect of goods or services, the supply of which has not been completed.

A further VAT invoice must be issued, at the latest, by the fifteenth day immediately following agreement between the parties where an increased consideration is paid or is payable in respect of the supply previously invoiced.

A credit note must be issued, at the latest, by the fifteenth day of the month immediately following agreement between the parties where a reduced consideration is paid or is payable in respect of the supply previously invoiced.

5.2.4   What details must a VAT invoice contain?

A VAT invoice must contain the following information:

- the name, address and VAT registration number of the person supplying the goods or services to which the invoice relates;

- the name and address of the person to whom the supply of goods and services is made;

- a sequential number, which uniquely identifies the invoice;

- where appropriate, the VAT registration number of the person in the other EU Member State to whom the goods/services are supplied and an indication that the customer must self-account for the VAT;

- the date of issue;

- the date of supply;

- a description of the goods or services supplied and, in the case of hiring, a description of the goods hired;

- the unit price exclusive of VAT and details of price reductions not included in the unit price;

- the consideration payable, exclusive of VAT;

- the rate(s) of VAT and the amount of VAT chargeable at each rate.

The amount of VAT indicated on the invoice issued by accountable persons must be specified in euro (€).

The amount of the consideration may be expressed in any currency.

5.2.5   Electronic invoicing

s17(14) VA 72 Since 1 January 2004, additional rules in relation to electronic invoicing have come into effect.

It is important to understand the mechanics. A physical invoice is no longer required to be issued. However, for the purpose of accountability and deductibility of VAT, an invoice must exist. While the supplier sends the details electronically to the customer, it is the customer who issues the invoice by printing a copy or by storing it in a legible form in his/her records. This invoice printed by the customer is deemed to have been issued by the supplier, provided the following four conditions are fulfilled:

(i) there must be agreement between the supplier and the customer allowing the customer to draw up and issue such an invoice;

(ii) the customer must be registered for value-added tax;

(iii) any conditions imposed by legislation on the supplier in relation to the form, content or issue of the invoice must be met by the customer;

(iv) agreed procedures must be in place for the acceptance by the supplier of the validity of the invoice.

With a paper invoice, it is very easy to establish whether the copy held by the supplier and that held by the customer are identical. This comparability must be capable of being carried out in the case of electronic invoicing.

The supplier is deemed to have issued the invoice and must retain a copy of it. The same details as are required on a physical invoice must also appear on an electronically issued invoice.

A specific regulation, Regulation 10, Value-Added Tax Regulations, 2006, lays down the conditions and system specifications governing the use and storage of electronic invoices.

Currently the invoice issued or received electronically must be transmitted by way of an electronic data interchange system or by an entity using an advanced electronic signature. The electronic data interchange system or the advanced electronic signature must satisfy certain criteria laid down in the above-mentioned regulation.

5.2.6 Settlement vouchers

A settlement voucher is an invoice issued by the customer on behalf of a supplier (not to be confused with electronic invoices). This mechanism is often used by large customers (e.g., retail chains) who buy goods from a large number of smaller suppliers. The customers must be VAT-registered. The settlement voucher becomes an invoice once accepted by the supplier.

5.2.7 Debit notes

A debit note is a credit note issued by a VAT-registered customer and becomes a credit note once accepted by the supplier.

5.3 Deductibility of Input VAT

s12(1)(a)
VA 72

Section 12(1), VAT Acts 1972–2009 states:

> *"In computing the amount of tax payable by him in respect of a taxable period, a accountable person may, insofar as the goods and services are used by him for the purposes of his taxable supplies or of any of the qualifying activities, deduct ..."*

A VAT-registered person may deduct input VAT incurred by him/her with the exception of certain non-deductible VAT (see 5.3.2). Sometimes, the word "recover" is alternated with the word "deduct". In the context of input VAT, they have the same meaning.

Deduction of input VAT is an essential part of the VAT system. Deduction of input VAT ensures that only the end-user pays VAT. In order to deduct input VAT, the VAT-registered trader must be in possession of a valid VAT invoice, issued by his/her supplier, in respect of the VAT, that he/she proposes to deduct.

A deduction of input VAT can be made in relation to VAT incurred on goods and services acquired, which are being sold on, and in relation to VAT incurred on capital and expense items, which are used by the business for the purpose of its taxable supplies.

Among the items in respect of which an accountable person may make a deduction are:

- VAT charged by other accountable persons in the taxable period, where supported by invoices;

- VAT charged on goods bought under a hire-purchase agreement;

- VAT charged on the importation of goods (see Chapter 4, Cross-Border Trade);

- VAT applicable on the intra-Community acquisition of goods (equal to the output VAT accountable on the acquisition) (see Chapter 4, Cross-Border Trade);

- VAT charged on goods, which a business has used for a taxable activity and then applied for the purposes of an exempt activity, or which have been appropriated to private use (see Chapter 3, The General Principles);

- VAT applicable to the acquisition of developed property which is chargeable to VAT by virtue of a joint option for taxation (equal to the output VAT accountable on the supply) (see Chapter 6 Property Transactions and Building Services);

- VAT applicable to the surrender/assignment of a legacy lease (equal to the output VAT accountable on the supply – see Chapter 6, Property Transactions and Building Services);

- VAT applicable to the receipt of certain services received from abroad (Fourth Schedule services – see Chapter 4, Cross-Border Trade);

■ the flat-rate addition (which is deemed to be VAT) paid by him/her to flat-rate farmers (see 5.5.2).

This list is not exhaustive but does include the main items in respect of which input VAT is deductible by an accountable person.

5.3.1 Qualifying activities

s12(1)(b)
VA 72

A deduction may be made for input VAT incurred on goods and services purchased to carry out (supply) certain "qualifying activities". Among such qualifying activities are:

■ the transport of passengers and their accompanying baggage outside Ireland;

You will recall that passenger transport in Ireland is VAT-exempt, which precludes deduction of input VAT incurred, e.g., VAT on the cost of buying a bus, VAT on diesel, etc. However, input VAT may be recovered where the passengers are transported outside the State, e.g., by train to/from Belfast, by ferry to/from France, by plane to/from UK, USA, etc.

■ the supply of goods in another EU Member State under the distance selling regime (see 4.2.4, Chapter 4);

■ financial and insurance services and related intermediary services supplied to persons outside the EU;

■ supplies of goods and services, the place of supply of which is outside Ireland and, which, if supplied in Ireland, would be liable to VAT;

■ the issue of new stocks, new shares, new debentures or new securities.

For example, where an Irish architect who designs a building in London (place of supply is the UK) incurs Irish VAT (e.g., the rent of his office in Dublin, stationery, etc.), he may deduct input VAT incurred. This is on the basis that his services, which are liable to VAT in the UK, would be liable to VAT in Ireland were it place of supply.

5.3.2 Non-deductible VAT

s12(3)
VA 72

A deduction of input VAT incurred on the purchase, importation and intra-Community acquisition of cars may not be made unless they are used as stock-in-trade (car-dealers), by a driving school for driving instruction, or by a car-hire firm.

A deduction of input VAT incurred on the purchase, importation and intra-Community acquisition of petrol may not be made unless it is used as stock-in-trade, i.e., it is for resale by petrol distributors, garages, etc.

A deduction of input VAT may not be made in relation to the purchase of accommodation, food and drink, entertainment, and personal services. However, with effect from

1 July 2007, a deduction may be made in respect of VAT incurred on accommodation provided during attendance at a 'qualifying' conference by VAT registered persons.

Input VAT may not be deducted where the goods or services concerned are used exclusively for VAT-exempt or non-taxable supplies.

Example 5.1

A garage may deduct input VAT on a car because it is in the business of selling cars. However, a manufacturing company that buys a car for an employee cannot recover the input VAT incurred, as it is not in the business of buying and selling cars.

Example 5.2

A VAT-registered firm holds a Christmas party for its employees. It incurs input VAT on the hotel bill (drinks, hire of room, entertainment, meals, etc.). It cannot recover (deduct) the VAT incurred.

Example 5.3

An insurance company buys a computer. It cannot recover (deduct) the input VAT because the computer is used for a VAT-exempt activity.

5.3.3   Partial deduction of input VAT

s12(4) VA 72 Where VAT has been incurred on goods and services that are used for both taxable and non-taxable supplies, referred to in legislation as "dual-use inputs", then special procedures must be put in place to ensure partial deduction (recovery) of input VAT incurred. Non-taxable supplies include exempt supplies and supplies outside the scope of VAT.

The cost should be directly attributed first, i.e., input VAT incurred on costs that can be directly attributed to taxable supplies may be fully deducted and input VAT incurred on costs that can be directly attributed to non-taxable supplies may not be deducted.

Where costs cannot be directly attributed, a partial deduction ratio must be agreed with the Revenue Commissioners. The ratio can be calculated on any basis

"…which correctly reflects the extent to which the dual-use inputs are used for the purposes of that person's deductible supplies or activities and has due regard to the rang e of that person's total supplies and activities".

Example 5.4

A bank uses a computer for its exempt activities (bank account transactions, lending, etc.) and its taxable activities (car leasing, debt factoring, etc). It may recover (deduct) a portion of the input VAT incurred. Where the turnover from the exempt activities is €9m and the turnover from the taxable activities is €1m, then it may be possible to agree a recovery ratio of 10% with the Revenue Commissioners in relation to the VAT incurred on the computer.

Thus, where input VAT on the computer amounted to, say, €200,000, only €20,000 may be deducted.

However, where the computer processed, say, 150,000 transactions, of which 50,000 related to exempt transactions and 100,000 related to taxable transactions, it may be possible to seek a 66% recovery ratio in relation to the input VAT. Recovery ratios must be by way of agreement with the Revenue Commissioners.

5.3.4 Deduction of input VAT – Motor Cars

A proportion of input VAT may be deducted on the purchase, hire, intra-EU acquisition or importation of certain motor vehicles, subject to the following conditions:

- The car (inc SUVs) must be first registered for VRT purposes on or after 1 January 2009

- It must have a level of CO_2 emissions of less than 156g/km (i.e. CO_2 emission bands A, B and C).

- It must be used primarily for business purposes. [Business purposes are defined as at least 60% business use].

- It must be used for business purposes for a period of two years or more.

If circumstances change within the two year period, i.e. the car is disposed of within two years, or it is used for less than 60% business purposes, and VAT credit has been claimed, then the accountable person is required to make an adjustment in the relevant taxable period, and repay a portion of the input VAT previously reclaimed.

If the car is disposed of or if 'business use' of the car by the accountable person drops below 60% then the claw-back of previously recovered VAT is calculated as follows:

Disposal or business use discontinues (or is used for less than 60% business use) within six months from date of purchase, acquisition or importation of the car	Clawback of all VAT deducted
Disposal or business use discontinues (or is used for less than 60% business use) in the period six to 12 months from date of purchase, acquisition or importation of the car	75% clawback of VAT deducted
Disposal or business use discontinues (or is used for less than 60% business use) in the period 12 to 18 months from date of purchase, acquisition or importation of the car	50% clawback of VAT deducted
Disposal or business use discontinues (or is used for less than 60% business use) in the period 18 to 24 months from date of purchase, acquisition or importation of the car	25% clawback of VAT deducted
Disposal or business use discontinues (or is used for less than 60% business use) after 24 months from date of purchase, acquisition or importation of the car	No clawback

Example 5.5

An accountable person purchases a new car for €30,000 in January 2009. He estimated that in excess of 60% of usage will be for business purposes. [Assume the VRT included in the price is €3,000.00]

The VAT included in the price is €4,777.77 (((30,000 – 3,000)/121.5) × 21.5) – note VRT is applied to the VAT-inclusive price of the car.

The VAT recoverable by the purchaser is €955.55 (4,777.77 × 20%).

5.4   Accounting for VAT

s19 VA 72   Every accountable person is obliged to account for the VAT charged by him/her to others and to account for any VAT arising on intra-Community acquisitions made. An accountable person must also account for any VAT arising on the basis of a 'reverse charge' (see section 4.3.1) (e.g. certain property acquisitions, receipt of Fourth Schedule services from abroad, etc) and must also account for any VAT arising on the basis of a "self-supply" (e.g., the appropriation of goods from the business).

An accountable person accounts for VAT charged by completing a periodic VAT return and including on it the details of the output VAT arising on the transactions outlined above.

The general rule is that a person accounts for VAT on the invoice basis, i.e., by reference to invoices issued in a particular taxable period. However, certain persons may account for VAT on the basis of monies received (see 5.3.6).

5.4.1   When is VAT due?

In the case where a VAT invoice is required to be issued, VAT chargeable is due when the invoice in respect of the supply is issued, or, if an invoice does not issue in due time, the VAT is due within the period in which the invoice should have issued, i.e., on or before the fifteenth day of the month immediately following the month in which the goods or services were supplied.

Where there is no requirement to issue a VAT invoice, the VAT is due at the time the goods or services are supplied.

In the case of intra-Community acquisitions, the VAT is due on the fifteenth day of the month immediately following that during which the acquisition occurs.

Where a stage payment/advance payment is received prior to the supply/completion of the goods or services, the VAT is due when the part-payment is received.

In the case of the receipt of Fourth Schedule services, the VAT is due when payment is made for the services.

In cases where goods is made for the services where goods are applied for the purposes of an exempt activity or where goods are appropriated for personal use, the tax is due when the exempt use or appropriation occurs.

5.4.2   VAT due on basis of cash receipts

Where more than 90% of an accountable person's turnover derives from supplies to persons who are not registered for VAT, or where an accountable person's total turnover does not exceed €1m in twelve continuous months, then such an accountable person may be authorised by the Revenue Commissioners to calculate the VAT due on the basis of monies received in each taxable period.

A person must apply to the Revenue Commissioner for this authorisation.

5.4.3   Bad-debt relief

Bad-debt relief applies where an accountable person has accounted for VAT on a supply of goods or services in respect of which he/she has issued a VAT invoice and subsequently the debtor defaults, i.e. fails to pay the accountable person for the supply. There is no relief in the case of a debt relating to property.

Obviously, the relief will not apply to an accountable person who accounts for VAT on the cash receipts basis, as failure by a debtor to pay will not require adjustment to the VAT payable.

In the case of an accountable person accounting for VAT on the invoice basis, VAT is due in the period in which the invoice is issued. Where, subsequent to the issue of the invoice, the debtor defaults and the supplier takes all reasonable steps to collect the debt but fails, then the supplier may reduce his/her VAT liability in the period in which the debt is being written off by the amount of the VAT on the bad debt.

As the purchaser will have deducted input VAT (remember, he/she has a valid VAT invoice), Revenue monitors the write-off of bad debts very closely, as the VAT amount involved is lost to the Exchequer.

5.4.4   Change of basis for calculating VAT due

An accountable person may change from the monies-received basis to the invoice basis at any time.

An accountable person may do this once he/she makes an application to the Revenue Commissioners and qualifies for the monies-received basis.

Adjustments are required in the event of a change of basis. Such adjustments are outlined in the Revenue Information Leaflet No. 22/01: "Moneys Received Basis of Accounting".

5.4.5   When is VAT payable?

It is very important to distinguish between VAT due and VAT payable. In the first instance, the VAT due and the VAT payable will rarely be the same amounts. This is due to the fact that the VAT due is the total output VAT as outlined above and the VAT payable is the VAT due less any input VAT that is deductible during the period.

In general, VAT payable must be paid to the Collector-General not later than the nineteenth day of the month immediately following a taxable period or an accounting period, whichever is appropriate.

In the case of a person who is obliged to account for VAT in respect of the intra-Community acquisition of a new means of transport, VAT is payable at the time of payment of vehicle registration tax (VRT) or, if VRT is not payable, at the time of registration of the vehicle.

5.4.6   A taxable period

A taxable period consists of two calendar months, commencing on the first day of January, March, May, July, September, November.

5.4.7   An accounting period

For most VAT-registered persons, an accounting period is the same as a taxable period, i.e. two months. The VAT return filed by the VAT-registered person is known as a Form VAT 3. A sample form can be found at Appendix I to this chapter. From time to time, the Collector-General may authorise accountable persons to make VAT returns and remit VAT payment for periods other than taxable periods.

Biannual VAT returns

Where a trader has an annual liability of less than €3,000 he may file two biannual returns each year.

Quarterly VAT returns

Where a trader has an annual liability of less than €14,000 but greater than €3,000 he may file four quarterly returns each year.

Monthly VAT returns

Where an accountable person is in a permanent VAT repayment position, he/she may be authorised to make monthly VAT returns. This is of cash-flow benefit to the accountable person.

Annual VAT returns

The Collector-General may authorise accountable persons to file annual VAT returns, i.e., one VAT return per year.

In the case of certain authorised small traders, the VAT payable must be remitted not later than the nineteenth day of the month immediately following the annual accounting period.

In the case of all traders, an application may be made to the Collector-General to account for VAT payable on an annual basis. In order to avail of this treatment, the accountable person is obliged to set up a direct debit facility and make a monthly payment on account to the Collector-General.

Once the annual VAT return is filed, the balance of VAT payable, if any, must be paid by the nineteenth day of the month immediately following the annual accounting period. Where the balancing payment is in excess of 20% of the tax payable for the year, then an interest charge of c.5.88% is applied to the balancing payment. This measure is to ensure that an accountable person does not postpone payment of what may be a very substantial VAT liability until the end of the accounting period.

5.4.8 Relief for non-refundable deposits

Where VAT has been accounted for on a deposit received in advance of a supply and where, due to a cancellation by the customer, the supply does not subsequently take place, then an adjustment may be made in the accounting period in which the cancellation occurs, reducing the amount of VAT due by the amount of VAT previously accounted for on the deposit, irrespective of whether or not the deposit is refunded to the customer. This is a new provision resulting from a recent decision of the ECJ. The reason for this relief is that as there has not been a supply (of goods or services) then there is not a transaction and therefore a charge to VAT cannot arise.

If a VAT invoice has been issued for the deposit received then a document, which the customer must treat as a credit note, must be issued by the supplier.

5.5 Margin & Special Schemes

VAT legislation provides for the use of 'Margin Schemes' and 'Special Schemes' in certain instances. In general such schemes are used to prevent distortions which may arise in the VAT system and generally apply to the final link in the supply, i.e. the end supply of certain goods and services to consumers. In the case of margin schemes, as the name implies VAT is charged, levied and paid on the 'margin' applied by the vendor to his sale to the consumer. We will briefly look at some of the schemes currently available below.

5.5.1 Second-hand goods (excluding cars) – margin scheme

The margin scheme allows dealers to apply VAT to the difference between the sale price and the purchase price of certain second-hand goods, works of art, antiques and collectors' items. [Note a separate scheme applies to used cars – see below]. The use of the scheme is at the discretion of the dealer. If he chooses not to use the scheme then normal VAT rules apply.

Margin-scheme goods include the following:

■ second-hand movable goods;

- certain works of art, collectors items and antiques,

- specified precious metals and precious stones (excluding, diamonds, rubies, sapphires, emeralds, gold, silver and platinum).

The Standard rate of VAT, currently 21.5%, applies to all supplies under the second-hand margin scheme.

The margin scheme applies to second-hand goods acquired, from consumers, from taxable persons who were not entitled to recover VAT on their acquisition of the goods and from other dealers who applied the margin scheme to their sale of the goods (i.e. they did not mention VAT on their sales invoice issue in respect of their supply of the goods to another dealer).

The scheme can also be extended to include the above indicated items where they have been imported from outside the EU.

In effect therefore the margin scheme applies to goods where the dealer was not charged VAT on his purchase of the goods. The dealer cannot deduct any input VAT included in the price of the goods purchased by him.

When the dealer sells second-hand goods under the margin scheme he cannot issue a VAT invoice in respect of such sale, irrespective of his customer.

The margin scheme operates by applying VAT, at the Standard rate, to the margin between the purchase price and the sales price.

A simplified arrangement is in place for individual items purchased and sold for less than €635. This provides that the dealer accounts for VAT on his 'global margin' in the taxable period, i.e. he does not have to account for VAT on an item by item basis.

Example 5.6 – sale by dealer under margin scheme

Item purchased by dealer for €600.00 from a consumer (no VAT charged)

The item is subsequently sold for €1,500.00 under the margin scheme

The margin is €900.00 including VAT.

The VAT included in the sale price is €159.25 ((900 / 121.5) × 21.5)

In this example the 'profit' made by the dealer is €740.75 (900 – 159.25). Where second-hand goods are sold to a person who cannot recover VAT the margin-scheme is used as this minimises the amount of VAT payable by the dealer.

Example 5.7 – sale by dealer outside the margin scheme

Item purchased by dealer for €600 from a consumer (no VAT charged)

The item is subsequently sold for €1,500.00 + VAT outside the margin scheme

The VAT on the sale price is €322.50 (1,500 × 21.5)

In this example the 'profit' made by the dealer is €900 (1,500 – 600). Generally where second-hand goods are sold to a person who can recover VAT then the margin-scheme is not used, e.g. selling antiques to a publican who wants to use them in his pub to create a certain ambiance as he can recover the VAT charged by the dealer.

5.5.2 Second-hand goods – Cars & Agricultural Machinery – Special scheme

Purchase and sale of second-hand motor vehicles under Special Scheme rules

Where a motor dealer purchases a second-hand motor vehicle from a person who was not entitled to reclaim VAT on his or her original purchase of the vehicle or accepts the trade-in of such a second hand motor vehicle, the dealer is still obliged to charge VAT on the resale of the vehicle. Therefore, the original VAT charged on the first sale of the vehicle is regarded as 'trapped' or 'residual'. However, a Special Scheme for second-hand motor vehicles has been put in place to allow the dealer to recover some or all of this trapped or residual VAT. The rules and procedures relating to this Scheme are complex but a brief summary is set out below.

If a car dealer accepts a vehicle as a trade-in against the purchase of another vehicle, this is treated as two separate transactions for the purpose of accounting for VAT: the sale of a vehicle by the dealer, and the purchase of the 'trade-in' by the dealer. The dealer treats the trade-in as the simple purchase of a second-hand vehicle.

The following vehicles qualify for the scheme:

- Cars sold (or traded-in) to a dealer by a person who was not entitled to deduct any VAT in relation to the original purchase of the vehicle, or

- Cars sold (or traded-in) by another dealer who took a deduction of residual VAT on the original purchase of the vehicle.

These are referred to in Irish law as *'qualifying vehicles'*.

Qualifying vehicles are bought (or taken as trade-ins) by the dealer as stock-in-trade for resale, from the following:

- Private individuals in Ireland or in another Member State of the European Union;

- Businesses in Ireland or in other Member State of the European Union which could not claim a VAT credit on its purchase of the vehicle or which are not obliged to issue a VAT invoice in respect of the sale of the vehicle;

- Businesses which are exempt, insurance companies which took possession of the goods in connection with the settlement of a claim under a policy of insurance from a person who was not entitled to input credit in respect of the goods.

- Businesses which are hire-purchase providers and have claimed residual VAT on the vehicle;

- Other motor dealers in Ireland who claimed residual VAT on the purchase of the vehicle;

- Motor dealer in other Member States selling the vehA motor dealer in another state selling the vehicle under the special scheme/margin scheme for taxation of second-hand goods in that other Member State.

A motor dealer may deduct the residual VAT included in the purchase price of any qualifying vehicle which s/he buys, whether as a straight purchase or as a trade-in. Residual VAT is deductible in the VAT period in which the vehicle is purchased by way of the VAT return for that period.

The amount of the residual VAT is calculated on the basis that the purchase price is VAT-inclusive. The rate at which the VAT should be calculated is the rate at which it is chargeable on the supply of motor vehicles in the EU Member State where the person selling the qualifying vehicle to the Irish dealer is based. That is, if the dealer purchases the vehicle from an Irish source, the rate used for the calculation is the Irish VAT rate of 21.5%. If the dealer purchases the vehicle from a UK source, the rate used for the calculation is the UK VAT rate, currently 15%.

Example 5.8 – second-hand vehicle purchased from an Irish vendor

If the qualifying vehicle is bought from an individual or business in Ireland, where the current VAT rate is 21.5%, the residual VAT is calculated as follows:

Purchase price   =   €10,000

Residual VAT   =   € 1,769 (10,000 × 21.5)/121.5

Example 5.9 – second-hand vehicle purchased from a U.K. vendor

If the qualifying vehicle is bought from an individual or business in the UK, the residual VAT calculation is based on the UK VAT rate, currently 15%, as follows:

€ equivalent of stg £ purchase price   =   €10,000

Residual VAT   =   € 1,304 (10,000 × 15)/115

5.5.3   Travel Agents – Margin scheme

With effect from 1 January 2010 a Travel Agents Margin Scheme (TAMS) has been introduced to Ireland. This brings Ireland into line with the rest of the EU where TAMS (more often called TOMS, Travel Operators Margin Schemes), have operated for some time. [Until relatively recently supplies of services by tour operators and travel agents were treated as being VAT-exempt. However, at a relatively recent Appeal Commissioners hearing the services of tour operators were held to be liable to VAT. This prompted the introduction of the TAMS in Ireland. (section 10C, VAT Acts, 1972–2009 refer).

In effect VAT will be charged at the standard rate on the supply of 'margin scheme services' by travel agents (including tour operators). The margin is the difference between the selling price (which must include all cobetweeen the selling price (which must include all costs, charges, taxes, etc) and the cost of 'bought-in' services, i.e. services which the travel agent purchases for the direct benefit of the customer, including, travel and accommodation services. [Note that a travel agent is a person who acts as principal in the supply of 'margin scheme services' to travellers].

The margin is inclusive of VAT and therefore the VAT arising on the margin is calculated by dividing the Margin amount by 121.5 and multiplying the result by 21.5.

The travel agent (including tour operator) cannot deduct input VAT arising on the 'bought-in' services. However, travel agents can recover input VAT incurred on overheads which are not 'bought-in' services and which have been incurred by the travel agent in operating the business. Thus the travel agent (including tour operator) can recover input VAT arising on rent, light, heat, travel agents commissions, etc, as any normal trader would.

The place of supply of the service by the travel agent is where the agent is established. However, if the service is supplied from a fixed establishment of the travel agent elsewhere, then the place of supply is where that fixed establishment is located. The TAMS only applies to margin scheme services supplied in the State.

The TAMS does not apply to margin scheme services supplied outside the State.

Example 5.6

A tour operator arranges a holiday in Ireland and sells the entire package for €900 to the traveller. In arranging the package the tour operator buys a hotel room for three nights for €300 + VAT and also breakfasts and evening meals to the value of €200 + VAT. In addition airport transfers and a tour to the value €150 is purchased.

The total cost of the bought-in services is:

Accommodation   €340.50 (inc VAT at 13.5%)
Meals   €227.00 (inc VAT at 13.5%)
Travel   €150.00 (exempt from VAT)
Cost   717.50

The 'margin' is €182.50 (900.00 – 717.50)

The amount of VAT payable on the margin IS €32.30 ((182.5/121.5) × 21.5)

Thus we can see from the above example that of the €900 paid by the traveler, the yield to the Exchequer is €99.80. [€32.30 paid over by the travel agent on his margin, €40.50 paid by the hotelier in respect of accommodation (which VAT cannot be reclaimed by the travel agent) and €27.00 paid by the restaurants supplying the meals to the traveller (which VAT also cannot be reclaimed by the travel agent).

5.5.4   Schemes for Retailers – Special scheme

Imagine a supermarket at the day's end. There is a cash register containing €15,000 upon which the retailer must account for VAT. During the course of the day, the retailer has sold goods at 0%, 13.5% and 21.5%. He/she must determine the proportion of his/her turnover on which he/she must account for VAT at each of the three rates.

In the case of large outlets with EPOS (Electronic Point of Sales systems), the calculation is very simple. As each item is scanned, it is allocated one of the three VAT codes so that, at the end of the day, all the sales have been allocated to one of the three VAT rates. There is no need for any element of estimation.

However, in the case of smaller outlets, such pinpoint accuracy is not possible and the retailer must have some way of estimating what proportion of his/her sales are chargeable to VAT at each of the three rates. Such estimation must be fair and equitable to both the trader and the Exchequer. With this in mind, Revenue has approved three

"Schemes for Retailers". In general, the schemes apportion the turnover on the basis of purchases. The most basic scheme apportions turnover exactly on the basis of purchases and the more developed schemes allow the trader to apply margins to goods at each of the three VAT rates before apportionment.

There is also a special scheme available for chemists.

All of the above schemes, both margin and special, are explained fully on the Revenue web-site.

5.6   Local Authorities

Article 13 of the Council Directive 2006/112/EC states:

> *"States, regional and local government authorities and other bodies governed by public law shall not be considered taxable persons in respect of the activities or transactions in which they engage as public authorities ..."*

In Ireland, all Government departments, local authorities and non-commercial statutory bodies are outside the scope of VAT and in general cannot register for VAT. Thus, they must bear as a cost any VAT charged to them by suppliers.

However, it is important to remember that local authorities in Ireland are obliged to register for VAT in certain circumstances. There are three circumstances where local authorities are obliged to register and account for output VAT. These are:

(i)   where a Fourth Schedule service (see 4.3.5, Chapter 4) is received from abroad by the local authority (as they are not "in business", they may not deduct input VAT);

(ii)   where intra-Community acquisitions (see 4.2.5, Chapter 4) are made and the combined value exceeds €41,000 in a twelve-month period (as they are not "in business", they may not deduct input VAT);

(iii) where the local authority operates a golf course (liable at 13.5%).

Where distortion of competition occurs due to a local authority not charging VAT, the Minister for Finance may make an order deeming the local authority to be an accountable person and liable to charge VAT on the supply of goods/services specified in the order.

Currently the European Commissions is taking Infraction Proceedings (see 2.6.3) against the Irish Government at the European Court of Justice in relation to the way in which State bodies are taxed in Ireland. The case has yet to be heard by the ECJ. The Commission is not satisfied that Article 13 of the VAT Directive has been properly transposed into domestic VAT legislation.

5.7 Farmers

s12A VA 72 From the outset, the VAT treatment of farmers can cause unnecessary confusion. Some basic information should ensure that this is not the case. One of the main reasons for the confusion that surrounds farmers and VAT is the use of the VAT system as an instrument of social policy. Council Directive 2006/112/EC allows Member States to implement special schemes to compensate groups such as farmers for VAT incurred.

In the first instance, we categorise farmers into two groups, those who have elected, or are obliged, to register for VAT and those who are not registered, the latter group being referred to as "flat-rate farmers". Flat-rate farmers constitute the majority of farmers in Ireland.

A farmer is a person who engages in one or more of the activities listed in the Fifth Schedule, VAT Acts 1972–2009. Broadly speaking, the activities are crop production, stock farming, cultivation, forestry and fisheries.

Very often, a farmer may engage in activities other than farming (as defined in the Fifth Schedule). Where a farmer also carries out one of the activities listed below and the turnover from the activity or a combination of activities does not reach the prescribed threshold, the farmer is not obliged to register and can continue to be a flat-rate farmer. Where the turnover exceeds the prescribed threshold, the farmer is obliged to register for VAT.

The relevant turnover thresholds are as follows:

- Where the farmer supplies agricultural services, the threshold is €37,500.

- Where the farmer is engaged in the supply of bovine semen, the threshold is €75,000.

- Where the farmer supplies nursery or garden-centre stock, the threshold is €75,000.

- Where the farmer is engaged in a combination of the above, the threshold is €37,500.

5.7.1 VAT-registered farmers

VAT-registered farmers have the same obligations and rights as any other accountable persons. Their sales are liable to VAT at a variety of VAT rates, depending on the goods and services being supplied, e.g., wool (21.5%), live cattle, sheep, etc. (4.8%), milk, grass, barley, wheat, etc. (0%), and live poultry (13.5%).

5.7.2 Flat-rate farmers

A flat-rate farmer is defined as a farmer who is not registered for VAT. A flat-rate farmer is nonetheless obliged to register for VAT in respect of intra-Community acquisitions and receipt of Fourth Schedule services (as any person in business is obliged to), but he/she is not registered in respect of his/her farming activities. Freshwater fishermen and fish farmers are regarded as flat-rate farmers; sea fishermen are not (see 5.6).

A flat-rate farmer applies the "flat-rate addition" of 5.2% when he/she makes sales to VAT-registered persons. This amount is not VAT, but is processed through the VAT system. The flat-rate addition is paid to the farmer by the VAT-registered customer.

For example:

■ Cattle are sold in the mart for €20,000. A flat-rate addition of €1,040 is paid to the farmer in addition to the €20,000.

■ Milk is sold to the creamery for €3,000. A flat-rate addition of €156 is paid to the farmer in addition to the €3,000.

■ Cabbage is sold to a retailer for €500. A flat-rate addition of €26 is paid to the farmer in addition to the €500.

■ Wool is sold to a wool merchant for €15,000. A flat-rate addition of €780 is paid to the farmer in addition to the €15,000.

The VAT-registered customer recoups the flat-rate addition by deducting the sum of the flat-rate additions paid to farmers in a taxable period from the amount of VAT due in arriving at the amount of VAT payable. The flat-rate addition is deemed to be VAT so as to enable the VAT-registered customer to reclaim the amount on his/her VAT return (see 5.3).

Albeit that the flat-rate addition is deemed to be VAT paid by a VAT-registered customer, it is not deemed to be VAT in the hands of the farmer and, consequently, the amount accrues for the benefit of the farmer. Accordingly, the purpose of the flat-rate addition is to compensate unregistered farmers for VAT incurred on farm expenses.

5.7.3 Invoicing by flat-rate farmers

s17(2) VA 72 A flat-rate farmer is obliged to issue an invoice to a VAT-registered customer and show the consideration for the sale and, separately, the flat-rate addition. Legislation provides that the purchaser may prepare the invoice and give a copy to the farmer. In this case, the farmer is deemed to have fulfilled his/her obligations. This is the most common method of invoicing, as the purchaser is the person who will have to recoup the amount from Revenue and it gives him/her greater control and flexibility over issuing the invoice.

5.7.4 Direct VAT repayments to flat-rate farmers

In addition to the 5.2% flat-rate addition, a flat-rate farmer may apply directly to the Revenue Commissioners for repayment of input VAT incurred on the construction, extension and alteration of farm buildings and land reclamation.

5.8   Sea Fishermen

s8(3)(b)
VA 72

A sea fisherman whose sales consist of unprocessed fish to VAT-registered customers is not obliged to register for VAT but may elect to do so.

In addition, an unregistered fisherman is allowed to sell equipment used by him in his business and other goods (e.g., sales of fish to the general public) up to a value of €70,000 before he is obliged to register for VAT.

Where a sea fisherman elects, or is obliged to register for VAT, he/she has the same obligations and rights as any other VAT-registered person.

5.9   Agricultural Contractors

6th Sch
VA 72

Agricultural contracting is the supply of a service which is liable to VAT at the reduced rate, currently 13.5%. Such services include fieldwork, reaping and mowing, threshing, baling, collecting, harvesting, sowing, planting, spraying, land drainage, hedge trimming and tree felling.

5.10   Hire Purchase Transactions

Hire purchase transactions have a unique VAT treatment because they combine a taxable supply of goods and a VAT exempt supply of financial services, the finance/interest charge.

The supply of goods to a HP Company, such goods being hired by the HP Company to a customer by way of a hire purchase agreement, is a taxable supply on which the supplier is obliged to account for VAT. However the onward supply of the goods by the HP Company, at the end of the hire period, to the customer is not a supply for VAT. The finance/interest charge levied by the HP Company is exempt from VAT. The supplier will invoice the HP Company, who in turn will invoice the customer at the outset of the hire period.

However if the customer defaults and the HP Company is obliged to sell the repossessed goods then it will charge VAT on the supply and will also be entitled to deduct the VAT originally charged by the garage on the goods. This has the effect of giving bad-debt relief to the HP Company in the case of customer default.

A HP Company can avail of the margin scheme for second-hand means of transport. (see 5.3.13 for definition).

[Note: HP transactions should not be confused with lease transactions, which for VAT purposes is the supply of a service].

5.11   Summary

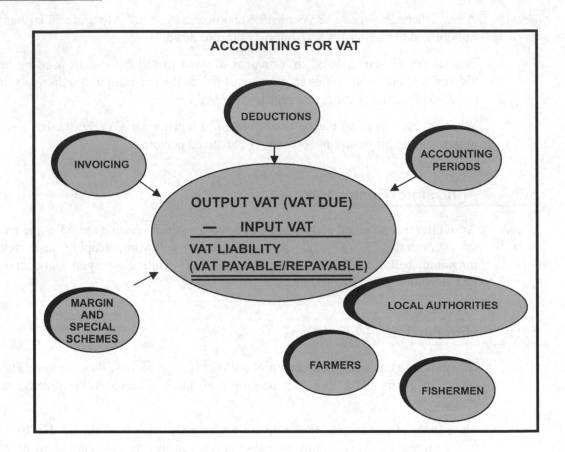

ACCOUNTING FOR VAT

DEDUCTIONS

INVOICING

ACCOUNTING PERIODS

OUTPUT VAT (VAT DUE)
— INPUT VAT
VAT LIABILITY
(VAT PAYABLE/REPAYABLE)

MARGIN AND SPECIAL SCHEMES

LOCAL AUTHORITIES

FARMERS

FISHERMEN

WHAT YOU SHOULD NOW KNOW

On completion of this chapter, you should be able to:

- ✓ Identify who may issue a VAT invoice.

- ✓ Describe when an invoice should be issued and what it should contain.

- ✓ Describe the procedure in place for electronic invoicing.

- ✓ Explain what deductions may be made by VAT-registered persons.

- ✓ List the qualifying activities in respect of which VAT deduction is allowed.

- ✓ List the items of expenditure in respect of which no input VAT deduction is allowable.

- ✓ Explain the concept of partial deduction.

- ✓ Identify who must account for VAT.

- ✓ Explain when VAT is due and payable.

- ✓ Explain when bad-debt relief and non-refundable deposit relief applies

- ✓ Describe the cash receipts basis of accounting for VAT and the circumstances in which it may be used.

- ✓ Distinguish between a VAT period and an accounting period.

- ✓ Comment upon and understand the special schemes available for second-hand goods, cars and travel agents.

- ✓ Discuss the application of the VAT system to local authorities.

- ✓ Explain the VAT treatment of VAT-registered farmers, flat-rate farmers, sea fishermen and agricultural contractors.

- ✓ Discuss the application of VAT to hire-purchase transactions.

- ✓ Complete Questions and the Assignments in Irish Taxation Law and Practice, Volume 2.

Appendix I

Specimen of VAT 3 form

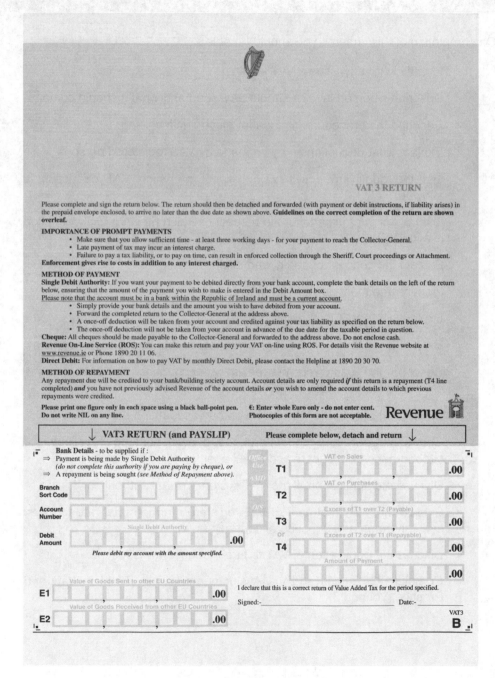

VAT 3 RETURN

Please complete and sign the return below. The return should then be detached and forwarded (with payment or debit instructions, if liability arises) in the prepaid envelope enclosed, to arrive no later than the due date as shown above. **Guidelines on the correct completion of the return are shown overleaf.**

IMPORTANCE OF PROMPT PAYMENTS
- Make sure that you allow sufficient time - at least three working days - for your payment to reach the Collector-General.
- Late payment of tax may incur an interest charge.
- Failure to pay a tax liability, or to pay on time, can result in enforced collection through the Sheriff, Court proceedings or Attachment.

Enforcement gives rise to costs in addition to any interest charged.

METHOD OF PAYMENT
Single Debit Authority: If you want your payment to be debited directly from your bank account, complete the bank details on the left of the return below, ensuring that the amount of the payment you wish to make is entered in the Debit Amount box.
Please note that the account must be in a bank within the Republic of Ireland and must be a current account.
- Simply provide your bank details and the amount you wish to have debited from your account.
- Forward the completed return to the Collector-General at the address above.
- A once-off deduction will be taken from your account and credited against your tax liability as specified on the return below.
- The once-off deduction will not be taken from your account in advance of the due date for the taxable period in question.

Cheque: All cheques should be made payable to the Collector-General and forwarded to the address above. Do not enclose cash.
Revenue On-Line Service (ROS): You can make this return and pay your VAT on-line using ROS. For details visit the Revenue website at www.revenue.ie or Phone 1890 20 11 06.
Direct Debit: For information on how to pay VAT by monthly Direct Debit, please contact the Helpline at 1890 20 30 70.

METHOD OF REPAYMENT
Any repayment due will be credited to your bank/building society account. Account details are only required *if* this return is a repayment (T4 line completed) *and* you have not previously advised Revenue of the account details *or* you wish to amend the account details to which previous repayments were credited.

Please print one figure only in each space using a black ball-point pen.   **€: Enter whole Euro only - do not enter cent.**
Do not write NIL on any line.   **Photocopies of this form are not acceptable.**   **Revenue**

↓ **VAT3 RETURN (and PAYSLIP)**	**Please complete below, detach and return ↓**

Bank Details - to be supplied if :
⇒ Payment is being made by Single Debit Authority
   (do not complete this authority if you are paying by cheque), or
⇒ A repayment is being sought *(see Method of Repayment above).*

Branch Sort Code

Account Number

Debit Amount   *Single Debit Authority*   .00
Please debit my account with the amount specified.

Value of Goods Sent to other EU Countries
E1   .00

Value of Goods Received from other EU Countries
E2   .00

VAT on Sales
T1   .00

VAT on Purchases
T2   .00

Excess of T1 over T2 (Payable)
T3   .00

or   Excess of T2 over T1 (Repayable)
T4   .00

Amount of Payment
.00

I declare that this is a correct return of Value Added Tax for the period specified.
Signed:-_____ Date:-

VAT3
B

GUIDE TO COMPLETION OF RETURN

Debit Amount
Complete this line if you wish to make a payment by Single Debit Authority. Please ensure that you have also provided your bank details.
Leave this line blank if paying by cheque or the return is a repayment claim.

Bank Details
Payment (T3): If your wish to pay your liability by Single Debit Authority, please enter the bank details of the account you wish to have debited. You must also enter the amount you wish to pay in the 'debit amount' line below.

Repayment (T4): If this return is a repayment and you have not previously advised us of the account details or you wish to amend the account details to which previous repayments were credited, please enter bank details here. If this return is not a repayment and you still wish to change your VAT repayment bank details please fax details to VAT Repayments Section Fax No. 065 6841366.

T1
Enter total VAT liability in respect of goods & services + intra-EU acquisitions + parcels imported VAT free.

T2
Enter total deductible VAT in respect of purchases + intra-EU acquisitions + imports.

Bank Details - to be supplied if :
⇒ Payment is being made by Single Debit Authority *(do not complete this authority if you are paying by cheque)*, or
⇒ A repayment is being sought *(see Method of Repayment above)*.

Branch Sort Code
Account Number
Debit Amount .00

Please debit my account with the amount specified.

SAMPLE

VAT on Sales
T1 .00

VAT on Purchases
T2 .00

Excess of T1 over T2 (Payable)
T3 .00

or

Excess of T2 over T1 (Repayable)
T4 .00

Amount of Payment
.00

Value of Goods sent to other EU Countries
E1 .00

Value of Goods received from other EU Countries
E2 .00

I declare that this is a correct return of Value Added Tax for the period specified.

Signed:- _____ Date:- _____
Name:
Reg No.: Period:

VAT3
B

E1/E2
Please enter the total value of goods sent to (E1 line) or received from (E2 line) other EU countries.

T3
If T1 amount exceeds T2 amount, please enter the difference on this line. You are required to submit full payment with this return.

Payment may be made by Single Debit Authority or cheque.

T4
If T2 amount exceeds T1 amount, please enter the difference on this line.

Subject to verification checks, this is the repayment amount due to you from Revenue and will be offset or repaid as appropriate.

Please Note:
Please print one figure only in each space using a black ball-point pen. Enter whole Euro only - do not enter cent. Do not write NIL on any line. Photocopies of this form are not acceptable.

Amount of Payment
Please enter the amount of your payment here. *In the case of repayment claim, leave this line blank.*

6

PROPERTY TRANSACTIONS AND BUILDING SERVICES

In this Chapter, you will deal with the following:

- Introduction to new definitions

- The Supply of Developed Property

- The Letting of Property

- Transitional Provisions relating to the Supply and Letting of Property

- The Capital Goods Scheme and the implications for the disposal of a Capital Good

- Building Services

6.1 Introduction

The VAT legislation relating to various property transactions has changed fundamentally with effect from 1 July 2008.

In 2005 the Revenue Commissioners commenced a review of the application of VAT to property transactions. What started off in 1972, at the introduction of VAT, as a relatively straightforward application of VAT law had become, by 2005, very complex and a specialised area within the VAT system; so much so that the virtuality and property transaction of substance required the advice of a VAT specialist.

The new legislative provisions relating to VAT are an attempt to simplify the application of VAT to transactions concerning the sale and letting of commercial property. Only time will tell if the new legislation has serviced this purpose.

While simplification was one of the driving forces in introducing the change, a key consideration was to protect the source of revenue for the State. Thus it should be borne in mind that, while simplification has been introduced, the new provisions ensure that the revenue accruing from VAT on property-related transactions is not reduced.

Additionally the new legislation brings our treatment of transactions relating to property broadly into line with the provisions of Council Directive 2006/112/EC, the recently recast VAT directive.

Broadly speaking, and for ease of understanding, the new provisions can be broken into five categories, as follows:

- The supply of property

- The letting of property

- Transitional provisions relating to the each of the above categories

- The Capital Goods Scheme

- Building Services

At this point it is important to recall that VAT is applicable only to transactions carried out in the course or furtherance of business. Therefore, for example, a person selling their place of residence will not fall within the scope of VAT as it is not carried out for a business purpose.

Therefore the introduction to VAT as it relates to property transactions will, in this publication, be dealt with systematically under each of the above categories.

6.2 Some New Definitions

The new provisions have introduced some new terms and definitions with which you should be familiar and which we will refer to throughout this chapter. While some of the old terms are now redundant many more of the old terms used are still relevant. Below is a selection of the new terms:

- **Capital Goods** – this term refers to developed immovable goods, i.e., developed property. Thus the property must have been developed in order for it to be categorised as a "Capital Good".

- **Development** includes the construction, demolition, alteration, or reconstruction of any building on land or the carrying out of any engineering works in, on, over or under the lands which adapts it for a materially altered use. It is important to note that maintenance and repair does not constitute development.

- **Minor Development** in relation to property does not make a property "New" (see below). Two conditions are necessary before any development of property can be classified as "Minor":

  - The development must not adapt the property for materially altered use, and

  - The cost of such development must not exceed 25% of the sale value of the property.

- **Completed Property** – means that development of the property has reached a stage whereby the property can be used for the purpose for which it has been designed. It should be noted that the development in relation to a "completed property" may vary depending on the property concerned. Thus, for example, in the case of a residential property, completion would entail developing the property to the point where a person could reasonable expect to move in and use it without any further development being necessary. However, in the case of a unit in a shopping centre, development to "shell and core" would constitute completion of the property. By "shell and core" we mean developed to a stage whereby the tenant can complete the development to his/her own requirement. It is generally the case that tenants will "fit out" retail units to their own specifications/requirements.

- **New Property** – Following completion, a property is considered to be a "New Property" for a period of five years following such completion. Minor development work on a property, which costs less than 25% of the value of the property and which work has not adapted the property for a materially altered use, will not render the property "new" for VAT purposes.

  However, where the property is disposed of within the first five years following completion to an unconnected person, the property only remains a "New Property" for a period of 24 months following first occupation.

- **Joint Option for Taxation** – This term refers to the joint exercise of an option by the vendor and purchaser to have VAT charged on the supply of a property, which supply would otherwise be exempt from VAT.

- *Landlords Option to Taxation* – this term refers to an option exercised solely by the landlord to charge VAT (at 21.5%) on the letting of a certain property, which letting would otherwise be exempt from VAT.

- *Connected Person* – in relation to the letting of property, the question of whether or not the lessor and the lessee are connected persons is relevant (see 6.4). In addition, in relation to determining the period during which a property remains 'New', a disposal to a Connected person is relevant. A 'connected person' is defined at section 7A(3), VAT Acts 1972–2009. It is quite complex and covers a variety of relationships between the lessor/lessee and vendor/purchaser.

Individuals are connected with:

- Their spouse;

- Their relatives or relatives of their spouses;

- Individuals (or spouses of individuals) with whom they are in partnership;

- The beneficiary of a trust where the individual is a trustee.

Companies (including bodies of persons) are connected with:

- Persons who control that company;

- Other companies that act in pursuit of a common purpose with that company;

- A person(s) with a reasonable commonality of interests who have the power to determine the activities of two or more companies.

- *Capital Goods Owner* – For the purposes of the Capital Goods Scheme a Capital Goods Owner is any person who acting in the course or furtherance of business, incurs expenditure on the acquisition or development of a Capital Good. In the case of a flat-rate farmer (see 5.5.2) the acquisition or development of a building or structure designed for use in, and used in, a farming enterprise is excluded.

- *Capital Goods Scheme* – is a mechanism for regulating VAT deductibility over the "VAT life" of a Capital Good. See 6.7.

6.3   The Supply of Developed Property

6.3.1   What Constitutes "Development"?

It is important to understand what constitutes "development" for VAT purposes. "Development" is defined as follows:

s1 VA 72 *"development"* in relation to any land, means—

(a) The construction, demolition, extension, alteration or reconstruction of any building on the land, or

(b) the carrying out of any engineering or other operation in, on, over or under the land to adapt it for a materially altered use,

and *"developed"* shall be construed correspondingly ..."

The definition is very broad and it may be more appropriate at this stage to say what does not constitute development. The following does not constitute development in relation to land (property):

- essential repairs and maintenance (e.g., painting, cleaning, repairing structural defects, etc.);

Development makes a property 'new' for VAT purposes. Therefore if a property is not already 'new' and the work carried out is considered to be a 'minor development', then the supply of the property is exempt from VAT.

If a property is a 'new', property and 'minor development' is carried out then the supply is liable to VAT so long as it occurs in the period when property is 'new', notwithstanding that the development is minor.

6.3.2 The supply of property

The supply includes the supply of a freehold or the supply of a "freehold equivalent" i.e., an interest in property which amounts, in substance, to a freehold interest, e.g., a very long lease.

A supply of property involves the transfer of ownership or the transfer in substance of the right to dispose of the property as owner or otherwise. It is not necessary that legal title be transferred.

6.3.3 The charge of VAT

Two conditions must be fulfilled for such supply to come within the charge of VAT:

(1) The property must have been developed, and

(2) The supply must be for consideration in the course or furtherance of business.

Thus, any property supplied prior to completion, which fulfills both of the above conditions, is liable to VAT at 13.5%.

In the case of a completed property (see 6.2 for definition) a third condition must be fulfilled, namely the property must be a New Property (see 6.2 for definition). This condition does not apply in the case of the sale of residential property, which sale by the developer or a person connected with the developer will always be liable to VAT at 13.5%.

6.3.4 The exempt supply of property

When a completed property is no longer a new property, then the supply of such property is exempt from VAT.

Thus, the first or subsequent sale of a completed property after a period of five years from completion, is exempt from VAT.

The subsequent sale of a property within the five-year period, but following two years of occupation, is also exempt from VAT. However, a joint option for taxation may be exercised upon agreement by both parties to the sale. This will render the sale liable to VAT at the reduced rate, 13.5%.

A Capital Goods Scheme adjustment will have to be made by the Capital Goods Owner in respect of a VAT exempt supply affected within the "VAT life" of the completed property (see Capital Goods Scheme – section 6.7).

6.3.5 Making an exempt supply of property liable to VAT

Where both parties to the transaction exercising an option, in writing, to tax the transaction then the supply of completed property which would otherwise be exempt from VAT, is liable to VAT at 13.5%.

6.3.6 Supply of property in connection with a contract to develop the property

The supply of property in connection with an agreement to develop the property is always liable to VAT regardless of whether or not the property is developed or whether the transaction is carried out in the course or furtherance of business.

This is an anti-avoidance provision.

6.3.7 Who accounts for the VAT on the taxable supply of property?

In almost all cases it is the vendor who must account for any VAT charged on the supply of property. However, the notable exception is in the case where a joint option for taxation has been exercised. In such cases it is the purchaser who is obliged to account for the VAT charged on the supply, on a 'reverse charge' basis (see Chapter 4, section 4.3.1).

6.3.8 The application of the Capital Goods Scheme

Where the supply of property is exempt from VAT, then an adjustment under the Capital Goods Scheme ('CGS') must be made by the vendor, where such adjustment is required (see 6.7).

6.4 Transitional Provisions Relating to the Supply of Developed Property

6.4.1 Why the need for transitional provisions?

Completed Properties which are held (by the 'holder') under freehold, freehold equivalent or long lease (i.e., a lease of 10 years or more and referred to as a 'legacy lease' in this chapter) prior to 1 July 2008 (i.e., acquired or developed under the 'old' VAT rules applying to property), are referred to as "transitional properties" and the rules outlined below apply to the supply, on or after 1 July 2008, of such properties. Such supplies are always treated as supplies of goods.

6.4.2 The "VAT life" of transitional property

The "VAT life" of a completed property is the period in which a Capital Goods Scheme adjustment must be made, should such adjustment be required, upon the supply of such completed property. In the VAT legislation it is referred to as the 'adjustment period' (see 6.7).

In the case of a freehold or freehold equivalent, the "VAT life" is a period of 20 years from the date such interest in the property was acquired. If the property was developed subsequent to such acquisition (but prior to 1 July 2008) then the "VAT life" is for a period of 20 years from such development.

In the case of a "legacy lease", i.e., a lease of 10 years or more, which was created and held by a person in business prior to 1 July 2008, the "VAT life" is a period of 20 years from the creation of the lease or the number of years in the term of the lease, if less than 20, whichever is the shorter.

In the case of a "legacy lease", i.e., a lease of 10 years or more obtained by way of assignment or surrender prior to 1 July 2008 and the current assignor is a person in business; the "VAT life" is the period remaining in the lease (unexpired part of the term) from the date of the then assignment or 20 years, whichever is the shorter.

6.4.3 VAT treatment of freeholds and freehold equivalents where the holder was entitled to deduct any part of the input VAT incurred on the acquisition or development of the property

The same rules apply as are outlined at 6.3 in respect of the supply of the completed property on or after 1 July 2008.

6.4.4 VAT treatment of freeholds and freehold equivalents where the holder was not entitled to deduct any part of the input VAT incurred on the acquisition and/or development of the property

The supply of the completed property, on or after 1 July 2008, is exempt from VAT. However, where both the seller and buyer are accountable persons, i.e., in business, then they may exercise a joint option for taxation (see 6.2 for definition).

Such a joint option for taxation will release, under a Capital Goods Scheme adjustment, (see 6.7), a portion of the input VAT previously denied to the vendor.

6.4.5 VAT treatment of legacy leases where the holder was entitled to deduct any part of the input VAT incurred on the acquisition of the lease or development subsequent to acquiring the lease

The assignment or surrender of a legacy lease, on or after 1 July 2008, is taxable as a supply of goods, where it occurs within the "VAT life" of the lease (see 6.4.2).

The same rules apply to any subsequent assignment or surrender of an assigned legacy lease.

6.4.6 VAT treatment of legacy leases where the holder was not entitled to deduct any part of the input VAT incurred on the acquisition of the lease

The assignment or surrender is an exempt supply of goods.

However, as in the case of transitional freeholds/freehold equivalents, where, in the case of an assignment, both the assignor and assignee are accountable persons, i.e., in business, then they may exercise a joint option for taxation (see 6.2) of the supply of goods. Where, in the case of a surrender, both the surrenderor and the landlord are accountable persons, then they may exercise a joint option for taxation of the supply of goods.

6.4.7 The application of the Capital Goods Scheme

Where the supply of a transitional property is exempt from VAT, then an adjustment under the capital goods scheme must be made by the vendor, where it is necessary to do so (see 6.7).

6.4.8 Who accounts for VAT on the supply of a transitional property?

In the case of the sale of a freehold or freehold equivalent transitional property which is liable to VAT, it is the vendor who must account for any VAT charged on the supply of property.

In the case of the sale of a freehold or freehold equivalent transitional property which would normally be exempt from VAT, but where a joint option for taxation has been exercised, then the purchaser is obliged to account for the VAT charged on the supply on the 'reverse charge' basis.

In the case of the assignment or surrender of a legacy lease it is the assignee (in the case of an assignment) or the landlord (in the case of a surrender) who must account for any VAT charged on the supply of property, where such person is an accountable person, i.e., is in business or is a Department of State or a Local Authority. Otherwise it is for the assignor or surrenderor to account for any VAT charged.

6.4.9   What is the amount liable to VAT on the supply of a transitional property?

In the case of the supply of a freehold or a freehold equivalent, the consideration passing from the purchaser to the vendor is the amount which is liable to VAT (at 13.5%).

In the case of an assignment or a surrender of a legacy lease a formula is used to determine the amount of VAT chargeable.

The equation is VAT due $= \dfrac{T \times N}{Y}$

Where:–

T = the total amount of VAT incurred on the acquisition of the legacy lease or on the development of the property

N = the number of full years plus 1, that remained in the VAT life of the property when the legacy lease is being assigned or surrendered

Y = the total number of years in the VAT life of the property or 20, whichever is the lesser

Example 6.1

> *Company A grants Company B a 30-year lease on 1 July 2001. VAT of €2m was charged on the then capitalised value of the long lease. Company B deducted this VAT as it used the property to make taxable supplies of goods/services.*
>
> *Company B assigns the lease to Company C on 1 July 2010.*
>
> *This is a "legacy lease" as the interest was held by Company B on 1 July 2008. The "VAT life" or adjustment period of the legacy lease is 20 years from 1 July 2001. The assignment is taxable, on the reverse charge basis, as it occurs within the VAT life of the legacy lease.*
>
> *Using the above formula, T = €2m, N = 12 (year 2021 – year 2010 + 1), Y = 20*
>
> *Therefore the VAT due and payable on the lease by Company C (under reverse charge) is €1,200,000 and that taxable amount, or consideration for VAT purposes is €8,888,888.80 (1,200,000/13.5 × 100). [The input VAT deductible by Company C will depend on its use of the property].*

6.4.10   The sale of a 'legacy lease' reversion

Each 'legacy lease' will have a reversion, i.e., the interest in the property held by the person (the landlord) who created the lease. Where the landlord sells a reversionary interest (which will generally consist of the property and the right to collect rent on the legacy lease) on or after 1 July 2008, then such sale will be exempt from VAT where no development work has been carried out on the property subsequent to the creation of the legacy lease either by or for the benefit of the landlord.

If the completed property was developed by or on behalf of the landlord subsequent to the creation of the legacy lease, then if the property is a 'new property' (see 6.2 for definition) at the time of sale, the supply will be liable to VAT.

6.4.11 The sale of a reversion following surrender of the legacy lease

Where the completed property is sold by the landlord following the surrender of a legacy lease then, until such time as the surrendered lease would have expired, the rules as set out at 6.3.2 – 6.3.4 will apply to the sale.

6.5 The Letting of Property

6.5.1 Introduction

The letting of property is a supply of a service for VAT purposes. In the first instance the letting of all property is exempt from VAT. [However, a very long lease which is considered to be freehold equivalent is a supply of goods and this sub-section does not apply to such lease (see 6.3.1)].

6.5.2 Option to tax

A landlord may exercise an option to tax rents. Once the option is exercised then the rents are no longer exempt from VAT but liable to VAT at 21.5%. The landlord charges the VAT and issues a VAT invoice in accordance with legislation.

There are however, a number of circumstances where a landlord may not exercise on option to tax rents, which are:

- Where the property is occupied for residential purposes

- Where the tenant is a 'connected person' (see 6.2) and where the tenant has a VAT recovery rate in excess of 90% (see Chapters 5.3.1 – 5.3.3)

- Where the let property is occupied by a connected person, even if the letting agreement is with an unconnected person

The option to tax rents is specific to each letting. Thus it must be exercised individually for each letting. A landlord may therefore have a mix of taxable and exempt lettings.

The landlords's option to tax a letting is exercised in the following ways:

- By claiming a deduction for input VAT incurred on the development or acquisition of property which is intended to be used for letting

- By agreeing with the tenant in writing that the letting will be taxable

■ By notifying the tenant in writing that the letting will be taxable

6.5.3 Terminating an option to tax

An option to tax must be terminated in the following circumstances:

■ Where the landlord and the tenant become connected persons and where the tenant has a VAT recovery ratio of less than 90% (see Chapters 5.3.1 – 5.3.3)

■ Where the property becomes occupied by a person connected to the landlord and where that connected person has a recovery ratio of less than 90%

■ Where the property is used for residential purposes

An option to tax may be terminated at any stage by the landlord notifying the tenant in writing. However, the cancellation of the option to tax cannot be earlier that the date the tenant is so notified.

Where an option to tax is terminated during the VAT life* of the property concerned then an adjustment under the Capital Goods Scheme ('CGS') must be made by the landlord (see 6.7).

*The "VAT life" of a capital good is the period during which a Capital Goods Scheme adjustment must be made, should such adjustment be required In VAT legislation it is referred to as the 'adjustment period' (see 6.7).

6.5.4 Amount on which VAT is chargeable upon opting to tax

All of the consideration attributable to the service of letting the property is liable to VAT. Obviously the rents are liable to VAT at 21.5%. The table below indicates the VAT treatment of other payments associated with a letting.

Table 6.1

Nature of payment	Landlord opts to tax rents	Rents exempt from VAT
Premium payable by tenant to landlord for grant of lease	Liable to VAT at 21.5%	Exempt from VAT
Premium payable by landlord to tenant as inducement to enter lease	Not a supply – therefore no VAT applicable	Not a supply – therefore no VAT applicable
Premium payable by landlord to tenant other than as inducement to enter lease	Liable to VAT at 21.5%	Liable to VAT at 21.5%
Premium payable by tenant to landlord upon surrender	Liable to VAT at 21.5%	Exempt from VAT
Premium payable by existing tenant upon assignment to another person	Liable to VAT at 21.5%	Liable to VAT at 21.5%
Premium received by existing tenant upon assignment to another person	Liable to VAT at 21.5%	Liable to VAT at 21.5%

6.6 Transitional Provisions Relating to the Letting of Property

6.6.1 Waiver of exemption

Where prior to 1 July 2008, the landlord had in place a 'waiver of exemption',[1] then certain transitional measures apply to such lettings.

Thus you will appreciate there are many lettings currently in place where the landlord, prior to 1 July 2008, waived exemption in relation to such lettings.

From 1 July 2008 a new waiver of exemption cannot be put in place.

An existing waiver of exemption does not extend to any property acquired or developed after 1 July 2008. However a waiver of exemption can be extended to a letting created after 1 July 2008, where the development of the property had commenced on 18 February 2008 and the waiver was in place prior to 18 February 2008.

A waiver of exemption in respect of a property let to a connected person (see 6.2, for definition), must, subject to certain exceptions[2], be cancelled on 1 July 2008. Upon cancellation, the landlord must pay to the Revenue the excess, if any, of the VAT deducted upon the acquisition and/or development of the property concerned, over the VAT charged on rental of the property concerned, during the operation of the waiver (called the cancellation amount). [Where there are properties let to unconnected tenants then the waiver will continue in force for such properties].

A waiver of exemption in respect of property let to unconnected persons or to connected persons in the circumstances outlined in footnote 2 may be cancelled at any time by the landlord, upon the payment of the cancellation amount, if such sum is due, i.e., if the input VAT on acquisition/development exceeds the output VAT on rents.

The Capital Goods Scheme ('CGS') does not apply to the properties which are within the waiver of exemption. This is because VAT incurred on acquisition and/or development of the properties concerned is taken into account in calculating the cancellation amount payable, if and when the waiver is cancelled.

---

[1] Prior to 1 July 2008 where a letting was for a period of less than 10 years it was considered to be a supply of a service and as such it was exempt from VAT. However the landlord was able to waive such exemption and thereafter apply VAT at 21.5% to the rents received. The waiver by the landlord extended to all rents in respect of all letting of less than 10 years which he made. [By waiving the exemption the landlord was able to deduct input VAT on the acquisition/development of the property].

[2] Where the VAT on the rents charged to a connected person exceeds a certain amount, as determined by a formula in VAT legislation, then the landlord is not obliged to cancel his waiver in respect of a letting to a connected person. The cancellation of a waiver is not obligatory where the waiver relates to a letting of a property held by a landlord under a legacy lease acquired between 18 February and 30 June 2008 from an unconnected landlord.

6.7 The Capital Goods Scheme – Implications for the Ongoing Use of a Capital Good

6.7.1 Introduction

The Capital Goods Scheme ('CGS') is a mechanism for regulating VAT deductibility in relation to a Capital Good over the "VAT life" (see 6.7.3 for definition) of the developed property. The VAT life and consequently the application of the CGS is unique to each property.

Not every accountable person will have to make a VAT deductibility adjustment under the CGS. In fact, only those accountable persons, who make an exempt use or exempt supply of the property, will be obliged to make an adjustment. Additionally, persons not previously registered for VAT who exercise a joint option for taxation in respect of the supply of property may be able to obtain a refund of VAT, by way of a deductibility adjustment, under the CGS.

6.7.2 Who does the scheme apply to?

The CGS applies to the following categories of persons:

- Any person in business (an accountable person) who was charged VAT on the acquisition or development of immovable goods.

- Any person in business (an accountable person) who, on 1 July 2008, held a legacy lease and who, subsequent to that date, assigned or surrendered a such legacy lease.

- Any person in business (an accountable person) who, subsequent to 1 July 2008, was charged VAT on the assignment or surrender of a legacy lease.

Any of the above categories of persons is known as a Capital Goods Owner.

The CGS does not apply to a person who acquired property in a private capacity (i.e., other than in the course or furtherance of business). Also the scheme does not apply to persons who acquired property upon which VAT was not charged. However, the CGS does apply to property acquired by way of a transfer of a business, upon which VAT was not chargeable.

6.7.3 The VAT life of a property

In general the VAT life, the 'adjustment period', of a property, for each owner, is as follows:

- 10 intervals, i.e., 10 years in the case of redevelopment (refurbishment) of a previously completed property

- 20 intervals, i.e., 20 years in the case of developed capital goods

■ 20 or less intervals in the case of a legacy lease (see 6.4.2)

The intervals in the adjustment period are as follows:

■ The initial interval is for a period of one year from the completion of the property by the owner or, in the case of a purchaser, one year from the date of purchase

■ The second interval begins on the day the initial interval ends and ends at the end of the capital goods owner's accounting year end during which the initial interval ends. This shorter interval is to align the subsequent intervals with the initial interval.

■ A number of subsequent intervals, each for a period of one year commencing at the end of the previous interval, until the end of the adjustment period.

In the case of a property developer the initial interval commences on the date the property is completed (see 6.2 for definition).

In the case of a purchaser of developed property the initial interval begins on the date the property is purchased.

6.7.4   Obligation for the owner at the end of the initial interval

At the end of the initial interval, the owner must review his/her use of the property in that period. He/she must divide the usage as between exempt and taxable use. For example a bank might have both taxable and exempt supplies. In another situation, the owner may be letting the property and may have opted to tax some of the leases and opted not to tax others. Again there is both taxable and exempt use.

Where the proportion of taxable use in this interval was less than the proportion of input VAT recovered on the acquisition/development of the property, then an adjustment is required. An amount of VAT will be payable by the owner.

Where the proportion of taxable use in this interval was greater than the proportion of input VAT recovered on the acquisition/development of the property, then an adjustment is also required. An amount of VAT will be repayable by Revenue to the owner.

Where the proportion of taxable use in this interval was equal to the proportion of input VAT recovered on the acquisition/development of the property, then an adjustment is not required.

Any adjustment made is made to the total amount of tax incurred, i.e., the tax charged on the acquisition/development of the property.

In the case of a property developer who builds residential units and who in the first interval lets them (exempt), then there is no obligation on him to carry out an adjustment at the end of the initial interval.

Example 6.2

VAT of €1,500,000 was charged by a vendor on the sale of the property to Compco. Compco, the owner, recovered all the VAT on the acquisition of a property (The new owner intended using the property to make taxable supplies). Circumstances changed and, in the initial interval, the entire property was let without opting to tax. Therefore there was no taxable use of the property in the initial interval.

Initial interval adjustment

The total tax incurred = €1.5m

The amount of total tax deducted = €1.5m

The initial interval proportion of deductible use = 0% (it is used fully for exempt purposes)

The total reviewed deductible amount = the total tax incurred × the initial interval proportion of deductible use

$$= 1.5 \times 0 = 0$$

An adjustment using the formula A − B must be made, where

A = the amount of total tax deducted   = €1.5m

B = the total reviewed deductible amount = 0

Adjustment = A − B = €1.5m − 0 = €1.5m

Compco must pay, as output VAT, all of the input VAT previously recovered, i.e., €1,500,000.

Example 6.3

VAT of €2,500,000 was charged by a vendor on the sale of a completed property to Colco, a trading company. Colco recovered all the VAT on the acquisition of a property (it intended to make fully taxable supplies). At the end of the initial interval, it calculated that 80% of its supplies were taxable or qualifying activities; the other 20% were exempt supplies. Therefore there was both taxable and exempt use of the property in the initial interval.

Initial Interval adjustment

The total tax incurred = €2.5m

The amount of total tax deducted = €2.5m.

The initial interval proportion of deductible use = 80%

The total reviewed deductible amount = the total tax incurred × the initial interval proportion of deductible use

$$= 2.5 \times 80\% = €2m$$

An adjustment using the formula A − B must be made, where

A = the amount of total tax deducted = €2.5m

B = the total reviewed deductible amount = €2m

Adjustment = A − B = €2.5m − €2m = €500,000

Colco must pay, as output VAT, the excess of A over B, i.e., €500,000.

6.7.5   Obligation for the owner at the end of the Second and Subsequent intervals

The owner must carry out the same review as between taxable and exempt usage for each interval. A comparison should then be made with the proportion of taxable usage in the initial interval.

Where the proportion differs an adjustment must be carried out.

Any adjustment made is the difference between the base tax amount and the reference deduction amount. As the computations under the CGS are complex perhaps this is best illustrated by way of example. Let us use the details in Example 6.3 and extend it to the next two intervals.

Example 6.4

VAT of €2,500,000 was charged by a vendor on the sale of a new property to Colco, an accountable person. Colco recovered all of the VAT charged by the vendor on the acquisition of the property (it intended to make taxable supplies).

At the end of the initial interval it calculated that 80% of its supplies were taxable or qualifying activities. The other 20% were exempt supplies. [See above example for initial interval deduction for Colco].

At the end of the second interval Colco calculated that, for that period, 90% of its supplies were taxable or qualifying activities; the other 10% were exempt supplies.

At the end of the third (subsequent) interval it calculated that 60% of its supplies were taxable or qualifying activities; the other 40% were exempt supplies.

The number of intervals in the adjustment period is 20.

Initial Interval adjustment

[See previous example 6.3 for initial interval deduction for Colco].

Second Interval adjustment

The total tax incurred = €2.5m

The amount of total tax deducted = €2.5m.

The initial interval proportion of deductible use = 80%

The total reviewed deductible amount = the total tax incurred × the initial interval proportion of deductible use

$$= 2.5 \times 80\% = €2m$$

The base tax amount = amount of total tax incurred/no of intervals = €2.5m/20 = €125,000.

The reference deduction amount = total reviewed deductible amount/no of intervals = €2m/20

$$= €100,000$$

Proportion of deductible use = 90% (taxable use/total use for the interval)

The interval deductible amount = base tax amount × proportion of deductible use = €125,000 × 90%

$$= €112,500$$

An adjustment using the formula C − D must be made, where

C = the reference deduction amount, and

D = the interval deductible amount

$C - D = -€12,500 (100,000 - 112,500)$

As $D > C$, VAT credit of €12,500 is due to Colco in the VAT period immediately following the interval.

Third Interval adjustment

The total tax incurred = €2.5m

The amount of total tax deducted = €2.5m.

The initial interval proportion of deductible use = 80%

The total reviewed deductible amount = the total tax incurred × the initial interval proportion of deductible use

$$= 2.5 × 80\% = €2m$$

The base tax amount = amount of total tax incurred/no of intervals = €2.5m/20 = €125,000.

The reference deduction amount = total reviewed deductible amount/no of intervals = 2m/20

$$= €100,000$$

Proportion of deductible use = 60% (taxable use/total use for the interval)

The interval deductible amount = base tax amount × proportion of deductible use = 125,000 × 60%

$$= €75,000$$

The adjustment using the formula $C - D$ must be made, where C = the reference deduction amount, and

D = the interval deductible amount

$C - D = €25,000 (100,000 - 75,000)$

As $C > D$, VAT of €25,000 is due by Colco in the VAT period immediately following the interval.

6.7.6 Obligation for the owner with 'big swings' in taxable use

Where taxable use varies in any interval by greater than 50% points from that in the initial interval, then an adjustment based on the full VAT incurred on acquisition/development must be made. [This is not within the scope of this chapter].

6.7.7 Development by the tenant

Where the tenant has a leasehold interest in a completed property (see 6.2 for definition) and carries out development (not minor development) then the tenant creates a Capital Good, of which he is the Capital Good Owner. This development is refurbishment and the adjustment period consists of 10 intervals.

The same obligations as outlined above also rest with the tenant in respect of any necessary adjustments at the end of each interval.

6.7.8 The Capital Goods Record

Every Capital Good Owner is obliged to create and maintain a "capital goods record" in respect of each property owned. Among the details which must be maintained are:

- The amount of VAT charged to the owner upon acquisition/development

- The amount of VAT deducted initially

- The commencement date of the adjustment period

- The number of intervals in the adjustment period

- The initial interval proportion of deductible use (see Example 6.2)

- The total reviewed deductible amount (see Example 6.3)

- The proportion of deductible use for each interval (see Example 6.3 and 6.4)

- Details of any adjustments under the scheme

- Details of any sale of the property.

6.8   The Capital Goods Scheme – Implications for Disposal of a Capital Good

6.8.1   Introduction

When a capital good (a developed property) is disposed of (sold, or in the case of a legacy lease, assigned or surrendered) during the VAT life of the property (the adjustment period) then account must be taken of the effects of the Capital Goods Scheme.

It is important to remember that the VAT life of the property will have been determined prior to the time of the sale (generally it will be 10 or 20 years) and where the property is sold, it is highly likely that the VAT life will not have expired.

Broadly speaking, the disposal of the capital goods will fit into one of the following categories:

- If the sale of the property is taxable, either because of the five-year rule (see 6.3.1) or because the joint option for taxation is invoked (see 6.2) then for the remaining periods in the VAT life of the property (the remaining intervals), the property is treated as having been used for fully taxable purposes by the vendor.

- If the sale of the property is exempt from VAT, either because of the five-year rule (see 6.3.1) or because the joint option for taxation is not invoked (see 6.2) then for the remaining periods in the VAT life of the property (the remaining intervals) the property is treated as having been used for exempt purposes by the vendor.

It is important to understand that the "VAT life" of the property is for the duration in which the property is owned by a person. Where the property is sold within its current "VAT life" to another person and the sale is liable to VAT, then a new "VAT life" for the property begins upon acquisition of the property by the new owner.

6.8.2 Taxable sale of a Capital Good during its VAT life

Where the sale of the property is liable to VAT, for whatever reason (see 6.8.1), then one of four possible events under the CGS will occur:

- If the vendor had been entitled to deduct all of the input VAT on his/her acquisition of the property (or the assignor in the case of a legacy lease on the property) and used the property for fully taxable activities in the initial interval, then no adjustment under the CGS is required.

- If the vendor had not been entitled to deduct any of the input VAT on his/her acquisition of the property (or the assignor in the case of a legacy lease on the property) then an adjustment under the CGS is required.

- If the vendor had deducted all of the input VAT on his/her acquisition of the property (or the assignor in the case of a legacy lease on the property) and had not used the property for fully taxable activities in the initial interval, then an adjustment under the CGS is required.

- If the vendor had deducted some of the input VAT (partial deduction) on his/her acquisition of the property (or the assignor in the case of a legacy lease on the property) then an adjustment under the CGS is required.

Example 6.5

Chargemore, an accountancy firm, has a purpose built office completed in October 2009 at a cost of €2.5m with VAT charged of €337,500. As it used the property for taxable supplies it deducted all of the input VAT and did not need to make any adjustments under the CGS during the course of its ownership of the building. It merges with another firm in May 2016 and sells the property for €8m.

As the property is no longer 'new' (i.e., it is over 5-years old) the sale is exempt from VAT. Therefore the options are to sell the property without VAT or for the vendor and purchaser to exercise the joint option for taxation and apply VAT at 13½% to the sale. We will assume a taxable sale of the property.

As the property is over 5-years old a joint option for taxation must be exercised and the purchaser must self-account for the VAT arising on the sale. As VAT is being charged on the sale and as the property was used for fully taxable purposes during the six intervals prior to the sale, no adjustment under the capital goods scheme is required.

Thus VAT of €1,080,000 will apply to the sale (€8m × 13.5%). The purchaser must account for this VAT and the amount of it which may be deducted as input VAT by the purchaser will depend on the use to which the purchaser puts the property. Chargemore will have to pay €337,500 × 15/20 = €253,125 to the Revenue as output upon sale of the premises.

6.8.3 VAT exempt sale of a Capital Good during its VAT life

Where the sale of the property is exempt from VAT, for whatever reason (see 6.8.1), then one of two possible events under the CGS will occur:

(1) Where the vendor (or the assignor in the case of a legacy lease on the property) was not entitled to deduct any of the input VAT incurred on acquisition of the property, then no adjustment is required.

(2) Where the vendor (or the assignor in the case of a legacy lease on the property) was entitled to deduct some or all of the input VAT on acquisition then an adjustment, based on the VAT use by the vendor and the number of intervals remaining, must be carried out under the CGS.

Example 6.6

Chargemore, an accountancy firm, has a purpose built office completed in October 2009 at a cost of €2.5m with VAT charged of €337,500. As it used the property for taxable supplies it deducted all of the input VAT and did not need to make any adjustments under the CGS during the course of its ownership of the building. It merges with another firm in May 2016 and sells the property for €8m.

As the property is no longer 'new' (i.e., it is over 5-years old) the sale is exempt from VAT. Therefore the options are to sell the property without VAT or for the vendor and purchaser to exercise the joint option for taxation and apply VAT at 13½% to the sale. We will assume an exempt sale of the property.

In this case there will be a claw-back of a portion of the input VAT initially recovered by Chargemore to reflect the fact that the property was only used for taxable purposes during six full years (2009-2016) of the VAT life (adjustment period).

The adjustment is computed by using the formula $\dfrac{B \times N}{T}$

Where B = the total reviewed deductible amount = €337,500

N = number of full intervals remaining + 1 = 15

T = total number of intervals in the adjustment period (VAT life) = 20

Adjustment = €337,500 × 15/20 = €253,125

Thus Chargemore will have to pay €253,125 to the Revenue as output upon sale of the premises. It will not charge VAT to the purchaser.

6.8.4   Taxable v Exempt sale of the property – Commercial Considerations

Consider the above two Examples 6.5 and 6.6.

In Example 6.5 VAT in the amount of €1,080,000 will apply to the sale of the property. In addition the vendor will be able to recover all input VAT incurred on Costs associated with the sale. Given that the joint option for taxation was exercised by both parties a new 'VAT life', this time for the purchaser, commences in 2016 and will extend for a 20-year period, or until such time as the purchaser sells the property, if within this 20-year period.

In Example 6.6 a CGS adjustment in the amount of €253,125 must be made by Chargemore. Additionally it cannot recover input VAT on costs associated with the sale. The sale of the property will be exempt from VAT and there will not be a new 'VAT life' for the property in the hands of the purchaser.

Exercise 6.1

> Imaging you are the registered tax consultant to Chargemore. Chargemore tells you it has an offer from another accountancy firm for the office and also an offer from an insurance provider.
>
> What VAT advice might you give to Chargemore in relation to the sale of the property? [Hint: one purchaser is a fully taxable supplier and the other is a fully VAT-exempt supplier].

6.8.5 Tenant development – CGS Implications

It is a very common occurrence now for a tenant to carry out certain works to an already completed building in order to prepare it for opening. Such works may involve putting in a mezzanine floor, individualised wall claddings, displays, lighting, etc. Under the new rules such work constitutes refurbishment and in itself creates a "VAT life" for a 10-year period for the tenant who carried out the refurbishment.

The property in question could therefore have two parallel "VAT lives"; a 20-year VAT life for the owner who is letting the property to the tenant in relation to the property itself, and a 10-year VAT life for the tenant in respect of the refurbishment carried out by the tenant.

The general rule is that where the tenant vacates the property during the VAT life of the refurbishments, then a claw-back of a proportion of the VAT incurred on the refurbishment will occur. However there are two ways in which this claw-back can be avoided:

- Where the tenant uses the property for fully taxable use in the initial interval and enters a written agreement with the person to whom the lease is assigned/surrendered that such person will "take over" his obligations under the CGS. The tenant must issue a copy of the 'capital goods record' (see 6.7.7 for definition) and such information is used to enable the person who acquired the fit-out to operate the CGS. In these circumstances an adjustment by the tenant under the CGS is not required.

- Where the refurbishment carried out is removed prior to assignment/surrender then an adjustment by the tenant under the CGS is not required.

6.8.6 Exercising and terminating the Landlords' option to tax – Implications for the CGS

As you will be aware the letting of immovable goods is, in the first instance, exempt from VAT. Where a landlord exercised an option to tax then the use of the property in his hands, i.e., the letting, is liable to VAT at 21.5%. You can therefore understand that by exercising the option to tax and thereafter terminating the option during the course of the VAT life of the property, you will create the necessity for a VAT adjustment under the CGS in the period(s) in which the option is exercised (if previously there was an exempt letting) or cancelled (where previously there was a taxable letting).

A landlord might decide to exercise or terminate an option to tax the lease any number of times during the course of the VAT life for a variety of reasons. Perhaps the most likely cause for a change would be a change in tenancy whereby a tenant with full VAT recovery is replaced by a tenant with no/limited VAT recovery, or vice versa.

You can imagine that for an accountant renting an office block, they will be VAT neutral, i.e., he/she would be entitled to deduct in full the VAT charged by the landlord. Whereas in the case of change of tenancy to say a crèche or a medical centre that VAT on rents for the new tenant would be a cost, as such VAT would not be deductible.

Example 6.7

Rentco Ltd buys an office building in 2008 for €3m upon which VAT of €405,000 has been charged and fully recovered by Rentco Ltd (on the basis that it will make fully taxable supplies). It rents the office to Haulco in 2008 and having opted to tax the rents charges VAT at 21.5% on the annual rent of €500,000. [Haulco, a haulage company, is able to recover this VAT in full].

In 2012 Haulco surrenders its lease and Rentco Ltd looks for a new tenant. In February 2013, Busco Limited, a company which operates a fleet of buses, rents the premises. It will not be in a position to recover the €107,500 VAT (500,000 × 21.5%) which it will be the charge each year on the rents (its supplies are VAT exempt) and asks Rentco Ltd to consider not applying VAT to the rents.

If Rentco Ltd decides not to apply VAT to the rents (as may well be necessary to attract Busco Limited to take up the lease) it must carry out an adjustment under the CGS to see what the cost to it will be.

[We will assume that no adjustments were made by Rentco Ltd in the previous periods as the property was used fully for taxable use, i.e., rented with an option to tax exercised by Rentco Ltd].

The adjustment will be made using the formula C − D

Where C = the reference deduction amount = total reviewed deductible amount/no of intervals

= €405,000/20 = €20,250

And D = the interval deduction amount = base tax amount × proportion of deductible use

= €405,000/20 × 0% = 0

C − D = €20,250 − 0 = €20,250

Thus at the end of the interval in which the exempt letting is made, Rentco Ltd will have to make an adjustment of €20,250 and pay this as output VAT. It will thereafter have to make the same adjustment every year.

Exercise 6.2

As the registered tax consultant to Rentco Ltd what would you advise in relation to the request by Busco Ltd to exempt the rental charge? Are there any tax implications for Rentco Ltd, other than VAT?

6.8.7 Letting of residential property by a developer prior to sale – Implications for the CGS

Where a property developer sets out to build residential accommodation for supply, he is entitled to deduct all input VAT as his intention at the time that it is incurred (generally the construction phase) is to make a VATable supply of property.

For whatever reason the developer may not be able to realise sales and, as a temporary Measure, may be forced to let the property on a short-term basis for a period of time. The letting of residential property is exempt from VAT and, as we have seen earlier, it is not possible for a landlord to opt to tax lettings of residential property (see 6.5.2).

In the case of the letting of residential property, the landlord does not have to carry out the initial interval adjustment but must carry out the subsequent interval adjustments over the period of letting of the property prior to sale.

[Note if he sets out to develop property for rental only and not for sale then he would not be entitled to register for and recover input VAT from the outset].

Example 6.8

Devco Ltd builds 70 houses over a period of time. In January 2010, 20 houses are completed and remain unsold. In order to defray costs, Devco lets them to tenants on a renewable yearly lease until such time as they can be sold. All of the VAT incurred on construction was recovered by Devco. [The VAT incurred on construction of the 20 houses remaining was €600,000.]

For the initial interval Devco is not obliged to make an adjustment under the Capital Goods Scheme.

For the second and each subsequent interval for which the houses are let Devco must make an adjustment under the CGS.

The adjustment in the second and subsequent intervals is as follows (assuming all 20 houses remain let):

Total tax incurred = €600,000

Initial interval of deductible use	*= 100% (as the houses are built with the intention to sell and the initial interval exempt use is disregarded)*
Total Reviewed Deductible amount	*= Total tax incurred $\times$ initial interval of deductible use*
	= €600,000 $\times$ 100% = €600,000
Reference deductible amount (C)	*= Total Reviewed Deductible amount/20 intervals = €30,000*
Base tax amount	*= €30,000 (600,000/20 intervals)*
Proportion of deductible use	*= 0% (as the property is used for fully exempt lettings in each subsequent interval)*
Interval deductible amount (D)	*= Base tax amount $\times$ Proportion of deductible use = 0*
Adjustment	*= C − D = 30,000 − 0 = €30,000*

Therefore in the second and each subsequent interval Devco will be obliged to repay €30,000 under the CGS in respect of the exempt use of the property.

6.8.8   The transfer of a business as a going concern – implications for the CGS

As we noted earlier, the transfer of a business is not considered to be a supply for VAT purposes. Thus the price received for the transfer, which will most likely include both tangible and intangible assets, will not carry the charge of VAT. This will have implications for the CGS.

Where a property is included in the transfer of the business, two scenarios present themselves transfer when the completed property is 'new' or 'not new' for VAT papers.

6.8.8.1   Transfer when a completed property is 'new' for VAT purposes

In these circumstances the vendor is considered to have made a taxable supply of the property (even though VAT is not charged) and his 'adjustment period' for the property is ended. It is important to note that where the vendor did not have full input VAT recovery in respect of the acquisition or development of the property, that the transfer will result in a payment to him of some of the input VAT incurred at the outset.

The purchaser is deemed to have been charged VAT (on the value of the property) and is deemed to have recovered this to the extent that he will use the property for taxable supplies. A 20-year adjustment period for the purchaser begins upon his acquisition of the business.

Example 6.9

Transco Ltd built a new warehouse and office which were completed in October 2009. It used them fully for its taxable transport and warehousing activities. In December 2011, the business was taken over by Haulco Ltd for €25m of which €12m referred to the premises. VAT was not charged on the sale price as this was the transfer of a business. The property, being less than five-years old, is 'new' for VAT purposes.

For Transco Ltd its adjustment period ended upon sale of the premises. It has already deducted all of the input VAT on the property and makes no further adjustment.

For Haulco Ltd its adjustment period is for 20 years from December 2011 (when it acquired the property). VAT in the amount of €1.62m (12m × 13.5%) is deemed to have been charged on the property; as Haulco uses the property fully for its taxable activity, it would be entitled to recover this VAT in full were it charged.

Therefore using the formula F − G to calculate any VAT payable by Haulco on the acquisition where F = the deemed VAT chargeable , i.e., €1.62m and G = the deemed VAT deductible, i.e., also €1.62m we see that no VAT is payable on the property by Haulco Ltd on acquisition of the business.

Example 6.10

Lylo Ltd, a firm of undertakers purchased new premises in January 2008. It paid €5m for the premises and incurred VAT of €675,000 which was irrecoverable because Lylo's activity undertaking is exempt from VAT. In March 2011, it sold the business to a competitor Morelo Ltd for €15m of which €8m referred to the premises. VAT was not charged on the sale price as this was the transfer of a business. The property, being less than five-years old, is 'new' for VAT purposes.

There is a CGS adjustment for both parties upon transfer because if the transfer of business rules did not apply the sale of the property would be liable to VAT.

For Lylo Ltd the CGS adjustment is as follows:

$$\frac{E \times N}{T}$$

Where E = the non-deductible VAT (€675,000)

    N = the number of intervals remaining for Lylo + 1 (17 + 1 = 18)

    T = total number of intervals in the adjustment period. (20)

Using the formula VAT in the amount of €607,500 can be claimed by Lylo Ltd in the VAT period in which it sold the business.

For Morelo Ltd the CGS adjustment is as follows:

F – G

Where F = the amount of VAT that would have been charged were the supply liable to VAT (€1.08m, being €8m × 13.5%)

G = the amount of VAT that would have been deductible by Morelo (€0, as the premises are used for an exempt activity by Morelo)

Using the formula the amount of VAT payable by Morelo on its acquisition of the property is €1.08m (1.08 − 0).

6.8.8.2   Transfer when a completed property is not 'new' for VAT purposes

In these circumstances a joint option for taxation between the vendor and the purchaser cannot be put in place (see 6.2). In these circumstances where the transfer of the property occurs within the adjustment period, the purchaser essentially "steps into the shoes" of the vendor and must comply with all of the vendors obligations for the remainder of the adjustment period. In essence, the purchaser is treated as having owned the property from the date it was acquired by the vendor. The vendor must hand over his Capital Goods Record to the purchaser at the time of the transfer. The subsequent use to which the property is put by the purchaser will determine if he has to make any ongoing annual adjustments under the CGS.

Example 6.11

A Ltd acquired a new completed property in January 2010. A Ltd used it for the purpose of a taxable activity until he sold his business in April 2017 to B Ltd for €10m. As the property is seven-years old on transfer, it would be exempt from VAT if it was not the transfer of a business.

VAT is not charged on the transfer, A Ltd is obliged to hand over its Capital Goods Record to B Ltd.

The adjustment period for A Ltd was from January 2010 to April 2017 and for B Ltd is from April 2017 to January 2030, i.e., 20 years in total from January 2010.

6.9   Building Services

6.9.1   Introduction

Work consisting of the development of immovable goods (land and buildings), including the installation of fixtures, is considered to be the supply of a service and not the supply of goods. Thus, where a builder supplies concrete blocks and builds a wall with the blocks, he has made a supply of a service for VAT purposes. The rate of VAT applicable will be the rate determined by section 11 VAT Acts 1972–2009 and the appropriate schedule to the Act.

In the case of a supply of labour only (no materials included), the appropriate rate of VAT is 13.5%.

In the case of a supply of labour and materials, the appropriate rate of VAT is determined by the "Two-Thirds Rule". (See Chapter 3, section 3.10.)

6.9.2   The "Two-Thirds Rule"

Where the value (cost) of movable goods (materials) used in the supply of a service consisting of the development of immovable goods (land and buildings) exceeds two-thirds of the total amount on which VAT is chargeable in respect of the supply, then the rate of VAT applicable to the supply is 21.5%.[3]

Where the value (cost) of movable goods (materials) used in the supply of a service consisting of the development of immovable goods (land and buildings) does not exceed two-thirds of the total amount on which VAT is chargeable in respect of the supply, then the rate of VAT applicable to the supply is 13.5%.

The "Two-thirds Rule" is an anti-avoidance mechanism to ensure that a supply which is correctly one of goods is not treated as a supply of a service.

Example 6.12

A property developer contracts with a plumber to supply and lay pipes for a number of houses which he is building. The plumber quotes a price of €225,000 plus VAT for the job.

The pipes and fittings cost the plumber €148,000 plus VAT. He prices his labour at €77,000.

As the cost of the materials to the builder does not exceed €150,000 (two-thirds of €225,000), the rate applicable to the service, 13.5%, is applied to the entire supply by the plumber. Thus, he will invoice the property developer for €225,000 plus €30,375 VAT.

Example 6.13

A bank contracts with a specialist supplier for the supply and installation of a safe at its premises. The specialist installer quotes a price of €500,000 for the supply and installation of the safe.

The cost of the safe to the installer is €400,000 and the installation charge amounts to €100,000.

As the cost of the safe to the installer exceeds two-thirds of €500,000, the rate applicable to the entire supply is 21.5%. However, as the recipient of the service is a bank, which is carrying on a

---

[3]   In the case where the "Two-thirds Rule" is broken, i.e., where the cost of materials exceed two-thirds of the charge for the service, the service provider can split his/her charge and invoice the labour amount at 13.5% and the materials amount at 21.5%.

VAT-exempt activity and as such cannot recover input VAT, the installer should apply 13.5% VAT to the installation charges and 21.5% to the charge for the supply of the safe.

Thus, he will invoice the bank for €400,000 plus €86,000 VAT (for the supply of the safe) and for €100,000 plus €13,500 VAT (for the installation of the fixture).

6.9.3 Place of supply

As discussed in detail at in Chapter 3 (Section 3.6.2), the place of supply of services connected with property is where the property is located. This includes all building services.

Where an Irish VAT-registered builder supplies services for a building being built in Germany, the place of supply is Germany.

Where a French VAT-registered builder supplies services for a building being built in Denmark, the place of supply is Denmark.

6.9.4 Person who must account for VAT

With effect from 1 September 2008, the accountable person in respect of building services may be either: (i) the supplier of the services or (ii) the recipient of the services. Which person accounts for the VAT depends on certain rules, as outlined below.

Where the relationship between the building service provider and the person who receives the building service is a contractor/sub-contractor relationship, i.e., Relevant Contracts Tax legislation applies, the recipient of the service (the principal contractor) is the accountable person for VAT. The service provider (the sub-contractor) does not charge VAT on the supply of his services, rather the recipient of the building service must self-account for VAT on the building service received. The service supplier must nonetheless issue an invoice to the principal contractor, which, in addition to the usual items which appear on a VAT invoice, must include the narrative "*VAT ON THIS SUPPLY TO BE ACCOUNTED FOR BY THE PRINCIPAL CONTRACTOR*".

Where the relationship between the building service provider and the person who receives the building service is not that of a contractor/sub-contractor nature, i.e., Relevant Contracts Tax legislation does not apply, then the supplier is the accountable person for VAT. The service provider charges VAT on the supply of his services, and issues the usual VAT invoice.

WHAT YOU SHOULD NOW KNOW

On completion of this chapter, you should be able to:

- ✓ Broadly understand the new rules and new terms relating to VAT and property.

- ✓ Identify dealings in property that may constitute taxable supplies.

- ✓ Know what constitutes development in relation to property.

- ✓ Distinguish between supplies of goods and supplies of services in relation to property transactions.

- ✓ Distinguish between taxable and exempt property supplies and understand the importance of the joint option for taxation.

- ✓ Distinguish between taxable and exempt letting services and understand the importance of the landlords's option to tax.

- ✓ Know who accounts for VAT on the taxable supply of property.

- ✓ Have an understanding of the transitional rules relating to the supply of developed property and the letting of property.

- ✓ Have a broad understanding of the operation of the Capital Goods Scheme.

- ✓ Describe the VAT treatment of building services.

- ✓ Explain the two-thirds rule and its application to the development of immoveable goods.

- ✓ Know who accounts for VAT on a building service.

- ✓ Complete Questions and the Assignments in Irish Taxation Law and Practice, Volume 2.

7

RIGHTS AND OBLIGATIONS OF ACCOUNTABLE PERSONS AND THE ROLE OF REVENUE

In this chapter, you will deal with the following:

- The Rights and obligations of accountable persons
- The powers of the Revenue Commissioners
- The role and structure of the Revenue Commissioners

7.1 Introduction

The VAT system is completely dependent on the goodwill and participation of accountable persons, i.e., the VAT-registered traders who operate the VAT system and collect the tax on behalf of the Collector-General, as is their obligation under domestic VAT legislation.

So far in the chapters on VAT, we have discussed the European context, the charge of VAT and how VAT is applied to transactions. We have also examined the legislation and how VAT-registered traders arrive at their VAT liability.

To ensure the smooth operation of the VAT system, many rights and obligations are enshrined in legislation. In this chapter, we will discuss some such rights and obligations. The chapter is also concerned with Revenue powers and the role of the Revenue Commissioners with regard to the operation of the VAT system.

The Revenue Commissioners, sometime ago, published a Charter of Rights for taxpayers (see Appendix IV to this chapter).

With effect from 24 December 2008 fundamental changes to the 'penalty regime' applicable in the case of non-compliance with VAT legislation have taken effect. (See 7.4.7 Penalties)

7.2 Rights and Obligations

7.2.1 Keeping records

s16 VA 72

"Every accountable person shall, in accordance with regulations, keep full and true records of all transactions which affect or may affect his liability to tax".

A VAT-registered person is obliged to retain records for six years. However, the Revenue Commissioners may authorise a person to destroy records within this period. This authorisation may be granted on foot of a request from the VAT-registered person and will generally be preceded by an inspection of the records concerned.

The records which must be retained are specified in Regulations 8–14, Value-Added Tax Regulations, 2006 [SI No 548 of 2006]. (An extract is included at Appendix I, to this chapter). Previous VAT regulations were replaced by these regulations, effective from 1 November 2006.

In the case of a person who acquires or develops taxable property or a person who has, prior to 1 July 2008 waived exemption in relation to short leases, there is a further obligation to retain records for a six-year period following disposal of the property or cancellation of the waiver.

7.2.2   Responsible officer

s33 VA 72   In the case of a body of persons (e.g., a company), the responsible person for the body is the secretary or the person acting as secretary. Any notification served on the secretary is deemed to be served on the company. Any obligation of the company with regard to VAT is also an obligation of the secretary.

The secretary may retain from the company an amount of money necessary for the payment of VAT should the matter arise, and the secretary is indemnified in respect of such retention.

7.2.3   Foreign trader's/promoter's declaration

S8(2)(d)
VA 72   Where a foreign (non-established) trader (referred to as a "mobile trader") proposes to sell goods in the State, there is an obligation on the owner or controller of the premises (the premises provider), from which the goods will be sold, to notify Revenue in advance. Additionally, when a foreign (non-established) promoter of cultural, musical or entertainment services supplies services in the State, there is an obligation on the owner or controller of the premises, from which the service will be supplied, to notify Revenue in advance.

The details which must be supplied in relation to such mobile traders and promoters are:

■ the name and address of the mobile trader/promoter;

■ the date on which the goods and services will be supplied;

■ the venue where the goods or services will be supplied; and

■ the address of the premises from which such supplies will be made.

Failure to notify Revenue in advance may have very serious consequences for the premises provider:

> *"... the Revenue Commissioners may, where it appears necessary to them to do so for the protection of the revenue, make such premises provider jointly and severally liable with a mobile trader or promoter, as the case may be, for the tax chargeable in respect of supplies made by that mobile trader or promoter on the premises provider's land ..."*

7.2.4   Letter of expression of doubt

s19B VA 72   Where a VAT-registered person has a doubt as to the correct VAT treatment applicable to a particular transaction, which may have a bearing on his/her liability to VAT, then he or she may file an expression of doubt with the Revenue Commissioners at the same time as he/she files their periodic VAT return.

The letter, which must be in written form, should be accompanied by any necessary documentation in support of it. Where Revenue issues a notification to the person concerned in response to an expression of doubt, which results in a greater liability to VAT in respect of the particular transaction concerned, and where the person pays such an amount in the same VAT period in which the notification is received, then interest will not be applied to such additional amount.

Revenue may refuse to accept a letter of expression of doubt where they believe the VAT treatment is straightforward. A VAT-registered person may appeal such a refusal.

7.2.5   VAT registration

s9 A 72   A person who is obliged to register for VAT is obliged to furnish the details required by regulation to the Revenue Commissioners, to enable them to register the person for VAT.

Liquidators and receivers are obliged to register for VAT when they dispose of the assets of a company. There is no registration threshold.

In the case of small traders, Form STR1 must be completed and filed.

In the case of sole traders/partnerships/joint ventures, Form TR1 must be completed and filed.

In the case of limited/unlimited companies, Form TR2 must be completed and filed.

A copy of Form TR1 and Form TR2 are included at Appendix II, to this chapter.

7.2.6   Interest payable on VAT due

s21 VA 72   Where an amount of tax is payable and the accountable person has not paid the amount, simple interest at 0.0322% per day is applied to the amount until such time as payment is made. This roughly equates to 1% per month or 12% per year.

In the case of a person who is authorised to make an annual return for VAT and who, at the end of the year, owes in excess of 20% of the VAT payable for the year, then interest at the rate of 0.0322% × 183 (6%) is applied to the outstanding balance.

As interest is statutory (i.e., determined by law to be payable), it is not negotiable.

In the case of a detection of underpaid VAT going back for a number of years, the interest charge can be very high. For instance, if an underpayment of VAT of €10,000 for the year 1996 is detected, the interest charge (at *c.* 12% × seven years) amounts to approximately €8,400.

7.2.7   Refund of VAT

s20 VA 72   Where an accountable person's input VAT exceeds the output VAT, the excess is repaid to the person by Revenue. This payment by Revenue is commonly referred to as a "VAT repayment". Additionally, where an accountable person overpaid VAT, Revenue may repay the overpaid amount.

For tax periods commencing on or after 1 May 2003, the prior period for which a refund may be claimed is four years. Thus, if an accountable person realises that he/she has overpaid VAT for some reason or other, the claim for repayment must be lodged within four years of the end of the tax period concerned.

7.2.8   Unjust enrichment

s20 VA 72   This is a somewhat controversial area and the subject of litigation. Where Revenue believes that by refunding an amount of VAT to an accountable person, such person will be unjustly enriched, it can refuse to make the refund.

Consider a mechanic who charged VAT at 21.5% on car repairs for a period of time and calculated the VAT payable on this basis. Some years later his registered tax consultant spots the mistake and advises him that the appropriate rate of VAT was 13.5%. He prepares a claim and lodges it with Revenue for the difference of 7.5%. Where there is no evidence that he will reimburse the customers he overcharged, Revenue may refuse to repay the overpayment, as the person will have been "unjustly enriched".

The matter is highly complex and has not as yet been fully explored. After all, the mechanic may argue that he is simply increasing profits, on which he may have to pay additional income tax.

The Finance (No. 2) Act, 2008 has amended the VAT Act with regard to claims for a refund of overpaid VAT by an accountable person. [Note that the notion of unjust enrichment arises where a claimant seeks a refund of VAT which, due to a mistaken assumption on his part, he has paid to the Revenue as VAT]. Any such claims must be submitted in writing setting out the full details of the claim. Before repaying the amount the Revenue Commissioners may determine whether or not the claimant would be 'unjustly enriched' by such refund and in this regard they may have regard to the following:

■ The extent to which the cost of the overpaid amount was passed on by the claimant to others in the price charged for the goods/services

■ Any loss of profit borne by the claimant due to the mistaken assumption made in relation to the operation of the tax

■ Any other factors which the claimant may bring to their attention.

7.2.9   Interest on refunds of VAT

s21A VA 72   The Revenue Commissioners are obliged to pay interest at 0.011% per day (4% per year) on VAT repayments due to taxpayers who have not been repaid. This follows a specific period. This obligation was brought about by a high-profile High Court case in which Revenue was compelled to pay substantial interest in a case where it was obliged to repay large sums of VAT following an earlier, successful Supreme Court challenge by a VAT-registered person.

Interest is payable by Revenue:

> ... *"Where a mistaken assumption in the operation of the tax is made by the Revenue Commissioners and, as a result, a refundable amount is payable to a claimant ..."*

In any case involving undue delay, other than a "mistaken assumption" on the part of Revenue, in making a VAT repayment, interest is also payable following the expiry of a six-month period immediately following the tax period in which the repayment was due.

7.2.10 Appeals

s25 VA 72   By far the most important right available to accountable persons is the right of appeal. The right of appeal acts as a check on the power of the Revenue Commissioners, and their use of that power. It also serves to link the tax system and the Courts. A right of appeal exists in relation to the following:

- an assessment raised by Revenue in relation to overstating an amount of VAT on an invoice;

- an assessment raised by Revenue in relation to a person not registered for VAT issuing a VAT invoice;

- the compulsory VAT group registration of a number of companies;

- the assessing of a premises provider in respect of VAT payable by the mobile trader/ promoter;

- a refusal to make a VAT repayment;

- the compulsory registration of a person for VAT by the Revenue Commissioners.

- a determination by the Revenue Commissioners in relation to the value, upon which VAT is chargeable, of certain transactions between connected persons

Time limits are set down for appeals, and the procedures applying to income and corporation tax appeals are applicable in the case of VAT appeals.

Where an accountable person is dissatisfied with the outcome of a hearing before the Appeal Commissioner, he/she may apply to have the appeal reheard *de novo* at the Circuit Court. This facility is not available to the Revenue Commissioners.

Either party, the accountable person or the Revenue Commissioners, may refer a case from the Appeal Commissioners or the Circuit Court to the High Court on a point of law.

The Appeal Commissioner may refer a case to the European Court of Justice for clarification in relation to interpretation or implementation of Community provisions (Council Directive 2006/112/EC– see Chapter 2). The Appeal Commissioners in Ireland have only very recently availed of this avenue. In the UK, by contrast, the equivalent of the Appeal Commissioner, the VAT Tribunal, sends cases to the ECJ on a regular basis.

The Appeal Commissioners

There are two Appeal Commissioners. They sit individually at appeal hearings. The Appeal Commissioners are appointed by the Minister for Finance and are completely independent of the Revenue Commissioners. They hear cases where there is a dispute between an appellant and Revenue.

7.3 The Role and Structure of the Revenue Commissioners

A VAT system would not be complete without a monitoring and policing function. Such a function is carried out by the Revenue Commissioners, who are entrusted with the "care and management" of VAT. Their duties extend to drafting legislation, making determinations, auditing taxpayers, dealing with appeals, maintaining a register of taxpayers and managing the system generally. We will now examine the divisions of the Revenue Commissioners which deal with VAT matters in a variety of ways.

With effect from 1 January 2003 the separate division in the Revenue Commissioners known as the Office of the Chief Inspector of Taxes has been integrated with the General Civil Service.

The Board of the Revenue Commissioners is composed of three Commissioners who are appointed by the Minister for Finance.

A number of divisions within the Office of the Revenue Commissioners deal with the day-to-day monitoring and policing of the VAT system. Certain divisions retain files on accountable persons. They also carry out VAT audits, verify VAT repayments and give assistance to accountable persons in dealing with their VAT affairs. There are five divisions dealing with the day-to-day policing and monitoring of the VAT system: the "Large Cases" division and four geographically arranged divisions.

A separate division, known as the "Indirect Taxes" division, co-ordinates policy, legislation and international functions for all indirect taxes (including VAT).

The Collector-General's division collects VAT and any interest charges, and makes VAT repayments.

The "Customs and Excise" division applies and collects VAT on imports and on the intra-Community acquisition of private means of transport (private cars, pleasure boats and small planes).

7.4   The Powers of Revenue

The Revenue Commissioners have very wide-ranging powers in relation to both accountable persons and records of transactions (supplies). We have outlined below the more common powers; there are additional powers, which are not discussed here.

7.4.1   Inspection of records

s18 VA 72   Authorised officers of the Revenue Commissioners have extensive and wide-ranging powers with regard to the inspection of records. VAT-registered persons have certain obligations when it comes to presenting records and assisting Revenue:

- A VAT-registered person or his/her employees or associates are required to produce records of the business requested by an authorised officer.

- A VAT-registered person or his/her employees or associates are required to provide all reasonable assistance to an authorised officer.

- A VAT-registered person or his/her employees or associates may not "wilfully obstruct or delay" an authorised officer in the course of his/her duties.

- A person is not obliged to disclose any professional advice rendered to a VAT-registered client.

The authorised officer is obliged to produce his/her authorisation on request. Generally speaking, advance notice will be given to the accountable person in respect of a proposed audit/inspection. Once notification has been received, the accountable person has the opportunity to present a written notification to Revenue of any underpayments of VAT of which he/she is aware. Where such disclosure is complete, Revenue will mitigate penalties, which they will apply in the event of additional VAT being payable.

7.4.2   Removal of records

An authorised officer of the Revenue Commissioners may search, without a warrant, any premises where he has reason to believe a business is being carried on and may remove any records from the premises for the purpose of examination.

7.4.3   Search of the person

An authorised officer of the Revenue Commissioners may search any person for any records that he believes are on the person and which he believes may be used in criminal proceedings.

7.4.4   Raising assessments/estimates

Revenue may raise assessments where it believes there has been an under-declaration of VAT liability.

Section 22 estimates

s22 VA 72   Where an accountable person fails to lodge a VAT return for a taxable period, Revenue may estimate the amount of VAT payable and raise an estimate for that amount. Also where a person fails to register for VAT then the Revenue may register such person and raise a s22 estimate where they form the opinion that he/she is an accountable person.

An accountable person may appeal a s22 estimate where he/she claims not to be a accountable person only within a 14-day period of being notified of the estimate.

Where a VAT return is not lodged, the amount of the s22 estimate may be pursued by Revenue. Where a VAT return is subsequently filed for the period and where the liability is paid, the s22 assessment is discharged.

Section 23 assessments

s23 VA 72   Where Revenue believes that the VAT paid in a taxable period(s) is less than the VAT it considers payable, or where the VAT refunded exceeds the VAT it considers refundable, it may raise an assessment for the amount it considers payable.

The accountable person may appeal such an assessment to the Appeal Commissioners, in the first instance, within a 21-day period of being notified of the assessment.

7.4.5   Determinations by Revenue

s8(3E) VA 72   The provision of facilities for taking part in sporting and physical education activities, and services closely related thereto, by non-profit-making organisations or local authorities is exempt from VAT.

However, where Revenue is satisfied that such exemption results in a distortion of competition, Revenue may determine that such bodies are accountable persons and their supplies of services are liable to VAT.

s11(1B)
VA 72   Where requested by an accountable person, Revenue may determine whether a particular supply of goods or services is exempt from VAT or liable to VAT.

Where requested by an accountable person, Revenue may determine the rate of VAT applicable to a supply of goods or services.

7.4.6 The making of VAT regulations

Revenue is empowered to make regulations

"... as seem to them to be necessary for the purpose of giving effect to this Act [VAT Act] and of enabling them to discharge their functions thereunder ..."

7.4.7 Penalties

Penalties, for failure to comply with certain obligations are broadly broken down into two categories insofar as VAT is concerned.

In the first instance, there are the specific fixed penalties consisting of a fixed amount of €4,000 (increased with effect from 24 December 2008) for certain defined offences. Thus failure to register for VAT, failure to retain specific records, failure to issue a proper invoice (by an accountable person or by a flat-rate farmer) or failure to file a VAT return by the due date can each result in a fine of €4,000 for each offence. Likewise, failure to produce records, failure to assist an authorised officer, charging VAT while not registered, obstructing a person whom Revenue has required to value a premises, etc are liable to a fine of €4,000 upon conviction.

Such penalties can be pursued by way of summary proceedings (summons), and Revenue may institute proceedings for a period of up to three years after the date of the offence.

With effect from 24th December 2008 a new section 27A, VAT Acts, 1972–2009 provides for Penalties in the case of 'deliberately' or 'carelessly' making incorrect VAT returns. Prior to then, the penalty regime dealt with the concepts of negligence or fraud and the new legislation would appear to replace the concept of negligence with the act of doing something carelessly and the concept of fraud, with the act of doing something deliberately.

Prior to 24 December 2008, the penalty regime dealt with the concepts of negligence or fraud and the new legislation would appear to replace the concept of negligence with the act of doing something carelessly and the concept of fraud with the act of doing something deliberately.

A scale of penalties, which were previously set out in the Revenue publication *Code of Practice for Revenue Auditors* have now been incorporated into VAT legislation at section 27A. Broadly speaking an accountable person may make an 'unprompted voluntary disclosure' or a 'prompted voluntary disclosure' prior to the actual commencement of a revenue audit. The former category applies where the Revenue have not notified the taxpayer of the commencement of a revenue audit, the latter category applies from the time of notification until the actual commencement of the audit. In each case a window of opportunity is afforded to an accountable person to make a disclosure to the Revenue Commissioners in relation to any incorrect VAT return which has been made either deliberately or carelessly. Mitigated penalties range from 3% to 75% of the undeclared amount of output VAT (or the overclaimed amount of input VAT) as the case may be. [In the case of persistent infringement the penalty, set at 100% of the tax, will not be mitigated].

In addition, where a person 'carelessly' makes use of any VAT record, a penalty of €3,000 may be imposed. Where a person 'deliberately' makes use of any VAT record a penalty of €5,000 may be imposed.

The new penalty regime also provides that an authorised officer of the Revenue Commissioners or a member of the Garda Síochána may, where they have reason to believe that a criminal tax offence has been committed, arrest a person who is not established in the State, or arrest a person who is likely to flee the State.

Technical issues

Where Revenue determines that additional VAT is payable in relation to a certain transaction or series of transactions (either supplies received or supplies made), and it can be established that what was at issue was of a technical nature and therefore subject to the possibility of differing interpretation, then a penalty should not be applied as the commission/omission was neither deliberately nor carelessly made. It may be necessary to draw the Revenue official's attention to such circumstances at the conclusion of an audit/inspection. It remains to be seen, in light of the new legislation, how the Revenue will deal with such situations.

TAX-GEARED PENALTIES[1]				
			% Mitigation of base penalty	
Default category	*Base Penalty*	*Co-operation only*	*Co-operation only Co-operation + prompted qualifying disclosure*	*Co-operation + unprompted qualifying disclosure Deliberate behaviour*
Deliberate behaviour	100% of under declaration	75%	50%	10%
Careless behaviour with significant consequences	40% of under declaration	30%	20%	5%
Careless behaviour with less than significant consequences	20% of under declaration	15%	10%	3%

[1]Note that second and third defaults (i.e. under declaration/over claim of VAT) With effect from 24 December 2008 a new section 27A, VAT Acts, 1972–2009 provides for Penalties in the case of those who 'deliberately' or 'carelessly' make incorrect returns within a five-year period may not avail of full mitigation.

WHAT YOU SHOULD NOW KNOW

On completion of this chapter, you should be able to:

- ✓ General understanding of certain rights and obligations that pertain to VAT-registered persons.

- ✓ Describe the role and structure of the Revenue Commissioners in relation to VAT.

- ✓ Describe the powers and sanctions available to Revenue in managing and policing the VAT system, and in dealing with VAT-registered persons.

- ✓ Complete the Assignments in Irish Taxation Law and Practice, Volume 2.

References and Recommended Further Reading

CASSIDY, B. & SOMERS, J. (ed.) (2008), *Law of Value-Added Tax,* Irish Taxation Institute

GANNON, F. (2006), *VAT on Property,* Irish Taxation Institute

MARTYN, J. and P. RECK (2008), *Taxation Summary,* Irish Taxation Institute

BRODIE and DILLON (2008), *Value Added Tax,* Irish Taxation Institute

Appendix I

Value-Added Tax Regulations 2006
Regulation 8

Accounts

8. (1) The full and true records of all transactions which affect or may affect the taxable person's liability to tax, which every taxable person is required to keep in accordance with section 16 of the Act, shall be entered up to date and include—

    (a)   in relation to consideration receivable from registered persons—

        (i)   the amount receivable from each such person in respect of each transaction for which an invoice or other document is required to be issued under section 17 of the Act, and

        (ii)   a cross-reference to the copy of the relevant invoice or other document,

    (b)   in relation to consideration receivable from unregistered persons—

        (i)   a daily total of the consideration receivable from all such persons, and

        (ii)   a cross-reference to the relevant counter books, copies of sales dockets, cash register tally rolls or other documents which are in use for the purposes of the business,

    (c)   in relation to consideration receivable from persons registered for value-added tax in another Member State—

        (i)   the amount receivable from each such person in respect of each transaction for which an invoice is required to be issued under section 17 of the Act, and

        (ii)   a cross-reference to the copy of the relevant invoice,

    (d)   in relation to intra-Community acquisitions of goods, in respect of which the taxable person is liable to pay the tax chargeable—

        (i)   the amount of the consideration relating to those acquisitions, and

        (ii)   a cross-reference to the relevant invoice,

    (e)   in relation to importations of goods, a description of those goods together with particulars of their value as determined in accordance with—

        (i)   the amount of the consideration relating to the purchase of the goods if purchased in connection with the importation,

(ii)   the amount of tax, if any, paid on importation, and

(iii)   a cross-reference to the invoices and customs documents used in connection with the importation,

(f)   in relation to goods supplied in accordance with section (3)(1)(e) of the Act, being goods developed, constructed, assembled, manufactured, produced, extracted, purchased, imported or otherwise acquired by the taxable person or by another person on his or her behalf, and applied by the taxable person (otherwise than by way of disposal to another person) for the purposes of any business carried on by him or her—

(i)   a description of the goods in question, and

(ii)   the cost, excluding tax, to the taxable person of acquiring or producing them except where tax chargeable in relation to the application of the goods would, if it were charged, be wholly deductible under section 12 of the Act,

(g)   in relation to goods supplied in accordance with section (3)(1)(f) of the Act, being goods appropriated by a taxable person for any purpose other than the purpose of his or her business or disposed of free of charge, where tax chargeable in relation to the goods—

(i)   on their purchase, intra-Community acquisition or importation by the taxable person, or on their development, construction, assembly, manufacture, production, extraction, or application in accordance with section 3(1)(e) of the Act, as the case may be, was wholly or partly deductible under section 12 of the Act, or

(ii)   where the ownership of those goods was transferred to the taxable person in the course of a transfer of a totality of assets, or part thereof, of a business and that transfer of ownership was deemed not to be a supply of goods in accordance with section 3(5)(b) of the Act,

a description of the goods in question and the cost, excluding tax, to the taxable person, of acquiring or producing them,

(h)   in relation to services deemed to be supplied by a person in the course or furtherance of business in accordance with section 5(3) of the Act—

(i)   a description of the services in question, and

(ii)   particulars of the cost, excluding tax, to the taxable person of supplying the services and of the consideration, if any, receivable by him or her in respect of the supply,

(i)   in the case of the supply of services in circumstances that, by virtue of any of the provisions of section 5 of the Act, are deemed to be supplied outside the State—

    (i)   the name and address of the person to whom the services are supplied,

    (ii)   the nature of the services,

    (iii)   the amount of consideration receivable in respect of the supply, and

    (iv)   a cross-reference to the copy of the relevant invoice or other document,

(j)   in the case of the receipt of goods and services in the State in respect of which the recipient of those goods and services is liable to pay the tax chargeable —

    (i)   a description of the goods and services in question, and

    (ii)   a cross-reference to the relevant invoice,

(k)   in relation to discounts allowed or price reductions made to a registered person subsequent to the issue of an invoice to such person—

    (i)   the amount credited to such person, and

    (ii)   except in a case in which section 17(9)(a) of the Act applies, a cross-reference to the corresponding credit note,

(l)   in relation to discounts allowed or price reductions made to unregistered persons—

    (i)   a daily total of the amount so allowed, and

    (ii)   a cross-reference to the goods returned book, cash book or other record used in connection with the matter,

(m)   in relation to bad debts written off, —

    (i)   particulars of the name and address of the debtor,

    (ii)   the nature of the goods or services to which the debt relates,

    (iii)   the date or dates on which the debt was incurred, and

    (iv)   the date or dates on which the debt was written off,

(n)   in relation to goods and services supplied to the taxable person by another taxable person—

    (i)   the amount of the consideration payable,

    (ii)   the corresponding tax invoiced by the other taxable person, and

    (iii)   a cross-reference to the corresponding invoice,

(o) in relation to goods and services supplied to the taxable person by unregistered persons, other than a means of transport supplied under the special scheme in accordance with Regulation 31 and goods and services in respect of which flat-rate farmers are required in accordance with section 12A(1) of the Act to issue invoices—

    (i) a daily total of the consideration payable to such persons, and

    (ii) a cross-reference to the purchases book, cash book, purchases dockets or other records which are in use in connection with the business,

(p) in relation to goods and services supplied to the taxable person by flat-rate farmers who are required, in accordance with section 12A(1) of the Act, to issue invoices-

    (i) the amount of the consideration payable (exclusive of the flat-rate addition) and the amount of the flat-rate addition invoiced by each such farmer, and

    (ii) a cross-reference to the corresponding invoice,

(q) in relation to agricultural machinery supplied to the taxable person by flat-rate farmers who are required, in accordance with section 12C(2) of the Act, to issue invoices, a full and true record entered up to date of all acquisitions and disposals of agricultural machinery by him or her,

(r) in relation to discounts or price reductions received from registered persons, subsequent to the receipt of invoices from such persons, except in a case in which section 17(9)(a) of the Act applies—

    (i) the amount of the discount or price reduction, and the corresponding tax received from each such person, and

    (ii) a cross-reference to the corresponding credit note,

(s) in relation to discounts or price reductions in relation to goods and services supplied to the taxable person by flat-rate farmers who are required, in accordance with section 12A(1) of the Act, to issue invoices—

    (i) the amount of the discount or price reduction (exclusive of the flat-rate addition) and the amount of the corresponding flat-rate addition, and

    (ii) a cross-reference to the invoice issued in connection with the goods and services in question,

(t) in relation to discounts or price reductions received other than those referred to in subparagraphs (r) and (s)—

    (i) a daily total of the amounts so received, and

       (ii)   a cross-reference to the cash book or other record used in connection with such matters,

    and

(u)   in respect of supplies of goods specified in paragraph (i) of the Second Schedule to the Act—

       (i)   the name and address of the person to whom the goods are supplied,

       (ii)   a description of the goods supplied,

       (iii)   the amount of the consideration,

       (iv)   a cross-reference to the copy of the relevant invoice, and

       (v)   a cross-reference to the relevant Customs and transport documents.

(2)   The accounts kept in accordance with paragraph (1) are required to set out separately, the consideration, discounts, price reductions, bad debts and values at importation under separate headings in relation to—

    (a)   exempted activities, and

    (b)   goods and services chargeable at each rate of tax including the zero rate.

(3)   In relation to a person authorised in accordance with section 14(1) of the Act to determine the amount of tax which becomes due by such person by reference to the amount of moneys which he or she receives, references in this Regulation to consideration in respect of the supply of goods or services are construed as references to such moneys received in respect of such supply.

Appendix II

Specimen of Form TR1.

TAX REGISTRATION — **TR1**

This form can be used to register 'Persons', i.e., Individuals, Partnerships, Trusts or Unincorporated Bodies for Income Tax, VAT, and as an Employer for PAYE/PRSI.

Companies (including foreign companies) requiring to register for Corporation Tax, VAT and PAYE/PRSI (as an employer) should complete **Form TR2**.

PAYE employees taking up their first employment should complete **Form 12A**.

Please complete ALL parts of this form as required IN BLOCK CAPITALS, sign the declaration below and return it to your Revenue District Office. Without accurate information the registration(s) will be delayed and/or you may experience delays in receipt of Returns and other forms.

Part A. — General Details

1. State the full name of the person, *(including a trust, partnership, club or society),* who is to be registered

2. If trading under a business name, state — Trading as

3. Legal Format (please tick the appropriate box) — Sole Trader | Partnership | Other (specify)

4. If you, *(or the trust, partnership, club or society),* were registered for any tax in this country previously, what reference numbers did you hold?
   - PPS Number
   - Employer (PAYE/PRSI)
   - Value Added Tax (VAT)

5. *(Individuals only)* State
   - If married, your pre-marriage name, where different
   - Your date of birth — DD / MM / YYYY
   - Your mother's maiden name

6. Marital Status
   Tick ☑ the relevant box — Single | Married | Widowed | Married but living apart | Divorced

7. If you are married, give the following information
   - Spouse's forename
   - Spouse's surname
   - Spouse's PPS number
   - Date of Marriage — DD / MM / YYYY

8. Business Address — Private Address *(if different)*
   - Phone: Area Code — Number
   - Fax: Area Code — Number
   - Mobile Phone Number

9. If you want your tax affairs to be dealt with in Irish, tick ☑ the box

Declaration — This must be made in every case before you can be registered for any tax

I declare that the particulars supplied by me in this application are true in every respect

NAME *(in BLOCK LETTERS)* — SIGNATURE

CAPACITY *(individual, secretary, partner, trustee etc.)* — DATE DD / MM / YYYY

Page 1

Part A. continued　　　　*General Details*

10. Type of business
(a) is the business

☐ mainly retail　　　☐ mainly wholesale　　　☐ mainly manufacturing

☐ building & construction　　　☐ service and other

(b) Describe the business conducted in as much detail as possible. Give a precise description such as 'newsagent', 'clothing manufacturer', 'property letting', 'dairy farmer', 'investment income', etc. **Do not** use general terms such as 'shopkeeper', 'manufacturer', 'computers', 'consultant', etc.

If the application is a property related activity you may also need to complete Panel 27.

11. When did the business or activity commence?　　　DD / MM / YYYY

12. To what date will annual accounts be made up?　　　DD / MM / YYYY

13. Adviser Details
Give the following details of your accountant or tax adviser, if any, who will prepare the accounts and tax returns of the business.

Name
Address

Phone: Area Code	Number		Mobile Phone Number	
Fax: Area Code	Number		Tax Adviser Identification Number (TAIN)	
Client's Reference				

If correspondence relating to VAT (ie VAT 3's) is being dealt with by the acountant or tax adviser tick ☑ the box

14. Partnership, Trust or Other Body
Give the following information in respect of all partners, trustees or other officers. Under 'Capacity', state whether precedent acting partner, partner, trustee, treasurer, etc. If necessary please continue on a separate sheet.

	Name	Private Address	Capacity	PPS number (Partners only)
(i)				
(ii)				
(iii)				
(iv)				

15. If you rent your business premises, state

The name and address of the landlord (not an estate agent or rent collector)

The amount of rent paid per week ☐ , month ☐ or year ☐ (Tick ☑ frequency)　　€

The date on which you started paying the rent　　　DD / MM / YYYY

The length of the agreed rental/lease period.

16. If you acquired the business from a previous owner, state

The name and current address of the person from whom you acquired it

The VAT / registered number of that person.

Part B.   *Registration for Income Tax (non-PAYE)*

17. Are you registering for Income Tax? (Tick ☑)   Yes [ ]   No [ ]

Part C.   *Registration as an Employer for PAYE / PRSI*

18. Are you registering as an employer for PAYE/PRSI? (Tick ☑)   Yes [ ]   No [ ]

If your answer is 'No', there is no need to answer questions 19, 20 or 21. Continue to PART D.

19. Persons Engaged
(i) How many **employees** are: **Full time -** usually working 30 hours or more per week? [ ]

                               Part time - usually working less than 30 hours per week? [ ]

(ii) State the date your first employee commenced or will commence in your employment   DD / MM / YYYY

20. What payroll and PAYE/PRSI record system will you use? (Tick ☑ the relevant box)

Tax Deduction Cards (Revenue Supplied) [ ]   Other Manual System [ ]   Computer System [ ]   Disk [ ]

21. Correspondence on PAYE/PRSI

If correspondence relating to PAYE/PRSI is being dealt with by an agent, tick ☑ this box [ ] and give the following details if different from 13 above.

Name

Address

Phone: Area Code [ ]	Number [ ]	Mobile Phone Number [ ]
Fax: Area Code [ ]	Number [ ]	Tax Adviser Identification Number (TAIN) [ ]
Client's Reference [ ]		

Part D.   *Registration for VAT*

22. Are you registering for VAT? (Tick ☑)   Yes [ ]   No [ ]

If your answer is 'No', there is no need to answer questions 23 to 28.

23. Registration

(i) State the **date** from which you require to register   DD / MM / YYYY

(ii) Is registration being sought only in respect of **European Union (EU) acquisitions?** (This applies only to farmers and non-taxable entities) (Tick ☑)   Yes [ ]   No [ ]

(iii) Are you registering

     (a) because your **turnover exceeds** or is likely to exceed the **limits** prescribed by law for registration?   (a) [ ]

       or

     (b) because you wish to **elect to be a taxable person**, (although not obliged by law to be registered)?   (b) [ ]   (Tick either (a), (b) or (c) as appropriate)

       or

     (c) because you are in receipt of **Fourth Schedule Services?**   (c) [ ]

(iv) State your expected turnover for the next 12 months   € [ ]

Part D. continued   *Registration for VAT*

**24. Are you applying for the moneys received basis
of accounting for goods and services?** (Tick ☑)   Yes [ ]   No [ ]

If your answer is 'Yes', is this because

(a) expected annual turnover will be less than €635,000   (a) [ ]

   or   (Tick either
                                                           (a) or (b) as

(b) at least 90% of your expected annual turnover will come from
supplying goods and services to persons who are not registered   (b) [ ]   appropriate)
e.g. hospitals, schools or the general public.

25. If your business is a foreign business registering in this State
State the expected annual turnover from supplies of taxable goods or services within the State   € [ ]

26. State your bank or building society account to which VAT refunds can be made (compulsory)

Bank/Building Society [ ]

Branch Address [ ]

Sorting Code [ ][ ][ ] [ ][ ][ ]

Account Number [ ][ ][ ][ ][ ][ ][ ][ ]

27. Property Details for VAT purposes

(a) Address of the property [ ]

(b) Date purchased or when development commenced   [DD / MM / YYYY]

(c) Planning permission reference number, if applicable   [ ]

(d) A signed statement from your client confirming that the property in question will be purchased and/or
developed and will be disposed of or used in a manner which will give rise to a VAT liability i.e.

    – by outright sale of the property or
    – by creation of a long term lease i.e. lease more than ten years or
    – by waiver of exemption in respect of short term lettings i.e. less than 10 years.

28. Exemption Waiver (in respect of the letting of property only)

(Such services are normally exempt from VAT).

Do you wish to waive exemption from VAT in respect of property letting? (Tick ☑)   Yes [ ]   No [ ]

Note the waiver of exemption applies to all rents receivable from short-term lettings including those from properties
other than that mentioned above. An option to 'Waiver of Exemption' cannot be backdated.

Additional Information

The following leaflets will provide additional information on the taxation aspects of running your own business. They are
available from your local revenue office or from Revenue's Form's and Leaflets service at **LoCall 1890 30 67 06** or at
www.revenue.ie

     IT48   Starting in Business – A Revenue Guide
     IT50   PAYE/PRSI for Small Employers
                  Employers Guide to operating PAYE and PRSI for certain benefits

If you have further information queries or concerns contact your Revenue District Office or Employer PAYE Enquiries at
LoCall 1890 23 63 36.

If you wish to receive an employer pack tick ☑ here. [ ]

If you want information on payment options, including **Direct Debit,** contact the **Collector General** at **LoCall 1890 20 30 70**.

Revenue On-Line Service (ROS) Save time – File On-Line
Once registered, you can access your tax details and file returns on-line using Revenue On-Line Service (ROS). ROS is
available 24 hours a day, 365 days a year. It is easy, instant and secure.

For further details on ROS, visit our website at **www.revenue.ie** or call the ROS Information Desk at **LoCall 1890 20 11 06.**

Specimen of Form TR2

TAX REGISTRATION   *TR2*

This form can be used to register a limited company for Corporation Tax, for PAYE/PRSI (as an employer), and/or for VAT.

*Persons, other than companies requiring to register, should complete **Form TR1** or **PAYE employees** taking up their first employment should complete **Form 12A**.*

Please complete all parts of this form as required IN BLOCK CAPITALS, sign the declaration below and return it to your Revenue District. Without accurate information the registration(s) will be delayed and/or you may experience delays in receipt of Returns and other forms.

Part A.   *General Details*

1. **State the full name of the company as it is registered under the Companies' Acts**

2. **If trading under a business name, state**   Trading as

3. **Business Address**

   Phone: Area Code   Number   Fax: Area Code   Number   Mobile No.

4. **Registered Office Address**

   Phone: Area Code   Number   Fax: Area Code   Number

5. **Legal Format** (please tick ☑ appropriate box)

Co-operative Society	Private Unlimited Company	Statutory Body
Public Limited Company	Private Limited Company	Branch of Foreign Company
Other (specify)		

6. **Date company was registered** *(Irish registered companies)*   DD / MM / YYYY

7. **Companies registration office (CRO) number** *(Irish registered companies)*

8. **When did the business or activity commence?**   DD / MM / YYYY

9. **To what date will annual accounts be made up?**   DD / MM / YYYY

10. **Foreign registered company**
    (i)   Address in this State of fixed place of business

    Phone Area Code   Number   Fax: Area Code   Number

    (ii)   Is trading stock held at this address?(Tick ☑)   Yes   No

    (iii)   Address in this State where the company's books and records will be produced for inspection by Revenue Officials

    Phone Area Code   Number   Fax: Area Code   Number

10. **If you want your tax affairs to be dealt with in Irish, tick ☑ the box**

Declaration   *This must be made in every case before the company can be registered for any tax.*

I declare that the particulars supplied by me in this application are true in every respect

NAME *(IN BLOCK LETTERS)*

SIGNATURE   **DATE** DD / MM / YYYY
(To be signed by the company secretary or other officer authorised)

Part A. continued   **General Details**

12. If the company was registered for any tax in this country previously what reference numbers did it hold?

Corporation Tax

Employer (PAYE/PRSI)

Value Added Tax

13. Type of Business

(a) is the business   ☐ mainly retail   ☐ mainly wholesale   ☐ mainly manufacturing

      ☐ building & construction   ☐ service and other

(b) Describe the business conducted in as much detail as possible. Give a precise description such as 'newsagent', 'dairy farmer', 'textile manufacturer', 'property letting', 'investment income' etc. **Do not** use general terms such as 'shopkeeper', 'manufacturer', 'computers', 'consultant' etc.

If the application is a property related activity you may also need to complete Panel 30.

14. Directors Give the following information in relation to each director. If necessary, continue on a separate sheet.

	Name	Private Address	Shareholding	PPS No.
(i)			%	
(ii)			%	
(iii)			%	

15. Company Secretary If this is one of the directors above the name will suffice.

Name	Private Address	PPS No.

16. Shareholders Give the details of any shareholder (other than a director whose details are shown above) who has 50% or more beneficial interest in the issued capital.

Name	Private Address	Shareholding	PPS No.
		%	

17. Adviser Details

Give the following details of the company's accountant or tax adviser, if any, who will prepare the accounts and tax returns of the company.

Name
Address

Phone: Area Code		Number		Mobile Phone Number	
Fax: Area Code		Number		Tax Adviser Identification Number (TAIN)	
Client's Reference					

If correspondence relating to VAT (ie VAT 3's) is being dealt with by the acountant or tax adviser tick ☑ the box

18. If the business premises is rented, state

(i)   The name and address of the landlord (not an estate agent or rent collector)

(ii)   The amount of rent paid per week ☐, month ☐ or year ☐ (Tick ☑ frequency)   €

(iii)   The date on which the company started paying the rent   DD / MM / YYYY

(iv)   The length of the agreed rental/lease period

19. If the business was acquired from a previous owner state

(i)   The name and current address of the person from whom it was acquired

(ii)   The VAT/ registered number of that person

Part B.   Registration for Corporation Tax

20.   **Are you registering for Corporation Tax (Tick ☑ the relevant box)**   Yes ☐   No ☐

Part C.   Registration as an Employer for PAYE/PRSI

21.   **Are you registering as an employer for PAYE/PRSI (Tick ☑ the relevant box)**   Yes ☐   No ☐
      If the answer is 'No', there is no need to answer questions 22, 23 or 24. Continue to Part D.

22.   **Persons Engaged**

      (i)   How many **employees** are: **Full time** - usually working 30 hours or more per week?   ☐

                               Part time - usually working less than 30 hours per week?   ☐

      (ii) State the date your first employee commenced or will commence in your employment   DD **/** MM **/** YYYY

23.   **What payroll and PAYE/PRSI record system will be used (Tick ☑ the relevant box)**
      Tax deduction card system (Revenue Supplied) ☐   Other manual system ☐   Computer system ☐   Disk ☐

24.   **Correspondence on PAYE/PRSI**
      If correspondence relating to PAYE/PRSI is being dealt with by an agent, tick ☑ this box ☐   and give
      the following details, if different from 17 above.

      Name
      Address

Phone: Area Code	**Number**	**Mobile Phone Number**
Fax: Area Code	**Number**	**Tax Adviser Identification Number (TAIN)**
Client's Reference		

Part D.   Registration for VAT

25.   **Are you registering for VAT? (Tick ☑ the relevant box)**   Yes ☐   No ☐
      If your answer is 'No', there is no need to answer questions 26 to 31.

26.   **Registration**

      (i)   State the **date** from which you require to register the company   DD **/** MM **/** YYYY

      (ii)   Is registration being sought only in respect of **European Union
            (EU) acquisitions**? (This applies only to farmers and non-taxable
            entities) (Tick ☑ the relevant box)   Yes ☐   No ☐

      (iii) Are you registering the company
                (a) because **turnover exceeds** or is likely to exceed the **limits**
                    prescribed by law for registration?   (a) ☐
          or **(b)** because you wish to **elect it to be a taxable person** (although   (b) ☐
                    not obliged by law to be registered)?
          or **(c)** because it is in receipt of **Fourth Schedule services**   (c) ☐

                 *Tick ☑ either
                 (a), (b) or (c) as
                 appropriate*

      (iv) State the expected turnover for the next 12 months   € ☐

27.   **Are you applying for the moneys received basis of accounting for
      goods and services?** (Tick ☑ the relevant box)   Yes ☐   No ☐
      If your answer is 'Yes', is this because

      (a) expected annual turnover will be less than €635,000   (a) ☐
      or
      (b) at least 90% of your expected annual turnover will come
           from supplying goods and services to persons who are   (b) ☐
           not registered, e.g. hospitals, schools or the general public

                 *Tick ☑ either
                 (a) or (b) as
                 appropriate*

Part D. continued	Registration for VAT

28. If your business is a foreign business registering in this State
State the expected annual turnover from
supplies of taxable goods or services within the State. €

29. State the bank or building society account to which VAT refunds can be made (Compulsory)

Bank/Building Society

Branch Address

Sorting Code

Account Number

30. Property Details for VAT purposes

(a) Address of the property

(b) Date purchased or when development commenced   DD / MM / YYYY

(c) Planning permission reference number, if applicable

(d) A copy of the minutes* of the meeting/meeting of the partners, where it was resolved that the property in question would be purchased and/or developed and would be disposed of or used in a manner which would give rise to a VAT liability i.e.
– by outright sale of the property, or
– by creation of a long term lease i.e. lease more than ten years, or
– by waiver of exemption in respect of short term lettings i.e. less than 10 years.

31. Exemption Waiver (in respect of the letting of property only)
(Such services are normally exempt from VAT).

Do you wish to waive exemption from VAT in respect of property letting? Tick ☑   Yes   No

(**Note:** the waiver of exemption applies to all rents receivable from short-term lettings including those from properties other than that mentioned above. An option to 'Waiver of Exemption' cannot be backdated.)

*The minutes should show the date of the meeting, the names of all those present at the meeting and should be signed by the company secretary or precedent acting partner in the case of a partnership.

Additional Information

The following leaflets will provide additional information on the taxation aspects of running a business. They are available from your local revenue office or from Revenue's Form's and Leaflets service at **LoCall 1890 30 67 06** or at **www.revenue.ie**

IT48   Starting in Business – A Revenue Guide
IT50   PAYE/PRSI for Small Employers
Employers Guide to operating PAYE and PRSI for certain benefits

If you have further information queries or concerns contact your Revenue District Office or Employer PAYE Enquiries at **LoCall 1890 23 63 36**.

If you want information on payment options, including **Direct Debit**, contact the **Collector General** at **LoCall 1890 20 30 70**.

Revenue On-Line Service (ROS) Save time – File On-Line

Once registered, you can access your tax details and file returns on-line using Revenue On-Line Service (ROS). ROS is available 24 hours a day, 365 days a year. It is easy, instant and secure.

For further details on ROS, visit our website at **www.revenue.ie** or call the ROS Information Desk at **LoCall 1890 20 11 06**.

Appendix III

Extract from the Revenue publication *Code of Practice for Revenue Auditors*

The following table sets out the net penalty after mitigation appropriate to each category of tax default:

Category of Tax Default	Tax-geared Penalty	Net Penalty *after* mitigation where there is:		
		Co-operation only	Co-operation and a Prompted Qualifying Disclosure	Co-operation and an Unprompted Qualifying Disclosure
Deliberate Default	100%	75%	50%	10%
Gross Carelessness	40%	30%	20%	5%
Insufficient Care	20%	15%	10%	3%

Appendix IV

Revenue's Customer Service Charter

Revenue collects taxes and duties which fund the provision of public services for the benefit of all citizens.

Revenue protects society through its Customs Service working on frontier control.

The effective and fair administration of tax and customs law requires Revenue and citizens to recognise certain basic rights and responsibilities.

This Customer Charter sets out mutual expectations in this context.

Consistency, Equity and Confidentiality

- Revenue will administer the law fairly, reasonably and consistently and will seek to collect no more than the correct amount of tax or duty

- Revenue will treat the information you give us in confidence and ensure that it will not be used or disclosed except as provided for by law

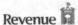

Courtesy and Consideration	**You can expect** ■ to be treated courteously, with consideration and in a non- discriminatory way in your dealings with Revenue.	**We expect you** ■ to treat Revenue officials with courtesy and to give them all reasonable co-operation
Information and Assistance	**You can expect** ■ to be given the necessary information and all reasonable assistance to enable you to clearly understand and meet your tax and customs obligations and to claim your entitlements and credits	**We expect you** ■ to provide true and correct information in all your contacts with Revenue and to advise Revenue in a timely manner of developments (such as change of address, commencement or cessation of business) that are relevant to your tax and customs affairs
Presumption of Honesty	**You can expect** ■ to be treated as honest in your dealings with Revenue unless there is clear reason to believe otherwise and subject to Revenue's responsibility for ensuring compliance with tax and customs law	**We expect you** ■ to deal in an honest way with Revenue by returning the tax and duty which you are due to pay and seeking only those entitlements and credits to which you are due
Compliance Costs	**You can expect** ■ that Revenue will administer the tax and duty regimes in a way that will minimise, as far as possible, compliance costs	**We expect you** ■ to maintain proper records and accounts and to ensure that your Returns and Declarations are completed fully, accurately and in a timely manner

Complaints, Review and Appeal

There are comprehensive complaints and appeal procedures open to all customers of Revenue and we encourage you to avail of these if you are in any way dissatisfied with the service you receive from us.

You can expect

- That if you make a complaint, Revenue will deal with it promptly, impartially and in confidence.

- That availing of Revenue's own complaints procedures will never prejudice your rights to raise issues with the Ombudsman or lodge, within the statutory time limits, a formal appeal to the Office of the Appeal Commissioners against an assessment raised by Revenue or against certain determinations made by Revenue officials.

Full details, including contact points, are contained in Leaflet CS4 which is available in any Revenue public office, from our Forms and Leaflets LoCall number 1890 30 67 06 and on our website, www.revenue.ie.

Section III

Income Tax

FONS AEQUI INTELLECTUS

The Institute would like to acknowledge the kind permission given by Gearóid Deegan, William McAteer and George Reddin for the use of some material from *Income Tax** in this section; such material has been adapted specifically for students with the addition of focused commentary and examples.

* Published by the Irish Taxation Institute (2008)

8

OVERVIEW OF THE IRISH INCOME TAX SYSTEM

In this chapter, you will deal with the following:

- Legislative framework of income tax

- Methods of collecting income tax

- Withholding taxes

- Classification of income in accordance with correct Cases and Schedules

- Exempt sources of income

- *Pro forma* income tax computation

8.1   Introduction

Income tax is the cornerstone of the Irish system of taxation. The net receipts from income tax in 2008, as reported in the Revenue Commissioners' 2008 Annual Report, amounted to €16,593 million (See chapter 1, section 1.6). Accordingly, income tax accounted for 28% of total net tax receipts for 2008 – more than the combined take from all other direct taxation measures, namely corporation tax, stamp duties, capital acquisitions tax and capital gains tax. Thus, though criticised for not being sufficiently comprehensive,[1] income tax has the broadest base of all direct taxes applicable in Ireland and, consequently, a significant part of the tax legislation is concerned with income tax measures. In addition, it is important to bear in mind that many of the definitions and provisions found in the income tax code also extend to other tax heads. This is particularly obvious in the context of corporation tax.

This chapter broadly considers the key income tax principles. It is concerned with distinguishing between the different sources of income that are liable to income tax and with how such sources of income are taxed. The chapter sets out a comprehensive *pro forma* income tax computation, which provides a framework for consolidating the many component computations of an individual's overall income tax liability. The remainder of Section III is concerned with the detailed rules relating to many of these component computations.

8.2   Income Tax Framework

Gladstone first introduced Peel's system of income tax to Ireland in 1853. The Income Tax Act 1967 was, in effect, a consolidation of the original measures introduced by Gladstone and subsequent adaptations necessitated by the establishment of the Free State, the Constitution of 1937 and Finance Acts from 1923 onwards. Readers are referred to the commentary at 1.1.2 above.

The 1967 Act is now consolidated with subsequent Finance Acts from 1968 to 1997 into the Taxes Consolidation Act 1997 (TCA 1997). The 1967 Income Tax Act had been amended by almost every annual Finance Act since 1967 and therefore, consolidation was required. In fact, TCA 1997 brings together three areas of tax law, these being Income Tax, Corporation Tax and Capital Gains Tax. It is important to note that TCA 1997 in no way changed the existing tax law that was in force prior to the consolidation process. The aim of the consolidation was to combine all the legislation relevant to a particular area of tax law into one section of an Act as opposed to having to refer to the

---

1   In 1982, the Irish Commission on Taxation argued in favour of a more comprehensive definition of income that would include capital sums received. Under the Irish system, such sums are distinguished from other sources of income and may be separately subject to capital gains tax and/or capital acquisitions tax. Readers are referred to the commentary in 1.6.

original Act and subsequent Finance Acts to find the particular applicable provisions. Amendments to TCA 1997 are included in subsequent Finance Acts.

In addition to the income tax legislation, readers should also be aware of decided case law which assists in the interpretation of the legislation. Documented details of Revenue practice in specific areas are also helpful.

8.3   Introduction to Income Tax Principles

Income tax is a tax on the income and profits of an individual for a year of assessment. Up until 5 April 2001, the tax year ran from 6 April to the following 5 April, e.g., the 2000/01 year of assessment ran from 6 April 2000 to 5 April 2001. With effect from 1 January 2002, the tax year is now aligned to the calendar year. Thus, the year 2001 was a "short" transitional tax year, which ran from 6 April 2001 to 31 December 2001.

Income tax is payable by all individuals (save for some exceptions). Broadly speaking, there are two methods of paying income tax:

- through the "pay as you earn" (PAYE) system, i.e., by deduction at source from salary/wages (considered in detail in Chapter 22); and/or

- through the self-assessment system, i.e., for "non-PAYE" individuals who make direct payments of tax to the Revenue Commissioners to cover their liability for a year of assessment (considered in detail in Chapter 10).

It is important to also bear in mind that companies and other statutory bodies may have an obligation to account for income tax to the Revenue Commissioners. Such entities are required to withhold income tax from certain payments and to pay amounts withheld to the Collector-General.

8.4   Withholding Taxes

In certain circumstances, a payment in discharge of a liability for services rendered or annual payments must be paid under the deduction of income tax at source. Examples of such withholding taxes are as follows:

- **PAYE (payroll taxes)** – An employer or payer of an occupational pension must deduct tax, PRSI (not applicable for pensions) and the health contribution levy, where appropriate, from the salaries/wages or pension payments to employees. Readers are referred to Chapter 23.

- **Professional services withholding tax (PSWT)** – Tax at the standard rate is deducted from payments made for professional services by Government Departments, State bodies, local authorities, health boards, etc. Examples of professional services include medical, dental, pharmaceutical, optical, architectural, auditing and legal services. Readers are referred to Chapter 15 (15.5) for further commentary on this system of withholding tax.

■ **Relevant contract tax (RCT)** – Payments made by a principal contractor to a sub-contractor in respect of payments on foot of contracts in the construction, forestry and meat-processing industries are subject to withholding tax at a rate of 35%. Where the principal contractor receives appropriate authorisation, RCT need not be deducted from the gross payment.

■ **Standard rate income tax** – The payer of certain annual payments must deduct tax at the standard rate of income tax from such payments. Examples of annual payments subject to this withholding tax are deeds of covenant and patent royalties.

Where tax is deducted under any of the above headings, the recipient may claim credit for such tax in calculating the tax liability that arises on receipt of the payment. The withholding tax may be allowed as a credit against:

– Corporation tax – where the recipient is a corporate entity;

– Income tax – where the recipient is a sole trader or a partner in a partnership.

8.5   Income Categorisation

Income is classified into different Schedules for tax purposes. Originally there were six such Schedules – Schedules A to F inclusive.

Schedule A was concerned with the taxation of imputed rent from property owned irrespective of whether or not such property was actually let. Similarly, Schedule B was concerned with measuring income from farming as the imputed rental value of the land. Both of these Schedules were abolished in 1969. The existing legislation ensures that rents only actually received are subject to tax and also that income from farming is calculated on a more objective basis.

Schedule C is concerned with tax at source levied on banks and other agents that collect and cash foreign dividends and that pay government interest and dividends from public revenue. These provisions are outside the scope of the analysis in this text and, accordingly, readers should concern themselves only with Schedules D, E and F. Schedule D is the most comprehensive of the categories and is consequently further classified into five Cases – Cases I – V.

Correct categorisation of income is essential to ensure that the appropriate rules are applied in determining:

■ how much income is taxed in a year of assessment;

■ how the income is taxed; and

■ how the losses, if any, arising from such income may be utilised.

A summary of the various income classifications, all of which are considered in detail in the chapters to follow, is set out below:

Schedule D	Case I	■ Trading income of self-employed sole traders and partners
	Case II	■ Professional and vocational income of self-employed sole practitioners and partners
	Case III	■ Investment income (not subject to deduction of tax at source) ■ Income from foreign employments and foreign investments (not subject to deduction of tax at source)
	Case IV	■ Irish deposit interest (subject to deduction of tax at source) ■ Foreign investment income (subject to deduction of Irish tax at source) ■ Covenant income ■ Miscellaneous sources of income not specifically taxable under any other Case or Schedule
	Case V	■ Rents from Irish property
Schedule E		■ Income from Irish employments and directorships ■ Irish pensions
Schedule F		■ Dividends from Irish resident companies

8.6   Exempt Sources of Income

A number of income sources are exempt from income tax in accordance with specific statutory measures. These are summarised as follows:

TCA97 s195 **Artists**

Certain earnings of individuals, which in the opinion of the Revenue Commissioners are derived from a work or works adjudged to have cultural or artistic merit, are exempted from tax. "A Work" is defined as an original and creative work, whether written, composed or executed as the case may be, which falls into one of the following categories:

■ a book or other writing;

■ a play;

■ a musical composition;

■ a painting or other like picture;

■ a sculpture

The individual must be resident in Ireland and not resident elsewhere, or ordinarily resident and domiciled in Ireland and not resident elsewhere. A formal claim for exemption must be made to Revenue and the exemption only applies from the tax year in which the claim is made.

Even though the above income is exempt from tax, nevertheless, such income must be included in the individual's annual tax return.

TCA97 s234 Patent Royalties*

In limited circumstances, income from a qualifying patent is exempt from tax. The exemption applies where the royalty is paid in respect of:

- a manufacturing activity of a company (whether carried on in the State or elsewhere); or

- a non-manufacturing activity, to the extent that the income arises from *bona fide* third-party payments, i.e. where the payer and recipient of the royalty are not connected.

The exemption from income tax also applies to dividends paid out of manufacturing royalties and *bona fide* third-party exempt royalties in respect of eligible shares in a patent company.

Even though the above income is exempt from tax, nevertheless, such income must be included in the individual's annual tax return.

TCA97 s231 Stallion fees*

The following income is exempt from tax:

- income arising to the owner/part-owner of a stallion, which is normally kept on land in the State, from the sale of services (or the rights to such services) of mares within the State, or

- income arising to the part owner of a stallion, which is normally kept on land outside the State, from the sale of services (or rights to services) of mares by the stallion. To qualify for the exemption, the part owner must carry on a trade in the State which consists of, or includes, bloodstock breeding, and it must be shown to the satisfaction of the Revenue Commissioners that the part owner acquired the stallion and held it primarily for the purposes of the servicing of mares owned or partly owned by the part owner of the stallion in the course of his/her trade.

Even though the above income is exempt from tax, nevertheless, such income must be included in the individual's annual tax return. This tax exemption was abolished with effect from 1 July 2008.

TCA97 s233 Greyhound stud fees*

Income arising to the owner/part owner of a stud greyhound from fees arising from the sale of services to female greyhounds is exempt from tax. This tax exemption was abolished with effect from 1 July 2008.

Even though the above income is exempt from tax, nevertheless, such income must be included in the individual's annual tax return.

TCA97 s232 Forests/Woodlands*

Profits or gains arising from the occupation of woodlands managed on a commercial basis and with a view to the realisation of profits are exempt from tax. Dividends paid out of such tax-free income are also exempt from tax.

From 1 January 2004, even though the above income is exempt from tax, nevertheless, such income must be included in the individual's annual tax return.

TCA97 s189 Payment in respect of personal injuries to permanently incapacitated individuals

Any payments made to, or in respect of, an individual by a Court order or under "out of court" settlements in respect of damages received for personal injury, where the individual is permanently and totally incapacitated by reason of mental or physical infirmity from maintaining themselves as a result of such injury, are exempt from income tax. Likewise, any income, including rental income arising from the investment of such awards, is exempt from tax. However, the amount of any such income must be included in the individual's annual tax return.

TCA97 s189A Trusts for permanently incapacitated individuals

Income arising to the trustees of a trust, which has been set up for the benefit of a permanently incapacitated individual and which has been funded by subscriptions from the general public, is exempt from tax. The income paid by the trustees to the incapacitated individual is also exempt from tax.

Even though the above income is exempt from tax, nevertheless, such income must be included in the individual's annual tax return.

TCA97 s190 Payments made by the Haemophilia HIV Trust

Income payments made by the Haemophilia HIV Trust to beneficiaries under the Trust are exempt from tax.

TCA97 s191 Hepatitis C compensation

Compensation payments made by the "Hepatitis C Tribunal" or received through the courts are exempt from tax. Any investment income arising from the compensation payments is also exempt from income tax, provided that the income is the individual's sole or main income and that the person is permanently and totally incapacitated. "Sole or main income" means that the total of such "compensation" income must be in excess of 50% of the aggregate of the individual's total income from all sources for the year concerned.

Even though the above income is exempt from tax, nevertheless, such income must be included in the individual's annual tax return.

---

* Readers are referred to Section 8.7 for restriction on reliefs for high income earners.

TCA97 s192 Payments in respect of Thalidomide children

Compensation payments made to Thalidomide children, and the income derived from the investment of such payments, are exempt from tax.

TCA97 s192A Compensation payments under employment law

Compensation awards paid following a formal hearing by a relevant authority under employment law in respect of the infringement of employees' rights and entitlements under that law are exempt from income tax.

TCA97 s192B Payments to foster parents

Payments made by the Health Service Executive to foster parents in respect of the care of foster children are exempt from income tax. Also exempt are certain discretionary payments by the Health Service Executive to carers relating to the care of former foster children (those aged 18 or over) who suffer from a disability, or until such children reach 21 years or complete their full-time education course.

TCA97 s216B Payments under Scéim na bhFoghlaimeoirí Gaeilge

Income received for the provision of student accommodation by persons in Gaeltacht areas under the Irish language student scheme known as Scéim na bhFoghlaimeori Gaeilge is exempt from tax.

TCA97 s216 Profits from lotteries

Profits from a lottery to which a licence under the Gaming and Lotteries Act 1956 applies are exempt from tax.

TCA97 s865 Interest paid on tax overpaid

Interest paid by the Revenue Commissioners on tax overpaid is exempt from tax.

TCA97 s42   Savings certificates

Interest payable on savings certificates issued by the Minister for Finance is not liable to tax, provided the amount invested does not exceed the amount which the recipient is authorised to hold. At the time of going to print, up to €120,000 worth of each issue of savings certificates may be held by an individual (€240,000 per joint holding).

TCA97 s197 An Post savings schemes

Any bonus or interest payable to an individual under An Post savings schemes (i.e., Index-Linked Savings Bond and Index-Linked National Instalment Savings) is not liable to tax provided the amount invested does not exceed the amount which the recipient is authorised to hold. At the time of going to print, the maximum subscription is €120,000 per individual (€240,000 per joint holding) for Savings Bonds and €1,000 per individual per month for Instalment Savings.

TCA97 s200 **Foreign pensions**

Certain foreign pensions are exempt from tax provided:

- it is a pension awarded for past services in a foreign employment, or is payable under the law of the foreign country in which it arises, and this law corresponds to the provisions of Chapters 12, 16 or 17 of Part II of or Chapters 4 or 6 of Part III of the Social Welfare (Consolidation) Act 1993, or any subsequent Act together with which that Act may be cited, apply, and

- it would have been exempt from tax in the foreign country, had it been received by a person resident in that foreign country.

TCA97 s204/205 **Military and other pensions, gratuities and allowances**

The following are exempt from tax:

- all pensions and gratuities awarded in respect of wounds and disabilities granted under the Army Pensions Act, 1923 to 1980 and any related Acts. The relief is restricted only to the amount of the pension solely attributable to the disability and is certified by the Minister for Defence;

- military gratuities and demobilisation pay granted to officers of the National Forces or the Defence Forces of Ireland on demobilisation;

- deferred pay within the meaning of the Defence Act 1954;

- gratuities granted in respect of service with the Defence Forces;

- military service pensions payable to Veterans of the War of Independence, their widows and dependants.

8.7 Restriction of Certain Reliefs for High Income Earners

Section 17 Finance Act 2006 introduced a restriction on the amount of reliefs available to "high income earners" effective from 1 January 2007. The maximum amount of reliefs an individual can use in a year is limited to the greater of €250,000 and 50% of "adjusted income". Any relief denied is carried forward to the following year(s). Adjusted income means taxable income after adding back the restricted reliefs. The restricted reliefs are as follows:

- capital allowances and losses from property incentive schemes;

- BES and Film Relief;

- patent royalty income and patent distributions;

- exempt artists income;

- interest on money to buy shares in certain companies and partnerships;

- exempt distributors and exempt income from forests/woodlands, greyhound stud fees, stallion fees and certain mining profits; and

- donations to charities and sports bodies.

Example 8.1

	€	
Case I	255,000	
Case V	500,000	
	755,000	
Less		
"Section 23" relief	(500,000)	
Trade Capital Allowances	(5,000)	Note 1
Taxable Income	250,000	
Add back restricted relief	500,000	
Adjusted Income	750,000	
Less "Section 23" relief	(375,000)	Note 2
Taxable Income	375,000	

Note 1: Ordinary Trade Capital Allowances are not subject to the restriction.

Note 2: Relief restricted to greater of 50% of adjusted income (€750,000) and €250,000.

8.8   Calculation of Income Tax Liability

An income tax liability for an individual should be presented in accordance with the prescribed *pro forma* computation set out at Appendix I to this chapter. Calculating a liability involves firstly calculating the taxable amount of income from various sources and then classifying these amounts in accordance with the correct Case or Schedule. Broadly speaking, tax is applied to the sum total of income from all sources subject to the proviso that there are deductions for certain reliefs and payments. The following terms are relevant:

- **Gross income** is the sum of the individual amounts of income from all sources less deductions or losses that can specifically be set off against that income.

- **Total income** is gross income after the deduction of certain "charges". Relief for charges paid is considered in detail in Chapter 12.

- **Taxable income** is total income, as defined above, less personal allowances and reliefs allowable at the marginal rate of tax. Readers are referred to Chapter 11 for a discussion of the reliefs available at the marginal rate of tax.

In general, income tax is applied to "taxable income" as defined above at rates of 20% and 41%. The 20% rate applies to the standard rate band of income and the amount of this band varies depending on the marital status of the taxpayer and, in the case of married couples, depending on whether or not both spouses earn income.

The balance of taxable income is taxed at the higher rate of 41%. Tax credits are deducted from the income tax amount so calculated. In general, non-refundable tax credits are granted on the basis of the personal circumstances of the taxpayer and, in respect of certain payments made by the taxpayer, while refundable tax credits are available for taxes already deducted at source from income received, e.g., PAYE, RCT, PSWT, etc.

Effective from 1 January 2009 a new levy was introduced known as an income levy. The levy is applied to income before capital allowances and pensions deductions. Readers are referred to Chapter 11 for further analysis of the levy and applicable rates.

Tax Facts

Due to the economic downturn the government was forced to bring the December 2008 budget forward to October 2008 (to become Finance (No. 2) Act 2008) and to introduce a supplementary budget on 7 April 2009. The main feature of the latter was the doubling of the income levy rates, which had been introduced in the Finance (No. 2) Act 2008.

8.9 Summary of Chapters to Follow

The foregoing is, as the name of the chapter suggests, an **overview** of the income tax system. In the chapters to follow, more detailed analysis is provided:

- Chapter 9 is concerned with the territorial scope of income tax.

- Chapter 10 deals with the administration of the self-assessment system. Much of the analysis has application for taxpayers assessed to corporation tax as well as for individuals and partners assessed to income tax.

- Chapters 11, 12 and 13 deal with the basis of taxation of single, widowed and married individuals, and examine the allowances, reliefs and tax credits to which they may be entitled.

- Chapters 14 to 17 deal with the tax treatment of business profits and losses, whether derived from a trade or profession.

- Chapter 18 deals with partnerships.

- Chapter 19 deals with the taxation of investment or "passive" income and foreign-earned income.

- Chapters 20 to 23 deal with the taxation of employment income and provide an analysis of how the PAYE system operates.

WHAT YOU SHOULD NOW KNOW

On completion of this chapter, you should be able to:

- ✓ Explain the legislative framework of income tax.

- ✓ Identify the two main methods of collecting income tax in Ireland.

- ✓ Explain how companies and other bodies may be obliged to account for income tax payments to Revenue.

- ✓ Classify various sources of income in accordance with the correct Case or Schedule.

- ✓ Explain the terms "gross income", "total income" and "taxable income".

- ✓ Identify sources of income that are exempt from income tax.

- ✓ Compute the restriction of certain reliefs for "high income earners."

- ✓ Draft a *pro forma* tax computation similar to that presented in Appendix I.

- ✓ Complete Questions and the Assignments in Irish Taxation Law and Practice, Volume 2.

Appendix I

Pro Forma Income Tax Computation

Income Tax Computation for the year 2009

	€	€
Schedule D		
Case I (Self-Employed Traders)		
Adjusted Case I profit in basis period	X	
Less: Case I losses carried forward	(X)	
Case I capital allowances	(X)	
Allowable retirement annuity premium	(X)	X
Case II (Self-Employed Professionals)	X	
Adjusted Case II profit in basis period	X	
Less: Case II losses carried forward	(X)	
Case II capital allowances	(X)	
Allowable retirement annuity premiums	(X)	X
Case III		
e.g., Government security interest, income from abroad	(X)	X
Case IV		
e.g., Irish building society and commercial bank interest	X	
income received under deduction of tax at the standard rate	X	
miscellaneous income	X	X
Case V		
Rents from property situated in the Republic of Ireland, i.e., Case V profit after allowable expenses	X	
Less: Case V losses carried forward	(X)	X

Schedule E: Income from Employments/Offices:

Salary/wages/directors' fees/pensions	X	
Bonus/commission	X	
Benefits-in-kind	X	
Taxable lump sums	X	
Less: Employee's contributions to a Revenue-approved scheme	(X)	
Less: Allowable retirement annuity premiums (in respect of non-pensionable employment)	(X)	X
Schedule F		
Distributions/dividends from companies resident in the Republic of Ireland		X
Gross Income		X
Less: Case I/II losses arising in 2009 (s381 TCA 1997)	(X)	(X)
Deduct: Relief for charges paid during 2009		
Qualifying covenants/annuities paid in 2009	(X)	
Patent royalties paid in 2009	(X)	(X)
TOTAL INCOME		X
Deduct: Personal allowances/reliefs *(available at marginal rate)*, e.g., medical expenses	(X)	(X)
TAXABLE INCOME		X
Taxed as follows (assume married and two incomes):		
First €72,800 @ 20%		X
Balance @ 41%		X
Total tax		X

Deduct:	**Non-refundable tax credits**		
	e.g., married persons' tax credit	(X)	
	Employee's tax credit (PAYE credit)		
	Deposit interest retention tax	(X)	
Add	Income tax deducted from payments *made*, e.g., tax deducted from covenants/annuities	X	(X)
Add	PRSI	X	
	Health contribution levy	X	
Add	Income levy	X	

Deduct: Refundable tax credits

e.g., tax withheld on covenant/annuities received under deduction of income tax	(X)	
PAYE paid	(X)	
Dividend withholding tax	(X)	
Net Income Tax Due		X

9

THE SCOPE OF INCOME TAX

In this chapter, you will deal with the following:

- Concepts of residence, ordinary residence and domicile

- Employment income reliefs

- Implications of residence, ordinary residence and domicile

9.1 Introduction

The purpose of this chapter is to establish how residence and domicile impact on the Irish taxation system. The extent of an individual's liability to Irish income tax depends on whether the individual is:

- resident in Ireland;

- ordinarily resident in Ireland; or

- domiciled in Ireland.

All the concepts mentioned above, i.e., resident, ordinarily resident and domiciled, have a very precise meaning, the former two being defined in tax legislation, the latter, not having a statutory meaning, being based on precedents and case law.

This chapter details the issues of relevance in determining an individual's residence status for Irish tax purposes and examines the implications of residence and domicile on Irish tax liabilities. The chapter also expands on further concepts, such as:

- Domicile of origin

- Domicile of choice

- Domicile of dependence

- Remittance basis of taxation

- Reliefs available for foreign employment income

9.2 Residence

9.2.1 Background

s819 TCA 97 Prior to 6 April 1994, the residence and ordinary residence position of an individual was based largely on tests and practices, that evolved from UK court decisions over the course of a number of years. The 1994 Finance Act effectively abolished the use of these tests and practices and replaced them with statutory rules. The "new" residence rules took effect from 6 April 1994.

9.2.2 Position with effect from 6 April 1994

An individual is regarded as resident in Ireland for a tax year if he/she is present in the State:

- at any one time or several times in the year of assessment for a period which in total amounts to 183 days or more; or

- at any one time or several times in the year of assessment and the preceding year for a period which in total amounts to 280 days or more.

However, he/she will not be regarded as resident for any tax year in which he/she spends a period in the whole amounting to 30 days or less in the State, and no account shall be taken of such a period for the purpose of the 280-day test. In determining days present in Ireland, an individual was deemed to be present if he/she is in the country at the end of the day, i.e., at midnight. Finance (No. 2) Act 2008 amended the definition of a day to include any part of a day, therefore day of departure from Ireland is counted as a day.

Alternatively, where the above rules are not satisfied an individual may elect to be Irish-resident in any year of assessment in which he/she is present in the State with the intention and in such circumstances that he/she will be resident in the State in the following year of assessment. The main advantage of electing to be Irish-resident in these circumstances is that the individual will have full entitlement to Irish personal allowances, reliefs and tax credits (see Chapter 11).

There is no facility to elect for non-residence; where the 183-day and 280-day tests outlined above are satisfied, residence status cannot be avoided.

Example 9.1

Eric Bertrand was seconded to Ireland on 15 July 2008 on a 12-month contract. During that period he did not return to his home in France or visit any other country. He left Ireland on 1 August 2009.

Residence position

2008
From 15 July to 31 December 2008 he spent 170 days in Ireland. He is not resident in Ireland in 2008 since he did not spend 183 days or more in Ireland during 2008, nor did he spend 280 days in Ireland during the current and the preceding tax years, i.e., during the years ended 31 December 2007 and 2008. However, he may elect to be Irish-resident if he is in a position to demonstrate that he came to Ireland in 2008 with the intention and in circumstances such that he would be resident in Ireland in 2009.

2009
From 1 January 2009 to 31 July 2009, he spent 212 days in Ireland. He is resident in Ireland for 2009 since he spent more than 183 days in the State in 2009. There is no facility to elect for non-residence albeit that he may intend returning to France at the end of the 12-month contract.

Example 9.2

Assume the same facts as Example 1 except that Eric had to return to France permanently on 1 May due to ill health.

Residence position:

2008

As above – no change.

2009

From 1 January 2009 to 1 May 2009, he spent 121 days in Ireland. This is less than 183 days. However, he is resident in Ireland in 2009 by virtue of the 280-day rule, i.e., since he spent more than 280 days in Ireland on combining the current and previous years' days of presence in the State (170 + 121 = 291).

Example 9.3

Mariola de la Fuente was seconded to Ireland from Spain on a 12-month contract with effect from 1 February 2008. She left Ireland and returned to Spain on 28 January 2009.

Residence position:

2008

She is resident in Ireland in 2008 under the 183-day rule since she spent 334 days in the State in that year.

2009

She is not resident in Ireland in 2009 under the 183-day rule since she only spent 28 days in the State in that year. She has spent 361 days in the State in the current and preceding tax years and would appear to satisfy the 280-day test. However, as she cannot be regarded as resident for any tax year in which she spends a period in the whole amounting to 30 days or less in the State, she is not Irish resident in 2009.

9.2.3   Ordinary residence

s820 TCA 97 An individual is ordinarily resident in Ireland for a year of assessment if he/she has been resident for each of the three years of assessment preceding that year.

An individual will not cease to be ordinarily resident for a year of assessment until such time as the individual has three consecutive years of non-residence. Thus, an ordinarily resident individual will become non-ordinarily resident for a year of assessment when he/she has been non-resident for each of the three years preceding that year of assessment. In effect, it is necessary to have been non-resident in Ireland in each of the three years of assessment following the year of departure from Ireland.

Example 9.4

Michael Reilly has lived and worked in Ireland all his life. He moved to Australia permanently on 1 August 2008. Thus, he will be regarded as Irish-resident in 2008, but non-Irish-resident thereafter. He will remain ordinarily resident in Ireland for the years of assessment 2009, 2010 and 2011 and will become non-ordinarily resident in 2012, i.e., in the year of assessment following three consecutive years of non-residence.

Example 9.5

Miguel Tito was seconded to Ireland on 16 July 2008 on a five-year contract. He had previously been resident in Spain where he had worked and lived all his life. On the assumption that he does not elect to be Irish-resident in 2008, he will be regarded as non-Irish resident in 2008. He will remain non-ordinarily resident for the years 2009, 2010 and 2011. He will become ordinarily resident in Ireland in 2012 on the basis that he will be Irish-resident in the years 2009, 2010 and 2011.

9.2.4 Domicile

Domicile is not defined in the Income Tax Acts. It is a complex legal concept. Generally, a person is domiciled in the country of which he/she is a national and in which he/she spends his/her life. However, it is not always possible to equate domicile to home, as in certain circumstances an individual may be domiciled in a country which is not and has never been his home. A person may have two homes but he can only have one domicile. There is a considerable volume of case law on the subject of domicile.

There are three general principles in relation to domicile:

(i) No person can be without a domicile.

(ii) No person can have more than one domicile at the same time, at any rate for the same purpose.

(iii) An existing domicile is presumed to continue until it has been proved that a new domicile has been acquired.

Domicile of origin

An individual is born with a domicile known as a domicile of origin. Normally, this is the domicile of his/her father. However, where the parents have not married, or if the father dies before his birth, the child's domicile will be the same as that of his/her mother. If, before he/she has reached the age of majority, the parent from whom he/she has taken his/her domicile changes his/her domicile, the minor's domicile will also change.

Once an individual has reached the age of majority, he/she can reject his/her domicile of origin and acquire a new domicile. In order to abandon his/her domicile of origin, the individual must prove conclusively that he/she has severed all links with the country in which his/her domicile of origin lies. A domicile cannot be lost by a mere abandonment. It can only be lost by the positive acquisition of a domicile of choice.

Domicile of choice

A domicile of choice is the domicile that any independent person can acquire for himself/herself by a combination of residence and intention. To acquire a domicile of choice, an individual must establish a physical presence in the new jurisdiction and have an intention to reside there indefinitely.

A domicile of choice can in turn be abandoned. This will involve either the acquisition of a new domicile of choice or the revival of the domicile of origin. Here, again, the two factors of presence and intention will be required. In this regard, decisions from a number of cases are relevant.

Case law

In *Revenue Commissioners v Shaw & Anor H.C.* [1982 ILR] ILR, McWilliam J. stated:

> *"In order to acquire another domicile, a person must have the intention of doing so together with actual residence in the country of his choice. The intention must be an intention to reside in that country for an unlimited time. A domicile of origin persists until it has been shown to have been abandoned and another acquired and the onus of proving a change of domicile is on the person alleging it."*

In the case of *Claire Proes v Revenue*, it was held in a judgment delivered in the High Court in June 1997 that, having previously acquired a domicile of choice in the UK, the appellant, Mrs Proes, while having resided in Ireland for a period of 10 years, did not revive her domicile of origin. This was on the basis that Mrs Proes never ceased to have an intention to return to reside permanently in the UK.

It should be noted that any question as to whether or not an individual who was Irish-domiciled has acquired a foreign domicile of choice is to be determined by reference to Irish law and not by reference to the law of the "foreign" country.

9.3   Implications of Residence, Ordinary Residence and Domicile

Broadly speaking, an individual's residence status determines his entitlement to the personal allowances, reliefs and tax credits discussed in Chapter 11. In general, an Irish-resident individual will have full entitlement to the basic tax reliefs available in calculating his/her Irish tax liability, while a non-resident individual will not. However, there are some exceptions to this rule in the case of Irish citizens, individuals who move abroad for health reasons and individuals resident in certain countries with which Ireland has a double taxation agreement.

Residence status (together with ordinary residence status and domicile) also determines the territorial scope of Irish taxation, i.e., the extent to which various sources of income are subject to Irish tax. Having examined the meaning of the terms residence, ordinary residence and domicile, the effect which they have upon the scope of an individual's income tax liability is now considered.

9.3.1   Individual resident and domiciled

In general, an individual who is resident and domiciled in Ireland is liable to Irish income tax on all his/her worldwide income as it arises. There is an exception to this rule in the case of non-ordinarily resident citizens (see 9.3.2 below).

Example 9.6

Tom Jones, who is married and is the sole earner, has the following sources of income in the 2009 tax year:

	€	
Salary paid by Irish company	*20,000*	
UK dividends	*5,000*	
USA rents	*6,000*	*(retained in USA bank account)*
Total	*31,000*	

Tom Jones is resident and domiciled in Ireland. He is therefore liable to income tax on his worldwide income of € 31,000 for 2009 regardless of the fact that the USA rents are not remitted to Ireland.

9.3.2 Individual resident but not domiciled/not ordinarily resident

s71 TCA 97 An individual who is resident but not domiciled in Ireland (e.g., a citizen of the United States working in Ireland for a temporary period of two years, who is regarded as tax-resident in Ireland) is liable to Irish income tax in full on:

■ income arising in Ireland, and

■ foreign income only to the extent that it is remitted to Ireland.

This is known as the remittance basis of taxation and is considered below in greater detail. Note that prior to 1 January 2008, income which arose in the UK was excluded from the remittance basis of taxation and was liable to Irish tax in full. The remittance basis of taxation also applies to Irish citizens (irrespective of domicile) who are not ordinarily resident in Ireland (e.g., an Irish citizen who has been living abroad for many years and who returns to Ireland for a temporary period without becoming ordinarily resident).

Example 9.7

Alex Smith, who is married, has the following sources of income in 2009:

	€
Salary paid by Irish company	*25,000*
UK dividends	*10,000*
USA rents	*15,000*
Total	*50,000*

Alex Smith is resident but not domiciled in Ireland. He remits €5,000 of his USA rental income to Ireland but none of his UK income.

He is liable to Irish tax on income arising in Ireland and remittances out of foreign income.

Assessable Income 2009:	€
Schedule E	*25,000*
Schedule D Case III:	
USA rents	*5,000*
Total	*30,000*

9.3.3 Individual not resident but ordinarily resident

s821 TCA 97 An individual who is not resident but is ordinarily resident and domiciled is taxable on the same basis as a resident and domiciled individual (i.e., on worldwide income) with the exception of income from:

- a trade or profession, no part of which is carried on in Ireland

- an office or employment all the duties of which are performed outside Ireland (apart from "incidental duties" – see below)

- other sources (i.e., other foreign income) the total of which do not exceed €3,810.

Where an individual, who is not resident but who is ordinarily resident, has other income exceeding €3,810, the full amount of that other income is taxable and not just the excess.

An individual who is not resident and not domiciled, but who is ordinarily resident, is taxable on the same basis as a resident, non-domiciled individual (i.e., on Irish income as it arises and on other foreign income remitted to Ireland), with the exception of income from any of the three sources listed above.

When determining what fulfils the condition of an office or employment "all the duties of which are performed outside the State", the Revenue Commissioners concessionally accept that no charge to Irish tax will arise where the Irish duties of an employment are merely incidental. Normally, any number of days up to a maximum of 30 in a tax year is regarded as incidental days.

While the Irish Revenue Commissioners have stated their willingness to "normally" look at the number of days in quantifying incidental duties, in the UK case of *Robson v Dixon* 48 TC 527, it was held that duties were not merely incidental if they formed an essential or critical element of the duties of the employee (even if only of brief duration).

Example 9.8

An Irish engineer goes to work in Saudi Arabia on a long-term contract. While abroad and still ordinarily resident in Ireland, he receives foreign rental income of €3,000 per annum and other foreign investment income of €600 per annum. He has no other sources of investment income. As he does not carry out his profession in the State and as his foreign income falls below the €3,810 threshold, he does not have a tax liability in Ireland in respect of the foreign income.

On the other hand, if the other foreign investment income was more than €3,810, then he would have an exposure to Irish tax in respect of all his foreign rental and investment income while he remains ordinarily resident. This is because other foreign income would have exceeded the limit of €3,810.

9.3.4 Individual not resident and not ordinarily resident

s18(3) TCA 97 An individual who is neither resident nor ordinarily resident, irrespective of domicile, is liable to Irish income tax only on income arising in Ireland, i.e., income from property located in the State and income from employments, trades and professions the duties of which are exercised in Ireland.

9.3.5 Summary table of tax implications of residence, ordinary residence and domicile

Residence, ordinary residence and domicile status	Extent of liability to Irish tax
Resident, ordinarily resident and Irish-domiciled	Taxable on all Irish and worldwide income.
Not resident, but ordinarily resident in Ireland and Irish-domiciled	Taxable on all Irish and foreign-sourced income in full. However, income from the following sources is exempt from tax: (a) income from a trade, profession, office or employment all the duties of which are exercised outside Ireland; and (b) other foreign income, provided that it does not exceed €3,810.
Not resident, but ordinarily resident in Ireland and not Irish-domiciled	Taxable on Irish source income in full and other foreign income only to the extent that it is remitted to Ireland. Income from the following sources is exempt from tax: (a) income from a trade, profession, office or employment all the duties of which are exercised outside Ireland; and (b) other foreign income, provided that it does not exceed €3,810.
Resident and ordinarily resident in Ireland but not Irish-domiciled	Taxable on Irish source income in full and foreign income only to the extent that it is remitted to Ireland.
Irish citizens, resident but not ordinarily resident	Taxable on Irish source income in full and foreign income only to the extent that it is remitted to Ireland.
Not resident, not ordinarily resident, irrespective of domicile	Taxable on Irish-sourced income in full and taxable on income from a trade, profession or employment exercised in Ireland.

9.3.6   Remittances

s71(3)
TCA 97

As mentioned above, certain individuals are liable to Irish income tax on remittances to Ireland out of "foreign income". Such remittances are assessed to tax under Case III of Schedule D. Only remittances out of income are liable to income tax.

Finance Act 2008 introduced a new provision whereby income from a UK source now qualifies for the Remittance Basis of Taxation Employees of foreign employers are subject to tax in Ireland in respect of the income attributed to the duties of employment carried out in Ireland.

9.3.6.1   UK Income position prior to 31 December 2007

UK source income was specifically excluded from the remittance basis. Therefore, a resident of Ireland for any tax year was always liable on his full income from UK sources. However, while UK source income was excluded from the remittance basis, this did not preclude a UK-domiciled individual, resident in Ireland, from entitlement to the remittance basis in respect of any non-Irish, non-UK source income. A remittance of such foreign income to the UK did not constitute a taxable remittance for Irish tax purposes so long as it was retained outside Ireland.

Example 9.9

Vincent Regan had the following sources of income in 2007:

	€
Salary paid by Irish company	*25,000*
UK dividends	*10,000*
USA rents	*15,000*
Total	*50,000*

Vincent Regan is resident but not domiciled in Ireland. He remitted €5,000 of his UK dividend income to Ireland €10,000 of his USA rental income was remitted to the UK. The remainder of the USA rental income was retained in a USA bank account.

He was liable to Irish tax on income arising both in Ireland and the UK and remittances to Ireland out of foreign income.

Assessable Income 2007:	*€*	
Schedule E	*25,000*	
Schedule D Case III:		
UK dividends	*10,000*	*(taxable in full albeit that only €5,000 was remitted)*
USA rents	*Nil*	*(remitted to the UK, not remitted to Ireland)*
Total	*35,000*	

9.3.6.2 Limited Remittance Basis Relief

Finance (No. 2) Act 2008 introduced a new "assignment relief" effective from 1 January 2009. The relief is available to certain employees who are assigned from abroad to work in Ireland for a period of at least three years. The new relief applies (subject to certain conditions being met) where employees earn more than €100,000. To qualify for relief the employee must:

■ Be non Irish domiciled,

■ Be employed by a company incorporated and resident in a country outside the EEA but with which Ireland has a double tax treaty,

■ Have been employed by an associated company of the Irish entity to which he/she is assigned prior to arrival in Ireland and continue to be paid by the overseas employer,

■ Have been tax resident and exercised the greater part of the employment in the overseas jurisdiction.

The employer must operate PAYE (and PRSI where relevant) in Ireland. The relief is calculated by only assessing the higher of the following:

■ The amount remitted to Ireland and

■ €100,000 plus 50% of the excess salary over €100,000.

Example 9.10

Tim Greenspan has worked for many years for a USA multi-national company. On 1 January 2009 he was seconded to Ireland for four years to carry out duties on behaf of the Irish subsidiary. In 2009 his gross salary was €300,000 on which PAYE was applied. He remitted €160,000 to Ireland. Tax relief is applied by only assessing the higher of:

■ *€160,000 and*

■ *€100,000 + (€200,000 × 50%) = €200,000.*

Therefore Tim may claim a tax refund on the salary of €100,000 (i.e. €300,000 – €200,000).

9.4   Employment Income Reliefs

Generally, being tax-resident in Ireland means that most sources of income are assessable to Irish tax. However, there are some reliefs which are available to reduce the Irish tax payable on employment income earned outside Ireland. These reliefs are considered below.

9.4.1 Cross-border relief

s825A
TCA 97

This is sometimes known as "Trans-Border Relief". The relief is typically aimed at employees who are resident in Ireland but carry out the duties of their employment in another country. In these circumstances, in the absence of any special relief, the employee is taxable in both countries. For example, an employee living in Dundalk and working in Newry would be taxable in both the UK and Ireland.

Subject to certain conditions being met, cross-border relief extends to duties carried out in the UK. While the relief applies to the UK, it is not confined exclusively to the UK. The main conditions to qualify for the relief are as follows:

- The employee must be present in the State for at least one day in each week.

- The office or employment must be a "qualifying employment".

- The duties of the qualifying employment must be performed wholly outside the State in a country with which Ireland has a double taxation agreement. The full amount of the income from the qualifying employment must be subject to tax in the foreign country and must not be exempt or relieved from tax in that country.

- The foreign tax due on the income from the qualifying employment must have been paid, and the individual must not have any right to any repayment of that foreign tax.

- The income from the qualifying employment must not qualify for any of the following reliefs:

  – remittance basis of taxation

  – split-year treatment (see 9.4.2 below).

"Qualifying employment" is defined as an office or employment held outside the State in a country with which Ireland has a double taxation treaty, but only if, for the tax year for which the relief is claimed, the office or employment is held for a continuous period of not less than 13 weeks. The relief does not apply to employees of the State or semi-State bodies. While qualification for the relief is dependent on the duties of the office or employment being performed outside the State, duties carried out within the State, that are incidental to the performance of the duties outside the State are nevertheless ignored. The individual must return to the State and be physically present there at the end of at least one day in every relevant week in a tax year. A relevant week is one in which the individual is absent from the State for one or more days for the purposes of performing duties of the employment. There is no requirement for the individual to be back in the State for a day in a week in which the employee is on holidays outside the State.

Relief is granted using the following formula:

$$\frac{A \times B}{C}$$

where:

A = the individual's liability to Irish income tax before deduction of credit for foreign tax paid,

B = the individual's total income excluding the income from the qualifying employment, and

C = the individual's total income including the income from the qualifying employment.

Example 9.11

Jack Daly is married and resident in the State. His wife works in the home looking after their two children, aged five and nine. He earned a salary of €60,000 in 2009 from a qualifying employment in Northern Ireland. He travelled home for at least one day every weekend. He took up this foreign employment during the year and, before he did so, had income from an employment in the State of €10,000. During 2009, he received Irish rental income of €4,200.

Jack Daly is liable to tax in the UK on the salary of €60,000 and paid the tax due in full in the sum of €10,000. He satisfied the other conditions for relief under s825A for 2009.

	€	€
Income from qualifying employment (before foreign tax)		60,000
Other employment income		10,000
Case V		4,200
Gross income **(C)**		74,200
Tax payable:		
€45,400 @ 20%	9,080	
€28,800 @ 41%	11,808	20,888
€74,200		
Less:		
Non-refundable tax credits		
Married person's credit	(3,660)	
Home-carer's credit	(900)	
PAYE allowance credit	(1,830)	(6,390)
Income tax liability **(A)**		14,498

Having calculated the income tax chargeable, the other elements in the formula for the "specified amount" are:

	€
Total income for year **(C)**	74,200
Total income for year excluding income from qualifying foreign employment **(B)**, *i.e., €74,200 - €60,000*	14,200
Income tax liability **(A)**	14,498

The "specified amount" is: $€14,498 \times \dfrac{€14,200}{€74,200} = €2,775$

Section 825A grants the relief by reducing Jack Daly's tax payable (A) so that it equals the specified amount, i.e., in effect, the relief restricts the Irish tax liability to €2,775, which is the portion of the tax charge referable to the non-qualifying employment income.

9.4.2   Split-year residence

s825A
TCA 97

This section sets out the specific rules relating to the Irish income tax treatment of an individual both in the year of departure from Ireland and in the year of arrival in Ireland.

Year of Arrival

The individual who takes up residence in Ireland during a tax year is treated as not being resident for that part of the tax year prior to the date of arrival. This treatment is applied only to employment income from an office or employment exercised outside the State prior to the date of arrival. In order to qualify for split-year residence treatment, the Revenue Commissioners must be satisfied that the individual took up residence in Ireland with the intention that he/she would be resident in Ireland for the following tax year. The individual must also not have been resident in Ireland for the tax year prior to that in which he/she takes up residence.

Example 9.12

John returns to Ireland on 1 July 2009 to commence a three-year contract with Multinational plc. He worked in the USA for the previous five years. In the period 1 January 2009 to 30 June 2009, John earned €50,000 from his foreign employment. He also earned foreign rental income in the amount of €2,000 in the same period. From 1 July 2009 to 31 December 2009, his Irish employment earnings were €40,000. All the foreign income has been remitted to Ireland.

John is liable to Irish income tax on all his income with the exception of the foreign employment income of €50,000 earned between 1 January 2009 and 30 June 2009.

Year of Departure

In the tax year in which an individual ceases to be resident in Ireland, he will be treated as not liable in respect of any foreign employment income arising after the date of departure. This applies provided he was tax-resident in Ireland prior to departure. To qualify for the relief, the individual must not be resident in Ireland in the following tax year.

Example 9.13

Mary, who is Irish-domiciled, has been resident in Ireland for more than five years. She leaves Ireland on 1 July 2009 to take up permanent residence in Spain. In the period 1 January 2009 to 30 June 2009, she received €30,000 employment income and €10,000 rental income from an Irish property. Following her departure, she earned €20,000 employment income in Spain and €500 deposit interest from her savings, which she invested in Spain. Provided Mary can demonstrate that she will not be tax-resident in Ireland in 2010, she will not be liable to Irish tax on the employment income of €20,000 earned from 1 July 2009 to 31 December 2009. She will be liable to Irish tax and on all other income as follows:

	€
Schedule D:	
Case III	*500*
Case V	*10,000*
Schedule E	*30,000*
Total	*40,500*

Tax Facts

Following the introduction of the application of PAYE to foreign employees working in Ireland (who were paid from abroad), some foreign employers encountered staffing and operational difficulties. The introduction of the (limited) Remittance Basis Tax Relief was seen as an attempt to counteract these difficulties.

WHAT YOU SHOULD NOW KNOW

On completion of this chapter, you should be able to:

✓ Define important concepts such as residence and ordinary residence.

✓ Discuss the criteria used to determine the domicile of an individual.

✓ Explain what impact residence, ordinary residence and domicile have on the charge to Irish taxation.

✓ Describe the reliefs from Irish taxation which are available for foreign employment income and calculate the amount of any such reliefs.

✓ Complete Questions and the Assignments in Irish Taxation Law and Practice, Volume 2.

10

THE SELF-ASSESSMENT SYSTEM

In this chapter, you will deal with the following:

- Introduction
- Pay and File system
- Payment of tax and penalties for late payment
- Tax returns and penalties for late filing

- Interest on tax overpaid
- Expressions of doubt
- Maintenance of records
- Revenue audits
- Appeal procedures

10.1   Introduction

The purpose of this chapter is to identify which categories of taxpayer come within the self-assessment system, what are its implications and what rights, if any, a taxpayer has under the system.

Broadly speaking, two alternative collection/assessment systems apply in Ireland:

- self-assessment; and

- PAYE ("pay as you earn") (considered in Chapter 23).

With the latter, the responsibility for the collection of the tax and payment of the tax to the Revenue Commissioners lies with the employer. Therefore, an employee who has no income other than wages/salaries has no tax-return filing obligations or tax payment obligations since the tax deducted at source satisfies the responsibility for both.

Taxpayers subject to the self-assessment system, unlike their PAYE counterparts, must pay their respective tax and file their tax returns on a specified date. Failure to do so will result in:

- interest on the late payment of tax;

- interest on the inadequate payment of tax; and

- a penalty for the late filing of a tax return (known as a surcharge). These concepts are considered in the following paragraphs.

10.2   The Pay and File System

Section 78 Finance Act 2001 introduced a common date for tax-return filing and payment of income tax, which is known as the "Pay and File" system. The changes were introduced to simplify the income tax system and make it work more effectively.

The Pay and File system provides for a single date, 31 October, for the:

- payment of preliminary income tax due for the current tax year;

- payment of the balance of income tax due for the previous tax year;

- filing of a tax return for the previous year.

31 October is also the relevant date for payment of capital gains tax due. The self-assessment system as it applies to capital gains tax is covered in detail in Chapter 24.

Example 10.1

31 October 2009 is the specified date for the:

- *payment of preliminary income tax for the year of assessment 2009;*
- *payment of the balance of income tax for the year of assessment 2008;*
- *filing of a tax return for the year of assessment 2008.*

10.3   Payment of Tax and Penalties for Late Payment

Income from which tax is not deducted at source must be accounted for on a self-assessment basis. Examples of such sources of income are trading income, investment income, rental income, etc. A feature of the self-assessment system is the requirement that liabilities to the Health Contribution levy and PRSI for the self-employed are fully integrated into the income tax system. Therefore, in arriving at the amount of income tax to be paid, the liability for these items must be included.

10.3.1   Chargeable persons

s915(5) TCA 97   Income tax is paid under the self-assessment system by "chargeable persons". Generally speaking, a chargeable person can be described as one whose income tax liability is not collected through the PAYE system. However, a "proprietary" director is regarded as a chargeable person even where the director's only income is a salary subject to PAYE. The term "proprietary director" means a director of a company who is the beneficial owner of, or is able, either directly or indirectly, to control more than 15% of the ordinary share capital of the company.

10.3.2   Preliminary tax

s952 TCA 97   Preliminary tax is due for payment on 31 October in a year of assessment. It is effectively a payment on account of the ultimate income tax liability for that year of assessment. Thus, preliminary tax due on 31 October 2009 is a provision against the ultimate income tax liability for the year of assessment 2009. In arriving at the amount of preliminary tax to be paid, the liability for the Health Contribution levy and PRSI for the self-employed must be included.

The payment could be better described as an "up-front payment", since the tax is being paid before the year of assessment has expired. As a result, there can be uncertainty in calculating the amount of tax due. To address this uncertainty, the legislation allows the taxpayer to use one of the following options in estimating the tax payable:

(a) 90% of the ultimate tax liability for the relevant tax year; or

(b) 100% of the tax liability for the preceding tax year; or

(c) 105% of the tax liability for the pre-preceding year (but only if paying the tax by direct debit).

In order to avoid interest charges arising, the preliminary tax payment must be:

- at least equal to an amount using the lowest of the above three options; and

- paid by 31 October in the relevant tax year (except in the case of option (c), where tax may be paid by direct debit over 12 months ending on 31 December).

Example 10.2

Preliminary tax due on 31 October 2009 may be calculated using the lower of the following options:

(a)   90% of the ultimate tax liability for the year of assessment 2009; or

(b)   100% of the tax liability for the year of assessment 2008; or

(c)   105% of the tax liability for the year of assessment 2007 (but only if paying the tax by direct debit).

If a taxpayer is using either of options (b) or (c) above, i.e., 100% of the previous year's liability or 105% of the pre-preceding year's liability, BES relief and Film Investment relief must be excluded in calculating the tax due.

10.3.3   The charge to interest on late payment of tax

Preliminary tax is due on 31 October in the year of assessment, and the amount paid must be in accordance with one of the three options outlined at 10.3.2 above. Payment of the balance of income tax for a year of assessment must be paid by 31 October in the following year. Failure to do so will result in interest being charged from 31 October in the year that the tax fell due to the date of eventual payment. From 1 April 2005, the rate of interest chargeable on tax underpaid is 0.0273%. With effect from 1 July 2009 the rate reduces to 0.0219%.

10.3.4   Margin of error

s958(3A)
TCA 97

The responsibility is on the taxpayer to adequately calculate the amount of the preliminary tax liability. However, there are tolerances built into the legislation that allow for a small margin of error. The tolerance level has been set at the greater of €635 or 5% of the tax payable (subject to a maximum of €3,175). The relief for computational error will be available only where:

- an assessment has not been made on or before the specified date;

- a tax return was delivered by the specified return date;

- the tax return contained a full and true disclosure for making a correct assessment; and

- the level of error was within the limits outlined above.

Where the relief applies, the balance of tax due (representing the error) will be due and payable on or before 31 December. Any additional preliminary tax payable for the subsequent tax year, consequent upon the computational error, should also be paid by 31 December to avoid exposure to interest charges.

Example 10.3

An individual submits his 2008 tax return on 1 October 2009. He calculates his tax liability for the year 2008 to be €20,000. He has already paid preliminary tax of €17,000 for 2008. He wishes to make a payment of preliminary tax for 2009 using the "100% of the tax liability for the preceding tax year" option. He therefore makes the following payments with his tax return:

	€
Balance of income tax 2008	*3,000*
Preliminary tax 2009	*20,000*
Total	*23,000*

When an assessment for 2008 issues from the Inspector of Taxes, the liability is in fact €21,000 and not €20,000 as previously calculated.

Since the €1,000 difference is less than 5% of the liability (i.e., €21,000 × 5% = €1,050) and not greater than €3,175, the margin of error relief may be applied. The additional tax of €1,000 should be paid on or before 31 December 2009.

Preliminary Tax 2009

Since the Preliminary Tax payment was meant to represent 100% of the tax liability for 2008, the amount paid of €20,000 is understated by €1,000. The additional tax of €1,000 should also be paid on or before 31 December 2009.

The margin of error relief deems the additional two payments of €1,000 each to have been made on 31 October 2009.

10.4 Tax Returns and Penalties for Late Filing — "surcharge"

All chargeable persons are required to submit a tax return to the Collector-General not later than 31 October following the year of assessment. This applies whether or not the Revenue Commissioners issue a tax return form to the individual for completion. Thus, 31 October 2009 is the specified date for the filing of tax returns for the year of assessment 2008.

The Inspector of Taxes is obliged to issue an income tax assessment following receipt of a tax return. The particulars to be stated on an assessment should include the amounts of income assessed under each of the different Schedules D, E and F. However, the tax payable may be stated in one sum.

10.4.1 Surcharge for late filing of tax returns

If a tax return is not submitted by the specified date, a surcharge on the liability arising for the year (after credit for PAYE already paid, but before credit for tax paid directly) is applied regardless of the fact that the tax liability may have been paid in full and on time.

s1084
TCA 97

Tax returns, if not submitted on time, will be liable to a surcharge calculated as follows:

- 5% of the tax liability for the year of assessment to which the tax return relates, subject to a maximum of €12,695. This applies where the tax return is delivered within two months of the filing date (e.g., for the year of assessment 2008, this means any date between 1 November 2009 and 31 December 2009 inclusive).

- 10% of the tax liability for the year of assessment to which the tax return relates, up to a maximum of €63,485. This applies where the tax return is not delivered within two months of the filing date (e.g., for the year of assessment 2008, a tax return filed after 31 December 2009 is liable to a surcharge of 10%).

10.5   Interest on Tax Overpaid

s865
TCA 97

Interest on tax overpaid only applies where there is a "valid claim" for repayment. A valid claim will only be deemed to be made where all necessary information, which the Revenue Commissioners reasonably require to certify the claim, has been submitted by the individual. Where Revenue forms the view that a valid claim has not been made, it is up to the individual to submit whatever information the Revenue Commissioners feel they reasonably require before a valid claim is deemed to have been made.

The rate of interest is calculated on a daily basis at the rate of 0.011%. The period from which interest runs depends on whether the overpayment is as a result of a mistake by the individual or by Revenue. Where the overpayment arises because of a mistaken application of the law by the Revenue Commissioners, and the claim for repayment is made within the requisite time limit, interest shall commence to run from the day after the end of the chargeable period in which the overpayment arises, or if later, the date of payment.

Where the overpayment cannot be ascribed to a mistaken application of the law by the Revenue Commissioners, the overpayment will carry interest from a day which is 93 days after the day on which a "valid claim" for the repayment had been filed with the Revenue Commissioners. Interest will not be paid where the overall amount due is less than €10. The Minister for Finance may change the rate of interest on overpayment of tax from time to time by Ministerial Order.

Interest paid to a taxpayer on the overpayment of tax is not subject to withholding tax and is exempt from income tax.

10.6   Expressions of Doubt

s955(4)
TCA 97

Where a taxpayer is in doubt as regards an item to be included in a return of income, he is regarded as having made a full disclosure if he draws to the attention of the Inspector of Taxes the doubtful item. A doubt may arise in relation to the tax treatment of a number of issues, e.g., as to whether:

- a particular source of income is taxable; or

- a particular expense deductible for Schedule D Case I/II purposes; or

- expenditure which qualifies for relief as a tax credit/tax allowance.

However, this provision will not apply where the Inspector of Taxes or the Appeal Commissioner are of the opinion that the doubt was not genuine and that the taxpayer was acting to avoid or evade tax.

10.7   Maintenance of Records

s886 TCA 97 Every taxpayer who carries on a trade, profession or other activity, the profits or gains of which are chargeable under Schedule D, or who is chargeable to tax under Schedule D or Schedule F in respect of any other sources of income, or has chargeable gains is obliged to retain records which will enable true returns to be made of such profits or gains. Linking documents, that is documents which are drawn up in the making up of accounts and which show details of the calculations linking the records to the accounts, must also be retained.

Records include accounts, books of account, documents and any other data maintained manually or by any electronic, photographic or other process relating to:

- all sums of money received and expended in the course of the trade, profession or other activity and the matters in respect of which the receipt and expenditure take place

- all sales and purchases of goods and services

- the assets and liabilities of the trade, profession or other activity.

Records must be kept in written form in an official language of the State and may, with the consent of the Revenue Commissioners (in accordance with s887 TCA 1997), be kept by means of any electronic, photographic or other process.

Records and linking documents must be retained for a period of six years after the completion of the transactions to which they relate.

s887(5) A person who fails to comply with the above will be liable to a penalty of €1,520.
TCA 97 A person who preserves records by electronic, photographic or other methods must furnish details relating to the process to the Revenue Commissioners if so requested. The penalty for failure to do so is €1,265.

10.8   Revenue Audits

s951 Under s951 TCA 1997, all chargeable persons are required to make a tax return to the
TCA 97 Revenue Commissioners for each year of assessment that they are so chargeable. The information sought in the tax return is at the discretion of the Revenue Commissioners but must:

- show all sources of income and any deductions/tax credits claimed for the year of assessment; and

- be signed by the taxpayer.

Following receipt of the tax return, the Inspector of Taxes issues an assessment to the taxpayer in accordance with the tax return filed for that year of assessment. The issue *empêcher* *par la suite*

of such an assessment does not preclude the Inspector of Taxes from subsequently examining the tax return. The purpose of the examination of the tax return by the Inspector of Taxes is to establish whether or not the entries are accurate. If he is not satisfied that the entries are accurate, the tax return is selected for a Revenue audit. The Inspector of Taxes is entitled to take whatever actions within his powers are deemed necessary to meet this objective.

Unless the Inspector of Taxes suspects that the tax return has been filed on a negligent or fraudulent basis, he is subject to a time limit within which to begin an examination of the tax return. The relevant time limit is four years from the end of the year of assessment within which the return was filed.

Example 10.4

A taxpayer files his tax return for the year of assessment 2008 on 15 October 2009. The Inspector of Taxes has until the end of 2013 (four years from the end of the period in which the tax return was filed) to examine this tax return. If the Inspector of Taxes suspects that the tax return was filed on a fraudulent or negligent basis, he is not subject to any time limit.

10.8.1   Types of Revenue audit

There are basically two types of audit:

- desk audit

- field audit

Desk Audit

This type of audit applies where verification of specific claims for expenses, allowances or reliefs is required. The procedure generally applies to straightforward issues. The audit is conducted by letter or telephone enquiries.

Field Audit

A field audit is conducted at the business premises of the taxpayer. Advance notice must be given in writing to the taxpayer.

10.8.2   Inspection of documents and records

s905
TCA 97

Section 905 TCA 1997 is the most widely used power by an Inspector of Taxes to test the accuracy of tax returns; it is the section that permits him/her to inspect supporting records on the taxpayer's premises.

The Inspector of Taxes may:

- examine all records that the taxpayer is obliged to retain for tax purposes which relate to any trade, profession, other source of profits, any tax liability or any repayments of tax, or any property (defined as "any asset relating to a tax liability");

- require any person present on the business premises, other than a customer, to produce any records or property;

- search for any records or property if he/she believes that they have not been produced;

- examine and take copies or extracts from any records;

- remove any records and retain them for a reasonable time for the purposes of inspection;

- request information from a third party (e.g., a financial institution, a supplier, or a customer). Where a request for such information is not forthcoming, he/she may apply to the High Court for an order to secure such information.

10.8.3 Where additional tax is due

If an Inspector of Taxes, having examined the books and records of the taxpayer, establishes that there is additional tax payable, he will advise the taxpayer of such tax. Where a taxpayer is dissatisfied with the findings of the Inspector of Taxes, he/she has the right to seek a review. This review may be undertaken by:

- another Revenue official at a local level, i.e., either by the appropriate District Inspector or by the Regional Director; or

- where a taxpayer does not wish the review to be undertaken locally, he or she can request that the review be undertaken either by the Director of Customer Services alone, or jointly by the Director of Customer Services and an external reviewer.

If the taxpayer is still dissatisfied following a review, he may ask the Inspector of Taxes to issue an assessment. On receipt of the assessment, he may appeal against the assessment. Lodging an appeal gives the taxpayer the right to have the case heard before the Appeal Commissioners. Appeal procedures are considered at 10.9 below.

10.8.4 Audit settlement

If, having examined the books and records of the taxpayer, additional tax becomes payable, interest and possibly penalties are added to the additional tax.

Interest

Statutory interest is payable and is charged at a daily rate of 0.0273% (0.0219% with effect from 1 July 2009).

Recovery of Penalties

The Inspector of Taxes and the taxpayer may reach agreement on a cash settlement, which includes a sum in lieu of Revenue instigating penalty proceedings through the courts.

Finance (No. 2) Act 2008 provides that where the Revenue Commissioners and the taxpayer cannot agree on the level of penalty (or the taxpayer fails to pay an agreed penalty) the Revenue Commissioners may apply to the courts (District, Circuit or High court depending on the level of penalty) for a determination as to whether a penalty arises.

The rate of the penalty ultimately payable by the taxpayer depends on the category of the tax default. Penalties range from 3% to 100% of the tax payable.

Tax Facts

As an incentive for taxpayers to file and pay tax electronically, Revenue have extended the pay and file deadline date of 31 October 2009 to 16 November 2009.

Following Finance (No. 2) Act 2008, where cases are referred to the courts for determination on the amount of penalty payable, such cases will no longer be held in camera.

10.9   Appeal Procedures

s933(1)(a) TCA 97

Section 933(1)(a) TCA 1997 entitles a taxpayer to appeal against any assessment to income tax made by an Inspector of Taxes if the taxpayer does not agree that the assessment is correct. Such an appeal must be made by giving notice in writing to the Inspector of Taxes, and the notice must specify the grounds of the appeal. Lodging an appeal does not preclude the taxpayer and the Inspector of Taxes from reaching agreement on the content of the assessment subsequently. Where no such mutual agreement arises, the Appeal Commissioner is responsible for appointing the time and place of the appeal hearing. This information is conveyed to the Inspector of Taxes who in turn advises the taxpayer. An appeal must be lodged against an assessment within 30 days of the date of issue of the assessment. The time limit may be extended to 12 months where the taxpayer was prevented by absence, sickness or other reasonable cause from making the appeal on time.

Appeal Commissioners are appointed by the Minister for Finance to act as arbiters between the Inspector of Taxes and the taxpayer in cases of dispute. Where an estimated assessment is made in the absence of a tax return, an appeal will be allowed only after:

■ the tax return has been submitted; and

■ the tax due on the basis of the tax return has been paid.

Where a taxpayer feels that there is a delay by the Inspector of Taxes in listing an appeal, he will be able to apply to the Appeal Commissioners for an early listing. The Appeal Commissioners may dismiss an appeal where there is evidence of non-co-operation by the taxpayer for requests for information by the Appeal Commissioners.

Where appeals against assessments to income tax are heard by the Appeal Commissioners, the determination of the Commissioners is final and conclusive.

A taxpayer aggrieved by a decision of the Appeal Commissioners may apply for a rehearing before a Circuit Court judge. The taxpayer may apply to a higher court, e.g., the High Court or Supreme Court, but may only do so on a point of law.

WHAT YOU SHOULD NOW KNOW

On completion of this chapter, you should be able to:

- ✓ Discuss the criteria used to determine if an individual is a chargeable person.

- ✓ Explain what impact "pay and file" obligations have for a chargeable person.

- ✓ Describe the two types of Revenue audit and their implications for a chargeable person.

- ✓ Discuss the mechanics of appeal procedures.

- ✓ Complete Questions and the Assignments in Irish Taxation Law and Practice, Volume 2.

TAX CREDITS, TAX BANDS AND INCOME LEVY

In this chapter, you will deal with the following: yah boo

- Personal tax credits – non-refundable

- Other tax credits – non-refundable

- Tax credits – refundable

- Allowances/reliefs deductible at marginal rate

- Allowances/reliefs deductible at marginal rate

- Tax rates and tax bands

- Low income exemption and marginal relief

- Income Levy

11.1   Introduction

dwils

The purpose of this chapter is to establish what entitlements a taxpayer has in terms of allowances, reliefs, rate bands and tax rates. It is important to understand the different key concepts and how they impact on a taxpayer's tax liability.

Personal tax credits – non-refundable

These are non-refundable credits which are available based on personal circumstances for example, the married person's tax credit and the single parent tax credit.

Non-personal tax credits – non-refundable

These are credits based on certain payments by the taxpayer. Unlike personal tax credits these can arise only where a taxpayer has actually made a payment towards something specific – for example, service charges or trade union subscriptions. Like personal tax credits, these are also non-refundable.

Refundable tax credits

These credits arise in relation to specific tax amounts already paid to Revenue in respect of specific sources of income, such as payroll taxes or PAYE ("pay as you earn"), dividend withholding tax and professional fees withholding tax. These credits are refundable where they exceed the actual liability of the taxpayer.

Reliefs available as deductions

déduchible

Such reliefs are deducted from income and are allowable at the taxpayer's marginal rate of tax. For example, relief as a deduction is available for certain qualifying health expenses. For taxpayers liable to tax at 41%, such reliefs are more worthwhile than tax credits since tax credits are available only at the standard rate of tax.

Tax rates and tax bands

There are two tax rates currently in operation, the standard rate of 20% and the higher rate of 41%. A tax band is the amount of income taxable at a specified rate. Thus the standard rate band is the amount of income taxable at the standard rate of 20%. The tax bands that currently apply depend on the taxpayer's circumstances (e.g., single, widowed or married) and, in the case of married couples, on whether or not both parties are working.

Low income exemption and marginal relief

Taxpayers in receipt of low income, where this income is below a "specified amount", may be exempt from income tax. Where the income exceeds a specified amount, full exemption from income tax is not available; however, marginal relief may apply. The specified amount is determined by reference to the taxpayer's personal circumstances, Including whether they are single, under or over 65 years of age, married or single.

Income levy

The income levy was introduced effective from 1 January 2009. The levy is applied to income, but the definition of income is broader than that for income tax. Initially the rates were 1%, 2%, and 3% by reference to certain income levels. These rates were increased to 2%, 4% and 6% effective from 1 May 2009.

11.1.1 *Pro forma* income tax computation

Below is a *pro forma* computation, which shows where both refundable and non-refundable tax credits are included in the computation of tax liability. Before addressing the detail of the computation, three important concepts require further commentary. These are:

- gross income;

- total income; and

- taxable income.

Gross income

This is the aggregate of the various sources of income which have been computed in accordance with the Taxes Acts.

Total income

This is gross income less charges. Charges will be covered in more detail in Chapter 12.

Taxable income

This is total income less allowances/reliefs allowable at the individual's marginal rate of tax.

Income tax computation of Mr X for 2009			€
Income	Schedule D	– Case I	X
		– Case III	X
	Schedule E		X
Gross income			X
Less: Charges (covered in Chapter 12)			(X)
Total income			X
Less: Deductible reliefs			(X)
Taxable income			X
Tax thereon			X

Less: Non-refundable tax credits	(X)
	X
Less: Refundable tax credits	(X)
Net income tax due/(refundable)	X

The various components of the above, i.e., credits and reliefs, are discussed in more detail throughout the remainder of this chapter.

11.2 Personal Tax Credits – Non-Refundable

Personal tax credits are determined by reference to the individual's personal tax circumstances. Personal tax credits are non-refundable.

Example 11.1

Pat is single and an Irish resident. In 2009 he will receive interest from government stock of €5,000 (tax not deducted at source). He has no other income. His tax assessment will be as follows:

	€
Tax on €5,000 20% =	*1,000*
Less:	
Single Person Tax Credit	*(1,830)*
Excess credit	*(830)*

The excess credit of €830 is non-refundable.

Details of the main personal tax credits for 2009 are set out in the reference material in Appendix I to this chapter.

11.2.1 Basic Personal Tax Credits

There are three categories of personal tax credits:

(i) single

(ii) married

(iii) widowed

11.2.2 Single Person's Tax Credit: €1,830

S461
TCA 97

The Single Person's Tax Credit is available to an individual who is:

■ single;

s1023
TCA 97

■ married but has elected under s1023 TCA 1997 for separate assessment (see Chapter 13 on taxation of married couples);

s1018(4)
TCA 97

■ married but has elected under s1018(4) for single assessment;

separated without a legally binding document (see Chapter 13 on taxation of married couples).

11.2.3 Married Person's Tax Credit: €3,660

s461
TCA 97

The Married Person's Tax Credit is available to an individual who is:

■ married, living with his/her spouse and assessed to tax under joint assessment;

■ widowed in the year of assessment, where the deceased spouse was the assessable spouse;

s1026
TCA 97

■ separate or divorced but has elected under s1026 TCA 1997 to remain jointly assessed.

11.2.4 Widowed Person's Tax Credit: €2,430

s461A
TCA 97

The Widowed Person's Tax Credit is available to an individual who is a widow or widower and who has no dependent children. The credit is granted in the year of assessment following the year of bereavement. (See 11.2.6 below for the Widowed Parent Tax Credit that applies in the five years following the year of bereavement.)

11.2.5 One-Parent Family Credit: €3,660

s462
TCA 97

An increase in credit is available to an individual who is not entitled to the married credit but who maintains a "qualifying child" during the year of assessment. The amount of credit depends on whether the individual is:

■ single (or separated/divorced and not qualifying for the Married Person's Credit); or

■ widowed.

A "qualifying child" is a child who:

■ is under the age of 18 years; or

■ if over 18 years, is receiving full-time education at any university, college, school or other educational establishment; or

■ is permanently incapacitated by reasons of mental or physical infirmity from maintaining himself/herself and, where the child has reached 21 years of age, was incapacitated before reaching that age; and *sous la garde de*

- is in the custody of and is maintained by the claimant at his/her own expense for the whole or part of the year of assessment.

Any income that the qualifying child may have is disregarded for the purposes of entitlement to the credit. The inclusion of the One-Parent Family Credit has the effect of increasing the total credit of the single/widowed parent to bring it in line with the Married Persons' Credit:

	Single €	Widowed €
Basic personal tax credit with no qualifying child	1,830	2,430
Above with One-Parent Family Tax Credit	3,660	3,660

There is no entitlement to the One-Parent Family Tax Credit in the case of a husband or a wife where the wife is living with her husband or in the case of a man and woman living together as man and wife.

11.2.6   Widowed Parent Tax Credit

s463
TCA 97

A widow who maintains a qualifying child (as described above) receives the Widowed Parent Tax Credit for the five years immediately following the year of bereavement. The additional credit is as follows:

- Year one following bereavement – €4,000

- Year two following bereavement – €3,500

- Year three following bereavement – €3,000

- Year four following bereavement – €2,500

- Year five following bereavement – €2,000

The individual is entitled to claim the tax credit for each of the five years after the year of bereavement provided that, in relation to each year for which the credit is claimed, the following conditions are met:

a)   the individual has at least one qualifying child residing with him/her for the whole or part of the year;

b)   the individual has not remarried before the commencement of the year; and

c)   the individual has not been living as man or wife with another person in the year.

A qualifying child for the purposes of the condition at a) above is as defined for the purposes of the One-Parent Family Credit at 11.2.5 above.

Example 11.2

A widow (bereaved in 2007) has one dependent child who is in full-time education. She has not remarried and lives alone with her child.

Her entitlements for the tax year 2009 are as follows:

	€	
Single Person's Tax Credit and One-Parent Family Tax Credit	*3,660*	
Widowed Parent additional credit	*3,500*	*(Year two following bereavement)*
Total	*7,160*	

Example 11.3

Assume the same facts as above, except that the widow during 2009 co-habits with a partner "as man and wife". She will be entitled to neither the Widowed Parent Tax Credit nor the One-Parent Family Tax Credit. She is entitled to only €2,430 (that being the Widowed Parent Tax Credit without a dependent child).

11.2.7   Home Carer's Tax Credit: €900

s466A
TCA 97

The Home Carer's Tax Credit is available to a spouse who "works at home" to care for children, the aged or incapacitated persons. The amount of the credit is €900. The conditions which must be met to qualify are as follows:

■ The married couple must be jointly assessed to tax.

■ The home carer must care for one or more dependent persons. A dependent person is:

– a child for whom social welfare child benefit is payable, i.e., children under 16 years, or children over 16 but under 19, who are in full-time education, or

– a person aged 65 years or over, or

– a person who is permanently incapacitated by reason of physical or mental infirmity.

The dependant(s) must normally reside with the married couple for the tax year.

A relative may, however, reside in a neighbouring residence on the same property or within two kilometres of the claimant where there is a direct system of communication between the home carer's residence and the residence of the dependant.

If the home carer has income of €5,080 or less, the full €770 credit is available. Where the income is more than €6,880, there is no credit available. For income between €5,080 and €6,880, the credit is restricted by half of the excess of the home carer's income over the limit of €5,080. The following table illustrates some examples of the amount of the restriction for given levels of income:

	Income of Home Carer	Tax Credit Due	Restriction of Tax Credit
1.	€5,080	€900	Nil
2.	€5,250	€815	€5,250 – €5,080 = €170 ÷ 2 = €85
3.	€5,500	€690	€5,500 – €5,080 = €420 ÷ 2 = €210
4.	€5,750	€565	€5,750 – €5,080 = €670 ÷ 2 = €335
5.	€6,000	€440	€6,000 – €5,080 = €920 ÷ 2 = €460
6.	€6,250	€315	€6,250 – €5,080 = €1,170 ÷ 2 = €585
7.	€6,500	€190	€6,500 – €5,080 = €1,420 ÷ 2 = €710
8.	€6,750	€65	€6,750 – €5,080 = €1,670 ÷ 2 = €835
9.	€7,000	Nil	€7,000 – €5,080 = €1,920 ÷ 2 = €960

For example in 3 above, 'Income of the Home Carer', let us assume that the home carer is in receipt of interest on government stock to the amount of €5,500 each year.

The restriction is calculated as half of the excess of the home carer's income of €5,500 over €5,080, i.e., (€5,500 – €5,080) / 2 = €420 / 2 = €210.

Thus, the tax credit due is €900 – €210 = €690.

The Home Carer Credit and the increased rate band may not be claimed together. The claimant may choose whichever of the two is more beneficial. Readers are referred to Chapter 13, Example 13.1 for an illustration of this point.

11.2.8   Incapacitated Child Tax Credit: €3,660

s465 TCA 97 A tax credit of €3,660 is granted to an individual for each incapacitated child of the individual. "Child" includes any child who is in the custody of the claimant and who is maintained by the claimant. The credit is granted if, in the year of assessment, the child:

- is under 18 years of age and is permanently incapacitated by reason of mental or physical infirmity; or

- if over the age of 18, is permanently incapacitated by reason of mental or physical infirmity from maintaining himself/herself and has become so before he or she reached the age of 21 years. Alternatively, if the child became permanently incapacitated after the age of 21 years, he or she must have been in full-time education at the time.

The income of the child is not taken into account in determining entitlement to the credit.

11.2.9   Age Tax Credit: €325/€650

s464 TCA 97 A tax credit is available to an individual if the individual or their spouse is 65 years of age or over in the year of assessment. In the case of a married individual, the tax credit is €650 regardless of whether one or both are over 65 years. For single individuals, the tax credit is €325.

11.2.10 Blind Person's Tax Credit: €1,830

s468 TCA 97 A credit of €1,830 is available to an individual if that individual or his/her spouse is blind during the whole or part of the year of assessment. Where both parties are blind, the credit is €3,660.

A blind person who is a registered owner with the Irish Guide Dog Association may claim €825 for the maintenance of a guide dog. This allowance is granted at the claimant's marginal rate of tax.

11.2.11 Employee Tax Credit: €1,830 (maximum)

s472 TCA 97 The Employee Tax Credit is sometimes known as the PAYE Tax Credit. It is granted to an individual who is in receipt of "emoluments" subject to PAYE deductions. Emoluments are salary, fees, bonus, holiday pay, overtime, etc.

A proprietary director (or the spouse of a proprietary director), i.e., a director who owns more than 15% of the ordinary share capital of the company, is excluded from entitlement to the credit.

In addition, emoluments paid by self-employed individuals (or by a partnership in which the individual is a partner) to his/her spouse or child will not qualify the recipient for relief.

A child of a proprietary director/self-employed individual is entitled to the relief where:

- the child works full-time throughout the year of assessment; and

- the child's income for the year of assessment from this employment is at least €4,572.

The employee tax credit is also available to recipients of certain pensions and benefits payable by the Department of Social and Family Affairs and to certain individuals who are liable to Irish tax on foreign employment income. If the individual suffers withholding tax similar to PAYE in his/her home country, the credit is granted as if the emoluments were subject to Irish PAYE.

A maximum credit of €1,830 is available for 2009. If tax at the standard rate on the qualifying emoluments for the year of assessment is less than this amount, the credit is restricted to that lower amount. For example, if emoluments for 2009 amount to only €5,000, then the employee tax credit is calculated as €1,000 (€5,000 × 20%).

11.2.12 Dependent Relative Tax Credit: €80

s466 TCA 97 A credit of €80 is available to an individual who proves that he/she maintains at his/her own expense any person who is:

- a relative or a spouse's relative who is incapacitated by old age or infirmity from maintaining himself/herself; or

- a widowed parent or the widowed parent of a spouse whether incapacitated or not; or

- a son or daughter who resides with the claimant and whose services the claimant is compelled to depend on by reason of old age or infirmity.

The credit will not be due if the income of the person for whom the claim is made exceeds the maximum rate of the old age contributory pension for a person aged over 80 years living alone. For 2009, the income limit was €13,837.

If two or more people jointly support the relative, the tax credit is apportioned according to the amount expended by each individual on the maintenance of the relative.

11.3   Other Tax Credits – Non-Refundable

At 11.2 above, personal tax credits, which are automatically available depending on an individual's circumstances, were covered in detail. Other tax credits exist where the individual makes payments for certain types of expenditure. Again, as with personal tax credits, these credits are non-refundable. They are considered in detail in the following paragraphs.

11.3.1   Tax credit for rents paid by certain tenants

s473 TCA 97 A tax credit is available to an individual for rent paid (subject to maximum limits) on private rented accommodation which forms his/her only or main residence. The maximum limits for 2009 are:

	Under 55 years of age	Over 55 years of age
	€	€
Married/widowed	4,000	8,000
Single	2,000	4,000

"Rent" for the purposes of the tax credit does not include:

- any amount relating to the cost of maintenance or repairs which, in the absence of an agreement to the contrary, would normally be the responsibility of the tenant;

- any amount relating to the provision of goods or services;

- any amount which relates to a right or benefit other than the right to use the premises;

- any amount subject to a right of reimbursement or a subsidy from any source enjoyed by the person making the payment, unless such reimbursement or subsidy cannot be claimed.

Example 11.4

A single individual aged 40 pays rent of €3,000 in the year ended 31 December 2009.
The relief granted by way of a tax credit will be €2,000 @ 20% = €400.
(Note: The tax credit is confined to 20% of the maximum limit.)

Example 11.5

A single individual aged 40 pays rent of €1,000 in the year ended 31 December 2009.
The relief granted by way of tax credit will be €1,000 × 20% = €200.
(Note: The tax credit is confined to 20% of the amount of rent actually paid.)

Example 11.6

A single individual aged 70 pays rent of €4,000 in the year ended 31 December 2009.
The relief granted by way of tax credit will be €4,000 × 20% = €800.
(Note: The tax credit is confined to 20% of the maximum limit.)

11.3.2 Relief for fees paid for third-level education

s474 TCA 97 Relief is available in respect of "qualifying fees" paid by an individual on his/her own behalf or on behalf of other persons* in respect of an "approved course" for the academic year when that course commences in the year of assessment. The relief is by way of a tax credit calculated as the fees paid at the standard rate of tax. The credit is non-refundable.

"Qualifying fees" in relation to an approved course and an academic year means the amount of fees chargeable in respect of tuition to be provided in relation to that course in that year which, with the consent of the Minister for Finance, the Minister for Education and Science approves for the purposes of this section. Relief will not be available in respect of any amount of the fees recoverable, directly or indirectly, by the individual or by other persons, from any source.

An "approved course" means:

- a full-time or part-time undergraduate course of study in an approved college which:

  - is of at least two academic years' duration, and

  - which has been approved by the Minister for Education and Science, having regard to the code of standards laid down in relation to the quality of education to be offered on approved courses;

or:

- a postgraduate course of study in an approved college which must be at least one academic year but not more than four academic years in duration and must lead to a postgraduate award based on either a thesis or an examination.

An "approved college" for the purposes of this section means a college or institution of higher education in the State, or a college, university or similar institution outside the State where certain additional conditions are fulfilled.

For the purposes of the relief, the Minister for Education and Science will approve the colleges, courses and the level of fees in respect of each course that will qualify for the relief. The Minister must provide this information to the Revenue Commissioners by 1 July in each year.

Where the Minister is satisfied that an approved college or an approved course in that college no longer meets the appropriate code of standards laid down, the Minister may, by notice given in writing to the approved college, withdraw the approval of that college or course. Notice of withdrawal must be published in *Iris Oifigiúil* and will only have effect from the following tax year.

Any claim for relief under this section must be accompanied by a statement in writing from the college stating the following:

- that the college is an approved college for the purposes of this section;

- the details of the course undertaken by the individual or other persons;

- the duration of the course; and

- the amount of fees paid in respect of the course.

The maximum amount of qualifying fees allowable is €5,000.

* Prior to 2007, tuition fees paid on behalf of "other persons" only qualified for relief if such persons were dependants of the claimant. Section 9 Finance Act 2007 removed the requirement that they be dependant. The change is effective from 1 January 2007.

11.3.3 Tax credit for service charges

s477 TCA 97 An individual may claim a tax credit for a year of assessment in respect of service charges paid on time to a local authority or private concerns (i.e., persons other than local authorities) in the year ending 31 December preceding the year of assessment.

The tax credit is limited to a maximum of €400 at the standard rate for domestic refuse collection or disposal services, which are provided by a local authority or by private concerns. "Service" means the provision by or on behalf of a local authority of:

- a supply of water for domestic purposes;
- domestic refuse collection or disposal; and
- domestic sewage disposal facilities.

The tax credit is given to the individual who is liable for the service charges. Alternatively, the tax credit may be granted to an individual who resides full-time in the premises to which the service charges relate and who pays such service charges, provided the individual who is liable has disclaimed the relief in favour of the payer.

An individual who wishes to claim this tax credit must furnish his or her PPS number to the local authority to whom the service charges are paid and the local authority must then provide a certificate containing the following details:

■ the name, address and PPS number of the claimant;

■ the name and address of the local authority;

■ the amount paid and the financial year in respect of which it was paid; and

■ confirmation that the payment was made on time and represents the full amount of the service charges which the claimant was liable to pay for the financial year for which the certificate was given.

Each local authority must, within one month of the end of every financial year, provide the Revenue Commissioners with a return showing the name of every claimant and each claimant's PPS number. Where a local authority makes a return in accordance with these provisions, the above certificate need not be issued to those claiming the relief.

Example 11.7

John paid €150 to his local county council for refuse collection on 1 July 2008. The amount paid was due "on or before 31 July 2008".
In the year of assessment 2009, John is entitled to a tax credit of €150 × 20% = €30.

11.3.4 Relief for trade union subscriptions

s472C
TCA 97

An individual may claim a tax credit in respect of subscriptions paid for membership of trade unions.

The maximum relief for 2009 is €350 at the standard rate of tax, i.e., a tax credit of €70.

11.3.5 Medical and dental insurance

Medical

s470

Relief is available only for payments made to an authorised insurer (e.g., VHI, Quinn Healthcare, Hibernian Healthcare).

TCA 97

The contract of insurance must provide for the reimbursement of medical, surgical or nursing expenses resulting from sickness or accident to the individual, his/her spouse, children or other dependants.

Tax relief at source (TRS)

Tax relief for medical insurance is granted at source (TRS). With a standard rate of income tax of 20% for the 2009 tax year, the policy-holder pays a reduced premium

(80% of the gross amount) to the medical insurer. Revenue will give a credit for the remaining 20% to the medical insurer.

The effect of the TRS is that an individual who might not otherwise be in a position to claim tax relief on medical insurance premiums (e.g., an individual exempt from tax), can obtain tax relief at source by paying a reduced premium.

Example 11.8

Audrey has been a member of VHI for many years. She pays tax at the top rate of 41%. She receives her VHI subscription renewal for €1,000 on 1 July 2009.

	€	
Amount paid by Audrey to VHI	*800*	*(Net of TRS)*
Amount recovered by VHI from Revenue	*200*	*(€1,000 × 20%)*
Total	*1,000*	

Audrey does not have to make any further claim to Revenue. The fact that she pays tax at 41% is irrelevant. She has received the only tax relief due to her at the standard rate of tax under TRS.

Example 11.9

Julie is exempt from income tax. She receives her Quinn Healthcare subscription renewal for €1,000 on 1 July 2009.

	€	
Amount paid by Julie to Quinn Healthcare	*800*	*(Net of TRS)*
Amount recovered by Quinn Healthcare from Revenue	*200*	*(€1,000 × 20%)*
Total	*1,000*	

Despite the fact that Julie pays no tax, she is still entitled to pay her Quinn Healthcare subscription net of the standard rate relief.

Dental

Finance Act 2004 introduced tax relief for premiums paid for non-routine dental cover on policies, providing dental insurance only. The tax relief is calculated in the same way as that for medical insurance.

11.3.6 Relief for premiums under qualifying long-term policies

s470A
TCA 97

Tax relief is available in respect of premiums on qualifying insurance policies designed to provide cover, in whole or in part, for future care needs of individuals who are unable to perform at least two activities of daily living or are suffering from severe cognitive impairment. The relief is similar to that available for medical insurance premiums.

The relief is at the standard rate and is given under a relief-at-source system, i.e., the subscriber can deduct the relief from the gross premium due. The amount deducted is refunded by Revenue to the insurer. Benefits payable under a qualifying policy are not taxable. Qualifying policies, which must be approved by Revenue, may be taken out by an individual in relation to him/herself, his/her spouse, children and/or other relatives. Policies must generally be renewable and stand alone and must not provide for a termination lump-sum payment or surrender for cash.

11.4   Tax Credits – Refundable

Refundable tax credits arise in respect of specific tax payments. They represent tax actually paid and are therefore refundable where they exceed the net tax liability after the deduction of non-refundable credits. Examples of refundable tax credits are as follows:

PAYE

These are payroll taxes which an employer is obliged to deduct under the "pay as you earn" system.

Dividend withholding tax

Dividends payable to Irish-resident shareholders suffer dividend withholding tax (DWT) at source. Tax is deducted at the standard rate and the net dividend is paid to the shareholder.

Professional services withholding tax

Tax at the standard rate is deducted from payments made for professional services by Government Departments, State bodies, local authorities, health boards, etc. Examples of professional services are medical, dental, architectural, engineering, accountancy services, etc.

Relevant contracts tax (RCT)

Principal contractors must deduct tax at a rate of 35% from certain payments to sub-contractors. This tax must be deducted where the payee has not submitted a certificate (called a C2) authorising the payer to make the payment gross. Examples of the types of payments subject to this tax are payments in respect of building contracts, forestry operations and meat-processing operations.

Tax on annual payments

There is an obligation on the payer of annual payments to deduct tax at the standard rate of tax. A Deed of Covenant is an example of an annual payment (see Chapter 12).

Deposit interest retention tax (DIRT)

DIRT is deducted from deposit interest at source by the financial institution or deposit-taker. Up to 31 December 2008 the DIRT rate was 20%. From 1 January 2009, the rate is 23% and from 8 April 2009 the rate is 25%. For cease of illustration, the example below is by reference to the tax year 2008. DIRT, it is only refundable in the case of individuals who are aged 65 years or older. For individuals under 65 years of age, DIRT is available as a non-refundable credit. An example of a tax computation where there is a combination of refundable and non-refundable tax credits is set out below.

Example 11.10

Pat is single. In the year of assessment 2008, he received interest on government stock in the amount of €3,000 and other income of €2,000 from which tax was deducted at source at the standard rate of 20%, i.e., €400.

His tax assessment is as follows:

	€
Tax on €5,000 at 20%	*1,000*
Less:	
Non-refundable tax credit –	
Single Person's Tax Credit	*(1,830)*
Tax liability	*Nil*
Tax deducted at source	*(400)*
Refund due	*400*

The excess credit of €830 is non-refundable. Only the actual tax deducted at source of €400 is refundable.

11.5 Allowances and Reliefs Deductible at Marginal Rate

Allowances, which are not deductible as tax credits at the standard rate, are allowed as deductions from total income and accordingly are relieved at the individual's higher rate of tax, i.e., the marginal rate of tax.

Examples of such reliefs include expenditure on a Business Expansion Scheme investment and on the Film Investment Scheme.

The allowances deductible at the marginal rate are described below, together with the criteria for qualifying for the tax deduction.

11.5.1 Employed person taking care of an incapacitated individual: €50,000

s467
T CA 97

This is sometimes known as a "housekeeper" allowance. The allowance is available when the claimant employs a person to take care of an incapacitated individual. The allowance is available if the claimant or a relative of the claimant is totally incapacitated owing to physical or mental infirmity. In the case of a married person who is jointly assessed, the relief also applies if either the spouse or a relative of the spouse is incapacitated.

s465, 466
TCA 97

If an allowance is claimed under this section, a tax credit may not be claimed under s465 TCA 1997 (Incapacitated Child Tax Credit) or s466 TCA 1997 (Dependent Relative Tax Credit) in respect of the employed person.

The amount of the allowance is the lower of the expense actually borne by the claimant or €50,000. It is allowed at the individual's marginal rate of tax.

Where two or more individuals are entitled to the allowance:

- the aggregate of the deductions may not exceed €50,000; and

- the allowance granted is apportioned between them in proportion to the amount borne by each of them in employing the employed person.

11.5.2   Medical expenses

s469 TCA 97 Relief is available for health expenses incurred on the provision of healthcare in respect of an individual, his/her spouse and other persons*. Relief is not available for medical expenses which have been (or will be) reimbursed under a contract of insurance (e.g., VHI, Quinn Healthcare), from any public or local authority by way of compensation, or from other sources.

"Health expenses" include expenses incurred on:

- services of a practitioner

- diagnostic procedures carried out on the advice of a practitioner

- maintenance or treatment in a hospital or approved nursing home

- drugs or medicine supplied on the prescription of a practitioner

- physiotherapy prescribed by a practitioner

- orthopaedic treatment prescribed by a practitioner

- transport by ambulance

- supply or repair of medical, surgical or dental appliances used on the advice of a practitioner

- maternity care

- educational psychological assessments and speech and language therapy services for children

The legislation specifically excludes expenses relating to:

- routine ophthalmic treatment (sight-testing, advice on use of spectacles/contact lenses, and the provision and repairing of spectacles/contact lenses); and

- routine dental treatment (extraction, scaling and filling of teeth, and the provision and repairing of artificial teeth/dentures).

Up until 2008, all medical expenses were granted at the individual's marginal rate of tax. However, from the tax year 2009 medical expenses with the exception of nursing home expenses are granted at the standard rate of tax. The relief is normally granted in the year of assessment in which the expenses are paid. However, if the individual so wishes, he/she may apply to have the relief granted in the year of assessment in which the expenses were incurred.

Example 11.11

Michael, who is single, incurs expenditure in 2009 as follows:

	€	
Pharmacy	300	*(prescribed drugs €200, non-prescribed medication €100)*
Dentist	250	*(€50 for check-up and polishing, €200 being balance due for orthodontic treatment)*
GP bills	190	
Hospital bill	1,050	*(€1,000 for operation/maintenance, €50 for telephone calls and laundry)*

Michael is due relief as follows:

	€	
Pharmacy	200	*(only prescribed drugs are allowed)*
Dentist	200	*(routine treatment not allowed)*
GP	190	
Hospital bill	1,000	*(non-medical expenditure not allowed)*
	1,590	

* Prior to 2007, health expenses paid on behalf of "other persons" only qualified for relief if such persons were dependants of the claimant. Section 9 Finance Act 2007 removed the requirement that they be dependant. The change is effective from 1 January 2007.

11.5.3   Permanent health benefit schemes

s471 TCA 97 Relief is available in respect of premiums paid under a permanent health benefit scheme approved by the Revenue Commissioners which provides for periodic payments to an individual in the event of loss or diminution of income resulting from ill health.

The amount of the premium allowable is limited to 10% of the individual's "total income". "Total income" is gross income from all sources less specific deductions and allowances (e.g., losses, capital allowances) and charges on income (e.g., annual payments such as payments under Deeds of Covenant).

Example 11.12

Mary earned €30,000 salary in 2009. She has no other income. She paid €3,500 in permanent health premiums.

She may claim only €3,000 due to the restriction of 10% of income.

Any benefit receivable by the employee under a permanent health scheme which has been approved by the Revenue Commissioners is normally taxable as emoluments under Schedule E. The person paying the benefit is required to deduct income tax from the benefit under the PAYE system. If the individual paying the premiums is assessed to tax under Schedule D, Revenue may agree to tax the benefits as part of the income of the trade or profession.

Tax relief is granted at source on contributions to Revenue-approved permanent health benefit schemes where the contributions are deducted from an individual's pay. The employer may deduct the premiums from gross pay for tax and PRSI purposes. If the contributions are not paid through the payroll, tax relief may be claimed as described above.

11.5.4 Tax relief for donations to eligible charities and other approved bodies

s848A
TCA 97

Tax relief is granted for donations to "eligible charities" and other "approved bodies". For the purposes of this relief, an "eligible charity" is any charity which is authorised as such in writing by the Revenue Commissioners. There are certain conditions the "charity" must meet to enable it to qualify under the scheme.

An "approved body" is one named in a list as issued by the Revenue Commissioners.

Prior to 2007, to be an eligible charity, the charity had to be established in the State. Section 27 of the Finance Act 2007 removed this requirement, the change is effective from 1 February 2007.

Conditions of relief

A number of conditions must be satisfied, as follows:

- The minimum qualifying donation is €250; there is no maximum figure.

- The donation must be in the form of money and must not be repayable.

- The donation must not confer any benefit on the donor or any person connected with the donor.

- The donation must not be conditional on, or associated with, any arrangements involving the acquisition of property by the charity or the approved body.

Relief

The method of granting tax relief on donations will depend on whether the donor is:

- a PAYE individual; or

- an individual taxed under the self-assessment system.

PAYE individual

The relief will be given on a "grossed-up" basis to the eligible charity or approved body, rather than by way of a tax credit to the donor. This in effect means that the charity will be treated as having received a donation net of income tax.

Example 11.13

An individual donates €500 to an eligible charity.

(a) If the individual is on the standard rate of income tax, i.e., 20%, the value of the donation to the charity will be €625. The charity receives €500 from the individual and can claim a repayment of €125 from Revenue at the end of the tax year. Thus, the individual has effectively given the charity an amount of €625 before tax relief at a rate of 20%.

(b) If the individual pays tax at the higher rate of 41%, the value to the charity will be €847. The charity receives €500 from the individual and can claim a repayment of €347 from Revenue at the end of the tax year. Thus, the individual has effectively given the charity an amount of €847 before tax relief at a rate of 41%.

Thus, if a higher-rate taxpayer on the PAYE system wants to donate €1,000 to a charity, he/she can accomplish this by simply paying an amount of €590 to the charity. The tax relief is, in effect, given at source as a deduction from the amount of the donation.

The PAYE individual must complete an "Appropriate Certificate" (CHY 2 Cert.) and forward it to the eligible charity or approved body so that it can claim the amount of tax on the grossed-up donation.

Self-assessment

The individual claims the relief for the amount paid. There is no grossing-up and therefore no tax repayment due to the charity, i.e., the donation is treated as paid gross to the charity.

Example 11.14

A donation of €500 is paid by an individual liable to tax at 20%. The value to the charity is €500. The individual has a tax saving of €100 (€500 × 20%); the donation costs the individual only €400. If the individual paid tax at the higher rate of 41%, he/she would have a tax saving of €205 (€500 × 41%), and the donation would cost the individual only €295.

The charity has already received €500 and no further amount is due to the charity.

Limit on Donations

There is a limit on the amount of tax relief an individual can claim in respect of donations to approved bodies where the individual is associated with that body. The limit is set at 10% of the individual's total income for that year of assessment.

An individual is deemed for the purposes of the new section to be associated with an approved body if that individual is an employee or member of that body or of a body with which the approved body is associated. Another body is associated with the approved body broadly if they are both under common control or the same persons can direct the activities of both bodies.

11.5.5   Relief for gifts of money to the State

s483 TCA 97 When a person makes a gift of money to the Minister for Finance for use for any purpose for, or towards the cost of which, public monies are provided, tax relief is available to the donor. The relief is based on the full amount gifted in the relevant tax year and accepted by the Minister. The donor claims a deduction equal to the amount of the gift in computing total income for the year.

The donor does not, however, retain power to stipulate how any funds donated must be used. How public monies are used is entirely at the discretion of the Minister.

11.5.6 Donations to certain sports bodies*

s874A
TCA 97

Tax relief is available for donations to approved sports bodies for the funding of capital projects. In order to qualify for this relief, the following conditions must be met:

- The body must be approved by the Minister for Arts, Sport and Tourism.

- The estimated aggregate cost of the project must not be greater than €40 million.

s235
TCA 97

- The sports body must hold a certificate from the Revenue Commissioners stating that the body is, in the opinion of Revenue, a body of persons to which s235 TCA 1997 applies, i.e., its income is exempt from tax because it is a body established for and existing for the sole purpose of promoting athletic or amateur games or sports, and such income is applied solely for those purposes.

- The body must also hold a valid tax clearance certificate.

*Readers are referred to Chapter 8 (Section 8.7) for restriction on reliefs for high income earners.

The minimum qualifying donation in any year to any sports body will be €250 and will be available at the individual's marginal rate of tax.

Relief

The method of granting tax relief on donations depends on whether the donor is a PAYE individual or an individual taxed under the self-assessment system. In both cases, the relief is granted in the same way as for eligible charities, and the analysis and examples at 11.5.4 above are relevant.

11.5.7 Relief for the long-term unemployed

s472A
TCA 97

Section 16 Finance Act 1998 introduced a tax incentive designed to help deal with the problem of the long-term unemployed.

Broadly speaking, an allowance is granted to those who return to work following a period of long-term unemployment. In order for this allowance to be granted, the employment must be a "qualifying employment", i.e., one which:

- commenced after 5 April 1998;

- is of at least 30 hour's duration per week; and

■ is capable of lasting at least 12 months.

The individual who takes up the qualifying employment must be a "qualifying individual", i.e., one who:

■ immediately prior to the commencement of the qualifying employment has been continuously unemployed for a period of at least 312 days (in effect 52 six-day weeks) and has been in receipt of unemployment benefit, unemployment assistance, or the one-parent family allowance under the Social Welfare Acts; or

■ is in any other special category approved by the Minister for Social, and Family Affairs.

"Qualifying individuals" who take up a "qualifying employment" may claim, for a three-year period, both a tapering personal deduction from total income and a tapering deduction in respect of each qualifying child. The amounts which may be claimed are as follows:

	Personal Tax Deduction	*Child Tax Deduction*
	€	*€*
Year 1	3,810	1,270 for each qualifying child
Year 2	2,540	850 for each qualifying child
Year 3	1,270	425 for each qualifying child

The relief is due at the individual's marginal rate of tax.

Section 16 Finance Act 1998 also provides for the following where relief is being claimed:

■ Where appropriate, the child tax deduction may be apportioned between more than one claimant.

■ The three-year period for the employee may commence with either the tax year in which the employment commences or the following year.

■ The employee's tax deduction under this section can be set only against the income from the qualifying employment.

■ An employee can change jobs once (to another "qualifying employment") and retain the balance of the deduction.

Example 11.15

John returned to work on 1 November 2009 following a period of two years on jobseeker's assistance. He has two qualifying children. His salary under the new contract of employment is €30,000 per annum. The employment is a "qualifying employment" for the purposes of relief for the long-term unemployed.

In Year 1, John's personal allowance will be calculated as (€3,810 + (€1,270 × 2)), i.e., €6,350. This allowance will be deductible at John's marginal rate of income tax but is limited in that it can only be set against income from the qualifying employment.

As John will earn only €5,000 from the employment in the 2009 year of assessment, he will not be able to use the Year 1 personal allowance in full. However, he may elect to have the relief

commence in the following year, i.e., 2010 instead. In this case, his personal allowances for each of the three relevant years will be as follows:

	Tax Year	Personal Allowance
€		€
Year 1	2010	6,350
Year 2	2011	4,240
Year 3	2012	2,120

11.5.8 Relief for investment in corporate trades (BES)

Position up to 31/12/2006

s488-508
TCA 97

This relief is more commonly known as Business Expansion Scheme Relief or BES. Relief is given as a deduction from total income and the maximum amount which qualifies for relief in any one tax year is €31,750 (minimum investment must be €250). The relief is available to each spouse, subject to availability of income in his/her own right. The relief is available to "qualifying individuals" who subscribe for "qualifying shares" in a "qualifying company" only. The expiry date for the relief is 31 December 2006. The conditions which must be satisfied to qualify for the relief are quite extensive, and some of the important concepts are explained at Appendix II.

Position post 1/1/2007

Section 19 Finance Act 2007 extended the relief and made a number of changes. The main changes are:

■ Relief extended for seven years to 31/12/2013.

■ Company limit for investment increased from €1m to €2m subject to a maximum of 1.5m raised in any 12 month period.

■ Investor limit increased from €31,750 to €150,000.

Example 11.16

Lisa Wiley who is single, made an investment of €150,000 in a qualifying BES company on 30 December 2009. Her salary for 2009 was €375,000 with tax deducted of €142,656 and she had no other income in 2009.

The calculation of the relief due is as follows (ignoring the income levy):

	€	€	€
Schedule E			375,000
			—
Less BES relief*			150,000
Taxable Income			225,000
36,400 × 20%	7,280.00		
188,600 × 41%	77,326.00		
			84,606.00

Less non refundable credits

Single	*1,830.00*
PAYE	*1,830.00*
	−3,660.00
	80,946.00

Less refundable credits

	–
PAYE paid	*142,656.00*
Refund due	*−61,710.00*

* *Restriction on reliefs for high income earners does not apply in this case.*

11.5.9 Seed capital investment (SCS)

Position up to 31/12/2006

s488-50
TCA 97

This relief was introduced to encourage individuals to set up their own business. The relief is deductible from total income and may be claimed for any of the six years immediately prior to the tax year in which the investment takes place. The individual must subscribe for shares in a new company. The new company must be carrying on trading operations of a BES nature. The maximum relief in any one tax year is €31,750. The expiry date for the relief was 31 December 2006.

To qualify for the relief, the individual must:

- be a full-time employee or a full-time director with the new company at any time up to six months after the end of the tax year in which the business is established;

- derive not less than 75% of his/her total income from Schedule E sources, income from other sources not being more than €25,000 in each of the three years of assessment preceding the year of assessment immediately prior to the year of assessment in which the employment commences;

- not have possessed or have been entitled to acquire more than 15% of the ordinary share capital, loan capital or voting power of a company other than a seed capital company except where the individual owns more than 15% of only one other company, provided:

  - the company's turnover in each of the three accounting periods (prior to the accounting period in which the investment is made in the seed capital company) did not exceed €127,000, and

  - the company is a trading company other than a company trading in land or financial services;

- acquire at least 15% of the issued ordinary share capital of the seed capital company and retain that 15% for two years from the date of the investment or from the date on which the company commences to trade, whichever is later.

Position post 1/1/2007

Section 19 Finance Act 2007 introduced the same proposed changes as for BES. However, the investor limit has been increased to €100,000 (€150,000 for BES).

Example 11.17

John Granger who is single was made redundant on 1 May 2009. He received a lump sum payment on termination of €160,000. He set up a manufacturing company and invested €100,000 in the company by buying 100,000 €1 shares.

His income and tax paid in previous years are as follows:

	2008	2007	2006	2005	2004	2003
	€	€	€	€	€	€
Salary	75,000	73,000	69,000	65,000	35,000	30,000
Other Income	2,000	1,800	1,500	1,000	500	300
Tax Paid	21,340	21,256	20,292	19,800	6,340	4,386

The relief is calculated as follows:

	2008	2007	2006	Total
	€	€	€	€
Salary	75,000	73,000	69,000	
Other Income	2,000	1,800	1,500	
Total	77,000	74,800	70,500	
Less SCR	77,000	23,000	0	
Taxable Income	0	51,800	70,500	
Tax due (A)	0	11,596	20,292	
Tax paid (B)	21,340	21,256	20,292	
Refund due (B–A)	21,340	9,660	0	**31,000**

11.5.10 Investment in films

s481 TCA 97 An individual who makes an investment in a company to produce a film is entitled to claim tax relief at his/her marginal rate of tax. The maximum amount of relief is the lower of 80% of the investment or 80% of €31,750, i.e., €25,400. The expiry date for the relief is 31 December 2012. Subject to Ministerial order this relief is increased to €50,000 (from €31,750) and is not subject to the 80% restriction for 2009 onwards.

The qualifying film company must be either incorporated and resident in the State or incorporated or resident outside the State but carrying on its trade in the State through a branch or agency. Not more than 60% of the cost of production may be obtained from investor companies qualifying for relief under this section.

11.5.11 Share subscription schemes

s479 TCA 97 Where an eligible employee of a qualifying company subscribes for eligible shares in that company, he/she may claim a deduction from total income for an amount equal to the amount of the subscription.

The maximum deduction for the tax year 2009 is €6,350. The conditions for this relief are as follows:

- the individual subscribes for the shares;

- the deduction is granted for the tax year in which the shares are issued;

- the individual takes up new ordinary shares in the company;

- the shares are issued in a company which is resident and incorporated in the State and is a trading company or a holding company;

- when the individual sells the shares within three years of the date of acquisition, any income tax relief granted is withdrawn by reference to the tax year in which it was originally given;

- the relief will not be withdrawn where the employee ceases employment with the particular company, where he ceases to be a resident or where he ceases to be a full-time employee;

- an amount equivalent to the tax deduction granted is excluded from the base cost of the asset in calculating the capital gains tax liability on the sale of the shares.

11.5.12 Retirement relief for sportspersons

s480A
TCA 97
A tax relief is available to certain retiring sportspersons who are resident in the State. The relief is given by way of a repayment of tax in the year in which the sportsperson ceases permanently to be engaged in that sport.

The relief is granted by allowing a deduction from earnings equal to 40% of those earnings derived directly from actual participation in the sport concerned for up to 10 years of assessment for which the sportperson was resident in the State. The deduction is calculated by reference to 40% of gross receipts (i.e., before deducting expenses) and may be claimed for any 10 years after the year of assessment 1990/91.

The relief has a number of conditions attaching to it:

- The individual must be resident in the State in the year of retirement.

- The relief is applied by allowing a deduction of 40% of the gross earnings (before deducting expenses) from the income from that sport.

- The claim for the deduction may be made in respect of consecutive years of assessment, up to 10 preceding tax years, for which the sportsperson was resident in the State.

- The relief is given in respect of earnings derived directly from the participation in the sport, such as prize money and performance fees.

- Other earnings, such as sponsorship fees, advertisement income, newspaper or magazine articles, etc., are excluded.

- If the sportsperson recommences to engage in that sport, the relief will be clawed back.

- The repayment will not carry interest.

- The relief cannot create or augment a loss.

- The relief will not affect the calculation of "net relevant earnings" for the purpose of ascertaining maximum pension contributions.

11.6   Tax Rates and Rate Bands 2009

The following table illustrates the rates and bands which apply for the 2009 year of assessment:

	Rate Band €	Rate of Tax	Description of Rate
Single/Widow(er):			
no dependent children			
First	36,400	20%	Standard
Balance		41%	Higher
Single/Widow(er):			
with dependent children			
First	40,400	20%	Standard
Balance		41%	Higher
Married couple:			
one income			
First	45,400	20%	Standard
Balance		41%	Higher
Married couple:			
two incomes			
First	72,800 *	20%	Standard
Balance		41%	Higher

* Note: The maximum standard rate tax band for a married couple with one spouse earning is €45,400. However, where both spouses are assessed to income tax in the year of assessment, the standard rate tax band may be increased up to a maximum of €72,800, provided the spouse with the lower income has assessible income of at least €27,400. If that spouse's assessible income is less than €27,400 for the year of

assessment, then the increase in the standard rate band above €45,400 is restricted to the amount of that spouse's income.

In determining the income of a spouse for the purposes of increasing the standard rate tax band, capital allowances, trading losses and pension contributions applicable to that income must be deducted first.

Income from deposit interest, which is subject to deposit interest retention tax (DIRT) of the spouse, is also deducted from the spouse's income in determining the increase in the standard rate band.

The following examples will best demonstrate the above:

Example 11.18

A married couple, with one spouse working and earning €80,000, is jointly assessed. The couple's income tax liability will be as follows:

		€	€
Taxable income			<u>80,000</u>
Tax thereon	€45,400 × 20% **Note 1**	9,080	
	€34,600 × 41%	<u>14,186</u>	
			<u>23,266</u>

Note 1: *The rate band is restricted to €45,400 since this is the maximum rate band for a single income couple.*

Example 11.19

A married couple is jointly assessed, with one spouse earning €50,000 and the other spouse earning €30,000. The couple's income tax liability will be as follows:

		€	€
Taxable income	(€50,000 + €30,000)		<u>80,000</u>
Tax thereon	€72,800 × 20% (€45,400 + €27,400) **Note 2**	14,560	
	€7,200 × 41%	<u>2,952</u>	
			<u>17,512</u>

Note 2: *The maximum rate band of income of €72,800 is utilised as the spouse with the lower income has assessable income of at least €27,400.*

Both Examples 11.18 and 11.19 above show total income of €80,000. However, the tax liability in Example 11.19 is €5,754 less than the liability in Example 11.18 (i.e., €23,266 – €17,512). This tax saving is achieved due to the couple in Example 11.19 having an additional €27,400 of taxable income charged at the standard rate instead of the higher rate of 41%. The tax saving is therefore €27,400 × (41 –20)% = €5,754.

Example 11.20

A married couple is jointly assessed, with one spouse earning €70,000 and the other spouse earning €10,000. The couple's income tax liability will be as follows:

		€	€
Taxable income	*(€70,000 + €10,000)*		80,000
Tax thereon	*€55,400 × 20% (€45,400 + €10,000)* **Note 3**	11,080	
	€24,600 × 41%	10,086	
			21,166

Note 3: *The maximum rate band of €72,800 is not utilised, as the accessible income of the spouse with the lower income is less than €27,400. The married couple band of €45,400 can be increased only by the actual income, in this case €10,000.*

Example 11.21

John and Jamie are jointly assessed. John has Schedule E employment income of €50,000. Jamie is self-employed. Her assessable profit for 2009 is €32,900. Her capital allowances for 2009 are €12,900. She pays allowable pension contributions in the amount of €3,000.

John and Jamie's assessable income and rate bands for 2009 are as follows:

	Jamie €	John €
Schedule E employment income (net)	–	50,000
Schedule D Case I income-tax adjusted profit	32,900	–
Less: *Capital allowances*	(12,900)	
	20,000	
Less: *Pension contributions*	(3,000)	
		–
	17,000	50,000
Total joint assessable income		67,000
Tax thereon *€62,400 (€45,400 + €17,000) × 20%* **Note 4**	12,480	
€4,600 × 41%	1886	
		14,366

Note 4: *The married couple band of €45,400 can be increased only by the actual income, in this case €17,000.*

11.7   Low Income Exemption and Marginal Relief

Exemptions from income tax are available to individuals with small incomes. The exemption limits are increased for individuals aged over 65 years. Marginal relief applies where the income does not greatly exceed the relevant exemption limit.

11.7.1 Low Income - Age exemption

s188 TCA 97 There is total exemption from income tax for an individual over 65 years if gross income does not exceed the following limits:

€20,000 – single person/widow(er)
€40,000 – married couple (jointly assessed)

The appropriate age limits are satisfied if either the individual (or his/her spouse) attains the relevant age at any time during the tax year.

The above exemption limits are increased by €575 for each of the first two dependent children maintained by the individual/married couple and by €830 for each dependent child in excess of two.

Example 11.22

> A married couple, both aged 65 have three dependent children. The exemption limit is increased by €1,980 ((€575 × 2) + €830) to €41,980.

The definition of dependent child is the same as that used for the purposes of the one-parent family tax credit.

11.7.2 Marginal relief

s188 TCA 97 Marginal relief will apply where the total income (i.e., gross income less charges of the individual) exceeds the specified income limit, but is not greater than twice the specified income limit. In such cases, the maximum income tax liability for the year may not exceed 40% of the difference between his/her total income and the specified income limit.

$-(45,100 - 41,150) \times 0.4 = 1,580$

Example 11.23

$limit = 41,150$

> Tom is married, aged 66 and has two dependent children. His gross income for 2009 is €45,100 and he pays qualifying charges of €1,000 and permanent health insurance premiums of €100.

	€
Income tax computation (ignoring marginal relief)	
Income	45,100
Less: Charges	(1,000)
Total income	44,100
Less: Deductible reliefs	(100)
Taxable income	44,000
Tax at 20%	8,800
Less:	
Married tax credit	(3,660)
Tax due	5,140

Less marginal relief (see below)	*(3,960)*
Net tax due	*1180*

€

Marginal relief computation

Income	*45,100*
Less: Charges (as above)	*(1,000)*
Total income (for exemption purposes only)	*44,100*
Less: Specified limit (married, over 65, with two dependent children)	
	(41,150)
	2950
Maximum final tax liability restricted to €2950 × 40%	*1180*

Marginal relief is further complicated if the individual is in receipt of deposit interest, which is subject to deposit interest retention tax (DIRT). Marginal relief is available if the taxpayer's total income does not exceed twice the appropriate specified income limit plus the gross interest received. If marginal relief is available, then it is calculated in the normal way. The maximum tax payable is the lower of the tax calculated per the income tax computation after deducting the DIRT paid or the 40% tax using the marginal relief calculation.

11.8   Relief for Pension Contributions

Tax relief is available at the marginal rate for pension contributions paid by individuals. There are different types of pension schemes, which can be loosely divided into two categories:

- pensions schemes for employed individuals;

- pensions schemes for self-employed individuals.

The maximum amount of pension contributions for which an individual may receive tax relief varies with age and is as follows:

Age	% of earnings
Up to 29	15%
30 to 39	20%
40 to 49	25%
50 to 54	30%
55 to 60	35%
Over 60	40%

In addition to the above limits, there is an overall earnings cap of €150,000 for 2009 (€275,239 for 2008).

Example 11.24

Mary Kate, aged 31, paid €60,000 pension contributions in 2009. Her assessiable income as a barrister in 2009 was €295,000.

	€
Case II Income	295,000
Subject to earnings cap	150,000
Maximum percentage allowed for	
age range 30 to 39	20%
Maximum allowed	30,000
Amount paid	60,000
Balance	30,000

The unutilised balance of €30,000 may be carried forward and claimed in the following year(s).

11.8.1 Contributions by self-employed individuals

This category also extends to individuals employed in a non-pensionable employment, i.e., an employment where there is no pension scheme in place for the employees. The maximum allowable contributions and earnings cap referred to above are applied to "net relevant earnings". Net relevant earnings are earnings from trades, professions and non-pensionable employment after deducting capital allowances, losses and charges (to the extent that they exceed non-trade income).

Example 11.25

Eddie Fox, aged 55, is single and self-employed. He pays €8,000 (gross) per year under a deed of convenant to his aunt who is permanently incapacitated. His Case I profit for 2009 is €130,000, capital allowances are €4,000 and he also pays €6,000 pension contributions.

	€	€
Case I income		120,000
Less:		
Capital allowances	(4,000)	
Payment under deed of convenant	(8,000)	
		(12,000)
"Net relevant earnings"		108,000
Less pension contributions		(6,000)
		102,000

Taxed as follows:

€36,400 × 20%	*7,280*
€65,600 × 41%	*26,896*
	34,176

Add: tax due on deed of convenant

€8,000 × 20%	*1,600*
	35,776

Less: non refundable credit

Single credit	*(1,830)*
Tax liability (ignoring Income Levy)	*33,946*

A further example illustrating the methodology for calculating net relevant earnings and the allowable pension contribution is included at Appendix III to this chapter.

11.8.2   Pensionable employment

Pensionable employment is one where the employer has put a pension scheme in place for the benefit of his/her employees. This is known as an "occupational pension scheme". Such schemes are generally Revenue-approved.

For the pension schemes which do not have Revenue approval, contributions made by the employer on behalf of the employee are treated as a taxable benefit in the hands of the employee. Furthermore any contributions made by the employee are not tax deductible. Conversely, for Revenue-approved schemes, any contributions made by the employer are not treated as a taxable benefit in the hands of the employee and the contributions made by the employee are tax-deductible for both PAYE and PRSI purposes. The contribution limits and earnings cap referred to above at 11.8 also apply to contributions to an occupational pension scheme.

Example 11.26

Mary Jane earns €3,000 per month from her employment with Zed Co Ltd. Zed Co Ltd has a Revenue-approved pension scheme in place into which Mary Jane pays 3% of her salary:

	€
Gross salary	*3,000*
Less pension contribution	*(90)*
Net pay	*2,910*

For PAYE/PRSI purposes, Mary Jane's "pay" is €2,910 and not €3,000. Her pension contributions are therefore effective for tax and PRSI purposes. However, for Income Levy purposes "Pay" is €3000.

Readers should note that pension contributions payable by self-employed individuals and individuals in non-pensionable employment are not effective for PRSI purposes.

Employees generally pay a fixed percentage to a pension scheme, e.g., 3% of pensionable salary. For some employees this contribution may not be sufficient, and such employees have the option of making an additional pension contribution. These top-up contributions are known as "Additional Voluntary Contributions" (AVCs). In determining the maximum contributions allowable, AVCs are added to the regular pension contribution.

11.9   Income Levy

11.9.1   Application of Income Levy

The income levy was introduced with effect from 1 January 2009 through the Finance (No. 2) Act 2008. The section introduced a new Part 18A to TCA 1997 and sixteen sections of legislation – Section 531A to 531N.

The levy is applied to "relevant emoluments" and "relevant income".

"Relevant emoluments" means emoluments to which PAYE is applied but excludes social welfare payments and payments similar in character to social welfare payments. Details of such payments are included at Appendix IV.

"Relevant income" is income from all sources apart from exempt income (referred to below). An interesting feature of the income levy is that certain income which is exempt or otherwise relieved from income tax is not exempt from the income levy, namely:

- Dividends from companies' exempt income from stallion fees, stud greyhound service fees, woodlands occupation, patent royalties, certain mining operations.

- Profits or gains from exempt income from stallion fees, stud greyhound service fees, woodlands occupation, patent royalties, certain mining operation.

- Exempt income from farmland leasing.

- Income qualifying for Artist's exemption.

Also the income levy is applied to income before deducting losses, capital allowances and pensions contributions. This contrasts with income tax rules where income, after deducting losses, capital allowances and pensions, is liable to income tax.

The income levy is collected in the same way as income tax, i.e. through the PAYE system for employees/recipients of occupational pensions and the self assessment system.

11.9.2   Exempt Income

The following income is exempt from the income levy:

- All social welfare payments including social welfare payments from abroad.

- Payments in lieu of social welfare payment, e.g. Community Employment Schemes etc (as included at Appendix IV).

- Income subject to DIRT (deposit interest retention tax).

- Income which does not exceed the exempt annual amount (referred to at 11.9.3 below).

- Miscellaneous income as included at Appendix V.

11.9.3 Exempt Individuals

The following are exempt from the income levy:

- Where the individual's income does not exceed the exempt amount (€18,304 up to 30 April 2009 and €15,028 from 1 May 2009).

- Where individuals are 65 years or older and their income does not exceed €20,000 for single individuals and €40,000 for married individuals.

- Medical card holders.

11.9.4 Rates and Income Thresholds

From 1 May 2009 the levy amounts were doubled and the exempt income level lowered. This is best illustrated by using the following table:

		From 1/1/09 to 30/4/09	From 1/5/09 to 31/12/09
		€	€
No levy if income below*		18,304	15,028
Annual income up to		100,100	75,036
	Liable @	1%	2%
Annual income		> 100,100	> 75,036
	Liable @	2%	4%
Annual income		> 250,120	> 174,980
	Liable @	3%	6%

*If income exceeds these limits the exemption does not apply.

The annualised table representing the above is:

First €75,036	1.67%
Between €75,037 and €100,100	3%
Between €100,101 and €174,980	3.33%
Between €174,981 and €250,120	4.67%
Greater than €250,120	5%

Example 11.27

George Jones has an adjusted profit of €400,000 for year ended 31 December 2009. His capital allowances for 2009 are €55,000 and he paid pension contributions of €45,000, also in 2009.

For income tax purposes he is assessed on €300,000 (€400,000 - €55,000 - €45,000). However, for income levy purposes he is assessed on €400,000 as follows:

€	€
75,036 × 1.67%	1,253.10
25,064 × 3.00%	751.92
74,880 × 3.33%	2,493.50
75,140 × 4.67%	3,509.04
149,880 × 5.00%	7,494.00
Total	15,501.56

Tax Facts

An Irish-resident, non-domiciled individual is not taxable on foreign income unless remitted to the State. For marginal relief purposes, "total income" is deemed to include all foreign income, even if it is not remitted to the State and is not taxable. This also applies to a non-resident individual who is liable to Irish income tax arising on income in Ireland.

WHAT YOU SHOULD NOW KNOW

On completion of this chapter, you should be able to:

✓ Explain the difference between refundable and non-refundable tax credits.

✓ List the various tax credits and allowances for the 2009 income tax year and describe the criteria for determining entitlement to relief for allowances/reliefs/tax credits.

✓ Explain how tax bands are applied in different circumstances.

✓ Calculate marginal relief where total exemption from income tax is not due.

✓ Calculate a net tax liability/refund using the above.

✓ Explain how the Income Levy operates.

✓ Understand the difference between definition of income for Income Tax purposes and that for Income Levy purposes.

✓ Complete Questions and the Assignments in Irish Taxation Law and Practice, Volume 2.

Appendix I

Main Personal Tax Credits

	Tax Year 2004	Tax Year 2005	Tax Year 2006	Tax Year 2007	Tax Year 2008	Tax Year 2009
	€	€	€	€	€	€
Single Person	1,520	1,580	1,630	1,760	1,830	1,830
Married Couple	3,040	3,160	3,260	3,520	3,660	3,660
Widowed Person						
– in year of bereavement	3,040	3,160	3,260	3,520	3,660	3,660
– without dependent children	1,820	1,980	2,130	2,310	2,430	2,430
– with dependent children	1,520	1,580	1,630	1,760	1,830	1,830
Widowed Parent						
– first year after bereavement	2,600	2,800	3,100	3,250	4,000	4,000
– second year after bereavement	2,100	2,300	2,600	2,750	3,500	3,500
– third year after bereavement	1,600	1,800	2,100	2,250	3,000	3,000
– fourth year after bereavement	1,100	1,300	1,600	1,750	2,500	2,500
– fifth year after bereavement	600	800	1,100	1,100	2,000	2,000
One-Parent Family						
– widowed person	1,520	1,580	1,630	1,760	1,830	1,830
– other person	1,520	1,580	1,630	1,760	1,830	1,830

Incapacitated Child Max.	500	1,000	1,500	3,000	3,660	3,660
Dependent Relative Max.	60	60	80	80	80	80
Income Limit	10,373	10,997	11,913	12,745	13,473	13,837
Blind Person	800	1,000	1,500	1,760	1,830	1,830
Both Spouses Blind	1,600	2,000	3,000	3,520	3,660	3,660
Age Credit: Single/ Widowed Person	205	205 410	250 500	275 550	325 650	325 650
Married/ Couple	410					
PAYE Max.	1,040	1,270	1,490	1,760	1,830	1,830
Home-carer Max.	770	770	770	770	900	900
Trade Union Subscriptions	40	40	60	60	70	70
Employment of Carer for Incapacitated Person Max.	30,000 @ Marginal Rate	30,000 @ Marginal Rate	50,000 @ Marginal Rate	50,000 @ Marginal Rate	50,000 @ Marginal Rate	50,000 @ Marginal Rate

Appendix II

Conditions for BES Relief

Qualifying Individual

The individual must not be connected with the BES company during a period starting with the incorporation of the company (or if later, two years before the shares are issued) and ending five years after the shares are issued. In determining whether an individual is connected with the company, it is necessary to take into account any interest held by his associates. Associates do not include spouses or relatives.

Qualifying Companies

In order for the individual to obtain tax relief, the investment must be made in a qualifying company. The company must be incorporated in the State and for a period of three years from the date the shares are issued (or if later, three years from the company commencing to trade), the company must satisfy a number of conditions which include the following:

- The company must be resident in the State.

- The company must not be quoted on a stock exchange. For this purpose a company trading on the Unlisted Securities Market is regarded as quoted.

- The company must not have a group connection with another company unless it has subsidiaries which would also all fulfil the required conditions. However, with effect from 6 April 1997, companies can enter both the Developing Companies Market (DCM) of the Irish Stock Exchange and similar or corresponding markets in other EU Member States without its status as a BES-qualifying company being affected, provided that it enters the DCM before or at the same time as it first enters one of the other EU unlisted markets.

- The company must be carrying on (or intend to carry on) a qualifying trade on a commercial basis, principally in the State, or be a company whose business consists wholly of:
  - the holding of shares or securities of, or the making of loans to one or more qualifying subsidiaries, or
  - both the holding of shares or securities, or the making of such loans and the carrying on principally in the State of one or more qualifying trades.

The maximum amount that may be raised by a company through the issue of eligible shares is €2m, subject to a maximum of €1.5m being raised in any 12 month period.

Qualifying Trade

A qualifying trade is one consisting wholly or mainly of the following operations:

- The manufacture of goods and certain other trades within the meaning of s443. The company must therefore claim and be entitled to the 10% rate of corporation tax.

- The rendering of services in the course of a service undertaking in respect of which an employment grant was made by the IDA, or which has received grant aid from *Údarás na Gaeltachta*.

- Tourist traffic undertakings.

- Qualifying shipping activities.

- The export sale of Irish manufactured goods by a special trading house.

- Construction and leasing of advance factories promoted by local community groups.

- The cultivation of plants in the State as defined by s443.

- Certain research and development activities.

- The cultivation of horticultural produce in greenhouses.

- The production, publication, marketing and promotion of qualifying musical recordings.

- Trading activities on an exchange facility established in the Custom House Docks Area.

If the company is not carrying on a trade at the time the shares are issued, it will be regarded as carrying on a trade if it has expended at least 80% of the money subscribed for the shares on research and development which is connected with an undertaking with a view to the carrying on of the trade, and begins to carry on the trade within three years after that time. In all other cases, the company must commence trading within two years of the date of issue of the shares.

Where the company carries on qualifying trading operations and other trading operations, the total amount receivable from sales made and services rendered in the course of qualifying trading operations must not be less than 75% of the total amount receivable by the company from all sales made and services rendered.

Qualifying Shares

The shares eligible for relief must be fully paid ordinary shares.

During a five-year period commencing with the date on which they were issued, the shares must not carry a present or future preferential right to dividends or to the company's assets on its winding up and no present or future preferential right to be redeemed.

No relief is available on shares issued after 12 April 1989 which are the subject of either a put or call option at a price other than their market value at the date at which the option is exercised.

The shares must be issued for the purpose of raising money for a qualifying trade which is being carried on by the company or which it intends to carry on.

The company must provide satisfactory evidence to the Revenue Commissioners that the money was used for any of the following purposes:

- enabling the company or enlarging its capacity to undertake qualifying trading operations;

- enabling the company to engage in research and development, the acquisition of technological information and data, the development of new or existing services or products, or the provision of new products or services;

- enabling the company to identify new markets and to develop new and existing markets for the products and services;

- enabling the company to increase its sale of products or provision of services.

In all cases, the money must be used with a view to the creation or maintenance of employment in the company.

A claim for relief must be made within two years of the end of the year of assessment in which the shares are issued. The company must issue a certificate certifying that the conditions for the relief have been satisfied (usually Form RICT 3 or RICT 5).

Where an individual receives any value from the company during a period beginning with the incorporation of the company (or if later, two years before the issue of the shares) and ending five years after the issue of the shares, the amount of the relief granted on the shares will be reduced by the value received.

For example: an individual receives value from the company in the following situations:

- the company repays, redeems or repurchases any of its share capital or securities which belong to the individual, or

- the company makes any payment to him/her for giving up his/her right to any of the company's share capital or any security on its cancellation or extinguishment;

- the company repays any debt to the individual other than a debt which was:

  - an ordinary trade debt incurred by the company, or

  - any other debt which was incurred by the company on or after the earliest date on which the subscription for the shares in respect of which the relief is claimed otherwise than in consideration of the extinguishment of a debt incurred before that date;

- the company makes to him/her any other payment except a payment of the kind mentioned in connection with payments to directors or employees, or a payment in discharge of an ordinary trade debt.

Appendix III

Methodology for calculating tax deductible self-employed pension contribution

Income Tax Computation of Belinda for 2009

Schedule D	€
Case I	*95,000*
Less capital allowances	*(3,000)*
Less losses	*(4,500)*
Relevant earnings	*87,500*
Deduct pension contribution	*(21,375)*
	66,125
Case III	*8,000*
Gross Income	*74,125*
Less charges	*(10,000)*
TOTAL (NET STATUTORY) INCOME	*64,125*

Step 1

"Net relevant earnings" is calculated as "relevant earnings" less charges to the extent that they may not be relieved against other non-trading sources of income.

Non-trading income (Case III income) of €8,000 absorbs €8,000 of charges. Therefore, additional charges of €2,000 (€10,000 – €8,000) are offset against relevant earnings of €87,500, giving "net relevant earnings" of €85,500

Step 2

Age 40, % applied is 25%

Step 3

She can subtract the lower of:

Amount paid

   OR

% net relevant earnings

25% €85,500 = €21,375

Appendix IV

List of Social-Welfare-Like Payments

Payments made by the Dept of Enterprise, Trade and Employment

- Community Employment Scheme

- FAS (non apprentice payments)

Payments made by the Health Service Executive (HSE):-

- Infectious Diseases Maintenance Allowance

- Blind Welfare Supplementary Allowance

- Domiciliary Care Allowance

- Mobility Allowance

Payments made by the Dept of Education:

- VTOS Training Allowances

- Youthreach Training Allowances

- Senior Traveller Training Allowances

- Back to Education Initiative (BTEI) Training Allowances paid to Youthreach, STTC or VTOS eligible participants on a pro-rata basis.

- Vocational Education Committees' Scholarship Scheme

- Fund for Students with Disabilities

- Student Assistance Fund

- Millennium Partnership Fund for Disadvantage

Payments made by the Dept of Agriculture:

- Farm Retirement Pensions

- Farm Retirement Workers' Pensions

Payments made by the Dept of Community Rural and Gaeltacht Affairs

- Rural Social Scheme

    - Farm/Fish Assist Jobseekers Allowance or Jobseekers Benefit

    - One-Parent Family Payment, Widow(er)'s Pension or Disability Allowance

    - Adult Dependent of a recipient of the non-contributory State Pension

Appendix V

Section	Title
42	Interest on savings certificates
188	Exemption from BIK - Travel Pass, new bicycle scheme, share options
189	Payments in respect of personal injuries
189A	Special trust for permanently incapacitated
190	Haemophilia Trust
191	Hepatitis C
192	Thalidomide
192A	Exemption in respect of certain payment under employment law
192B	Foster Care Payment
193	Income from Scholarships
194	Child benefit
194A	Early Childcare Supplement
195A	Exemption in respect of certain expense payments
196	Expenses of members of Judiciary
196A	State Employees: Foreign Service Allowance
196B	Employee of certain agencies: foreign service allowances
197	Bonus or interest paid under instalment savings schemes
198	Certain interest not to be chargeable
199	Interest on certain securities
200	Certain foreign pensions
201	Exemptions and reliefs in respect of tax under section 123 (Redundancy)
202	Relief for agreed pay restructuring
203	Payments in respect of Redundancy
204	Military & other pensions, gratuities and allowances
205	Veterans of war of independence
216A	Rent a Room relief
216B	Scéim na bhFoghlaimeoiri Gaeilge
216C	Childcare service relief
42	Interest on savings certificates
188	Exemption from BIK - Travel Pass, new bicycle scheme, share options
189	Payments in respect of personal injuries
189A	Special trust for permanently incapacitated
190	Haemophilia Trust
191	Hepatitis C
192	Thalidomide
192A	Exemption in respect of certain payment under employment law
192B	Foster Care Payment
193	Income from Scholarships
194	Child benefit
194A	Early Childcare Supplement
195A	Exemption in respect of certain expense payments

12

RELIEF FOR CHARGES AND INTEREST

In this chapter, you will deal with the following:

- Deeds of Covenant
- Patent royalties
- Interest as a charge
- Mortgage interest relief

12.1   Introduction

The term "charges" is given primarily to annual sums which a person is under a legal obligation to pay and from which income tax is deductible at source. Examples of such charges are patent royalties and payments under Deeds of Covenant (considered at 12.2 below). Income tax at the standard rate is deducted from these payments and is remitted to the Revenue Commissioners.

The term "charges" is also applied to certain sums which a person is under a legal obligation to pay, but which may be paid gross, i.e., without the deduction of tax at source. This chapter considers the various charges, differentiating between those requiring payment to be made:

■ under the deduction of income tax; and

■ without the deduction of income tax.

The basic principle is that "charges on income" are deducted in arriving at the individual's total or statutory income. In the case of charges paid under deduction of tax, the payer of the charges is accountable for the tax deducted.

This chapter also considers the tax treatment of certain interest payments. 12.3.1 below deals with relief as a charge for interest paid on certain loans to invest in companies or partnerships. Such interest payments constitute sums that may be paid without deduction of tax. 12.3.2 below deals with "mortgage interest relief", i.e., relief for interest on borrowings to fund the borrower's principal private residence. This relief, previously granted as a tax credit, is now available at source as a reduction in the amount of the periodic mortgage repayment.

12.2   Deeds of Covenant and Patent Royalties

Payments in respect of Deeds of Covenant and patent royalties are made under deduction of tax at the standard rate.

12.2.1   Deeds of covenant

A Deed of Covenant is a legal instrument by which a person binds himself/herself (the covenantor) to make periodic payments of income to another person (the covenantee).

The advantage to be derived from such a deed is that it enables the covenantor to divest part of his/her statutory income by transferring it to the covenantee. Any amount may be paid under a Deed of Covenant; however, only covenants in favour of certain individuals qualify for tax relief.

The covenantor's total income is reduced by the gross amount that he/she covenants to pay. Tax relief is therefore obtained at the marginal rate. However, he/she must account for the tax deducted at source. The covenantee is taxed under Schedule D Case IV at the marginal rate on income from covenants. The covenantee may obtain the benefit of personal reliefs and tax credits (to the extent that these are not covered by other income) against the income received under the covenant, and, depending upon the amount of the gross payment, may receive a repayment of the tax deducted at source.

Example 12.1

Edward Cox (covenantor) is single and self-employed. He pays €8,000 (gross) per year under Deed of Covenant to his aunt (covenantee) who is permanently incapacitated.

	€	€
Covenantor		
Case II income		*120,000*
Less payment under Deed of Covenant		*(8,000)*
		112,000
Taxed at:		
€36,400 × 20%	*7,280*	
€75,600 × 41%	*30,996*	
	38,276	
Add tax due on Deed of Covenant		
€8,000 × 20%	*1,600*	
	39,876	
Less non-refundable credit		
Single credit	*(1,830)*	
Tax liability	*38,046*	

	€	€
Covenantee		
(Assume single, incapacitated with no other income)		
Income under Deed of Covenant		*8,000*
Taxed as follows:		
€8,000 × 20%	*1,600*	
Less credits:		
Single Person's Credit	*(1,830)*	
Tax liability	*Nil*	
Less		
Tax deducted on Deed of Covenant	*(1,600)*	
Tax overpaid	*(1,600)*	

The covenantee may claim a tax refund of €1,600.

12.2.2 Covenants qualifying for relief as a charge

Minor Children

s795(1)
TCA 97

Covenants in favour of the covenantor's own minor children are ineffective for tax purposes. A minor child for this purpose is an unmarried individual under 18 years. Section 795(1) TCA 1997 treats the income from the covenant as being that of the covenantor, i.e., the parent. However, unrestricted tax relief may be claimed on covenants in favour of permanently incapacitated minors, other than from parents to their own minor incapacitated children.

Adults

s792
TCA 97

Section 792 TCA 1997 provides for tax relief as follows:

- unrestricted tax relief may be claimed on covenants in favour of permanently incapacitated adults;

- tax relief may be claimed on covenants in favour of adults aged over 65, but the relief is restricted to 5% of the covenantor's total income, i.e., gross income less certain deductions, such as expenses, capital allowances, etc.

All covenants must be capable of lasting more than six years. In practice, for a covenant to be tax effective it should be drawn up to cover a minimum period of seven years. Also, it should not contain a provision for revocation of the covenant within the seven-year period.

Covenants other than those in favour of individuals

s848A
TCA 97

Tax relief was available for the conduct of research, teaching of natural sciences, promotion of human rights and payments to universities and other approved bodies for research in or teaching of approved subjects. However, s45 Finance Act 2001 repealed this relief. Tax relief for such payments is now provided for by s848A TCA 1997. Readers are referred to Chapter 11 (11.5.4) for an analysis of the relevant relief.

12.2.3 Patent royalties

The payment of royalties and other sums for the use of a patent are generally made under deduction of standard rate tax. The gross royalty is allowed as a deduction in arriving at the statutory income of the taxpayer, but the taxpayer is accountable for the tax deducted.

It should be noted that annuities, annual payments and patent royalties are not allowable deductions in arriving at the trade or professional profits under the rules of Cases I and II Schedule D, but are treated as charges to be deducted in arriving at statutory income. The tax treatment is similar to that of covenants.

Example 12.2

John Rogers is single. His only source of income is from a trade and amounts to €120,000. He paid patent royalties of €10,000 in 2009.

His tax calculation for 2009 is as follows:

	€	€	€
Case I income			*120,000*
Less patent royalty payment			*(10,000)*
			110,000
Taxed as follows:			
€36,400 × 20%		*7,280*	
€73,600 × 41%		*30,176*	
		37,456	

Add tax due on patent royalty:
€10,000 × 20%   *2,000*
       39,456

Less credits:
Single Person's Credit   *(1,830)*
Tax liability   *37,626*

12.3   Interest

Tax relief is granted in different ways for different types of interest. Broadly speaking, the following interest payments will qualify for some form of income tax relief:

- Certain interest expenses will be deductible as trading or professional expenses in arriving at taxable Case I or Case II income. In this regard, readers are referred to the relevant commentary in Chapter 15, which is concerned with calculating taxable Case I and Case II income.

- Interest incurred on loans used to purchase both residential and commercial rental properties will generally be available as a deduction in calculating taxable Case V income. Readers are referred to the commentary in Chapter 19.

- Interest paid on money to invest in certain companies and partnerships is deductible as a charge. This issue is considered in detail at 12.3.1 below.

- Interest paid on money to fund the borrower's principal private residence is granted at the standard rate of tax either as a tax credit or under the "tax relief at source" system. This is considered in 12.3.2 below.

12.3.1   Interest on loans to acquire shares in a company or partnership

The following types of interest are eligible for relief as charges on income:

s248
TCA 97
- Section 248 TCA 1997 provides for relief on interest on loans to acquire shares in companies

s253
TCA 97
- Section 253 TCA 1997 provides for relief on interest on loans to acquire a share in a partnership

Payment of such interest is not subject to the deduction of tax at source.

12.3.1.1   Relief for individuals on interest on loans applied in acquiring interests in companies

s258
TCA 97
Tax relief is granted as a charge to individuals for interest paid on loans to acquire ordinary shares in or to lend money to certain "qualifying companies". Interest relief is not given on loans to acquire shares in quoted companies. A quoted company is a company whose shares are listed on the Irish Stock Exchange or any other stock exchange, or are quoted on an unlisted securities market of any stock exchange.

The relief is given by way of a charge in arriving at the individual's statutory or total income, provided the individual holds a "material interest" in the qualifying company.

A "qualifying company" is a company:

- which exists wholly or mainly for the purpose of carrying on a trade or trades ("a trading company");

- whose income consists wholly or mainly of profits chargeable under Case V of Schedule D ("a rental company")*; or

- whose business consists wholly or mainly of holding shares or securities of a "trading" or a "rental" company ("a holding company").

s247 TCA 97 "Material interest" in relation to a company is defined in s247 TCA 1997, as meaning the beneficial ownership of or the ability to control, directly or through the medium of a connected company or connected companies, or by any other indirect means, more than 5% of the ordinary share capital of the company.

s248 TCA 97 To qualify for relief under s248 TCA 1997, the following conditions must be met:

- The company is a trading/rental company* or a holding company.

- The individual has a material interest in the company or in a connected company.

- The individual employee/director of the company works on a full-time basis with the company.

Tax relief on borrowings under ss248 and 250 TCA 1997 is prohibited where the monies are used by a company to purchase a commercial or industrial building that has a remaining tax life.

*Section 9 Finance Act 2006 abolished relief on loans taken out after 7 December 2005 for investments in a company whose income arises wholly or mainly from rents or other income from property.

Example 12.3

Kevin Glennon, who is single, is a full-time employee of Horwath Candies Ltd., a private trading company. He owns 8% of the ordinary share capital of the company and borrowed €100,000 to lend to the company. In 2009, he paid interest of €9,000 on the loan. His salary for 2009 was €120,000 and PAYE of €41,680 was deducted. He is entitled to tax relief as follows:

	€	€	€
Schedule E			*120,000*
Less charges: interest payment			*(9,000)*
			111,000
Taxed as follows:			
€36,400 × 20%	*7,280*		
€74,600 × 41%	*30,586*		
			37,866

Less non-refundable credits:
Single Person's Credit   *(1,830)*
PAYE Credit   *(1,830)*
     (3,660)
Tax liability   *34,206*
Less refundable credits
Tax deducted under PAYE   *(41,680)*
Tax overpaid   *(7,474)*

Where the proceeds of the loan are applied in lending money to the company, relief is available only if the money lent is used wholly and exclusively for the purpose of the trade or business of the company or of a connected company. Relief is not granted if, during the period from the application of the loan to the date the interest is paid, the company makes any loans or advances any money to the individual, unless the loan or advance is made in the ordinary course of a business, which includes the lending of money. Readers are referred to "Rules relating to recovery of capital and replacement loans" below.

s250
TCA 97

Section 250 TCA 1997 extends the relief under s248 TCA 1997 to certain individuals who do not satisfy:

- the "material interest" test; or

- are not working full-time for the company.

The section also extends (restricted) relief to investment in certain non-private, i.e., "public" companies. There is no definition of a public company in TCA 1997. However, it is taken to have the same meaning as that assigned to it in the Companies Act 1963, i.e., any company which is not a private company within that Act.

A "private company" is given the same meaning as s33 of the Companies Act 1963, i.e., a company which by its Articles:

- restricts the right to transfer its shares;

- limits the number of its members to 50 (excluding employees and former employees who hold shares in the company); and

- prohibits any invitation to the public to subscribe for any shares or debentures of the company.

The table below best illustrates the application of the relief:

Individual	Private Trading/ Rental* Company	Private Holding Company	Non-Private Trading/ Rental* Company	Non-Private Holding Company
Full-time working director/employee with no material interest	Unrestricted relief	Unrestricted relief	Max. relief €3,050	Max. relief €3,050
Part-time working director/employee with no material interest	Unrestricted relief	No relief	No relief	No relief

*No relief on loans taken out after 7 December 2005 (s9 Finance Act 2006)

Rules relating to recovery of capital and replacement loans

s249
TCA 97

Where the individual recovers any amount of capital from the company (or from a connected company) without using that amount in repayment of the loan, he/she is treated as if, at that time, an equivalent amount of the loan was repaid. Accordingly, a portion of the qualifying loan equal to the amount of capital recovered is no longer eligible for relief.

An individual is treated as having recovered an amount of capital from the company (or from a connected company) if:

- he/she receives consideration of that amount or value for the sale of any part of the ordinary share capital of the company or of a connected company;

- he/she receives consideration of that amount or value by way of repayment of any part of the ordinary share capital;

- the company or a connected company repays that amount of the loan advanced by him/her; or

- he/she receives consideration of that amount or value for assigning any debt due to him/her from the company or from a connected company. Where a sale or assignment is not at arm's length, market value is imposed.

12.3.1.2 Relief to individuals on loans applied in acquiring an interest in a partnership

s253
TCA 97

Tax relief is available to an individual who obtains a loan to purchase a share in a partnership or to advance money to a partnership. The money advanced must be used wholly and exclusively for the purposes of the trade or profession carried on by the partnership. Any interest paid on the loan is available for relief if, throughout the period from the application of the proceeds of the loan until the interest is paid:

- the individual personally acts in the conduct of the trade or profession carried on by the partnership; and

- the individual has not recovered any capital from the partnership.

If the individual recovers any amount of capital from the partnership without using that amount to pay off the loan, he/she will be treated as if he/she had repaid that amount out of the loan, and accordingly, the interest on the amount of capital so recovered no longer qualifies for relief.

The individual is treated as having recovered an amount of capital from the partnership if:

- he/she receives a consideration of that amount for the sale of any part of his/her interest in the partnership;

- the partnership returns any amount advanced by him/her; or

- he/she receives a consideration of that amount for assigning any debt due to him/her from the partnership.

For a summary of the tax treatment of interest on loans to invest in partnerships and companies, readers are referred to Appendix I of this chapter.

12.3.2 Mortgage interest relief

s244
TCA 97

Relief is available under s244 TCA 1997 in respect of interest paid on a "qualifying loan". The interest eligible for relief on a "qualifying loan" is confined to:

- yearly interest charged to tax under Schedule D; or

- interest (whether short or annual) paid to banks, building societies, stockbrokers or discount houses,

- in respect of a loan taken out for the purchase, repair, development or improvement of a residential premises situated in the State, Northern Ireland or Great Britain which is the sole or main residence of:

    - the claimant,

    - a former or separated spouse,

    - a dependent relative.

Interest under these provisions is often referred to as "home loan" interest.

12.3.2.1 Mortgage interest restrictions

Relief is subject to an upper limit based on whether the claimant is single or married/ widowed. The maximum relief allowable is also higher in the case of first-time buyers.

Qualifying interest is restricted to €3,000 for single persons and €6,000 in the case of married for widowed persons. For those in their first seven years of entitlement to mortgage interest relief, the aforementioned limits are increased to €10,000 and €20,000 respectively.

The annual ceiling on the amount of qualifying interest, for 2009 is as follows:

	First-Time Buyer	All Other
Single	€10,000	€3,000
Widowed/Married	€20,000	€6,000

Tax relief is granted at rates varying between 15% and 25%, depending on the year the mortgage was taken out (see table below).

12.3.2.2 Tax relief at source (TRS)

Mortgage interest relief is not given through the tax system but is, instead, granted "at source". As a result, the tax relief is given when the borrower makes a mortgage payment to the mortgage lender. The qualifying interest element of the repayment is reduced by a percentage depending on whether the tax payer is a first time buyer or not and depending on the year the mortgage was taken out (see table below) (thereby giving the tax relief to the borrower) while the mortgage lender will be repaid an equivalent amount by the Revenue Commissioners.

Tax Facts

2009 saw the introduction of a tax credit system that was not based on the standard rate of income tax (currently 20%). Relief on home loan interest is available at varying rates; 15%, 20%, 22.5% to 25%.

From 1 January 2009, the rate at which relief is given depends on whether the borrower is a "first" time buyer or not. For non-first time buyers tax relief is granted at 15% of interest paid, subject to a maximum relief of €900 (€6,000@ 15%) for married or widowed persons and €450 (€3,000@15%) for single persons. For first time buyers the relief is as follows:

Years	1 - 2	Married or widowed	Lower of €5,000 or 25% of interest paid
		Single Person	Lower of €2,500 or 25% of interest paid
Years	3 - 5	Married or widowed	Lower of €4,500 or 22.5% of interest paid
		Single Person	Lower of €2,250 or 22.5% of interest paid
Years	6 - 7	Married or widowed	Lower of €4,000 or 20% of interest paid
		Single Person	Lower of €2,000 or 20% of interest paid
Years	8 and >	Married or widowed	Lower of €900 or 15% of interest paid
		Single Person	Lower of €450 or 15% of interest paid

Tax relief at source (TRS) arrangements do not change the basic qualifying conditions for mortgage interest relief (already outlined at 12.3.2). However, under the TRS scheme, the residence must be situated in the State. Relief for qualifying interest on a sole or main residence in Northern Ireland or Great Britain continues to be given, but outside of TRS.

Example 12.4

Mary Costello, who is single, bought her first home in Dublin in 2004. Her mortgage provider, Ace Mortgages Ltd., calculates that her monthly gross repayments for 2009 will be €900, of which €850 represents interest. Her estimated interest for 2009 is €850 @ 12, i.e., €10,200. As a single first-time buyer, Mary Costello may claim maximum interest relief of €10,000 in 2009. Relief under TRS will be granted as follows:

	€
Gross repayment per month	900.00
Less TRS (€10,000 @ 20%/12 months)	166.67
Net repayment to Ace Mortgages Ltd.	733.33
The Revenue Commissioners will refund Ace Mortgages Ltd. the TRS amount of €166.67.	

The same upper limits to the relief, which depend on the marital status of the claimant and on whether or not the claimant is a first-time buyer, apply under TRS. While a qualifying loan is one which must be used solely for the purchase, repair, development or improvement of a qualifying residence, loans within the scope of TRS are those which are secured on the residence (i.e., mortgage loans). Interest on non-mortgage loans qualifying for tax relief continue to be relieved through the tax system rather than through TRS. All banks and building societies operating in the State, as well as local authorities, are within the TRS system, as are mortgage lenders in other EU Member States which lend on the security of properties based in the State.

The net effect of the TRS scheme means that the tax relief is granted in an efficient manner. The borrower obtains the tax relief in the form of reduced mortgage repayments when the repayments are made. It is not necessary to claim the relief on an annual tax return. Adjustments to the tax relief (for example, as a result of changes in interest rates) are made automatically by the mortgage lender. The TRS system results in an extension of the relief to persons who have qualifying loans but would not otherwise get any relief because their taxable income is insufficient to avail of the tax relief. Under the TRS arrangements, a person who pays no tax is entitled to the same reduced interest payments as someone who has a liability to income tax.

Home Loan Interest on Prinicpal Private Residence from 1 May 2009

The Finance Act 2009 amended the above. From 1 May 2009 tax relief is not available on home loans taken out over seven years ago (i.e. in their eighth and subsequent years). Therefore loans which were taken out more than seven years ago only qualify for tax relief in 2009 on the basis of interest paid from 1 January 2009 to 30 April 2009. The relief will continue to be available on interest payments made for the first seven years of any new qualifying loans taken out from 1 May 2009.

WHAT YOU SHOULD NOW KNOW

On completion of this chapter, you should be able to:

✓ Explain the meaning of the word "charge" and describe how tax relief is granted for charges.

✓ Discuss the criteria required to qualify for tax relief on borrowings to invest in a company or partnership.

✓ Describe the circumstances in which tax relief may be granted under the TRS system and identify interest payments outside the scope of TRS.

✓ Complete Questions and the Assignments in Irish Taxation Law and Practice, Volume 2.

Appendix I

Charges Paid	Tax Treatment
Interest PAID on loan used to buy into or lend to a partnership where taxpayer is an active partner	Deduct the full interest as a charge
Interest PAID on loan used to buy shares or lend to **private or non private** trading/Rental*/holding company in which taxpayer is an employee/director and **has a >5% interest**	Deduct the full interest as a charge
Interest PAID on loan used to buy shares or lend to **private** trading/Rental*/holding company in which taxpayer is an employee/director and **has NOT GOT a >5% interest**	Deduct the full interest as a charge (excl. part-timers who invest in a holding company)
Interest PAID on loan used to buy shares or lend to **non private** trading/Rental*/holding company in which taxpayer is an employee/director and **has NOT GOT a >5% interest**	Deduct interest as a charge up to €3,050 (excl. part-timers)
Interest PAID on loan used to buy shares or lend to **quoted company under any circumstances**	No relief for the charge

*Only applies to loans taken out before 7 December 2005 (S9 Finance Act 2006)

13

TAXATION OF MARRIED COUPLES

In this chapter, you will deal with the following:

- Basis of assessment for married couples
- Taxation treatment in year of death
- Relief in year of marriage
- Effects of separation and divorce

13.1   Introduction

The purpose of this chapter is to explain the basis of assessment for married couples. Complexities arise where couples separate or divorce, or where one spouse dies. Often, one party is left with custody of dependent children. This chapter addresses the tax treatment of these categories of "spouses". The specific areas covered in this analysis are therefore as follows:

- methods of assessment
- year of marriage
- year of death separated/divorced spouses
- year of separation.

For ease of illustration, all examples in this chapter ignore income levy, PRSI and the health levy.

13.2   Basis of Assessment

It is important to be aware that for a couple to be taxed as a married couple, it is not sufficient to be just legally married. Irish tax law states that the couple must be "living together as man and wife". Therefore, a married couple who by choice decide to live apart may not be taxed as a married couple.

Married couples have three options as to how they wish to be assessed to income tax:

(i)   Joint assessment

(ii) Separate assessment

(iii) Single assessment.

13.2.1   Joint assessment

s1017,
s1018
TCA 97

Under s1017 TCA 1997, a husband and wife may be assessed to income tax on the combined incomes of both. An election for such treatment is made under s1018 TCA 1997. The Revenue Commissioners deem an election to have been made for joint assessment where there is no specific evidence to support the election.

Married couples who are assessed to tax on the basis of joint assessment may elect to have either spouse regarded as the assessable spouse. The election must be made to the Inspector of Taxes in writing before 1 April in the year of assessment. The assessable spouse assumes responsibility for the joint tax liability. The assessable spouse:

- is assessed on the combined total income;
- receives the combined tax credits; and

■ files a joint tax return, which includes full details of the couple's joint income.

The assessable spouse is deemed to be the spouse with the greater total income.

Under joint assessment, a married couple is entitled to:

■ a personal tax credit which is double the Single Person's Tax Credit;

■ the Home Carer's Tax Credit (subject to certain conditions);

■ double the maximum mortgage interest relief available to a single person; and

■ an increased standard rate band.

With the introduction of "individualisation", the band of income taxable at the standard rate has been restricted somewhat in recent years in the case of married couples. The standard rate band available to married couples is now as follows:

■ where only one spouse has income in his/her own right, the standard rate band is €45,400;

■ where each spouse has income in his/her own right, the maximum standard rate band is €72,800 (i.e., €45,400 + €27,400). The increase above the standard rate band of €45,400 is the lower of:

(a) €27,400; or

(b) the specified income of the lower-earning spouse.

The increased standard rate band is available as an alternative to the Home Carer's Tax Credit. A married couple may claim whichever of the two is more beneficial to them. The specific circumstances of each couple must be considered independently in determining this.

Example 13.1

Option 1 – not claiming Home Carer Tax Credit

	€	€
Income – husband		*90,000*
Income – wife		*4,000*
		94,000
Taxed as follows:		
€49,400 at 20%	*9,880*	
€44,600 at 41%	*18,286*	
		28,166
Less non-refundable tax credits:		
Married Person's Credit	*(3,660)*	
PAYE Credits – husband	*(1,830)*	
* – wife (Note 1)*	*(800)*	*(6,290)*
Tax liability		**21,876**

Note 1: The PAYE Credit cannot exceed the amount of PAYE income taxed at the standard rate – in this instance, €4,000 @ 20%, i.e., €800.

Option 2 – claiming Home Carer Tax Credit

	€	€
Income – husband		90,000
Income – wife		4,000
		94,000
Taxed as follows:		
€45,400 at 20%	9,080	
€48,600 at 41%	19,926	
		29,006
Less non-refundable tax credits:		
Married Persons' Credit	(3,660)	
PAYE Credits (€1,830 + €800)	(2,630)	
Home Carer's Credit	(900)	
		(7,190)
Tax liability		**21,816**

Difference is (€21,816 – €21,876), i.e., €60.

Therefore, Option 2, i.e., availing of the Home Carer's Tax Credit, is more beneficial in this case.

Readers are referred to Chapter 11 (11.2.7) for a detailed analysis of the criteria for entitlement to the Home Carer's Tax Credit.

13.2.2 Separate assessment

Separate assessment is available to couples who have opted or who are deemed to have opted for joint assessment. Under separate assessment, income tax is assessed, charged and recovered separately from each spouse.

Where either a husband or wife elects for separate assessment, they can retain the tax saving, if any, of joint assessment and at the same time have their income tax assessments and returns of income dealt with separately. The personal credits and reliefs available to both husband and wife are the same as in the case of joint assessment and the total tax payable cannot be greater than the amount payable if an application for separate assessment had not been made.

s1023
TCA 97

An election for separate assessment under s1023 TCA 1997 must be made not later than 1 April in the year of assessment. An application applies for the year of claim and subsequent years and may be withdrawn only by the spouse who made the application.

Where separate assessment for income tax is claimed, the personal tax credit, Incapacitated Child Tax Credit (where applicable), Age Tax Credit and Blind Person's Tax Credit are divided equally between the spouses. Other tax credits and reliefs are generally granted to the spouse who actually bears the cost. Any unused balances of tax credits and reliefs of one spouse are set against the income of the other. Also, any unused standard rate band of one spouse may be transferred to the other.

Readers are referred to Example 13.2 below, which illustrates that the combined liability under separate assessment is the same as the joint assessment liability.

13.2.3   Single assessment

s1016,
s1018
TCA 97

Single assessment is also known as separate treatment. This form of assessment treats each spouse as a single person, i.e., as if they had not married. In view of the fact that it is normally beneficial for married couples to be jointly assessed for income tax, s1018 TCA 1997 deems an election to have been made for joint assessment. For single assessment to apply, either spouse must, before the end of the tax year, give notice in writing to the Inspector of Taxes that they wish to be assessed as single persons under s1016 TCA 1997. Where such a notice is given to the Inspector of Taxes, both spouses are assessed as single persons until such time as the election is withdrawn by the spouse who made it.

Since both spouses are effectively treated as single persons, there are no provisions whereby one spouse may transfer any balance of unused standard band or tax credits to the other spouse. The benefit of any unused tax credits is therefore lost and for this reason, single assessment is generally less advantageous than joint assessment or separate assessment.

Example 13.2

A married man has a salary of €90,000 and his wife has a salary of €6,000. They have no children. If an election for single assessment was sought under s1016 TCA 1997, their income tax liabilities for the tax year 2009 would be as follows:

Single Assessment

	Husband				**Wife**	
	€	€			€	€
Income		90,000	Income			6,000
Taxed as follows:			Taxed as follows:			
€36,400 @ 20%	7,280		€6,000 @ 20%	1,200		
€53,600 @ 41%	21,976					
		29,256				1,200
Less non-refundable credits:			Less non-refundable credits:			
Single Person's Credit	(1,830)		Single Person's Credit	(1,830)		
PAYE Credit	(1,830)		PAYE Credit	(1,200)		(Note 1)
		(3,660)				(3,030)
Tax liability		**25,596**	Tax liability			**Nil**

Note 1: The PAYE credit is limited to the PAYE income @ 20%.

Contrast the above with the following where, using the same facts, the married couple did not elect to be singly assessed:

Joint Assessment

	€	€
Income – husband		90,000
Income – wife		6,000
		96,000

	€	€
Taxed as follows:		
€51,400 @ 20%	10,280	
€44,600 @ 41%	<u>18,286</u>	
		28,566
Less non-refundable credits:		
Married Person's Credit	(3,660)	
PAYE Credits	<u>(3,030)</u>	
		<u>(6,690)</u>
Tax liability		**<u>21,876</u>**

The difference between the two calculations is €3,720, which may be explained as follows:

	€
■ *Wife has unabsorbed tax credits of (€3,030 – €1,200)*	1,830
■ *The standard rate band for a married couple is €45,400 + value of other spouse's income (subject to max. €27,400). Under joint assessment, the Husband has therefore decreased his 41% rate band by €9,000 @ 21% [(41–20)%]*	<u>1,890</u>
Total tax saving	**<u>3,720</u>**

Separate Assessment

Husband			**Wife**		
	€	€		€	€
Income		90,000	*Income*		6,000
Taxed as follows:			*Taxed as follows:*		
€36,400 @ 20%	7,280		€6,000 @ 20%	<u>1,200</u>	
€9,000* @ 20%	1,800				
€44,600 @ 41%	<u>18,286</u>				
		27,366			1,200
Less non-refundable credits:			*Less non-refundable credits:*		
Single Person's Credit	(1,830)		Single Person's Credit	(1,830)	
PAYE Credit	(1,830)		PAYE Credit	(1,200)	
Surplus credits of spouse	<u>(1,830)</u>			<u> </u>	
		<u>(5,490)</u>			<u>(3,030)</u>
Tax liability		**<u>21,876</u>**	Tax liability		**<u>Nil</u>**

* *Surplus 20% band of spouse. €45,400*

Readers will observe from the above workings that the combined liability under separate assessment (€21,876 + Nil) is the same as for joint assessment (€21,876).

13.2.4 Year of marriage

s1020
TCA 97

Married couples are taxed as single persons in the year of assessment in which the marriage takes place. If the total of the tax payable as single persons exceeds the amount which would have been payable if they were married and jointly assessed for the whole year, they are entitled, on making a joint claim, to additional tax relief. The relief is calculated by the formula:

$$A \times \frac{B}{12}$$

where:

A = the additional tax payable when comparing the combined single person's assessments with the joint assessment for the year in which the marriage takes place, and

B = the number of income tax months from the date of marriage to the end of the income tax year (part of a month being treated as a month).

Example 13.3

Assume date of marriage is 1 October 2009.

	Husband €	Wife €	Total €
Tax payable under single basis	10,000	1,000	11,000
Tax payable under joint basis			(9,900)
Excess tax liability			1,100

Therefore, the year of marriage relief is calculated as follows:

€1,100 @ $\frac{3}{12}$ = €275

The tax liability of €11,000 is therefore reduced by €275 to €10,725.

A claim for relief must be made jointly and in writing after the end of the tax year in which the marriage took place.

13.3 Year of Death

Where a party to a marriage dies, the taxation treatment of his/her income for that year depends on the method of tax assessment in force and also on which party to the marriage dies.

s1018
TCA 97

If a married couple is taxed under the single assessment provisions, the death of one spouse does not affect the taxation of the other spouse in that year. The surviving spouse continues to be taxed as a single person on his/her own income. However, the surviving spouse may elect under s1018 TCA 1997 before the end of that tax year for joint assessment for the year of death.

Where a couple is jointly assessed, the tax treatment in the year of death will vary depending on whether or not the deceased spouse was the assessable party. The position where the assessed spouse dies is considered at 13.3.1 below, while 13.3.2 below deals with the provisions that apply on the death of a non-assessable spouse.

Death results in a cessation for tax purposes of all the sources of income of the deceased spouse, and assessments are made for the period to the date of death. Earlier years may be revised according to the cessation rules of each Case and Schedule (readers are referred to Chapter 14 for commentary on the cessation rules that apply to Case I/Case II).

Where there is a cessation of the non-assessable spouse's sources of income on his/her death. If the deceased spouse possessed a source of income which was assessable under Schedule D Case I/II, and the source of income passes in its entirety to the surviving spouse, the Revenue Commissioners will as a concession, allow the income source to be treated as a continuing source, provided the surviving spouse did not previously possess any such sources of income and provided it is more beneficial to the couple.

Example 13.4

John Joe and Mary Farrelly are jointly assessed. They have no children. John Joe dies on 1 July 2009. He was self-employed as a shop-owner and prepared accounts to 30 September. Mary opts to continue with the trade. The couple's income for the year of death and the preceding year is as follows:

2009   *€*
John Joe: *Case I*   *90,000*   *(based on accounts to year ended 30/09/2009)*
Mary: *Salary*   *60,000*
             UK dividends   *1,000*

2008
John Joe: *Case I*   *78,000*   *(based on accounts to year ended 30/09/2008)*
Mary: *Salary*   *20,500*
             UK dividends   *600*

The income tax liabilities for 2009, assuming the concessional basis is applied, are as follows:

Period 1 January 2009 to 1 July 2009:
Assessment for John Joe

	€	€	€
Case I (Note 1) – Self			45,000
Salary – Spouse			30,000
UK dividends – Spouse			500
			75,500
Taxed as follows:			
€72,800 @ 20%		14,560	
€2,700 @ 41%		1,107	
		15,667	
Less tax credits:			
Personal tax credit	(3,660)		
PAYE Tax Credit	(1,830)		
		(5,490)	
Tax due		10,177	

Period 1 July 2009 to 31 December 2009:

Assessment for Mary

	€	€	€
Case I (Note 1)			*45,000*
Salary			*30,000*
UK dividends			*500*
			75,500

	€	€	€
Taxed as follows:			
€36,400 @ 20% (Note 2)		*7,280*	
€39,100 @ 41%		*16,031*	
		23,311	
Less: tax credits:			
Personal tax credit	*(3,660)*		
PAYE Tax Credit	*(1,830) (Note 3)*		
		(5,490)	
Tax due		*17,821*	

Note 1: Since the Case I income is to be treated as a continuing source, John Joe is assessable on six months of the income of the accounting period which forms the basis period for 2009, i.e., year ended 30 September 2009. The remaining six months are assessed on Mary.

Had the cessation of trade provisions been applied, the Case I assessable figure for 2008 would have been increased by €3,000 (€81,000* – €78,000) on revision to actual basis for the year. This would have resulted in an additional liability of €1,230. Readers are again referred to Chapter 14 for relevant commentary on the cessation provisions.

*Calculated as (€90,000 * 3/12) + (€78,000 * 9/12).

Note 2: Since the couple have no dependent children, the standard rate band is €36,400. If John Joe and Mary had dependent children, the standard rate band of €40,400 would apply.

Note 3: Mary is entitled to the full year's PAYE Tax Credit post-death.

13.3.1 Death of an assessable spouse

On the death of an assessable spouse:

■ An assessment is made on the income of both spouses from the beginning of the relevant tax year to the date of death with the full Married Person's Tax Credits and rate bands applying.

■ The surviving non-assessable spouse is assessed on his/her income from the date of death to the end of the year of assessment and is granted the full Married Person's Tax Credits but the single standard rate band.

Example 13.5

John and Martina, a married couple, are taxed under joint assessment. John, the assessable spouse, dies on 1 October 2009. The following is the couple's income for 2009:

	€
John (from 01/01/2009 to 01/10/2009):	
Salary	*155,000*
UK interest	*4,000*
Irish dividends (gross)	*1,000*

Martina (for full year)

Salary	120,000
UK dividends	6,000

The calculation of the tax liability is therefore as follows (ignoring PRSI and tax deducted at source):

Joint Assessment

John

	€	€
Salary – self		155,000
UK interest – self		4,000
Irish dividends – self		1,000
Salary – spouse		90,000
UK dividends – spouse		4,500
		254,500

Taxed as follows:

€72,800 × 20%	14,560	
€181,700 × 41%	74,497	
		89,057

Less non-refundable credits:

Married Person's Credit	(3,660)	
PAYE Credit	(3,660)	
		(7,320)

Tax liability (before deduction of refundable tax credits) **81,737**

Martina

Salary ($^1/_4$)	30,000
UK dividends ($^1/_4$)	1,500
	31,500

Taxed as follows:

€31,500 × 20%	6,300	
		6,300

Less non-refundable credits:

Married Person's Credit	(3,660)	
PAYE Credit	(1,830)	
		(5,490)

Tax liability **810**

The combined liability for 2009 is €82,547.

13.3.2 Death of a non-assessable spouse

On the death of a non-assessable spouse:

- The surviving spouse is assessed for the full tax year on his/her own income for the full year and on the non-assessable spouse's income for the period to the date of death.

- The assessable spouse is granted the Married Person's Tax Credit and standard rate band.

Example 13.6

Assume the same facts as at Example 13.5 except that Martina was the assessable spouse prior to John's death.

The calculations of the tax liabilities are therefore as follows (again ignoring PRSI and tax deducted at source):

Joint Assessment

Martina	€	€
Salary – spouse		*155,000*
UK interest – spouse		*4,000*
Irish dividends – spouse		*1,000*
Salary – self		*120,000*
UK dividends – self		*6,000*
		286,000
Taxed as follows:		
€72,800 × 20%	*14,560*	
€213,200 × 41%	*87,412*	
		101,972
Less non-refundable credits:		
Married Person's Credit	*(3,660)*	
PAYE Credits	*(3,660)*	
		(7,320)
Tax liability		***94,652***

Example 13.6 shows an uplift in the tax liability of €12,105 (i.e., €94,652 – €84,547), notwithstanding that the same level of income has been assessed in both examples.

13.4   Effects of Separation and Divorce

The provisions relating to the taxation of married couples apply to a situation where a husband and wife are "living together". A husband and wife are treated, for income tax purposes, as living together unless:

■ they are separated or divorced; or

■ they are separated in such circumstances that the separation is likely to be permanent.

Tax is not deducted at source from maintenance payments following a separation or divorce.

13.4.1   Separation

A separation is treated as "likely to be permanent" where the husband and wife are living apart by mutual consent or by force of circumstances, and their separation has continued for a considerable period of time – usually taken as a minimum of one year. If a husband and wife are not treated as living together, then they are treated as separated spouses and are taxed as single persons. However, there are options that they may consider as to how they wish to be assessed for tax purposes.

Maintenance payments from one spouse to the other where the payments are made under maintenance arrangements drawn up on or after 8 June 1983 (which are legally enforceable) may be treated as:

Income of the payee

s1025 TCA 97 Under s1025 TCA 1997, such payments are allowed as a deduction from the income of the payer for tax purposes and chargeable to income tax under Case IV of Schedule D in the hands of the recipient. In these circumstances, both parties are taxed as single individuals.

Income of the payer

s1026 TCA 97 An election may be made under s1026 TCA 1997 to be jointly assessed. The maintenance payments are regarded as income of the payer and are therefore ignored for tax purposes. The couple is effectively taxed as if the separation had not taken place.

Example 13.7

Assume a couple separated in 2005. During the year of assessment 2009, the husband earned €90,000 from his employment. He paid €15,000 in maintenance payments to his ex-wife who has no other source of income. The calculation below determines which of the two taxation options is more beneficial:

Option (a)

Single Assessment – Husband	€	€	Single Assessment – Ex-Wife	€	€
Income – husband		90,000	Income – ex-wife		_15,000_
Income – ex-wife		_–_			
		90,000			
Less maintenance payment		_(15,000)_			
		75,000			
Taxed as follows:			Taxed as follows:		
€36,400 @ 20%	7,280		€15,000 @ 20%		3,000
€38,600 @ 41%	_15,826_				
		23,106			
Less non-refundable credits:			Less non-refundable credits:		
Single Person's Credit	(1,830)		Single Person's Credit	(1,830)	
PAYE Credit	_(1,830)_	_(3,660)_	PAYE Credit	_–_	_(1,830)_
Tax liability		_19,446_	Tax liability		_1,170_
Combined liability:	**20,616**				

Option (b)

Joint Assessment

	€	€
Income – husband		*90,000*
Income – ex-wife		*–*
		90,000
Taxed as follows:		
€45,400 @ 20%	*9,080*	
€44,600 @ 41%	*18,286*	
		27,366
Less non-refundable credits:		
Single Person's Credit	*(3,660)*	
PAYE Credit	*(1,830)*	
		(5,490)
Tax liability		*21,876*
Difference		**1,260**

In the above example, it is more beneficial to opt for single assessment with the husband claiming a deduction for the maintenance payments.

Maintenance payments for the benefit of children of the marriage are always ignored, regardless of whether the couple is taxed under s1025 or s1026 TCA 1997.

If an individual wholly or mainly maintains a former spouse, but does not qualify for a tax deduction for the maintenance (e.g., not paid pursuant to a legal agreement), the Married Person's Tax Credit may still be claimed but without the additional standard rate band.

13.4.2 Year of separation

In Example 13.7 above, we observed that where a taxpayer claims a deduction for maintenance payments, the Married Person's Tax Credit is unavailable. However, in the year of separation, an individual who had been entitled to the Married Person's Credit is entitled to claim a deduction for legally enforceable maintenance payments and the Married Person's Tax Credit. This is because the entitlement to the Married Person's Credit preceded the maintenance payments.

s1026
TCA 97

The provisions relating to the taxation of separated spouses come into immediate effect on the date of separation. Except in the case of an election for joint assessment under s1026 TCA 1997, each spouse is taxed as a single person from the date of separation. Where a couple was jointly assessed prior to the date of separation, special rules apply for the year of separation. The rules are somewhat similar to those applying for the year of death (see 13.3 above), except that there is no cessation of any sources of income merely by virtue of the separation.

An assessment is made on the assessable spouse for the full year to include the income of both spouses to the date of separation and his/her own income for the period from the date of separation to the following 31 December. Since the assessable spouse is assessable on the income of the other spouse for part of the year, he/she is granted the Married Person's Tax Credit and the married person's standard rate tax band for the full year.

The other spouse is assessed as a single person on his/her income from the date of separation to the following 31 December. The Single Person's Tax Credit and the single rate band are granted against the income for that period.

Example 13.8

Michael and Margaret Brennan are formally separated by a Deed of Separation dated 1 October 2009. They have no children. They were jointly assessed for all years prior to separation. They had the following income in 2009:

2009	€
Michael	
Salary	55,000
UK interest	4,000
Irish dividends (gross)	1,000
Margaret:	
Salary	45,000
UK dividends	6,000

The income tax liabilities for 2009 are as follows (ignoring PRSI and tax deductions at source):

Joint Assessment

Michael (full year)

	€	€
Salary – self		55,000
UK interest – self		4,000
Irish-taxed dividends		1,000
Salary – spouse		33,750
UK dividends – spouse		4,500
		98,250
Taxed as follows:		
€72,800 @ 20%	14,560	
€25,450 @ 41%	10,434	
		24,994
Less non-refundable credits:		
Married Person's Credit	(3,660)	
PAYE Credit	(3,660)	
		(7,320)
Tax liability		**17,674**

Margaret (from 1/10/2009 to 31/12/2009)

	€	€
Salary ($^1/_4$)		11,250
UK dividends ($^1/_4$)		1,500
		12,750
Taxed as follows:		
€12,750 @ 20%		2,550
Less non-refundable credits:		
Single Person's Credit	(1,830)	
PAYE Credit	(1,830)	
		(3,660)
Tax liability		**Nil**

13.4.3   Divorce

The Fifteenth Amendment to the Irish Constitution repealed the constitutional ban on divorce, enabling the Oireachtas to legislate so as to give individuals whose marriage had irretrievably broken down the right to divorce and remarry. The Family Law (Divorce) Act 1996 provides the necessary statutory framework to give effect to the constitutional amendment. The Act makes a number of specific provisions in relation to taxation.

s1026
TCA 97

The joint assessment provisions (under s1026 TCA 1997) are extended to couples whose marriage has been dissolved under either s5 of the Family Law (Divorce) Act 1996 or under the law of another country, recognised as valid Ireland. Both spouses must be resident in the State and not have remarried.

If the election for assessment is made under s1026, the couple is assessed to income tax without regard to maintenance payments and is granted the Married Person's Tax Credit. If the spouses each have income in their own right, apart from the maintenance payments, the income tax applicable to their respective incomes is calculated by the separate assessment procedure but treats the payer's income as undiminished by the maintenance payments (i.e., maintenance payments are ignored). These provisions apply to payments made under maintenance arrangements made after 7 June 1983. In the case of maintenance arrangements made before that date, these provisions will not apply unless:

■ the maintenance is varied or a new arrangement is entered into; or

■ both parties jointly elect in writing.

WHAT YOU SHOULD NOW KNOW

On completion of this chapter, you should be able to:

✓ Describe the different assessment options available to married couples.

✓ Calculate the tax relief available to couples in the year of marriage.

✓ Discuss the tax impact which the death of a spouse has on the surviving spouse.

✓ Explain how a separated couple might qualify for joint assessment.

✓ Describe how divorced couples are taxed and what options for assessment are available to them.

✓ Complete Questions and the Assignments in Irish Taxation Law and Practice, Volume 2.

14

INCOME FROM TRADES AND PROFESSIONS

In this chapter, you will deal with the following:

- The Badges of Trade

- Basis of assessment for Case I/
  Case II income

- Commencement rules

- Cessation rules

- Change in accounting date

14.1   Introduction

Income from a trade is assessed to tax under Schedule D Case I. Examples of traders include electrical contractors, plumbers, carpenters, etc.

Income from a profession is assessed to tax under Schedule D Case II. Examples of professionals include tax consultants, accountants, solicitors, etc.

The rules for determining taxable income for Cases I and II are identical and are considered in detail in Chapter 15. This chapter is concerned with identifying those activities that constitute trading. It also deals with the basis of assessment rules for Case I and Case II.

14.2   Trade

Tax is charged under Schedule D Cases I and II on "the full amount of the profits or gains" of trades and professions respectively. Section 3 TCA 1997 defines trade as follows:

> "'trade' includes every trade, manufacture, adventure or concern in the nature of trade."

This definition does not provide much assistance in deciding whether or not a particular activity constitutes a trade. It is important to determine if a particular activity constitutes a trade because, if a trade does not exist, the profit from that activity may not be within the charge to income tax. If a particular activity is not held to be a trade, the profit from the activity could be within the charge to capital gains tax.

In deciding if an activity constitutes a trade, we are guided by:

- a large body of cases on this subject

- the Badges of Trade, set down by a Royal Commission (UK) established in 1954.

It is sometimes difficult to decide whether a particular activity constitutes trading and is therefore liable to income tax or constitutes a transaction liable to capital gains tax. Given the fact that trading is liable to income tax at marginal rates, which can be (ignoring income levy) 46% including PRSI and the health contribution, while capital gains tax is payable at 25%, the distinction is very important. In addition, there are certain exemptions available under the capital gains tax legislation, which have no parallel in the income tax code. For example, gains on disposals of wasting assets, i.e., assets with an expected life of less than 50 years are exempt from capital gains tax but would be subject to income tax where they accrue to an individual who trades in such assets.

In 1954, a Royal Commission was set up in the UK to consider the practical factors that should be taken into account in deciding whether trading is being carried on. The factors recommended by the Royal Commission to be taken into account are commonly known as the "Badges of Trade".

They are stated in the report of the Royal Commission as follows:

1. The subject matter

While almost any form of property can be acquired to be dealt in, those forms of property such as commodities or manufactured articles, which are normally the subject of trading, are only very exceptionally the subject of investment.

Again, property that does not yield to its owner an income or personal enjoyment merely by virtue of its ownership is more likely to have been acquired with the object of a deal than property that does.

2. The length of period of ownership

Generally speaking, property meant to be dealt in is realised within a short time after acquisition. But there are many exceptions to this as a universal rule.[1]

3. The frequency or number of transactions by the same person

If realisations of the same sort of property occur in succession over a period of years, or there are several such realisations at about the same date, a presumption arises that there has been dealing in respect of each.

4. Supplementary work on, or in connection with, the property realised

If the property is worked on in any way during the ownership so as to bring it into a more marketable condition, or if any special exertions are made to find or attract purchasers, such as the opening of an office or large-scale advertising, there is some evidence of dealing. For when there is an organised effort to obtain profit, there is a source of taxable income. But if nothing at all is done, the suggestion tends the other way.

5. Circumstances of sale

There may be some explanation, such as a sudden emergency or opportunity calling for ready money, that negates the idea that any plan of dealing prompted the original purchase.

6. Motive

There are cases in which the purpose of the transaction or the sale is clearly discernible. Motive is never irrelevant in any of these cases. What is desirable is that it should be clearly realised that the purpose of the transaction could be inferred from surrounding circumstances in the absence of the seller's intentions and even, if necessary, in the face of his/her own evidence.

A number of the important tax cases on this question are now considered.

---

1   For example, a distillery that distils whiskey may require a number of years of ownership before the product is sold.

In *Erichsen v Last* 4 TC 422, Lord Justice Cotton gave the following definition of trading:

> *"... where a person habitually does and contracts to do a thing capable of producing a profit, and for the purpose of producing a profit, he carries on a trade or business".*

In the case of *Martin v Lowry* 11 TC 297, an agricultural machinery merchant who had never had any connection with the linen trade, purchased from the UK government the whole of its surplus stock of aeroplane linen.

Failing in his original endeavour to sell the linen in one lot, the agricultural machinery merchant engaged in an advertising campaign, rented offices and employed staff to sell the linen to the public. The House of Lords held that the profit arising from the sale of the linen arose from a trade. The judges referred repeatedly to the mantle of trading which the merchant had donned as a result of the elaborate selling organisation employed by him.

In the case of *Wisdom v Chamberlain* 45 TC 93, the taxpayer purchased silver bullion as a hedge against devaluation. It was held by the Court of Appeal that the transaction in question constituted an adventure in the nature of trade. Harman LJ stated:

> *"In the first place it seems to me that supposing it was a hedge against devaluation, it was nevertheless a transaction entered into on a short-term basis for the purpose of making a profit out of the purchase and sale of a commodity, and if that is not an adventure in the nature of a trade I do not really know what is. The whole object of the transaction was to make a profit."*

The profit objective is not an infallible test in deciding whether or not a particular transaction is an adventure in the nature of a trade, as can be seen from the following statement by Donovan LJ in the case of *Jenkinson v Freedland* 39 TC 636:

> *"It cannot be right, therefore, to assert, as the Crown did before us, that whenever something is bought to resell at a profit an adventure or concern in the nature of trade necessarily results, and any finding of the Commissioners to the contrary must be perverse. Otherwise there would hardly be any need to introduce capital gains tax. It would virtually be here already. The true position in my opinion, is that all the facts in each case must be considered, not merely the motive of acquisition, and a conclusion arrived at from such a comprehensive review."*

In the case of *Rutledge v The Commissioners of the Inland Revenue* 14 TC 490, the taxpayer was a moneylender who purchased a large quantity of toilet paper while in

Berlin on a totally separate matter. Lord Sands, in considering the matter, stated in relation to the appellant:

> *"He made a large purchase and brought the toilet paper to this country and effected a sale at a profit. The nature and quantity of the subject dealt with exclude the suggestion that it could have been disposed otherwise than as a trade transaction. Neither the purchaser nor any purchaser from him was likely to require such a quantity for his private use. Accordingly, it appears to me a quite reasonable view for the Commissioners to have taken that this transaction was in the nature of trade. From beginning to end the intention was simply to buy and resell. Your Lordship in the Chair has indicated that there may be cases of purchase and resale at a profit where the transaction cannot be said to be in the nature of trade. In particular, this may be the case where there is no definite intention of reselling when the purchase is made. But I do not think we can regard what was done here as other than 'an adventure ... in the nature of trade' within the meaning of the Act."*

No single test is decisive in establishing trading, and in the case of *Marson v Morton* (1986) 59 TC 381, the judge reviewed and broadened the Badges to some degree by identifying the following key questions:

- Has the taxpayer undertaken a similar transaction?

- Is the transaction related to the trade the taxpayer otherwise carries on?

- How is the transaction financed?

- Was the item normally the subject of trading?

- Was the transaction typical of the trade in an item of that nature?

- Was work carried out on the item for the purposes of resale?

- Was the item sold as it was bought, or broken down into saleable lots?

- Did the item provide enjoyment, pride of possession or produce an income?

- What was the taxpayer's intention when the item was purchased?

- The judge summed up the issue as follows:

> *"Was the taxpayer investing money or was he doing a deal?"*

14.3   When Does a Trade Commence?

The date on which the trade or profession commences is a question of fact. There are no specific rules for determining when a trade commences. However, there is a distinction between commencing to trade and preparing to commence trading. The leading case concerning this issue is *Birmingham & District Cattle By-Products v CIR* [1919].

In this case, a company carried on the business of processing and marketing butchers' by-products. From June to October 1913, its directors were engaged in securing premises and plant and arranging for the supply of by-products. A works manager was taken on in August. Actual processing commenced in October. It was held that the company had commenced to trade in October. Trade was held to commence when the company first received raw materials for manufacture.

14.4   When Does a Trade Cease?

In general, it can be said that a trade ceases when all of its trading stock has been disposed of or when it ceases to manufacture. The fact that a person ceases to purchase more stock does not of itself constitute a cessation. This point was highlighted in *Gordon and Blair Ltd. v IRC* [1962].

In that case, a brewing company ceased brewing but continued to sell beer, which was supplied by another company. It was held that the company had ceased the trade of brewing beer and had commenced the trade of selling beer.

14.5   Illegal Trades

Profits or gains arising from an unlawful activity are within the charge to income tax under Case IV. This applies not only to trading income but to all income.

14.6   Basis of Assessment

The rules for determining the basis of assessment for Case I and Case II are identical, and no distinction between the two applies in the commentary that follows.

A trader will usually prepare accounts for a 12-month period. It is necessary to consider which accounts and profits are taken into account ("assessed") in particular tax years. In examining the basis of assessment rules, a number of different scenarios need to be examined:

- ongoing business

- commencing business

- ceasing business

- business changing its accounting period

14.6.1 Ongoing business

Ongoing businesses are subject to a "current year" basis of assessment. This means that the profits of the 12-month accounting period ending in the income tax year of assessment are taxable in that year.

Example 14.1: Ongoing Business

Romeo has traded for many years. His tax-adjusted profits are:

	€
Year ended 30 June 2007	*120,000*
Year ended 30 June 2008	*130,000*
Year ended 30 June 2009	*150,000*

Assessable:	
2007 – year ended 30 June 2007	*120,000*
2008 – year ended 30 June 2008	*130,000*
2009 – year ended 30 June 2009	*150,000*

There are special rules in the legislation to deal with traders who are commencing and ceasing in business.

14.6.2 Commencing business

When a business commences trading, the taxable profits assessable for the first three years of trading are as follows:

First Year

Profits are assessable on an actual basis, i.e., the profits assessable are those from the date of commencement until the following 31 December.

Second Year

Profits to be assessed in the second year are as follows:

- If there is only one set of accounts made up to date within that year and these accounts are for a full 12 months, the full amount of the profits of the 12 months ending on that date should be included.

- If the accounts are for less than one year or there is more than one set of accounts made up to a date or dates within that tax year, the full amount of the profits of the 12 months ending on the later or latest of those dates should be included.

- In any other case, the actual profits for the tax year must be accounted for.

Third and subsequent years

The assessment for these years is on a current year basis. However, if the actual profits of the second year (i.e., the profits attributable to the income tax year, which runs from 1 January to 31 December) are lower than those assessable in accordance with the rules for year two, as set out above, the taxpayer may elect to offset that difference against the profits of the third year of assessment.

When the profits of the third year of assessment are insufficient to absorb the full amount of the difference, any balance can be carried forward as a loss available to be offset against profits of subsequent years of assessment.

These rules are best illustrated by the following examples:

Example 14.2: Commencing to Trade

Don commenced to trade on 1 September 2007. He prepared his first accounts to 31 August 2008 and his second set of accounts to 31 August 2009.

Tax-adjusted Case I profits for both of these periods are as follows:

Year ended 31 August 2008	*€100,000*
Year ended 31 August 2009	*€150,000*

Assessable:

2007

Profits from 1 September 2007 to 31 December 2007, i.e., tax-adjusted accounting profit for the year to 31 August 2008 @ 4/12 = €100,000 @ 4/12 = €33,333.

2008

As there is only one set of accounts made up to a date within the year and it is for a full 12 months, the profits assessable are those for the 12 months to 31 August 2008, i.e., €100,000.*

2009

Tax-adjusted accounting profit for the year to 31 August 2009, i.e., €150,000.

*2008 – Actual

($^{8}/_{12}$ @ €100,000) + ($^{4}/_{12}$ @ €150,000)

€66,667 + €50,000 = €116,667

As the actual profits for year two are greater than the assessed profits, the taxpayer's option may not be exercised in this case and thus, no adjustment is required to year three.

Example 14.3

John commenced to trade on 1 April 2007.

His profits for the first two years of trading are as follows:

	€
Tax-adjusted Case I for year to 31 March 2008	*60,000*
Tax-adjusted Case I for year to 31 March 2009	*40,000*

John's assessments for the three years are as follows:

Basis of assessment		€
Year 1 – 2007	*Actual* ($^9/_{12}$ × €60,000)	_45,000_
Year 2 – 2008	*Profits to 31 March 2008*	_60,000_
Year 3 – 2009	*Current year basis*	40,000
	Deduct: Third year option relief	_(15,000)_*
		_25,000_

* *Third year option:*	€
– *Assessed – Year 2*	60,000
– *Actual – Year 2* ($^3/_{12}$ @ €60,000) + ($^9/_{12}$ @ €40,000)	_45,000_
Excess	_15,000_

14.6.3 Ceasing business

Section 67 TCA 1997 provides for the following basis of assessment in the final years of a business up to cessation.

Year of cessation:	— actual profits from 1 January to date of cessation
Penultimate year:	— revised by the Revenue Commissioners to "actual" profits if these exceed the profits previously assessed on a current year basis

Example 14.4: Ceasing Business

Brooklyn will cease to trade on 31 August 2009. Results will be as follows:

	€
Year ended 30 April 2008	*80,000*
Year ended 30 April 2009	*50,000*
Period ended 31 August 2009	*20,000*

	€
Assessable:	
2009 (year of cessation) – actual	
$^4/_4$ @ €20,000	*20,000*
$^4/_{12}$ @ €50,000	_16,667_
	_36,667_
2008 (penultimate year)	
Normal basis	
Year ended 30 April 2008	_80,000_
Actual basis:	
€50,000 @ $^8/_{12}$	*33,333*
€80,000 @ $^4/_{12}$	_26,667_
	_60,000_

As the profits assessed on a normal (current year) basis are greater than the profits that arise on an actual basis, there will be no revision of the penultimate year by the Revenue Commissioners in this case.

Example 14.5

Michael ceased to trade as a sole trader on 30 June 2009.

His tax-adjusted Case I profits for recent years are as follows:

	€
Year to 30 June 2009	*100,000*
Year to 30 June 2008	*80,000*
Year to 30 June 2007	*50,000*

His assessments for the three years up to the date of cessation are as follows:

Year	*Basis of Assessment*	*€*	*€*
2009	*Actual (€100,000 × $^6/_{12}$)*		*50,000*
2008	*Original – current year basis*	*80,000*	
	Actual ($^6/_{12}$ × €100,000) + ($^6/_{12}$ × €80,000)	*90,000*	
	As the actual assessment is higher, Revenue will assess Michael on an actual basis.		
	Final assessment		*90,000*
2007	*Current year basis*		*50,000*

14.6.3.1 Post-cessation receipts

Where a trade has ceased, accounts will be prepared to the date of cessation as determined using the principles set out above. However, it can happen that after the business has ceased, income is received. This income is known as post-cessation receipts and the following rules apply:

■ Post-cessation receipts are assessed under Case IV and the receipt of such income does not affect the cessation rules.

■ A deduction may be made against the post-cessation receipts for any expenses incurred which would have been allowed if the trade had not ceased. (Readers are referred to Chapter 15 for commentary on the deductibility of certain expenses.)

■ Unused capital allowances at the date of cessation may be set against the post-cessation receipts. (Readers are referred to Chapter 16 for commentary on the calculation of capital allowances.)

14.6.4 Business changing its accounting period

A business, for a variety of reasons, may change its accounting period. For the purposes of basis of assessment, three situations can arise where there is a change in accounting date:

i) There may be more than one accounting period ending in any given tax year.

ii) The accounting period ending in the tax year may be shorter/longer than 12 months in duration.

iii) There may be no accounting period ending in the tax year.

Where any of the above occurs, the following rules apply:

■ The profits assessable in the tax year in which the change occurs are the profits of the 12 months to the latest accounting year-end. If there is no accounting period ending in the tax year, the assessable profits are the actual profits for the income tax year, i.e., the profits attributable to the period from 1 January to 31 December.

■ The profits of the preceding tax year will be revised on the basis of the new accounting year-end of the tax year in which the change occurs, if those profits are higher than the profits originally assessed.

Example 14.6: Change of Accounting Period

1. More than one accounting period ending in the year of assessment

Results are as follows:	€	€
12 months ended 30 September 2008	*35,000*	
12 months ended 30 September 2009	*23,400*	
2 months ended 30 November 2009	*36,000*	

Assessable:
2009 – 2 accounting periods
Profits assessed are those for the 12 months
to the later accounting date.

	€	€
$^2/_2$ @ €36,000	*36,000*	
$^{10}/_{12}$ @ €23,400	*19,500*	*55,500*

2008 – Original assessment		*35,000*
Corresponding period:		
$^2/_{12}$ @ €23,400	*3,900*	
$^{10}/_{12}$ @ €35,000	*29,167*	*33,067*

As the profits originally assessed in 2008 are higher, no revision of the assessment is applied.

2. Short/Long accounting period

Results are as follows:	€	€
Year to 30 September 2007	*100,000*	
Year to 30 September 2008	*255,500*	
8 months to 31 May 2009	*120,000*	

Assessable:

2009		€	€
	$^8/_8$ @ €120,000	*120,000*	
	$^4/_{12}$ @ €255,500	*85,167*	*205,167*

2008 – Original assessment		*255,500*
Revision to corresponding accounting period		
(i.e., 31 May):		
$^4/_{12}$ @ €100,000	*33,333*	
$^8/_{12}$ @ €255,500	*170,333*	
		203,666

As the profits originally assessed in 2008 are higher, no revision of the assessment is applied.

3. No accounting period ending in year of assessment

Results are as follows:	*€*
12 months ended 31 October 2007	*120,000*
24 months ended 31 October 2009	*275,000*

Assessable:
2008 – No accounting period
Assessment based on actual profits to 31 December 2008:

$^{12}/_{24}$ @ €275,000	*137,500*

2007 – Original assessment	*120,000*

Revise to actual basis:

$^{10}/_{12}$ @ €120,000	€100,000	
$^{2}/_{24}$ @ €275,000	€22,917	*122,917*

As the revised assessment on an actual basis is higher than the original assessment, Revenue will exercise the option to revise the assessable profits for 2007 in this case.

WHAT YOU SHOULD NOW KNOW

On completion of this chapter, you should be able to:

- ✓ Describe the six 'Badges of Trade' and discuss the associated case law.

- ✓ Explain the basis of assessment for Case I/II in an ongoing business.

- ✓ Calculate assessable Case I/II for the first three years after commencement.

- ✓ Calculate assessable Case I/II for the final year of cessation and for the penultimate year.

- ✓ Calculate assessable Case I/II where a business changes its accounting date.

- ✓ Complete Questions and the Assignments in Irish Taxation Law and Practice, Volume 2.

15

ADJUSTED INCOME TAX COMPUTATION

In this chapter, you will deal with the following:

- Methodology for calculating the profits of a trade or profession

- Distinction between items of a capital nature and items of a revenue nature

- Meaning of the term "wholly and exclusively"

- Treatment of movements in provisions

- Statutory adjustments

15.1   Introduction

This chapter examines the calculation of profits assessable to tax for a sole trader or a professional. It looks at the general process involved in arriving at a taxable figure by examining the tax principles involved. The specific legislative provisions are discussed in detail.

In theory, one of two approaches could be used to calculate the assessable profits of a sole trader:

(i) Using the source information of the business, it is possible to recreate all the income of that type earned in the year and work out all the tax-deductible expenses for that type of income

(ii) Alternatively, one could use a "shortcut" and work from the figures that will already have been prepared for the business accounts adjusting these to arrive at the total taxable profits.

Method (ii) is the easiest and quickest method. It is the method that is used in practice and the recommended approach for examination questions.

The remainder of this chapter is concerned with using the financial statements of a business as a starting point and with the various adjustments necessary to arrive at taxable profits.

The skill is in identifying all of the tax adjustments required. This requires a familiarity with:

■ the vast body of specific legislative provisions which operate to prohibit certain expense deductions, or otherwise adjust the treatment for tax purposes from the accounting treatment;

■ various court decisions in Ireland, the UK and the EU. While UK legislation is not binding in Ireland it may be persuasive, particularly where the legislation in the UK is similar to that in Ireland and particularly where there is no equivalent Irish interpretation;

■ established Revenue practice, such as Statements of Practice, Information Leaflets and Guidance Notes issued by Revenue, together with Revenue precedents.

15.2   Using the Financial Statements to Calculate Taxable Income

This approach involves effectively taking the "profit before tax" figure in the profit and loss account or income statement and adjusting it to arrive at taxable profits. The "profit before tax" figure is the total accounting income booked to the profit and loss account or income statement net of the total expenses booked in accordance with accounting rules and generally accepted accounting practice (GAAP).

In the vast majority of cases, the accounts will not show the final figure to be taxed for the period. While the Revenue Commissioners require GAAP to be used in the computation of taxable profits, a number of established tax principles, which derive from both case law, and specific legislative provisions give rise to differences between the accounting and taxable profit. The main reasons for these differences are specifically disallowed items (e.g., business entertainment – see 15.3.4.1 below) and adjustments necessary to counter the lack of consistency and objectivity in the accounting treatment of many items, such as depreciation and general provisions.

To overcome these differences, the accounting profits are adjusted such that non-taxable income and non-deductible expenses are stripped out. Thus, an adjustment to the profit-before-tax figure will be made because:

(a) there are expenses in the profit and loss account or income statement which are not deductible in arriving at Case I income and which must therefore be added back for tax purposes;

(b) there is income in the profit and loss account or income statement which is not taxable as Case I income and which must therefore be deducted in arriving at taxable Case I; or

(c) there are costs which are not deductible in the profit and loss account or income statement but which are allowable in calculating Case I income.

To establish the adjustments required for parts (a) and (b) above, a review of all the income and expense items that are included in the detailed profit and loss account or income statement should be undertaken. In light of the criteria at 15.3 below, it is then a question of determining whether each of the items is taxable as Case I income or an allowable Case I deduction as appropriate.

The adjustments required for the items listed at (c) are potentially more difficult to establish as these expense items are not already in the profit and loss account but nevertheless are Case I adjustments, e.g., double rent allowance in a designated area.

15.3   Adjusting Items

For the purposes of this analysis, all references are to the profit and loss account albeit that some sole trade businesses may choose to adopt the terminology and accounting practices of international accounting.

There are four very important considerations to bear in mind when examining the items included in the profit and loss account or income statement:

1. It is necessary to consider whether the item is capital in nature or income/revenue related. In general, an adjustment is required for capital items. A number of Irish and UK decisions help to clarify the distinction between "capital" and "revenue". It is important to bear in mind that some capital expenses, which are disallowed

for the purposes of calculating Case I, may be deductible in calculating chargeable gains.

2. The item must be "trade" related. In general, items that do not relate to the trade are adjusted for in arriving at taxable Case I. The legislation specifically requires that for amounts to be deductible under Case I, the expenditure must be incurred "wholly and exclusively" for the purposes of carrying on the trade. This concept of "wholly and exclusively" is a complex area and has been the subject of much case law in Ireland and the UK over many years. It is explained in more detail below, and one of the main cases is outlined.

3. In general, items of expenditure must have been incurred in the period. An adjustment will be required if an item relates to a movement on a general provision. Movements in provisions are only allowable where they relate to specific items, the amount of which can be determined with exactitude. Rough estimates of future expenditure are not allowable.

4. Certain specific items of expenditure are disallowed by statute notwithstanding that they are revenue in nature and may have been incurred wholly and exclusively for the purposes of the trade. The main provisions disallowing specific types of expenditure are addressed at 15.3.4 below.

The commentary that follows is concerned with elaborating on these considerations and with presenting examples of matters which may be addressed under the four headings as described. It is important to bear in mind that many of the issues addressed in this context are more relevant for companies. This is particularly true in the case of adjustments arising as a consequence of the application of accounting standards. Readers are referred to Chapter 29 for detailed commentary on the subtle differences between the adjusted profits computations of sole traders and those of companies.

The application of the four considerations in determining the deductibility of an expense item in the profit and loss account can be summarised diagrammatically as follows:

ELIGIBILITY TEST TO CLAIM A TAX-DEDUCTIBLE EXPENSE

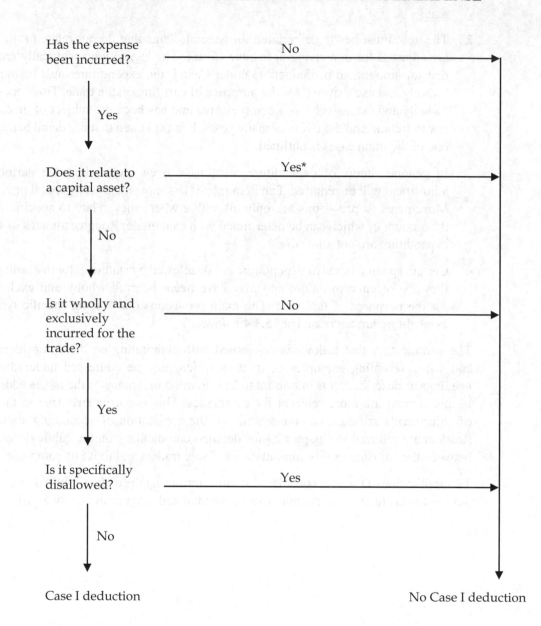

Has the expense
been incurred? ——————— No ——————→

Yes ↓

Does it relate to
a capital asset? ——————— Yes* ——————→

No ↓

Is it wholly and
exclusively
incurred for the
trade? ——————— No ——————→

Yes ↓

Is it specifically
disallowed? ——————— Yes ——————→

No ↓

Case I deduction   No Case I deduction

* Consider capital allowances

15.3.1 Income or capital

Income tax is not assessed on capital profits; it is only assessed on income profits. Therefore, the only expenses which will be allowed in its calculation are income expenses. This is supported by the fact that, under ordinary accounting principles, capital expenditure is not ordinarily charged to the profit and loss account in arriving at net profit. However, in certain incidences, businesses will charge capital expenditure to the profit and loss account, either because the amount is small and immaterial from an accounting perspective or because the distinction between capital and revenue is not always clear. It is therefore necessary to establish whether particular items in the profit and loss account are capital or revenue in nature. There are some factors that should be considered when deciding whether an expense item is capital or revenue in nature. These factors are:

- the treatment of the expenditure in the accounts

- the reason for the expenditure and a common-sense approach

- the lasting quality of the asset/item on which expenditure has been incurred

- the form in which the transaction is carried out.

Capital expenditure is generally taken to be expenditure incurred by a business on an item which is used in the trade (rather than consumed by the trade) and which is expected to have a certain useful life. The key requirement derived from case law is that there must be "an enduring benefit for the trade". Obvious examples of this would be the purchase of new machinery, buildings, etc.

In most situations, the legislation grants capital allowances at 12.5% or 4% for capital expenditure incurred. (In this regard, readers are referred to Chapter 16.) However, a full tax deduction for this type of expenditure could take eight years (12.5% per annum over 8 years = 100%). Therefore, businesses naturally seek to write off certain purchases as trade deductions. Readers should always bear in mind that capital items are commonly included in profit and loss repair charges and that these should be properly reclassified as capital for the purposes of the tax computation.

A number of common items that need to be adjusted for on the basis that they are capital as opposed to revenue in nature are now discussed in turn.

15.3.1.1 Repairs and renewals versus improvements

It is important to distinguish between repairs and improvements, as improvements will generally be regarded as capital in nature while repairs will be allowed as a revenue expense.

s81(2)(g)
TCA 97

Section 81(2)(g) TCA 1997 specifically disallows a deduction for "any capital employed in improvements of premises occupied for the purposes of the trade or profession".

In addition, the replacement of an asset in its entirety will generally be regarded as capital expenditure, while the replacement of a component part will be classified as tax-deductible repairs.

Due to the nature of claims by taxpayers and disagreements with tax inspectors over the distinction between repairs and improvements, numerous cases have been referred to the courts over the years. In the case of *JT Hodgins v Plunder & Pollak* (Supreme Court 19 January 1955, ITR Vol. 2 p. 267), a large building covering a weighbridge on the grounds of a factory was destroyed in a storm. The company built a much smaller building as a replacement and sought a tax deduction, which the Inspector disallowed. The Supreme Court decided that no improvement had occurred as the new building was considerably smaller than the previous one and was only a small part of the factory as a whole. Therefore, the expenditure was allowable.

15.3.1.2 Depreciation/Write-off of goodwill

Depreciation represents a notional write-off against profits for accounting purposes of the cost of the capital asset over its useful economic life. Depreciation rates for accounting purposes can be quite arbitrary, and policies can vary between businesses. Accordingly, accounting depreciation must be added back for tax purposes. A system of capital allowances or tax depreciation calculated on a more objective basis in accordance with clearly defined rules compensates for the add-back in relation to accounting depreciation. Readers are referred to Chapter 16 for further commentary on capital allowance claims.

Goodwill is generally taken to be the difference between the overall purchase price paid for a trade and the sum of the assets actually bought. Thus, it may be perceived as the price of purchasing the trade "name". Purchased goodwill is an intangible asset, which is capitalised in the balance sheet and usually written off over a period of 20 years or less. Like depreciation, the write-off represents a notional expense in relation to a capital item and, accordingly, is not allowable for tax purposes and must be added back in arriving at tax-adjusted Case I.

15.3.1.3 Amortisation of government grants

Capital grants are treated as deferred revenue for accounts purposes and are amortised or credited to the profit and loss account over the useful life of the asset purchased with the grant. Thus, their treatment is a mirror image of the treatment of depreciation. As the deferred revenue credited to the profit and loss account is a notional amount based on the perceived useful economic life of the asset, the amount amortised is not taxable and, accordingly, is deducted from the accounting profit figure for the purposes of arriving at tax-adjusted Case I. The benefit of the grant is effectively taxed through the capital allowance system, as the capital allowance claim on the asset is generally calculated on a net-of-government-grant basis.

15.3.1.4 Disposal of fixed assets

Profits or losses that arise on the sale of fixed assets arise as a result of a capital transaction. Consequently, under the general principles outlined in s81 TCA 1997, such profits/losses would not qualify as a Case I receipt/deduction and must be deducted/added back in the computation. Instead, relief may be given for any inherent loss on disposal through the capital allowances system in the form of a balancing allowance.

Where the sales proceeds exceed the written down value of the asset for capital allowance purposes, capital allowances claimed to date may be clawed back. In addition, it is possible that the transaction in question gives rise to a chargeable gain/loss, and this must always be borne in mind. For example, a loss recorded in the accounts on the sale of a building indicates that a chargeable transaction has taken place, and the chargeable gain or loss will need to be calculated in accordance with the capital gains tax principles outlined in Section IV of this book.

15.3.1.5 Expenses relating to the acquisition/disposal of capital assets

Expenses relating to capital transactions, e.g., legal fees, professional fees, estate agents, fees, etc., are not allowable Case I deductions and, accordingly, must be added back. However, these costs may be relieved under the capital gains tax system when the assets to which they relate are ultimately sold. It is important to bear in mind that professional fees, legal expenses, etc., of a revenue or trading nature are tax-deductible, e.g., debt-collection costs or preparation of legal contracts with suppliers or customers.

By concession, Revenue allows a deduction for interest on funds used to finance capital expenditure for the purposes of a trade.

15.3.2 "Wholly and exclusively"

s81
TCA 97

In order to be allowed as a deduction, expenditure must be "wholly and exclusively" incurred for the purposes of carrying on the trade. This is legislated for in s81 TCA 1997 under the heading "General rule as to deductions".

It provides that:

> "(1) The tax under Cases I and II of Schedule D shall be charged without any deduction other than is allowed by the Tax Acts.
>
> (2) Subject to the Tax Acts, in computing the amount of the profit or gains to be charged to tax under Case I or II of Schedule D, no sum shall be deducted in respect of –
>
> (a)   any disbursements or expenses, not being money wholly and exclusively laid out or expended for the purpose of the trade or profession …"

The word "wholly" refers to the amount of money expended. If only part of the money was spent for the purposes of the trade, then in principle it is not deductible. However, in practice, if it is possible to distinguish between the business and private expenses, Revenue will permit the business element to be deductible. Typically this apportionment is carried out on motor expenses, telephone and light and heat. The word "exclusively" refers to the motivation behind incurring the expense. The expense must be incurred solely for the purpose of the trade and there must be no other purpose or requirement involved.

It is important to note that where a business-owner incurs expenses which relate to the personal or private lives of employees of the business, such expenses are fully deductible on the basis that they are costs of rewarding employees and as such are a business expense. Thus, only the private elements of expenses relating to the owner of a business are disallowed. Such expenses, and indeed the owner's salary, are simply appropriations of the trading profit. Allowing a tax deduction for these amounts on the basis that they constitute salary or remuneration of some sort would involve incorrectly classifying the profits of the sole trade operation as Schedule E income.

Example 15.1

John's profit and loss account for the year ended 31 December 2009 is as follows:

	€	€
Sales		300,000
Cost of sales		(100,000)
Gross Profit		200,000
Less Expenses:		
Depreciation	20,000	
Salaries and wages*	65,000	
Light and heat	1,000	
Telephone	1,500	
Motor expenses	3,000	
Miscellaneous	4,000	(94,500)
Profit before tax		105,500

*The salaries and wages include a salary of €25,000 paid to John.

John operates from a room in his own home. The light and heat expense relates to the expense for the house as a whole for the year. John has agreed with his Inspector of Taxes that one-fifth of this amount is business related.

The telephone expense relates to a separate line, which John has put in place exclusively for business purposes.

The motor expenses comprise an amount of €1,000 in respect of John's own car, which is used 50% for business purposes (as agreed with the Inspector of Taxes), and €2,000 in respect of a salesman's car which is used 60% for business purposes.

The miscellaneous expenses are all allowable.

John's Case I computation is as follows:

	€	
Profit before tax	*105,500*	
Add back:		
Depreciation	*20,000*	
Drawings	*25,000*	
Light and heat	*800*	*(4/5 private)*
Motor expenses	*500*	*(private element of owner's motor expenses)*
Tax-adjusted Case I	*151,800*	

> *Note:* *The owner cannot pay himself a salary and the amount paid is in effect drawings or an appropriation of the profits of the business. He is not taxed under Schedule E on this amount or on any other benefits accruing from his involvement in the business.*
>
> *The private element of the salesman's motor expenses are allowable on the basis that they are a cost of rewarding an employee. The benefit accruing to the salesman would be taxable in his hands under Schedule E as a benefit-in-kind. In this regard, readers are referred to Chapter 21.*

The meaning of the term "wholly and exclusively" has been considered frequently in both Irish and UK case law. The case of *Mallalieu v Drummond* ([1981] STC 391) illustrates the rigid application of the principle by the courts. In this case, a barrister was seeking a deduction for the cost of the black clothing that she wore in court. Her main argument was that as she would not ordinarily wear such clothing, she was using it "wholly and exclusively" for her trade. Therefore, the expenditure on the clothing should be deductible. The case was ultimately referred to the House of Lords where it was held that as decent human beings must wear clothing, the expenditure was not incurred "wholly and exclusively" for the trade, even though she would not normally wear this type of clothing.

It is important to bear in mind that expenses, which are not wholly and exclusively for the purpose of the trade, may be deductible against another specific category of income or gain. For example, a rates charge on a property rented out by the sole trader will be disallowed against Case I but may be allowed against Case V income. Alternatively, the expense may be deductible against total income as a charge. For example, a deed of covenant payment by a sole trader to his 70-year-old widowed mother will not be an allowable Case I deduction. Accordingly, if booked to the business profit and loss account, the amount will have to be added back for the purposes of arriving at taxable Case I. However, the amount will be deductible from total income as a charge. In this regard, readers are referred to Chapter 12.

A useful approach in dealing with the issues considered thus far may be to look at adjustments to the profit before tax figure (i.e., add-backs and deductions) from the point of view of income or capital and then further apply the wholly and exclusively test in each case. The following diagram illustrates the suggested approach.

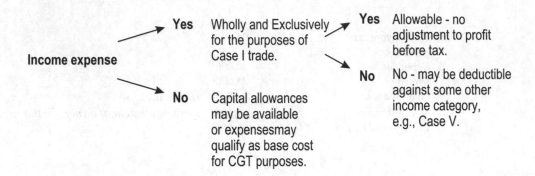

Further adjustments must be looked at in the light of the treatment of movements on provisions and specific legislative principles.

15.3.3   Movements in general provisions and accruals

Any general provisions that do not relate to specific transactions or events will not be allowed as a deduction and should be added back in the tax computation. An example of a general provision is a provision for bad debts calculated as a percentage of debtors. Only bad debts written off in the accounts as irrecoverable and provisions for bad debts, which can be reliably estimated and which relate to specific identifiable debtor balances, will be allowed as a deduction.

This logic also applies to other provisions. For example, a general stock obsolescence provision calculated as a percentage of closing stock would not be allowable, but a provision relating to some specific items of damaged or non-saleable stock would be allowed in full. However, standard examination questions generally tend to focus on movements in bad debt provisions as such provisions are commonly encountered in practice. An understanding of the underlying effect of movements on provisions on the final profit figure is imperative to an understanding of the tax adjustments necessary. Thus, readers are advised to study the commentary in Appendix 1 in relation to the accounting and tax treatment of bad debts and bad debt provisions before considering the following examples.

Example 15.2

The bad debts charge in the profit and loss account of Mr Andrews is €120,000 and can be broken down as follows:

	€	€
Trade debts written off as irrecoverable		*60,000*
Debts previously written off now recovered		*(15,000)*
Movement in Specific Bad Debt Provision		
– Opening provision	*25,000*	
– Closing provision	*40,000*	*15,000*

	€	€
Movement in General Bad Debt Provision		
– Opening provision	*30,000*	
– Closing provision	*90,000*	*60,000*
		120,000

Tax Implications

1. The bad debts written off are allowed as a Case I deduction in full, while the bad debts recovered are taxed as trading income.

2. The increase in the Specific Bad Debt Provision of €15,000 is allowed in full as a Case I deduction.

3. The increase in the General Bad Debt Provision of €60,000 is disallowed in full and must be added back in the Case I tax-adjusted profit computation.

Example 15.3

Included in the profit and loss account of Ms Simpson is a bad debts charge of €90,000. This charge can be broken down as follows:

		€	€
Bad debts written off			*55,000*
Bad debts recovered			*(10,000)*
Specific Bad Debt Provision	*– Opening*	*20,000*	
	–	*90,000*	*70,000*
Closing			
General Bad Debt Provision	*– Opening*	*65,000*	*(25,000)*
	–	*40,000*	*(25,000)*
Closing			
			90,000

Assess the components of the above expense for tax purposes.

The tax consequences of the above bad debt charge of €90,000 are as follows:

■ Bad debts written off as a fully allowable expense against Case I (no add-back);

■ Bad debts recovered is taxed as trading income (no deduction);

■ An increase in Specific Bad Debt Provision of €70,000 is allowed in full as a Case I deduction (no add-back);

■ A decrease in General Bad Debt Provision of €25,000 is not taxable, as a corresponding increase in a general provision is not an allowable expense. Therefore, the amount of the decrease should be deducted from the accounting profit to arrive at the amount of tax-adjusted Case I income.

Readers should bear in mind that general bad debt provisions are unlikely to feature in company accounts prepared under IFRS in the future. Readers are referred to the commentary in Chapter 29 (29.3) for further commentary on the treatment of bad debt provisions under IFRS.

15.3.3.1 Accounting treatment of provisions

Where businesses adopt the accounting treatment of provisions recommended by either Financial Reporting Standard (FRS) 12 or International Accounting Standard (IAS) 37, concerns over adjustments of profits in respect of provisions are to some extent eliminated. However, in general the provisions of accounting standards only apply to companies. Prior to the introduction of FRS 12 in 1999, it was common practice for companies to include general provisions in their accounts based on "roughly" estimated future liabilities.

FRS 12 deals with the accounting treatment of provisions and contingent liabilities in company accounts. It deals only with provisions for expected liabilities and not with provisions for impairment of assets, such as provisions for depreciation and bad debts. The standard only allows a provision to be charged to the profit and loss account when the following conditions are met:

(a) there is a present obligation;

(b) arising as a result of a past event;

(c) it is probable that expenditure will be required;

(d) the expenditure can be reliably estimated.

Recent case law has strengthened the links between accounting standards and accounts for taxation purposes. In *Herbert Smith v Honour* ([1999], STC 173), the UK tax authorities sought to disallow a provision for future rents of a building, which the company was no longer occupying. This provision was allowable under FRS 12 as it met all four conditions noted above. In his decision allowing the provision as a tax deduction, the judge stated "if a particular statute provision applies to the situation, commercial accounting must give way". Therefore, as there was no specific legislation dealing with the company's provision, it was deemed to be an allowable expense. The Irish Revenue Commissioners issued a statement in September 2000 stating that provisions for losses in accordance with FRS 12 are now allowable, whereas they may previously have sought to disallow them. It is anticipated that this guidance will also apply to provisions in accordance with IAS 37.

Thus, if a company intends repairing a roof in the next 12 months at an expected cost of €7,000 and has signed a contract for this work, the creation of a provision for such repairs this year is fully allowable for tax purposes.

The reader should bear in mind that even if GAAP are followed in creating provisions, the deduction must still pass the "wholly and exclusively" test of s81 to ensure that relief is granted. In addition, provisions in accounts for capital expenditure would not be allowed whereas a provision for an item, which is revenue in nature (e.g., a provision for redundancies), may be allowable.

15.3.4 Specific adjustments

Notwithstanding what has already been said regarding provisions, the income/capital distinction and the "wholly and exclusively" test, there are certain items, that although revenue in nature and incurred for the purposes of carrying on the trade, are disallowed for tax purposes. Further, adjustments must be looked at in the light of specific legislative principles. Some of the common "statutory" adjustments are considered below. The analysis below also looks at certain adjusting items, which may fall within one of the categories already addressed at 15.3.1 and 15.3.2 above, but which nonetheless merit separate discussion because of the frequency with which they are found in the profit and loss account.

15.3.4.1 Entertainment expenses

s840
TCA 97

The legislation prohibits a tax deduction in respect of business entertainment.

Business entertainment is defined in the legislation as:

"... entertainment (including the provision of accommodation, food and drink and any other form of hospitality in any circumstances whatsoever) provided directly or indirectly – in connection with a trade".

This disallowance will operate where the entertainment is provided by a person carrying on the trade, or by a member of staff or any other person performing services for the proprietor. Thus, amounts expended on the entertainment of customers, suppliers, professional advisors, etc, must be added back for tax purposes.

The term "business entertainment" does not extend to the provision of facilities for members of staff unless the provision to them of these facilities is incidental to the entertainment of clients. Hence, expenses such as the provision of a canteen primarily for the staff is allowable, as is specific entertainment of staff, e.g., a staff Christmas party. However, the expense of providing entertainment for staff members, which is merely incidental to the provision of entertainment for clients or customers, is disallowed.

Example 15.4

Tom incurred the following costs relating to the launch of a new product:

	€
Staff dinner after final testing of product	*1,000*
Hotel room hire for launch	*2,000*
Food and drink for clients at launch	*1,500*
Dinner for staff and selected clients	*3,000*
	7,500

The costs relating to client entertainment are not allowed and are added back, being the amounts of €1,500 and €3,000.

The distinction between business entertainment and business development is an important one and while it may be considered that attracting potential customers is business development, careful consideration needs to be given to each item of expenditure. The following types of expenditure will generally be allowed as business development:

- promotion of events;

- sponsorship of competitions;

- associations with business seminars, including hiring of facilities.

15.3.4.2 Gifts to customers

s840(5)
TCA 97

The disallowance of business entertainment also extends to gifts. This would appear to extend to the cost of making gifts to customers at Christmas. This disallowance operates even though the making of such gifts may be considered important in maintaining the goodwill of the business. However, a distinction may however be drawn between entertainment and promotion and Revenue will not normally seek to disallow the handing out of free samples of products to customers or potential customers.

15.3.4.3 Interest on under-/over- and late payment of taxes

In general, interest is charged at a daily rate of 0.0273% (0.0219% from 1 July 2009) on the late payment of taxes. Such interest is not an allowable deduction for tax purposes. Correspondingly, any interest received as a result of a tax overpayment is refunded at a daily rate of 0.011% and is exempt from tax. This interest income should be deducted from the accounting profits in arriving at tax-adjusted Case I.

15.3.4.4 Patent royalties

s243
TCA 97

Patent royalties are treated as charges for tax purposes (see Chapter 12). As such they are not allowed as a trade expense and must be added back in calculating tax-adjusted figures.

Case I.

15.3.4.5 Political subscriptions and donations

Political subscriptions and non-trade contributions are not allowable as they would not be "wholly and exclusively" for the trade under s81. Thus, they must be added back. Trade subscriptions are allowable.

Relief is available for certain charitable donations and donations to sporting bodies where certain conditions are met. These conditions have already been discussed in Chapter 11 and are reproduced here in Appendix II.

15.3.4.6 Taxes and penalties

Any taxes or penalties charged to the profit and loss account, such as stamp duty, parking fines, etc, are not allowed and must therefore be added back.

15.3.4.7 Motor leasing expenses restriction

s377
TCA 97

Motor lease repayments (interest and capital) are reduced to the proportion which a €24,000 ceiling bears to the list price of the car.

Leasing charges for car $\times$ $\dfrac{\text{Retail Price when manufactured} - €24,000}{\text{Retail Price}}$ = Restriction

The €24,000* limit applies for the tax year 2007 onwards.

(A full list of the historical limits is given in Chapter 16.)

Example 15.5

List price of car: €25,000

Leasing charges: €4,500

Restriction = €4,500 $\times$ $\dfrac{(€25,000 - €24,000)}{€25,000}$ = €180

Example 15.6

Mr. Gamma had bought a new car for €25,000 under a finance lease in June 2005 for the purposes of his trade. The total running costs for the car for the accounting period to 31 May 2009* were €2,300 while the finance lease repayments for the car were €1,800.

s377
TCA 97

The motor leasing charge restriction under s377 TCA 97 is calculated as follows:

€1,800 $\times$ $\dfrac{€25,000 - €24,000}{€25,000}$ = €72

Therefore the leasing restriction to be added back is €72.

It is important to note that it is the retail price of the car when it was manufactured that is included in the formula and not the cost to the company of acquiring the car in the case of second-hand cars.

* With effect from 1 July 2008, a new regime for calculating leasing charges on business car was introduced by reference to the carbon emissions level of the car.

Categories of cars:

    – Up to 155g/km (AB & C)

    – Between 156 and 190g/km (D & E)

    – Above 190g/km (F & G)

The specified limit remains at €24,000, however, there are changes to its application:

Categories A, B & C

• The limit of €24,000 is applied even where the actual cost is less than €24,000.

Categories D & E

- Limit is 50% of the lower of cost and €24,000.

Categories F & G

- No allowances are available.

Example 15.7

John White leases a business car with carbon emissions level of 150g/km (Category C). The list price of the car is €36,000 and annual leasing charges of €5,000. The allowable leasing charges are:

$$5,000 \times \frac{36,000 - 24,000}{36,000} = \frac{\begin{array}{c} 5,000 \\ (1,667) \end{array}}{3,333}$$

If the list price had been €12,000 (assume same leasing charges), the allowable charges would be doubled. The leasing charges are proportionally increased by reference to the specified limit as a multiple of the list price, i.e., 24,000/12,000.

15.3.4.8 Finance lease payments

A business is entitled to a full deduction for finance lease payments including both capital and interest elements (this is adjusted by adding back the lease interest and allowing the lease payment/rental in full, or by simply allowing a deduction for the capital element of the payment).

For a detailed commentary on the accounting treatment of finance leases and a worked example of the necessary adjustments for tax purposes, readers are referred to Appendix III.

15.3.4.9 Operating leases

The total lease rentals are charged to the profit and loss account over the period of the lease. As with a finance lease, the lessee is entitled to tax relief for the total rentals arising, but in this case no adjustment is required to the computation as the full rentals have already been deducted in arriving at profit before tax. There is no capital element in the lease rentals.

15.3.4.10 Pension fund contributions

s774
TCA 97

Contributions to a Revenue-approved Pension Scheme are allowed on a paid basis. This differs from the accountancy treatment under FRS 17 which ensures that the charge to the profit and loss is the annual contribution whether paid in the period or not. Any contribution not actually paid in the period is disallowed for tax purposes. The contribution will only be allowed in the period in which it is actually paid. Additionally, where an employer makes abnormally high "special" contributions, Revenue will determine a period over which the deduction will be allowed depending on the circumstances. The "spread" is usually calculated by dividing the special contribution by the normal annual contribution.

Example 15.7

The normal annual contribution of a company, which is allowed as a Case I deduction, is €50,000. During the year, the company made an additional special lump sum contribution of €150,000 to the Approved Scheme. The special contribution will be allowable over a three-year period. Therefore €100,000 will be added back and €50,000 claimed in each of the next two years.

15.3.4.11 Insurance expenses

The main focus in considering insurance expenses should be to ensure that all insurance premiums have been incurred for the purposes of the trade and do not contain any elements of private expenditure, e.g., private house insurance being included on a business policy.

Certain insurance expenditure incurred on capital items will be allowable, e.g., building and contents insurance for the premises from which the business trades. Thus, there are certain cases where although an item is capital in nature, or the underlying asset is capital, the expense will be allowed. The same holds true for the interest expense incurred in acquiring a trading premises. Such deductions are allowed due to a Revenue concession as opposed to strict legislative interpretation.

For example, Keyperson insurance has insurance on the lives of key individuals in the business – for example, an employee who is central to the management and control of the business and who may be responsible for a large element of the goodwill of the business. It may be considered that the death, sickness or disability of such an individual could give rise to a substantial loss of profits or trade of the business. Notwithstanding that, the taxpayer is really insuring against loss of profits, the triggering event would be the death of the key individual. Keyperson insurance is allowed as a deduction for the purposes of the tax computation where certain conditions are met. However, it should be noted that any benefit paid under such a policy will be treated as a trading receipt for the period in which it is paid. If the payment does not qualify for a deduction, then any receipt/payment from the proceeds of the policy will not be taxable.

15.3.4.12 Embezzlement

As a broad rule, losses arising as a result of embezzlement or misappropriation by an employee are likely to be allowed, but not those arising from the misdeeds of a proprietor.

15.3.4.13 Illegal payment

A new s83A TCA 97 effective from 1 January 2008 disallows expenditure (e.g., bribes), the making of which constitutes a criminal offence. The disallowance of the expenditure extends to payments both inside and outside the State.

15.3.4.14 Pre-trading expenditure

s82 TCA 97 Section 82 TCA 97, provides that Revenue expenditure incurred within three years prior to the commencement of trading is deductible where the following conditions are met:

- The expense must be of a type which would otherwise be allowable as a trading expense.

- The expense and charges can only be offset against income from the trade or profession and not against any other income.

- The relief is only available for new businesses.

The expenditure falling within the provisions will be deemed to have been incurred at the time when the trade or profession is commenced.

15.3.4.15 Trademark registration

s86 TCA 97 A specific deduction is provided by s86 TCA 97 for the cost of the registration of trademarks. The accounting treatment may have been to capitalise this amount and write it off over a period. This can be reversed and a deduction taken in the year to which the expenditure relates.

15.3.4.16 Double rent deduction

A double rent deduction may be allowed for rent paid by businesses in respect of certain properties eligible for special schemes of relief, generally on the basis of geographical location, e.g., Temple Bar and other urban renewal areas. Thus, a business paying a rent of €100,000 is entitled to charge another €100,000 in calculating its taxable trading income.

15.3.4.17 Employee expenses

The following items are discussed in turn:

(i) wages and salaries;

(ii) long-term unemployed relief;

(iii) redundancy payments;

(iv) travel and subsistence.

(i) Wages and salaries

Wages and salaries of employees are normally allowed in full on the basis that they are wholly and exclusively incurred for the purposes of carrying on the trade. However, where payments are deemed to be "excessive", the full payment may be disallowed on the basis that it is not necessary for the carrying on of the trade.

In the case of *Copeman (HM Inspector of Taxes) v William Flood & Sons Ltd,* 24 TC 53, it was held that remuneration paid to directors of a company was not wholly, exclusively and necessarily incurred for the purposes of the trade.

As already illustrated in 15.3.2 above, any withdrawals taken by the trader (even though they might refer to this as "wages") are not allowable and must be added back in the computation. One of the important things to note is that a sole trader is assessed to income tax on profit; the drawings are irrelevant to the trader's tax position. If wages are paid to the trader's spouse or family, they are allowable provided they are "wholly and exclusively" for the purpose of the trade.

(ii) Long-term unemployed

s88A
TCA 97

Section 88A TCA 97 provides a double deduction for employee salaries and employer's PRSI contributions where long-term unemployed individuals are employed. Employers can claim this double deduction for the first three years during which salaries are paid to qualifying employees.

To be a qualifying employee, the individual must have been unemployed for at least 12 months and must have been in receipt of specified social welfare payments or must be in a category approved for the purposes of the scheme by the Minister for Social, Community and Family Affairs.

A double deduction is claimed by allowing the expense in calculating accounting profit, and by granting a further deduction for the expense in the tax computation.

(iii) Redundancy payments

s203
TCA 97

Where an employer pays a lump sum under s46 Redundancy Payments Act 1967 to an employee, that sum is an allowable deduction in computing taxable profits. The deduction is available in computing profits under Case I. Where the Minister makes the payment in the first instance but is reimbursed by the employer, it is regarded as being paid by the employer.

Where the employer is entitled to a rebate from the Department of Enterprise and Employment, any rebate must be treated as a trade receipt. Rebates of up to 60% of the termination payment are granted in the case of a genuine redundancy, i.e., where the function that the employee performed is no longer required by the employer.

Where the payment is made after the discontinuance of the trade or profession it is regarded as made on the last day of the trade or profession.

(iv) Travel and subsistence

Payments for travel and subsistence may be made on the basis of vouched receipts or under Revenue-approved rates. Payments in excess of Revenue-approved amounts should be cleared in advance. Travel between home and the office is not treated as an allowable business expense.

A businessman who pays for his own lunch does not spend his money exclusively for the purposes of his business – *Caillebotte (HM Inspector of Taxes) v Quinn,* 50 TC 222.

15.4   Income not Taxable under Case I/II

While the commentary on the distinction between revenue and capital, the principle of "wholly and exclusively", movements on provisions and statutory adjustments is relevant to both income and expense items, the analysis thus far has focussed on expense items. The purpose of this section is to focus attention on certain receipts and items of income, which regularly appear in the profit and loss account.

All items of income, which do not relate to Case I trading activities must be deducted and instead categorised under the appropriate case, or alternatively, classified as a capital receipt for capital gains tax purposes, or alternatively classified as tax-exempt income. It is important to note that the figure deducted is that which is credited to the profit and loss account. This may be different from the figure to be included under the relevant case heading.

■ Deposit interest is taxable under Case III if no DIRT was deducted at source and under Case IV if tax was deducted at source.

■ Irish source rental income is taxable under Case V.

■ Irish dividends or distributions received are taxable under Schedule F and accordingly, must be deducted from the "profit before tax" figure in arriving at tax-adjusted Case I/II.

s44 TCA 97   ■ Interest on Government Securities (s44 TCA 97): interest received on securities issued by the Minister of Finance is exempt. Other interest received on Government Securities is paid without deduction of tax at source and is therefore taxable under Schedule D Case III.

■ Revenue Grants

s223, 224, 225, 226 TCA 97   Revenue grants are taxable apart from the following, which are specifically exempt from tax (s226 TCA 97): the Employment Incentive Scheme, the Market Development Fund, the Employment Subsidy Scheme, EU Programme for Peace and Reconciliation in Northern Ireland and Border Counties (s226 TCA 97), initiatives of the International Fund for Ireland (s226 TCA 97), Údarás na Gaeltachta Employment Grants (s223 TCA 97 and s224 TCA 97).

■ Employment grants given under s25 of the Industrial Development Act 1986 or under s12 of the Industrial Development Act 1993 are not taxable.

■ There may be other exempt receipts included in a trader's accounts that should be excluded for the purposes of income tax. These include:

■ certain income from stallions* (s231 TCA 97),

- profits or gains arising from the occupation of woodlands managed commercially with a view to profits* (s232 TCA 97),

- income from greyhound stud fees* arising after 6 April 1996 (s233 TCA 97).

- Insurance proceeds of a revenue nature are fully taxable, whereas if they relate to capital items, i.e., buildings or machinery, they must be adjusted for (i.e., deducted from the "profit before tax" figure). In these circumstances, they may give rise to a chargeable gain.

- Compensation and damages will very often be classified as capital in nature and accordingly, should be deducted in arriving at tax-adjusted Case I. However, where receipts are in respect of revenue items, e.g., loss of earnings, they are taxable in full and no adjustment is necessary.

Readers are referred to Chapter 8, Section 8.6 for dates from which this exemption is abolished.

15.5   Professional Services Withholding Tax

s520   The Finance Act 1987 introduced rules for the operation of a withholding tax on professional

TCA 97   fees paid by Government and other semi-State bodies. The withholding tax is deducted at the standard rate of income tax on fees paid. The individual (or company) who suffers having to pay a withholding tax can claim a credit (or a refund – subject to certain conditions).

15.5.1   Who deducts the withholding tax?

All "accountable persons" are required to deduct withholding tax. "Accountable persons" include Government Departments, health boards and semi-State bodies.

15.5.2   On what fees is the withholding tax operated?

The withholding tax will be operated on all professional fees. These include:

- services of a medical, dental, pharmaceutical, optical, aural or veterinary nature;

- services of an architectural, engineering, or surveying nature and related services;

- services of an accountancy, auditing, or finance nature and services of financial, economic, marketing, advertising firms or other consultancies;

- services of a solicitor or barrister or other legal services;

- geological services;

- training services on behalf of FÁS.

15.5.3 Credit for withholding tax

Credit for withholding tax is allowed by reference to the withholding tax deducted in the basis period for the relevant tax year.

Example 15.8

Dr. Purcell is a medical doctor. He completes medical examinations on behalf of the gardaí. The amount of fee income relating to this work in his accounts year ended 31 December 2009 was €10,000. The withholding tax deducted at source was €2,000. The gross income of €10,000 will be incorporated into his fee income for the year and a credit will be given for the retention tax withheld.

Consequently Dr. Purcell will receive a net cheque of €8,000 from the Gardaí. Assuming Dr. Purcell pays income tax at a marginal rate of 41%, his tax position will be as follows (ignoring Income Levy, PRSI and Health Levy):

	€
Income	*10,000*
Taxed at 41%	*4,100*
Less Credit for withholding tax deducted	*(2,000)*
Net Liability	*2,100*

WHAT YOU SHOULD NOW KNOW

On completion of this chapter, you should be able to:

- ✓ Describe the method used in practice to calculate the profits of a trade or profession.

- ✓ Calculate the tax-adjusted Case I/II income for a sole trader/professional.

- ✓ Describe the treatment of various items included in the profit and loss account.

- ✓ Explain how movements in provisions are treated for tax purposes.

- ✓ Discuss the meaning of the term "wholly and exclusively".

- ✓ Distinguish between capital items and items that are revenue in nature.

- ✓ Complete Questions and the Assignments in Irish Taxation Law and Practice, Volume 2.

Appendix I

Bad and Doubtful Trade Debts

The accounting treatment of "Bad Debts" can be categorised as follows:

(a) Bad debts, i.e., amounts due that are considered irrecoverable, are written off against accounting profit as a trade expense.

(b) Bad debts subsequently recovered are credited to the profit and loss account as a trade receipt.

(c) An increase in the Specific Bad Debt Provision is treated as a trade expense against the accounting profit, as is an increase in the General Bad Debt Provision.

(d) A decrease in the Specific Bad Debt Provision is treated as a trade receipt, as is a decrease in the General Bad Debt Provision. Thus, such amounts are credited to the profit and loss account (i.e., they increase accounting profit).

The tax implications of each element of the overall charge can be identified as follows:

(1) Bad debts written off are allowable in full as a Case I deduction, e.g., if the debtor has gone into liquidation without paying the debt, it is written off as irrecoverable.

(2) Bad debts recovered are treated as taxable Case I income. For example, if a liquidator of a debtor company recovers monies from the sale of assets and distributes this to the creditors, the debt which was written off, but which has been recovered, or is known to be recoverable, is now taxable.

(3) An increase in the Specific Bad Debt Provision is an allowable Case I deduction, e.g., an amount provided for specifically, debt by debt against those debts which are genuinely considered doubtful.

For example:	€
Opening Specific Bad Debt Provision 1/1/2009	10,000
Closing Specific Bad Debt Provision 31/12/2009	25,000
Increase in Specific Bad Debt Provision (expense)	15,000

This expense charged to profit and loss account is fully allowable as a Case I deduction.

(4) A decrease in the Specific Bad Debt Provision is treated as taxable Case I income, i.e., the amount credited to profit and loss account is treated as a fully taxable trade receipt.

(5) An increase in the General Bad Debt Provision is not an allowable Case I deduction and must therefore be added back. This provision is an amount of the total debtors at the period end (usually a percentage of the total debtors) which the trader feels will be "bad" based on previous experience.

	€
Opening General Bad Debt Provision 1/1/2009	(9,000)
Closing General Bad Debt Provision 31/12/2009	16,000
Increase in General Bad Debt Provision	7,000

This expense charged to profit and loss account is not allowable as a Case I deduction.

6) A decrease in the General Bad Debt Provision is not treated as taxable income and is therefore deducted from the accounting profit.

Appendix II

Donations

Approved Bodies

s848A
TCA 97

Up to 2001 various reliefs existed for donations to different bodies. The Finance Act 2001 introduced a new s848A and Sch. 26A into the TCA 97, which effectively consolidated all of the legislation relating to donations, to provide for relief in a uniform manner for donations to "approved bodies". These include bodies already eligible to receive tax-deductible donations (e.g., bodies providing education in the arts, certain bodies approved for research, etc., and educational bodies authorised by the Revenue Commissioners as meeting certain conditions).

Qualifying Donation

A donation must also satisfy the following conditions:

■ minimum donation of €250, no maximum* figure except where associated with the charity and a 10% cap on income applies;

■ it must not be subject to any condition of repayment;

■ neither the donor nor any person connected with him/her can receive a benefit in consequence of making the donation directly or indirectly;

■ it is not conditional on, nor associated with or part of an arrangement involving the acquisition of property by the approved body otherwise than by way of gift from the donor or person connected with him;

■ the donation is not otherwise deductible for tax.

Readers are referred to Chapter 8, Section 8.7 for restriction on reliefs for high income earners.

Approved Bodies

The following are the types of "approved bodies" that qualify for tax relief:

■ eligible charities (who have been tax-exempt for at least two years);

■ educational institutions or bodies including primary, second-level or third-level, if they meet certain conditions (e.g., their programmes are approved by the Minister for Education and Science or the institution provides courses which are validated by the Higher Education Training and Awards Council);

■ the Scientific and Technological Education (Investment) Fund;

- a body approved for Education in the Arts by the Minister for Finance;

- First Step Limited;
- certain other named bodies, including the following:

    - The Equine Foundation,

    - The Institute of Ophthalmology,

    - The Mater College for Research and Postgraduate Education,

    - St. Luke's Institute of Cancer Research.

A body to which s209 of the Taxes Consolidation Act 1997 applies, i.e., a body for the promotion of the observance of the Universal Declaration of Human Rights or the implementation of the European Convention for the protection of Human Rights and Fundamental Freedoms or both,

    - The Foundation for Investing in Communities Limited or any of its 90% subsidiaries as may be approved by the Minister for Finance.

    - US-Alliance Limited.

Donations to Certain Sports Bodies

**s847A
TCA 97**

Section 41 Finance Act 2002 introduced a new section, s847A, to the TCA 97, which operates in a similar manner to s848A as outlined above.

Section 847A provides for relief for qualifying donations to approved sports bodies, to enable the sports body to construct facilities, purchase significant equipment or to repay a loan to carry out any of these transactions.

Approved Body

An approved body is one which is established to promote athletic or amateur games or sports. In order to qualify as an approved sports body, the organisation must hold a valid tax clearance certificate, and also a valid certificate from Revenue stating that the organisation qualifies for the exemption from income tax/corporation tax set out in s235 TCA 97 (i.e., bodies established to promote athletic or amateur games or sports).

The Relief

For a donation to qualify for relief it must be at least €250 in the year of assessment; there is no upper limit on the qualifying donation. The donation does not reduce the individual's income for the purposes of determining his or her net relevant earnings.

Approved Project

To qualify for relief the donation must be used to fund a project, which has been approved by the Minister for Tourism, Sports and Recreation, and for which the sports body holds a valid certificate. The Minister will not certify projects costing in excess of €40 million. To be approved the project must fall into one of the following categories:

■ purchase of land or buildings (or the construction or refurbishment of a building or part of a building) to be used for sporting activities by the approved sports body;

■ purchase of permanently based equipment to be used for sporting activities by the approved sports body;

■ the improvement of playing pitches, surfaces or facilities by the approved sports body;

■ the payment of loan interest on funds borrowed by the approved sports body for any of the above activities.

Appendix III

Finance Lease Repayments

Under GAAP, a finance lease is a contract between a lessor and a lessee for the hire of a specific asset whereby substantially all of the **risks and rewards** of ownership of that asset are transferred to the lessee. It usually involves payment by the lessee to a lessor of the **full** cost of the capital asset together with a return on the finance provided by the lessor. The accounting treatment of such a finance lease is as follows:

1. The capital cost of the fixed asset is capitalised with a corresponding liability created for the "capital element" of the finance lease.

2. Each lease repayment to the lessor includes a "capital" and "finance charge" element. The capital element is used to reduce the lease liability while the finance charge element is debited to the Profit and Loss Account as a trading expense.

For tax purposes, because assets held under finance leases will generally not qualify for capital allowances, the full amount of the finance lease repayment, i.e., both the capital and the interest element, will be deductible in arriving at taxable Case I. Thus, the appropriate treatment is as follows:

1. The amount of finance lease charges which have been debited to the profit and loss account as a trading expense are added back in the Case I computation.

2. The company is allowed a deduction against Case I income for the total of the finance lease repayments (capital and interest element) made during the accounting period.

This figure is derived as follows:

		€
	Opening leasing liabilities per balance sheet due within one year and after more than one year	X
Plus:	Capital cost of fixed asset additions acquired under finance leases during the period	X
Plus:	Finance lease charges to the profit and loss account	X
Less:	Closing leasing liabilities per balance sheet due within one year and after more than one year	(X)
■	Finance lease repayments made in period	X

It is this final figure, which is allowed as a deduction against Case I profits.

Example Appendix III.1:

B Limited:

The following information is relevant for the accounting period ended 31 March 2009:

			€
1.	1 April 2008: Opening Lease Liabilities	< 1 year	6,000
		> 1 year	12,000
2.	A machine was acquired under a finance lease in October 2008. The capitalised cost of this fixed asset is €14,000.		
3.	Total finance lease charges included in the profit and loss account for the year is €7,700.		
4.	31 March 2009: Closing Lease Liabilities	< 1 year	10,000
		> 1 year	16,000

Tax consequences

1. The figure of €7,700 for the finance lease charges is added back to the accounting profit in the tax-adjusted profits computation.

2. The company is allowed a deduction for the total finance lease repayments, calculated as follows:

		€
1/4/2008	Opening Lease Liabilities	18,000
Plus:	Machine acquired under finance lease	14,000
Plus:	Finance lease charges expensed	7,700
Less:	Closing Lease Liabilities at 31/3/2009	(26,000)
■	Total finance lease repayments	13,700

Assets acquired under a hire-purchase agreement qualify for capital allowances on the cost of the asset with no allowance for the lease payments made.

16

CAPITAL ALLOWANCES

In this chapter, you will deal with the following:

- Meaning of plant and machinery and industrial buildings

- Allowances available for capital expenditure

- Basis for relief

- Implications of disposal of assets

16.1 Introduction

In computing taxable profits, generally no deduction is allowable for capital expenditure or the depreciation of capital assets. To compensate for this statutory disallowance, capital allowances are available in respect of certain capital expenditure on plant and machinery, motor cars and industrial buildings.

In addition, capital allowances have been offered as a 'carrot' to encourage investment in certain types of capital expenditure projects, e.g., hotels, private nursing homes, urban renewal buildings, private convalescent homes, buildings used for certain childcare facilities, buildings used for third-level educational purposes and buildings used as private hospitals. Readers are referred to *Income Tax* by McAteer, Reddin and Deegan for commentary on the specific regimes applicable to these incentive measures. The analysis here is concerned with the more general rules, which apply to the broad categories of expenditure, namely, plant and machinery, motor vehicles and industrial buildings. Each category of asset is considered separately as capital allowances are calculated in different ways for different types of asset.

16.2 Plant and Machinery

16.2.1 Case law

There is no definition of plant and machinery in the Income Tax Acts. In theory, the term should therefore be given its ordinary meaning. However, over the years, the term "plant" has acquired an artificial and largely judge-made meaning. One of the earliest definitions of plant was given by Lindley L.J. in the case of *Yarmouth v France* (19 QBD647) when he stated:

> *"In its ordinary sense, it includes whatever apparatus is used by a businessman for carrying on his business, not his stock in trade which he buys or makes for sale; but all goods and chattels, fixed or movable, live or dead, which he keeps for permanent employment in his business."*

Lindley's definition contains three important elements:

(i) The item must be an "apparatus".

(ii) It must be used for the carrying on of a business.

(iii) It must be kept for permanent use in the business.

This test was further refined in the case of *J Lyons & Co Ltd v Attorney-General* (1944 1 All ER 477) by Uthwatt J. who posed the question as to whether the lamps which were the subject matter of that case were "properly to be regarded as part of the setting in which the business is carried on, or as part of the apparatus used for carrying on the business?"

In the case of *Jarrold v John Good & Sons Ltd* (40 TC 681), it was recognised that "setting" and "plant" are not mutually exclusive concepts. That case decided that the fundamental test as to whether an apparatus constitutes "plant" is whether it fulfils the function of plant, in that it is the means by which a trading operation is carried out. Applying the test in that case, it was found that special partitioning used by the taxpayer to subdivide floor space to accommodate fluctuating office accommodation requirements was plant.

The "functional" test set out in *Jarrold v Good* has been applied in many subsequent tax cases. The cases fall into two broad categories. The first category consists of cases where the point at issue is whether or not a whole structure constitutes plant. In the case of *Schofield v R & H Hall Ltd* (40 TC 538) the company had built silos on the dockside. Grain could be delivered from ships to the silos from which, in turn, it could be dispensed to customers easily. It was decided that the silos were plant for the purposes of capital allowances. In the case of *IRC v Barclay Curle & Co Ltd* (45 TC 221), the taxpayer had constructed a dry dock, a process requiring the excavation of the site and the construction of a concrete lining. The Revenue agreed that such expenditure as that incurred on the dock gate, the operating gear and the electrical and pumping installations related to plant, but argued that the expenses of excavation and concreting did not.

However, the expenditure on the concrete lining was held to be in respect of plant because it could not be regarded as the mere setting in which the trade was carried on but was an integral part of the means required for the trading operation. Hence, a structure, which fulfils the function of plant, is *prima facie*, plant.

The second category of cases concerns the application of the functional test so as to distinguish between setting and plant. The operation of the functional test in these circumstances is well illustrated by three important UK tax cases:

- *Benson v Yard Arm Club Ltd* ([1979] STC 266);

- *IRC v Scottish & Newcastle Breweries Ltd* ([1982] STC 296); and

- *Wimpy International Ltd v Warland* ([1988] STC 149).

In the case of *Benson v Yard Arm Club Ltd*, the taxpayer acquired a ship and incurred expenditure for the purpose of converting it into a floating restaurant. The taxpayer claimed that the expenditure was on plant and claimed capital allowances on it. It was held that the ship was not plant as it played no part in the carrying on of the business activities but was merely the place in which they were carried on. The ship failed therefore to be regarded as plant on the functional test in that it was not part of the apparatus employed in the commercial activities of the business. Templeman L.J. stated:

> *"There are borderline cases in which a structure forming part of business premises has been held to be plant because it does not merely consist of premises providing accommodation for the businesses but also performs a function in the actual carrying on of the business. Premises or structures forming part of premises, which have the characteristics and perform the function of plant, merit the claim for capital allowances. In my judgment it follows that if a chattel such as a ship or a hulk only provides accommodation for a business and has the characteristics and only performs the function of premises that chattel does not qualify as plant for the purposes of capital allowances."*

This case can be contrasted with that of *IRC v Scottish and Newcastle Breweries Ltd*. In this case the taxpayer incurred expenditure on electric light fittings, decor and "murals" for its hotels and public houses. The decor consisted of pictures, plaques, tapestries and other items which were either hung on or screwed to the wall and were movable. The "murals" were panels, which were screwed to the wall and were removable. It was held that as hotel-keepers, the taxpayer provided an "atmosphere" conducive to the comfort and well-being of its customers and any items intended to create or enhance that atmosphere fulfilled a function in the carrying on of the business.

Lord Lowry went on to explain that not everything which provided atmosphere in a hotel trade was necessarily plant. Contrasting the position of wallpaper and murals painted on a wall with the detachable "murals" in the case under appeal, he said:

> *"... the mural paintings and the wallpaper when executed or applied, are part of the walls and not plant, whereas the 'murals', being apparatus, are plant. The fact that two things perform the same function or role is not the point. One thing functions as part of the premises, the other as part of the plant."*

In *Wimpy International Ltd v Warland*, the taxpayer company operated a chain of restaurants providing "fast food". The company was losing money and following a takeover, the new management decided to make major changes to the premises and incurred expenditure on the installation of, *inter alia*, shop fronts, light fittings and wiring, raised floors, floor and wall tiles, suspended ceilings, balustrade and stairs. The company claimed that the items installed were "plant". Fox L.J. stated:

> *"There is a well established distinction, in general terms, between the premises in which the business is carried on and the plant with which the business is carried on. The premises are not plant."*

He went on to explain the "functional" test as follows:

"It is proper to consider the function of the item in dispute. But the question is what does it function as? If it functions as part of the premises it is not plant. The fact that the building in which a business is carried on is, by its construction, particularly well suited to the business, or indeed was specially built for that business, does not make it plant. Its suitability is simply the reason why the business is carried on there. But it remains the place in which the business is carried on and is not something with which the business is carried on ..."

The Court upheld the Special Commissioners' decision that the disputed items were not plant.

The distinction between buildings and apparatus remains difficult. In the UK it has been held that the following items were not plant since they performed no function in the particular trade:

(i) a prefabricated building at a school used to accommodate a chemical laboratory *St John's School v Ward* [1974] STC 69;

(ii) a false ceiling in a restaurant *Hampton v Forte's Autogrill Ltd* [1980] STC 80; and

(iii) an inflatable cover over a tennis court *Thomas v Reynolds* [1987] STC 135.

On the other hand, it has been held that a swimming pool at a caravan site was plant since it was part of the apparatus of the business, *Cooke v Beach Station Caravans Ltd* [1974] STC 402. Decorative screens placed in the window of a building society's offices were held to be plant because the screens were not the structure within which the business was carried on, *Leeds Permanent Building Society v Proctor* [1982] STC 821.

Furthermore, it is interesting to note that the Irish Courts could well take a different view from their UK counterparts. For instance, in the UK case of *Dixon v Fitch's Garage Limited* [1975] STC 480 it was held that a canopy over a petrol station was not plant. However, in the Irish case of *S O Cullacháin v McMullan Bros* (HC 1991), it was held by the Supreme Court that such a canopy was plant.

There are a number of items which are incorporated into buildings and which are normally regarded as plant for the purposes of capital allowances. The principal items are:

■ lifts;

■ electrical installations and fittings;

■ heating and ventilation systems;

■ special housing for machinery and equipment;

■ sprinkler systems;

■ special foundations or reinforced flooring for machinery and equipment;

■ boilers;

■ movable partitioning.

Whether an item qualifies as plant must be determined by reference to the facts of the particular case. An item, which may qualify as plant in one situation, may not qualify in another.

Machinery and plant are not confined to things used physically but extend to the intellectual apparatus of the trade or profession. Thus it was held in the Irish case of *Breathnach v McCann* (4 ITC 121) that a barrister's law books were plant.

16.2.2 Amount of capital allowances on plant and machinery

For expenditure incurred prior to 1 January 2001, there is an annual wear & tear allowance of 15% which is given on a straight-line basis for six years and a 10% allowance in year seven for plant and machinery (other than road vehicles). For vehicles suitable for the conveyance by road of persons or goods or the haulage by road of other vehicles, i.e., lorries, trucks, vans, motor cars, etc., the allowance was given at a rate of 20% on a reducing balance basis.

Section 284(2) TCA provided for a single rate of annual wear & tear allowance of 20% on a straight-line basis for capital expenditure incurred on or after 1 January 2001 on plant and machinery, including motor vehicles.

Section 284(2)(ab) provides that, for chargeable periods ending on or after 1 January 2002, a taxpayer may elect to pool together the combined tax written down value of pre-1 January 2001 qualifying expenditure, and to claim wear & tear allowances for this amount on a straight-line basis at 20% per year.

Finance Act 2003 increased the write off period for capital allowances on plant and machinery and motor vehicles from five to eight years in respect of expenditure incurred on or after 4 December 2002. Therefore, capital expenditure on such assets is now allowed on a straight-line basis at 12.5% per annum.

Thus, the position with regard to the amount of capital allowances on plant and machinery has been complicated by the fact that three separate possible regimes may apply to assets purchased in recent years. Thus, in the past, it has been necessary to pay careful attention to the date of acquisition of an asset in order to ascertain which regime applies. On the assumption that no further changes to the regime are made, only the 12.5% rate will apply. A simple example illustrating a *pro forma* allowance computation is as follows:

Example 16.1

"A" is a printer who operates as a sole trader and makes up his accounts to 31 December each year. He acquired three printing machines at a cost of €500,000 on 10/1/2006.

2006	12.5% Machine
Addition	500,000
Wear & Tear 2006	(62,500)
TWDV 31/12/2006	437,500
Wear & Tear 2007	(62,500)
TWDV 31/12/2007	375,000
Wear & Tear 2008	(62,500)
TWDV 31/12/2008	312,500
Wear & Tear 2009	(62,500)
TWDV 31/12/2009	250,000

16.2.3 Qualifying conditions for wear & tear allowance

s284
TCA 97

To qualify for a wear & tear allowance:

- a person must carry on a trade, profession, employment or office;

- a person must have incurred capital expenditure on the provision of plant or machinery for the purposes of the trade, profession, or employment; and

- the plant or machinery must be in use for the purposes of the trade, etc., at the end of the person's basis period, in order to qualify for the wear & tear allowance for a year of assessment.

16.2.4 Part private use

Section 284(1) TCA 97 provides that in order to qualify for a wear & tear allowance, the machinery or plant, while used for the purpose of the trade, must be wholly and exclusively so used. This section does not prevent the making of an allowance where an item of plant is used partly for business purposes and partly for other purposes. Where an item of plant is used partly for business purposes and partly for private use, only the part of the wear & tear allowance relating to the business use is allowable for capital allowances purposes.

Example 16.2

A trader acquired a Volkswagen Golf for €19,000 on 1 June 2007. He travels a total mileage of 20,000 miles and estimated private mileage of 5,000 miles (three-quarters of total mileage is business). He makes up accounts to 31 December each year.

	€	Allowance ¾ €
Cost	19,000	
Wear & tear 2007	(2,375)	1,781
TWDV 31/12/2007	16,625	

	€	Allowance ¾ €
Wear & tear 2008	*(2,375)*	*1,781*
TWDV 31/12/2008	*14,250*	
Wear & tear 2009	*(2,375)*	*1,781*
TWDV 31/12/2009	*11,875*	

16.2.5 Qualifying expenditure

Section 316(1) TCA 97 provides that capital expenditure does not include any expenditure allowable as a deduction in computing the profits or gains of the person incurring the expenditure.

The total allowances claimed over the life of the asset cannot exceed the actual cost of the plant or machinery purchased. Only expenditure net of grants is taken into account for the purposes of capital allowances.

Example 16.3

A trader acquired a machine in June 2009 for €700,000 and obtained a government grant of €100,000. His capital allowances will be based on €600,000 and the capital allowances available in 2009 will be €75,000 (i.e., €600,000 × 12.5%).

16.2.6 Basis of assessment

It is important to note that capital allowances are given for years of assessment. The capital allowances for a year of assessment are calculated by reference to the plant or machinery put into use in the basis period for the year of assessment (in addition, of course, to unclaimed balances coming forward referable to expenditure in preceding periods). For example, the expenditure in the accounts year ended 31 December 2009 would qualify for 2009 capital allowances in a continuing business.

Example 16.4

A butcher has a year-end of 30 June. He had the following purchases of assets in 2008 and 2009:

		€
1 August 2008	*Refrigerator*	*10,000*
1 September 2008	*Meat-cutter*	*4,000*
1 January 2009	*New sign*	*2,000*
15 August 2009	*New cash register*	*3,000*
20 December 2009	*Desk for office*	*500*

The Capital Allowances for 2009 would be as follows:

	€
Cost	16,000
Wear & tear 2009	*(2,000)*
TWDV 31/12/2009	*14,000*

Even though the refrigerator and the meat-cutter were purchased in the 2008 income tax year, they will qualify for capital allowances for the first time in 2009. This is on the basis that they were purchased in the accounting period to 30 June 2009, which forms the basis period for the 2009 income tax year.

Even though the cash register and desk for the office were acquired in the tax year 2009, they form part of the assets acquired for the accounting year ended 30 June 2010 (basis period for the 2010 tax year). Consequently, no tax write-off will be obtained in the 2009 tax year for these assets.

Unusual situations may arise however, where one accounting period forms the basis of assessment for more than one tax year (commencement situations) and where an accounting period forms the basis of assessment of no year of assessment (cessation situations or change of accounting date). The legislation contained in s306 TCA 97 provides for such situations as follows:

"(a)   Where two basis periods overlap, the period common to both shall be deemed to fall in the first basis period only;

(b)   Where there is an interval between the end of the basis period for one year of assessment and the basis period for the next year of assessment then, unless the second mentioned year of assessment is the year of the permanent discontinuance of the trade, the interval shall be deemed to be part of the second basis period;

(c)   Where there is an interval between the end of the basis period for the year of assessment preceding that in which the trade is permanently discontinued and the basis period for the year in which it is permanently discontinued, the interval shall be deemed to form part of the first basis period."

In addition, it is important to bear in mind that where an asset is in use for less than 12 months, in general a full year's wear & tear will nonetheless be available. For example, an asset purchased and put in use on 31 December 2009, i.e., on the last day of the basis period for 2009, will qualify for a full year's wear & tear in 2009, albeit that it was only used for one day of the basis period. It is only where the basis period for a year of assessment is less than one year in duration that the allowance is proportionally reduced. This generally only arises in a commencement situation or where there has been a change in accounting date.

These aspects are best illustrated by the following series of examples.

Example 16.5: Commencement

A trader commences business on 1 December 2008. He incurs expenditure on an item of plant in December 2008. The first accounts to 30 November 2009 will form the basis of assessment for 2008 (1/12/2008 to 31/12/2008) and 2009 (1/12/2008 to 30/11/2009). There is an overlap for the period 1 December 2008 to 31 December 2008. Therefore the expenditure in that period qualifies for allowances in 2008.

As the basis period for 2008 is from 1 December to 31 December, then the wear & tear allowable for 2008 must be restricted to one-twelfth.

Example 16.6

Jane commenced trading on 1 October 2007 and makes up accounts to 30 September each year. In the year ended 30 September 2008, she purchased the following assets which were put to use immediately:

		€
1 October 2007	*Desk and chairs*	*2,000*
1 October 2007	*Computers and printers*	*5,000*
10 January 2008	*Telephone system*	*6,000*
30 June 2008	*Projector and screen for presentations*	*2,000*

There were no additions during the year ended 30 September 2009. The adjusted Case I profits were as follows:

	€
30 September 2008	*100,000*
30 September 2009	*150,000*

Calculate the assessable profits and capital allowances for the first three years of assessment.

Jane's first year of assessment will be 2007 and the basis period will be 1 October 2007 to 31 December 2007. The assessable profits will be €100,000 × 3/12 = €25,000.

It is necessary to identify for capital allowance purposes the assets in use at the end of the basis period, i.e., 31 December 2007. The assets acquired were the desk and chairs, €2,000, and computers and printers, €5,000, on 1 October 2007. The length of the basis period is three months and therefore the capital allowances will have to be reduced proportionately as the basis period is less than one year.

Wear & tear Computation 2007	12½%
	€
Additions	*7,000*
Wear & tear ($^3/_{12}$)	*(219)*
TWDV at 31/12/2007	*€6,781*

Jane's second year of assessment will be 2008 and the basis period will be the 12 months ending 30 September 2008. Again, it is necessary to identify the assets in use at the end of the basis period. The desk and chairs, €2,000, computers and printers, €5,000, telephone system, €6,000, and projector and screen, €2,000, were all in use.

As the basis period is of 12 months' duration, there is no reduction necessary in the capital allowances. Consequently, a full year's wear & tear will be granted.

Wear & tear Computation 2008	*€*	*€*	Total
TWDV at 1/1/2008	*6,781*		
Additions		*8,000*	
Wear & tear	*(875)*	*(1,000)*	*1,875*
TWDV at 31/12/2008	*5,906*	*7,000*	

The profits assessable in 2008 will be the profits of the first 12 months to 30 September 2008, i.e., €100,000.

Jane's third year of assessment will be 2009, and the basis period will be the 12-month accounting period ending in the year of assessment, i.e., year ended 30 September 2009. There were no additions for this period.

Wear & tear Computation 2009	€	€	Total
TWDV 1/1/2009	*5,906*	*7,000*	
Wear & tear	*(875)*	*(1,000)*	*1,875*
TWDV 31/12/2009	*5,031*	*6,000*	

The assessable profit will be the tax-adjusted accounting profits for the year ended 30 September 2009, i.e., €150,000.

SUMMARY:		
	Case I	Capital Allowances
	€	€
2007	*25,000*	*219*
2008	*100,000*	*1,875*
2009	*150,000*	*1,875*

Example 16.7: Cessation

A trader ceases business on 31 December 2009. He makes up his accounts as follows:

Year ended 30 September 2006

Year ended 30 September 2007

Year ended 30 September 2008

15 months to 31 December 2009

Assuming no revision to actual for 2008, the period from 1 October 2008 to 31 December 2008 will not be used as the basis for any year of assessment. Expenditure in that period will qualify for an allowance claim for 2008.

Example 16.8: Cessation

Mary has been trading for many years but due to ill-health has decided to cease to trade on 31 May 2009. Mary makes up accounts to 30 September each year.

Her adjusted trading profits were as follows:

	€
Period to 30/9/2007	*100,000*
Period to 30/9/2008	*120,000*
Period to 31/5/2009	*10,000*

Details of Mary's capital allowance computations are as follows:

Cost and TWDV 31 December 2006	Cost	TWDV
	€	€
Machine A (12.5% rate of wear & tear)	*10,667*	*8,000*
Machine B (12.5% rate of wear & tear)	*24,000*	*18,000*

Mary also acquired Machine C on 1/10/2008 for €10,000.

Given that Mary had falling profits, the Inspector of Taxes will not seek to revise to "actual" the assessable profits for the penultimate year. Thus, the basis period for 2008 is the 12 months to 30 September 2008 and the basis period for 2009 is the period from 1 January 2009 to 31 May 2009. Accordingly, the profits of the period 1 October 2008 to 31 December 2008 are not assessed to tax. For capital allowances, this period is treated as part of the 2008 penultimate year and the machine purchased on 1 October 2008 is treated as an addition in the capital allowance computation for 2008.

2008	Machine A	Machine B	Machine C
	12.5%	12.5%	12.5%
	€	€	€
TWDV 1/1/2008	8,000	18,000	–
Additions			10,000
	8,000	18,000	10,000
Wear & tear	(3,000)	(1,333)	(1,250)
TWDV 31/12/2008	5,000	16,667	8,750

Note: A permanent discontinuance of the trade by Mary requires consideration as to whether a balancing allowance/charge arises in 2009.

Example 16.9

David decided to change his accounting date from 30 April to 30 September in 2008. His profits were as follows:

Year ended 30 April 2007	€50,000
Year ended 30 April 2008	€80,000
5 Months ending 30 September 2008	€15,000
Year ended 30 September 2009	€45,000

The 2008 assessment will be based on the 12-month period to 30 September 2008 (the later of the two accounting dates ending in the year).

2007 will be based on the 12 months to 30 September 2007, if greater than the profits for the 12 months to 30 April 2007.

2008

Originally based on 30 April 2007 – €50,000

Year ended 30 September 2007:

(7/12 × €50,000) + (5/12 × €80,000)

€29,167 + €33,333 = €62,500

Basis period 1/10/2006 to 30/9/2007

2008

Basis period 1/10/2007 to 30/9/2008

(7/12 × €80,000) + €15,000

€46,667 + €15,000 = €61,667

2009

Basis period 1/10/2008 to 30/9/2009

€45,000

The details of David's capital allowances are as follows:

	Cost	TWDV 1/1/2007
	€	€
Machine A (W+T 12.5%)	16,000	6,000
Machine B (W+T 12.5%)	32,000	12,000
Machine C acquired 1/6/2007	50,000	

As Machine "C" was acquired in the revised basis period for 2007, it therefore qualifies for capital allowances in 2007.

2007	Machine A	Machine B	Machine C
	€	€	€
TWDV 1/1/2007	*6,000*	*12,000*	*–*
Additions	*–*	*–*	*50,000*
	6,000	*12,000*	*50,000*
Wear & tear 2007	*(2,000)*	*(4,000)*	*(6,250)*
TWDV 31/12/2007	*4,000*	*8,000*	*43,750*

2008 and 2009	Machine A	Machine B	Machine C
	€	€	€
TWDV 1/1/2008	*4,000*	*8,000*	*43,750*
Wear & tear 2008	*(2,000)*	*(4,000)*	*(6,250)*
TWDV 31/12/2008	*2,000*	*4,000*	*37,500*
Wear & tear 2009	*(2,000)*	*(4,000)*	*(6,250)*
TWDV 31/12/2009	*–*	*–*	*31,250*

16.2.7 Balancing charges/allowances

The purpose of capital allowances is to give the trader a tax deduction for his/her net capital outlay on the plant used in his/her business. The net outlay of a trader, who spends €100 on a piece of plant and who receives €30 on the sale of the plant a few years later, is €70 (€100 – €30). Capital allowances are given on the original cost (i.e., €100) and these are adjusted to the net capital outlay of the trader when the plant is sold and the proceeds of the sale become known.

If the net capital outlay is more than the capital allowances given, additional capital allowances are given by way of a balancing allowance. If the net capital outlay is less than the capital allowances granted, the excess capital allowances are restricted by way of a balancing charge.

A balancing charge or allowance is calculated by comparing the tax written down value of the asset disposed of with the proceeds. If the tax written down value is higher than the proceeds, a balancing allowance arises and if the proceeds are higher, a balancing charge arises.

A balancing charge or allowance for a year of assessment is made by reference to events occurring in the basis period for the year of assessment. Where basis periods overlap or there is an interval between basis periods, the rules as outlined previously apply.

Any of the following events gives rise to a balancing charge or balancing allowance:

■ the machinery or plant ceases to belong to the trader;

■ the machinery or plant permanently ceases to be used for the purposes of the trade;

■ the permanent discontinuance of the trade.

Money received on the sale of plant or machinery after the cessation of a trade may be taken into account when computing balancing allowances or charges.

Balancing charges and allowances are to be computed as if machinery or plant had been sold at open market price, where:

- a trade ceases and the trader does not sell the plant or machinery;

- machinery is sold at less than market price or given away;

- machinery is transferred from business to private use.

Example 16.10

John makes up his accounts to 30 June each year. In the year to 30 June 2009 he sold a machine for €50,000. The TWDV of the asset was €30,000. The asset originally cost €70,000.

	€
Proceeds	50,000
TWDV	(30,000)
Balancing charge	20,000

If the sales proceeds were €25,000, a balancing allowance of €5,000 would occur.

A balancing charge in effect claws back the excess of capital allowances given over the net capital outlay by the trader. The balancing charge can therefore never exceed the capital allowances granted.

Example 16.11

A machine cost €6,000. The trader sold the asset for €10,000. The TWDV of the asset was €3,300.

The calculation is as follows:

	€
Sales proceeds	10,000
TWDV	(3,300)
Apparent balancing charge	6,700

The balancing charge of €6,700 is greater than the actual allowances claimed, and is restricted to the amount claimed, €2,700 (i.e., cost €6,000 – TWDV €3,300).

A balancing charge will not arise in respect of disposals of plant and machinery occurring on or after 1 January 2002, where the disposal proceeds are less than €2,000.

Example 16.12

The sales proceeds of a machine on 1 June 2009 was €1,500. The TWDV was €1,200. Technically a balancing charge of €300 would occur but as the sales proceeds are less than €2,000, no balancing charge will arise.

Where plant or machinery disposed of is replaced by the owner, he/she may elect for the cost of the replacement plant or machinery to be reduced by the amount of the balancing charge rather than being assessed immediately on the balancing charge.

This reduction in the cost of the replacement plant will be treated as if an initial allowance of that amount was given.

Example 16.13

Jenny prepares accounts to 30 June each year. During the year to 30 June 2009, she disposed of an asset and replaced it with a similar asset. The details were as follows:

	€
Original cost of asset	10,000
TWDV at 31/12/2008	7,000
Sale proceeds	9,000
Cost of replacement asset	15,000

The calculation is as follows:

	€
Proceeds	9,000
Less	
TWDV	(7,000)
Balancing charge	2,000

If the replacement option is claimed, the balancing charge of €2,000 will not be levied in 2009 and capital allowances will be claimed on the replacement asset as follows:

Capital allowances 2009	€
Additions	15,000
Less	
Balancing charge on original asset	(2,000)
Qualifying cost of replacement asset	13,000
Wear & tear 2009	(1,625)
TWDV 31/12/2009	11,375

16.2.8 Leasing

Capital allowances are available to persons who incur expenditure on plant and use the plant for trading purposes. However, it is not unusual for traders to lease plant rather than purchase it. Persons who purchase plant and lease it to traders are entitled to claim the capital allowances on the cost of the plant, if the plant is leased on such terms that the burden of wear & tear falls directly on the lessor. The lessee of course cannot claim capital allowances in this situation but would instead claim deductions for the payments as noted in paragraphs 15.3.4.8 and 15.3.4.9 and in Appendix III of Chapter 15.

16.2.9 Motor vehicles

General

Motor vehicles are defined as vehicles used for the conveyance by road of persons or goods or the haulage by road of other vehicles. The rate of wear & tear for expenditure incurred on motor vehicles prior to 1 January 2001 is 20%, calculated on a reducing balance, but the rate is 40% for taxis and for cars used for short-term hire to the public (see below). There is a five-year straight-line write-off period for wear & tear capital allowances for expenditure incurred between 1 January 2001 and 3 December 2002 inclusive.

There now exists an eight-year straight-line write off period for wear & tear capital allowances for expenditure incurred on or after 4 December 2002 in respect of motor vehicles.

Restriction for "expensive" cars

s373
TCA 97 Under s373 TCA 97, expenditure on cars is restricted for the purposes of capital allowances. The limit has been increased on a number of occasions. From 1 January 2007, the limit for both new and second-hand cars is €24,000.

The limits were lower in the past. A summary of the limits is included in Appendix I.

Example 16.14

A (Category A) car was acquired on 30 June 2009 for €40,000. The capital allowances are restricted to a maximum relevant limit of €24,000.

Consequently, the capital allowances in 2009 are €24,000 × 12.5% = €3,000.

Any proceeds arising on the disposal of such cars will be similarly restricted when calculating balancing allowances or balancing charges. This restriction does not apply to cars which are used in the ordinary course of trade for hiring to the general public.

Where a car is used partly for business purposes and partly for private use by an individual, only the part of the capital allowance relative to the business use is allowable as a set-off against the individual's trading income.

An example best illustrates the points made above.

Example 16.15

Mr McCarthy has been in business for many years. He purchased a car costing €40,000 on 1 June 2008. It has been agreed with the Inspector of Taxes that 25% of the usage of the car is private. He sells the car on 1 June 2009 for €30,000.

Mr McCarthy makes up his accounts to 31 December each year.

His capital allowances on the car are as follows:

2008	€
Cost of car	*40,000*
Restrict to relevant limit at that time	*24,000*
Wear & tear 12.5%	*(3,000)*
Tax written down value at 31/12/2008	*21,000*

Wear & tear 2008 = €3,000 × 75% = €2,250, as only the wear & tear attributable to business use is allowable.

2009

The car was disposed of in the basis period for €30,000 and therefore a balancing allowance or charge arises as follows:

Only that portion of the total proceeds of €30,000 which relates to that part of the car on which capital allowances were granted is taken into account in calculating the balancing charge or allowance, i.e.,

	€
Restricted proceeds:	
$€30,000 \times \dfrac{€24,000}{€40,000} =$	*18,000*
Less tax written down value	*(21,000)*
Balancing allowance	*3,000*
Restrict to part attributable to business use, i.e., 75%	*2,250*

With effect from 1 July 2008, a new regime for calculating capital allowances on business cars was introduced by reference to the carbon emissions level of the car.

Categories of cars:

- Up to 155 g/km (A, B & C)

- Between 156 and 190 g/km (D & E)

- Above 190 g/km (F & G)

However, the specified limit remains at €24,000 and there are changes to its application:

Categories A, B & C

- The limit of €24,000 is applied even where the actual cost is less than €24,000.

Categories D & E

- Limit is 50% of the lower of cost and €24,000.

Categories F & G

- No allowances are available.

Example 16.16

Seamus Smith purchases a business car on 1 September 2009 with a carbon emissions level of 150 g/km (a category C car). The cost price is €36,000, however, the amount on which allowances are available is restricted to €24,000 (the specified amount).

The car is disposed of for €21,000 a few years later. The calculation of the balancing allowance/ charge on the disposal will be calculated by comparing the TWDV with the proceeds as adjusted i.e., €21,000 × €24,000/36,000 = adjusted proceeds of €14,000.

Example 16.17

John O'Carroll purchases a business car on 1 November 2009 with a carbon emissions level of 130 g/km (a category B car). The cost price is €12,000. However, the amount on which allowances are available is increased to €24,000 (the specified amount).

The car is disposed of for €6,000 a few years later. The calculation of the balancing allowance/ charge on the disposal will be calculated by comparing the TWDV with the proceeds as adjusted i.e., €6,000 × 24,000/12,000 = adjusted proceeds of €12,000.

Example 16.18

Aiden Finlay purchases a business car on 1 December 2009 with a carbon emissions level of 160 g/km (a category D car). The cost price is €36,000, however, the amount on which capital allowances are available is restricted to €12,000 (50% of the specified amount).

The car is subsequently disposed of for €18,000 a few years later. The calculation of the balancing allowance/charge on the disposal will be calculated by comparing the TWDV with the proceeds as adjusted i.e., €18,000 × 12,000/36,000 = adjusted proceeds of €6,000.

Example 16.19

Mike Brady purchases a business car on 1 December 2009 with a carbon emissions level of 250 g/km (a category G car). The cost price is €70,000, capital allowances are not claimable.

The car is subsequently disposed of for €40,000 a few years later – no balancing allowance/ charge will arise.

Taxis and short-term hires

s286
TCA 97

The rate of wear & tear allowance is 40% for cars used for qualifying purposes, which are defined as cars in use as taxis or for short-term hire to members of the public.

16.3   Industrial Buildings

Allowances are available on expenditure incurred on industrial buildings. The allowances are quite different from those available for expenditure on plant and machinery.

16.3.1   Definition of industrial building

Overview

An "industrial building or structure" is defined in s268 TCA 97 as a building or structure in use:

■ for the purpose of a trade carried on in a mill, factory or other similar premises;

■ for the purpose of a trade which consists of the operation or management of an airport and which is an airport runway or airport apron used solely or mainly by aircraft carrying passengers or cargo for hire or reward;

■ for the purpose of a trade which consists of the operation or management of an airport (other than airport runways and aprons);

■ for the purpose of a dock undertaking;

■ for the purpose of growing fruit, vegetables or other produce in the course of a trade of market gardening;

■ for the intensive production of cattle, sheep, pigs, poultry or eggs in the course of a trade other than the trade of farming;

- for the purpose of the trade of hotel-keeping;

- for the purpose of a trade consisting of the operation or management of a private registered nursing home within the meaning of s2 of the Health (Nursing Homes) Act 1990. Finance Act 2009 has provided for the phasing out of capital allowances for such expenditure;

- for the purpose of a trade consisting of the operation or management of a convalescent home providing treatment for acutely ill patients;

- for the purpose of a trade which consists of the operation or management of a qualifying hospital. Finance Act 2009 has provided for the phasing out of capital allowances for such expenditure;

- for the purpose of a trade which consists of the operation or management of a qualifying sports injury clinic; or

- for the purpose of a trade which consists of the operation or management of a qualifying mental health centre. Finance Act 2009 has provided for the phasing out of capital allowances for such expenditure;

- for purpose of a trade where consists of the operation of specialist palliative care.

- caravan sites and camping sites kept under the control of the Tourist Traffic Acts 1939 to 2003.

Specific exclusions

The definition of an industrial building specifically excludes any building or structure in use:

- as a dwelling house (other than a holiday cottage or residential unit);

- as a retail shop;

- as a showroom or office;

- for a purpose ancillary to any of the above.

s268(8)
TCA 97

Where part of a building or structure is, and part is not, an industrial building or structure, and the capital expenditure on the non-industrial section does not exceed one-tenth of the total capital expenditure incurred on the whole building, then the whole building will be treated as an industrial building. Where the cost of the office or shop, etc., exceeds 10% of the total expenditure, the full cost of the office or shop is disallowed and not just the excess over the 10%.

Example 16.20

	€
Site cost	*100,000*
Cost of factory	*410,000*
Cost of offices	*40,000*
	550,000

$$\frac{\text{Cost of offices}}{\text{Total cost (excluding site cost)}} = \frac{€40,000}{€450,000} = 8.89\%$$

Therefore the offices will qualify for capital allowances.

If the position were as follows:	€
Site cost	*100,000*
Cost of factory	*410,000*
Cost of offices	*50,000*
	560,000

$$\frac{\text{Cost of offices}}{\text{Total cost (excluding site cost)}} = \frac{€50,000}{€460,000} = 10.87\%$$

As the fraction exceeds 10%, no part of the expenditure on the office qualifies for capital allowances.

"Office" is not defined. In the case of *Inland Revenue Commissioners v Lambhill Ironworks Limited* (31 TC 393), it was held that the drawing office of a firm of structural steel engineers was an "industrial building or structure" being on the industrial side of the concern rather than on the managerial side. The Lord President commented in this case that a drawing office of a certain type was no more an "office" within the meaning of the Income Tax Act than a machine shop was a shop.

In looking at s268(8) TCA 97, the first thing to be determined is what exactly constitutes "the whole of a building or structure".

In the case of *Abbott Laboratories Limited v Carmody* (44 TC 569), a factory had been built on a large site. The factory was built in four main blocks: a chemical block: a pharmaceutical block, a maintenance block and an administration block. The blocks were connected to each other by pipes and roadways and all shared a common boilerhouse. The administration block was connected to the pharmaceutical block by means of a covered passageway. The company claimed an industrial building allowance in respect of the cost of construction of the entire factory. The Revenue resisted an allowance on the cost of the administration block. On appeal to the Special Commissioners, the company contended that all of the buildings constituted an industrial building for the purposes of the industrial building allowance. The Special Commissioners held that the definition of industrial building or structure was "not apt to apply to an extensive factory site so that it falls to be treated as one unit for the purpose of an industrial building allowance". The matter went to the High Court but was ultimately decided in favour of the Revenue.

16.3.2 Qualifying expenditure

Qualifying expenditure is capital expenditure incurred on the construction of an industrial building or structure. The expression "capital expenditure on the construction of an industrial building or structure" includes expenditure on part of a building or structure. The expenditure need not be on the construction of a building or structure, which is complete in itself. The expression includes capital expenditure on items such as the following:

- preparing, tunnelling and levelling land for foundations;

- strengthening the structure of an existing building, for example, to make it safe to increase the load put upon a floor;

- the erection of additional interior walls in an industrial building; and

- additions to, and improvements of, entrances, stairways, ramps, access roads and main supplies of water gas and electricity.

It should be noted that the expenditure must be of a capital nature, and that it must be incurred on the construction of the building or structure.

The following expenditure is specifically excluded:

- acquisition cost of land;

- expenditure on the provision of machinery or plant or any asset which is treated as machinery or plant;

- any expenditure, which qualifies for an allowance as being capital expenditure on scientific research or mining development allowance.

Expenditure is incurred on the day on which the relevant sum becomes payable.

Although the legislation is silent on the meaning of the date when the sum becomes payable, it may be interpreted as the agreed date for payment as specified in the agreement between the buyer and seller. If the date of payment is not specified in the agreement, then it may be acceptable to assume that the payment is due one month from the date of the invoice. In practice, the date of issue of the invoice is frequently taken as the date the sum becomes payable.

16.3.3 Industrial buildings annual allowance

This analysis is primarily concerned with the calculation of an Industrial Buildings writing down allowance (usually referred to as Industrial Buildings annual allowance or IBAA). Initial allowances and free depreciation may be claimed in certain incidences in respect of urban renewal properties. In this regard, readers are referred to the commentary in *Income Tax* by McAteer, Reddin and Deegan.

An IBAA may be claimed each year, on expenditure incurred on an industrial building until the cost of the building is fully allowed. This allowance is calculated on a straight-line basis. It is calculated on the expenditure net of any grants received, but before deducting any industrial building initial allowance which may have been claimed.

An IBAA may be claimed by the person who is entitled to the relevant interest, i.e., the person who has incurred the expenditure, provided the building is an industrial building as already defined and is in use for that purpose. Generally, expenditure on industrial buildings is written off on a straight-line basis over a 25 year period, so that a trader may claim an IBAA of 4% of the qualifying cost each year. Where an individual incurs expenditure on certain items, such as nursing homes, crèches etc., the write off is 15% per annum for six years and 10% in year seven.

16.3.4   Purchasers of certain buildings

The allowance is made primarily to the person who incurs expenditure on the construction of an industrial building. However, Section 279 TCA 97 however extended the allowance to persons who buy an industrial building before it has been used or within one year after it commences to be used, provided the allowance has not been claimed by any other person.

The purchaser of such a building is deemed to incur expenditure at the time when the purchase price becomes payable and not when the actual construction expenditure was incurred.

The amount on which the allowance is granted depends on whether the expenditure on the construction of the building was incurred by a builder or non-builder.

16.3.4.1 Construction incurred by a builder

If the sale by the builder is the only sale of the relevant interest, before the building is used or within one year after it commences to be used, the allowance is granted on the "net price paid" to the builder. Where there is more than one such sale, before the building is used or within one year after it commences to be used, the allowance is granted by reference to the "net price paid" on the first sale by the builder (unless the last purchaser pays a lower price).

In other words, the "net price paid" to the builder remains the figure by reference to which allowances are given unless the last purchaser pays a lower price.

The cost of land is excluded from the "net price paid" by the operation of the following:

$$\text{Amount paid} \quad \times \quad \frac{\text{Actual Construction Costs}}{\text{Actual Construction Costs} + \text{Cost of Land}}$$

16.3.4.2 Construction expenditure incurred by a non-builder

The purchaser is deemed to incur expenditure, on the date when the purchase price becomes payable, equal to the lower of the actual construction costs incurred by the non-builder or the "net price paid" by the purchaser of the building.

Where there is more than one sale, before the building is used or within one year after it commences to be used, the allowance is based on the lower of the actual construction costs incurred by the non-builder or the "net price paid" by the last purchaser.

The cost of land is excluded from the "net price paid" by the operation of the following:

$$\text{Amount paid} \quad \times \quad \frac{\text{Actual Construction Costs}}{\text{Actual Construction Costs} + \text{Cost of Land}}$$

16.3.5   Balancing allowances and balancing charges

A balancing charge or allowance may arise:

(a) where the relevant interest in an industrial building is sold; or

(b) where the building is demolished or destroyed or ceases altogether to be used; or

(c) where the relevant interest is a leasehold one and comes to an end except by the person entitled to that interest acquiring the reversionary interest.

No balancing charge or allowance can arise when any of the above events occurs after the tax life of the building has expired. In the case of industrial buildings where the qualifying expenditure was incurred after 16 January 1975, the tax life is generally 25 years. Thus, where such buildings are disposed of within that 25 year period, a balancing allowance or charge may arise.

Example 16.21

An industrial building, which cost €500,000 in 1997 is sold in 2009 for €700,000. The tax written down value is €300,000.

The position would be as follows:

	€
Sales proceeds	*700,000*
TWDV	*(300,000)*
Balancing charge	*400,000*
Restricted to allowances granted	*200,000*

If the building was sold in 2023, no balancing charge would arise.

Where capital allowances are claimed in respect of the refurbishment of a building, the tax life of the building runs from the time the expenditure is incurred and not from the time the building is first used.

As in the case of plant and machinery, balancing charges and allowances are calculated by comparing the tax written down value of the building with the proceeds of sale. A balancing charge cannot exceed the allowances already granted.

Where a purchaser buys an industrial building on which capital allowances have already been claimed by the vendor, then the purchaser may be entitled to an annual allowance, depending on how long the building has been in use prior to his/her purchase of it. In the case of industrial buildings with a tax life of 25 years, a sale by a vendor after

25 years does not attract a balancing charge or allowance and the purchaser is not entitled to any allowances on the expenditure incurred by him/her. If such a building has been in use for less than twenty-five years, he/she will be entitled to industrial buildings annual allowance on the cost to the original purchaser or on his/her own cost, whichever is the lower. The annual allowance is calculated as follows:

- Calculate the residue after sale by the vendor:

  Where a balancing charge arises, the residue after sale is equal to the written down value of the building plus the balancing charge.

  Where a balancing allowance arises the residue after sale is equal to the written down value after deducting the balancing allowance.

- Calculate the number of unexpired years for which an industrial buildings annual allowance could have been claimed by the vendor.

- The annual allowance available to the purchaser is the residue divided by the number of unexpired years.

Thus in example 16.17 above, the second-hand purchaser may claim allowances on the residue, in this case €500,000, over a remaining unexpired tax life of 15 years. Thus, his industrial buildings annual allowance will be €33,333 each year for a period of 15 years.

16.3.6 Temporary disuse of industrial building or structure

A building is not deemed to cease to be an industrial building if it merely falls temporarily out of use. When a building or structure is an industrial building or structure immediately before any period of temporary disuse, it is deemed to continue to be an industrial building or structure during the period of temporary disuse. An annual allowance will continue to be granted during that period.

There is no statutory definition of the term "temporarily out of use". Thus, whether or not a building is temporarily out of use in particular circumstances is a question of fact to be decided in each case.

16.3.7 Lessors

A lessor of a building is entitled to claim the allowances if he/she lets the building to a lessee who uses it as an industrial building. Where a lessor incurs expenditure on a building and does not lease it to a lessee who uses it as an industrial building, capital allowances may still be claimed by the lessor provided the building is leased to:

- the IDA; or

- SFADCo; or

- Údarás na Gaeltachta,

and provided that they in turn lease it to a person who uses it as an industrial building.

WHAT YOU SHOULD NOW KNOW

On completion of this chapter, you should be able to:

- ✓ Explain the terms "plant" and "industrial buildings".

- ✓ Calculate the capital allowances available for expenditure on plant and machinery, motor vehicles and industrial buildings.

- ✓ Identify the income tax year in which assets are acquired and disposed of with particular reference to the rules that apply on commencement, cessation and change of accounting date.

- ✓ Calculate balancing allowances and charges on disposals of plant and motor vehicles.

- ✓ Explain the income tax implications of disposals of industrial buildings.

- ✓ Complete Questions and the Assignments in Irish Taxation Law and Practice, Volume 2.

Appendix I

Motor Car Restrictions

TCA s373   Under S.373 TCA expenditure on cars is restricted for the purposes of capital allowances. The limit has been increased on a number of occasions. For convenience, the limits and the periods to which they apply are summarised in the following table:

Period during which expenditure incurred	*Limit* €
(1) Before 16 May 1973	None
(2) 17 May 1973 to 28 January 1976	3,174.35
(3) 29 January 1976 to 5 April 1986	4,444.08
(4) 6 April 1986 to 27 January 1988	5,078.95
(5) 28 January 1988 to 25 January 1989	7,618.43
(6) 26 January 1989 to 29 January 1992	8,888.17
(7) 30 January 1992 to 26 January 1994	12,697.38
(8) 27 January 1994 to 8 February 1995	16,506.60
(9) 9 February 1995 to 22 January 1997	17,776.33
(10) 23 January 1997 to 2 December 1997	19,046.07
(11) 3 December 1997 to 1 December 1998	19,680.94
(12) 2 December 1998 to 30 November 1999	20,315.18
(13) From 1 December 1999 to 31 December 1999	20,950.68
(14) From 1 January 2001 to 31 December 2001	21,585.55
(15) From 1 January 2002 to 31 December 2005	22,000.00
(16) From 1 January 2006	23,000.00
(17) From 1 January 2007	24,000.00

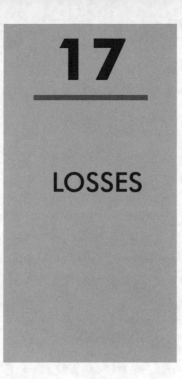

17

LOSSES

In this chapter, you will deal with the following:

- Relief for trading losses under s382 TCA 97

- Time limit for making loss-relief claims

- Relief for trading losses under s381 TCA 97

- Order of reliefs

- Interaction of loss reliefs with other reliefs

- Creating or augmenting losses with capital allowances

- Loss relief on commencement

- Loss relief under miscellaneous other Cases and Schedules.

17.1   Introduction

This chapter deals with the treatment of a loss sustained by an individual in carrying on a trade, profession or employment. Trading or professional losses may generally be relieved in one of two ways:

s381
TCA 97

■ against other sources of income in the year in which the loss arises under s381 TCA 97;

s382
TCA 97

■ against future Case I or Case II income from the same trade or profession under s382 TCA 97.

In addition, terminal loss relief may be available in certain circumstances on the cessation of a trade or profession.

17.2   Relief for Losses under s381 TCA 97

Relief is granted to a person who, in carrying on a trade, profession, vocation or employment, sustains a loss during a year of assessment. A loss for an accounting period is computed in the same manner as a profit would be computed under Cases I and II of Schedule D.

Strictly, relief for a loss under s381 should be calculated for the actual year of assessment, i.e., for the tax year 1 January to 31 December. In practice, a loss for a twelve-month accounting period, ending in the year of assessment, is normally taken as the loss for that year. The Revenue Commissioners will, however, insist upon the strict statutory basis (i.e., loss for the year to 31 December):

■ for the first three years of assessment on commencement of a trade or profession;

■ for any year of assessment following a year in which a claim has been made on the strict statutory basis;

■ for the year of cessation, i.e., the loss from 1 January to the date of cessation.

The taxpayer can always insist on obtaining relief for a loss on the strict statutory basis.

Relief under s381 is obtained by reducing the taxpayer's gross statutory income (i.e., gross income before charges on income and reliefs) for the year of assessment by the amount of the loss. Losses incurred in the tax year may be set-off against the other income of that tax year under this section.

Example 17.1

Mr Jones, who has traded for many years, incurred a trading loss of €20,000 in the year ended 31 July 2009. The other assessable income in the 2009 tax year was Irish rental income of €15,000 and UK dividends of €10,000.

2009	€
Trading Profit (Y/E 31/12/2008)	*Nil*
Schedule D Case III – UK dividends	*10,000*
Schedule D Case V – rental income	*15,000*
	25,000
Less s381 loss 2009	*(20,000)*
Income before deduction of charges on income and reliefs	*5,000*

A s381 loss is deemed first to reduce the earned income of the individual, then his/her unearned income, next the earned income of his wife/her husband, and finally the unearned income of his wife/her husband. This is relevant in calculating the maximum allowable for tax relief on pension contributions.

17.2.1 Claim

It is important to note that the taxpayer must make a claim to obtain the relief under s381. The claim must be made within two years of the end of the year of assessment to which the claim relates. In the above example, the claim for relief under s381 must be made on or before 31 December 2011. When a loss is utilised under s381 relief for the loss cannot be obtained under any other section.

It should be noted that the full amount of the loss must be claimed under s381 to the extent that it can be absorbed by the taxpayer's gross income. It is not possible to use only part of a loss under s381 so as to leave sufficient income to be covered by reliefs.

Example 17.2

Mr Mitchell sustained a loss as adjusted for tax purposes of €20,000 in the year ended 30 June 2009. The trader's other assessable income for 2009 consisted of UK rental income of €12,000 and he had reliefs of €5,000.

Relief for the trading loss is due as follows:

2009	€
UK rental Income – Schedule D Case III	*12,000*
Less s381(1) loss available	*(20,000)*
Assessable income	*Nil*
Available for relief under s382 for 2010	*8,000*

It is not possible to claim only €7,000 of the loss under s381(1) in 2009, leaving the balance of income to be covered by the 2009 reliefs of €5,000.

17.3   Creating or Augmenting a Loss with Capital Allowances

s392
TCA 97

Under s392 TCA 97, it is possible to create or augment a loss by having capital allowances deducted in computing the loss of the trade.

The capital allowances taken into account are the allowances due for the year of assessment, in which the loss arises, but only to the extent that they are not required to offset any balancing charges due for that year.

Example 17.3

Mr Ryan, who has traded for many years, has the following profits and capital allowances:

	€
Profit – year ended 30/9/2009	*4,000*
Capital allowances 2009	*17,000*
Balancing charge 2009	*3,000*

The s381 loss for 2009 is as follows:		€
Profit – year ended 30/9/2009		*4,000*
Less Capital allowances 2009	*(17,000)*	
* Balancing charge 2009*	*3,000*	*(14,000)*
s381 loss 2009		*(10,000)*

17.3.1   Capital allowances brought forward

Capital allowances brought forward cannot be used to create or augment a s381 loss. However, they can be used to reduce profits and offset balancing charges for the year.

Example 17.4

Mr Curran, who has been trading for many years, makes up his accounts annually to 30 September. His accounts for the year to 30 September 2009 show a profit for tax purposes of €10,000. He has capital allowances for 2009 as follows:

	€
Wear & tear	*15,000*
Balancing charge	*(1,000)*
The capital allowances forward are €5,000.	

The s381 loss for 2009 is	€
Capital allowances forward	*(5,000)*
Profit chargeable 2009	*10,000*
	5,000
Balancing charge 2009	*1,000*
	6,000
Capital allowances 2009	*(15,000)*
s381 loss 2009	*(9,000)*

17.3.2 Extent to which capital allowances are to be taken into account

Where, in a commencement situation, the capital allowances taken into account for creating or augmenting a s381 loss are allowances for the year of claim, they will be restricted to the excess over the profit of the basis period.

Example 17.5

Mr Purcell commenced trading on 1 June 2007. Recent results for tax purposes are as follows:

	€
Year ended 31/5/2008	*4,000*
Year ended 31/5/2009	*3,000*
Capital allowances were as follows:	*€*
2008	*4,800*
2009	*2,000*

Mr Purcell claimed relief under s381 for 2008.
As this is a commencement, the Revenue will insist on the actual loss being computed for s381 purposes.

		€
i.e.,	*($€4,000 \times {}^5/_{12}$) + ($€3,000 \times {}^7/_{12}$)*	*3,417*
Less capital allowances		*(4,800)*
Loss		*(1,383)*

This loss will be restricted to the amount by which the capital allowances exceed the assessable profits for 2008 i.e.,

2008 Assessment	*€*
Assessable 2008	*4,000*
Less capital allowances	*(4,800)*
Loss available for relief	*(800)*

17.4 Carry Forward of Losses under s382 TCA 97

Where a person carrying on a trade or profession sustains a loss in respect of which relief has not been wholly given under s381 or under any other provision of the Income Tax Acts, he/she may claim that any portion of the loss for which relief has not been given may be carried forward against subsequent assessments of profits of the same trade.

Relief under s382 is to be given as far as possible against the first subsequent year of assessment. For this purpose, the taxable profits for the next year available to cover the loss forward are the taxable profits for that year after deducting the relevant capital allowances. Any unrelieved balance of that loss is carried forward again to the next year of assessment and so on indefinitely so long as the trade or profession continues until the loss carried forward is fully used up.

Example 17.6

Mr McGrath has been in business for many years and makes up accounts to 31 December. Recent results are as follows:

	Profit/(Loss)
Year ended	*€*
31 December 2007	*(20,000)*
31 December 2008	*5,000*
31 December 2009	*6,000*

A claim was made for relief under s381 for 2007. Mr McGrath also had rental income in 2007 of €10,000.

Assessments are as follows:

		€	*€*
2007	*Rental income*	*10,000*	
	Less s381 loss	*(20,000)*	*Nil*
2008	*Case I*	*5,000*	
	Less s382 loss	*(5,000)*	*Nil*
2009	*Case I*	*6,000*	
	Less s382 loss (balance)	*(5,000)*	*1,000*

The loss in year ended 31 December 2007 has been utilised as follows:

		€
s381	*2007*	*10,000*
s382	*2008*	*5,000*
s382	*2009*	*5,000*
		20,000

A loss can be carried forward only to the extent that it has not been effectively allowed under s381 or in apportioning and aggregating profits and losses in computing an assessment.

Example 17.7

Mr Moran commenced business on 1 May 2007. His results for the first years were as follows:

	Profit/(loss)
	€
Seven months to 30 November 2007	*(40,000)*
Period to 31 October 2008	*5,000*
Period to 31 December 2009	*45,000*

Assessable profits for first three years of assessment:

			Assessment
2007	*01/05/2007 – 31/12/2007*	*€*	*€*
	(€40,000) + ($^{1}/_{11}$ × €5,000)	*(39,545)*	*Nil*
2008	*12 months to 31/10/2008*		

		€	€
	€5,000 + (¹/₇ × (€40,000))	(714)	_Nil_
2009	_Period ended 31 December 2009_		
	Profits €45,000 × ¹²/₁₄	38,571	
	Less loss forward (see Note):	<u>(34,545)</u>	<u>4,026</u>

Note:		_Total loss_	(40,000)
Less utilised:			
2007		455	
2008		<u>5,000</u>	<u>5,455</u>
			<u>(34,545)</u>

The profits assessable in the third year of assessment are based on the basis period of 12 months ending during the year of assessment, but this figure can be reduced by the excess of the profits of the 12 month period ending during the second year of assessment over the actual profits for the year. Where this deduction is greater than the amount of the original profits assessable for the third year, then the excess is treated as if it were a loss forward under s382.

Example 17.8

Mr Kearney commenced to trade on 1 October 2007. His results for the first years were as follows:

	Profit €
Period 1 October 2007 to 30 September 2008	_10,000_
Year ended 30 September 2009	_500_
Year ended 30 September 2010	_5,000_

Computation of assessable profits: **_Assessable_**

2007	_01/10/2007 – 31/12/2007_		**€**
	_€10,000 × ³/₁₂_		<u>2,500</u>
2008	_01/10/2007 – 30/09/2008_		
	_€10,000_		<u>10,000</u>
2009	_Year ended 30 September 2009_	_(Note)_	<u>Nil</u>

Note:	**€**
Amount assessable for second year 2008	_10,000_
Less actual profits 2008:	
_((⁹/₁₂ × €10,000) + (³/₁₂ × €500))_	<u>(7,625)</u>
Excess	<u>2,375</u>

Final 2009 assessment: (€500 − €2,375) = (€1,875), i.e., Nil.

The excess of €1,875 is carried forward under s382 against future trading profits for 2010 et seq.

In order to ensure that losses can be carried forward under s382, the same trade has to be continued without interruption. Losses forward cannot be set against the profits of a new trade and if trading has permanently ceased, then pre-cessation losses cannot be carried over to a later year when the trade is reactivated.

Whether a trade currently being carried on is the same trade as that in which the losses were incurred is a question of fact, as indeed is the question of whether or not a trade has permanently ceased and recommenced or has merely been suspended. When a trade has merely been suspended, losses can be carried forward and relieved under s382.

**s382
TCA 97**

It is interesting to note the UK tax case of *Gordon & Blair Limited v IRC* (40 TC 358). The appellant company carried on a business as brewers. In October 1953, it ceased brewing but continued to bottle and sell beer supplied to its specification by another brewery. The company claimed that it carried on the same trade before and after October 1953, so that losses sustained prior to that date could be set-off against subsequent profits. It was held that the company had ceased trading as brewers and commenced a fresh trade of selling beer. The losses prior to October 1953 could not be carried forward under the UK equivalent of s382 TCA 97.

**s69
TCA 97**

If a trade or profession ceases to be carried on by one person and is then carried on by another person or persons, s69 TCA 97 provides that the trade is to be treated as permanently discontinued at that time and a new trade has been set up. Accordingly, trading or professional losses at the date of deemed cessation cannot be carried forward.

By concession, the provisions of s69 do not apply where a person dies and the trade or profession is carried on by the surviving spouse.

17.5   Terminal Loss

Where a trade or profession is permanently discontinued and in the 12 months to the date of discontinuance a loss has been sustained (referred to as a "terminal loss"), the loss may be set-off against the trading profits for the three years of assessment prior to the year of cessation provided that relief is not claimed for the loss under any other section. For further commentary on the nature and calculation of this relief, readers are referred to the analysis in *Income Tax* by McAteer, Reddin and Deegan (2007), Irish Taxation Institute.

17.6   Schedule D Case III

**s382
TCA 97**

There is no statutory relief for Case III losses. By concession, Case III losses incurred in a foreign trade may be carried forward for offset against future profits of the same trade (assessed under Case III) in the same way as trading losses, etc., under s382 TCA 97.

17.7　Schedule D Case IV

A loss incurred in any activity, the income from which would be chargeable under Case IV, may be set-off against other Case IV assessments for the same year and any unused balance may be carried forward against Case IV assessments in future years.

17.8　Schedule D Case V

A Case V loss incurred in any year may be set-off against Case V profits assessed for the same year and any unused balance carried forward against subsequent Case V assessments.

Example 17.9

Mr Brown had the following net rents (after deduction of all allowable expenses) in respect of let properties situated in Ireland. The properties had been let for many years.

		Profit/(Loss)
	€	€
Period ended 31 December 2007		*(5,000)*
Year ended 31 December 2008		*2,000*
Year ended 31 December 2009		*8,000*

Assessments are as follows:

2007	*Period ended 31 December 2007*		*Nil*
2008	*Year ended 31 December 2008*	*2,000*	
	Less loss carried forward	*(5,000)*	*Nil*
2009	*Year ended 31 December 2009*	*8,000*	
	Less loss (balance)	*(3,000)*	*5,000*

17.9　Schedule E

A loss from an employment might arise in exceptional circumstances, for instance, where a manager remunerated on a share of profits has to suffer a share in a loss, or where a commercial traveller has guaranteed debts incurred and suffers a loss in one year because of a large bad debt.

It is important to note that relief for Schedule E losses can be claimed only under s381. There is no provision to claim relief under any of the other loss sections.

WHAT YOU SHOULD NOW KNOW

On completion of this chapter, you should be able to:

- ✓ Calculate the final income tax liability of an individual after claiming all possible loss relief.

- ✓ Describe how a loss relief claim under s381 can displace certain other personal reliefs and tax credits.

- ✓ Identify the due date for making a claim under s381.

- ✓ Describe the form of relief under s382 and identify the circumstances in which loss relief under s382 will be unavailable.

- ✓ Explain how a taxpayer may not benefit from double relief for aggregated losses.

- ✓ Calculate loss relief on commencement.

- ✓ Explain how Case I or Case II capital allowances may be used to create or augment a Case I or Case II loss.

- ✓ Describe the nature of relief for losses arising under other miscellaneous Cases and Schedules.

- ✓ Complete Questions and the Assignments in Irish Taxation Law and Practice, Volume 2.

18

TAXATION OF PARTNERSHIPS

In this chapter, you will deal with the following:

- The nature of a partnership
- The "precedent" partner
- The "relevant" period
- Apportionment of profits
- Capital allowances and charges

- Losses
- Interest on capital
- Partner's salaries
- Appeals
- Joining and leaving a partnership

18.1   Definition

Fundamental to understanding partnerships and taxation is the Partnership Act 1890 and the definition therein of exactly what is a partnership.

Section 1(1) sets out the definition as follows:

> *"Partnership is the relation which subsists between persons carrying on a business in common with a view of profit."*

18.2   Existence of Partnership

The leading case in respect of this is *Inspector of Taxes v Cafolla & Co*[1]. In this case, Joseph Cafolla converted his sole trader business in Dublin into a partnership with his sons. Under the terms of the partnership agreement, Mr Cafolla reserved to himself very extensive and far-reaching powers over the direction and control of the firm. In particular, he had the power to put an end to the partnership at any time, to reclaim the premises, the stock and the goodwill and to resume the carrying on of the business as a sole trader.

Nevertheless it was held by the Special Commissioner of the Revenue, and it was subsequently challenged in the High Court and the Supreme Court, that a partnership existed in this case. Indeed in the High Court, McGuire, J indicated that there was abundant evidence for such a finding. It was argued that Mr Cafolla was entitled at any time to obtain the beneficial entitlement of the income of the firm and therefore the income of the firm should be deemed to be Mr Cafolla's sole income under section 20(1) of the Finance Act 1922.

However, the Supreme Court held by 3:2 majority, that the income of the firm arose from the carrying on of the firm's business under the terms of the partnership agreement and under this agreement the sons undertook to devote the whole of their time to the business of the firm. Thus, although under the terms of the partnership agreement, Mr Cafolla was able to resume the restaurant business as a sole trader at any time, by doing so he would not be receiving the income of "the firm". Thus, the firm's income was not something of which he could have beneficial enjoyment at any time for the purpose of section 20(1) of the Finance Act 1922 and therefore it was incorrect to deem it be his income for income tax purposes. In this way, the Supreme Court maintained the strict distinction between the sole trader's business and that of the subsequent partnership.

The other leading case was *Macken v Revenue Commissioners*[2] which concerned an oral agreement between Mr Macken, his daughter and his son, whereby Mr Macken agreed

---

1   1949 IR210
2   1962 IR302

to admit his daughter and son as partners into his painting business which, up to then, he had operated as a sole trader. The question for the High Court was whether after the date of the oral agreement, the business continued to be carried on as a sole trade operation or whether the parties were carrying on the "business in common".

The Revenue Commissioners claimed that no partnership existed at the date of the oral agreement, but that the transfer of the father's business to his children took place on the date of the execution of the partnership agreement, a number of months later, and the estate duty was to be assessed on this basis.

The profits of the business were in fact shared between the three partners for the period between the oral agreement and the written agreement, and the Revenue Commissioners in assessing income tax treated the three parties as partners. Nonetheless, Teevan, J held that the oral agreement was simply an agreement to enter partnership at a future date and that the partnership did not commence at the date of the oral agreement. The parties were not carrying on a business in common since there was no perceptible change in the manner in which the business was carried on after the oral agreement. In addition, the parties had not reached agreement at that time on one of the vital terms of the agreement, namely a determination of which assets were to be brought into the partnership. The other factors considered by Teevan, J can be framed as questions, which may provide assistance in determining whether a business is being carried on in common after a pre existing business purportedly admits a partner. These are as follows:

1. Has the business name of the firm been changed?

2. Are the bank accounts in the name of the purported partners?

3. Have notices been issued to those parties who have been contracting with the pre-existing business to advise them of a change in structure?

4. Has the transfer of debts from the pre-existing business to the new business taken place?

5. If the pre-existing business was a partnership, has a registration in the Register of Business Names been effected?

6. How was the relationship between the parties treated by the Revenue Commissioners for tax purposes?

18.3   Relevant Legislation

The taxation of partnerships is covered in s1007 to 1012 of the Taxes Consolidation Act 1997.

Section 1013 deals with limited partnerships, which are outside the scope of this chapter.

Important aspects of partnerships covered in the legislation are as follows:

Section1007 – Interpretation

Section1008 – Separate assessment

Section1009 – Partnership involving companies

Section1010 – Capital allowances

Section1011 – Provision as to charges under s757

Section1012 – Modifications of provisions as to appeals.

Section1007, 1008, 1010 and 1012 are the subject matter of this analysis and explanations of these sections, followed by practical examples are set out below.

A partnership is not a legal entity *per se*. For taxation purposes all partners in a partnership are assessed on their share of the profits in the partnership, as if all are sole traders. Partners are individually liable for their respective taxation liabilities in connection with their share of the firm's profits.

Section 1007 sets out the definitions in relation to partnerships to ensure that profits are correctly taxed and collected by Revenue.

18.4   How are Partners Assessed?

John and Bernard are in partnership sharing profits/losses equally.

Profits of the partnership amount to €100,000. John is assessed for €50,000 and Bernard is assessed for €50,000.

How are these details returned to the Revenue or, if no returns are made, how are the profits assessed by Revenue?

The "precedent partner" is established in relation to a partnership. The precedent partner is the partner who, being resident in the State, is the first named in the partnership agreement.

If there is no agreement, the precedent partner is the partner named singly or with precedence over the other partners in the usual name of the firm. For example, in the case of Murphy, Smith & Jones, Murphy is the precedent partner.

If the person named with precedence is not an acting partner, then the precedent acting partner is the precedent partner.

Any reference to a precedent partner shall, in a case where no parties are resident in the State, be construed as a reference to the agent, manager or factor of the firm resident in the State.

The precedent partner is responsible for the preparation for the firm's annual return (Form 1– firms) for filing with the Revenue by the due date (31 October each year). This form can be downloaded from the Revenue website (www.revenue.ie.) and a copy is included at Appendix I.

In effect this return includes all the sources of income of the partnership. It also shows full details of any capital gains tax assessable and any capital assets acquired by the partnership.

The other important interpretation in Section 1007 (1) is that of a "relevant period". This definition is of fundamental importance and broadly means a continuing period, the whole or part of which is subsequent to 5 April 1965, during which a trade is carried on by two or more persons in partnership and during which a complete change of proprietorship did not occur at any time.

A relevant period in relation to a given partnership trade begins:

(a) when the trade is set up or commenced by two or more persons in a partnership, at the time when the trade is commenced, e.g., John & Bernard commenced business in partnership on 1 July 2008;

(b) where the trade having previously been carried on by a sole trader becomes carried on by a partnership (including the partnership of which the former sole trader is a member), at the time of succession, e.g., John and Bernard are sole practitioner solicitors who decide to cease as sole practitioners on 30 June 2008 and commence partnership on 1 July 2008 together;

(c) where the trade having previously been carried on by a partnership becomes carried on by another partnership, none of whose members was a member of the previous partnership at the time of succession, e.g., John and Bernard are carrying on a partnership and Shay and Ray are admitted to the partnership on 30 June 2008 and John and Bernard retire on that date.

A relevant period in relation to a partnership trade ends on the happening of whichever of the following events first occurs:

(a) The trade is in fact discontinued, e.g., John and Bernard are in partnership and decide to cease business on the 30 June 2008.

(b) The partnership is succeeded by a sole trader (including a sole trader who has been a member of the partnership), e.g., John and Bernard are in partnership and Bernard retires on 30 June 2008, with John continuing as a sole trader in business.

(c) The partnership is succeeded by a new partners and no member of the old partnership becomes a member of the new one, e.g., John and Bernard are in partnership and Shay and Ray are admitted to partnership on 1 July 2008 and John and Bernard retire on 30 June 2008.

For a relevant period, the partnership is regarded as an entity having a continued existence despite any changes in its constitution, e.g., if John and Bernard are in partnership and Shay is admitted as a partner on 1 July 2008, the partnership continues.

Example 18.1

When does the relevant period commence and cease in the following scenario?

John is a sole practitioner solicitor for many years. In 2004, he decides with Bernard to create a partnership to include both himself and Bernard.

In 2005, Shay is admitted into the partnership. John retires in 2006 and Ray is admitted to the partnership as a partner.

In 2007, Bernard dies and ceases to be a partner.

In 2008, Shay and Ray are unable to continue and they decide to go their separate ways.

In this example, the relevant period starts in 2004.

Shay's admission in 2005 and the retirement of John in 2005 have no effect. Nor does the death of Bernard in 2007.

The partnership ceases in 2008 and the relevant period ends.

18.5   Apportionment of Profits (losses)

Section 1008 Taxes Consolidated Act 1997 deals with separate assessment of partners.

This section provides that in the case of a trade (or profession) carried on by a partnership, profits arising to a partner in the trade (or losses sustained by a partner in the trade) are taxable (or relieved) as if they were, respectively, profits (or losses) of a separate trade carried on by him/her on his/her own account. The amount of any profits (or losses) attributable to a partner is determined in accordance with the partnership agreement in force for the accounting period. The tax-adjusted accounting profits of the partnership are calculated in the normal way (using the Case I/II rules addressed in Chapter 15). However, there are some additional features, which are unique to partnerships, and these are addressed in further detail at 18.8 below.

Where the profit sharing ratio is constant for the duration of the accounting period or basis period taxable in any given income tax year, then the tax adjusted accounting profits are split in that ratio for that basis period.

Example 18.2

John, Joan and Bernard have been in partnership for several years preparing accounts to 30 September each year and sharing profits and losses equally. On 1 October 2009, they changed the profit sharing ratio to 3:2:2 respectively (John:Joan:Bernard). Tax adjusted accounting profits for the year ended 30 September 2009 amounted to €420,000.

Assessable Case I/II for 2009 is as follows:

	€
John	140,000
Joan	140,000
Bernard	140,000

Albeit that the profit sharing ratio changed during the income tax year, the profits are split in the profit sharing ratio that applies for the basis period, i.e., the accounting year ended 30 September 2009.

Where the profit-sharing ratio changes during the basis period, it is necessary to time-apportion the tax-adjusted accounting profits and to apply the relevant profit-sharing ratios to each component amount.

Example 18.3

Facts as per example 18.2 above, except in this instance, the profit sharing ratio changes to 3:2:2 on 1 April 2009.

Assessable Case I/II for 2009 are as follows:

	Total	*John*	*Joan*	*Bernard*
	€	*€*	*€*	*€*
Tax-adjusted profits from 1/10/2008–31/3/2009	*210,000*	*70,000*	*70,000*	*70,000*
Tax-adjusted profits from 1/4/2009–30/9/2009	*210,000*	*90,000*	*60,000*	*60,000*
Total assessable Case I/II for 2009	*420,000*	*160,000*	*130,000*	*130,000*

18.6   Capital Allowances and Charges

Capital allowances are calculated for the partnership in the normal way, i.e., in accordance with the rules addressed in Chapter 16. The total capital allowance claim is split between the partners on the basis of the profit-sharing ratio that applies in the actual income tax year.

Similarly, charges paid during the year are allocated between the partners in their profit-sharing ratio for the income tax year. Thus, where the profit sharing ratio changes during the income tax year, it is necessary to time apportion the total claim.

This differs from the treatment of tax-adjusted accounting profits, which are split by reference to the ratio that applies during the basis period.

Example 18.4

Facts as per Example 18.2 above except in this instance, a capital allowance claim has been calculated for the partnership in the amount of €84,000.

The profit-sharing ratio changes to 3:2:2 on 1 October 2009.

The capital allowance claim for 2009 must be time apportioned and allocated as follows:

	Total	*John*	*Joan*	*Bernard*
	€	*€*	*€*	*€*
Capital allowance claim 1/1/2009–30/9/2009 (9/12ths)	*63,000*	*21,000*	*21,000*	*21,000*
Capital allowance claim 1/10/2009–31/12/2009 (3/12ths)	*21,000*	*9,000*	*6,000*	*6,000*
Total capital allowance claim 2009	*84,000*	*30,000*	*27,000*	*27,000*

Example 18.5

As above, except in this instance, the profit-sharing ratio changes to 3:2:2 on 1 April 2009

The capital allowance claim for 2009 must be time-apportioned and allocated as follows:

	Total	*John*	*Joan*	*Bernard*
	€	€	€	€
Capital allowance claim 1/1/2009–31/3/2009	21,000	7,000	7,000	7,000
Capital allowance claim 1/4/2009–31/12/2009	63,000	27,000	18,000	18,000
	84,000	34,000	25,000	25,000

18.7 Losses

Losses are apportioned in a similar manner to profits, i.e., in the profit-sharing ratio that applies for the basis period.

Example 18.6

John and Bernard are in partnership sharing profits/losses 2:1.

The partnership results for the year ended 31/12/2009 show a loss of (€90,000)

Apportioned

John – Loss	*(60,000)*
Bernard – Loss	*(30,000)*

Losses may also be created or augmented by capital allowances either to convert a small profit to a loss or to increase the loss incurred for the particular period.

Example 18.7

Bernard and John are in partnership sharing profits/losses 2:1.

The partnership results for the year ended 31/12/2009 are as follows:

Profit	€3,000	
Capital allowances	€6,000	

Apportioned	**Profit**	**Capital allowances**	**Net loss**
John	*2,000*	*(4,000)*	*(2,000)*
Bernard	*1,000*	*(2,000)*	*(1,000)*

The partnership results for the year ended 31/12/2009 are as follows:

Loss	*(€9,000)*
Capital allowances	€6,000

Apportioned	Loss	Capital allowances	Increased loss
	€	€	€
John	(6,000)	(4,000)	(10,000)
Bernard	(3,000)	(2,000)	(5,000)

Each partner has discretion as to how he may utilise his losses in a particular period.

The options available are:

1. The loss may be offset against other income in the year of assessment (s381), or

2. The loss may be carried forward and set off against profits arising from the partner's several trade in future years (s382).

How losses are utilised will depend on the additional income and credits available in the year of assessment in which the loss was incurred and the tax bands at which the partners may be taxed.

Example 18.8

John and Bernard are in partnership sharing profits/losses 2:1

The partnership results for the year ended 31/12/2009 are as follows.

Schedule D, Case I Loss   (€90,000)

Apportioned	€
John	(60,000)
Bernard	(30,000)

John also has Schedule E income for the year ended 31/12/2009 of €90,000. He therefore has the option to:

1. Offset the partnership loss against Schedule E income under section381;

or

2. Carry the loss forward against Schedule D, Case I/II profits in future years under section382.

Scenario 1 (John's tax credits amount to €5,000)

	€
Schedule E – Income	90,000
Loss relief – Section381	(60,000)
Assessable income	€30,000
Taxable @ 20% =	6,000
Credits/reliefs	(5,000)
Net tax payable	1,000

Scenario 2 (John's tax credits amount to €8,000)

	€
Schedule E – Income	*90,000*
Loss relief – Section381	*(60,000)*
Assessable income	*30,000*
Taxable @20% =	*6,000*
Credits	*(8,000)*
Loss of credits	*(2,000)*

In this option the excess of credits cannot be utilised and are therefore lost for the year of assessment.

It would therefore be appropriate to carry forward the Schedule D loss to be offset against Schedule D profits in the future years.

It should be borne in mind that, while capital allowances augment a loss for s381 purposes, unutilised capital allowances may not be carried forward by a partner who has insufficient income to absorb his share of the capital allowances. In these circumstances, the unutilised capital allowances revert to the partnership and are added to the capital allowance claim of the subsequent period and are subdivided again in that period in accordance with the profit-sharing ratio for that subsequent period.

Example 18.9

Ann and Mary share profits of a partnership equally. Ann has no other sources of income, but Mary has sufficient other income to utilise partnership losses and capital allowances in full. Partnership results for 2008 and 2009 are as follows:

		€
2008:	*Tax adjusted loss*	*(40,000)*
	Capital allowances	*6,000*
2009:	*Tax adjusted profit*	*15,000*
	Capital allowances	*8,000*

In 2008, Ann is allocated a loss of €20,000 and capital allowances of €3,000. She is unable to utilise either of these amounts under s381. She may carry forward the unutilised loss of €20,000 against her Case I/II income for 2009 of €7,500 (50% of €15,000). However, her capital allowance claim for 2008 of €3,000 reverts to the partnership and is added to the claim for 2009. Thus, the total capital allowance claim for 2009 available for allocation is €11,000. (€8,000 from 2009 + €3,000 from 2008). This is split in the profit-sharing ratio for 2008, i.e., equally between both partners. Accordingly, Ann loses 50% of her 2008 allocation. In these circumstances, the Revenue may give relief to Ann by making a new apportionment, provided that all partners agree to such a re-apportionment in writing.

18.8   Adjustments Unique to Partnerships

There are two further areas to be examined in relation to partnership taxation:

1.   Interest on capital.

2.   Partners' salaries.

Both of these items constitute adjustments to accounting profits and have implications for the total amount of income attributable to individual partners.

18.8.1   Interest on capital

Partnership agreements can have a clause which states that the partners are entitled to interest on capital invested by them in the partnership. As such, interest on capital is simply an appropriation of profits. It is not an allowable deduction for Case I/II purposes.

This interest is charged against the profits of the partnership before apportionment of the profits and is added back to the individual partner's share of profits for the purposes of determining the total amount assessable on that partner.

Example 18.10

John and Bernard invested €300,000 and €100,000 respectively in the partnership and they agreed to pay 5% of the capital by way of interest before apportioning profits/losses, which are agreed at 2:1.

		€	€
Profits for year ended 31/12/2009			*80,000*
Interest on capital	*– John*	*15,000*	
	– Bernard	*5,000*	
			(20,000)
Profit per accounts			*€60,000*
Apportionment:	*John*	*40,000*	
	Bernard	*20,000*	

Adjusted profit computation: 31/12/2009

Profit per accounts		*60,000*
Add: Interest on capital		*20,000*
Adjusted profit		*80,000*

Apportionment:	**John**	**Bernard**
Interest on capital	*15,000*	*5,000*
Share of profits 2:1	*40,000*	*20,000*
Assessable income	*€55,000*	*€25,000*

18.8.2   Partners' salaries

Again, partnership agreements will usually contain a clause that partners will receive a salary prior to the apportionment of profits/losses. This is particularly the case where there may be a dormant (or sleeping) partner in the firm who has only invested capital in the partnership and who does not take any active part in the trade of the partnership.

Example 18.11

John, Bernard and Aisling are in partnership. John does not take any active part in the business of the firm. It was agreed that Bernard would receive a salary of €30,000 per annum and Aisling a salary of €50,000.

Profits/losses were shared equally.

Net profit after charging salaries for year ended 31/12/2009 amounted to €210,000.

Tax Computation:	*€*
Profit per accounts	*210,000*
Add: Partners' salaries	*80,000*
Adjusted profit	*€290,000*

Apportionment:	*John*	*Bernard*	*Aisling*	*Total*
	€	*€*	*€*	*€*
Partners salaries	*–*	*30,000*	*50,000*	*80,000*
Profits 1:1:1	*70,000*	*70,000*	*70,000*	*210,000*
Assessable	*€70,000*	*€100,000*	*€120,000*	*€290,000*

18.9   Modification of Provision as to Appeals

Where the Inspector of Taxes has made a determination, he/she may give notice of it to the precedent partner.

If the determination is not appealed against or if any appeal against it has been settled, it is to be binding on all the partners and no question as to its correctness can be raised by any partner on an appeal against an assessment made on him/her.

Where the Inspector of Taxes' apportionment of partnership profit/joint allowances is not accepted by one or more of the partners, all the partners and not only the one who appeals, have the right to be informed of, and to be present at, the hearing of the matter by the Appeal Commissioners.

18.10   Joining and Leaving an Existing Partnership

Where a new partner joins an existing partnership, the new partner will be commencing to trade and accordingly, the commencement rules (addressed in Chapter 14) will apply to the new partner in respect of the assessment of his share of partnership profits. The commencement rules will not apply to the other partners who will be subject to the normal current year basis of assessment applicable for individuals continuing in business. Where a partner leaves a partnership which continues in business after his leaving, then the cessation provisions will apply to that partner, but not to the other partners who are continuing to trade. Obviously, in both of these cases, there may be a change in the profit-sharing ratio, which would require that profits and capital allowances be time-apportioned as in the case of Examples 18.3, 18.4 and 18.5 above.

WHAT YOU SHOULD NOW KNOW

On completion of this chapter, you should be able to:

- Identify the existence of a partnership.

- Explain how partners are assessed for income tax.

- Calculate the amount assessable on each partner, including where there is a change in the profit-sharing ratio.

- Calculate the capital allowances and charges due to each partner, including where there is a charge in the profit-sharing ratio.

- Explain the treatment of losses.

- Calculate the amount assessable on each partner where there is interest on capital and/or salaries paid to partner(s).

- Explain the rules that apply where a partner joins or leaves the partnership.

- Complete Questions and the Assignments in Irish Taxation Law and Practice, Volume 2.

Appendix I

Form 1 (Firms)
Partnership Tax Return 2008

Tax Reference Number
Remember to quote this number in all correspondence or when calling at your Revenue office

GCD

TAIN

Return Address

Office of the Revenue Commissioners,
Collector-General's Division,
PO Box 354,
Limerick.

This Tax Return is for use by partnerships.
The Return should be made by the partner

- who is the first named in the agreement of partnership, or
- who is named singly or with precedence in the usual name of the firm if there is no agreement, or
- if the partner named with precedence is not an acting partner then by the precedent acting partner.

If no partner is resident in the State the Return should be made by the firm's agent, manager or factor resident in the State.

RETURN OF INCOME AND CAPITAL GAINS OF THE PARTNERSHIP IN THE YEAR ENDED 31 DECEMBER 2008
RETURN OF CHARGEABLE ASSETS ACQUIRED BY THE PARTNERSHIP IN THE YEAR ENDED 31 DECEMBER 2008

The **Precedent partner** is required by Section 951 Taxes Consolidation Act, as amended, to prepare and deliver a Return of partnership income and gains for 2008 on or before 31 October 2009.

Individual partners should make separate returns on Form 11, in addition to this Return.
Revenue On-Line Service (ROS) allows you to file this form electronically. Access ROS at **www.revenue.ie**

When completing this Return, remember:

- Write clearly and accurately within boxes,
- Any panel(s) or section(s) that do not require an entry should be left blank,
- In date boxes enter the format of Day / Month / Year - 31/10/2008,
- Use BLUE ink when completing this form,
- If there is not enough space in any of the panels provided on the form, attach a separate schedule set out in the same format as the relevant panel(s),
- If submitting this return use any envelope and write "Freepost" above the Return Address. You do not need to attach a stamp.

YOU MUST SIGN THIS DECLARATION

I DECLARE that, to the best of my knowledge and belief, this form contains a correct statement for the purposes of assessment to tax for the year 2008 and a correct statement of capital gains which accrued and of chargeable assets acquired in the year 2008.

Signature

(DD/MM/YYYY)

Date

Capacity of Signatory

Full Name of Partnership/Firm
(if different from above)

Contact Details (in case of query about this return)

Agent's TAIN

Contact Name

Client's Ref.

Telephone or E-Mail

Tax Reference Number ☐☐☐☐☐☐☐☐

Any panel(s) or section(s) that do not require an entry should be left blank.

A - PARTNERSHIP DETAILS [1 - 4]

Panel A is set out on pages 2 and 3; entries should be made on both pages where relevant.

1. If there are any changes under the following headings, not already notified to Revenue, enter the new details here

   (a) **Nature of Primary Trade / Profession**

   (c) **Business Address of Primary Trade / Profession**

Particulars of the Several Partners during Accounting Period(s) covered in Panel B

Complete columns **(i)** to **(vi)** on behalf of all partners

3. Partners **resident** in Ireland

	PPS No. of Partner (i)	Partners share of Case I/II (ii)	Partners share of other income (iii)	If salary received, tick ☑ box (iv)	If interest on capital received, tick ☑ box (v)
(a)		·00	·00	☐	☐
(b)		·00	·00	☐	☐
(c)		·00	·00	☐	☐
(d)		·00	·00	☐	☐
(e)		·00	·00	☐	☐
(f)		·00	·00	☐	☐

4. Partners **not resident** in Ireland

	PPS No. of Partner or Name & Address of Partner (i)	Partners share of Case I/II (ii)	Partners share of other income (iii)	If salary received, tick ☑ box (iv)	If interest on capital received, tick ☑ box (v)
(a)		·00	·00	☐	☐
(b)		·00	·00	☐	☐

Income Tax

Tax Reference Number ☐☐☐☐☐☐☐☐

Any panel(s) or section(s) that do not require an entry should be left blank.

Panel A is set out on pages 2 and 3; entries should be made on both pages where relevant.

1. (b) **Name and Address of Precedent Acting Partner**

Expression of Doubt

2. If you have a genuine doubt about the tax treatment of any item in the Return, tick ☑ this box ☐ and enclose a letter setting out clearly the point at issue.

   Note: Individual partners affected by this tax treatment should also indicate an Expression of Doubt on their own tax return.

Complete columns **(vii)** to **(xi)** if there were changes in the Partnership or in the Basis of Distribution of Profits in this Accounting Period

3. Partners **resident** in Ireland

	Basis of distribution of profits* at start of period (%) (vi)	If partner commenced, tick ☑ box (vii)	If partner ceased, tick ☑ box (viii)	If there was a change in the basis of distribution of profits, tick ☑ box (ix)	Date of Event (DD/MM/YYYY) (x)	Basis of distribution of profits* at end of period (%) (xi)
(a)	☐☐☐.☐☐	☐	☐	☐	☐☐/☐☐/☐☐☐☐	☐☐☐☐.☐☐
(b)	☐☐☐.☐☐	☐	☐	☐	☐☐/☐☐/☐☐☐☐	☐☐☐☐.☐☐
(c)	☐☐☐.☐☐	☐	☐	☐	☐☐/☐☐/☐☐☐☐	☐☐☐.☐☐
(d)	☐☐☐.☐☐	☐	☐	☐	☐☐/☐☐/☐☐☐☐	☐☐☐.☐☐
(e)	☐☐☐.☐☐	☐	☐	☐	☐☐/☐☐/☐☐☐☐	☐☐☐.☐☐
(f)	☐☐☐.☐☐	☐	☐	☐	☐☐/☐☐/☐☐☐☐	☐☐☐☐.☐☐

*after salary and interest on capital

4. Partners **not resident** in Ireland

	Basis of distribution of profits* at start of period (%) (vi)	If partner commenced, tick ☑ box (vii)	If partner ceased, tick ☑ box (viii)	If there was a change in the basis of distribution of profits, tick ☑ box (ix)	Date of Event (DD/MM/YYYY) (x)	Basis of distribution of profits* at end of period (%) (xi)
(a)	☐☐☐.☐☐	☐	☐	☐	☐☐/☐☐/☐☐☐☐	☐☐☐.☐☐
(b)	☐☐☐.☐☐	☐	☐	☐	☐☐/☐☐/☐☐☐☐	☐☐☐.☐☐

*after salary and interest on capital

Tax Reference Number ☐☐☐☐☐☐☐☐☐

Any panel(s) or section(s) that do not require an entry should be left blank.

B - PROFITS FROM TRADES, PROFESSIONS OR VOCATIONS [101 - 145]

	Primary Trade	**Subsidiary Trade**
101. Description of Trade, Profession or Vocation	☐☐☐☐☐☐☐☐☐☐	☐☐☐☐☐☐☐☐☐☐

Do not submit accounts with this Return. Instead you must give an extract of information from the accounts in Extracts From Accounts, Lines 111 - 145.

	Primary Trade	Subsidiary Trade
102. If this source of income ceased during 2008 state the date of cessation (DD/MM/YYYY)	☐☐/☐☐/☐☐☐☐	☐☐/☐☐/☐☐☐☐
103. (a) Amount of adjusted net profit for accounting period	☐☐☐☐☐☐☐ ·00	☐☐☐☐☐☐☐ ·00
(b) If any of the profits entered at Line 103(a) refer to **Stallion Fees,** enter that amount here	☐☐☐☐☐☐☐ ·00	☐☐☐☐☐☐☐ ·00
(c) If any of the profits entered at Line 103(a) refer to **Greyhound Stud Fees,** enter that amount here	☐☐☐☐☐☐☐ ·00	☐☐☐☐☐☐☐ ·00
104. Amount of adjusted net loss for accounting period	☐☐☐☐☐☐☐ ·00	☐☐☐☐☐☐☐ ·00
105. Income assessable under Section 98A(4) TCA 1997, (Reverse Premiums in trading situations) (if not already included above)	☐☐☐☐☐☐☐ ·00	☐☐☐☐☐☐☐ ·00
106. Balancing Charges	☐☐☐☐☐☐☐ ·00	☐☐☐☐☐☐☐ ·00

Capital Allowances for 2008 [107 - 109]

	Primary Trade	Subsidiary Trade
107. Machinery and Plant	☐☐☐☐☐☐☐ ·00	☐☐☐☐☐☐☐ ·00
108. Industrial Buildings and/or Farm Buildings Allowance	☐☐☐☐☐☐☐ ·00	☐☐☐☐☐☐☐ ·00
109. Other	☐☐☐☐☐☐☐ ·00	☐☐☐☐☐☐☐ ·00

Profit or Gains from Dealing in or Developing Land (including Buildings)

110. Profit assessable to Income Tax for the year ended 31 December 2008 (if a loss, show **0.00**)   ☐☐☐☐☐☐☐ ·00

EXTRACTS FROM ACCOUNTS [111 -145]

Accounts Information Period (must be completed)

			Primary Trade	Subsidiary Trade
111.	**From**	(DD/MM/YYYY)	☐☐/☐☐/☐☐☐☐	☐☐/☐☐/☐☐☐☐
112.	**To**	(DD/MM/YYYY)	☐☐/☐☐/☐☐☐☐	☐☐/☐☐/☐☐☐☐

Extracts From Accounts must be completed in all cases where the partnership is in receipt of trading or professional income, except where Line 113 applies.

113. If the partnership has previously submitted accounts information relating to this return state the income tax return with which accounts were submitted (YYYY)   ☐☐☐☐   ☐☐☐☐

Income

	Primary Trade	Subsidiary Trade
114. Sales/Receipts/Turnover	☐☐☐☐☐☐☐ ·00	☐☐☐☐☐☐☐ ·00
115. Receipts from Government Agencies (GMS, etc.)	☐☐☐☐☐☐☐ ·00	☐☐☐☐☐☐☐ ·00
116. Other Income including tax exempt income	☐☐☐☐☐☐☐ ·00	☐☐☐☐☐☐☐ ·00

Tax Reference Number [ ][ ][ ][ ][ ][ ][ ][ ]

Any panel(s) or section(s) that do not require an entry should be left blank.

Trading Account Items	Primary Trade	Subsidiary Trade
117. Purchases	▭·00	▭·00
118. Gross Trading Profits	▭·00	▭·00

Expenses and Deductions

	Primary Trade	Subsidiary Trade
119. Salaries/Wages, Staff costs	▭·00	▭·00
120. Sub-Contractors	▭·00	▭·00
121. Consultancy, Professional fees	▭·00	▭·00
122. Motor, Travel and Subsistence	▭·00	▭·00
123. Repairs/Renewals	▭·00	▭·00
124. Depreciation, Goodwill/Capital write-off	▭·00	▭·00
125. (a) Provisions including bad debts – positive	▭·00	▭·00
(b) If negative, state amount here	▭·00	▭·00
126. Other Expenses (Total)	▭·00	▭·00

Capital Account and Balance Sheet Items

	Primary Trade	Subsidiary Trade
127. Cash/Capital introduced	▭·00	▭·00
128. Drawings (Net of Tax and Pension contributions)	▭·00	▭·00
129. (a) Closing Capital Balance – positive	▭·00	▭·00
(b) If negative, state amount here	▭·00	▭·00
130. Stock, Work in progress, Finished goods	▭·00	▭·00
131. Debtors and Prepayments	▭·00	▭·00
132. Cash/Bank (Debit)	▭·00	▭·00
133. Bank/Loans/Overdraft (Credit)	▭·00	▭·00
134. Client Account Balances (Debit)	▭·00	▭·00
135. Client Account Balances (Credit)	▭·00	▭·00
136. Creditors and Accruals	▭·00	▭·00
137. Tax Creditors	▭·00	▭·00
138. (a) Net Assets – positive	▭·00	▭·00
(b) If negative, state amount here	▭·00	▭·00

Tax Reference Number ☐☐☐☐☐☐☐☐

Any panel(s) or section(s) that do not require an entry should be left blank.

Extracts from Adjusted Profit Computation

	Primary Trade	Subsidiary Trade

Profit/Loss

139. Net Profit per Accounts ☐☐☐☐☐☐☐☐ .00 ☐☐☐☐☐☐☐☐ .00

140. Net Loss per Accounts ☐☐☐☐☐☐☐☐ .00 ☐☐☐☐☐☐☐☐ .00

Adjustments

141. Motor Expenses ☐☐☐☐☐☐☐☐ .00 ☐☐☐☐☐☐☐☐ .00

142. Donations (Political and Charitable)/Entertainment ☐☐☐☐☐☐☐☐ .00 ☐☐☐☐☐☐☐☐ .00

143. Light, Heat and Phone ☐☐☐☐☐☐☐☐ .00 ☐☐☐☐☐☐☐☐ .00

144. Net gain on sale of fixed/chargeable assets ☐☐☐☐☐☐☐☐ .00 ☐☐☐☐☐☐☐☐ .00

145. Net loss on sale of fixed/chargeable assets ☐☐☐☐☐☐☐☐ .00 ☐☐☐☐☐☐☐☐ .00

C - EXEMPT INCOME [201 - 204]

Income from Sources Exempt from Tax

201. (a) Profit, gains or distributions from **Stallion Fees** prior to 1 August 2008 ☐☐☐☐☐☐☐☐ .00

(b) If a loss, enter the amount of the loss prior to 1 August 2008 ☐☐☐☐☐☐☐☐ .00

202. (a) Profit, gains or distributions from **Woodlands** ☐☐☐☐☐☐☐☐ .00

(b) If a loss, enter the amount of the loss ☐☐☐☐☐☐☐☐ .00

203. (a) Profit, gains or distributions from **Greyhound Stud Fees** prior to 1 August 2008 ☐☐☐☐☐☐☐☐ .00

(b) If a loss, enter the amount of the loss prior to 1 August 2008 ☐☐☐☐☐☐☐☐ .00

204. Exempt **Patent Income** including distributions from exempt Patent Income ☐☐☐☐☐☐☐☐ .00

D - IRISH RENTAL INCOME [301 - 308]

Rental Income from Land and Property in the State

301. Where the registration requirements of Part 7 of the Residential Tenancies Act 2004 have been complied with in respect of all residential premises tick ☑ the box ☐

302. Number of properties let ☐☐☐☐☐☐

303. Area in hectares, if applicable ☐☐☐☐☐☐

304. Gross Rent Receivable ☐☐☐☐☐☐☐ .00

305. **Expenses**
(a) Repairs ☐☐☐☐☐☐☐ .00

(b) Interest ☐☐☐☐☐☐☐ .00

(c) "Section 23" type relief where 2008 is the **first** year of claim ☐☐☐☐☐☐☐ .00

(d) Other ☐☐☐☐☐☐☐ .00

306. Amount of **chargeable income** after expenses **but** before Capital Allowances (If a loss, show **0.00**) ☐☐☐☐☐☐☐ .00

307. Total Capital Allowances available for 2008 ☐☐☐☐☐☐☐ .00

308. Amount of unused losses from a prior year ☐☐☐☐☐☐☐ .00

Tax Reference Number ⬚⬚⬚⬚⬚⬚⬚⬚

Any panel(s) or section(s) that do not require an entry should be left blank.

E - OTHER IRISH INCOME [309 - 312]

Income from which Irish income tax was not deducted

309. Interest - (interest on Government or other loans, deposit accounts, etc. and discounts, payable without deduction of Irish income tax) — `,    ,    . 00`

Income from which Irish income tax was deducted

310. Interest paid or credited on deposits with the Commercial Banks, Building Societies, the ACC Bank, the Industrial Credit Corp. and An Post (other than interest on Special Savings Accounts) (Show the **gross** amount paid or credited **before** the application of retention tax) — `,    ,    . 00`

311. Gross Distributions (i.e. distributions **plus** dividend withholding tax) — `,    ,    . 00`

312. Other income, including Patent Royalties, received in 2008 where the partnership is not the original inventor — `,    ,    . 00`

F - FOREIGN INCOME [401 - 417] (Enter amounts in €)

Securities and Possessions outside the State

401. Income from securities and possessions outside the State — `,    ,    . 00`

Foreign Bank Accounts (Section 895 TCA 1997)

Give the following details for each foreign bank account opened in 2008 of which the partnership was the beneficial owner of the deposits held.

402. Name & address of deposit holder (bank, etc.)

403. Date account was opened (DD/MM/YYYY) — ⬚⬚ / ⬚⬚ / ⬚⬚⬚⬚

404. Amount of money deposited on opening the account — `,    ,    . 00`

405. Name & address of intermediary through whom account was opened

(Include details of interest received from these accounts at Line 401)

Foreign Life Policies (Sections 730H, 730I, 730J, 730K TCA 1997)

Give the following details in respect of policies issued in 2008 from ANY Member State of the EU or EEA, or from a Member State of the OECD with which Ireland has a Double Taxation Agreement.

406. Name & address of person who commenced the Foreign Life Policy

407. Terms of the policy

408. Annual premiums payable — `,    ,    . 00`

409. Name & address of the person through whom the Foreign Life Policy was acquired

(Include details of income received from these accounts at Line 401)

Tax Reference Number ⬚⬚⬚⬚⬚⬚⬚⬚

Any panel(s) or section(s) that do not require an entry should be left blank.

Offshore Funds

Give the following details in respect of each material interest in 'regulated offshore fund(s)' [those coming within Sec. 747B(2A) TCA 1997] acquired in 2008 IN the EU or EEA, or in a Member State of the OECD with which Ireland has a Double Taxation Agreement.

410. Name & address of Offshore Fund(s)

411. Date material interest was acquired (DD/MM/YYYY)   ⬚⬚ / ⬚⬚ / ⬚⬚⬚⬚

412. Amount of capital invested in acquiring the material interest   ⬚⬚⬚⬚⬚⬚⬚ · 00

413. Name & address of intermediary (if any) through whom the material interest was acquired

[Include details of income received from these accounts at Line 401]

Other Offshore Products

Give the following details for each material interest acquired in 2008 in (i) other offshore products (including foreign life assurance policies) OUTSIDE the EU or EEA, or outside a Member State of the OECD with which Ireland has a Double Taxation Agreement and in (ii) 'unregulated funds' [those not coming within Sec. 747B(2A) TCA 1997] within the EU or EEA, or within any Member State of the OECD with which Ireland has a Double Taxation Agreement.

414. Name & address of Offshore Products

415. Date material interest was acquired (DD/MM/YYYY)   ⬚⬚ / ⬚⬚ / ⬚⬚⬚⬚

416. Amount of payment made in acquiring the material interest   ⬚⬚⬚⬚⬚⬚⬚ · 00

417. Name & address of intermediary (if any) through whom the material interest was acquired

(Include details of income received from these accounts at Line 401)

G - INCOME/PROFIT FROM SOURCES NOT SHOWN ELSEWHERE

(Include sums received after discontinuance of trade or profession and sums deemed to be income of the partnership under Section 806 TCA 1997)

501. (a) Gross amount of income/profit from sources not shown elsewhere   ⬚⬚⬚⬚⬚⬚⬚ · 00

(b) Detail(s) of income/profit source(s)

Tax Reference Number ⬚⬚⬚⬚⬚⬚⬚⬚

H - ANNUAL PAYMENTS, CHARGES, INTEREST PAID AND DONATIONS [601 - 606]

601. Gross amount of **Rents, etc. payable to Non-Residents** in 2008 · 00

602. **Clawback of Employer's Tax Relief at Source (TRS)**
If you **are an employer** enter gross amount of Medical Insurance premiums paid, if any, on behalf of employees · 00

603. (a) Gross amount of payment of **Charges/Annuities, incl. Patent Royalties** where tax was deducted · 00

(b) Type of payment

604. Interest on mortgage or loan (including bank overdraft interest) · 00

605. Amount of Donations made to **Approved Bodies** · 00

606. Amount of Donations made to **Approved Sports Bodies** · 00

I - PARTNERSHIP PROFITS ASSESSABLE UNDER SEC. 1008(2)(a)(ii) TCA 1997 [701 - 703]

701. Amount of profits assessable under Sec. 1008(2)(a)(ii) TCA 1997 · 00

702. Apportionment required under Sec. 1008(2)(a)(ii) TCA 1997

703. State why the aggregate of profits arising to partners is less than the full amount of the partnership profits

J - CHARGEABLE ASSETS ACQUIRED IN 2008 [801 - 808]

Enter the number of assets acquired and the consideration given

Description of Asset	Number of Acquisitions	Consideration
801. Shares (quoted & unquoted)		· 00
802. Residential Premises		· 00
803. Commercial Premises		· 00
804. Agricultural Land		· 00
805. Development Land		· 00
806. Business Assets		· 00
807. Antiques / Works of Art		· 00
808. Other		· 00

Tax Reference Number

Any panel(s) or section(s) that do not require an entry should be left blank.

K - CAPITAL GAINS ACCRUED IN 2008 [901 - 915]

Details of Assets Disposed of	No. of Disposals	Disposals between connected persons ☑	Aggregate Area in Hectares	Aggregate Consideration (Substitute market value where disposal not made at arm's length)
901. Shares/Securities - Quoted		☐		·00
902. Shares/Securities - Unquoted		☐		·00
903. Agricultural Land/Buildings		☐		·00
904. Development Land		☐		·00
905. Commercial Premises		☐		·00
906. Residential Premises		☐		·00
907. Other Assets		☐		·00
908. **Total Consideration on Disposals**				·00

909. Incidental cost(s) of disposal(s) — ·00

910. Aggregate net consideration (after incidental costs of disposals) — ·00

911. (a) Cost of acquisition (If assets acquired prior to 6/4/1974 or acquired otherwise not at arm's length substitute market value for cost) - indexed where appropriate — ·00

(b) Indicate ☑ if not at arm's length ☐

912. Amount of enhancement expenditure claimed (indexed where appropriate) — ·00

913. Amount of Chargeable Gain/s — ·00

Particulars of Distribution between Partners of Capital Gains Accrued in 2008

914. Partners **resident** in Ireland

PPS No. of Partner	Basis of Distribution (%)	Amount of Chargeable Gain
	·	·00
	·	·00
	·	·00
	·	·00
	·	·00

915. Partners **not resident** in Ireland

Name, address and PPS No. (if any) of Partner	Basis of Distribution (%)
	·
	·

19

TAXATION OF INTEREST, DIVIDENDS AND RENTAL INCOME

In this chapter, you will deal with the following:

- Interest income received without deduction of tax

- Tax treatment of UK dividends and interest

- Tax treatment of scrip dividends

- Taxation of interest received under deduction of tax

- Relief for DIRT

- Savings incentive schemes

- Miscellaneous sources of income taxable under Case IV

- Rental income and allowable deductions

- Irish dividend income

- Dividend withholding tax system

19.1　Introduction

Income may be divided into two categories:

- "earned", and

- "unearned".

"Earned" income is essentially derived from two sources, namely employment and self-employment. The tax treatment of these sources is dealt with elsewhere in this publication.

This chapter addresses the tax treatment of "unearned" income, e.g., interest, dividends, rental and investment income and foreign sourced "earned" income. The same rates of income tax apply to both earned and unearned income. This is to be contrasted with the corporation tax position, whereby the rate of corporation tax applicable to passive or unearned income is generally twice that applicable to earned or trading income.

The chapter is divided as follows:

- Paragraph 19.2 deals with Schedule D Case III. This includes interest received without deduction of tax and foreign-sourced income.

- Paragraph 19.3 deals with Schedule D Case IV. This includes investment income subject to tax at source and miscellaneous other sources of income not taxable under any other Case or Schedule.

- Paragraph 19.4 is concerned with Schedule D Case V, i.e., the tax treatment of rental income from property in the State.

- Paragraph 19.5 deals with Schedule F, i.e., the tax treatment of dividends and distributions received from Irish resident companies.

19.2　Schedule D Case III

The following are the main categories of income assessable under Schedule D Case III:

- interest, annuities and other annual payments not liable to Irish tax at source;

- all "discounts" – a profit on a discount transaction may be realised either by holding a bill (e.g., a bill of exchange, a promissory note, etc.) until its maturity, or by selling it earlier at a price in excess of that paid for it;

- interest on any securities issued under the authority of the Minister for Finance where such interest is paid without deduction of tax – examples include National Loan Stock or securities issued by such bodies as Bord na Móna and the ESB;

■ dividends paid on ordinary credit union share accounts only (dividends/interest paid on credit union special share accounts are liable to DIRT);

■ income arising from foreign securities and possessions to the extent that it has not suffered Irish tax at source – examples include rents from property situated abroad, dividends and interest from UK companies, income from foreign employments or businesses and interest from foreign securities. Readers are referred to 19.3.5.1 for the tax treatment of interest from EU Countries effective from 1 January 2005;

■ shares issued in lieu of dividends receivable from a non-resident company. The cash dividend foregone is liable to tax under Case III without any tax credit.

19.2.1 Basis of assessment

s70 TCA 97 Case III income is assessed to tax on the income arising in the year of assessment. Income arises for Case III purposes when it is received, unlike Cases I, II and V, where income arises when it is earned (and not necessarily received). For the purposes of determining when an individual first becomes taxable under Case III, it is the date on which income first arises from the Case III source that is relevant and not the date on which the Case III source is acquired. The cessation of a Case III source is the date on which the source is disposed of and not the date on which the income ceases. If a source continues to exist but does not produce income in any particular year, there is no cessation. Death constitutes a cessation of a Case III source. Where a husband and wife both have Case III income, they are regarded as having two separate sources of Case III income.

19.2.2 United Kingdom dividends and interest

UK dividends

The assessment is based on the cash amount received exclusive of any tax credit in respect of the dividends received.

Example 19.1

An Irish-resident individual receives a dividend payment from a UK plc. The information on the voucher (i.e., dividend counterfoil) reads:

Net dividend   *stg£99*

Tax credit   *stg£10*

The individual is assessed to tax under Schedule D Case III on the euro equivalent of stg£99. The tax credit is ignored and may not be refunded.

UK interest

Interest from UK securities is assessable under Schedule D Case III. Under the terms of the Ireland/United Kingdom Double Taxation Agreement (Article 12), the interest is liable only to Irish tax where the recipient is a resident of Ireland. Any UK tax deducted at source may be recovered in full on foot of an appropriate claim to the UK tax authorities.

Example 19.2

An Irish-resident individual receives an interest payment from UK debenture stock. The information on the voucher (i.e., interest counterfoil) reads:

Gross interest	*stg£100*
Tax deducted	*stg£20*
Net interest	*stg£80*

The individual is assessed to tax under Case III on the euro equivalent of stg£100. The UK tax deducted of stg£20 may be recovered in full on foot of an appropriate claim to the UK tax authorities.

19.2.3 Allowable deductions

The allowable deductions which may be set against Case III income for tax purposes are limited – the main one being a deduction for foreign tax borne on foreign income to the extent that it is not allowed as a credit under a double taxation agreement. However, in the case of foreign rents, deductions are normally allowed for interest, rates, repairs, insurance, management and collection expenses. Similarly, in the case of foreign trades, deductions are normally allowed for trading expenses. For commentary on allowable trading expenses, readers are referred to Chapter 15.

19.3 Schedule D Case IV

Tax is charged under Schedule D Case IV on any annual profits or gains not falling under any other Case of Schedule D and not falling under any other Schedule. In addition to certain specific sources directed by the legislation to be charged under Case IV, the Case embraces all profits and gains not otherwise chargeable under another Schedule.

19.3.1 Basis of assessment

s74 TCA 97 The basis of assessment for Case IV is normally the actual profits arising in the year of assessment. The amount assessable under Case IV is "the full amount of the profits or gains arising". There is no specific direction as to how these profits or gains are to be determined.

19.3.2 Losses

s383 TCA 97 Where in any year of assessment a person sustains a loss on a transaction (being a transaction which, had a profit arisen would have been assessable under Schedule D Case IV), then such loss may be set off against other profits assessable under Case IV for that year of assessment. Any portion of the loss for which relief is not so given may be carried forward and relieved against subsequent profits assessed under Case IV.

19.3.3 Statutory sources of Case IV income

The following are the main categories of income specifically assessable under Case IV on the basis of the legislation:

(a) income subject to tax at source;

(b) sale of patent rights for a capital sum;

(c) partnership profits not allocated to partners; (readers are referred to (c) overleaf for F.A. 2007 changes)

(d) income subject to deposit interest retention tax (DIRT);

(e) certain dividend payments by credit unions;

(f) post-cessation receipts;

(g) shares in lieu of dividends;

(h) profits from unlawful activities.

Income received by an individual under deduction of income tax is charged to tax under Schedule D Case IV. Section 59 TCA 97 provides that credit is given for the tax deducted, against the tax payable by the individual. The assessment is on the gross amount of the income. An example of income chargeable under this case is a payment received under a Deed of Covenant. The payer deducts tax at the standard rate from the payment due to the payee and the payee claims credit for it against his/her own tax liability.

Example 19.3

Malachy Jones pays €8,000 (gross) per year under a Deed of Covenant to his aunt. He must deduct standard rate tax in the amount of €1,600 from the gross payment. Thus, his aunt receives a net amount of €6,400 on an annual basis. In 2009, his aunt is assessed to tax under Schedule D Case IV as follows:

	€	€
Income under Deed of Covenant		*8,000*
Taxed as follows:		
€8,000 × 20%		*1,600*
Less non-refundable credits:		
Single person's credit		*(1,830)*
Tax liability		*Nil*
Less		
Tax deducted on Deed of Covenant		*(1,600)*
Tax overpaid		***(1,600)***

Malachy Jones' aunt may claim a refund of €1,600.

(b) Sale of patent rights for a capital sum

s757
TCA 97

Section 757 TCA 97 provides that where a person resident in Ireland sells any patent rights and the net proceeds of the sale consist wholly or partly of a capital sum, he/she is assessable to tax under Schedule D Case IV. The amount receivable is spread over six years, i.e., one-sixth of the lump sum is assessed in each year. The taxpayer may elect to have the total amount receivable charged to tax in the year in which it is received.

A person not resident in Ireland who sells Irish patent rights is also liable to tax under Schedule D Case IV on the amount receivable, provided the proceeds of the sale consist wholly or partly of a capital sum. However, the purchaser of the patent rights is obliged to deduct income tax at the standard rate on the amount payable to the non-resident. The non-resident may elect to have the sum receivable spread over six years for the purposes of being assessed to tax.

(c) Partnership profits not allocated to partners

s1008 TCA 97   Section 1008 TCA provided that undistributed profits of a partnership were assessed on the precedent acting partner under Schedule D Case IV at 20%. Section 30 Finance Act 2007 amended this, effective from 1 January 2007, whereby the undistributed profits are allocated for tax purposes to each partner and taxed at the marginal rate.

(d) Income subject to Deposit Interest Retention Tax (DIRT)

s256 TCA 97   Section 256 TCA 97 provides that interest paid on deposits held in banks, building societies and other similar institutions is, in most cases, subject to DIRT. This means that the interest is paid under deduction of tax and, as such, is assessable in the hands of the recipient under Case IV. (DIRT is considered in more detail at 19.3.5.)

(e) Dividend payments by credit unions

Credit union members are obliged to declare dividends received and are liable to marginal rate tax on the full amount of the dividend. While this system continues for dividends from which tax is not deducted at source, s57 provides the credit union member with a facility to elect for tax treatment in any of the following ways:

(a) Given that credit unions are now deemed "Relevant Deposit-Takers" the member may be liable to DIRT on deposit interest at source.

(b) The member may elect, in writing, to open a Special Share Account. Where such an election is made the value of the shares held in the account at any time is treated as a relevant deposit. The value of any dividend paid on the shares is treated as if the dividend was interest and appropriate tax is levied on such interest. Appropriate tax (DIRT) in this instance has the same meaning as that defined in s256 (I) TCA 97 and is considered at paragraph 19.3.5.

(c) The member may elect in writing to open a medium or long-term share account. The conditions relating to these accounts and the tax treatment of the accounts are identical to those pertaining to Special Term Accounts, which are considered in detail at paragraph 19.3.7.

(f) Post-cessation receipts

s95 TCA 97   Section 95 TCA 97 provides that sums received after the cessation of a trade or profession, which could not be brought into account while the business or profession was being carried on, are taxed under Schedule D Case IV. The charge is extended to consideration received for the transfer of the right to receive post-cessation receipts.

(g) Shares in lieu of dividends

It is common for companies when declaring dividends to give their shareholders the option of receiving additional share capital in the company rather than the cash dividend. Readers will recall that where such shares are received from non-resident companies, the receipt is taxable under Case III. Section 816 TCA 97 provides that where the paying company is an Irish-resident company, which is not a quoted company, the individual is taxed on an amount equal to the cash distribution (net of any tax credit) that he/she would have received had the option not been exercised to take the additional share capital. There is no entitlement to a tax credit against the tax on income assessable. For the tax treatment of shares in lieu of dividends from quoted resident companies, readers are referred to the analysis at 19.5.5 below.

(h) Profits from unlawful activities

Profits or gains may be charged to tax notwithstanding that:

■ the source from which the profits or gains arose is not known to the Revenue Commissioners;

■ the profits or gains are not known to have arisen wholly or partly from a lawful source of activity.

Such profits or gains are charged as miscellaneous income under Schedule D Case IV. This provision effectively nullifies the decision of the Supreme Court in the case of *Hayes v Duggan* (1 ITC 269). These provisions were further extended by DCITPA 1996 Disclosure of Certain Information for Taxation and Other Purposes Act 1996 in relation to income or gains, which derive, or are suspected to derive, from criminal activity.

19.3.4   Non-statutory instances of Case IV

The following are examples of sources of income liable to tax under Schedule D Case IV. The legislation does not specifically state that these sources of income are liable to tax under Case IV, but case law has held that they are so assessable:

■ casual profits, i.e., profits of a casual nature not chargeable to tax under Schedule E or Schedule D Cases I or II;

■ profits from the hire of movable assets where a similar trade is not carried on;

■ fees, etc., not arising from land, e.g., shipping dues;

■ lettings of premises in such circumstances that the relationship of landlord and tenant does not exist between the owner and the lessee, e.g., lettings of halls for dances, meetings, etc.;

■ casual literary activities that do not constitute the exercise of a profession;

■ fees from sporting or fishing rights;

- green fees from non-members received by a golf club, if not amounting to a trade assessable under Schedule D Case I;

- copyright royalties.

19.3.5 Deposit interest retention tax (DIRT)

s257
TCA 97

Deposit interest retention tax is charged on the payment of certain interest by specified institutions. Section 257 TCA 97 provides for the deduction of "appropriate tax" (DIRT) on the payment of deposit interest by a "relevant deposit-taker".

The following are "relevant deposit-takers" for the purposes of the DIRT provisions:

(a) a bank which has been granted a licence under s9 Central Bank Act 1971 or under a similar law of another EC Member State;

(b) a building society (within the meaning of the Building Society Act 1989 or established under a similar law of another EC Member State);

(c) a credit union (from 1/1/2002);

(d) Trustee Savings Bank;

(e) the Post Office Savings Bank.

Rates of DIRT

Prior to 1 January 2009, where interest was paid at intervals which did not exceed 12 months, the rate of DIRT was 20% (where interest payments were at intervals which exceeded 12 months, the rate was 20% + 3%). The following rates now apply:

from 1/1/2009 23% (Plus 3% where appropriate)

from 8/4/2009 25% (Plus 3% where appropriate)

Treatment in hands of recipient

s261
TCA 97

Under the provisions of s261 TCA 97, DIRT paid on a relevant deposit account is deemed to be in full settlement of the income tax liability on that income, even if the individual is liable to tax at the higher rate. However, the gross interest is liable for the health contribution levy, but not for the income levy.

Refunds of DIRT

A relevant deposit-taker must deduct DIRT unless instructed otherwise by the Revenue Commissioners. Certain categories of deposit-holders, although subject to the deduction of DIRT at source, may be entitled to a refund if the DIRT exceeds their overall tax liability. Examples of such categories are considered below.

s267
TCA 97

(a) **Charities** (as recognised for tax purposes) are entitled to a refund of DIRT by virtue of s267(2) TCA 97. However they may avoid the need to reclaim DIRT deducted on interest received by arranging with the Revenue Commissioners to have interest paid gross.

s263
TCA 97

(b) **Individuals who are not resident in Ireland** may elect to have Irish deposit interest paid to them free of DIRT by making an appropriate written declaration of non-residency to the deposit-holder (s263 TCA 97). In the past, false declarations of non-residency were commonplace in Ireland with many taxpayers using bogus non-resident accounts to evade liability to DIRT.

s189A(2)
TCA 97

(c) **Special trusts for permanently incapacitated individuals** are entitled to refunds of DIRT where interest income is exempt from income tax under s189A (2) TCA 97.

s267(1)(a)
TCA 97

(d) **An individual who was**, or whose spouse was, at some time during the relevant tax year, **aged 65 or older** (s267(1)(a) TCA 97) is entitled to a refund of DIRT. Section 34 Finance Act 2007 provides that the deposit taker may pay the interest gross, i.e., without the deduction of DIRT, where:

■ at any time in a year of assessment, the individual beneficially entitled to the interest or his or her spouse is 65 years of age or over and their total income does not exceed the relevant income exemption limit; and

■ such individual makes a declaration to that effect to the relevant deposit taker.

s267(1)(b)
TCA 97

(e) A refund of DIRT is also granted to an individual who was, or whose spouse was, throughout the relevant tax year, or from some time during the tax year, permanently incapacitated by reason of mental or physical infirmity, from maintaining himself/herself (s267(1)(b) TCA 97). Section 34 Finance Act 2007 also provides that the deposit taker may pay the interest gross i.e. without the deduction of DIRT, where:

■ the individual beneficially entitled to the interest or his or her spouse is permanently incapacitated or where the persons entitled to the interest are trustees of a special trust are permanently incapacitated individuals who are exempt from tax under Section 189A (2); and

■ the deposit taker receives the appropriate notification from the Revenue Commissioners.

An individual not within any of the above categories (e.g., an individual under 65 years and not permanently incapacitated by reason of mental or physical infirmity, from maintaining himself/herself) is not entitled to a refund of DIRT even if he/she is in a repayment situation for the tax year or is otherwise completely exempt from income tax.

Tax Facts

Deposit Interest: 2009 Onwards

For the first time since the introduction of DIRT, the withholding tax on interest (paid at intervals of 12 months or less) is greater than the standard rate of tax – (currently 20%).

Example 19.4

Ethel Jones is 64 years old and has been a widow for many years. Her only source of income is derived from deposit interest. The net interest paid to her in March 2009 is €15,064. Her assessment to tax for 2009 is as follows:

	€	€
Schedule D Case IV		*19,564*
Taxed as follows:		
€19,564 × 23%		*4,500*
Less non-refundable credits:		
Widowed person's tax credit	*(2,310)*	
DIRT	*(4,500)*	
		(6,810)
Excess tax credits (non-refundable)		*(2,310)*
Tax liability		*Nil*

Ethel Jones may not claim a refund of the excess tax credit of €2,310. However, if she was permanently incapacitated by reason of mental or physical infirmity from maintaining herself, she would be entitled to the refund.

Example 19.5

Assume the same facts, as above in Example 19.4 except that Ethel Jones is over 65 years of age and DIRT is deducted at source. Her assessment to tax for 2009 is as follows:

	€	€
Schedule D Case IV		*19,564*
Taxed as follows:		
€19,564 × 20%	*4,500*	
Less non-refundable credits:		
Widowed person's tax credit	*(2,310)*	
Tax liability	*2,190*	
Less refundable credits:		
DIRT	*(4,500)*	
Tax overpaid	*(2,310)*	

In these circumstances, Ethel Jones may claim a refund of the excess DIRT of €2,310.

Ethel Jones may also arrange to have such interest paid without the deduction of DIRT, subject to making the appropriate declaration to the deposit taker.

19.3.5.1 Deposit Interest

Prior to 1 January 2005 deposit interest paid by financial institutions outside Ireland was liable to tax under Schedule D Case III.

Section 20 Finance Act 2005 introduced changes to the tax treatment of interest paid by EU Banks, Building Societies etc. Previously such interest was liable to tax (under Schedule D Case III) at the depositor's marginal rate. From 1 January 2005 the interest is liable only to tax at the standard rate of tax, provided the tax due is paid by the tax return filing date for the year concerned.

19.3.6 Special term accounts

s261A
TCA 97

Section 57 of the Finance Act 2001, which came into effect on 1/1/2002 by Ministerial Order, made provisions for the introduction of two new deposit-based accounts, which attract favourable tax treatment.

There are two types of account to choose from:

- a medium-term account; and

- a long-term account.

A medium-term account is for a term of at least three years' duration and a long-term account is for a term of at least five years' duration.

s256
TCA 97

These accounts are deposit-based and the legislation specifically prohibits returns that are linked in any way to stocks, shares, debentures and listed or unlisted securities. The list of relevant is set out in s256 TCA 97 and includes credit unions.

There are a number of conditions relating to Special Term Accounts:

- the account may not be denominated in foreign currency;

- the account holder must be aged over 16;

- the account must be in the name of the beneficial owner;

- the maximum monthly contribution is €635. However, a once-off contribution of €7,620 may be added to the fund;

- the individual may only hold one account. However, married individuals may hold two joint accounts simultaneously;

- withdrawals from the account may not be made within the three-year or five-year period, except:

    (a) an individual whose account commenced before his/her sixtieth birthday may make a single withdrawal without penalty on or after his/her sixtieth birthday.

    (b) withdrawals may be made without penalty on the death of the account-holder.

- the deposit interest rate may not be guaranteed for a period of more than 12 months;

- interest may accumulate within the account. The deposit-holder may elect to withdraw the interest provided that he/she does so within 12 months of it being credited to the account.

19.3.6.1 Taxation of special term accounts

Medium-term account

A charge to tax arises on a medium term account if the interest realised on the account exceeds €480 per annum. Interest up to €480 is not taken into account in computing total income. Interest realised in excess of this amount is charged to DIRT.

Long-term account

A charge to tax arises on a long-term account if the interest realised on the account exceeds €635 per annum. Interest up to €635 is not taken into account in computing total income. Interest realised in excess of this amount is charged to DIRT.

If the conditions regarding the accounts are breached within the three- or five-year terms, the legislation makes provisions for the taxation of the amounts, which were previously exempt on the basis of being below the €480 or €635 thresholds.

19.4   Schedule D Case V

This section details the taxation implications on the receipt of income from property and easements, which are chargeable to income tax under Schedule D Case V.

19.4.1   Income assessable

s18 TCA 97   Section 18 TCA 97 charges to tax rent arising from Irish property and receipts from easements. The term "easement" includes any right, privilege or benefit in, over or derived from premises - e.g., a right-of-way. Foreign rents are assessable under Case III of Schedule D.

19.4.2   Basis of assessment

s75(3)
TCA 97

The basis of assessment for Case V is the income arising in the year of assessment. For example, the rental income receivable during the year ended 31 December 2008 is assessable in the tax year 2008. Unlike Schedule D Cases I and II, there are no special rules for calculating Case V in the years of commencement and cessation.

It is the date on which income first arises from the Case V source, and not when the Case V source is acquired, that creates a commencement. Income arises when the person chargeable becomes entitled to it, even though the income may not necessarily be received.

Example 19.8:

Brendan Smith who owns an apartment enters into a lease agreement with a tenant. The lease is effective from 1 February 2009 at an agreed rent of €1,500 per month. The rent due for February and March is paid on time. However, the rent for April to December inclusive remains unpaid at 31 December 2009. The arrears of €13,500 are eventually paid in February 2010.

Brendan Smith is assessable on Case V income of €16,500 for 2009 (i.e., €1,500 × 11 months).

The date of cessation of a Case V source is the date on which the source is disposed of, not the date on which the income ceases. If a source continues to exist, but does not produce income in any particular year, there is no cessation.

Death constitutes a cessation of a Case V source.

19.4.3 Deductions

s384
TCA 97

Section 97(2) TCA 97 sets out the types of deduction which may be made from the gross rents received. In computing the net rents assessable under Case V, the following expenses may be deducted:

- "rent" payable in respect of the property (e.g., ground rent);

- rates payable on the property;

- cost of goods provided, or services rendered, in connection with the letting;

- cost of maintenance, repairs, insurance and management of the property;

- interest on monies borrowed for the purchase, improvement or repair of the property (see 19.4.3.1 for restrictions);

- mortgage protection policy premia.

A deduction is not allowed in computing net rents for any capital expenditure (with the exception of the capital expenditure referred to in paragraph 19.4.5).

While not provided for in the legislation, the Revenue Commissioners allow accountancy on a concession basis, fees incurred for the purposes of preparing a rent account as an allowable deduction in computing Case V income for income tax purposes.

Only the expenses relating directly to that portion of a property which is let are allowable deductions for Case V purposes. If only part of a property is let, expenses incurred on the property as a whole are apportioned. An example of a Case V computation illustrating the apportionment of deductions from the rental income of a property, which is partially let, and partially occupied, is set out below.

Example 19.9

A landlord has owned a property for some time. Half of the property is let and the landlord occupies the other half. In 2009 the rents receivable were €6,000, the expenses on the house as a whole were as follows:

	€
Insurance	*500*
Rates	*700*
Cleaning	*300*
Repairs	*2,000*

The following is the Case V computation for 2009:

	€	€
Gross rents		6,000
Allowable expenditure		
Insurance	250	
Rates	350	
Cleaning	150	
Repairs	1,000	
		(1,750)
Case V		4,250

*As half the property is let, only half of the relevant expenditure is allowed as a deduction.

19.4.3.1 Interest on borrowed monies

Interest paid on monies borrowed for the purchase, improvement or repair of the let property is allowed as a deduction. However, there are some restrictions. Section 16 Finance Act 2003 was introduced to counter contrived arrangements between spouses. Where one spouse buys out the interest of the other spouse in the family home, then moves to another property and lets the original family home, the interest on the borrowed monies (to buy out the other spouse's interest) is not allowed as a deduction against the rental income from the original family home. This restriction only applies to residential lettings.

Section 11 Finance Act 2006 introduced a new provision whereby relief for interest paid is conditional on the borrower meeting the registration requirements of the Residential Tenancies Act 2004. This condition is effective from 1 January 2006.

Finance Act 2009 provides that interest on monies borrowed to purchase, improve or repair a residential premises is restricted to 75% of qualifying expenditure with effect from Budget Day, 7 April 2009. The restriction applies regardless of whether the loan was taken out before or after 7 April 2009.

19.4.3.2 Pre-letting expenses and expenses between lettings

In computing the net rents assessable, no deduction is allowed for pre-letting expenses incurred prior to first occupancy. Thus, no deduction is available for any rent payable or interest paid on monies borrowed for the purchase, improvement or repair of any property to the extent that such expenses are incurred prior to the date on which the premises are first occupied by a lessee. However, it should be borne in mind that expenses incurred by the lessor in negotiating a lease for the property are allowable deductions in computing the assessable rental income. This is in accordance with the ruling in the Irish case of *Stephen Court Ltd v J A Brown* (H.C. 1982 No. 293 S.S.).

In this case a letting agent was appointed by the lessor to negotiate a lease for the property and to prepare the necessary documents. The letting agent was not entitled to any fee until a letting had been agreed. It was held by McWilliam J. in the High Court that the expenses of negotiating the lease and preparing the necessary documents were incurred during the currency of the lease and not for the purpose of setting up the lease. It was also held that such expenses were not expenses of a capital nature but were expenses of management.

Expenses incurred in the period between the termination of one lease and the granting of a new lease of the same premises are allowed provided the following two conditions are met:

(i) the person who was the lessor of the premises immediately before the termination of the lease did not occupy the premises during the post-termination period but was entitled to possession of the premises; and

(ii) the premises became subject to another lease granted by the same lessor at end of that period.

19.4.4 Losses

A loss or deficiency arises when the total allowable deductions exceed the gross rental income receivable for the year of assessment. A deficiency arising on a Case V computation in any year of assessment is carried forward and set-off against Case V profits in subsequent year(s) of assessment.

In the case of a loss arising from lettings outside the State (and therefore assessable under Schedule D of Case III), it is understood that in practice, the Revenue Commissioners concessionally allow such a loss to be carried forward and set against future profits from the same property.

19.4.4.1 Favoured lettings

s75 TCA 97   Where a property is let other than at an arm's length arrangement and the rent receivable is insufficient to cover the outgoings on the property, any loss arising will only be allowed against profits from that property only. "Favoured" lettings usually occur between connected persons e.g., relatives of the landlord.

19.4.5 Capital allowances

s284(7) TCA 97   In the case of furnished lettings, capital allowances may be claimed on expenditure incurred on fixtures and fittings, e.g., furniture, fitted kitchens, carpets, curtains, etc. For expenditure incurred on or after 1 January 2001 and before 4 December 2002, the wear & tear allowance is 20% per annum of the cost of the furniture/fittings on a straight-line basis. For expenditure incurred post-4 December 2002, the rate is 12.5% per annum, also on a straight-line basis. These capital allowances may only be offset against Case V income.

Example 19.10

A landlord spent €1,000 on fixtures and fittings on 1 February 2009 for use in a rented residential property, which has been let continuously since 2002. He may claim capital allowances as follows:

2009

€1,000 × 12.5% = €125.00

For each year thereafter he may claim €125 until the full expenditure of €1,000 is written off.

Capital allowances are considered in detail in Chapter 16.

19.4.6 "Rent a room" relief

s216A TCA 97 Section 32 Finance Act 2001 inserted a new section, s216A TCA 97, which exempts from income tax, "relevant sums" (€10,000 for 2008 and following years of assessment), derived from the renting out of a room in a "qualifying residence".

"Relevant sums" are defined as all sums received for the use of the accommodation, and include sums arising in respect of goods and services, for example, meals, cleaning, laundry, etc.

A "qualifying residence" is defined as a private residence situated in the State which is occupied by the owner as his/her principal private residence during the tax year.

Profits or gains or any losses in respect of relevant sums are ignored for the purpose of the Income Tax Acts. Relevant sums are calculated without any deduction for expenses.

It is important to note that should the relevant sums exceed the above limits, all of the income is taxable and not just the excess. An individual is obliged to disclose relevant sums when filing a tax return and also has the choice of electing not to claim this relief each tax year. Wear & tear allowances are deemed to be granted unless an election to not claim this relief has been made. If an individual elects not to claim this relief, the election must be made to the Inspector of Taxes, in writing, on or before the return-filing deadline for the year.

The receipt of relevant sums does not affect an individual's entitlement to mortgage interest relief (see Chapter 12) and capital gains tax relief on the disposal of a principal private residence (see Chapter 27). Section 14 of the Finance Act 2007 removed the exemption for children residing with their parents who pay "rent" to their parents.

s216B TCA 97 Section 12 Finance Act 2004 introduced a form of "Rent a Room" relief for households in Gaeltacht areas. A scheme known as Scéim na bhFoghlaimeoirí Gaeilge exempts such income from tax with no income limit.

Example 19.11

Margaret Kelly has lived alone for many years. Due to diminishing returns on her investments she finds that her income is not sufficient to meet her day-to-day living needs. Her only recourse is to let part of her own home. She is not happy with the idea of a stranger using her cooking and washing facilities. Therefore she decides to offer accommodation on a full-board basis, which includes providing laundry facilities. She registers with a local college and a student is recommended to her. The guidelines for the weekly provision of accommodation and related services given to her are as follows:

	€
Bed and breakfast only	*85.00*
Lunch and evening meal	*30.00*
Laundry	*5.50*
Total	*120.50*

Margaret Kelly charged the recommended amount of €120.50 per week. In 2009, she received €120.50 per week from Student A for 30 weeks and €120.50 per week from Student B for 25 weeks.

The total gross amount received in 2009 is €6,627.50. The related costs are €2,305. Since the gross amount is below the exempt threshold of €10,000, Margaret Kelly is not liable to tax under Schedule D Case V.

Had she received €10,700 gross, even though the allowable expenses would reduce the profit figure to under €10,000, she would be liable to tax under Schedule D Case V on the net rental profit.

19.4.7 Taxation of reverse premiums

s98 TCA 97   In recent times, it has become more popular for property developers to offer some type of inducement to prospective tenants to encourage them to enter into a lease for a commercial premises. This would especially have been the case with "anchor tenants". Such an inducement usually consisted of a direct payment to the prospective tenant and was not subject to income tax in the hands of the tenant.

s98A(2) TCA 97   Section 18 Finance Act 2002 was introduced to redress this position. Where an inducement to enter into a lease is made to a prospective tenant, such inducement is treated as a taxable receipt under Case V Schedule D (or Case I or II where the prospective tenant carries on a trade or profession). Section 98A(2) TCA 97 treats a reverse premium as a receipt of a revenue nature and hence, the amount is taxed as if it were an amount of rent.

However, where the person enters into such a transaction for the purpose of a trade or profession either carried on or shortly to be carried on by that individual, then the reverse premium is treated as a taxable receipt of the profession or trade and is assessed to tax under Schedule D Case I or II.

19.4.8 Favoured lettings

s75(4) TCA 97   Where the rent receivable under a lease is insufficient, taking one year with another, to meet the allowable expenses of the letting, any losses arising in respect of that lease may not be relieved either by carry forward or by set-off against other rental income. An example of such a situation arises where property is let to a connected person, e.g., a relative.

19.4.9   Exemption of income from leasing of farmland

**s664
TCA 97**

Exemption from income tax is granted in respect of certain leasing income obtained by a lessor of agricultural land. The conditions attaching to the relief are:

(a) the income must arise from the leasing of farmland;

(b) the lease must be in writing and for a definite term of five years or more;

(c) the land must be leased to an individual who is not connected with the lessor and who uses the farmland leased for the purpose of a trade of farming carried on solely by him or in partnership;

(d) (i)   the land must be leased by an individual who is aged 40 years or more or who without reference to age, is permanently incapacitated by reason of mental or physical infirmity from carrying on a trade of farming, and

   (ii)   The land may not be leased to a connected person on terms which are not at arm's length.

For any qualifying leases entered into on or after 1 January 2006, the limits are:

■ €15,000 for a lease of seven years or more;

■ €12,000 for a lease of between five and seven years.

Section 16 Finance Act 2007 introduced an additional threshold of relief of €20,000 per annum for leases exceeding 10 years' duration.

The leasing income of a husband and wife is treated separately for the purposes of the relief, whether they are jointly assessed or not.

19.4.10 Property-based tax incentives

Various incentive measures apply under many property schemes, which have been introduced over the course of the last 20 years. A detailed analysis of the various schemes is outside the scope of this publication. However, a short resumé of one measure, which is commonly known as "Section 23" relief, is included.

Expenditure on rented accommodation

Expenditure incurred on the construction, refurbishment or conversion of a house or flat for letting is allowable as a deduction against the rental income from the property or other properties.

The relief applies to new, refurbished or converted properties measuring between 35 sq.m. and 125 sq.m. in the case of a house and 30 sq.m. to 90 sq.m. in the case of a flat which, without having been used for owner-occupation, is let by its owner to a tenant on an arm's length basis.

A clawback of relief arises where the property ceases to be a qualifying premises or the lessor's interest passes to another party (including on death) within ten years of the first letting of the premises under a qualifying lease.

In calculating the relief, the site cost together with a proportion of the builder's profit is not allowable as qualifying expenditure. Qualifying expenditure is arrived at by applying the formula:

$$\text{Purchase Price} \quad \times \quad \frac{\text{Builder's Development Cost}}{\text{Builder's Site Cost} + \text{Builder's Development Cost}}$$

An example of how to compute qualifying expenditure is as follows:

Example 19.11

	€
Cost of site	*5,000*
Site development costs	*2,000*
Building costs	*20,000*
Builders profit	*3,000*
Purchase price	*30,000*

Qualifying expenditure is, therefore:

$$€30,000 \quad \times \quad \frac{(€2,000 + €20,000)}{(€5,000 + €2,000 + €20,000)} \quad = \quad \mathbf{€24,444}$$

Assuming the assessable Case V figure in the year in which the above expenditure is incurred is €20,000, the net tax position is as follows:

	€
Case V	*20,000*
"Section 23" relief	*(24,444)*
Case V loss	*(4,444)*

The loss arising may be carried forward to future years.

19.5   Schedule F

19.5.1   Income assessable

s20 TCA 97   Tax under Schedule F is charged on dividends and other distributions received from Irish-resident companies. The term "distribution" is widely defined and it includes any distribution out of profits of a company except distributions in respect of a company's share capital on the winding-up of that company. A comprehensive list of items to be treated as a distribution is reproduced at Appendix I.

19.5.2 Basis of assessment

The basis of assessment for Schedule F for any year of assessment is the actual dividends or distributions received in that year of assessment.

19.5.3 Dividend withholding tax (DWT)

s172A
TCA 97

Withholding tax equal to the standard rate of tax applies to dividends (including scrip dividends and non-cash dividends) and other distributions (referred to as relevant distributions) paid by an Irish-resident company.

Dividends paid to Ministers of Government in their capacity as such Ministers and distributions made by an Irish-resident subsidiary company to its parent in another EU Member State are excluded from the provisions of dividend withholding tax. An Irish resident individual in receipt of distributions from an Irish-resident company is entitled to offset the withholding tax deducted against his/her total tax liability. Where the withholding tax deducted exceeds the recipient's tax liability, the excess may be reclaimed from the Revenue Commissioners. Thus, dividend withholding tax constitutes a refundable tax credit.

Example 19.12

Brian Jones is single. In 2009 he received €24,000 net dividends from Irish quoted companies. Ignoring PRSI, the Health Contribution levy and income levy, his assessment to tax is as follows:

	€
Schedule F	*30,000*
Taxed as follows:	
€30,000 × 20%	*6,000*
Less non-refundable credits:	
Single person's credit	*(1,830)*
Tax liability	*4,170*
Less refundable credits:	
Dividend withholding tax	*(6,000)*
Tax overpaid	***(1,830)***

Brian Jones is entitled to a repayment of €1,830.

Dividends may be paid gross (i.e., without the need to deduct DWT) to the following recipients:

(a) other Irish-resident companies;

(b) charities;

(c) pension funds;

(d) certain collective investment undertakings;

(e) certain employee share-ownership trusts;

(f) certain residents of the EU Members States or Tax Treaty countries;

(g) distributions made to designate brokers for the benefit of a holder of a special portfolio investment account;

(h) fund managers of approved retirement fund or approved minimum retirement fund;

(i) savings managers of special savings incentive accounts;

(j) permanently incapacitated individual exempt from income tax on income from investment of compensation awards from personal injury claim;

(k) certain amateur and athletic sports bodies;

(l) trustees of tax-exempt trust funds set up by public funds on behalf of permanently incapacitated individuals and permanently incapacitated individuals in receipt of income from such trusts.

19.5.4   Non-resident individuals

Sch 2A
TCA 97

An exemption from dividend withholding tax applies to individuals who are neither resident nor ordinarily resident in the State and who are resident in a country with which Ireland has a tax treaty or in another EU Member State. To qualify for the exemption, the individual must make a declaration of entitlement and provide a certificate given by the tax authority in that country confirming that the person is resident in that State.

Non-resident individuals who are in receipt of dividends, but are not resident in either another EU Member State or a country with which Ireland has a tax treaty are only chargeable to income tax on the dividend income at the standard rate of tax.

19.5.5   Shares in lieu of dividend

Dividends are assessable in full on the basis of the gross amount received, i.e., the net dividend received plus dividend withholding tax is subject to tax. The dividend withholding tax is allowed as a credit against the tax liability of the recipient for the year of assessment.

It is common for companies, when declaring dividends, to give their shareholders the option of receiving additional share capital in the company rather than the cash dividend. If the shareholder opts to receive the additional share capital in the company rather than the dividend, the shareholder is assessed to tax under Schedule F on the cash foregone. This tax treatment applies where the paying company is an Irish-resident quoted company. The individual is taxed on an amount equal to the distribution (plus the dividend withholding tax) that he/she would have received had the option to take additional shares not been exercised. Therefore the tax position of shareholders who take a cash dividend and those who take shares is identical.

Readers are referred to paragraph 19.3.3 for an analysis of the tax treatment of the dividend foregone where the paying company is Irish tax resident but is not a quoted company, and to paragraph 19.2 for an analysis of the tax treatment of the dividend foregone where the paying company is not Irish tax resident.

The following diagram summarises the tax treatment of scrip dividends:

19.5.6 Exempt distributions

Some distributions/dividends are exempt from tax in the hands of the shareholder. Certain types of income preserve their tax-free status when passed on to shareholders in the form of dividends. The following are the types of income from which dividend income is exempt:

s140 TCA 97   stallion services (s140 TCA 97);

woodlands occupied on a commercial basis, in order to realise a profit (s140 TCA 97);

s141 TCA 97   profits from qualifying patents (s141 TCA 97).

Dividend income, which is exempt under any of the above headings, is not regarded as income for any purpose of the Income Tax Acts.

19.5.7 Credit unions

s700
TCA 97
Dividends paid by credit unions are exempt from dividend withholding tax. Such dividends are assessable under Schedule D Case III (considered at paragraph 19.2 above).

Appendix I

The following matters are treated as distributions and amounts received by an individual are assessable to income tax in his/her hands under Schedule F:

- any dividend paid by a company, including a capital dividend;

- any distribution out of the assets of the company in respect of shares in the company except so much of the distribution, if any, as represents a repayment of share capital or is made for new consideration;

- scrip dividends (see 19.5.5);

- a redemption of bonus securities insofar as is not referable to new consideration;

- interest paid on bonus securities;

- interest on securities convertible into shares or carrying rights to shares or securities (unless they are quoted securities or securities issued on terms reasonably comparable with those of quoted securities);

- interest which depends on the results of the borrowing company's business;

- the excess of interest over a reasonable commercial rate;

- interest on securities which are connected with shares in the company;

- a bonus issue followed by a repayment of share capital –
  A bonus issue is not regarded as a distribution if:

  - the company is not a close company,

  - the bonus issue was of shares other than redeemable shares,

  - the repayment takes place more than 10 years after the bonus issue;

- a repayment of share capital followed by a bonus issue –
  The amount of the repayment is not treated as a distribution if:
  - (i)   the company is not a close company,
  - (ii)   the bonus issue is of share capital other than redeemable share capital,
  - (iii) the bonus issue takes place more than 10 years after the repayment of share capital;

- transfer of assets at undervalue or liabilities at overvalue by a company to its members;

- any expenses incurred by a close company (see Chapter 33) in providing benefits, or facilities of any kind for shareholders and their associates (other than directors or employees);

■ loan interest in excess of 13% paid to a director or to an associate of a director with a material interest in a close company (see Chapter 33):

– "Material interest" means the ability to control directly or indirectly more than 5% of the ordinary share capital.

– A close company, broadly speaking, is a company under the control of five or fewer shareholders or under the control of the directors regardless of their number.

WHAT YOU SHOULD NOW KNOW

On completion of this chapter, you should be able to:

✓ Describe the different sources of income assessable to tax under Schedule D Cases III, IV and V and Schedule F.

✓ Explain the basis of assessment for the different sources of income assessable to tax under Schedule D Cases III, IV and V and Schedule F.

✓ Explain how a taxpayer might claim credit for tax deducted at source from income assessable under Schedule D Case IV and Schedule F.

✓ In relation to Schedule D Cases III, IV and V and Schedule F, explain:

   ✓ what sources of income are exempt;

   ✓ how losses are treated;

   ✓ what deductions (if any) may be claimed.

✓ Describe the tax relief associated with 'special savings investment accounts' (SSIAs).

✓ Describe the tax treatment of shares issued in lieu of dividends.

✓ Calculate the tax liability of an individual in receipt of various sources of "passive" income.

✓ Complete Questions and the Assignments in Irish Taxation Law and Practice, Volume 2.

20

TAXATION OF INCOME FROM OFFICE AND EMPLOYMENT

In this chapter, you will deal with the following:

■ Scope of charge to Schedule E

■ Distinction between "employed" and "self-employed"

■ Expenses allowable as a deduction under Schedule E

20.1   Introduction

The purpose of this chapter is to identify the sources of income which are charged to tax under Schedule E.

In general, tax is charged under Schedule E:

- on every individual holding a public office or employment within the State;

- in the case of a resident individual, on profits arising from any employment wherever exercised;

- on employments exercised within the State (regardless of where the individual is resident).

Tax is also charged under Schedule E on pensions, including pensions payable out of the public Revenue of the State, pensions payable under occupational pension schemes and social welfare pensions.

The chapter also considers the difficulties in determining the distinction between an individual who is employed under a contract *of* service and an individual retained under a contract *for* service. Finally, the chapter considers expenses allowable as a deduction under Schedule E.

20.2   Scope of charge to Schedule E

s112 TCA 97   Schedule E charges to tax income from all "salaries, fees, wages, perquisites or profits whatever" arising from an office or employment. The definition also includes occupational pensions and certain social welfare payments. The term "emoluments" is used to cover any such amounts chargeable under this Schedule.

s123 TCA 97   In addition, Schedule E extends the charge to include specific types of income, e.g., payments on retirement or removal from office or employment (discussed in Chapter 22).

20.2.1   Meaning of "emoluments"

s112(2)(a) TCA 97   The term "emoluments" is used to describe anything assessable to tax under Schedule E. It is defined as including "all salaries, fees, wages, perquisites or profits whatever" arising from an office or employment. Benefits-in-kind and perquisites are considered in Chapter 21.

The terminology "arising from an office or employment" is important. In the case of *Seymour v Reed* (11 TC 625), Lord Cave stated:

> *"It must now (I think) be taken as settled that the words, 'salaries, fees, wages, perquisites or profits whatsoever' include all payments made to the holder of an office or employment as such, that is to say, by way of remuneration for his services, even*

though such payments may be voluntary, but they do not include a mere gift or present (such as a testimonial) which is made to him on personal grounds and not by way of payment for his services".

If a payment meets the above criteria, i.e., by reference to the service the employee renders by virtue of his office, and is in the nature of a reward for those services, then the payment is assessable under Schedule E, even if the payment is voluntary.

20.2.2 Office or employment

The first principle of Schedule E is to establish whether an office or employment exists.

There are two types of office and employment within the scope of Schedule E, namely "public" offices and employments and other employments.

There is no statutory definition of an office or employment. In this regard, decisions from a number of cases are relevant.

An "office" was defined by Rowlatt J. in *Great Western Railway Co. v Bater* (8TC 231) as "a subsisting, permanent, substantive position, which had an existence independent of the person who filled it, and which went on and was filled in succession by successive holders; an example of an office holder is a company director".

This definition was quoted with reserved approval in the more recent case of *Edwards v Clinch* ([1981] STC 617), where Lord Wilberforce questioned Rowlatt J.'s use of the word "permanent". However, Lord Wilberforce did say that "the word (office) must involve a degree of continuance (not necessarily continuity) and of independent existence".

In practice, there is no distinction between public offices and other offices.

20.2.3 Basis of assessment

s112 TCA 97 Tax is charged under Schedule E on the actual amount of all salaries, fees, wages, perquisites or profits whatsoever derived from the office, employment or pension for the year of assessment.

20.3 Distinction between "employed" and "self-employed"

The terms "employed" and "self-employed" are not defined in law. It is sometimes difficult to determine whether an individual is:

■ employed and consequently chargeable under Schedule E; or

■ self-employed and chargeable under Case I or II of Schedule D (considered in Chapter 14).

In this regard, decisions from a number of cases are relevant. The courts have treated as employed, individuals who operate under a contract of service, while self-employed individuals are those who operate under a contract for service.

20.3.1 Relevant case law

Cooke J.'s comment in *Market Investigations v Minister of Social Security* ([1968] 3 All ER 732) has been quoted with approval in subsequent cases:

"the fundamental test to be applied is this: Is the person who has engaged himself to perform these services performing them as a person in business on his own account? If the answer to that question is 'yes', then the contract is a contract for service. If the answer is 'no', then the contract is a contract of service."

There are no established criteria for determining whether a contract is one "of" service or "for" service. Relevant factors include pay arrangements, working hours, the degree of control held by the individual over his/her work, whether the individual may hire other people to do work he/she has undertaken, etc.

Whether a contract of service or a contract for service was in existence was discussed in the case of *Director of Public Prosecutions v Martin McLoughlin* (6 ILRM 493).

In this case, Mr McLoughlin skippered a boat which went on weekly fishing trips. Each weekly trip was a separate venture and although the same crew turned up regularly, no crew member had a contract which entitled him to participate in future trips. No wages were paid to the crew members but each member was entitled to a share of the profits, such share being decided by custom and agreement. If there was no profit, the crew did not suffer a share of the losses. It was held, on the facts of the case, that there was no contract of service between the crew members and the skipper. The profits paid to the crew members were accordingly not assessable under Schedule E.

In a recent Irish case, *Henry Denny & Sons (Ireland) Limited v Minister for Social Welfare* (1997), it was held by the High Court that a supermarket demonstrator was engaged under a contract of service. The case considered the various tests, which may be applied in determining whether a contract of service exists:

1. control test   – the demonstrator was subject to control, direction and dismissal by the company;

2. integration test   – the supermarket demonstrations were considered an integral part of the company's business;

3. economic relations test   – the terms of engagement were consistent with those of a contract of service;

4. entrepreneurial test   – the demonstrator was shown not to be in business on her own account.

This decision was upheld by the Supreme Court. In his judgment, Keane J. placed emphasis on the substance of the contract over its form.

20.3.2 Report of the employment status group

The Employment Status Group[1] delivered a report in August 2006. The group had been set up because of a growing concern that there may be increasing numbers of individuals categorised as self-employed when the indicators may be that "employee" status would be more appropriate.

The report was issued as a code of practice and is reported in the Revenue Commissioner's publication *Tax Briefing Issue 43*. While the code of practice does not have legislative effect, it is expected that its contents will be considered by those involved in disputes on the employment status of individuals. The report established the criteria to determine whether an individual is an employee. It advised that whilst all of the following factors may not be applicable, an individual would normally be an employee if he or she:

- is under the control of another who directs as to how, when and where the work is to be carried out;

- supplies labour only;

- receives a fixed hourly/weekly/monthly wage;

- cannot sub-contract the work;

- does not supply materials for the job;

- is not exposed to personal financial risk in carrying out the job;

- does not have the opportunity to profit from sound management;

- works set hours or a given number of hours per week; and

- receives expense payments to cover subsistence and/or travel expenses.

20.4 Expenses allowable as a deduction under Schedule E

s114
TCA 97

For a deduction to be allowed for travelling expenses, "the holder of an office or employment" must have been "necessarily obliged" to incur the expense "in the performance of the duties of the office or employment". A deduction is given for other expenses to the extent that they are incurred "wholly, exclusively and necessarily in the performance of the duties" of the office or employment. In both cases, a test of necessity is imposed and the expense must be incurred in "the performance of the duties" of the office or employment.

---

[1] This group was set up under the Programme for Prosperity and Fairness (PPF) and consisted of representatives from the Irish Congress of Trade Unions, the Irish Business and Employers Confederation, the Revenue Commissioners, the Department of Social, Community and Family Affairs, the Department of Enterprise, Trade and Employment and the Department of Finance.

Whether an expense is allowable usually hinges on the interpretation of one or more of the following phrases:

■ "in the performance of the duties of the office or employment;"

■ "necessarily obliged to incur and defray" (travelling expenses);

■ "wholly, exclusively and necessarily" (other expenses).

These phrases are now considered in turn.

20.4.1   "In the performance of the duties"

For an expense to be allowable, it must be incurred in the actual discharge or performance of the duties of the office or employment to which it relates. It is an established principle that expenses incurred by an employee in travelling to the place where he/she performs the duties of his/her office or employment are not expenses incurred in the actual performance of those duties, but merely expenses incurred in putting him/her in a position to perform those duties. In this regard, case law is relevant.

In the case of *Ricketts v Colquhoun* (10 TC 118), a barrister who was living and practising in London was appointed to the position of Recorder of Portsmouth. He was obliged to travel to Portsmouth four times a year to hold Court there and he claimed relief for the expenses of travelling to and from Portsmouth and his hotel expenses in Portsmouth. It was held that the expenses were not incurred in the performance of his duties as Recorder but partly before he entered upon his duties and partly after he had fulfilled these duties, and as such they were not allowable.

20.4.2   "Necessarily obliged to incur and defray"

This is a condition of the test which applies to travelling expenses. The full test is that "the holder of the office or employment is necessarily obliged to incur the expenses of travelling in the performance of the duties of the office or employment". The test is an objective one, not a personal one, i.e., the individual must be obliged to incur the expense by the very fact that he/she holds the office or employment and must perform its duties.

Returning to the case of *Ricketts v Colquhoun* (10 TC 118) already referred to above, the hotel expenses failed the objective test on the grounds that if an individual elects to live away from his/her work and must bear the expenses of staying away from home, it is by his/her own choice and not by reason of any necessity arising out of his/her employment.

20.4.3   "Wholly, exclusively and necessarily"

s114
TCA 97

This condition is substituted for the phrase "necessarily obliged to incur" in looking at the allowability of non-travelling expenses under s114 TCA 97 so that the test becomes: "the holder of the office or employment incurs the expense wholly, exclusively and necessarily in the performance of the duties of the office or employment". The objective test discussed above in connection with travelling expenses applies equally here.

The duties of the office or employment must impose the test of necessity, not the employer. In *Brown v Bullock* (40 TC 1), a bank manager joined a West End club, membership of such a club being virtually a requisite of his appointment. He claimed a deduction for the subscription to the club. It was disallowed on the grounds that the expense was not necessary to enable him to perform the duties of the office of bank manager. If he had not joined the club he could still have performed those duties.

In *Lupton v Potts* (45 TC 643), examination fees paid by a solicitor's apprentice were not allowed as they were not laid out "wholly, exclusively and necessarily" to carry out his duties. The fees could also have been disallowed on the grounds that they were not incurred in the performance of the duties of the employment.

Although the words "wholly and exclusively" might be held to prohibit the deduction of any part of an expense, where the expense as a whole is not incurred in the performance of the duties, in practice, if the nature of an expense is such that a definite part or proportion can be regarded as being expended "wholly, exclusively and necessarily" in the performance of the duties of the office or employment, then that part or proportion will be allowed.

It will be noted for the latter two tests above that the expense must actually be "incurred" by the holder of the office or employment, prohibiting a claim for notional or estimated expenses. The onus is on the taxpayer to prove that expenditure has been incurred.

The following expenses are generally allowable in practice:

■ expenditure on special clothing worn in the performance of the duties;

■ expenditure on tools used in the performance of the duties;

■ expenditure on books and newspapers for journalists;

■ expenses incurred by commercial travellers who are required to bear travelling and hotel expenses in the course of performing their duties.

WHAT YOU SHOULD NOW KNOW

On completion of this chapter, you should be able to:

✓ Explain the scope of the charge to income tax under Schedule E.

✓ Explain the difference between "employed" and "self-employed" and describe the criteria used to make the distinction.

✓ Describe the conditions necessary for expenses to be allowed as a deduction under Schedule E.

✓ Complete the Assignments in Irish Taxation Law and Practice, Volume 2.

21

BENEFITS-IN-KIND

In this chapter, you will deal with the following:

- Application of PAYE/PRSI to BIK
- Company Vehicles
- Living accommodation
- Valuation of employer-provided assets
- Preferential loans
- Proposed parking levy
- Exempt benefits-in-kind

21.1 Introduction

This chapter covers the charge to tax on the provision of various employer-provided assets, expense allowances and other benefits. The analysis is concerned with how such benefits are valued for assessment purposes. The typical types of employer-provided assets, expense allowances and benefits are as follows:

Company cars/vans

A tax charge is not confined to the provision of a company car. A tax charge may also arise on the provision of vans. This chapter explains how to calculate the amount assessable for both types of vehicle and also considers amounts that may be deducted to reduce the amount assessable to tax.

Living accommodation

This chapter explains how to value accommodation and also identifies the circumstances where accommodation can be provided tax-free.

Preferential loans

Where loans are provided by an employer at a rate of interest that is lower than that in the market place, a charge to tax arises. This chapter explains how to calculate the amount assessable to tax.

Expenses paid by employers

In addition to the above benefits, it is common for employers to pay certain expenses on behalf of employees, e.g., medical insurance (VHI/Quinn Healthcare/Hibernian Healthcare) and golf subscriptions. This chapter explains how to value these expenses for assessment purposes.

21.1.1 General

Tax is charged under Schedule E on every person having or exercising an office or employment in respect of "all salaries, fees, wages, perquisites or profits whatsoever arising from the office or employment". Income tax under Schedule E is therefore charged on the emoluments of an employment, which are paid either in cash or in a form which can be converted into money. Accordingly, benefits received by an employee, which cannot be converted into money, such as free accommodation, free travel or the use of certain company assets, cannot be assessed to tax under general principles. In order to counter this situation, the legislation contains special provisions to bring within the scope of Schedule E, expense allowances and benefits-in-kind (BIK), which are not otherwise chargeable to tax.

Where the benefit to the employee derives from the transfer of ownership of an asset (previously used by the employer) from the employer to the employee, the prevailing market value of the asset at the time of transfer (and not the original cost to the employer of acquiring the asset) is taken to be the benefit-in-kind.

Where the benefit involves the free use of property without the transfer of ownership, the annual value of the property is generally taken to be the benefit-in-kind. However, very specific rules exist for valuing benefits arising on the provision of living accommodation, motor cars and preferential loans and these are discussed in detail below.

Where the benefit derives from the provision of some service by the employer or from the payment of some expenses by the employer on behalf of the employee, the costs incurred by the employer are generally taken to be the benefit-in-kind. In Ireland, marginal cost as opposed to average cost is taken to be the normal measure of the BIK assessment. The precedent in the following UK case is interesting in this regard.

The UK case of *Pepper v Hart* ([1992] STC 898) raised an important point in relation to the valuation of "in-house" benefits where the employer permits employees to acquire goods or use facilities at a reduced price. The case concerned a number of schoolmasters who were entitled to have their sons educated at the college in which they were employed in return for a payment equal to 20% of the normal fees.

The schoolmasters contended that this payment covered all the additional costs incurred by the college in educating these boys and as such no BIK charge would arise. The Revenue took a different view, contending that the true cost to the college in providing this benefit had to be ascertained by taking the total cost to the college in educating all its pupils and dividing this cost rateably between all those pupils (i.e., the average cost). On this basis the benefit to the schoolmasters exceeded the amount reimbursed by them and a BIK charge arose on the excess.

The Revenue's view was upheld by the Court of Appeal. However, the taxpayers won a subsequent appeal to the House of Lords. In arriving at their decision, the Law Lords referred to statements made in Parliament during the passage of the relevant legislation (UK Finance Act 1976, s63, the equivalent of s118), which indicated that the intent of the legislation was to charge only the marginal cost as a BIK rather than the average cost. Lord Browne-Wilkinson, in the course of his judgment, remarked that were it not for the fact that such reference was permitted, the Revenue view would have to be upheld. The basis of the House of Lords' decision is essentially a point of UK constitutional law. Its applicability in this jurisdiction is doubtful. Irish Revenue practice continues to be that marginal cost is the normal measure of the BIK assessment in such cases.

21.1.2 Exemption from tax of certain benefits-in-kind

s118 TCA 97 Not all benefits are liable to tax. **The following are exempt from tax**:

- The provision by the employer of any accommodation, supplies or services for use by a director or employee in any of its business premises, where used by that director or employee solely in performing the duties of the employment;

- The provision of living accommodation for an employee (other than a director), who is required to live on the business premises, provided that such accommodation:

- is necessary for employees of that class because of the nature of their employer's trade, or

- has commonly been provided in trades of that kind since before 1948;

■ The provision of canteen meals, which are provided for all staff generally;

■ The provision of any pension, annuity, lump sum, gratuity or other like benefit accruing on the death or retirement of a director or employee;

■ Expenses incurred by an employer in providing a monthly or annual bus, Luas or train pass issued by or on behalf of CIE or any of its subsidiaries, or passes for travel on commuter ferries which operate in the State;

■ The provision of certain free or subsidised childcare facilities by employers for the benefit of their employees. The exemption does not apply if the employer simply pays or subsidises the cost to an employee of an independent crèche or nursery. The BIK exemption will only apply in respect of any expense incurred by an employer in connection with the provision of a childcare service in a "Qualifying Premises" for a child of an employee or director. "Qualifying Premises" in broad terms means premises which are made available solely by the employer or are made available by the employer jointly with other person(s) and the employer is wholly or partly responsible for financing and managing the service;

■ Employer-provided security services/assets are exempt where there is a risk to the personal safety of the employee/director while carrying out the duties of their employment;

■ With effect from 1 January 2009, an employer may provide a new bicycle and related safety equipment to a maximum value of €1,000 tax-free. The bicycle must be used mainly for 'qualifying journeys' i.e. from home to work or between places of work while carrying out the employment duties.

21.2   Application of PAYE/PRSI to Benefits-in-Kind

Finance Act 2003 introduced new provisions, which came into force on 1 January 2004. From that date, non-cash benefits and perquisites provided by an employer to an employee are effectively deemed to be emoluments to which PAYE rules apply.

Prior to 1 January 2004, calculation of and payment of the tax due on non-cash benefits and perquisites provided by an employer were the responsibility of the employee.

This chapter considers the valuation rules for all benefits post-1 January 2004. Readers are referred to Chapter 23 for details of how PAYE and PRSI applies to such benefits from 1 January 2004.

21.2.1   Valuation of benefits-in-kind from 1 January 2004

The following are considered:

- Valuation of company car;

- Valuation of company van;

- Valuation of employer-provided accommodation and land;

- Valuation of an employer-provided asset other than a car, van or accommodation;

- Valuation of a preferential loan from an employer;

- Discharge by an employer of employee personal expenses;

- Proposed introduction of a parking levy.

21.3   Company Vehicles

The tax treatment varies depending on whether the employee is provided with exclusive use of a motor car or commercial vehicle, or simply has the use of a pooled car.

21.3.1   The valuation of a company car

s121
TCA 97

An employee is charged to tax on the "cash equivalent" of the benefit of an employer-provided motor vehicle, otherwise known as a "company car". The BIK is calculated at 30% of the Original Market Value. "Original market value" (OMV) is defined as the price including any customs or excise duty or value-added tax chargeable on the car which the car might reasonably have been expected to fetch if sold in Ireland singly in a retail sale on the open market immediately before the date of its first registration. If the car was first registered abroad, the OMV is still taken as the price it would have retailed for if sold on the open market in Ireland and not the country of registration. In practice, the Revenue take the list price and allow a deduction (normally 10%) representing a cash discount.

If an employee is provided with a second-hand car, the original market value of the car when new is used in calculating the benefit-in-kind and not the amount paid by the employer. If an employee is supplied with a company car for only part of the year of assessment, the cash equivalent is reduced proportionately.

There is no mitigation of the 30% figure regardless of whether the employee bears the costs of private fuel, servicing and repairs, road tax and/or insurance. However, the figure of 30% is reduced where business travel exceeds 24,000 kilometres per annum.

Finance Act (No. 2) 2008 amends "miles" to read "kilometres". However, in the TCA '97 references to distance travelled is still referred to as "mileage" and this chapter mirrors those references.

Example 21.1

Jim McDonald is a top-rate taxpayer whose company car supplied to him in 2007 has an OMV of €40,000. Mr McDonald pays for his car insurance and also for private fuel costs

BIK 2009 (ignoring PRSI Health + Income levies)

	€
€40,000 @ 30% =	12,000
Tax due @ 41% =	**4,920**

If the employer incurred the expenditure on insurance and fuel and Jim McDonald reimbursed his employer, the calculation for 2009 would be as follows, assuming the reimbursement was €2,000:

BIK 2009 (ignoring PRSI Health + Income levies)

	€
€40,000 @ 30%	12,000
Less employee contribution	(2,000)
Assessable	10,000
Tax due @ 41% =	**4,100**

Business mileage relief is available where business mileage exceeds 24,000 kilometres per annum, as follows:

Business kilometres	Taxable % of OMV
24,000 kms or less	30%
24,001 to 32,000 kms	24%
32,001 to 40,000 kms	18%
40,001 to 48,000 kms	12%
over 48,000	6%

Example 21.2

Thomas Wilson is a top-rate taxpayer whose company car supplied to him in 2007 has an OMV of €40,000. He completed 50,000 business kms in the year and his employer bears all running costs on the car.

BIK 2009 (ignoring PRSI Health + Income levies)

	€
€40,000 @ 6% =	2,400
Tax due @ 41% =	**984**

Prior to Finance Act 2003, Revenue practice was to adjust the business mileage chart for an individual who did not have use of the company car for the full tax year. This was achieved by effectively annualising the business mileage.

From 1 January 2004, the annualisation process is provided for by legislation and is calculated as follows:

(a) Adjust the 24,000 kms threshold by reference to the number of days in the year the car was available for use; and

(b) Adjust all the figures in the five categories by reference to the following percentage:

<u>Result of (a)</u>
24,000

Example 21.3

Michael Ryan is provided with a fully expensed company car for nine months each year. For the months of June, July and August, the car in not available to Mr Ryan. The OMV is €50,000 and his business mileage in each nine-month period is 30,000 kms.

Adjustment of 30,000 kms for nine months, as follows:

• *24,000 × 273/365*	=	*17,950*
• *17,950/24,000*	=	*74.79%*

Business kilometres	Taxable % of OMV
17,949 or less	*22.43%*
17,950 to 23,933 kms	*17.95%*
23,934 to 29,916 kms	*13.46%*
29,917 to 35,898 kms	*8.97%*
> 35,898 kms	*4.48%*

Therefore, (as Mr Ryan's business mileage is 30,000 kms during the nine-month period), the appropriate % for Mr Ryan's BIK computation is 8.97%

€50,000 @ 8.97% = €4,485

There is an **alternative relief** for extensive use of a car for business purposes where an employee does not have significantly high business mileage. This relief is appropriate for employees who regularly use their cars for business purposes, but who are unable to avail of the conventional high business mileage relief, i.e., business mileage does not exceed 24,000 kms per annum, because, for example, they operate mainly in urban areas. The employee may choose whichever method produces the lower figure.

The alternative relief provides that the employee may elect to have the BIK charge on the company car reduced by 20% provided all of the following conditions are met:

■ He/she must spend at least 70% of his/her time working away from his/her employer's premises;

■ Annual business mileage must exceed 8,000 kms;

■ He/she must work on average at least 20 hours per week; and

■ A detailed logbook to record daily business travel must be maintained.

Example 21.4

Robbie Brown has the use of a company car. The car had an original market value of €30,000 when purchased new by his employer in 2006. All expenses relating to the car are borne by the employer with the exception of petrol for private use, which is borne by Robbie Brown. His business mileage in the tax year is 10,000 kms. He reimburses his employer €1,000 towards his private use of the car each year.

	€
Original market value (OMV)	*30,000*
Relevant percentage	*30%*
	9,000
Less:	
20% reduction	
Taxable percentage	*80%*
	7,200
Less reimbursement	*(1,000)*
Assessable benefit	***6,200***

To avail of the 20% reduction, Robbie Brown must spend at least 70% of his time working away from his employer's premises and work at least 20 hours per week.

Regardless of which method of calculation is used, it is important that each step is calculated in the correct order:

Step 1

Calculate the cash equivalent (i.e. OMV $\times$ 30%).

Step 2

Adjust to reflect actual use in year (e.g., if car is only provided on 1 July 2009, amount assessable for 2009 is 50% of figure at Step 1).

Step 3

Apply high business mileage reduction (or 20% reduction).

Step 4

Deduct amount of contribution by employee.

21.3.1.1 BIK by reference to C02 emissions - Proposed changes

Section 6 Finance (No. 2) Act 2008 proposes that the BIK charge for cars be increased if they fall within a particular C02 emissions category. The proposed changes only impact on new cars provided in 2009. Cars provided to employees prior to 1 January 2009 are not affected.

The changes are subject to a Commencement Order which at the time of writing is still awaited.

The effect of the changes means that the cash equivalent charge for cars in the category bands D to G will be increased as follows:

- OMV × A, where A is a percentage as determined by

  1. Business mileage (Table A), and

  2. C02 emissions category (Table B)

Table A

Lower Limit Kilometres	Upper Limit Kilometres	Category A,B,C %	Category D&E %	Category F&G %
	24,000	30	35	40
24,000	32,000	24	28	32
32,000	40,000	18	21	24
40,000	48,000	12	14	16
48,000	1	6	7	8

Table B (which follows VRT bands)

Vehicle Category	Co2 Emissions (g/km)
A	0 to 120
B	> 120 to 140
C	> 140 to 155
D	> 155 to 170
E	> 170 to 190
F	> 190 to 225
G	> 225

Example 21.5

Bert Kane is provided with a new car (following the Ministerial Order) in 2009 the OMV of which is €40,000 and is in vehicle category F. Bert Kane has annual business mileage of 30,000 kilometres.

Original market value (OMV)	*40,000*
Relevant percentage	*32%*
Assessable amount	*12,800*

Cars in the category bands A to C will be unchanged.

21.3.2 Pooled cars

Where an employee has the use of a car from a car pool no liability to tax arises provided that:

- The car is made available to, and actually used by, more than one employee and is not ordinarily used by one to the exclusion of the others;

- Any private use by the employees of the car is incidental to other use; and

- The car is not normally kept overnight in the vicinity of any of the employees' homes.

21.3.3 The valuation of a company van

s121A
TCA 97

A van is defined as follows:

"A mechanically propelled road vehicle which:

(a) is designed or constructed solely or mainly for the carriage of goods or other burden;

(b) has a roofed area to the rear of the drivers seat; and

(c) has no side windows or seating fitted in that roofed area."

The rules provide that the BIK valuation is 5% of the original market value ("OMV") of the van. The OMV is defined in the same manner as that applicable to a company car, which in effect means the VAT-inclusive amount is relevant.

Section 8 Finance Act 2004 provides that incidental private use of a van will be exempt from tax where:

- The vehicle is necessary in the performance of the duties of employment

- The employee is required to keep the van at his/her residence while not in use

- Apart from business travel, private travel is prohibited

- The employee spends at least 80% of his/her time away from the employer's premises

The section is therefore intended to exempt the private use of the van in travelling to/from work, which would otherwise be taxable.

21.4 The Valuation of an Employer-Provided Accommodation and Land

s118 TCA 97 The provision of living accommodation by an employer to an employee, such as the use of a house rent-free or at a reduced rent, is a taxable benefit unless the provision of such accommodation is within the exemptions outlined above at 21.1.2.

The BIK assessable on the employee is the annual open market rent for the house, together with expenses connected with the house (which are borne by the employer and not reimbursed by the employee), less any rent payable by the employee. In practice, where the employer owns the premises, Revenue takes the annual value of the accommodation provided as 8% of its current market value. This can often be higher than the "annual letting value". Otherwise, the value of the BIK is an amount equal to the actual rent payable by the employer.

Example 21.5

Peter McCartney is provided with a house by his employer for his private use. The employer pays a gardener €5,000 per annum. The employer does not own the house and pays rent of €10,500 a year. Mr McCartney pays rent of €2,500 to his employer. Mr McCartney is liable to pay tax on a benefit-in-kind arising from his use of the house and the provision by the company of a gardener for the tax year, as follows:

	€
Rent payable by employer	*10,500*
Gardener's wages	*5,000*
	15,500
Less: rent paid	*(2,500)*
Benefit-in-kind	*(13,000)*

With effect from 1 January 2005, where an employee enjoys the use of employer-provided land, the BIK is calculated at 5% of the market value of the land.

21.5 The Valuation of an Employer-Provided Asset other than a Car, Van or Accommodation

s122 TCA 97 With effect from 1 January 2004, the annual value of the use of an asset is 5% of its market value when first applied for the benefit of the employee.

Example 21.6

John McCarthy is provided with a computer for his private use. It was purchased on 1 January 2009 at a cost of €1,500 to his employer and was supplied to him on the same date. The amount assessable 2009 is:

€1,500 × 5% = €75

21.6 Preferential Loan from an Employer

s122 TCA 97 Where an employer provides a "preferential" loan to an employee (or former employee), a charge to tax may arise on the benefit to the employee of the low or nil rate of interest on the loan. A "preferential" loan is one in respect of which no interest is payable or interest is payable at a rate less than the "specified rate". For the tax year 2008, the specified rate is:

- 5% where the loan is used to fund the cost/repair of the employee's principal private residence;

- 12.5% in other cases.

The BIK charge is on the difference between the interest on the loan at the specified rate, and the interest actually paid on the loan for the year.

Where the loan is used to fund the cost/repair of the employee's principal private residence, the employee will obtain tax relief for the notional interest paid.

Example 21.7

Paul Gill received an interest-free loan of €26,000 from his employer on 1 January 2009, which he used to finance an extension to his house. He has no borrowings on his house. He repaid €3,000 off the loan on 1 April 2009 and a further €3,000 on 1 July 2009. The BIK charge for the 2009 tax year is as follows:

	€
€26,000 at 5% × 3/12	*325.00*
€23,000 at 5% × 3/12	*287.50*
€20,000 at 5% × 6/12	*500.00*
BIK charge	*1,112.50*

Mr Gill is entitled to claim tax relief under s244 TCA 1997 on the notional interest of €1,112.50. He must make a claim to the Inspector of Taxes since relief is not granted under the TRS system (tax relief at source).

A charge to tax also arises where a loan to an employee is released or written off by the employer. The loan in such a case need not be a preferential one.

Example 21.8

Jeff Best borrowed €20,000 from his employer, Big Bank plc. The rate of interest charged was the market rate (i.e., the loan was not at a preferential rate). Therefore no charge to tax arose on the provision of the loan. The balance of the loan outstanding at 31 December 2008 was €18,200. In recognition of the valuable contribution of Mr Best to his employer's business it was decided that the loan should be written off on 1 January 2009.

The amount assessable in the tax year 2009 is €18,200, being the amount written off.

21.7   The Discharge by an Employer of Employee Personal Expenses

The BIK assessable is the actual amount discharged by the employer. Examples of such expenditure are:

- Telephone rental,

- Club subscriptions, and

- Medical expenditure.

21.8   Expense Payments

Where an employee or director receives a payment in respect of expenses from his/her employer, he/she is charged to tax as if that payment were part of his/her salary, subject to the right of claiming deductible expenditure under general rules.

Where an employee incurs expenses in the course of carrying out the duties of his/her employment and is reimbursed by his/her employer based on individual vouchers submitted by him/her, no liability in practice arises on receipt of the payments from his/her employer. Note that vouched reimbursed expenses must be incurred "wholly, exclusively and necessarily" in the performance of the duties of the employment.

The legislation is designed to assess "round sum" expense allowances, which are paid to employees even though the expenses are designed to cover business expenses. Round sum expenses paid to employees are taxable as if they were another component of salary.

An example would be an employer paying €500 per month to an employee to cover travel and other "out of pocket" business expenses. Even though the employee may very well incur costs of approximately €500 per month, the payment by the employer must be taxed at source as it is a round sum expense and not specific to a vouched allowable claim. There are certain exceptions to the taxation of such amounts, e.g., the Revenue will in certain instances grant approval for the payment of tax-free round sum expense allowances. Such tax-free payments are discussed in further detail in 21.8.1 below. In general, this treatment only applies where the amounts are agreed in writing with the Revenue in advance.

21.8.1 "Tax-free" payments

The Revenue Commissioners permit the payment of certain expenses tax-free, provided they refer solely to expenses incurred in the actual performance of the employee's duties and do no more than reimburse the employee for the actual expense incurred. These expenses include:

■ Motoring expenses,

■ Subsistence expenses,

■ Removal expenses.

Motoring and subsistence expenses

Historically, the Revenue Commissioners required prior approval for the payment of these expenses tax-free. It is now possible to pay specific amounts tax-free without prior Revenue approval. Revenue has issued leaflets (IT51 for motor expenses and IT54 for subsistence expenses), which set out amounts that employers may pay to staff tax-free without the need for staff to provide receipts. All the conditions set out in the leaflets must be adhered to – otherwise the employer may not pay the amounts tax-free. The rates covered in the leaflets reflect the expense amounts payable to civil servants.

Removal expenses

The Revenue Commissioners have issued a Statement of Practice (SP IT/1/91) in relation to expenses incurred by an employee in moving home to take up a new employment either within the same organisation or with a new employer. Such expense payments may be made without deduction of tax provided they are within the guidelines set down in the Statement of Practice. The types of expense covered include auctioneer's and legal fees, removal and storage of furniture and effects and the payment of temporary subsistence allowances to the employee while he/she is looking for accommodation at the new location.

21.9   Parking Levy

Section 3 Finance (No. 2) Act 2008 proposes the introduction of a parking levy in designated areas where employers provide free car parking spaces to employees. The levy is a stand-alone levy and the amount is €200.

The designated areas are in the following five city councils:

- Dublin

- Cork

- Galway

- Limerick

- Waterford

There are exemptions to the imposition of the levy and the €200 charge is reduced for employees who are job sharing, work part time or are on maternity leave.

The introduction of the parking levy is subject to a Commencement Order which at the time of writing is still awaited.

WHAT YOU SHOULD NOW KNOW

On completion of this chapter, you should be able to:

✓ Explain the scope of the benefit-in-kind provisions and identify which benefits and expense payments are exempt from tax.

✓ Explain how different types of benefit-in-kind are valued.

✓ Calculate the amount assessable as benefit-in-kind in the case of employer-provided vehicles, living accommodation, preferential loans, etc.

✓ Describe the obligations of employers with respect to reporting the provision of benefits to employees.

✓ Complete Questions and the Assignments in Irish Taxation Law and Practice, Volume 2.

22

TERMINATION PAYMENTS

In this chapter, you will deal with the following:

- Elements of a severance package
- Foreign service

- Calculation of tax-free amount
- Top-slicing relief

22.1   Introduction

The termination of an employment can occur for various reasons:

- Redundancy;

- Dismissal;

- Death of the employee;

- Resignation;

- Retirement.

In cases of redundancy (whether voluntary or compulsory), it is quite common for employees to receive "termination payments". In these cases the payments are intended to represent a compensation for loss of office. Termination payments are sometimes made to employees who have been dismissed (known as a "golden boot" payment) and to employees on resigning or retiring in recognition of past performance (known as a "golden handshake" payment). The payments can therefore be put into two categories:

(a) compensation for loss of office (whether on dismissal or redundancy); and

(b) *ex gratia* payments in recognition of past performance.

The tax treatment for both types of payment is the same and hereinafter will be referred to only as termination payments.

This chapter examines the circumstances in which termination payments may be paid tax-free by the granting of exempt amounts. The analysis focuses on how the exempt amounts are calculated and also on how the final liability to tax on the taxable portion of a termination payment can be reduced in certain circumstances.

22.2   Elements of a Severance Package

A payment made to an employee in connection with the termination of an employment may be made up of the following components:

- Lump sums on retirement from Revenue-approved pension schemes;

- Payments on account of injury, disability or death in service;

- Statutory redundancy;

- *Ex gratia* termination payments;

- Pay in lieu of notice;

- Holiday pay.

In addition, an employer may agree to write off an outstanding loan or transfer an asset (e.g., a company car) to the employee as part of an agreed severance package.

Pension lump sums

Lump sums paid from Revenue-approved pension schemes are generally not taxable where the amount received is no more than 1.5 times the salary of the employee in his or her final year of employment. Whilst such amounts are themselves not taxable, they can have the effect of reducing the tax-free component of any *ex gratia* payment. In this regard, readers are referred to the analysis at 22.4 below.

Compensation for injury, disability or death in service

Any payments received on account of injury, disability or death in service are specifically exempt from tax. Section 19 Finance Act 2005 introduced a new reporting requirement, whereby details of such payments must be delivered to the Revenue Commissioners not later then 46 days after the end of the year of assessment in which the payments were made.

Statutory redundancy payments

These are payments an employee is entitled by law to receive provided certain conditions are met. They are, as the name suggests, only payable where the termination of the employment arises as a result of redundancy (whether voluntary or compulsory). These payments are exempt from tax.

Ex gratia termination payments

These are amounts, which the employer is not obliged to pay to the employee. The tax treatment of such '*ex gratia*' payments is covered in detail in paragraph 22.4 below.

Pay in lieu of notice

An employer is obliged by law to give notice in advance that an employment is to be terminated. The length of the notice depends on the employee's number of years of service and can range from one week to eight weeks. An employment contract usually states what the required period of notice is. It may happen that an employer will not want the employee to work out the notice period. In these circumstances, the employer must pay the employee in lieu of notice. The treatment of pay in lieu of notice is similar to that of *ex gratia* payments and accordingly, it may be paid tax-free provided it does not exceed a certain tax-free amount (covered in 22.4.1 below).

Holiday pay

Such pay is treated as forming part of normal salary and is taxed under general rules. It is not treated as a "termination payment" for tax purposes.

Loans written off or assets transferred

Where these form part of a severance package, they must be taken into account. They are valued and added to any other termination payments for the purposes of determining whether or not they are subject to tax. For loans, the cash value is the amount of the loan written off. Assets transferred are valued at their market value at the time of transfer.

22.3 Foreign Service

s201 TCA 97 Subject to certain conditions detailed below, termination payments may be paid tax-free if made in respect of an office or employment in which the holder's service included foreign service. The exemption applies where the period of "foreign service" was:

- Three-quarters of the whole period of service up to the date of termination; or

- Where the period of service exceeded 10 years, the whole of the last 10 years; or

- Where the period of service exceeded 20 years, one-half of that period including any ten of the last 20 years.

Foreign service means a period of employment, the emoluments in respect of which were not chargeable to Irish tax.

Example 22.1

> Liam Farrell was employed by Great Oceans Limited from 1 January 1985 until 30 June 2009, when he was made redundant. From 1 January 1994 until 30 June 2009, he worked and lived in India. He qualifies for "foreign service" relief since the period of service exceeded 20 years and one-half of that period was spent on foreign service, which included 10 of the last 20 years.

Where the individual has insufficient foreign service to qualify for the full exemption, a measure of relief is available under Sch3 Para 9 TCA 1997. The taxable payment is reduced further as follows:

$$P \times \frac{FS}{TS}$$

Where:

P   = Payment (as reduced by SCSB etc.)

FS = Number of foreign years service

TS = Number of total years service

22.4 Calculation of the Tax-Free Amount of *Ex Gratia* Payments

s112, s123, A payment made to an employee in connection with the termination of an employment
s201 is assessable as normal pay under the ordinary Schedule E rules (i.e., s112 TCA 97)
TCA 97 if it represents a payment under the terms of a contract of employment, or if it is in

consideration for services rendered by the employee in his/her capacity as such. However, a payment not made by virtue of a contract of employment but as a voluntary or *ex gratia* payment by the employer is treated as not having the nature of emoluments taxable under general Schedule E rules. Instead such payments are assessed under s123 TCA 97 and afforded certain exemptions and reliefs under s201 TCA 97 and Schedule 3, TCA 97.

Case law is often considered in determining whether a payment is to be assessed as an emolument under s112 or as a termination payment within s123. It is important to note at this stage that it is only payments specifically brought within the charge to tax by the termination payments provisions which may qualify for relief or exemption under s201 or Schedule 3. Other payments, such as holiday pay, are taxable under the general Schedule E rules and may not qualify for the exemptions and reliefs available for termination payments.

Case law

In *Henley v Murray* (31 TC 351), the Managing Director of a company was employed under a service agreement which was not terminable before a certain date. However, it became desirable from the company's point of view that he should leave the service of the company. The Managing Director subsequently left the company before the service agreement expired and was paid an amount equal to that to which he would have been entitled had his employment continued until the expiry of the service agreement. It was held that the payment was in consideration of the abrogation of his contract of employment and was not a payment under that contract and, as such, it was not assessable as an emolument of the employment.

In *Mairs v Haughey* [1993] STC 569, in advance of the privatisation of Harland & Wolff, employees were offered a lump sum to give up the enhanced redundancy rights which they had enjoyed as a condition of their employment with a nationalised company. The lump sum comprised two elements:

■ Element A: – a payment amounting to 30% of the amount the employee would have received under the scheme if he or she were made redundant at the time of the privatisation.

■ Element B: – an additional payment negotiated by the unions to obtain the consent of employees to the changed conditions of their employment.

The Inland Revenue contended that the lump sum was taxable in full as an emolument of the taxpayer's employment, or alternatively as an inducement to take up new employment with the privatised company. It was held that if the enhanced redundancy payment had been made, it would not have been an emolument assessable under Schedule E even though it formed part of the taxpayer's conditions of employment. Therefore the element of the lump sum, which bought out the right to the redundancy payment (i.e., Element A), was equally not an emolument. However, Element B was held to be taxable on the grounds that it was an inducement payment to enter into employment with the privatised company.

22.4.1 Exemptions for payments within s123

s201 TCA 97 Payments which fall within the definition of this section qualify for exemption if they are less than certain "tax-free amounts" under s201 TCA 97 as follows:

- Basic exemption;

- Increased exemption; and

- Standard Capital Superannuation Benefit (SCSB).

Basic exemption

The basic exemption is €10,160 plus €765 for each complete year of service.

Example 22.2

Jane Fitzsimons was made redundant after three years and 11 months of service with her employer. The amount which she can receive tax-free is:

$$€10,160 + (€765 \times 3) = €12,455$$

Note: Only complete years of service are taken into consideration. Thus, the period of 11 months is ignored.

Increased exemption

The basic exemption may be increased by a maximum of €10,000 if:

(i) No claim for relief (other than the basic exemption) has been made in respect of a previous lump sum payment within the previous 10 years; and

(ii) No tax-free lump sum has been received or is receivable under an approved superannuation scheme relating to the office or employment. If a tax-free lump sum of less than €10,000 has been received or is receivable from the scheme, the increased exemption will be the basic exemption plus €10,000, less that amount or, in the case of deferred benefits, the actuarial value of that amount. Thus, the following formula summarises the position:

Increased basic exemption = basic exemption + (€10,000 – pension lump sum entitlement).

Example 22.3

Assume the same facts as above except that Jane Fitzsimons was entitled to receive €3,000 of a tax-free lump sum pension payment. She had never made a previous claim for an increased exemption. The amount which she can receive tax-free is:

$$€10,160 + (€765 \times 3) + (€10,000 – €3,000) = €19,455$$

Standard Capital Superannuation Benefit (SCSB)

The Standard Capital Superannuation Benefit (SCSB) may be substituted for the basic or increased exemption, if it produces a higher figure. The SCSB is calculated by the formula:

$$A \times \frac{B}{15} - C$$

where

A = the average for 12 months of the emoluments of the employment for the last 36 months of service up to the date of termination. Emoluments for this purpose include salary, benefit-in-kind, etc., before deduction of superannuation contributions.

B = the number of complete years of service in the office or employment.

C = any tax-free lump sum received or receivable under an approved superannuation scheme.

The term "lump sum received or receivable" as used in the calculation of the increased exemption and SCSB does not include amounts received by an employee as refunds of personal contributions from a pension fund, which have borne tax at 20%.

Example 22.4

Jean Flood was made redundant on 31 October 2009 after 22 years' service with Jack Weldon Products Limited. On leaving, she was paid a lump sum of €30,000 comprised as follows:

	€
Statutory redundancy	*14,600*
Ex gratia payment	*15,400*

In addition, she is entitled to a tax-free lump sum from the pension fund of €3,000. Her average pay for the three years ending 31 October 2009 was €20,000.

Calculation of SCSB:

$$(€20,000\ (A) \times \frac{22\ (B))}{15} - €3,000\ (C) = €26,333$$

The tax-free amount is €26,333. Since this exceeds the termination payment of €15,400, the latter can be paid tax-free.

22.5 "Top-Slicing Relief"

Schedule 3, paragraph 10 TCA 97 gives a measure of relief to an employee by limiting the rate of tax payable on the taxable portion of a termination payment to the average rate of tax (i.e., tax paid/taxable income) borne by the individual over the previous three tax years.[1] This is more commonly known as "top-slicing relief".

The income tax on the taxable payment (treating the taxable payment as the highest part of the individual's income for that year) is reduced by an amount calculated by the following formula:

---

[1] Section 19 Finance Act 2005 reduced the number of years from five to three for 2005 year of assessment and onwards.

$$A - \frac{(P \times T)}{I} \quad \text{where,}$$

A = the tax which would be payable if the taxable lump sum were treated as income earned in the year of assessment, less the amount which would be payable if the lump sum had not been paid.

P = the taxable lump sum.

T = the aggregate of tax payable in respect of the total income of the payee for the three preceding years of assessment (note that the tax payable on total income excludes tax on charges).

I = the aggregate of the taxable income of the payee for the three preceding years of assessment. Note that it is the taxable income, which is taken into account for the purposes of the formula and not total income.

Example 22.5

Agnes Carroll was made redundant on 31 October 2009 after 20 years of service with Vincentie Enterprises Limited. She is married with two young children. Her husband stays at home to care for the children and he has no income. The following is the breakdown of Mrs Carroll's agreed redundancy package:

	€
Statutory redundancy	11,000
Pay in lieu of notice	2,000
Compensation payment	52,500
Company car (market value October 2009)	24,125

Mrs Carroll's salary and benefit-in-kind amounted to €48,822 in the period 1 January 2009 to 31 October 2009. She had no further income from 1 November 2009 to 31 December 2009. Her emoluments for the three years 2006 (i.e., 1/11/2006 to 31/12/2006), 2007 and 2008 were as follows:

Year	Salary	BIK	Total
	€	€	€
2006	3,167	1,000	
2007	20,720	2,590	
2008	25,000	3,000	
	48,887	6,590	55,477

Her taxable income and tax chargeable for the previous three years were as follows:

Year	Taxable income	Tax payable
	€	€
2006	27,000	10,106
2007	24,800	9,119
2008	28,500	10,439

At the date of termination of employment, the actuarial value of her tax-free lump sum pension entitlement amounted to €3,800. Mrs Carroll's tax liability for 2009 can be calculated using a step-by-step process as follows:

(1) Calculate the taxable portion of the redundancy package after the appropriate reliefs.

(2) Calculate the tax payable on her income assessable for 2009, including the taxable termination payment.

(3) Calculate the "top-slicing relief" available to Mrs Carroll on the taxable termination payment.

Deduct the relief at (3) from the tax payable at (2), to give the final liability for 2009.

Step 1

s123 TCA 97   The statutory redundancy of €11,000 is exempt. The pay in lieu of notice of €2,000 is within s123 TCA 97 as it is assumed not to have been paid under the terms of Mrs Carroll's contract of employment. The compensation payment and the value of the car transferred to Mrs Carroll are both within s123 TCA 97. Thus, the "termination payment" is €78,625 (€2,000 + €52,500 + €24,125). The tax-free amount is the higher of:

(a) **Basic exemption** of €25,460 (€10,160 + (€765 × 20 years))

or

(b) **Increased exemption** of €31,660 (€25,460 + (10,000 – €3,800))

or

(c) **SCSB**, which is calculated as follows:

$$\frac{(A \times B)}{15} - C$$

$A = 1/3 \ (€55,477 + €48,822) = €34,766$

$B = 20$

$C = €3,800$

$$€34,766 \times \frac{20}{15} - €3,800 = €42,555$$

(SCSB produces the highest tax-free figure.)

Termination payment chargeable to tax:

€78,625 – €42,555 = €36,070

Step 2

Mrs Carroll's 2009 income tax liability is calculated as follows:

(a)	**Without termination payment:**	€	€
	Salary and BIK		48,822
	Taxable as follows:		
	€45,400 at 20%		9,080
	€3,422 at 41%		1,403
			10,483
	Less credits:		
	Personal	(3,660)	
	PAYE	(1,830)	
	Home-carer's allowance	(900)	
			(6,390)
			4,093

(b) **_With termination payment:_**

Tax liability as above	_4,093_
Add:	
Taxable termination payment	
_€36,070 at 41%*_	_14,789_
Total tax liability	_18,882_

Step 3

Calculation of top-slicing relief:

$$A - \frac{(P \times T)}{I}$$

$A = $ _€18,882 – €4,093 = €14,789_

$P = $ _€36,070_

$T = $ _1/3 (€10,106 + €9,119 + €10,439) = €9,888_

$I = $ _1/3 (€27,000 + €24,800 + €28,500) = €26,767_

$$€14,789 - \frac{(€36,070 \times €9,888)}{€26,767} = €1,464$$

Step 4

Final tax liability for 2009

	€
Total tax liability per Step 2 (b)	_18,882_
Less top-slicing relief per Step 3	_(1,464)_
Final tax liability	_17,418_

*The taxable lump sum is also liable to the income levy and health levy but is not liable to PRSI. For ease of illustration both levies have not been included.

Tax Facts

Income levy on Termination Payments

The Finance Act (No. 2) 2008 as drafted was unclear as to whether the income levy applied to the gross termination payments or to the taxable portion only. The Revenue Commissioners have confirmed that the income levy only applies to the taxable portion.

WHAT YOU SHOULD NOW KNOW

On completion of this chapter, you should be able to:

✓ Identify the different elements of a termination package, separating taxable payments from non-taxable ones.

✓ Calculate the amount of the tax-free lump sum.

✓ Calculate and apply "Top-Slicing relief".

✓ Complete Questions and the Assignments in Irish Taxation Law and Practice, Volume 2.

23

OPERATION OF PAYE/PRSI SYSTEM

In this chapter, you will deal with the following:

- Operation of PAYE
- Calculation of PAYE
- Temporary basis/emergency basis
- Pensions

- Operation of PRSI
- PRSI rates
- Employer duties
- Application of PAYE/PRSI to benefits-in-kind

23.1   Introduction

The Pay As You Earn (PAYE) system is a method of tax deduction at source, which applies in the case of annuities, salaries, wages, certain benefits and pensions, etc. This chapter examines:

■ The types of income which are specifically within the PAYE system;

■ The obligations of an employer in relation to employees and the Revenue Commissioners;

■ How the PAYE system works; and

■ How Pay Related Social Insurance (PRSI), which is not a tax but a social security contribution, must be collected through the PAYE system.

23.2   Operation of PAYE

s986
TCA 97

The authority governing the operation of PAYE is contained within the Income Tax (Employments) (Consolidated) Regulations 2001. Such Regulations were made by the powers conferred on the Revenue Commissioners by s986 TCA 97 (No.39 of 97).

Tax is charged under Schedule E on the actual amount of all salaries, fees, wages, perquisites or profits whatsoever derived from the office, employment or pension for the year of assessment. The Pay As You Earn (PAYE) system is a method of tax deduction at source by the payer (usually the employer) whereby income tax is paid by deduction at source on amounts which come within the scope of the PAYE system. PAYE applies to all income chargeable under Schedule E except emoluments upon which the Revenue Commissioners consider the operation of PAYE to be "impractical", e.g.,

■ Emoluments paid from outside the State;*

■ Certain taxable social welfare benefits.

* Refer to 23.2.2 for Finance Act 2006 changes for foreign employers.

Where tax is collected under the PAYE system, the taxpayer effectively pays tax each week or month as he/she receives his/her wages or salary. It is also a method of collecting Pay-Related Social Insurance (PRSI) contributions (considered in more detail at 23.6 below).

The PAYE system is designed so that, as far as is possible, the correct amount of tax is deducted from an employee's pay, to meet his/her tax liability for the year. Therefore, the PAYE system removes, in the majority of cases, the necessity for raising formal assessments on employees in respect of Schedule E income. However, formal assessments may be made in the following situations:

- Where underpayments of tax cannot be recovered by adjusting the tax credits and standard rate cut-off point (tax credits and standard rate cut-off point are considered below);

- Where the employee has other income (e.g., investment income or rental income), which has not been effectively taxed by reducing the tax credits and standard rate cut-off point; or

- Where an assessment is requested by the taxpayer.

To ensure that the correct amount of tax is deducted for the year, PAYE is normally computed on a "cumulative basis". This means that when an employer computes the total tax of an employee, he/she actually calculates the total tax due from the beginning of the tax year to the date on which the payment is being made. The tax deducted in the particular week/month is the cumulative tax due to that date from the beginning of the tax year, reduced by the amount deducted up to the previous pay period. It also ensures that refunds can be made to an employee, where a revised Certificate of Tax Credits and Standard Rate Cut-Off Point is received, increasing the employee's tax credits and standard rate cut-off point.

23.2.1 Certificate of tax credits and standard rate cut-off point

A Certificate of Tax Credits (and Standard Rate Cut-Off Point) is a document which the Inspector of Taxes issues on behalf of an employee. There are two components within a certificate of tax credits:

Tax credits

The most common tax credits are personal tax credits and these are determined by reference to the individual's personal circumstances, e.g., married person's tax credit, single parent tax credit. The single tax credit amount for 2009 is €1,830. A single individual therefore may have his/her tax liability for 2009 reduced by €1,830. (Tax credits are considered in detail in Chapter 11.)

Another common tax credit available to employees is the employee tax credit. This is sometimes known as the PAYE tax credit. It is granted to an individual who is in receipt of "emoluments" subject to PAYE deductions. The employee tax credit amount for 2009 is €1,830.

Standard rate cut-off point

A standard rate cut-off point is the amount of the personal standard rate tax band as adjusted for any non-PAYE income, benefits-in-kind or tax reliefs due at the higher rate of tax, e.g., a single individual whose only income for 2009 is salary has a standard rate cut-off point of €36,400 for the year of assessment. Therefore the first €36,400 of his/her salary is taxed at the standard tax rate, i.e., 20% and the excess over €36,400 is taxed at higher tax rate, i.e., 41%. If an employee received €1,000 non-PAYE income per year, the standard rate cut-off point for 2009 would be €35,400. Tax rates and tax bands are considered in detail in Chapter 11.

As already stated, tax credits are non-refundable; they are used to reduce tax on gross pay for each pay period. However, any unused tax credits are carried forward on a cumulative basis and can be used in a subsequent pay period(s) in the same tax year. Tax refunds arise when the cumulative tax due and paid for the last pay period exceeds the cumulative tax due for the current pay period. Readers are referred to Appendix I for a worked example.

Some employees may have other income which is liable to tax and on which tax is collected through the PAYE system rather than through the self-assessment system.

Under the PAYE system other income is taxed by reducing:

- The tax credits by the amount of the income at the standard rate of tax; and

- The standard rate band by the amount of the income.

Reducing the tax credits ensures the non-PAYE income is taxed at the standard rate. Reducing the standard rate band ensures the income is taxed at the difference between the standard rate and the higher rate of tax, if appropriate. The combined effect is to collect tax due on the non-PAYE income at the higher rate of tax, when due.

With effect from 1 January 2004, PAYE/PRSI applies to all benefits-in-kind (considered in detail at 23.9) with deductions being made at source through the PAYE system.

Some employees may have deductions or reliefs on which tax relief is due at the higher rate of tax. The relief in respect of non-standard rated deductions is granted by increasing:

- The tax credits by the amount of the relief at the standard rate of tax; and

- The standard rate band by the amount of the relief.

Increasing the tax credits ensures relief is obtained at the standard rate of tax, while increasing the standard rate band ensures relief is obtained at the difference between the standard rate and the higher rate of tax. The combined effect ensures relief is obtained in full at the higher rate of tax, if applicable.

23.2.2 Obligation on employer to deduct PAYE

A person (or corporate body) who intends hiring staff for the first time must register as an employer with the Revenue Commissioners. The Revenue Commissioners allocate a tax registration number specific to the operation of PAYE and PRSI. Each employer who pays remuneration exceeding €8 per week to a full-time employee (or exceeding €2 per week where the employee has other employments) is obliged to register with the Revenue Commissioners and operate PAYE on all emoluments paid to the employee. The threshold is increased to €40 per week for employers with only one domestic employee. The Revenue Commissioners have the power to compulsorily register an employer who has neglected to register for PAYE.

Section 16 Finance Act 2006 imposed an obligation on foreign employers to deduct PAYE from individuals working in the State. Where the employee is carrying out duties in Ireland for someone other than the employer (e.g. an Irish subsidiary of a USA parent) there is an obligation to operate PAYE on the amount of emoluments which are applicable to the Irish duties.

Where the foreign employer fails to deduct PAYE, the Irish entity is held accountable.

Example 23.1

> John, an American citizen, has worked for JB (USA) Corp for many years. JB (USA) Corp's Irish subsidiary, JB (Irl) Ltd needs expertise in setting up a new computer system which they cannot source in Ireland. John is sent to Ireland to assist with the project. He spends four months in Ireland in 2009. He remains on the USA payroll for the duration of the time in Ireland.
>
> If JB (USA) Corp fail to register for and account for PAYE on John's emoluments, JB (Irl) Ltd, will be accountable for the PAYE due for John.

23.3   Calculation of Tax

s123
TCA 97

"Pay" for the purposes of PAYE includes salary, wages, benefits, pensions, fees, arrears of pay, bonuses, overtime, commissions, holiday pay, pay during illness, etc. It also covers termination payments chargeable under s123 TCA 97 (considered at Chapter 22) and expenses payments (to the extent that agreement has not been reached with the Inspector of Taxes to make the payments gross). PAYE must be operated on all emoluments (as set out above), which are paid during the tax year. This is so even if the emoluments were actually earned, but not paid, in a prior year, and therefore assessable in that prior year.

Example 23.2

> Mary Guinness is paid commissions based on quarterly sales. For the quarter ended 31 December 2008 she earned €2,000 which is payable with her salary on 31 January 2009. PAYE must be operated on the €2,000 by reference to 2009 tax and PRSI rates and not by reference to 2008 rates.

At the start of each year, the Inspector of Taxes issues a certificate of tax credits (and standard rate cut-off point) to each employee. A shortened version of the certificate is issued to the employer.

The certificate of tax credits which issues to the employer contains the following information:

■ The total amount of tax credits (but not itemised);

■ Standard rate cut-off point; and

■ Rates of tax prevailing for the year of assessment.

The calculation of tax for each pay period is made by applying the information supplied in the certificate of credits against the pay as follows:

- Gross pay (less superannuation deductions) is taxed at the appropriate tax rates to give gross tax;

- The standard rate of tax is applied to gross pay up to the standard rate cut-off point for that week or month. Any balance of pay over that amount in the pay period is taxed at the higher rate;

- The gross tax is reduced by the tax credit as advised in the certificate of tax credits to arrive at the net tax payable.

The rates of tax for 2009 are 20% on amounts up to the standard rate cut-off point (SRCOP) and 41% on any amount over the SRCOP.

Example 23.3

The Inspector of Taxes issues a certificate of tax credits to John's employer containing the following information:

tax credits of €305.00 per month;

SRCOP €3033.33 per month;

standard rate of tax 20%, higher rate 41%.

John earns €4,158.00 per month and pays €158 pension.

The tax calculation for each month (ignoring the income levy) is as follows:

	€	€
Gross pay		*4,158.00*
Less superannuation		*(158.00)*
Pay for tax purposes		*4,000.00*
Tax on €3033.33 × 20%	*606.67*	
Tax on €966.67 × 41%	*396.33*	
Gross tax due	*1003.00*	
Less tax credits	*(305.00)*	
Tax due for the month	*698.00*	

Tax credits are non-refundable, i.e., where the gross tax due is less than the tax credit, the difference is not refundable. In this case the employee has no liability for the period and any excess tax credit is carried forward for offset against future tax due on a cumulative basis. However, tax refunds arise when the cumulative tax due and paid for the last pay period exceeds the cumulative tax due for the current pay period. Readers are referred to Appendix I (months four and nine) for an example of a refund in these circumstances.

The cumulative basis also applies to the SRCOP. Where an individual's SRCOP exceeds the gross pay in a pay period, the unused amount is carried forward on a cumulative basis for use in the following pay period(s) in the same tax year. Again, readers are referred to Appendix I for an example of how the cumulative basis operates.

23.4   Temporary Basis/Emergency Basis

Where an employee remains with the same employer from year to year, there are seldom problems in relation to the issue of a certificate of tax credits. Problems can arise where an employee changes employment mid-year. On joining a new employer, if PAYE is to be operated on a cumulative basis, the new employer will require the following:

1.   Form P45 (considered at 23.8 below) from the employee's previous employer, and

2.   Certificate of tax credits.

In the absence of a form P45, the Inspector of Taxes may issue a statement advising the new employer of the employee's previous pay, tax, PRSI, tax credits and SRCOP details.

23.4.1   Week 1/Month 1 (non-cumulative) basis

A certificate of tax credits usually applies on a cumulative basis from the previous 1 January. However, there are occasions when the certificate is issued on a non-cumulative basis known as a Week 1/Month 1 certificate. If the Week 1/Month 1 basis applies, neither the pay, tax credits, nor the standard rate cut-off point are accumulated for tax purposes. The pay for each income tax week or month is dealt with separately. The tax credits and standard rate cut-off point for Week 1 (or Month 1) are used in the calculation of tax due, each week (or each month). No refunds may be made in such cases. Readers are referred to Appendix II for a worked example.

23.4.2   Temporary basis

Another method of operating PAYE is by using the "temporary basis". This is very similar in principle to the Week 1/Month 1 basis. An employer is obliged to operate this basis where a new employee joins, provides a form P45 but a certificate of tax credits has not yet been issued. The tax credits and SRCOP details on the P45 may be used on a non-cumulative basis.

23.4.3   Emergency basis

An individual must be taxed on the "emergency basis" if:

■ The employer has not received, in respect of the employee, either a certificate of tax credits (or TDC) or a form P45 for the current year; or

- The employee has given the employer a completed form P45 indicating that the emergency basis applies; or

- The employee has given the employer a completed P45 without a PPS number and not indicating that the emergency basis applies.

Tax is calculated on the gross pay (after deduction of pension contributions where relevant). Different rules apply depending on whether or not the employee provides the employer with a PPS number.

Where an employee provides a PPS number

The table below outlines the tax credits and standard rate cut-off points applicable where the employee provides a PPS number:

	SRCOP €	Tax Credit €
Weekly paid:		
Weeks 1 to 4	700.00	36.00
Weeks 5 to 8	700.00	0.00
Week 9 onwards	0.00	0.00
Monthly Paid:		
Month 1	3,034.00	153.00
Month 2	3,034.00	0.00
Month 3	0.00	0.00

Where an employee does not provide a PPS number

If the employee does not provide a PPS number, tax is calculated on all gross pay:

- At the higher rate (41%); and

- With no deduction for a tax credit.

23.5 Pensions

Tax is charged under Schedule E on the actual amount of all salaries, benefits, fees, wages, perquisites or profits whatsoever derived from the office, employment or pension for the year of assessment. The same PAYE rules apply equally to occupational pensions as they do to salary/wages. The application of PAYE does not apply to pensions payable by the State. Such pensions are paid without the deduction of tax at source.

23.6   Operation of PRSI

23.6.1   Overview

The principal act for pay-related social insurance (PRSI) is the Social Welfare (Consolidation) Act 1993. Most of the content of the Act is devoted to the benefits and entitlements of the insured individual. The material dealing with PRSI contributions and insurability of employment is concentrated in ss9-16 of the Act and Regulations made thereunder.

In the case of the vast majority of contributors (i.e., individuals who pay PRSI contributions), contributions are collected by the Revenue Commissioners through the PAYE system, and are then passed on to the Department of Social and Family Affairs for inclusion in the Social Insurance Fund. The PAYE system is also used for the collection and maintenance of information on the duration of the employee's insurable employment, on which his/her eligibility for virtually all the PRSI benefits depends.

The PRSI system applies to all individuals employed in the State under a contract of service. A fixed percentage of the worker's reckonable earnings is payable by both the employee and the employer. The precise percentage payable depends on the PRSI class under which the individual is insured.

In addition to deducting PAYE, employers are also obliged to deduct PRSI. The PRSI contribution is made up of two different components, including:

- The social insurance contribution, which varies depending on the earnings of the employee and the benefits for which the individual is insured; and

- The health contribution.

23.6.2   Health contribution

The health contribution of 4.00% (5% where income exceeds €1,443 per week) has a legislative basis entirely distinct from that of PRSI. The primary legislation is the Health Contributions Act 1979 as amended by subsequent Social Welfare Acts and supplemented by the Health Contributions Regulations 1979. The health contribution is more commonly referred to as a "levy". However, in the case of PAYE contributors, the levy is collected as part of the total PRSI deduction made from their emoluments. In the case of chargeable persons, the levy is assessed directly by the Revenue Commissioners and is payable as part of the preliminary tax payment under the self-assessment provisions. The levy is charged on the full amount of earnings, subject to certain income exemption thresholds.

23.6.2.1 Health contribution rates

Finance Act 2009 doubled the health contribution rates and lowered the income level above which the health contribution is increased. These increases are effective from 1 May 2009 and are best illustrated by use of the table below:

From 1 January 2009 to 30 April 2009

Income level	Rate
up to €500 per week	Exempt
€500.01 to €1,925	2%
more than €1,925	2.50%

From 1 May 2009 to 31 December 2009

Income level	Rate
up to €500 per week	Exempt
€500.01 to €1,443	4%
more than €1,443	5%

The annualised rates version of the above applicable to self-assessed individuals is:

From 1 January 2009 to 31 December 2009

Income level	Rate
First €75,036	3.33%
Next €25,064	4%
Excess over €100,100	4.17%

Tax Facts

The supplementary budget on 7 April 2009 announced changes to health contribution rates, PRSI ceiling etc. to be effective from 1 May 2009. The changes were passed into law. The short time span between the budget date and the implementation date of 1 May 2009 gave rise to unprecedented administrative difficulties for employers.

23.6.3 Insurable employment

The First Schedule to the Social Welfare (Consolidation) Act 1993 defines insurable employment as:

"Employment in the State under any contract of service or apprenticeship, written or oral, whether expressed or implied, and whether the employed person is paid by the employer or other person, and whether under one or more employers".

23.6.4 PRSI classes

There are different levels of PRSI contributions, each of which is given a particular letter code and called a contribution class. The particular type of contribution determines entitlement to the various social welfare benefits, e.g., civil servants who are insured at the "modified rates", i.e., lower rates, are not entitled to personal social welfare pensions or to unemployment benefits. The different classes are considered below:

Class A

This is the standard PRSI class, and includes more than 65% of the insured employee population. It comprises employees in commercial, service and agricultural employments. PRSI under class A provides cover for all social welfare benefits.

Classes B, C, D and H

These classes apply to permanent and pensionable public sector employees, such as civil servants, registered doctors and dentists employed in the Civil Service, gardaí, teachers, nurses, local authority staff, members of the Defence Forces, etc. Insured persons in these classes pay reduced rates of contribution since they are only covered for a reduced range of benefits, specifically widow's and orphan's pensions and deserted wife's benefit.

Class J

Class J contributions comprise an employee's contribution in respect of the levies, plus a small employer's contribution in respect of occupational injuries. This class applies to:

- Employed persons over 66 years of age;

- Persons employed under the Community Employment Scheme where such employment commenced prior to 6 April 1996;

- Persons in employment of a subsidiary nature – the term "subsidiary employment" is defined in the regulations as being an employment exercised by persons who are concurrently insurable at the modified rates (such persons are not permitted to pay full rate (Class A) contributions, any such employment is insured at Class J);

- Persons employed under a contract of service whose gross earnings per week are less than €38, i.e., the employment is deemed to be of inconsiderable extent (€38 limit applies to total earnings where an individual has a number of employments).

Class K

This class is used as a method for deducting the levies at source from the PAYE income of persons who are not insurably employed and therefore not liable to PRSI. Examples include:

■ Persons in receipt of an occupational pension who are not insurably employed;

■ Persons employed by a spouse.

Class S

This class is used for certain directors and self-employed contributors.

23.6.5 PRSI deduction for employees

The Social Welfare Acts provide for a deduction of €127 per week in calculating an individual's PRSI liability. The deduction is granted on a weekly, non-cumulative basis. In effect the first €127 of weekly earnings is exempt from employee PRSI contributions.

The deduction applies to the employee's element of the PRSI contribution only, i.e., the employer is not entitled to a deduction in calculating his/her share of the contribution.

PRSI is payable by an employee on earnings up to a certain ceiling. The earnings ceiling for the year of assessment 2009 is €75,036. Any income earned in excess of €75,036 is subject only to the 4%/5% health levy.

*From 1 January 2009 to 30 April 2009 the earnings ceiling was increased to €52,000. From 1 May 2009 the ceiling increased to €75,036.

Example 23.4

A class A individual has earnings of €2,480 per week and cumulative earnings to date are below €75,036. The PRSI and health levy liability for July 2009 is as follows:

	€				€
Gross weekly earnings	2,480				
PRSI deduction	(127)				
Employee PRSI contribution	2,353	×	4.00%	=	94.12
Employee health levy	1,443	×	4.00%	=	57.72
	1,037	×	5.00%	=	51.85
					203.69
Employer contribution	2,480	×	10.75%	=	**266.60**

The deduction of €127 only applies to persons insured at the higher rates of PRSI. For persons insured at modified rates, e.g., civil and public servants, the deduction is reduced to €26 per week.

23.6.6 Special exemption for low incomes

An employee who has weekly earnings of less than €352 in any week is exempt from payment of PRSI contributions for that week. The employer's share of the contribution is, however, payable as normal (see PRSI rates below). Notwithstanding the exemption, the employee is still credited with a PRSI contribution for social welfare benefit purposes.

Where an employee's income does not exceed €356 in any week, the employer's contribution is paid at the reduced rate of 8.5% rather than the normal rate of 10.75%.

23.7   PRSI Rates

Broadly speaking, employees are liable for PRSI at a rate of 4% on income up to €75,036, with no PRSI payable on amounts in excess of this income limit. Employer's PRSI is levied at a rate of 10.75%. The rate of PRSI for the self-employed is 3%.

Readers are referred to Appendix III for a summary of the PRSI rates applicable for each class.

23.8   Employer Duties

Monthly remittance

Employers must remit the tax and PRSI deducted by them under the PAYE system on a form P30 to the Collector-General (collection arm of the Revenue Commissioners) within 14 days of the end of each income tax month. Thus, tax and PRSI deducted from January 2009 salary must be remitted by 14 February 2009.

s991
TCA 97

Under s991 TCA 97 interest accrues at a daily rate of 0.0322% (0.0274% from 1 July 2009) Where the payment not made on time.

End-of-year returns

P35

After the end of each tax year, an employer must submit an end-of-year tax return (known as a P35) showing in relation to each employee:

■ Name of the employee;

■ PPS number of the employee (if known);

■ Date of commencement/leaving the employment, if same occurred during the tax year;

■ Total amount deducted in respect of:

    – pay (after pension deductions),

    – tax,

    – employee PRSI,

    – employer PRSI;

- Total number of insurable weeks.

The latest date for filing form P35 is 46 days after the end of the year of assessment, e.g., form P35 for 2008 must be filed by 15 February 2009. Failure to do so may result in a penalty imposition of €2,535.

P60

Each employee is entitled to receive a form P60 after the end of the year of assessment. The information on the form P60 mirrors that contained on form P35.

Employee leaving

Where an employee leaves an employment, the employer must provide the employee with a cessation certificate known as a form P45. Form P45 must contain the following information:

- Name of the employee;

- PPS number of the employee (if known);

- Date of leaving the employment;

- Amount of weekly/monthly tax credits;

- Amount of weekly/monthly SRCOP;

- Total pay (after pension deductions), tax, employee and employer PRSI deductions from the previous 1 January to date of leaving (or from date of commencement of employment if later than 1 January);

- Total number of insurable weeks.

Form P45 must indicate that emergency tax was applied, if relevant.

23.9   Application of PAYE/PRSI to Benefits-in-Kind

The Finance Act 2003 introduced new provisions, which came into force on 1 January 2004. From that date, non-cash benefits and perquisites provided by an employer to an employee are effectively deemed to be emoluments to which PAYE rules apply.

Prior to 1 January 2004, calculation of and payment of the tax due on non-cash benefits and perquisites provided by an employer was the responsibility of the employee.

An example of some of the more common benefits which are subject to PAYE/PRSI since 1 January 2004 are as follows:

- Preferential loans;

- Medical insurance premia;

- Company cars;

- Company vans.

It should be noted that benefits in respect of shares and/or contributions to personal retirement savings accounts (PRSAs) are specifically excluded from these new provisions.

s985A(3)
TCA 97

Employers have the onerous task of having to calculate the benefit-in-kind (BIK) figure assessable on each employee. This point is recognised by the new legislation which states that employers should operate PAYE on an amount, which is the "best estimate that can reasonably be made" of the amount "likely" to be chargeable under Schedule E. Having calculated the value of the BIK, the figure is then added to "normal" salary and PAYE and PRSI is applied. The BIK figure is known as "notional pay".

Where an employer is unable to withhold the full amount of tax due from the employee's cash salary (e.g., due to insufficiency of income in any particular pay period), the employer is responsible for remitting the full amount of the tax to the Revenue Commissioners. Where the employee does not make good the tax owing before the end of the tax year in question, the amount outstanding is treated as an emolument in the following year of assessment. This leads to an additional tax charge for employees.

Example 23.5

Jonny Laidlaw receives a holiday voucher worth €3,500 from his employer in December. His gross pay each month is €1,000, he has a monthly standard rate cut-off point of €2,950 and a tax credit of €305. The calculation (ignoring the income levy) is as follows:

			€	€
Pay				*1,000.00*
Notional pay				*3,500.00*
				4,500.00
Tax thereon:				
€2,950	×	*20%*	*590.00*	
€1,550	×	*41%*	*635.50*	
			1,225.50	
Less tax credit			*(305.00)*	
Tax due				*920.50*
PRSI				
(€4,500 – €551) ×		*4%*	*157.96*	
€1,443	×	*4%*	*57.72*	
€3,057	×	*5%*	*152.85*	
				368.53
Total deductions				*1,289.03*

Since the cash amount is only €1,000, the full liability of €1,181.30 cannot be collected:

	€
Cash	*1,000.00*
Less PRSI	*(368.53)*
Cash available to pay tax	**631.47**
Actual tax due	*(920.50)*
Balance uncollected	**(289.03)**

The €289.03 not collected from Jonny Laidlaw in 2009 becomes a further BIK in 2010.

Revenue practice is to allow the employee up until 31 March in the following year to reimburse the employer before the additional BIK arises. Therefore, if Jonny Laidlaw reimburses his employer the outstanding amount of €289.03 by 31 March 2010, no further liability will arise.

The employer must pay the following to the Revenue Commissioners by 14 January 2010:

	€
As above	*1,289.03*
Employer PRSI €4,500 × 10.75%	*483.75*
Total	*1,772.78*

Valuation of benefits-in-kind

The employer must value the particular BIK using stated rules and then add that value to salaries/wages as notional pay.

The following are considered in detail in Chapter 21:

- The valuation of an employer-provided car;
- The valuation of an employer-provided van;
- The valuation of employer-provided accommodation and land;
- The valuation of an employer-provided asset other than a car, van or accommodation;
- The valuation of a preferential loan from an employer;
- The discharge by an employer of employee's personal expenses.

WHAT YOU SHOULD NOW KNOW

On completion of this chapter, you should be able to:

- ✓ Explain how the PAYE system operates and describe its implications for an employer.

- ✓ Describe the difference between the "Cumulative", "Month 1", "Temporary" and "Emergency" basis of taxation.

- ✓ Explain how PRSI operates and describe the different classes of PRSI.

- ✓ Describe the rules for determining the valuation of benefits-in-kind and how such benefits are taxed through the payroll system.

- ✓ Complete Questions and the Assignments in Irish Taxation Law and Practice, Volume 2.

References and Recommended Further Reading

MAGUIRE, T. (2008), *Direct Tax Acts* Irish Taxation Institute.

DEEGAN, G., W. McATEER, G. REDDIN (2008), *Income Tax,* Irish Taxation Institute.

MARTYN, J. and RECK, P. (2008), *Taxation Summary,* Irish Taxation Institute.

Appendix I

Tax Calculation 2009
Cumulative Basis

Standard Rate	20%
Higher Rate	41%
Total Tax Credit	€3,660 per month
Total SRCOP	€36,400 per month

Month No.	Gross Pay this month €	Cum Gross Pay To Date €	Cum SRCOP €	Cum. Tax due 20% SR €	Cum Tax 41% HR €	Cum Gross Tax €	Cum. Tax Credit €	Cum. Tax €	Tax Ded. this Period €	Tax Refund this Month €
1	3200.00	3200.00	3033.33	606.67	68.33	675.00	305.00	370.00	370.00	0.00
2	3000.00	6200.00	6066.67	1213.33	54.67	1268.00	610.00	658.00	288.00	0.00
3	2900.00	9100.00	9100.00	1820.00	0.00	1820.00	915.00	905.00	247.00	0.00
4	1000.00	10100.00	12133.33	2020.00	0.00	2020.00	1220.00	800.00	0.00	-105.00
5	2900.00	13000.00	15166.67	2600.00	0.00	2600.00	1525.00	1075.00	275.00	0.00
6	2900.00	15900.00	18200.00	3180.00	0.00	3180.00	1830.00	1350.00	275.00	0.00
7	2900.00	18800.00	21233.33	3760.00	0.00	3760.00	2135.00	1625.00	275.00	0.00
8	2900.00	21700.00	24266.67	4340.00	0.00	4340.00	2440.00	1900.00	275.00	0.00
9	500.00	22200.00	27300.00	4440.00	0.00	4440.00	2745.00	1695.00	0.00	-205.00
10	2900.00	25100.00	30333.33	5020.00	0.00	5020.00	3050.00	1970.00	275.00	0.00
11	2900.00	28000.00	33366.67	5600.00	0.00	5600.00	3355.00	2245.00	275.00	0.00
12	2900.00	30900.00	36400.00	6180.00	0.00	6180.00	3660.00	2520.00	275.00	0.00

Glossary of abbreviations:

SR	Standard Rate
HR	Higher Rate
Cum	Cumulative
SRCOP	Standard Rate Cut-Off Point
Ded	Deducted

Appendix II

Tax Calculation 2009
Week 1/Month 1 Basis

Month No.	Gross Pay this month €	SRCOP €	Tax due 20% SR €	Tax 41% HR €	Gross Tax €	Tax Credit €	Cum Tax €	Tax Ded. this Period €	Tax Refund this Month €
1	3200.00	3033.33	606.67	68.33	675.00	305.00	370.00	370.00	0.00
2	3000.00	3033.33	600.00	0.00	600.00	305.00	295.00	295.00	0.00
3	2900.00	3033.33	580.00	0.00	580.00	305.00	275.00	275.00	0.00
4	1000.00	3033.33	200.00	0.00	200.00	305.00	0.00	0.00	0.00
5	2900.00	3033.33	580.00	0.00	580.00	305.00	275.00	275.00	0.00
6	2900.00	3033.33	580.00	0.00	580.00	305.00	275.00	275.00	0.00
7	2900.00	3033.33	580.00	0.00	580.00	305.00	275.00	275.00	0.00
8	2900.00	3033.33	580.00	0.00	580.00	305.00	275.00	275.00	0.00
9	500.00	3033.33	100.00	0.00	100.00	305.00	0.00	0.00	0.00
10	2900.00	3033.33	580.00	0.00	580.00	305.00	275.00	275.00	0.00
11	2900.00	3033.33	580.00	0.00	580.00	305.00	275.00	275.00	0.00
12	2900.00	3033.33	580.00	0.00	580.00	305.00	275.00	275.00	0.00

Glossary of abbreviations:

SR   Standard Rate
HR   Higher Rate
Cum.   Cumulative
SRCOP   Standard Rate Cut-Off Point
Ded.   Deducted

Appendix III

PRSI Rates 2009

Employee Class A1			
	PRSI		**Health Contribution**
	Employer	Employee	Employee
01/01/2009 - 30/04/2009	10.75%	4% (annual ceiling €52,000)	Exempt if < or = €500 p.w. Up to €1,925 p.w. 2% over €1,925 p.w. 2.5%
01/05/2009 - 31/12/2009	10.75%	4% (annual ceiling €75,036)	Exempt if < or = €500 p.w. Up to €1,443 p.w. 4% over €1,443 p.w. 5%

Self – Employed			
First €75,036		3% (minimum €353)	3.33%
Next €25,064		3%	4%
Excess over €100,100		3%	4.17%

Notes:

(a) **Employee**

2009   No PRSI on income of €352 p.w. or less
No Health Contribution on income of €500 p.w. or less

2009   First €127 p.w. (non-cumulative), €6,604 p.a. is ignored when calculating PRSI

2007 + 2008   Where income exceeds €100,100 per annum (€1,925 per week), the health contribution increases to 2.5% on the excess.

Recipients of a Social Welfare Widow's or Widower's Pension, Deserted Wives' Benefit/Allowance or One-Parent Family Payment and all Medical Card holders (including people 70 and over) are exempt from paying the Health Contribution.

(b) **Employer**

2009   Employer's PRSI is 8.5% on earnings of €356 p.w. or less

In the case of Schedule E income PRSI is calculated on net income after superannuation. In the case of Schedule D, income is after capital allowances but before pension contributions. There is no liability to PRSI where reckonable income is below €3,174. This test is applied separately to the income of husband and wife.

Section IV

Capital Gains Tax

FONS AEQUI INTELLECTUS

24

BASIC PRINCIPLES OF CAPITAL GAINS TAX

In this chapter, you will deal with the following:

- The charge to capital gains tax (CGT)

- Disposal of an asset

- Timing of disposal

- Chargeable/non-chargeable assets

- Chargeable persons

- Territorial scope of CGT

- Connected persons and married persons

- Due dates for payment of CGT and filing of returns

- Withholding tax rules

24.1   Introduction

Capital gains tax (CGT) was introduced in 1975 by the Capital Gains Tax Act 1975. CGT applies to capital gains arising on the disposal of chargeable assets made on or after 6 April 1974. The legislation has been amended by subsequent Finance Acts and it is now contained in the Taxes Consolidation Act 1997 (TCA 97). CGT was introduced as a means of collecting tax from persons disposing of assets, where the assets being disposed of have increased in value during the period of ownership. Therefore, it is the increase in the value of the asset that is subject to CGT. It is important to note that CGT only applies to realised gains; no CGT arises in respect of assets, which are not disposed of, albeit that those assets may have risen substantially in value since the date of acquisition. Furthermore, not all assets and not all persons are subject to CGT; certain exemptions and reliefs may apply. These matters are discussed in some detail in the paragraphs that follow. The final section of this chapter is concerned with some of the administrative requirements in relation to CGT, i.e., payment and filing dates and procedures relating to CGT withholding tax. Detailed rules regarding the computation of CGT liabilities are addressed in Chapter 25.

24.2   The Charge to Capital Gains Tax

s28 TCA 97   Section 28 TCA 97 provides that CGT:

> *"...shall be charged in accordance with the Capital Gains Tax Acts in respect of capital gains, that is, in respect of chargeable gains computed in accordance with those Acts and accruing to a person on the disposal of assets".*

Therefore, the principle for charging CGT is that the following must occur:

- a disposal,

- of an asset,

- by a chargeable person,

- triggering a chargeable gain.

Consequently, a charge to CGT arises where these four concepts are present. The way in which a chargeable gain is calculated is considered in detail in Chapter 25. The first three elements, i.e., the "disposal" of an "asset" by a "chargeable person" are considered in detail in the paragraphs that follow.

24.3   Disposal of an Asset

In order for a liability to CGT to arise, there must be a disposal of an asset. The term disposal is not defined in the legislation. For CGT purposes, a disposal is generally taken to arise when a person gives up the rights which he/she has in relation to certain assets. While in practice this usually involves a transfer of the ownership of an asset from one person to another, this is not always the case. Furthermore, the transfer of ownership of an asset may occur in different ways and does not necessarily require the physical disposal of the asset. "For example, an individual may receive a capital sum in exchange for the surrender of their rights to shares held at a fixed price at a fixed date in the future. The receipt of the capital sum constitutes the disposal of a right and so is deemed to be a disposal of an asset for capital gains tax purposes." With regard to the disposal of an asset, there are two main issues to be aware of and these are the types of disposal and the timing of the disposal.

24.3.1   Types of disposal

CGT is not charged on unrealised gains, i.e., a disposal or deemed disposal of an asset must take place in order for a charge to CGT to arise. There are many types of transaction which constitute an actual disposal of an asset for CGT purposes. Some examples are as follows:

- the sale of an asset;

- the sale of part of an asset (part-disposal), for example, where 10 acres of land are disposed out of a holding of 100 acres;

- the gift of an asset or part thereof;

- a compulsory purchase order;

- the receipt of a capital sum for the surrender of rights or for not exercising rights – an example of this is where a payment is made for the release of a person from a contract or restrictive covenant;

- an option ceasing to exist;

- the creation, sale or assignment of a leasehold interest;

- the purchase by a company of its own shares;

- the receipt of a capital sum as consideration for the use or exploitation of assets;

- the transfer of an asset by an individual to a trust or a corporate body;

- the exchange of assets in a barter transaction;

- the repayment or forgiveness of a debt.

The analysis in this book is concerned mainly with the sale and gift of assets and parts of assets. For commentary on the CGT treatment of other transactions referred to above, readers are referred to *The Taxation of Capital Gains* by Appleby, T. and O'Hanlon, F. (2009), Irish Taxation Institute.

In addition to the actual disposals referred to above, certain transactions can be classified as "deemed" disposals for CGT purposes albeit that there is no actual surrender of any right in relation to any asset. For example, a "deemed" disposal takes place when a company, which is resident in Ireland, becomes non-resident on or after 21 April 1997. Students are referred to 32.4.8 for further commentary on this issue. In addition, where a company ceases to be a member of a group, any assets which it acquired from other group members whilst it was a member of the group may be deemed to be disposed of and immediately reacquired by the company, leaving the group at market value at the date of acquisition from the other group company – see 32.4.4. A "deemed" disposal can also arise where a capital sum is received resulting from the ownership of an asset, e.g., where compensation is received under a policy of insurance for the loss/damage to property.

24.3.2 Death

Death does not give rise to a disposal for CGT purposes. Accordingly, any gain accruing up to the date of death is not subject to CGT. In this case, the ownership of the deceased's assets transfers to the beneficiaries and they are deemed to acquire the assets at their market value on the date of death of the original owner. Therefore, for subsequent disposal purposes, the date of acquisition of the assets for CGT purposes is the date of death of the original owner and the base cost of the assets is their market value at the original owner's date of death.

Example 24.1

Mr Boyle acquires 1,000 shares in December 1979 for €800. He dies in January 2001 and the market value of the shares at that date is €5,000. Mr Boyle's wife inherits the shareholding and subsequently disposes of the shares in March 2009 for €7,000. There is no CGT liability in respect of the gain accruing from December 1979 up to January 2001. When preparing her CGT computation for the disposal of the shares, the sales proceeds are €7,000 and the date of acquisition and the cost of the shares for inclusion in the calculation are January 2001 and €5,000 respectively.

s534 TCA 97 A part-disposal of an asset is chargeable to CGT. Section 534 TCA 97 provides that references to disposal of an asset in the CGT legislation include references to a part-disposal of an asset. A part-disposal of an asset occurs where, on a person making a disposal, any description of property derived from the asset remains undisposed of. There are special rules to calculate the part of the cost of the asset which is allowable as a deduction when calculating the chargeable gain or loss arising on the part-disposal of the asset. These rules are considered in detail at 25.13.

24.3.3 Timing of a disposal

The timing of a disposal of an asset for CGT purposes is important because it determines the tax year in which the disposal of an asset takes place and details of the disposal must 567 be returned to the Revenue for that tax year. In addition, the timing of the disposal has implications for the actual calculation of the gain. The rate of CGT and the amount of gains exempt from CGT vary between tax years. Inflation relief applies to assets acquired before 2003 and the level of relief available varies with the period of ownership of the asset and accordingly with the date of disposal. These issues are considered in further detail in Chapter 25.

s542 TCA 97 Section 542 TCA 97 sets out the basic rules to determine the date of disposal in certain types of transaction. These are set out as follows:

1. Unconditional Contract

   Where an asset is disposed of by unconditional contract, the date of disposal is the date of the contract.

2. Conditional Contract

   Where a contract is conditional, the date of disposal for CGT purposes is the date the condition is satisfied. For example, where the sale of a property is dependent on planning permission being granted, the date of disposal is the date the stipulated condition is satisfied, i.e., the date planning permission is granted.

3. Compulsory Purchase Order (CPO)

   Where an interest in land is acquired by a local authority by means of a CPO, the date of disposal is the earlier of:

   – the date on which the compensation for the acquisition of the land is agreed; or

   – the date on which the local authority enters the land.

   There are exceptions to this rule in the case of certain CPOs.

4. A Capital Sum Derived from an Asset

   Where a capital sum is derived from the ownership of an asset, the date of disposal is the date the capital sum is received.

5. Gifts

   In the case of gifts, the date of disposal is the date on which the asset passes to the beneficiary/recipient.

6. Receipt of a Compensation Payment

   The date of disposal is generally the date of receipt of the compensation payment.

24.4   Assets

s532 TCA 97   There must be a disposal of a chargeable asset in order to incur a charge to CGT. Section 532 TCA 97 defines a chargeable asset for CGT purposes. In general, a chargeable asset for CGT purposes includes all forms of property, whether situated in Ireland or not, with the exception of assets specifically exempt from CGT under the legislation. These non-chargeable assets are discussed in 24.4.1.

Specifically included in the legislative definition of assets are:

- options and debts;

- any currency, other than Irish currency (which is now the Euro); and

- intangible property, e.g., goodwill, patents, copyrights.

It is worth noting that an ordinary debt owed by a creditor to a person is not an asset for CGT purposes unless the debt is sold by the person to a third party.

Where there is a disposal of a chargeable asset, it is worth noting that the legislation provides exemptions and reliefs from a charge to CGT where qualifying conditions are satisfied. Examples include retirement relief and principal private residence (PPR) relief. Retirement relief is, in general, a relief granted to an individual on the sale of all or part of the qualifying assets of his/her business provided he/she is 55 years of age or more at the date of disposal. PPR relief provides for an exemption from CGT in respect of any gain arising on the disposal of an individual's principal private residence. These reliefs are discussed in more detail in Chapter 27.

24.4.1   Non-chargeable assets

The legislation specifically exempts certain types of assets and certain bodies from CGT. The following assets are generally not subject to CGT:

- government securities, i.e., those issued by the government, local authorities, semi-State bodies and other, similar organisations;

- life assurance policies and contracts for deferred annuities, or interests therein, except where the disposer is not the original beneficial owner of the policy;

- any gain accruing to a body with charitable status, provided the asset disposed of was applied for charitable purposes;

- any gain arising on approved superannuation funds;

- any gain on the disposal of growing timber;

- any gain arising on the disposal of a debt by an original creditor;

- prize bond winnings, national lottery winnings and sums received by way of compensation for or damages for any wrong or injury suffered by an individual in his/her person or in his/her profession;

- wasting chattels, except those used for the purposes of a trade and qualifying for capital allowances (see 24.4.2.1);

- non-wasting chattels sold for €2,540 or less (see 24.4.2.2).

Where an asset is not a chargeable asset for CGT purposes, there is no relief for any loss arising on the disposal of such an asset. Readers are referred to 25.14 for commentary on the relief available for losses arising on chargeable assets.

24.4.2 Chattels

The definition of a chattel is "tangible, movable property", i.e., it is an asset, which can be touched and which is capable of being moved from one place to another. Examples include a car, a painting, a piece of furniture, etc. Goodwill is not a chattel as it is intangible, nor are buildings or land as these are immovable. There are two types of chattel – wasting and non-wasting.

24.4.2.1 Wasting chattels

s603 TCA 97 A wasting chattel is defined as an asset that wastes away over its life and is taken to have a predictable life of less than 50 years. Examples include livestock, motor vehicles and plant and machinery. Section 603 TCA 97 provides an exemption from CGT for any item of tangible movable property, which is a wasting asset. The exemption applies to all taxpayers irrespective of the sales proceeds received on the disposal of the asset. However, there is an exception to the CGT exemption in respect of wasting chattels which are used for business purposes and which qualify for capital allowances. Such wasting chattels do not qualify for the exemption from CGT. Where capital allowances have not been claimed, the CGT exemption will not apply if capital allowances could have been claimed.

Accordingly, a gain arising on the disposal of a motor vehicle by a private individual is not subject to CGT. However, a gain arising on the disposal of a motor vehicle used by an individual for the purposes of his/her trade is subject to CGT to the extent that the motor vehicle qualifies for capital allowances.

No relief under CGT is available for losses arising on the disposal of wasting assets. Such losses are dealt with at 25.14.7.

24.4.2.2 Non-wasting chattels

s602 TCA 97 Conversely, a non-wasting chattel is defined as tangible, movable property, which has a predictable life of more than 50 years when acquired. Examples of non-wasting chattels include antique furniture, paintings and jewellery. In relation to non-wasting chattels, s602 TCA 97 provides an exemption from CGT where the consideration received on the disposal of the asset does not exceed €2,540. It is important to note that the CGT exemption for non-wasting chattels applies only to individuals.

Example 24.2

Mr X disposes of jewellery for €2,000. He had acquired this jewellery for €400 three years earlier. As this is the disposal of a non-wasting chattel for less than €2,540, the exemption from CGT applies. Therefore, the gain arising on the disposal is not liable to CGT.

The CGT exemption is not an annual exemption applying to the collective disposal of all non-wasting chattels in the tax year. The exemption applies to each separate non-wasting chattel disposed of in a year of assessment. Therefore, the number of non-wasting chattels disposed of in a tax year is irrelevant. Provided that the consideration received on each disposal does not exceed €2,540, each disposal is exempt (see 25.15.3 for rules regarding sets of chattels).

Where a non-wasting chattel is disposed of resulting in a capital loss, special rules apply to determine the allowable loss for CGT purposes. In addition, where a non-wasting chattel is sold for an amount slightly in excess of the exemption threshold of €2,540, marginal relief may apply. The application of these special rules and marginal relief is considered in greater detail in Chapter 25 (25.15.1 and 25.15.2).

24.4.3   Location of assets

s533 TCA 97   To determine whether a charge to Irish CGT arises on the disposal of a chargeable asset, it is necessary to know where the asset is located. Section 533 TCA 97 stipulates the location of certain assets where the location of the assets may not be self-evident. These provisions relating to the deemed location of various assets are as follows:

- rights or interests in or over immovable or tangible movable property are situated where the property is situated;

- debts (secured or unsecured) are situated in Ireland only if the creditor is resident in Ireland;

- shares or securities issued by a municipal or governmental authority are situated in the country where the authority is established;

- other registered shares and securities are situated where they are registered;

- a ship or aircraft is situated in Ireland only if the owner is resident in Ireland;

- goodwill of a trade, business or profession is situated in the place where that trade, business or profession is carried on;

- patents, trademarks and designs are situated in the country where they are registere

■ copyrights and licenses to use any copyright material, patents, trademarks or designs are situated in Ireland if the rights derived from them are exercisable in Ireland;

■ a judgment debt is situated where the judgment is recorded.

24.4.4 Specified assets

An individual who is neither resident nor ordinarily resident in Ireland is chargeable to Irish CGT on the disposal of a "specified" asset. Readers are referred to paragraph 24.5 below for further commentary on the territorial scope of CGT.

s29 TCA 97   Specified assets comprise:

(a) land and buildings in Ireland including any interest in land such as leases;

(b) minerals or any rights, interests or other assets in relation to mining or minerals or the searching for minerals in Ireland. Exploration or exploitation rights within the Irish Continental Shelf are also deemed to be assets situated in Ireland for CGT purposes;

(c) assets situated in Ireland, which were used in, or acquired for use for the purposes of a trade carried on in Ireland;

(d) unquoted shares deriving the greater part of their value from (a) or (b) – the greater part of their value is taken to be > 50%.

24.5 Chargeable Persons

At this stage, we have addressed the issues arising where there is a disposal of a chargeable asset. Therefore, issues involving the person making the disposal must now be considered. CGT is assessed on chargeable gains realised by individuals, partnerships and trusts. In limited cases it also applies to companies. Readers are referred to 29.6 for the detailed rules regarding the taxation of gains of companies. In the case of partnerships, gains are attributable not to the partnership or firm as a separate entity but rather to the individuals who form that partnership. For more detailed commentary on the CGT treatment of partners in partnership and for an analysis of the position in relation to trusts, readers are referred to the commentary in *The Taxation of Capital Gains* by Appleby, T. and O'Hanlon, F. (2009), Irish Taxation Institute. This text is concerned primarily with the scope of CGT for individuals and companies. In general, the scope of CGT varies with the residence status of the chargeable person.

24.5.1 Companies

An Irish-resident company is liable to CGT but only on gains arising on the disposal of development land. With regard to the disposal of other assets by a company, any chargeable gains realised on the disposal are subject to corporation tax and not CGT.

Readers are referred to Chapter 29 (29.6) for further commentary on the tax treatment of chargeable gains realised by companies.

24.5.2 Individuals

An individual's residence, ordinary residence and domicile status impact on his/her exposure to Irish CGT. The terms residence, ordinary residence and domicile have the same meaning as for income tax purposes. Readers are referred to Chapter 9 for a detailed explanation of these concepts.

24.5.2.1 Irish resident and/or ordinarily resident and domiciled individual

Where an individual is resident and/or ordinarily resident and domiciled in Ireland, he/she is liable to CGT on chargeable gains arising on the disposal of all assets wherever they are situated and whether or not the gains are remitted to Ireland.

24.5.2.2 Irish resident and/or ordinarily resident but non-domiciled individual

Where an individual is resident and/or ordinarily resident but not Irish-domiciled, he/she is liable to CGT on chargeable gains arising on the disposal of assets situated in Ireland and the UK and on gains arising on the disposal of assets situated outside Ireland and the UK to the extent that the proceeds of such gains are remitted to Ireland, i.e., transferred to Ireland. Where the gains are remitted to Ireland, the remitted gains are taxed in the year of assessment in which they are remitted to Ireland as opposed to in the tax year in which the disposal of the asset takes place. When preparing the CGT computation, the liability is calculated by reference to the rules applying in the tax year in which the disposal of the asset has taken place.

It is important to note that where an individual is assessed to CGT on the remittance basis, he/she will not receive relief for a capital loss realised on the disposal of an asset situated outside of Ireland and the UK.

Where only a portion of the sales proceeds in respect of an asset (subject to CGT on the remittance basis) is remitted to Ireland, then each euro of sales proceeds remitted will trigger €1 of a chargeable gain. The following example illustrates this point.

Example 24.3

John is resident in Ireland but domiciled in Germany. During the 2009 tax year, John disposed of his German shareholdings. The proceeds of disposal amounted to €10,000 and the chargeable gain arising on the disposals was €4,000. He remitted €2,000 of the sales proceeds to Ireland on 1 August 2009. John is chargeable to CGT on the full amount of €2,000 in 2009. Albeit that John has only remitted 20% of the proceeds, he is taxable on 50% of the gain arising. This is because each euro of sales proceeds remitted triggers €1 of the chargeable gain. If John had remitted sales proceeds of €4,000 or more, he would have been chargeable to CGT on all of the gain despite the fact that only a portion of the proceeds had been remitted.

24.5.2.3 Individual not resident and not ordinarily resident in Ireland

Where an individual is neither resident nor ordinarily resident in Ireland, irrespective of domicile, he/she is assessed to CGT on chargeable gains realised on the disposal of certain types of asset, known as specified assets. Specified assets are defined in paragraph 24.4.4 above.

24.5.2.4 Summary

The following chart summarises the scope of CGT for individuals.

Individual	Liable to CGT
Resident/ordinarily resident and domiciled	On worldwide gains (irrespective of whether the assets are situated in Ireland or not and irrespective of whether the gains are remitted to Ireland)
Resident/ordinarily resident but non-domiciled	On Irish and UK gains as they arise and on foreign gains only to the extent that they are remitted to Ireland. Foreign gains/proceeds remitted to the UK are ignored
Non-resident/non-ordinarily resident, irrespective of domicile	Gains on specified assets only

24.5.3 Exempt persons

The following bodies are not chargeable persons for the purposes of CGT:

■ Registered Trade Unions;

■ Friendly Societies;

■ Local Authorities;

■ County Councils;

■ The Health Service Executive;

■ Vocational Educational Committees and Committees of agriculture;

■ Regional tourism bodies;

■ Various government agencies, e.g., IDA, Enterprise Ireland, etc.;

■ The Commission for Communications Regulation (Comreg);

■ The Digital Hub Development Agency (effective from 1 January 2008).

Therefore, any gains realised by these bodies are exempt from a charge to CGT.

In addition, we have already identified that gains accruing to Revenue-approved pension funds and charities are exempt from CGT.

24.5.4   Connected persons

s10 TCA 97   Where there is a transaction between connected persons, the consideration is deemed to equal the open market value. Therefore, any consideration agreed between connected persons is replaced by the open market value for the purpose of calculating the chargeable gain or allowable loss arising on the transaction. Section 10 TCA 97 defines "connected". The following are connected persons:

Spouses and blood relatives

A husband, wife, or relative is a "connected" person. Relative includes brother, sister, uncle, aunt, niece, nephew, lineal ancestor, lineal descendant, step child or a person adopted under the Adoption Acts 1952 to 1991, including foreign adoptions.

The use of the term lineal descendant would include most children. It clearly includes a child born naturally to a couple. The question of a legally adopted child (under the specific Acts mentioned) is also clear.

"In-laws"

The husband or wife of a relative, or a relative of the individual's husband or wife is a "connected" person.

Trustees

A trustee of a trust is connected with the settlor if the settlor is an individual, but not if the settlor is not an individual, e.g., a company. The trustee is also connected with any person connected with that settlor.

A trustee of a settlement is connected with a body corporate, which is connected with the settlement. A body corporate is connected with the settlement in any year if it is a close company (or would be so if Irish resident) and the shareholders include either the trustees or a beneficiary of the settlement. Close companies are considered in Chapter 33.

Partners

A person is connected with any partners of his/hers and with the husband, or wife, or relatives of any of his/her partners. However, there is one important exception to this rule. A person is not connected with another person solely by reason of being that person's partner, where the transaction in question is the acquisition or disposal of partnership assets pursuant to *bona fide* commercial arrangements.

Company

A person is connected with any company he/she controls either on his/her own or together with other persons connected with him/her. In addition, companies under common control are connected persons.

Where a capital loss arises on the disposal of a chargeable asset to a connected person, the loss is available only for offset against chargeable gains arising on the disposal of other assets to the same connected person. Readers are referred to the analysis in 25.14.

24.5.5 Married persons

s1028
TCA 97

Section 1028 TCA 97 deals with married persons. In general, the CGT arising on chargeable gains accruing to a married woman living with her husband in any year of assessment are assessed and charged on her husband. The gains and losses realised by each spouse are calculated separately as if they were single persons and then assessed on a joint basis. Each spouse's residence status must be examined individually to determine whether that individual is chargeable to Irish CGT. It is possible, however, to have the CGT assessment issued in the wife's name if both spouses jointly elect in writing by 1 April in the year of assessment in respect of which the assessment is to be raised in the wife's name.

24.5.5.1 Separate assessment

An election for separate assessment can be made by either spouse by giving written notice to the Inspector of Taxes before 1 April following the end of the year of assessment in respect of which the separate assessment basis is to apply. The effect of the separate assessment election is that both spouses will be assessed separately in respect of any chargeable gains accruing to them. The election for separate assessment continues to have effect until it is withdrawn. In the event that a married couple wish to revert to the joint assessment basis at any time after they elect for separate assessment, an election must be made by the spouse who initially lodged the claim for separate assessment. The notice of withdrawal must be made before 1 April following the end of the year of assessment in which the joint assessment basis is to be effective.

24.5.5.2 Transactions between spouses

Broadly speaking, transactions between spouses are not subject to CGT. The manner in which this relief is applied and the CGT implications of disposing of an asset originally acquired from one's spouse are considered in greater detail in Chapter 25 (25.10).

24.6 Administration of CGT

24.6.1 Self-assessment system

The year of assessment for CGT purposes is the same as the year of assessment for income tax purposes. Therefore, the CGT year of assessment runs from 1 January to the following 31 December. For example, where an asset is disposed of in March 2009, the year of assessment for CGT purposes is the tax year 2009.

s913, s95

The self-assessment system applies to CGT. Section 913 TCA 97 stipulates that the TCA 97 provisions of the Income Tax Acts relating to the making or delivery of any return, statement, declaration, list, etc., subject to any necessary modification, apply to capital gains tax as the provisions apply to income tax. Section 951 TCA 97 imposes an obligation on all chargeable persons disposing of assets in a tax year to file a return of capital gains realised in the tax year. The return must be made in a form prescribed by the Revenue. In general, the capital gains tax return is made on the same form used to file an income tax return. It is the responsibility of the chargeable person to submit details of any chargeable gains realised in the tax year and to pay the CGT liability by the due date irrespective of whether the Revenue has requested it. In addition, any person requested by the Revenue to file a return is required to do so. The obligation to file a return to include details of the chargeable assets disposed of in the relevant period extends not only to individual taxpayers and trustees, but also to companies.

s1084
TCA 97

The return filing date for CGT is the same as for income tax. Therefore, the due date for filing a return of capital gains realised in a tax year is 31 October following the year of assessment in which the disposal of the asset occurs. Therefore, for capital gains realised in the tax year 2009, the due date for filing the 2009 return is 31 October 2010. As the return filing date for income tax and CGT is the same, therefore, the CGT reporting requirement is simplified by the inclusion of a section on the taxpayer's return for chargeable gains realised in the tax year. Forms 11 and 12 contain a section on which chargeable gains may be returned by a taxpayer. Where a taxpayer is not liable to income tax, he/she must file a form CG1 to return details of chargeable assets disposed of during the year of assessment. Where a taxpayer fails to submit a return of chargeable assets disposed of in the tax year, or alternatively, submits an incorrect return, the Revenue has the powers to impose a surcharge on the relevant amount of CGT due. The surcharge is treated as part of the total CGT liability for the year, and therefore, interest charges for late payment of the tax due will be applied to the CGT liability and the surcharge. The surcharge is calculated on the total CGT liability before taking into account any CGT payment on account. Section 1084 TCA 97 provides that the surcharge to be applied where a tax return is filed late is as follows:

- Where the return is filed within two months of the due date, a surcharge of 5% of the tax, or €12,695, if lower, is applied.

- Where the return is filed more than two months late, the surcharge to be applied is 10% of the tax, or €63,485, if lower.

Payment of a CGT liability is also determined under the self-assessment provisions. The adoption of the pay and file system, effective for the year of assessment 2001 and subsequent tax years, removed the application of preliminary tax to CGT.

Finance Act 2009 introduced changes to the CGT payment dates. The legislation stipulates that for 2009 and subsequent tax years, CGT is payable on the following dates:

- 15 December in the current year of assessment in respect of the disposal of chargeable assets made between 1 January and 30 November inclusive (described as the initial period); and

- 31 October in the following year of assessment in respect of the disposal of chargeable assets made between 1 December and 31 December (described as the later period).

- Prior to Finance Act 2009, disposals of chargeable assets made between 1 January and 30 September became payable on 31 October (initial period) in the current year and disposals of chargeable assets between 1 October and 31 December became payable by following 31 January (later period).

> **Tax Facts**
>
> This change in the date for 2009 will result in an estimated cash flow yield of €200 million for the government (www.budget.gov.ie/2009).

Example 24.4

Mary disposes of shares in ABC Limited on 1 April 2009 and she realises a gain of €10,000 on the disposal of the shares. On 1 December 2009, Mary disposes of more shares in ABC Limited, and this time, due to a significant increase in the company's share price, she realises a gain of €25,000.

Mary must file a return no later than 31 October 2010 to include details of the chargeable assets disposed of in the tax year 2009. With regard to paying the CGT liability arising on the disposals of the shares, she must make CGT payments by the following dates:

- *15 December 2009 in respect of the disposal made on 1 April 2009;*

- *31 October 2010 in respect of the disposal of shares made on 1 December 2009.*

When calculating the CGT liability arising on the disposal made on 1 April 2009, Mary is entitled to utilise her annual exemption in full for offset against the chargeable gain after deducting any Capital losses carried forward from prior tax years.

s1080
TCA 97

The relevant amount of CGT due must be paid by the due date to avoid an exposure to interest charges. The interest rate currently charged is 0.0273% per day or part of a day (s1080 TCA 97) where the CGT liability is not fully settled by the due date. Interest is charged from the due date and is payable until the relevant tax is paid.

24.6.2 Withholding tax

s980 TCA 97
s51 FA 2007

Section 980 TCA 97 provides that where certain types of asset are disposed of, the person by or through whom payment is made is obliged to withhold an amount from the sales proceeds and remit it to the Revenue. The requirement to withhold tax from the sales proceeds applies to certain types of asset as specified in the legislation and where the consideration received for the disposal of the asset exceeds the sum of €500,000 (with effect from 1 January 2002). The aim of this is to collect tax from a non-resident in the event that later collection of the tax due may prove impossible. However, the legislative provision with regard to the operation of withholding tax also applies to the disposal of specified assets by an Irish resident. The withholding tax requirement applies to the following types of asset:

(a) land and buildings in the State;

(b) minerals in the State or any rights, interests or other assets in relation to mining or minerals or the searching for minerals;

(c) exploration or exploitation rights in a designated area;

(d) unquoted shares in a company deriving their value or the greater part of their value directly or indirectly from assets specified in (a), (b) or (c) above;

(e) unquoted shares accepted in exchange for shar(e) Unquoted shares accepted in exchange for shares deriving their value, or the greater part of it, from (a), (b) or (c) above;

(f) goodwill of a trade carried on in the State.

The current rate of withholding tax is 15% and it is chargeable on the full consideration. Where the consideration exceeds the limit (currently €500,000), the full proceeds are subject to 15% and not just the excess over the specified limit. The onus to withhold tax at 15% of the consideration on the disposal rests with the purchaser. The purchaser is required to return the amount of tax withheld to the Revenue under the self-assessment rules within 30 days of the acquisition of the asset. If payment has not been made within 30 days, Revenue can assess the purchaser for that amount. A form CG50B should be provided to the individual disposing of the asset confirming the amount of tax deducted. The vendor can then use this form to obtain a refund of the tax withheld, if necessary, when the correct CGT liability has been agreed.

The purchaser need not withhold tax where the consideration for the disposal does not exceed €500,000 or where the vendor provides a form CG50A. A form CG50A is a clearance certificate from the Revenue authorising the purchaser to pay over the full proceeds to the vendor. The vendor can obtain a clearance certificate from the Revenue by completing an application form CG50. The application form should be accompanied by a copy of the contract of sale.

Where the consideration is not for cash and the vendor has not provided a form CG50A, the purchaser is obliged to provide the following details to the Revenue within 30 days of the acquisition:

- the asset acquired;

- the consideration for acquiring the asset;

- market value of the consideration;

- name and address of the person making the disposal.

The purchaser must also pay over 15% of the estimated market value of the consideration to the Revenue within 30 days of the acquisition. The purchaser then has a right to recover this amount from the person from whom he/she acquired the asset.

Where the amount is recovered from the vendor, the vendor is entitled to a credit for this amount against his/her possible capital gains tax liability, provided the amount required to be deducted is paid within the 30 days.

WHAT YOU SHOULD NOW KNOW

On completion of this chapter, you should be able to:

- ✓ Identify issues/transactions which give rise to a disposal of an asset for CGT purposes.

- ✓ Appreciate the importance of the timing of disposal and ascertain the correct timing of a disposal.

- ✓ Identify non-chargeable assets, i.e., those that are exempt from CGT.

- ✓ Explain the CGT treatment of wasting and non-wasting movable assets.

- ✓ Explain the implications of the residence, ordinary residence and domicile status of an individual on the scope of CGT.

- ✓ Discuss the remittance basis of taxation and identify the taxable portion of a gain where only a portion of the sales consideration is remitted to Ireland.

- ✓ Describe the scope of CGT for companies.

- ✓ List the bodies which are not chargeable persons for the purposes of CGT.

- ✓ Describe the CGT treatment of transactions between connected persons.

- ✓ Describe the CGT treatment of married persons.

- ✓ Identify the due dates for payment of CGT and for filing of returns.

- ✓ Describe the general rules and procedures in relation to CGT withholding tax.

- ✓ Complete Questions and the Assignments in Irish Taxation Law and Practice, Volume 2.

25

COMPUTATION OF GAIN
OR LOSS

In this chapter, you will deal with the following:

- Identifying sales consideration and acquisition cost

- CGT treatment of incidental costs of acquisition and disposal

- Capital grants

- Application of market value

- Relief for indexation

- Enhancement expenditure

- Treatment of transactions between spouses

- Calculation of a CGT liability

- Part-disposal rules

- Calculation and use of capital losses

- Non-wasting chattels

25.1   Introduction

In general, the chargeable gain or allowable loss arising on the disposal of an asset is calculated as the difference between the consideration received for the disposal of the asset and the cost of acquisition of the asset. Therefore, when preparing a capital gains tax computation, it is necessary to identify both the consideration and the costs that may be taken into account.

Where any part of the consideration received for the disposal of the asset is included as income for income tax or corporation tax purposes, it is excluded from the consideration figure for CGT purposes. Consequently, a taxpayer will never be liable to tax twice on the same income or gains. Similarly, any expenditure incurred on the acquisition of an asset or on enhancing the value of the asset will only be allowable as a deduction under one tax head. Hence, expenditure allowed as a deduction for income tax or corporation tax purposes will not be an allowable deduction for CGT purposes. The purpose of this chapter is to set out the rules used to determine the consideration or deemed consideration received on the disposal of an asset and also to identify the allowable cost of an asset for CGT purposes. Having established these elements, the remainder of the analysis is concerned with the general rules and basic reliefs applied in calculating CGT liabilities and allowable losses. More detailed rules unique to the disposal of certain types of asset, namely shares and development land, are the subject matter of Chapter 26. Chapter 27 is concerned with some additional more complex reliefs, which may apply in certain circumstances.

25.2   Consideration

s547
TCA 97
The legislation does not define "consideration". The general rule is that the actual consideration received for the disposal of an asset is included in the CGT computation. However, in certain circumstances, the legislation (s547 TCA 97) substitutes market value as the consideration for CGT purposes in place of the actual consideration received on the disposal of a chargeable asset (see 25.6). Other legislative provisions substitute base cost for the consideration received in certain scenarios, e.g., on the transfer of chargeable assets between spouses (see 25.10).

s563 TCA 97 Where the legislation does not substitute deemed consideration for actual consideration received, then the consideration to be taken into account is the actual consideration received by a person disposing of an asset.

25.3   Allowable Expenditure

s552 TCA 97 Section 552 TCA 97 sets out the deductions allowable in calculating the chargeable gain or allowable loss arising on the disposal of an asset. The legislation provides that *inter alia*, the following expenditure is allowable for CGT purposes:

■ the amount or value of the consideration in money or money's worth given by the individual wholly and exclusively for the acquisition of the asset, together with the incidental costs of acquisition;

■ expenditure wholly and exclusively incurred on the asset for the purpose of enhancing the value of the asset – the expenditure must be reflected in the state or nature of the asset at the time of disposal to be allowable for CGT purposes;

■ expenditure wholly and exclusively incurred in establishing, preserving or defending title to, or to a right over, the asset;

■ the incidental costs of making the disposal.

In respect of assets acquired prior to the introduction of CGT, i.e., pre-6 April 1974, such assets are deemed to have been disposed of and immediately reacquired at 6 April 1974. Therefore, the market value of the asset at 6 April 1974 is taken to be the cost of the asset for CGT purposes, irrespective of the actual acquisition cost pre-6 April 1974. This effectively ensures that the gain, which accrued prior to the introduction of CGT, is not taxed when the asset is ultimately sold. The deemed disposal of the asset at 6 April 1974 does not give rise to a disposal for CGT purposes.

Example 25.1

Mr Boyle acquired a property in 1963 for €5,000. The market value of the property was €15,000 on 6 April 1974. Mr Boyle disposes of the property in 2009 for €90,000. What is the acquisition cost of the property for CGT purposes?

As the property was acquired pre-6 April 1974, the cost is taken to be €15,000, i.e., the market value of the property at 6 April 1974. Hence, the gain of €10,000 that had accrued between 1963 and 1974 will not be taxed when the asset is disposed of in 2009.

Additional rules in relation to the substitution of market value on 6 April 1974 for base cost are considered in 25.9.

25.4   Incidental Costs

The legislation stipulates that incidental costs of acquisition or disposal must be incurred wholly and exclusively for the purpose of the acquisition or the disposal of the asset. Examples of incidental costs include:

■ fees, commission or remuneration paid for the professional services of any surveyor, valuer, auctioneer, accountant, agent or legal adviser;

■ costs of transfer or conveyance (including stamp duty);

■ costs of advertising to acquire the asset;

■ in the case of a disposal, costs of advertising to find a buyer and costs reasonably incurred in making a valuation necessary to compute the gain or loss arising on the disposal.

In effect, the allowable incidental costs will either:

(a) increase the cost of the asset – the incidental costs on acquisition are added to the original purchase price of the asset; or

(b) reduce the amount of consideration received – the incidental costs of disposal are deducted from the consideration received on the disposal.

Thus, when calculating the chargeable gain or allowable loss arising on the disposal of an asset, the amount of consideration paid by the taxpayer to acquire the asset, inclusive of any expenses of acquisition, is deducted from the proceeds received on disposal net of any selling expenses. An exception to this arises where incidental costs are incurred on the acquisition of an asset pre-6 April 1974. In this case, the incidental costs incurred on acquisition of the asset are deemed to be included in the market value of the asset at 6 April 1974.

s554 TCA 97 Section 554 TCA 97 provides that any expenditure allowable as a deduction for income tax purposes, or expenditure which would be allowed if the asset were used as a fixed asset for trade purposes, is not allowable for CGT purposes.

Example 25.2

John purchased a rental property in January 2009 for €240,000. Legal expenses in connection with the acquisition amounted to €2,950. In February 2009, he spent €20,000 on structural improvements to the property. In March 2009, he agreed to lease the property to a tenant for six months for €1,000 per month. Estate agent's fees in connection with the letting amounted to €300. Legal fees relating to the draft of this lease amounted to €350. Repairs to the property during the period of the lease amounted to €1,000. In December 2009, John sold the property for €320,000. Estate agent's fees (inclusive of advertising) in connection with the sale amounted to €4,300. Legal fees on selling amounted to €3,800.

John has also informed you that he was billed €3,200 by his tax advisors in connection with the property. This comprises €1,500 in respect of the calculation of taxable Case V rental income and €1,700 in respect of tax advice regarding the disposal of the property.

John's capital gains computation is as follows:

	€	€
Sales proceeds		*320,000*
Less selling expenses: – estate agent's fees		*(4,300)*
– legal fees		*(3,800)*
– tax fees		*(1,700)*
		310,200

	€	€
Cost – acquisition	*240,000*	
– acquisition expenses	*2,950*	
– enhancement	*20,000*	*(262,950)*
		47,250)

Note: There is no deduction for the expenses which relate to the letting of the property, i.e., estate agent's fees of €300, legal fees of €350, repairs of €1,000 and tax fees of €1,500. As these expenses are non-capital in nature, they are deductible from Case V income for income tax purposes.

Example 25.3

Michael purchased land in January 1970 for €30,000. Legal fees on acquisition amounted to €3,500. The market value of the land on 6 April 1974 was €45,000.

The legal fees incurred on acquiring the property in 1970 are deemed to be reflected in the value of the property on 6 April 1974, i.e., €45,000. Accordingly where market value on 6 April 1974 is substituted for original cost, there is no relief for expenses of acquisition.

25.5   Capital Grants

Where part of the acquisition cost of an asset is met by means of a capital grant or other type of subsidy, no deduction is available for that part. For example if an asset is acquired in June 1990 for €25,000 and qualifies for a grant of €3,000, the amount of the acquisition cost allowable for CGT purposes is €22,000.

Where an asset is acquired prior to 6 April 1974, the asset is deemed to have been disposed of and immediately reacquired at market value on that date, i.e., 6 April 1974. The market value of any asset on that date is to be reduced by any capital grant received in respect of the acquisition of that asset.

Example 25.4

Pat acquired a factory in July 1969 for €45,000. He received a grant from the IDA in the amount of €10,000 in respect of this factory. Expenses of acquisition amounted to €3,500. The market value of the factory on 6 April 1974 was €62,500.

Where market value on 6 April 1974 is substituted for original cost, the amount of the grant received on acquisition is deducted in full. Accordingly, in this case, the deemed base cost is €52,500.

25.6   Application of Market Value

s547 TCA 97 Section 547 TCA 97 provides that, in certain circumstances, the actual consideration received on the disposal of a chargeable asset is ignored and the market value of the asset is imposed in place of the actual proceeds received. The legislation sets out the rules to determine the type of transactions where the market value of an asset must be substituted for the actual consideration. In general, market value means the amount which the asset might reasonably be expected to fetch if sold on the "open market". A person is deemed to acquire an asset for a consideration equal to its market value where:

- the person acquires the asset otherwise than by way of a bargain made at arm's length (e.g., assets acquired as gifts, assets acquired on a death);

- the person acquires the asset by way of a distribution from a company in respect of shares in the company, e.g., by way of a distribution on a winding-up of a company;

- the asset is acquired wholly or partly for a consideration that cannot be valued, e.g., in a barter situation;

- the asset is acquired from a connected person (other than a spouse), e.g., an acquisition from a sibling, parent, etc. The concept of connected persons has already been dealt with in Chapter 24 (24.5.4);

- the asset is acquired in connection with loss of employment or diminution of emoluments or in recognition for services or past services.

In the above transactions, market value is deemed to equal the consideration for the purpose of calculating the chargeable gain or allowable loss for CGT purposes. It is important to note that transfers between spouses are not deemed to take place at market value. In this regard, readers are referred to the analysis at 25.10 below.

Example 25.5

Mr Crowley acquired 10,000 shares in ABC Ltd for €5,000 in 1988. In 2009, Mr Crowley gifted the entire shareholding with a market value of €60,000 to his daughter. For CGT purposes, Mr Crowley has made a disposal of a chargeable asset. The market value of the shares, i.e., €60,000 is deemed to be the consideration for inclusion in the CGT computation.

Where his daughter subsequently disposes of the shares in ABC Ltd, the base cost of the shareholding for CGT purposes is €60,000, i.e., the market value of the shares at the date of acquisition.

25.7   Indexation Relief

s556 TCA 97 Indexation relief was originally legislated for in the Capital Gains Tax Amendment Act 1978. It was introduced retrospectively to 6 April 1974, the date CGT was introduced. Section 556 TCA 97 provides that indexation relief operates by adjusting the acquisition cost of a chargeable asset for inflation by reference to the Consumer Price Index (CPI) over the period of ownership of the asset. Accordingly, the objective of indexation relief was to ensure that only real gains (i.e., gains on assets that appreciated in value by more than the cumulative rise in CPI throughout the period of ownership) were subject to capital gains tax. Where the relief is available, it may be claimed by all taxpayers irrespective of their residency position.

Section 556 TCA 97 has been amended by Finance Act 2003. The amendment provides that the application of indexation relief is now restricted to assets which were acquired prior to 1 January 2003. Thus, for assets acquired in 2003 and subsequently, indexation relief is no longer available. For assets acquired prior to 2003, indexation relief only eliminates the part of the gain attributable to inflation in the years up to and including 2003. Thus, there is no relief for inflation attributable to subsequent periods of ownership.

The relief operates by applying a multiplier to the base cost of the asset inclusive of expenses of acquisition. This results in the allowable base cost of the asset being increased in line with inflation, and accordingly, the gain (calculated as the difference between the sales consideration and the increased base cost) is lower. A table of multipliers issued by the Revenue Commissioners indicates the rate of relief to be applied to deductible acquisition costs for different periods of ownership. This table has been reproduced below to facilitate an understanding of the examples that follow.

INDEXATION FACTORS FOR CAPITAL GAINS TAX

Tax Year Expenditure Incurred	Indexation Factor for Disposals in Tax Year																	
	1987/88	1988/89	1989/90	1990/91	1991/92	1992/93	1993/94	1994/95	1995/96	1996/97	1997/98	1998/99	1999/00	2000/01	2001	2002	2003	2004 et seq.
1974/75	4.756	4.848	5.009	5.221	5.355	5.552	5.656	5.754	5.899	6.017	6.112	6.215	6.313	6.582	6.930	7.180	7.528	7.528
1975/76	3.842	3.916	4.046	4.217	4.326	4.484	4.568	4.647	4.764	4.860	4.936	5.020	5.099	5.316	5.597	5.799	6.080	6.080
1976/77	3.309	3.373	3.485	3.633	3.726	3.863	3.935	4.003	4.104	4.187	4.253	4.325	4.393	4.580	4.822	4.996	5.238	5.238
1977/78	2.837	2.892	2.988	3.114	3.194	3.312	3.373	3.432	3.518	3.589	3.646	3.707	3.766	3.926	4.133	4.283	4.490	4.490
1978/79	2.621	2.672	2.760	2.877	2.951	3.059	3.117	3.171	3.250	3.316	3.368	3.425	3.479	3.627	3.819	3.956	4.148	4.148
1979/80	2.365	2.410	2.490	2.596	2.663	2.760	2.812	2.861	2.933	2.992	3.039	3.090	3.139	3.272	3.445	3.570	3.742	3.742
1980/81	2.047	2.087	2.156	2.247	2.305	2.390	2.434	2.477	2.539	2.590	2.631	2.675	2.718	2.833	2.983	3.091	3.240	3.240
1981/82	1.692	1.725	1.782	1.857	1.905	1.975	2.012	2.047	2.099	2.141	2.174	2.211	2.246	2.342	2.465	2.554	2.678	2.678
1982/83	1.424	1.451	1.499	1.563	1.603	1.662	1.693	1.722	1.765	1.801	1.829	1.860	1.890	1.970	2.074	2.149	2.253	2.253
1983/84	1.266	1.290	1.333	1.390	1.425	1.478	1.505	1.531	1.570	1.601	1.627	1.654	1.680	1.752	1.844	1.911	2.003	2.003
1984/85	1.149	1.171	1.210	1.261	1.294	1.341	1.366	1.390	1.425	1.454	1.477	1.502	1.525	1.590	1.674	1.735	1.819	1.819
1985/86	1.082	1.103	1.140	1.188	1.218	1.263	1.287	1.309	1.342	1.369	1.390	1.414	1.436	1.497	1.577	1.633	1.713	1.713
1986/87	1.035	1.055	1.090	1.136	1.165	1.208	1.230	1.252	1.283	1.309	1.330	1.352	1.373	1.432	1.507	1.562	1.637	1.637
1987/88	–	1.020	1.054	1.098	1.126	1.168	1.190	1.210	1.241	1.266	1.285	1.307	1.328	1.384	1.457	1.510	1.583	1.583
1988/89	–	–	1.034	1.077	1.105	1.146	1.167	1.187	1.217	1.242	1.261	1.282	1.303	1.358	1.430	1.481	1.553	1.553
1989/90	–	–	–	1.043	1.070	1.109	1.130	1.149	1.178	1.202	1.221	1.241	1.261	1.314	1.384	1.434	1.503	1.503
1990/91	–	–	–	–	1.026	1.064	1.084	1.102	1.130	1.153	1.171	1.191	1.210	1.261	1.328	1.376	1.442	1.442
1991/92	–	–	–	–	–	1.037	1.056	1.075	1.102	1.124	1.142	1.161	1.179	1.229	1.294	1.341	1.406	1.406
1992/93	–	–	–	–	–	–	1.019	1.037	1.063	1.084	1.101	1.120	1.138	1.186	1.249	1.294	1.356	1.356
1993/94	–	–	–	–	–	–	–	1.018	1.043	1.064	1.081	1.099	1.117	1.164	1.226	1.270	1.331	1.331
1994/95	–	–	–	–	–	–	–	–	1.026	1.046	1.063	1.081	1.098	1.144	1.205	1.248	1.309	1.309
1995/96	–	–	–	–	–	–	–	–	–	1.021	1.037	1.054	1.071	1.116	1.175	1.218	1.277	1.277
1996/97	–	–	–	–	–	–	–	–	–	–	1.016	1.033	1.050	1.094	1.152	1.194	1.251	1.251
1997/98	–	–	–	–	–	–	–	–	–	–	–	1.017	1.033	1.077	1.134	1.175	1.232	1.232
1998/99	–	–	–	–	–	–	–	–	–	–	–	–	1.016	1.059	1.115	1.156	1.212	1.212
1999/00	–	–	–	–	–	–	–	–	–	–	–	–	–	1.043	1.098	1.138	1.193	1.193
2000/01	–	–	–	–	–	–	–	–	–	–	–	–	–	–	1.053	1.091	1.144	1.144
2001	–	–	–	–	–	–	–	–	–	–	–	–	–	–	–	1.037	1.087	1.087
2002	–	–	–	–	–	–	–	–	–	–	–	–	–	–	–	–	1.049	1.049
2003 et seq.	–	–	–	–	–	–	–	–	–	–	–	–	–	–	–	–	–	1.00

NOTE: No indexation is available for expenditure made within 12 months prior to the date of disposal.

When using the table of multipliers, the year in which the asset was acquired must be identified. This is located in the table in the column headed "Tax Year Expenditure Incurred" (A). The tax year in which the disposal of the chargeable asset took place must subsequently be identified. This is located at the top of the table under the heading "Indexation Factor for Disposals in Tax Year" (B).[1] To identify the indexation factor applicable to the disposal, trace from (A) to (B) to the point of intersection.

Example 25.6

Assuming that all of the following disposals took place in the tax year 2009, identify the relevant indexation factors:

1. *Asset acquired in March 1979.*
   Indexation factor: 4.148.

2. *Asset acquired in December 1983.*
   Indexation factor: 2.003.

3. *Asset acquired in May 2001.*
   Indexation factor: 1.087.

4. *Asset acquired in February 2003.*
   No Indexation.

On careful consideration of the table, a number of issues (some already addressed) become obvious. These are as follows:

■ There are no indexation factors for expenditure incurred prior to 1974/75, i.e., prior to 6 April 1974. This is because there is no capital gains tax on gains accruing prior to this date. Where assets were acquired prior to 6 April 1974, the market value of the asset on 6 April 1974 is substituted and indexed in calculating the deductible expenditure for CGT purposes.

■ The column of multipliers for 2003 applies for "2003 *et seq*" i.e., it applies for all years after 2003 also. Therefore the multipliers for 2009 are the same as those in 2003. In fact, the column of multipliers for all future years will be identical to that for 2003. This is because inflation relief has effectively been terminated for inflation attributable to subsequent periods. The Finance Act 2003 provides that there is no inflation relief for expenditure incurred on or after 1 January 2003.

■ There is no inflation relief for assets acquired and disposed of in the same income tax year. In fact, the legislation states that there is no indexation relief for expenditure incurred in the 12 months prior to disposal. This was an important point to note prior to 2003, as the multiplier table does not highlight this matter in cases where the acquisition and disposal take place in different income tax years. For example, assume an asset is acquired in December 2002 and disposed of in February 2003.

---

1   Where the table refers to a tax year by making reference to two calendar years, e.g., 1988/89, it is referring to the period from 6 April to the following 5 April, in this case, the period from 6 April 1988 to 5 April 1989. With effect from 6 April 2001 onwards, the tax year-end coincided with the calendar year-end. Prior to this, the tax year ended on 5 April.

No indexation relief can be applied to the cost of this asset because the cost was incurred less than 12 months prior to the date of sale. However, the table correctly indicates that a factor of 1.049 can apply to disposals in 2003 of assets acquired in 2002 and readers may find the table deceptive in such cases.

25.8   Indexation and Enhancement Expenditure

The acquisition cost of an asset together with any allowable incidental acquisition costs are indexed from the tax year in which the expenditure is incurred up to the tax year in which the asset is disposed of. Indexation relief may also be applied to enhancement expenditure. In general, enhancement expenditure is expenditure wholly and exclusively incurred on an asset for the purpose of enhancing the value of the asset. In addition, the expenditure must be reflected in the state or nature of the asset at the time of disposal of the asset. Therefore, to qualify as a deduction for CGT purposes, enhancement expenditure must increase the value of the asset and be reflected in the asset at the date of disposal. Enhancement expenditure is indexed from the date on which it is incurred. Thus, where there is a disposal of a chargeable asset and enhancement expenditure is incurred in some year or years subsequent to the original year of acquisition, two or more indexation factors may be applied when calculating the chargeable gain arising on the disposal.

Example 25.7

Joe acquired a rental property in 1970 for €16,000. Expenses of acquisition amounted to €1,000. He began letting the property immediately. In 1980, an extension was built at a cost of €8,000. In 1982, the local authority forced Joe to take down this extension as proper planning permission had not been obtained. In June 1985, Joe paid a builder €15,000 to construct another extension. Planning and design expenses paid to an architect in connection with this extension amounted to €4,000. In August 1990, the property was vandalised by the tenants and Joe spent €10,000 repairing broken fittings and windows and €2,000 on legal fees in an effort to recover costs from the tenants. In September 2003, Joe added a conservatory to the property at a total cost of €18,500. In February 2009, he sold the property for €550,000. Legal expenses and auctioneer's fees on sale amounted to €4,000 and €6,800 respectively. The market value of the property on 6 April 1974 was €22,000.

Joe's capital gain is calculated as follows:

	€	€
Sales proceeds		*550,000*
Deduct selling expenses (€4,000 + €6,800)		*(10,800)*
		539,200
M.V. 6/4/1974	*22,000*	
Indexed @ 7.528		*(165,616)*
Enhancement 1985/1986	*15,000*	
Expenses	*4,000*	
	19,000	
Indexed @ 1.713		*(32,547)*
Enhancement 2003		*(18,500)*
Gain		*322,537*

Notes:

1. *The expenses of acquisition were not added to the market value on 6 April 1974 on the basis that they are already deemed to be included therein.*

2. *There is no relief for costs incurred on the first extension which was taken down, on the basis that this expenditure was not reflected in the asset at the time of disposal.*

3. *There is no relief for the expenditure incurred on repairs on the basis that these repairs did not constitute improvements/enhancement expenditure and would in any event have been allowable against Case V rental income for income tax purposes.*

4. *There is no indexation of the enhancement expenditure incurred on the conservatory in 2003 as indexation does not apply to expenditure incurred on or after 1 January 2003.*

25.9   Restrictions on the Use of Indexation and the Market Value 1974 Rule

The rationale for indexation and the market value 1974 rule is to ensure that only real gains accruing from 1974 onwards are taxable and only real losses are allowable. A number of exceptions ensure that the application of these rules cannot:

1. increase the actual monetary loss suffered;

2. increase the actual monetary gain realised;

3. turn an actual monetary gain into a book or paper loss;

4. turn an actual monetary loss into a book or paper gain.

Examples of the restrictions on the use of indexation and the market value 1974 rule are set out below.

(1) Where the effect of the rules is to increase the actual loss arising on the disposal of an asset, the rules are ignored and the actual loss is taken as that arising on the disposal.

Example 25.8

An asset acquired in March 1988 for €40,000 is disposed of in December 2009 for €35,000. What is the allowable gain/loss arising on the disposal?

The gain/loss arising on the disposal is calculated as follows:

	€	€
Proceeds		*35,000*
Cost	*40,000*	
Indexation factor	*1.583*	
Indexed cost		*(63,320)*
Indexed loss		***(28,320)***

The actual monetary loss on this transaction is €5,000. In this case the application of indexation has had the effect of increasing the loss from €5,000 to €28,320. Accordingly, the allowable loss available for offset against any chargeable gains arising in the tax year 2009 and subsequent years is restricted to the monetary loss of €5,000.

(2) Similarly, for a gain, if after applying the rules, the resultant gain is higher than the actual gain arising, the effect of the rules is ignored. The actual gain replaces the indexed gain in the computation.

Example 25.9

An asset purchased in 1973 for €48,000 is disposed of in October 2009 for €50,000. The market value of the asset on 6 April 1974 was €6,000. What is the allowable gain/loss arising on the disposal?

	€	€
Proceeds		*50,000*
Cost	*6,000*	
Indexation factor	*7.528*	
Indexed cost		*(45,168)*
Indexed gain		***4,832***

The actual monetary gain is €2,000. Therefore, the taxpayer will be assessed to CGT on the lower actual gain of €2,000.

(3) If the effect of the rules is to turn a monetary gain into an indexed loss, this is treated as if neither a gain nor a loss arose on the transaction. This situation is known as a "no gain/no loss" situation.

Example 25.10

An asset purchased in June 1985 for €50,000 is disposed of in May 2009 for €70,000. What is the allowable gain/loss arising on the disposal of the asset?

	€	€
Proceeds		*70,000*
Cost	*50,000*	
Indexation factor	*1.713*	
Indexed cost		*(85,650)*
Indexed loss		***(15,650)***

In this example, there is an indexed loss even though a monetary gain arises on the transaction. Accordingly, this is treated as a "no gain/no loss" situation. The monetary gain is not assessable to CGT and the indexed loss is not available for offset against any chargeable gains.

(4) If the effect of the rules is to turn an actual monetary loss into an indexed gain, again this is deemed to be a "no gain/no loss" situation.

Example 25.11

An asset acquired in 1963 for €40,000 is disposed of in July 2009 for €30,000. The market value of the asset at 6 April 1974 was €2,500. What is the allowable gain/loss arising on the disposal of the asset?

	€	€
Proceeds		*30,000*
Cost	*2,500*	
Indexation factor	*7.528*	
Indexed cost		*(18,820)*
Indexed gain		***11,180***

In this example, there is an indexed gain. However, a monetary loss of €10,000 arises on the transaction. Accordingly, this is treated as a "no gain/no loss" situation. The indexed gain is not assessed to CGT and the monetary loss is not available for offset against any chargeable gains.

In addition to the restrictions outlined above, there is a restriction on the amount of indexation relief available on a disposal of development land. This will be dealt with in detail in Chapter 26 (26.2).

25.10   Transactions between Spouses

s1028(5)
TCA 97

Section 1028(5) TCA 97 provides that the disposal of an asset between spouses is treated as having been made at a price, which gives no gain and no loss to the spouse making the disposal. Therefore, the disposal does not give rise to a charge to CGT, nor does it create an allowable loss for the spouse who effects the transfer. Where the asset was acquired by the transferring spouse prior to 6 April 1974, the transfer is treated as being at market value on 6 April 1974.

The spouse who has acquired the asset from his/her partner takes over the period of ownership and the base cost from that partner. For subsequent disposals outside of the parties to the marriage, the acquiring spouse is deemed to have acquired the asset at the same cost and on the same date as the spouse who had originally acquired the asset. Enhancement expenditure incurred by either spouse is taken into consideration and attributed to the spouse making the disposal to the third party. (However, assets acquired from a spouse on death are acquired at market value, see 24.3.2.)

Example 25.12

Mr A acquires a painting in June 1989 for €5,000, which he gives to his wife in July 1993. Mrs A subsequently disposes of the asset for €15,000 in May 2009. At the date of the transfer of the painting in July 1993, the market value of the painting was €10,000.

The effects of the transactions are as follows:

The transfer by Mr A to Mrs A in July 1993 gives rise to a "no gain/no loss" transaction. For subsequent disposals, Mrs A is deemed to have acquired the asset on the original date of acquisition and at the original cost, i.e., in June 1989 for €5,000.

The gain by Mrs A on the subsequent disposal of the asset is calculated as follows:

	€	€
Proceeds		*15,000*
Less:		
Cost 1989/1990	*5,000*	
Indexation factor	*1.503*	
Indexed cost		*(7,515)*
Indexed gain		***7,485***

25.11　Annual Exemption

s601 TCA 97　Section 601 TCA 97 provides that the first €1,270 of chargeable gains realised by an individual in a year of assessment is exempt from CGT. The annual exemption of €1,270 is only available to individuals. Companies, trustees and partnerships cannot claim the annual exemption. Where an individual does not utilise his/her annual exemption in a year of assessment, the exemption is effectively lost, as it cannot be carried forward. An individual is entitled to claim the annual exemption irrespective of his/her residence position in a year of assessment.

Each spouse is entitled to a separate annual exemption.

25.12　Capital Gains Tax Rate

s28 TCA 97　Finance Act 2009 provides that the CGT rate to be applied to the disposal of chargeable assets from the 15 October 2008 to the 7 April 2009 inclusive is 22%. The CGT rate to be applied to the disposal of chargeable assets from the 8 April 2009 is 25%. It should be noted that a rate of 20% applied to the disposal of chargeable assets disposed of prior to 15 October 2008. In addition disposals of certain types of assets prior to 1 December 1999 were liable to different CGT rates. For example, in the case of development land, a rate of 40% applied to a disposal unless the land was zoned for residential use or had residential planning permission. The rate of 20% now applies to the disposal of all assets with the exception of foreign life policies and certain offshore funds, where the CGT rate applicable is 40%.

25.13　Part-Disposal of an Asset

The disposal of part of an asset is deemed to be chargeable to capital gains tax. A part-disposal occurs where a portion of an asset is sold. Where a part-disposal of an asset occurs, the sales proceeds are known. However, the cost of the portion of the asset disposed of must be determined to calculate the chargeable gain or allowable loss arising on the transaction.

s557 TCA 97　Section 557 TCA 97 provides that the portion of the original expenditure, which is allowed as a deduction against the sales proceeds received on the part-disposal, is restricted to the proportion of the original cost of the asset, which the value of the part being disposed of bears, at the date of disposal, to the market value of the full asset. The formula to calculate the acquisition cost of an asset part disposed of is as follows:

$$\textbf{Original Cost of Asset} \quad \times \quad \frac{\textbf{A}}{\textbf{A} + \textbf{B}}$$

Where:

A = the amount of sales proceeds received on the part-disposal of the asset (or market value if appropriate), and

B = the market value of the remaining part of the asset retained after the disposal.

Incidental costs of acquisition are also apportioned using the above formula where a part-disposal of an asset occurs.

The base cost of the remainder of the asset for the purposes of subsequent disposals is the full original cost less the portion attributed to the previous part disposal.

Where there is a disposal of shares, as each share is identical and of equal value, the fraction applied in the part-disposal formula may be modified to mean the following:

$$\frac{\text{Number of shares sold}}{(\text{Number of shares sold} + \text{number of shares retained})}$$

However, this modification is relevant only in the case of disposals of shares. For other assets, the component parts are not identical and use of a unit basis as opposed to a value basis for apportioning the original cost may yield an incorrect result.

Example 25.13

Paul purchased 10 acres of farmland in December 1990 for €30,000. Incidental costs of acquisition amounted to €2,000. In 2009, he disposed of five acres from this holding for €25,000. The market value of the remainder of the farm at the date of disposal was €75,000. Paul's gain arising on the 2009 part-disposal is calculated as follows:

	€
Sales proceeds	*25,000*
*Costs: (€30,000 + €2,000) * €25,000/(€25,000 + €75,000)*	
* = €8,000*	
Indexed @ 1.442	*(11,536)*
	13,464

*Note 1: **Albeit that half of the land has been sold, only 25% of the original costs are attributed to the part-disposal.***

*Note 2: **The base cost of the remaining five acres for the purposes of subsequent disposals is €24,000, comprising actual acquisition cost of €22,500 and expenses of acquisition of €1,500.***

Where a part-disposal of an asset occurs and enhancement expenditure has been incurred in respect of the asset in its entirety, the enhancement expenditure must also be apportioned for CGT purposes. The above formula is also used to apportion enhancement expenditure incurred between the part of the asset disposed of and the asset remaining.

Where enhancement expenditure relates only to a specific part of the asset, which part is readily identifiable, no apportionment of the enhancement expenditure is necessary. In the latter case, the enhancement expenditure attaches to that part of the asset in respect of which it is incurred. Accordingly, it is only taken into account for disposal purposes when that part of the asset is disposed of.

Example 25.14

Helen purchased an old period residence in Rathmines for €60,000 in March 1994. In June of 1995, she spent €45,000 on converting the entire property into four separate residential units. In August 2002, she sold the two ground-floor units for €600,000. The market value of the remaining first-floor units at this time was €800,000. In September 2009, she sold the remaining two first-floor units for €950,000. She had no other disposals in 2002 and 2009. Helen's capital gains tax liability for 2002 is calculated as follows:

		€
Sales proceeds		600,000
Cost 1993/1994:	€60,000 * €600,000 / (€600,000 + €800,000) = €25,714	
	Indexed @ 1.27	(32,657)
Enhancement 1995/1996:	€45,000 * €600,000 / (€600,000 + €800,000) = €19,286	
	Indexed @ 1.218	(23,490)
		543,853
Annual exemption		(1,270)
		542,583
CGT at 20%		108,517

Helen's capital gains tax liability on the disposal of the remainder of the property in 2009 is calculated as follows:

		€
Sales proceeds		950,000
Cost 1993/1994:	€60,000 – €25,714 = €34,286	
	Indexed @ 1.331	(45,635)
Enhancement 1995/1996:	€45,000 – €19,286 = €25,714	
	Indexed at 1.277	(32,837)
		871,528
Annual Exemption		(1,270)
		870,258
CGT at 25%		174,052

25.14   Losses

s546(2) TCA 97

Section 546(2) TCA 97 provides that "the amount of a loss accruing on a disposal of an asset shall be computed in the same way as the amount of a gain accruing on a disposal is computed". Therefore, when calculating the gain/loss arising on the disposal of an asset, the same rules apply as to the consideration and the allowable expenditure.

25.14.1 Indexation

There are restrictions on the use of indexation in calculating an allowable loss for CGT purposes. In effect, indexation cannot create or augment a loss.

Example 25.15

Tom purchased shares at a cost of €4,000. He disposed of them for €5,000. Assume that the effect of indexation is to increase the cost of acquisition by €2,000. The computation is as follows:

Acquisition cost	*€4,000*
Indexation increase	*€2,000*
Deductible cost	*€6,000*
Consideration for sale	*(€5,000)*
Loss	*€1,000*

This is not an allowable loss because it arises entirely due to indexation. The sales proceeds of €5,000 exceed the acquisition cost of €4,000, so there was in fact a gain, but for indexation. The indexation is allowed to eliminate the gain but it cannot create a loss. Therefore, the transaction gives rise to neither a chargeable gain nor an allowable loss.

25.14.2 Non-allowable losses

No loss relief is available for losses arising on the disposal of assets which are not chargeable assets for CGT purposes, e.g., government stock. In effect, where a gain arising on the disposal of an asset is not liable to CGT, then a loss incurred on the disposal of such an asset is not available for offset.

Losses available for relief against profits liable to income tax or corporation tax cannot be offset against chargeable gains. Conversely, capital losses are not available for offset against income taxable under corporation tax or income tax.

In relation to a person who is either resident or ordinarily resident in Ireland but not Irish domiciled, he/she is liable to Irish CGT on Irish and UK gains, and foreign gains to the extent the proceeds of such gains are remitted to Ireland.

Where a loss arises on the disposal of an asset situated outside Ireland and the UK, no loss relief is available in respect of that loss irrespective of whether the sales proceeds are remitted to Ireland or not.

In the case of an individual liable to Irish CGT on the disposal of specified assets, loss relief is available only in respect of gains arising on the disposal of specified assets.

25.14.3 Use of losses

Losses are relieved in the tax year in which the disposal takes place. They are offset against a chargeable gain prior to the deduction of the annual exemption. Therefore, the offset of capital losses in priority to the annual exemption may sometimes result in the loss of the benefit of the annual exemption. Where the loss remains unutilised in the year of disposal, it can be carried forward for offset against the earliest future chargeable gains. Relief cannot be given more than once for capital losses. For example, a taxpayer cannot utilise the losses in the year they arise and carry them forward for relief in subsequent tax years.

25.14.4 CGT – initial period (1 January 2009 to 30 November 2009)

For the initial period of 1 January 2009 to 30 November 2009, allowable capital losses incurred in the eleven-month period ended 30 November 2009 and/or any such losses carried forward from 2008 together with the annual exemption of €1,270 may first be deducted from the chargeable gains accruing in the period.

Example 25.16

Mary disposes of shares in March 2009 realises a chargeable gain of €4,000. She has unutilised capital losses carried forward of €1,500.

She is due to pay CGT in respect of the chargeable gain she made in March 2009 by 15 Decembeer 2009. The capital losses carried forward of €1,500 are first offset against the chargeable gain of €4,000, and her annual exemption of €1,270 is set against the balance of the gain of €2,500. Therefore, Mary is due to pay CGT on the net gain of €1,230 (i.e., €1,230 @ 22% = €270) by 15 December 2009. She will include details of the disposal on the 2009 tax return, which is due to be filed by 31 October 2010.

Losses cannot be carried back for offset against chargeable gains arising in earlier years of assessment. (However, there is an exception for the year of death – see Example 25.17 below).

The restriction on the carry-back of losses, however, does not preclude the offset of losses against gains, which arise earlier than the losses, but where both arise in the same year of assessment.

Example 25.17

John realises a gain on the disposal of an asset in June 2009 and then incurs a loss on a subsequent disposal in December 2009. The loss is available for offset against the gain. This results in only the net gain being assessed to CGT. The offset is available because both the gain and the loss arise in the same year of assessment.

There is an exception to this rule in respect of losses arising in the year of death of a taxpayer. In such cases, the losses can be carried back and offset against any gains arising in the three years of assessment preceding the year of assessment in which the death of the taxpayer arises. This is known as Terminal Loss Relief.

For example, if a taxpayer dies in June 2009, any capital losses arising in the tax year 2009, to the extent unutilised in that year, are available to be carried back and offset against gains arising in any of the three preceding tax years: 2008, 2007 and 2006.

It is important to note that it is only the current year losses, i.e., the losses arising in the year of death that can be carried back. Any aggregated losses carried forward from earlier years of assessment are not available for relief in this way.

For example, if capital losses arose in 1998/99 and remain unutilised, they will be carried forward and aggregated with any subsequent losses until they are relieved. However, if the taxpayer dies in the tax year 2009, the aggregated losses carried forward are lost and the only losses available for relief by means of carry-back under a Terminal Loss Relief claim are the losses arising in the year of death.

25.14.5 Connected persons

Where a capital loss arises on the disposal of a chargeable asset to a connected person, the loss is available only for offset against chargeable gains arising on the disposal of other assets to the same connected person.

25.14.6 Non-wasting chattels

Where a non-wasting chattel is disposed of resulting in a capital loss, special rules apply to determine the allowable loss for CGT purposes. Where the consideration is less than €2,540, for the purpose of determining the allowable loss, the consideration is deemed to equal €2,540. In this respect, the loss relief is restricted and is limited to the excess of the cost of the asset over the €2,540 limit. In such cases, it is important to note that any incidental costs incurred on the disposal of the asset are added to the allowable loss and are not deducted from the consideration. See 25.15.2 for worked examples.

25.14.7 Wasting chattels

As noted at 24.4.2.1, gains on disposals of wasting chattels are exempt, except where the wasting chattel has been used for business purposes and qualified for capital allowances. Losses on wasting chattels are never allowable losses, even in cases where a gain would be taxable. Where a wasting asset that qualifies for capital allowances is disposed of, any loss arising is not allowable for CGT purposes, as relief will have been given for the loss through the capital allowances system and relief cannot be given twice.

25.14.8 Married persons

The general rule is that where a married couple is jointly assessed, surplus losses of one spouse are offset against chargeable gains accruing to the other spouse in a year of assessment. The surplus losses taken into account include current year losses and losses carried forward from prior tax years. The exception to the general rule is where the married couple are separately assessed. In the latter case, it is not possible to transfer any surplus losses between spouses. In this case, the unutilised losses of the spouse are carried forward for offset against any future chargeable gains accruing to the spouse who incurred the losses.

It is possible to elect not to have losses transferred between spouses where the couple are jointly assessed. The election must be made before 1 April following the end of the year of assessment in which the losses are incurred.

25.14.9 Loss or destruction of an asset

s538
TCA 97

Section 538 TCA 97 provides that the entire loss, destruction, dissipation, or extinction of an asset constitutes a disposal of that asset for CGT purposes, which may give rise to a loss claim.

25.14.10 An asset of negligible value

s538
TCA 97

In general, only a realised loss is allowable for CGT purposes. However, if the Revenue is satisfied that the value of an asset has become negligible, they may allow loss relief as if the asset had been sold and reacquired at market value, and the loss in fact realised. (s538(2) TCA 97).

Where an inspector allows the loss relief claim, the loss arises not on the date at which the asset lost its value, but rather on the date on which the claim for the loss relief is made.

25.15 Chattels

The concept of chattels was initially dealt with in Chapter 24. Readers should refer to Chapter 24 (24.4.2) to refresh themselves on the definition of a wasting chattel and a non-wasting chattel. The legislation provides for an exemption from CGT where the consideration received on the disposal of a non-wasting chattel does not exceed €2,540. Where the consideration is in excess of €2,540, marginal relief may apply in calculating the final CGT liability. In addition, where the disposal of a non-wasting chattel results in a capital loss, special rules may apply in determining the allowable loss for CGT purposes. Finally, where non-wasting assets form part of a set, part-disposal rules need to be applied. Having considered the calculation of CGT liabilities, the treatment of losses and the part-disposal rules in detail, we are now in a position to revisit the CGT treatment of chattels and to consider each of these issues in turn.

25.15.1 Marginal relief – Non-wasting chattel

Where the consideration received on the disposal of a non-wasting chattel is slightly in excess of the €2,540 limit, marginal relief exists to restrict the tax payable to 50% of the excess of the consideration over the €2,540 limit. Where the actual CGT liability is lower than the CGT liability after applying the marginal relief, the lower amount will be payable.

Example 25.18

In February 2009, Mr Z disposes of a painting for €3,100. The painting cost €1,600 in the 1993/94 tax year. The CGT liability arising on the transaction is calculated as follows:

	€	€
Sales proceeds		*3,100*
Cost 1993/94	*1,600*	
Indexation factor	*1.331*	
Indexed cost		*(2,130)*
Gain		*970*

CGT at 22% (ignoring the annual exemption): €214.

Marginal relief works to restrict the CGT liability to 50% of the excess of the consideration over the €2,540 limit,

i.e., 50% × (€3,100 – €2,540) = €280.

The actual CGT liability is lower than the liability calculated using marginal relief, and therefore the actual CGT liability is the amount payable.

Alternatively, if in the above example, the actual CGT liability was €300, the marginal relief provisions would operate to restrict the CGT liability payable to €280.

25.15.2 Losses – non-wasting chattels

Where a non-wasting chattel is disposed of resulting in a capital loss, special rules apply to determine the allowable loss for CGT purposes. Where the consideration is less than €2,540, for the purpose of determining the allowable loss, the consideration is deemed to equal €2,540. In this respect, the loss relief is restricted and is limited to the excess of the cost of the asset over the €2,540 limit. In such cases, it is important to note that any incidental costs incurred on the disposal of the asset are added to the allowable loss and are not deducted from the consideration.

Example 25.19

Mr X acquired a painting for €2,800 in 2009 and he disposed of it in the same tax year for €2,400. A monetary loss of €400 arises on the disposal. However, as the asset disposed of is a non-wasting chattel and the consideration received on the disposal is €2,400, i.e., less than the €2,540 limit, the consideration is deemed to be €2,540, thus creating an allowable loss for CGT purposes of €260, i.e., €2,800 – €2,540.

If, in the above example, €50 of incidental costs were incurred on the disposal of the non-wasting chattel, the allowable loss would be €310, i.e., the incidental disposal costs would increase the allowable loss and would not reduce the consideration as normal.

Where a loss arises on the disposal of a non-wasting chattel, a monetary loss will not be converted into a notional gain by virtue of deeming the consideration received on the disposal of the asset to equal €2,540. The purpose of imposing the €2,540 limit in such loss scenarios is to reduce the amount of allowable loss available for offset against chargeable gains.

Example 25.20

Mr Y disposes of a painting for €1,200, which he acquired for €1,800 a number of years ago.

The transaction results in a monetary loss of €600. However, as the asset is a non-wasting chattel and the consideration is less than €2,540, the consideration received on the disposal is deemed to equal €2,540. By imposing the €2,540 limit, a gain of €740 arises and theoretically converts the actual monetary loss of €600 to a notional gain of €740.

As the imposition of the €2,540 limit as consideration converts the monetary loss arising on the disposal to a notional gain, no relief is available for the actual loss suffered, i.e., the loss cannot be offset against any chargeable gains. However, no assessment to CGT will be raised on the notional gain of €740. In effect, this transaction will be treated as a "no gain/no loss" situation.

25.15.3 Sets of non-wasting chattels

Where the non-wasting chattels form a set of assets, e.g., four antique chairs, the exemption from CGT cannot be gained by disposing of each asset separately for less than €2,540 to the same person or connected persons. In such circumstances, the disposal of each of the assets is treated as part of a single translation for the purpose of applying the CGT exemption for non-wasting chattels. The consideration on each separate disposal is aggregated to determine whether the €2,540 limit applies and whether a CGT liability arises.

The exemption from CGT on the disposal of a non-wasting chattel is only available on the part-disposal of a chattel (i.e., the disposal of a right or interest in the chattel) if, at the time of the disposal, the consideration received together with the value of the interest remaining is less than €2,540. Where the combined value of the consideration and the interest remaining does not exceed €2,540, no charge to CGT arises on the part-disposal. However, where the combined value exceeds €2,540, the normal part-disposal rules apply. Where the combined value does not exceed €2,540 and a loss arises, the loss is restricted.

For the purposes of the operation of the exemption, marginal relief and loss relief provisions, the consideration is taken to be the actual consideration received on the part-disposal together with the value of the interest remaining.

Example 25.21

Mr A sells an interest in a non-wasting chattel for €1,000. The value of the interest remaining in the chattel is €1,300. As the combined value of the consideration and the interest remaining is less than €2,540, the relief applies in full to the part-disposal, i.e., the part-disposal is exempt from CGT.

Example 25.22

Mr B sells an interest in a non-wasting chattel for €1,650. The value of the interest remaining is €1,100. In this example, the aggregate value of the consideration and the interest remaining is €2,750. It is this value that is used in the marginal relief calculation. Accordingly, the maximum tax payable ordinarily would be €105, i.e., ((€2,750 – €2,540) × 50%).

However, as the consideration figure used in the calculation above comprises a value relating to an interest in the asset not disposed of, the maximum tax payable, as calculated, must be divided between the asset disposed of and that remaining. The maximum tax payable on the part-disposal is arrived at by apportioning the amount calculated above by reference to the consideration received on the part-disposal as a percentage of the combined value of the consideration and the interest remaining, i.e., €105 × (€1,650 / €2,750) = €63.

WHAT YOU SHOULD NOW KNOW

On completion of this chapter, you should be able to:

- ✓ Identify the amount of consideration or "deemed" consideration and the amount of the allowable cost for CGT purposes.

- ✓ Describe the CGT treatment of enhancement expenditure and calculate CGT liabilities where enhancement expenditure has been incurred.

- ✓ Calculate gains after inflation relief on disposals and part-disposals of chargeable assets.

- ✓ Calculate losses arising on the disposal of chargeable assets and show how loss relief may be utilised.

- ✓ Describe the CGT treatment of married couples and the CGT implications of transfers between spouses.

- ✓ Calculate marginal relief from CGT on non-wasting chattels and calculate losses arising on the disposal of non-wasting chattels.

- ✓ Describe the implications of the €2,540 exemption limit for disposals of non-wasting chattels, which form part of a set.

- ✓ Complete Questions and the Assignments in Irish Taxation Law and Practice, Volume 2.

26

ADVANCED COMPUTATIONAL
ISSUES

In this chapter, you will deal with the following:

- Development land
- Share identification rules
- Bonus issues

- Rights issues
- Scrip dividends
- Bed-and-breakfast transactions

26.1　Introduction

The analysis so far has been concerned with the computational rules, which generally apply to disposals of chargeable assets. This chapter is concerned with certain refinements to these rules and certain additional considerations, which need to be taken into account in calculating gains and losses on the disposal of specific chargeable assets. The particular assets considered here are development land and shareholdings in companies.

Development land is defined as land, the consideration for the disposal of which exceeds the current use value (normally the agricultural value) of the land, i.e., land with development potential. Where land falls within this category, certain restrictions apply to the normal rules regarding the application of indexation relief and the use of losses. These restrictions and certain other issues relevant to transactions in development land are considered at 26.2.

With regard to disposals of shares, as with all assets, it is necessary to identify the date of acquisition and the cost of the shares for the purposes of preparing a capital gains tax computation. However, shares are unique in that each share of the same class in any company is identical despite the fact that the shares may have been acquired on different dates over a period of time. The most common method by which an individual acquires shares is through purchase. However, an individual can also increase a shareholding by means of a bonus issue or a rights issue. Special computational rules exist to enable us to identify which shares are the subject matter of the disposal, thereby facilitating the calculation of the base cost of the shares for CGT purposes. The remaining paragraphs in this chapter are concerned with those special rules and also with certain anti-avoidance legislation which applies in the case of disposals of shares.

26.2　Disposals of Development Land

26.2.1　Development land

In general, where there is a disposal of land and the consideration received for the disposal of the land exceeds the current-use value (CUV) of the land, it is development land.

The meaning of development land is not related in any way to the use to which the land is put. It is defined only in terms of its value on disposal.

s648
TCA 97

Section 648 TCA 97 defines development land as "land in the State, the consideration for the disposal of which, or the market value of which at the time at which the disposal is made, exceeds the current-use value of that land at the time at which the disposal is made, and includes shares deriving their value or the greater part of their value directly or indirectly from such land, other than shares quoted on a Stock Exchange."

The meaning given to current-use value differs in relation to land and shares deriving value from land.

Section 648 TCA 97 defines current-use value:

(a) Land:

"in relation to land at any particular time means the amount which would be the market value of the land at that time if the market value were calculated on the assumption that it was at that time and would remain unlawful to carry out any development (within the meaning of Section 3 of the Act of 1963 or, on or after 21 January 2002, within the meaning of Section 3 of the Act of 2000) in relation to the land other than development of a minor nature."

The Acts referred to are the Local Government (Planning and Development) Act 1963 and the Planning and Development Act 2000.

(b) Shares deriving their value from land:

"in relation to shares in a company (being shares deriving their value ... from land other than shares quoted on a Stock Exchange) at any particular time, means the amount which would be the market value of the shares at that time if the market value were calculated on the same assumption, in relation to the land from which the shares so derive value, as is mentioned in paragraph (a)."

Thus, the definition of development land requires the current-use value of the land to be compared with the consideration for the disposal or the market value of the land at the time of disposal. Where the market value of the land which is the subject matter of the disposal exceeds the current-use value of the land, the land constitutes development land and certain onerous restrictions apply.

26.2.2 Restriction on indexation

In computing a gain or loss on the disposal of development land, on or after 28 January 1982, the relief due in respect of indexation of expenditure incurred is restricted. The effect of the restriction is that indexation is only allowed in respect of the part of the cost (or market value at 6 April 1974) attributable to the current use value at the date of acquisition or 6 April 1974 (if later). In addition, no indexation is allowed on enhancement expenditure in the computation of a gain arising on the disposal of development land.

Example 26.1:

Land was acquired in 1972 at a cost of €25,395. Planning permission was obtained in 1973. Market value at 6 April 1974 was €253,947. Enhancement expenditure incurred in 1976 was €76,184. Current-use value at 6 April 1974 was €38,092. The land was sold in March 2009 for €900,000, when its current use value was €350,000.

The gain is calculated as follows:

	€	€	€
Sales proceeds (March 2009)			900,000
Market Value at 6 April 1974	253,947		
CUV at 6/4/1974	38,092		
Indexed @ 7.528		286,757	
Development Value	*€253,947 – €38,092*	215,855	
Enhancement Expenditure		76,184	
			(578,796)
Gain			321,204

26.2.3 Restriction on use of losses

s653 TCA 97   Section 653 TCA 97 provides for a restriction on the offset of losses against development land gains where the gain arises on or after 28 January 1982. The only losses which can be offset against gains arising on the disposal of development land are losses accruing on the disposal of development land. Other losses cannot be offset against such gains.

Losses arising on the disposal of development land are not required to be offset against development land gains in priority to other gains.

26.2.4 Scope of restrictions

Certain other restrictions in the context of "rollover relief" and "principal private residence relief" also apply to development land and these are considered in Chapter 27.

The restrictions relating to development land do not apply to an individual in a year of assessment if the total consideration from disposals of development land in that year do not exceed €19,050.

It should be noted that this exception to the normal rules is given by reference to the amount of the consideration for the disposal. The amount of the actual gain or loss is not relevant.

In applying this rule, husband and wife are treated separately.

26.3 Disposals of Shares

26.3.1 Share identification rules

Each shareholding acquired in a company on a separate date is treated as the acquisition of a separate asset for capital gains tax purposes.

s580 TCA 97   Section 580 TCA 97 provides that the principle of first in/first out (FIFO) applies to the disposal of shares of the same class, i.e., the shares acquired on the earliest date are deemed to be sold first.

Example 26.2:

Details of Ann's dealings in shares in XYZ Limited are as follows:

Date		Number	Cost
June 1984	Acquired	100	€200
August 1986	Acquired	200	€400
December 1989	Sold	(50)	–
May 1992	Acquired	150	€300
September 1995	Sold	(300)	–

The 50 shares disposed of in December of 1989 were sold for €600, i.e., €12 per share. The 300 shares disposed of in September 1995 were sold for €900, i.e., €3 per share.

Applying the FIFO rules, the disposals are dealt with as follows:

- *December 1989 disposal – The 50 shares disposed of are deemed to be out of the shares purchased in June 1984. This results in a remaining holding of June 1984 shares in the amount of 50 shares.*

- *September 1995 disposal – The 300 shares disposed of are deemed to be out of different blocks of shares and are deemed to be separate disposals as follows:*

  - *50 shares remaining out of the June 1984 purchase.*

  - *200 shares purchased in August 1986.*

  - *50 shares out of the purchase made in May 1992. This results in a remaining holding of May 1992 shares in the amount of 100 shares.*

For the purpose of tracking the share acquisitions and disposals, it may be easier to draw a table to follow the share transactions. Each shareholding acquired on a separate date is treated as a separate asset and is included in a separate row in the table.

Date	Original	Disposal 1989	Subtotal	Disposal 1995	Subtotal
June 1984	100	(50)	50	(50)	–
August 1986	200	–	200	(200)	–
May 1992	150	–	150	(50)	100
				(300)	

Using the table to track what happens to each of these shareholdings in chronological order enables us to clearly identify which asset is being disposed of at each particular point in time.

26.3.2 Part-disposals of shareholdings

The acquisition of each shareholding on a separate date constitutes a separate asset for capital gains tax purposes. Therefore, in Example 26.2, the disposal of 50 shares in 1989 is a part-disposal of the asset acquired in June 1984 and the disposal in 1995 of 300 shares out of three separate shareholdings is deemed to be three separate disposals as follows:

■ the disposal of the remainder of the asset acquired in 1984;

■ the disposal of all of the asset acquired in 1986;

■ the part-disposal of the asset acquired in May 1992, i.e., the disposal of 50 shares out of a total of 150 shares.

We have already considered the CGT treatment of part-disposals in Chapter 25. This commentary merits revisiting in the context of part-disposals of shares.

s557 TCA 97 Section 557 TCA 97 provides that the portion of the original expenditure which is allowed as a deduction against the sales proceeds received on the part-disposal is restricted to the proportion of the original cost of the asset, which the value of the part being disposed of bears, at the date of disposal, to the market value of the full asset. The formula to calculate the acquisition cost of an asset part-disposed of is as follows:

$$\textbf{Original Cost of Asset} \quad \times \quad \frac{\textbf{A}}{\textbf{A + B}}$$

Where:

A = the amount of sales proceeds received on the part-disposal of the asset (or market value, if appropriate), and

B = the market value of the remaining part of the asset retained after the disposal.

The base cost of the remainder of the asset for the purposes of subsequent disposals is the full original cost less the portion attributed to the previous part-disposal.

Where there is a disposal of shares, as each share is identical and of equal value, the fraction applied in the part-disposal formula may be modified to mean the following:

$$\frac{\textbf{Number of shares sold}}{\textbf{(Number of shares sold + number of shares retained)}}$$

On this basis, Ann's capital gains on each of the relevant disposals in Example 26.2 are as follows:

Capital Gains Computation 1989/1990
Disposal of 50 shares acquired in June 1984

	€
Sales proceeds	600
Less:	
*Allowable Cost: €200 * (50/100) = €100*	
Indexed @ 1.210	*(121)*
Chargeable gain	*479*

Capital Gains Computation 1995/1996
(1) *Disposal of remaining 50 shares acquired in June 1984*

	€
Sales proceeds (50 @ €3)	150
Less:	
Allowable Cost: €200 – €100 = €100	
Indexed @ 1.425	*(143)*
Chargeable gain	*7*

It is important to note that the 50 shares remaining out of the June 1984 acquisition are disposed of in September 1995. Therefore, the disposal of 50 shares involves the disposal of the remainder of an asset, which has been subjected to a previous part-disposal. Readers are referred to Chapter 25 for additional examples on this issue.

(2) *Disposal of 200 shares acquired in August 1986*

	€
Sales proceeds (200 @ €3)	600
Less:	
Allowable Cost: €400	
Indexed @ 1.283	(513)
Chargeable gain	87

(3) *Disposal of 50 shares acquired in May 1992*

	€
Sales proceeds (50 @ €3)	150
Less:	
Allowable Cost (Note 1): €100 indexed @ 1.063	(106)
Chargeable gain	44
Total Chargeable Gain	138

Note 1:

Cost of 50 shares disposed of is calculated as follows:

€300 × 50 / (50 + €100) = €100

26.3.3 Bonus issues

A bonus issue is also known as a scrip issue or a capitalisation. A bonus issue occurs when a company allocates shares to existing shareholders and no consideration is paid by the shareholders for the bonus shares. The issue of the shares is made in direct proportion to the existing shareholdings. For example, a bonus issue of one for two means that a shareholder will receive one new share for every two shares already held.

Shares acquired by means of a bonus issue are deemed to have been acquired on the same date as the original holding in respect of which they are issued. The bonus shares form part of this holding for subsequent disposal purposes and accordingly, the cost per share of the original holding is diluted as a result of the bonus issue. The reason for this is that the total number of shares has increased while the original cost of the shares remains the same.

Example 26.3:

Ann acquired 1,000 shares in ABC Ltd in July 1995 at a cost of €2 per share, i.e., €2,000 in total. In December 1998, ABC Ltd made a bonus issue of one for five (i.e., one new share for every five shares held at that date). As a result of the bonus issue, Ann now holds 1,200 shares at a cost of €2,000, i.e., €1.67 per share. In October 2003, Ann purchases 800 shares at a cost of €4,000. Ann subsequently disposes of 1,500 shares in May 2009 for €6 each.

Prior to Ann's disposal in May 2009, her shareholding was made up as follows:

Deemed Date of Acquisition	Number	Cost
July 1995	1,200*	€2,000
October 2003	800	€4,000

* Includes the bonus issue of 200 shares.

The disposal of the 1,500 shares is deemed to come out of the following holdings:

- *1,200 shares acquired in July 1995 for €2,000; and*

- *300 shares out of the holding of 800 shares acquired in October 2003 for €4,000.*

The disposal of 1,500 shares gives rise to two separate disposals of two separate assets, and therefore, two separate computations must be prepared, as each acquisition of shares in ABC Ltd is treated as the acquisition of a separate asset.

Date	Original	Bonus	Subtotal	Disposal	Subtotal
July 1995	1,000	200	1,200	(1,200)	–
October 2003	800	–	800	(300)	500
				(1,500)	

Capital Gains Computation 2009

	€
Sales proceeds (1,200 @ €6)	7,200
Less:	
Allowable cost: €2,000 indexed @ 1.277	(2,554)
Chargeable gain	4,646
Sales proceeds (300 @ €6)	1,800
Less:	
Allowable cost: €4,000 × 300/800 = €1,500*	(1,500)
Chargeable gain	300
Total Chargeable Gain	4,946

* No indexation is available, as indexation does not apply to expenditure incurred on or after 1 January 2003.

26.3.4 Rights issues

26.3.4.1 Disposals of shares acquired under a rights issue

s584 TCA 97 Section 584 TCA 97 deals with the capital gains tax treatment of reorganisations of share capital including rights issues. A rights issue occurs when a company offers its existing shareholders the opportunity to purchase additional shares at a discount on the market value of the shares. A rights issue is similar to a bonus issue in that it is offered in proportion to the shareholders' existing holdings. However, it differs in that the shareholders must subscribe some amount for the shares offered under the rights issue; in the case of a bonus issue, the bonus shares are granted without requiring any additional outlay from the shareholders. A rights issue generally takes place when a company is seeking to raise funds; it gives the company the necessary cash injection.

The treatment of shares acquired under a rights issue is the same as for a bonus issue, i.e., the shares are deemed to be part of the original holding in respect of which they are allocated. Therefore, for disposal purposes, the shares acquired under a rights issue merge with the shares of the original holding. The price paid by the shareholders for shares acquired under a rights issue is treated as enhancement expenditure incurred in respect of the original shareholding.

We have already observed, in Chapter 25 (25.8) that enhancement expenditure is indexed upwards from the date on which it is incurred. Thus, for the purposes of indexation, the cost of the original holding is indexed up from the date of acquisition of the original holding and the enhancement expenditure, i.e., the cost of the rights issue is indexed up from the date on which the enhancement expenditure is incurred, i.e., the date of the rights issue. Where such enhancement expenditure is incurred on or after 1 January 2003, no indexation will apply.

Example 26.4:

Mary acquired 2,000 shares in XYZ Ltd in July 1996 for €4,000, i.e., at a cost of €2 per share. In January 1998, Mary acquired a further 1,000 shares for €500, i.e., €0.50 per share. In February 1999, XYZ Ltd made a rights issue of one for two (i.e., one new share for every two shares held) at €1 per share. Mary takes up the rights issue, and she acquires 1,500 shares at a cost of €1,500. Mary disposes of 4,000 shares in June 2009 for €3 each.

Mary's shareholding is made up as follows (prior to the disposal):

Date	Original	Rights	Subtotal	Disposal	Subtotal
July 1996	2,000	1,000	3,000	(3,000)	–
January 1998	1,000	500	1,500	(1,000)	500
				(4,000)	

The shares acquired under the rights issue are split between the original shareholdings. The disposal of 4,000 shares is treated as two separate disposals. The disposal is deemed to come out of the following holdings:

- *3,000 shares acquired in July 1996; and*

- *1,000 shares out of the holding of 1,500 shares acquired in January 1998 (leaving 500 shares of this holding remaining).*

Capital Gains Computation 2009

Capital Gain on Disposal of 1996 Holding

Chapter 26 – Advanced Computational Issues

	€
Sales proceeds (3,000 × €3)	9,000
Less:	
Original cost: €4,000 indexed @ 1.251	(5,004)
Rights issue: €1,000 indexed @ 1.212	(1,212)
(enhancement expenditure)	
Chargeable gain	2,784

Capital Gain on Part-Disposal of 1998 Holding

		€
Sales proceeds (1,000 × €3)		3,000
Less:		
Original cost €500 × $\frac{1,000}{1,500}$ = 333		
Indexed @ 1.232		(410)
Rights issue €500 × $\frac{1,000}{1,500}$ = 333		
(enhancement expenditure)		
Indexed @ 1.212		(404)
Chargeable gain		2,186
Total Chargeable Gain		4,970

26.3.4.2 Scrip dividends

A company may offer its shareholders the option to take additional shares in the company in lieu of a cash dividend. Dividends taken in this way are known as scrip dividends. The capital gains tax treatment of disposals of shares acquired in lieu of dividends is the same as for disposals of shares acquired under a rights issue. Therefore, the shares acquired attach to the original holding of shares in respect of which they are issued for the purposes of determining the date of acquisition, and the cost of the shares, i.e., the dividend foregone, is treated as enhancement expenditure.

Example 26.5:

Bernadette acquired 1,000 shares in Setel Limited on 1 January 2000 for €2,000. On 30 June 2003, a dividend of €0.50 per share is proposed or alternatively, a scrip dividend of one share for every four shares held is offered. Bernadette opts for the scrip dividend and the shares are issued in July. On 30 May 2009, Bernadette sells 625 shares for €3,000.

Prior to the disposal, Bernadette's shareholding is comprised as follows:

Date	Original	Scrip	Subtotal	Disposal	Subtotal
January 2000	1,000	250	1,250	(625)	625

The scrip issue increases the size of the original holding to 1,250 and Bernadette sells half of this holding on 30 May 2009.

The cost of the scrip issue, i.e., the enhancement expenditure laid out at the date of issue, is the dividend foregone, i.e., €500 (1,000 × €0.50 per share).

Assuming no other disposals in 2009, Bernadette's chargeable gain for 2009 is as follows:

	€
Sales proceeds	*3,000*
Cost: €2,000 × (625/1,250) = €1,000	
Indexed @ 1.193	*(1,193)*
Scrip: €500 × (625/1,250) (Note)	*(250)*
Chargeable gain	*1,557*

Note: There is no indexation of the cost of the scrip issue (i.e., the enhancement expenditure), as indexation does not apply to expenditure incurred on or after 1 January 2003.

26.3.4.3 Disposal of rights

Shareholders entitled to subscribe for rights issues may elect to sell their rights. In such circumstances, the cash sum received in respect of the sale of the rights is a capital distribution and the original holding is deemed to have been disposed of in part. This will require the application of the formula A/(A + B) to the original cost of the Shareholding. In this case,

A = proceeds of the sale of rights, and

B = market value of the remainder of the holding, i.e., ex-rights price of the shares.

Example 26.6:

Tom acquired 5,000 shares in ABC Limited on 1 May 2000 for €10,000. In July 2009, the company makes a rights issue of two for five, which may be exercised at a cost of €3.00 per share. Tom sells all of his rights for €1 per share. The ex-rights price per share is €4.

Tom's capital gains computation for 2009 is as follows:

	€
July 2009 Consideration: 5,000 × 2/5 × €1	*2,000*
Cost 2000/01: €10,000 × 2,000 / (2,000 + (5,000 × 4)) = 909	
Indexed @ 1.144	*(1,040)*
Gain	*960*

26.3.5   Bed-and-Breakfast transactions

Loss relief is only available for realised capital losses, i.e., there is no relief available unless the asset which has fallen in value is actually sold. In the absence of anti-avoidance legislation, losses on shareholdings could be realised without, in substance, disposing of the shares, by simply putting in place a succession of paper transactions. Such transactions are known as "bed-and-breakfast" transactions and are very restricted by anti-avoidance legislation. The anti-avoidance legislation is two-fold it targets situations where shares are reacquired within four weeks of their disposal and also situations where shares are disposed of within four weeks of acquisition. The provisions also apply where shares disposed of by one spouse are reacquired by the other and vice versa.

26.3.5.1 Acquisition of shares within four weeks of disposal

s581 TCA 97 Section 581 TCA 97 was introduced to prevent individuals from using "bed-and-breakfast" transactions to create artificial losses for offset against chargeable gains. An example best illustrates the anti-avoidance provisions where there is an acquisition of shares within four weeks of disposal.

Example 26.7:

> Sharon acquired 10,000 shares in ABC plc on 1 December 2000 for €20,000, i.e., €2 per share. On 1 March 2009, the shares are quoted at €1 each. Sharon is confident that the share price will rise, and therefore, she does not wish to dispose of her shareholding in ABC plc. However, she would like to claim loss relief for the "paper loss" she has suffered as a result of the share price movement. The only way to realise a loss is for her to dispose of the shareholding. She makes an arrangement with her stockbroker whereby she disposes of the shares on 1 March 2009 for €1 per share and she repurchases 10,000 shares in ABC plc within the next few days.
>
> As a result of this, Sharon realises an "artificial loss" of €10,000 on the disposal of her shareholding in ABC plc which, in the absence of anti-avoidance legislation, would be available for offset against any chargeable gains she realises in the 2009 tax year. In addition, she will still own 10,000 shares in the company.

The legislation stipulates that where a disposal and reacquisition of the same class of shares takes place within four weeks, the loss arising on the disposal of the shares can only be set against a subsequent gain arising on the disposal of the shares that have been reacquired. Therefore, the loss cannot be offset against other chargeable gains realised in the tax year. Thus, in Example 26.7 above, Sharon may not claim relief for the artificial loss of €10,000 against gains on other assets disposed of in 2009.

26.3.5.2 Disposal of shares within four weeks of acquisition

Section 581 TCA 97 also provides that the FIFO rule does not apply where shares of the same class are bought and sold within a period of four weeks. Where shares are sold within four weeks of the date of acquisition, for capital gains tax purposes, the shares disposed of are identified with the shares of the same class acquired within the preceding four-week period. This is known as the last in/first out (LIFO) rule. This provision effectively covers situations where the "buy-back" for the purposes of "bed-and-breakfast" transactions precedes the disposal.

Example 26.8:

> Mary acquired 1,000 ordinary shares in DEF Limited in May of 1997 for €5,000. On 1 August 2000, she bought 500 shares for €1,250. On 15 July 2009, she bought 1,000 shares for €500. On 1 August 2009, she sold 1,000 shares for €495.
>
> If we apply the normal FIFO rules in this case, Mary will be deemed to be selling the 1,000 shares, which she acquired in May of 1997 and she will have a loss of €3,505 (i.e., €495 – €5,000).

However, because the shares are being sold within four weeks of their acquisition, the LIFO rules apply and Mary is deemed to be selling the shares acquired most recently. Accordingly, the loss is restricted to €5 (€495 – €500) and there is no benefit in engaging in such bed-and-breakfast transactions.

The usual FIFO rules will apply to disposals of the balance of the 1,500 shares.

There is no restriction on the losses arising in Example 26.8 above. The loss is limited by the LIFO rules to €5 and this may be used in the normal way. The provision which provides that the loss arising on the disposal of shares can only be set against subsequent gains arising on the disposal of the shares reacquired only applies where the sale precedes the repurchase.

WHAT YOU SHOULD NOW KNOW

On completion of this chapter, you should be able to:

- ✓ Explain what is meant by development land and describe the onerous CGT provisions that apply to disposals of development land.

- ✓ Calculate gains arising on the disposal of development land.

- ✓ Apply loss relief where there are disposals of development land.

- ✓ Calculate gains arising on the disposal of shares, whether acquired by direct purchase, under a rights issue, a bonus issue or a scrip issue.

- ✓ Calculate gains arising on the sale of rights under a rights issue.

- ✓ Describe what is meant by a "bed-and-breakfast" transaction and apply the relevant anti-avoidance rules.

- ✓ Complete Questions and the Assignments in Irish Taxation Law and Practice, Volume 2.

27

CGT RELIEFS

In this chapter, you will deal with the following:

- Principal private residence relief
- Transfer of a site to a child
- Rollover relief
- Retirement relief
- Relief from CGT on incorporation
- Relief on the disposal of shares by holding companies

27.1   Introduction

In Chapter 24, we observed that the gains on disposals of certain assets are exempt from CGT. The exemptions that we have already considered are very straightforward and in general, do not involve special computational rules. A number of additional reliefs are available in certain circumstances where detailed conditions are satisfied. These reliefs frequently involve exemption of only a portion of the gain from CGT and the calculation of the amount of relief available is generally quite complicated. The purpose of this chapter is to consider these more advanced reliefs in some detail as follows:

- paragraph 27.2 is concerned with principal private residence relief;

- paragraph 27.3 considers the relief available on the transfer of a site to a child of the owner;

- paragraph 27.4 deals with rollover relief,[1] i.e., relief from CGT on the disposal of certain assets where the proceeds are reinvested in replacement assets;

- paragraph 27.5 considers the relief available on conversion of a sole trade operation to a limited company;

- paragraph 27.6 deals with retirement relief; and

- paragraph 27.7 deals with relief on the disposal of shares in other companies by holding companies.

27.2   Principal Private Residence Relief

s604 TCA 97 Broadly speaking, the legislation provides for an exemption from CGT on the gain arising on the disposal by an individual of his or her principal private residence together with gardens or grounds of up to one acre. A person may not have more than one principal private residence at any one time. Furthermore, where a married couple are living together, they may only have one principal private residence for the purposes of the relief. Individuals and married couples who own two dwelling houses must therefore nominate which one should qualify for relief by giving notice to the Inspector of Taxes in writing within two years of acquiring the second property. Such an election is only valid with the agreement of the Inspector. The relief extends to properties owned by the taxpayer and occupied by a dependent relative of the taxpayer free of charge. The dependent relative must be the widowed parent of either the taxpayer or his or her spouse. Other dependent relatives may also qualify provided they are incapacitated by old age or infirmity.

The principal private residence exemption only applies where the property has been occupied by the individual as his or her main residence throughout the period of

---

1   Although rollover relief was effectively terminated by Finance Act 2003, it may continue to have implications for the calculation of CGT liabilities for a number of years.

ownership. There are some exceptions to this requirement and these are considered in greater detail in 27.2.1. In addition, the exemption may be lost in whole or in part where a building or a portion of it is used for trade or professional purposes. In these circumstances, it may be necessary to apportion the gain between the exempt and non-exempt elements. This issue is illustrated in Example 27.2. The relief is restricted if the house constitutes development land. The restriction is described in 27.2.2.

27.2.1 Period of ownership

Where an individual has not occupied the property as his principal private residence during his entire period of ownership, part of the gain may be chargeable. In such cases, the exempt part of the gain is the proportion, which the period of such occupation (during the period of ownership) bears to the total period of ownership. In making the calculations any period of occupation or ownership before 6 April 1974 is ignored.

In arriving at the period (post-5/4/1974) throughout which the property is occupied as a principal private residence, the legislation sets out certain circumstances in which the property is deemed to be so occupied. These are as follows:

- Foreign employment

s604(5)(b)(i)
TCA 97
"Any period of absence (after 5/4/1974) throughout which the individual worked in an employment or office all the duties of which were performed outside the State", may be deemed to be a period of occupation for principal private residence relief purposes.

- Condition of employment

s604(5)(b)(ii)
TCA 97
Any period (after 5/4/1974) of absence, not exceeding four years (or periods of absence which together do not exceed four years), throughout which the individual was prevented from residing in his/her house because of any condition imposed on him/her by his/her employer requiring him/her to reside elsewhere may be deemed to be a period of occupation of the property as a principal private residence provided the condition was reasonably imposed to secure the effective performance of his/her duties.

S604(5)
TCA 97
For both of the above periods of deemed occupation, the period of absence is treated as a period during which the house was occupied by the individual as a principal private residence "if both before and after the period, the dwelling house (or the part in question) was occupied by the individual as his or her only or main residence".

In addition, for both of the above periods to qualify as periods of deemed occupation, it is a requirement that the taxpayer should have no other residence eligible for the relief at the time.

- Last 12 Months

The last 12 months of ownership is deemed to be a period of residential occupation for the purpose of calculating the relief, provided the house was (at some time) his/her principal residence.

The "last 12 months" deemed residence applies without any other conditions provided the property is, or was, the taxpayer's main residence. However, as already observed, to avail of the deemed period of residence during an absence caused by employment, it is necessary for the taxpayer to actually reside in the premises after the absence. The "deemed" period of residence in the last twelve months of ownership is not sufficient in itself to satisfy this condition.

In summary, "period of ownership" and consequently "period of occupation" cannot include any period prior to 6 April 1974 and certain periods are deemed periods of occupation albeit that the individual does not actually reside in the house during those periods. Consequently, the following formula can be used to calculate the exempt portion of the gain:

$$\frac{\text{Periods of actual and "deemed" occupation post-6 April 1974}}{\text{Total period of ownership post-6 April 1974}} \times \text{chargeable gain}$$

Example 27.1

John is unmarried. He bought a house in Dublin for IR£10,000 on 1 January 1970. It was his home until 30 September 1981 when he was required to move to Cork to set up a new branch of his employer's business. He stayed in a rented house in Cork until 31 December 1983 and during that period let his Dublin home. On his return, he reoccupied his Dublin home. On 31 March 1994, he moved to Limerick permanently and let the house in Dublin. On 31 March 2009, he sold the house for €360,000. He has no other chargeable gains for 2009.

The market value of the property at 6 April 1974 was IR£25,000 (€31,743).

The chargeable gain is calculated as follows:

Period of Ownership	Years
6/4/1974 to 31/3/2009	35
Period of Occupation as residence	**Years**
Actual – 6/4/1974 to 30/9/1981	7.5
Deemed – 30/9/1981 to 31/12/1983	2.25
Actual – 1/1/1984 to 31/3/1994	10.25
Deemed – 1/4/2008 to 31/3/2009 (last year)	1
Total	21

Chargeable Gain – 2009	€
Sale price	360,000
Market value 6 April 1974 (as indexed)	
€31,743 indexed @ 7.528	(238,961)
Total gain	121,039
Chargeable gain €121,039 14/35	46,280

The chargeable gain is reduced by the annual exemption, and CGT is chargeable on the balance at 22% (March 2009).

Note: In calculating the fraction to be applied to the total gain, all periods of both occupation and ownership prior to 6 April 1974 are ignored. Twenty-one years out of the 35 years of ownership are exempt – 14/35 of the gain only is chargeable.

Example 27.2

On 1 July 2009, Grace sold a house in Dublin for €500,000. The house, which is on a 0.5-acre site, was purchased on 1 October 1988 for €60,000. Throughout Grace's period of actual occupation, she used a portion of the house (25% of the total area) exclusively for the purposes of a trade.

Details of the use of the house during the period of ownership are as follows:

1/10/1988 – 30/6/1995	*It was Grace's only private residence, with 25% used for the purposes of her trade.*
1/7/1995 – 31/12/1998	*It was let to a third party. During this period, Grace was employed by a company in France and lived in rental accommodation.*
1/1/1999 – 31/12/2001	*It was Grace's only private residence and 25% of the house was again used for the purposes of her trade.*
1/1/2002 onwards	*The house was again let to a third party and Grace purchased another property which became her principal private residence.*

The chargeable gain is calculated as follows:

Period of ownership	*Years*
1/10/1988 to 30/6/2009	*20.75*
Period of occupation as principal private residence	***Years***
Actual – 1/10/1988 to 30/6/1995	*6.75*
Deemed – 1/7/1995 to 31/12/1998	*3.5*
Actual – 1/1/1999 to 31/12/2001	*3*
Deemed – 1/7/2008 to 30/6/2009 (last year)	*1*
Total	*14.25*

Chargeable Gain – July 2009	*€*	*€*
Sale price		*500,000*
Cost	*60,000*	
Indexed @ 1.553		*(93,180)*
		406,820
Deduct principal private residence relief		*(209,537)*
(Note 1)		
		197,283
Less annual exemption		*(1,270)*
		196,013
CGT at 25%		*49,003*

(Note 1)	
Total gain	*406,820*
Less attributable to office	*(101,705)*
Attributable to residence	*305,115*
Attributable to period of occupation (14.25/20.75)	*209,537*

27.2.2 Restriction in the case of development land

S604(12)
TCA 97

The relief given to an individual on the sale of his/her residence does not apply to the part of the gain reflecting "development value". The relief is calculated only by reference to the gain, which would have arisen if the property was both bought and sold for its value solely as a residence. This restriction on the relief is contained in s604(12) TCA 97.

The gain on the disposal of the property is calculated in the normal way (as development land), and the resulting gain is reduced by the restricted residence relief. The balance of the gain is chargeable in full as a development land gain.

Example 27.3

Claire bought a property on 31 January 1987 for its residence value of €88,882. Incidental costs of acquisition amounted to €10,745. The asset was sold to a developer on 28 February 2009 for €900,000. Its value as a residence at that time was €300,000. The incidental costs of disposal were €15,000. Throughout her period of ownership of the property, it was her principal private residence.

The gain chargeable for February 2009 is calculated as follows:

		€	€
Sale proceeds (development land)			900,000
Cost (current-use value)		88,882	
Indexed @ 1.637		145,500	
Incidental costs	– acquisition €10,745		
	indexed @ 1.637	17,590	
	– disposal	15,000	(178,090)
GAIN			721,910
Less residence relief	(See below)		(131,910)
Gain taxable at 22%			590,000

Residence Relief:	€	€
Sale price as residence		300,000
"Residence" cost (as indexed above)	145,500	
Incidental cost of acquisition (as indexed above)	17,590	
Incidental cost of disposal (apportioned – see Note)		
€15,000 × €300,000 / €900,000	5,000	(168,090)
"Residence" gain (qualifying for full relief)		131,910

Note: In calculating the gain that would arise on the sale solely as a residence, the incidental costs of a disposal are apportioned proportionately.

Example 27.4

If, in Example 27.3, the facts were as stated save that the cost price of the residence in January 1987 was €177,764, of which the residential current-use value was €88,882, the computation would be as follows:

Development land computation:	€	€
Sales proceeds (development land)		*900,000*
Indexed current-use value €88,882 × 1.637	*145,500*	
Indexed incidental acquisition costs – €10,745 × €88,882/€177,764 × 1.637	*8,795*	
Development potential (no indexation relief) (177,764 – 88,882)	*88,882*	
Acquisition costs referable to development potential (no indexation) – €10,745 × (€88,882/€177,764)	*5,372*	
Incidental costs of disposal	*15,000*	*(263,549)*
Gain		*636,451*
Less residence relief (see below)		*(140,705)*
Gain taxable		*495,746*
Residence relief:		
Sale price as residence		*300,000*
"Residence" cost (indexed) €88,882 × 1.637	*145,500*	
Incidental cost of acquisition proportionate to residence cost – €10,745 × (€88,882/€177,764) × 1.637	*8,795*	
Incidental cost of disposal €15,000 × (€300,000/€900,000)	*5,000*	
Total		*(159,295)*
(Residence) gain (qualifying for full relief)		*140,705*

27.3 Transfer of a Site to a Child

s603A TCA 97
s93 FA 01
s53 FA 07

A CGT exemption applies on the transfer by a parent to a child (or certain foster children) of land, provided certain conditions are met. The exemption applies in respect of disposals on or after 6 December 2000.

The conditions that must be met are:

■ the open market value of the land being transferred must not exceed €500,000 (€254,000 for disposals prior to 5 December 2007) at the date of transfer;

■ the area of the site must not exceed 1 acre;

■ the transfer must be for the purpose of enabling the child to construct on the land a dwelling house to be occupied by the child as his/her only or main residence.

■ the €500,000 limit applies where both parents make a simultaneous disposal of a site to their child.

There is a claw-back of the relief if the child disposes of the land at a time when a dwelling house has not been built on it. The claw-back also applies where the dwelling house has been built but has not been occupied by the child as his or her only or main residence for a period of three years. In these circumstances, the gain, which would have arisen to the parent on the transfer, accrues instead to the child and is levied on the child at the time of his or her disposal of the property.

Example 27.5

Joe Smith owns a farm of land in Galway. On 1 January 2004, he transferred a one-acre site to his son to enable the son to build a house on the site for use as a principal private residence. At the date of transfer, the site was worth €70,000. Joe's CGT allowable cost of the site was €8,000.

The child, Peter, built a house upon the site and lived in it as his principal private residence for four years from 2005. As his family was growing, he felt he needed a larger house and wished to build a new house rather than extending the existing house. Accordingly, he sold the site and purchased from his father a further site in 2009. The market value of the second site at the date of its purchase by Peter from Joe in 2009 was €160,000. Peter built a new house on it and resided in it as his principal private residence.

Notwithstanding that the total value of land disposed of by the father to the son has not exceeded €500,000, the relief applies only to the first disposal. It does not apply to the second disposal in 2009 because the relief has already applied to a previous disposal from a parent to the child.

If, instead, Peter had disposed of the property in 2007, before it had been occupied by him for a three-year period as his principal private residence, the gain on which his father received relief in 2004 (a chargeable gain of €62,000) would have been treated as accruing to Peter at the time of its disposal. However, relief under the section would have been available to the father in relation to the second transfer in 2009. Depending on values, it might be a better result all around to have crystallised the first gain, and make the relief available in respect of the second gain.

27.4   Rollover Relief

In certain circumstances the legislation gave relief from an immediate charge to tax which would otherwise occur on the disposal of an asset where the consideration for the disposal of the asset was reinvested. Broadly speaking, the relief was available in respect of trading assets, certain shares, certain rental properties and compulsory purchase orders. The relief generally applied to sole traders and companies, but public authorities, bodies promoting games or sports (e.g., the GAA), farmers, persons occupying woodlands on a commercial basis with a view to profits, trade associations, non-profit-making bodies, employees and persons carrying on a profession were also eligible. In general, no relief was available in respect of gains on the disposal of "development land". However, there was an exception in the case of disposals of such land by bodies promoting amateur games or sports (e.g., the GAA) and also in the case of certain compulsory purchase orders.

Finance Act 2003 restricted the relief to disposals before 4 December 2002 (with limited transitional provisions). However, as the relief simply involved a deferral of the payment of the CGT liability, CGT liabilities relieved under the rollover relief provisions will continue to arise for some time into the future and accordingly, an understanding of the provisions that applied prior to 4 December 2002 is very important. The analysis here is concerned only with the rollover relief which applied to business assets.

27.4.1   Conditions

In order for the relief to apply, certain conditions had to be met. These were as follows:

- The old and the new asset, i.e., the asset sold and the replacement had to belong to one of the following classes:

    (i)   land and buildings occupied as well as used only for the purpose of the trade, generally excluding development land;

    (ii)   plant and machinery;

    (iii)   goodwill.

Financial assets also qualified for the relief where the assets were disposed of by a body established for the purposes of promoting amateur sports.

It was not necessary for the old and the new asset to belong to the same class of asset, e.g., a reinvestment in plant and machinery could qualify the owner for rollover relief on a disposal of land.

- The new assets had to be used in the same or in a similar trade carried on concurrently in a different locality. An exception existed where a person had been trading for 10 years or longer and ceased to trade but recommenced a different trade within two years. In these circumstances, both trades were regarded as the same for the purposes of rollover relief. Thus, gains arising on the disposal of the old trade could be deferred by investing in qualifying assets in the successor trade.

- In general, the reinvestment of the proceeds had to take effect within the period beginning 12 months before and ending three years after the date of the disposal or within such longer time as otherwise allowed at the discretion of the Revenue Commissioners.

27.4.2   Form of relief

Unlike some other reliefs that give relief by deeming "no disposal" of the asset with a corresponding adjustment to the qualifying cost of the replacement asset, with rollover relief, the gain was calculated in the normal way and simply held in abeyance until the happening of a specified future event. The gain on the "old" assets is deferred until the "new" replacement assets cease to be used for the trade. The relief only applies where the old assets are disposed of before 4 December 2002 (with, depending on the facts, an extension of the period up to 31 December 2003).

Where only a portion of the disposal proceeds was reinvested, deferral of any gain arising was restricted to the amount by which the gain exceeded the proceeds held back. Where the sales proceeds held back was equal to, or exceeded the gain, no relief could be claimed. In effect, each euro of proceeds not reinvested triggered €1 of chargeable gains, up to the amount of the gain.

Example 27.6

John sold his factory in June 2002 and the details are as follows:

	€
Sale proceeds	200,000
Cost (indexed)	(160,000)
Gain	40,000

In 2003 he bought a new factory for €190,000.

As only part of the sales proceeds was reinvested, the gain on the 2002 disposal was taxed up to the amount not reinvested, i.e., €10,000.

The balance of the gain is treated as not arising until the replacement asset ceases to be used by John for the purpose of the trade.

	€	
Gain	40,000	
Rollover relief	(30,000)	
Taxable (amount not reinvested)	10,000	
CGT at 20%	2,000	*(payable in respect of 2002)*

Example 27.7

Alan disposed of his factory premises for €470,000 on 1 December 2002 giving rise to a chargeable gain of €60,000. He spent €450,000 on a new premises.

Alan's CGT payable was calculated as follows:

	€
Chargeable gain arising	60,000
Proceeds not reinvested	(20,000)
Deferred gain	40,000
Taxable gain 2002 (€20,000 – annual allowance €1,270)	18,370
Taxed at 20%	3,674

The deferred gain of €40,000 will be chargeable when the new premises ceases to be used by Alan for the purposes of the trade.

Section 597(4)(b) extends the deferral further where the "new" replacement assets were themselves sold and the sale proceeds were used to acquire "further new" replacement assets. Thus, if the sales proceeds of the new premises were invested in further new qualifying assets, the gain of €40,000 might be further deferred, and so on.

Section 597(4)(b) effectively allowed the gain on the "old" assets to be deferred until the "further new" replacement assets ceased to be used for the trade. Finance Act 2003 did not change this part of the relief, allowing the continued deferral where the original gain arose on a qualifying asset disposal before 4 December 2002.

Example 27.8

Peter carries on a manufacturing trade. In March 1972, he acquired his factory premises for IR£60,000 (market value on 6/4/1974 was IR£80,000). In June 1999, he sold the premises for

IR£680,000 and purchased another for IR£750,000. In March 2000, he decided to change the location of his operation. He sold the 1999 premises for IR£800,000 and used the proceeds towards the cost of new plant costing IR£150,000 (€190,461) and a unit in a new industrial estate costing IR£650,000 (€825,330). The old plant was scrapped and a balancing allowance obtained for the loss.

In 2008, his health deteriorated and in September of that year he retired, selling the plant for €240,000 and the building for €990,000.

Peter's liability to tax on these transactions is calculated as follows:

Disposal June 1999

	IR£
Sale proceeds (March 1972 factory)	680,000
MV 6/4/1974 (indexed) IR£80,000 6.313	(505,040)
Gain IR£	174,960
Gain (€ equivalent)	222,153

The full proceeds of IR£680,000 were invested in 1999 in a new factory so that the gain is deemed not to arise until the 1999 factory ceases to be used for the purposes of the trade.

Disposal March 2000

	IR£
Sale proceeds (March 1999 factory)	800,000
Cost (no indexation – 12-month rule)	(750,000)
Gain IR£	50,000
Gain (€ equivalent)	63,487

Again, however, the full proceeds were invested in 2000 in new plant and factory buildings so that the gain arising in 2000, and that arising in 1999 are deferred.

Disposals September 2008

Sales proceeds			€	€
	Plant (2000)		240,000	
	Buildings (2000)			990,000
Cost:	Plant	IR£150,000		
		€190,461 @ 1.193	(227,220)	
	Buildings	IR£650,000		
		€825,330 @ 1.193		(984,619)
			12,780	5,381

Total gain on both assets	18,161

As the sale proceeds are not reinvested, all deferred gains (i.e., €222,153 from 1999 and €63,487 from March 2000) are now deemed to arise in addition to the €18,161 gain in September 2009.

Although the "plant" is a wasting chattel, and would normally have a life not exceeding 50 years, it is not treated as an exempt wasting chattel because it qualifies for capital allowances – see Chapter 24 (24.4.2.1).

It is important to note that if Peter had not retired in 2009 and if he had invested the full proceeds of the 2009 disposals in other qualifying assets, he would not have been able to claim rollover in respect of the 2009 gains of €18,161. However, the gains of €222,153 from 1999 and €63,487 from 2000 would continue to be deferred until such time as the new replacement assets ceased to be used for the trade. This is the case because unlike s597(4)(a) TCA 97, the continuing deferral under s597(4)(b) TCA 97 is unchanged by Finance Act 2003. The effect is to allow a continuing deferral of the gain on "old" assets already deferred under s597(4)(a) TCA 97 by reason of a disposal pre-4 December 2002.

Example 27.9

John carries on a manufacturing trade. He sold his factory premises in 2001 for €4m, realising a gain of €1m. On 31 January 2002, he reinvested the entire proceeds in a new factory premises costing €5m, deferring the full gain on disposal of the "old" asset. He found the new factory premises unsatisfactory, and on 18 January 2009 he sold it for €6m, and bought a further new premises for €6.5m in December 2009.

The gain on disposal of the "old" factory of €1m is deferred under s597(4)(a) TCA 97 as it was sold before 4 December 2002 and the full consideration for the sale was reinvested. On disposal of the "new" 2002 premises in January 2009 two gains arose – the deferred gain on the "old" property of €1m and the gain on the "new" 2002 premises of €500,000. As the sale proceeds of the "new" property have been reinvested (in full) in "further new assets" the gain of €1m is further deferred until the "further new assets" cease to be used for the trade. The gain of €500,000 on the 2009 disposal cannot be deferred as the property was disposed of after 4 December 2002.

27.4.3   Significance in future years

The rollover relief provisions will be relevant for some years yet, as the time allowed for reinvestment extends to three years after the qualifying disposal and the continuing rollover for existing deferrals could continue indefinitely. In addition, understanding the rollover relief provisions is key to identifying the crystallisation of any deferred gain and the amount of any such gains in future years.

27.5   Relief from CGT on Incorporation

s600
TCA 97

Where a non-corporate person (i.e., an individual, trust, or partnership) transfers a business (as a going concern) to a company, a measure of relief is given to the extent that the sale proceeds are taken by way of shares in the company. In the absence of this relief, capital gains tax would be payable in full on the gains arising on the disposal of the assets of the business to the company. The relief, in effect, consists of a deferral of the tax payable on the amount of the consideration taken in the form of shares in the company.

27.5.1   Conditions for relief

All of the following conditions must be complied with before the relief applies:

(a)   there must be a transfer of a business to a company from a person who is not a company;

(b)   the business must be transferred as a going concern;

(c)   the whole of the assets of the business or all of those assets other than cash must be transferred;

(d)   the transfer must be wholly or partly for shares in the company;

(e)   the transfer must be for *bona fide* commercial reasons and must not form part of any arrangement or scheme of which the main purpose or one of the main purposes is avoidance of tax.

There is no requirement that the person making the transfer should have worked in the business. A sleeping partner is as entitled to this relief on the incorporation of a business as is a full-time worker in the business.

27.5.2 Calculation of relief

Calculation of the relief involves the following process:

- The gain is calculated on the normal basis, ignoring any relief, which may be available under this provision.

- The gain is then apportioned (on the basis of market value) between:

  - the value of shares taken in consideration of the transfer, and

  - the value of other consideration (i.e., cash, assets, loan account, etc.).

- The relief is the amount of the gain apportioned to the value of the shares taken in the company and this amount is not assessed. The part of the gain apportioned to the other consideration is assessed, and the tax is collected in the normal manner.

- The relief claimed, i.e., the element of the gain not assessed, is deducted from the base cost of the shares taken in the company, thereby reducing the allowable cost of the shares for the purposes of calculating a gain or loss on their ultimate disposal. Unlike rollover relief, the gain is not merely held in abeyance; the cost of the shares is reduced. On a subsequent sale of the shares, with a reduced cost, the gain (if any) on the disposal of those shares will be increased, and the tax may, in effect, be payable at that stage. If, however, the value of the shares fell substantially before the disposal, the tax on the gain deferred on the transfer of the business may never be collected.

Example 27.10

Michael, who started in business on 30 June 1965, transferred his business (all of its assets) to "Aztec Limited" in exchange for 10,000 ordinary shares of €1 each in Aztec Limited and €30,000 cash on 31 March 1995. The value of the shares at 31 March 1995 is agreed at €95,000.

Michael's assets as shown by his balance at 31 March 1995 were:

			MV 6/4/1974
		€	€
Premises (at cost 30/6/1965)		7,000	15,000
Goodwill (*Michael's estimate at 1995)		12,000*	3,000
Debtors		4,000	N/A
Stock in trade		10,000	N/A
Cash		3,000	N/A
		36,000	
Less creditors	€6,000		N/A
Taxation due	€2,000	(8,000)	N/A
		28,000	

During the negotiations with Aztec Limited, the following market values (at 31 March 1995) were agreed:

	€
Premises	100,000
Goodwill	20,000
Debtors	3,000
Stock in trade	10,000
Agreed value of business and assets at 31/3/1995	133,000

The following were to be paid by Aztec Limited, on behalf of Michael:

	€	€
Creditors	6,000	
Taxation	2,000	8,000
Net consideration due to Michael		125,000

On 30 November 2009, Michael sold his €10,000 ordinary shares in Aztec Limited to Takeover Limited for €200,000.

The first matter to be looked at is the 1995 transfer of the business to the company:

	€	€
The value of the assets is		133,000
Taken in cash	30,000	
Debts paid on behalf of William	8,000	(38,000)
Value of shares (balance)		95,000

Gain on incorporation

Premises:
Sales proceeds		100,000	

		€	€
6/4/1974 value indexed	€15,000 5.754	(86,310)	13,690

Goodwill:
Sales proceeds		20,000	

6/4/1974 value indexed	€3,000 5.754	(17,262)	2,738
Debtors	– no chargeable gain		
Stock	– no chargeable gain		
Cash	– no chargeable gain		

TOTAL GAIN			16,428

DEFERRED GAIN	95/133 €16,428		11,734

This part of the gain is not taxed; instead, the cost of the shares is reduced by the deferred gain.

	€
i.e.,	95,000
Less: deferred gain	(11,734)
"Cost"	83,266

CGT Computation for 1994/1995:

Total gain	16,428
Relief from CGT on incorporation	(11,734)
CHARGEABLE GAIN: 38/133 €16,428	4,694

This part of the gain was taxed in the normal manner, at the appropriate rate.

The next step to complete the picture is the calculation of the gain on the subsequent sale of those shares in November 2009:

	€
Sale proceeds (November 2009)	200,000
March 1995 – cost €83,266	
Indexed @ 1.309	(108,995)
GAIN	91,005

Tax is calculated in the normal way on this gain.

Where the acquiring company takes over the liabilities of the business (on the transfer of the business to the company) the value of the liabilities taken over represents consideration other than shares, for the transfer. This is on the basis that the discharge of liabilities of the transferor by the transferee is equivalent to the payment of cash by the transferee to the transferor. Concessionally, the Revenue Commissioners may treat the transfer of *bona fide* trade liabilities as not being consideration in the form of cash equivalents for the purpose of calculating the relief, provided that the individual transfers the business in exchange for shares only and assets exceed liabilities.

27.6   Retirement Relief

s598 TCA 97 Retirement relief is something of a misnomer in that there is no actual requirement that the taxpayer retire. Broadly speaking, the relief provides for an absolute exemption from CGT on the disposal of certain qualifying assets (in general, business assets) by individuals who are aged 55 years or more on the date of disposal. The relief is available even though the owner, who disposes of all or part of his/her business assets, remains actively engaged in the business after the disposal. Where all conditions are met, the relief takes the form of a reduction in the tax (CGT) payable on gains accruing on the disposal of the qualifying assets. In most circumstances, the relief reduces the tax payable to nil. The relief is absolute in the sense that the gain relieved is not held in abeyance as in the case of rollover relief. However, it is important to note that the relief may only be temporary, and could, in effect, be withdrawn by reference to certain events happening subsequent to the relieved disposal.

Retirement relief only applies to individuals. A company, or person holding the business in a fiduciary or representative capacity (who would be deemed not to be an individual in that capacity) does not qualify for this relief. The relief extends to an individual sole trader, a farmer, an individual partner in a partnership, or an individual who holds his/ her business interests through a company (on the disposal of all or part of the shares in his/her family company). Where the relief is being claimed in respect of a disposal of shares held in the claimant's family company, additional conditions apply and the computation can be more complicated. For this reason, disposals of assets held in an unincorporated entity and disposals of shares in an incorporated entity are considered separately below in 27.6.1 and 27.6.2 respectively.

Note: Where an individual disposes of qualifying assets before his/her 55th birthday, the Revenue will consider a claim for relief where the individual is within 12 months of his/her 55th birthday and is disposing of qualifying assets due to chronic ill health.

27.6.1 Unincorporated business

The relief is available for disposals by qualifying individuals of "qualifying assets", i.e., "chargeable business assets" of an unincorporated business. A number of detailed conditions must be met. (Note: the relief also applies to certain farm related assets of farmers that do not satisfy the normal conditions.)

27.6.1.1 Conditions

- The claimant must be an individual and must be at least 55 years of age. The claimant need not actually retire.

- The relief is available in respect of disposals of "chargeable business assets". Chargeable business assets are assets (including goodwill but not including shares or securities or other assets held as investments), which are used by sole traders or partners in a partnership for the purposes of a trade, profession or farming. The relief also extends to assets used for the purpose of an employment.

- The claimant must have owned the chargeable business assets for at least 10 years prior to the date of disposal. This condition does not extend to movable chattels, (e.g., plant and machinery), which qualify for relief irrespective of the period of ownership. In determining the period of ownership for the purposes of this condition, the following rules apply:

  1. Where the claimant acquired the qualifying assets from his or her spouse, the latter's period of ownership is aggregated with his or her own period of ownership.

  2. Where assets (which qualified for rollover relief) were sold, and the proceeds were reinvested in further qualifying assets, the period of ownership of the assets that were sold is taken into account as if it were a period of ownership of the new assets.

27.6.1.2 Computation of relief

Before calculating the relief, any losses arising on chargeable business assets should be netted off against gains on chargeable business assets.

The annual allowance of €1,270 cannot be claimed by an individual in the same year of assessment in which he/she benefits from retirement relief.

s598(2)(b)
TCA 97

s52 FA 07

Full relief from CGT payable on the disposal of qualifying assets to parties other than a child of the claimant is available provided the aggregate sale proceeds of such assets does not exceed a current threshold of €750,000. For the position with regard to disposals of assets to a child of the claimant, readers are referred to 27.6.3.

Example 27.11

John sold a building used by him for the purpose of his business at arm's length to a total stranger. He had owned the building and used it for business purposes for the past seventeen years. He also sold a painting, which was not a business asset. The relevant details are as follows:

	Sale Price	*Gain*
	€	*€*
Building	*260,000*	*20,000*
Painting	*10,000*	*2,000*

John is unmarried, and has no other gains or losses to be taken into account in calculating the tax payable for that year. He is fifty-six years of age, and has never sold any other qualifying assets. Both sales took place during 2009.

The gain on the disposal of the building is exempt since the sales proceeds do not exceed €750,000 and the building is a chargeable business asset.

The gain of €2,000 on the disposal of the painting is taxable in full and since John is claiming retirement relief in 2009, he is not entitled to the annual exemption. Accordingly the CGT payable is €2,000 @ 22%, i.e., €440.

s598(2)
TCA 97

Marginal relief may be available where the aggregate sales proceeds exceeds the current limit. The effect of this marginal relief is to restrict the maximum CGT payable to a sum equal to half the difference between the limit of €750,000 and the consideration.

Example 27.12

If in example 27.11 above, the sales proceeds of the business premises were €751,000, and the gain remained the same at €20,000, the tax payable on the disposal of the premises would be reduced from €4,400 to a maximum of one-half of (€751,000 – €750,000), i.e., €500.

To this would be added the tax payable on the disposal of the painting of €440, making a total CGT payable by John for 2009 of €940.

Where an individual makes two or more disposals of qualifying assets, the consideration for all the disposals is aggregated for the purposes of considering whether they fall within the €750,000 limit and whether they qualify for marginal relief. Thus, the €750,000 limit is a lifetime limit. Both the full, and marginal reliefs are potentially subject to recomputation in the future if the taxpayer makes further disposals of qualifying assets, and increases the aggregate of such disposal proceeds. The revised sale proceeds aggregate applies to current and also to past years. Applying this revised aggregate to earlier years may result in a full or partial claw-back of relief already granted in those earlier years.

The €750,000 threshold is available to each spouse. It is important to note that disposals of qualifying assets to a spouse, although exempt in themselves, erode the €750,000 threshold.

27.6.2 Incorporated business

Where the subject matter of the disposal is shares in a "family company", retirement relief can also apply. Again, it is necessary for the claimant to be an individual aged 55 years or over. A number of additional conditions are relevant with regard to the shares in the "family company".

27.6.2.1 Conditions

Additional conditions where the subject matter of the disposal is shares in a "family company" are as follows:

- At least 25% of the voting rights in the company must be controlled by the claimant or alternatively at least 10% of the voting rights must be controlled by the claimant and not less than 75%, including his/her 10%, must be controlled by his/her family. "Family" in this context includes spouses, direct relatives (brothers, sisters, ancestors or lineal descendants) and direct relatives of spouses (brothers-in-law, etc.).

- The family company must have been engaged in either trading or farming for at least ten years ending with the date of disposal. Relief is also extended to holding companies of trading or farming companies.

- The claimant must have owned the shares in the family company for a period of at least 10 years ending with the date of disposal. Where the claimant had previously transferred his trade to the company and obtained incorporation relief, the shares will be treated as having been acquired on the same date as the original trade.

- The claimant must have been a working director for a period of at least 10 years and a full-time working director for at least five of those years. A "full-time working director" is one who is "required to devote substantially the whole of his time to the service of the company in a managerial or technical capacity" (s598(1) TCA 97). Where the claimant's spouse has previously died, the deceased's period of ownership and period of service as a full-time working director is attributed to the claimant. Where shares are disposed of to a spouse, while the transferor is alive, the period of ownership of the transferor is attributed to the spouse receiving the shares. However, this period of service as a working director is NOT attributed to the spouse receiving the shares.

27.6.2.2 Computation of relief

Where the disposal is of shares in a family company, then relief is only available for the portion of the gain on the shares that is equivalent to the proportion of "chargeable business assets" to total chargeable assets (taken at current market values).

Similarly, the consideration taken into account for the purposes of the determining whether or not the disposal is within the €750,000 threshold is restricted by reference to the ratio of chargeable business assets to total chargeable assets owned by the company (taken again at current market values).

Example 27.13

Joe is aged 60 years, and has decided to sell the shares in his family trading company. He has owned the shares in the company for the past 20 years and worked as a full-time working director of the company for the first 15 years of that period. He has been a part-time director for the last five years. Joe has had no previous disposals of qualifying business assets since his fifty-fifth birthday. Immediately prior to the disposal of the shares, the assets of the company were as follows:

	€
Land and buildings	*250,000*
Plant and machinery	*20,000*
Goodwill	*150,000*
Government stocks (investments)	*50,000*
Quoted shares (investments)	*5,000*
Trade stocks	*30,000*
Trade debtors	*40,000*
Cash at bank	*60,000*
TOTAL ASSETS	*605,000*

The total liabilities of the company amount to €155,000.

The agreed sale price of the shares in the company is €450,000. Joe paid the IR£ equivalent of €10,000 for the shares in May 1983.

The trade debtors, trade stocks and cash at bank are neither chargeable business assets nor chargeable assets.

The government stocks are not chargeable business assets and neither are they chargeable assets because they are exempt from CGT.

The quoted shares are chargeable assets since they are assets upon whose disposal a chargeable gain can arise, but they are not chargeable business assets since they have not been used for the purpose of a trade but rather were held for investment purposes.

The land and buildings, plant and machinery, and goodwill are all chargeable assets and also chargeable business assets being both chargeable to CGT and used in the trade.

The value of the chargeable business assets therefore in total amounts to €420,000 (€250,000 + €20,000 + €150,000).

The value of the chargeable assets amounts to €425,000 (the same as above, with the addition of the quoted shares of €5,000).

The gain on the disposal of these shares is calculated as follows:

CGT Computation for September 2009:

	€
Sales proceeds	*450,000*
Cost €10,000	
Indexed @ 2.003	*(20,030)*
	429,970
Retirement relief (Note 2)	*(424,912)*
Taxable gain	*5,058*
CGT @ 25% (Note 1)	*1,265*

Note 1:

The annual exemption is not available, as retirement relief is claimed.

Note 2:

The element of the gain eligible for retirement relief is calculated as:

$$€429,970 \; \frac{€420,000}{€425,000} \; = €424,912$$

27.6.3 Disposals to a child of the claimant

s599 TCA 97
S52 FA 07 Where the disposal is to a child of the claimant, there is no limit on the proceeds of disposal, or gain, which may qualify for relief. Furthermore, such disposals do not erode the €750,000 threshold for the purposes of disposals to third parties. A child for the purposes of this section includes the child of a deceased child, certain foster children and a nephew or niece who has worked substantially on a full-time basis for at least five years prior to the disposal in carrying on or assisting in carrying on the trade.

However, there is, in effect, a claw-back of the relief granted to the parent if the child does not retain the assets for a period of six years. This claw-back involves the tax, which would have arisen if the original relief under s599 TCA 97 had not applied, being levied on the child. Thus, the child will be liable to account for CGT on his or her own actual disposal and also for the CGT that would otherwise have been payable on the original transfer.

Example 27.14

William, who is entitled to retirement relief, transferred all his qualifying assets by way of gift to his son George in June 2004. The assets were valued at that time at €5,300,000. William's base cost of those assets to be deducted in computing the gain on the disposal was €100,000 (including indexation). In July 2009, George sold the assets (which were transferred to him by his father) for a total consideration of €6,000,000.

Because George disposed of the qualifying assets within six years of the transfer from his father, he is now liable to:

- *any CGT arising on his own disposal of those assets; and*

- *pay the CGT his father would have paid on the 2004 disposal if relief under s599 TCA 97 did not apply to the transfer.*

It is therefore necessary to calculate what amount of tax his father would have paid if no relief was available under s599 TCA 97 at the time of the transfer.

If retirement relief had not been available to William at the date of transfer to his son George, CGT of €1,039,746 (20% (€5,300,000 – €100,000 – €1,270)) would have been payable. This amount now becomes payable and is levied on George.

Additionally, George has of course to compute his own CGT liability by reference to the base cost of €5,300,000 and any enhancement expenditure, which may have arisen in the five-year period, and the consideration of €6,000,000 on the disposal.

It should be noted that there is no relief from this claw-back on a subsequent transfer by the child of his business to a company within the six-year period. The relief for such transfers applies only to the child's own gain on the transfer of assets. It does not prevent the claw-back of the parent's gain, which is chargeable on him by virtue of the disposal of the assets to a company.

27.6.4 Relief on Disposal of Asset Used by Company

A taxpayer claiming retirement relief in respect of the disposal of shares in a family company, may also claim retirement relief in respect of land and buildings and machinery and plant which the individual has owned for a period of at least 10 years ending on the date of the disposal provided that:

(i) the asset(s) was used by the company throughout the taxpayer's period of ownership, and

(ii) the asset(s) is disposed of at the same time and to the same person as the shares in the family company.

27.6.5 Retirement Relief and Decommissioning of Fishing Vessels

The Finance Act 2008 introduced retirement relief under s598 in respect of compensation payments made under the scheme for decommissioning fishing vessels. For retirement relief to apply, the person who received the compensation payment must have owned and used the fishing vessel for a period of six years prior to receipt of that payment and must have been at least 45 years of age at the time.

27.7 Relief on the Disposal of Shares in Other Companies

s626B
TCA97

Finance Act 2004 introduced a number of new exemptions/reliefs in order to make Ireland an attractive location for headquarter operations and holding companies. One of these exemptions is an exemption from corporation tax on gains on certain disposals of shares and assets related to shares.

In order for this exemption to apply, the following conditions must be satisfied:

■ First, the investor company must have a minimum shareholding of 5% in the investee company. The investor is required to have the minimum 5% holding in the investee company for a continuous period of at least 12 months in the three years prior to the disposal.

■ Second, the investee company must carry on a trade, or else the business of the investor company, its investee company and their "10 per cent" investee companies, taken as a whole, must consist wholly or mainly of the carrying on of a trade or trades.

■ Finally, at the time of the disposal, the investee company must be resident in an EU Member State or a country with which Ireland has a tax treaty. (This includes the Irish State, i.e., disposals of shares in Irish companies where the Irish company owns at least 5% of the other Irish company, and the trading test is satisfied, are exempt from Irish corporation tax.)

The exemption does not apply where the shares are part of a life assurance company's life business fund. Nor does it apply to shares which derive the greater part of their value from land in the State or from minerals, or rights or interests in relation to mining or minerals or the searching for minerals or deemed gains on change of residence.

The exemption also applies to gains on disposal of assets related to shares, e.g., an option to acquire or dispose of shares.

This exemption applies from 2 February 2004.

Example 27.15

Irish Limited sells its shares in Maith Limited, an Irish trading company, in which it has owned 10% of the shares for the last five years. Irish Limited also sells its shares in Paris Limited, a French trading company in which it owns 8% of the shares for the last four years.

The gains on disposal of shares in both of these companies are exempt from corporation tax.

WHAT YOU SHOULD NOW KNOW

On completion of this chapter, you should be able to:

- ✓ Identify the circumstances in which principal private residence relief applies.

- ✓ Calculate the partial principal private residence relief which applies when a residence has not been occupied by the claimant for all of the period of ownership.

- ✓ Understand the restrictions which apply when a principal private residence has development potential.

- ✓ Describe the relief available on the transfer of a site by a parent to a child.

- ✓ Explain how the relief on the transfer of a site to a child may be clawed back in certain circumstances.

- ✓ Describe the conditions that need to be satisfied to qualify for rollover relief and explain the form that this relief takes.

- ✓ Explain why the rollover relief provisions will continue to have implications for a number of years and identify any deferred gains as they become payable in future years.

- ✓ Describe the conditions that need to be satisfied to qualify for relief from CGT on incorporation.

- ✓ Calculate the amount of any gain deferred as relief from CGT on incorporation.

- ✓ Calculate the gain arising on a subsequent disposal of shares where relief from CGT on incorporation had previously been claimed.

- ✓ Describe the conditions that need to be satisfied to avail of retirement relief in respect of disposals of both business assets of an unincorporated entity and shares in an incorporated entity.

- ✓ Explain the form that retirement relief takes and calculate the amount of any marginal relief in the case of disposals of both business assets of an unincorporated entity and shares in an incorporated entity.

- ✓ Explain the retirement relief measures that apply on disposals to a child of the claimant and describe how this relief may be clawed back in certain circumstances.

- ✓ Describe the circumstances in a disposal of a 5% or greater shareholding can be exempt from Corporation Tax.

- ✓ Complete Questions and the Assignments in Irish Taxation Law and Practice, Volume 2.

References and Recommended Further Reading

APPLEBY, T. and F. O'HANLON (2009), *The Taxation of Capital Gains*, Irish Taxation Institute.

MAGUIRE, T. (2009), *Direct Tax Acts,* Irish Taxation Institute.

MARTYN, J. and P. RECK (2009), *Taxation Summary,* Irish Taxation Institute.

Section V

Corporation Tax

FONS AEQUI INTELLECTUS

The Institute would like to acknowledge the kind permission given by Frank Brennan, Paul Moore, Helen O'Sullivan and Michael Ryan for the use of some material from *Corporation Tax** for this section; such material has been adapted specifically for students, with the addition of focused commentary and examples.

* Published by the Irish Taxation Institute (2008)

28

GENERAL PRINCIPLES OF IRISH CORPORATION TAX

In this chapter, you will deal with the following:

- The system of corporation tax in Ireland

- The scope of corporation tax and territoriality

- The factors which determine company residence

- Administration of corporation tax and the self-assessment system

- Rates of corporation tax and the impact of the European Union on the Irish corporation tax regime

28.1   Introduction

Companies in Ireland pay corporation tax on their "profits" and have done so since 1976. It was in that year that the Corporation Tax Act 1976 was passed and "corporation tax" introduced.

The legislation behind our corporation tax regime is contained in the Taxes Consolidated Act 1997 (TCA 97). This legislation is based on the original Corporation Tax Act 1976. Prior to the introduction of corporation tax, companies were liable to income tax, corporation profits tax and capital gains tax. Much of the corporation tax legislation is based on the original Income Tax Act and Capital Gains Tax Act, the rules of which are still used primarily to compute taxable income and gains for corporation tax purposes.

Corporation tax is not the only tax which a company may be liable to pay – the following taxes may also apply depending on the company's circumstances and the transactions it carries out:

- Income tax;

- Capital gains tax;

- Dividend withholding tax;

- Value-added tax;

- Stamp duty;

- Capital duty;

- Capital acquisitions tax;

- Deposit interest retention tax;

- Encashment tax;

- Professional services withholding tax (F45);

- Relevant contracts tax (C45).

However, the focus of this part of the book is to examine the extent of a company's corporation tax liability and, to a very limited extent, any possible income tax and capital gains tax liabilities that may arise.

28.2   The System of Corporation Tax in Ireland

Corporation tax systems in general are built around one of two models, namely the classical system or the imputation system. Some countries may operate systems which have features of both, applying an imputation system which is not a "full" imputation system, i.e., a partial imputation system. The difference between the two systems is basically that the classical system does not give credit to shareholders for the underlying corporation tax paid by the company, whereas the imputation system does.

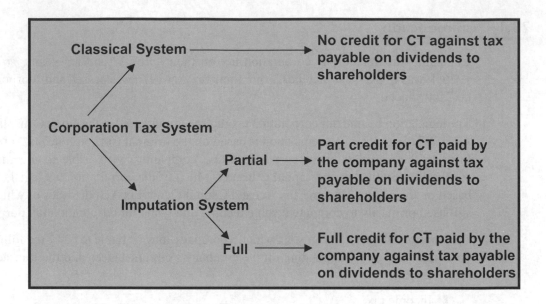

28.2.1 Classical system of corporation tax

Tax is assessed on an Irish resident company under a regime having the full characteristics of a classical corporation tax system. Corporation tax is levied at the company level on profits, i.e., income plus chargeable gains. When those profits are withdrawn by way of a distribution, a further tax levy will generally arise on the shareholders. No credit is given for any element of the underlying tax paid by the company.

The payment of such a distribution is subject to withholding tax at the standard income tax rate, currently 20%. Where the recipient is another Irish resident company or a company or individual resident in another EU country or a Tax Treaty country (or a company under the control of such persons), then withholding tax does not arise. Where the recipient is an Irish resident individual, he/she will be subject to income tax on the net dividend amount plus the withholding tax, i.e., the gross dividend and credit will be given for the tax withheld. In essence, the position for the individual, under the withholding tax system, is similar to that which applies for a credit system.

28.2.2 The imputation system

The classical system of corporation tax is a system where no credit is given to shareholders for underlying tax paid at the company level. This differs from an imputation system which gives credit for the underlying corporation tax paid against any further income tax liability of the shareholder arising on the dividend. A system of full imputation or partial imputation may operate to give shareholders either some credit or full credit for underlying tax paid by the company on the profits out of which the dividend is paid.

A full imputation system makes no distinction between distributed and undistributed profits and charges all company profits at the same rate of corporation tax. Part of the company tax is "imputed" to the shareholder by granting credit for tax paid by the company to the shareholder. This credit attaches to the dividend paid. The shareholders receive a net dividend from the company plus a tax credit. They are then subject to income tax on the gross amount received (the net dividend plus the tax credit amount), with credit granted for the tax already paid by the company.

The tax is imputed in terms of the rate applicable to corporate profits. If a company distributes all of its profits, with a tax rate of 12.5% and a personal tax rate of 41%, the effective rate of tax is 48.38% (12.5% + [41% of 87.5%]), whereas under a full imputation system the effective rate of tax is 41% regardless of the company rate.

28.2.3   History of the Irish tax system

Prior to 6 April 1999, Ireland operated an imputation system of corporation tax. The payment of tax on dividends was by way of a payment of "advance corporation tax" (ACT). This system was abolished in April 1999, effectively bringing the Irish system of imputation to an end, replacing it with a classical system and introducing dividend withholding tax (DWT). Withholding tax does not operate to impute any tax payment to the shareholder. It applies to dividends only after the profit out of which the dividend is paid has been subject to full corporation tax and is analogous to an advance payment of income tax as opposed to an advance payment of corporation tax.

The Irish corporation tax system effectively doubly taxes dividends which are distributed, while at the same time providing for a surcharge on the undistributed income of close companies. Most Irish companies are close companies (see Chapter 32 for a detailed discussion on close companies). The total effective rate of tax for such companies on distributed income is 48.38%, i.e., 12.5% + [41% of 87.5%], while the total effective rate of tax on undistributed income is 30%, i.e., 12.5% + [20% of 87.5%].

28.3   Scope of Corporation Tax

A company which is resident in Ireland is subject to corporation tax in respect of its worldwide profits. A company's profits are defined as its income plus its chargeable gains.

s25(1)
TCA 97

A non-resident company which carries on a trade in Ireland through a branch or an agency is liable to corporation tax on the income and any gains of the branch or agency (see paragraph 28.5 below for a more detailed discussion on territoriality and the definition of residence for corporation tax purposes).

The basic principle in calculating income and chargeable gains for corporation tax purposes is that, apart from certain specific provisions of the Corporation Tax Act 1976, the principles of income tax and capital gains tax law and practice apply. The calculation of such income and chargeable gains is discussed in detail in Chapter 29.

There are certain circumstances when a company's gains will be subject to capital gains tax instead of corporation tax. These are as follows:

1. Gains on development land are separately assessed to capital gains tax.

2. Gains from unquoted shares deriving the greater part of their value from development land are separately assessed to capital gains tax.

   Such gains do not form part of a company's profits and are assessed separately to capital gains tax, rather than to corporation tax on chargeable gains. There are restrictions on the reliefs that can be claimed against development land gains. The rate of capital gains tax on all development land gains is 20%.

3. Non-resident companies are liable to capital gains tax on disposals of certain specified assets including land in the State, minerals in the State or any rights, interest or other assets in relation to mining or minerals or the searching for minerals in the State.

s29(3)(a)(b) TCA 97 In addition to the tax on a company's profits, dividend withholding tax is also *prima facie* payable by a company on distributions or dividends paid from its "after tax profits". Dividend withholding tax applies at the standard rate of income tax, which is currently 20%.

While members of groups of companies, consortia and associated companies are each dealt with separately as stand-alone entities for the purposes of calculating corporation tax, special rules governing their association or relationship exist and certain reliefs may apply depending on the nature of the relationship (see Chapter 32 for a discussion on groups).

There are also special rules governing the taxation of close companies (see Chapter 33).

28.4   Who can expect to pay Corporation Tax?

All companies resident in Ireland are liable to corporation tax with some exceptions and exclusions from the charge.

s4(1) TCA 97 For corporation tax purposes, a company means any body corporate, including a Trustee Savings Bank within the meaning of the Trustee Savings Bank Act 1989. The term therefore includes companies formed under the Companies Acts 1963–2006, whether those companies are limited by shares, limited by guarantee or unlimited.

The term also includes societies registered under the Industrial and Provident Societies Act, friendly societies and companies established by statute or incorporated by charter, e.g., ESB, RTÉ, etc.

The most important concept to appreciate when dealing with companies is that their identity is separate from the identity of the owners of the company, i.e., the shareholders. The term "company" does not include partnerships even in circumstances where the partnership is limited. Each partner is assessed personally on his/her share of profits.

However, a company may form a partnership with a number of individuals, or with another company. Where a share of partnership profits is earned by a company, then that share of profits is liable to corporation tax.

As a company is a separate legal entity from its shareholders, the responsibility for the activities and actions of a company normally rests with the directors of a company and the company secretary. This is the case unless a liquidator has been appointed to the company.

Certain bodies (e.g., health boards, Vocational Educational Committees, and local authorities) are specifically excluded from the meaning of a company and accordingly will not pay corporation tax. In addition, certain companies (e.g., The Custom House Docks Development Authority, The Pensions Board, and The Irish Horse Racing Authority) have been granted exemption from corporation tax on certain or all sources of income.

All companies will be exempt from corporation tax on specific sources of income (e.g., certain grants, certain patent income, profits from commercially managed woodlands), which are excluded by reason of a statutory income tax exemption, which extends to corporation tax.

28.5   Territoriality

The scope of corporation tax will depend largely on whether a company is tax resident or not in Ireland. The charge to corporation tax by reference to a company's residence is fundamental.

The residence of a company, for taxation purposes was, prior to 11 February 1999, determined broadly by where central management and control were exercised. This has now been extended so that all companies incorporated in Ireland are also automatically considered resident here, with certain exceptions. This "incorporation test" as it is known, has been used in a number of other tax jurisdictions for many years. For a fuller discussion of these changes, see 28.5.5 below.

28.5.1   Irish resident company

s26 TCA 97   A company resident in the State is chargeable to corporation tax in respect of its total "profits", i.e., income and chargeable gains. This covers worldwide profits irrespective of where they arise and whether or not they are remitted to the State.

s129 TCA 97   The term "profits" includes income and chargeable gains, as noted above. Specifically excluded are distributions received from Irish resident companies, which are termed Franked Investment Income. This Franked Investment Income is exempt in the hands of the Irish recipient company because it has already been subject to Irish corporation tax. It should be noted, however, that distributions received by a close company (as defined) may in certain circumstances attract a surcharge or additional levy of corporation tax of 20% (see Chapter 32).

Example 28.1

Celtic Tiger Limited is an Irish resident company and has the following income and gains in 2009:

		Jurisdiction	€	Extent of Corporation Tax Charge
Trading Income				
a)	Profits from trading	(Ireland)	440,000	Liable on total profits
b)	Profits from trading	(Rest of Europe)	210,000	Liable, with credit for foreign tax paid on the branch/agency profits (may be subject to limitations).*
Capital Profits				
c)	Sale of premises	(Ireland)	48,000	Liable to corporation tax on chargeable gains
d)	Sale of investments	(Ireland)	75,000	Liable to corporation tax on chargeable gains
e)	Sale of development land	(Ireland)	120,000	Liable to capital gains tax
f)	Sale of premises	(Hungary)	92,000	Liable to corporation tax on chargeable gains with relief under the treaty for Hungarian tax paid (may be subject to limitations)*
Investment Income				
g)	Deposit accounts	(Ireland)	10,000	Liable on total income
h)	Deposit accounts	(Rest of Europe)	15,000	Liable with offset for local tax paid (may be subject to limitations)*
i)	Dividends	(Irish subsidiaries)	148,000	Not liable to corporation tax
j)	Dividends	(Hungary)	134,000	Liable with offset for tax credit or underlying tax depending on terms of the treaty or by reference to unilateral relief (may be subject to limitations)*

* Limitations can arise where the Irish tax liability on the income is lower than the overseas tax suffered, subject to pooling with tax paid in other foreign branches with tax lower than the Irish effective rate, A detailed discussion of this is beyond the scope of this publication. See also 29.5.1 regarding the taxation of certain foreign dividends.

28.5.2   Non-resident company

Where a company is not resident in Ireland, the extent of its Irish corporation tax liability is limited to:

s25(2) TCA 97
- Trading income arising directly or indirectly through a branch or agency, in the State; and

- Any income from property owned or used by, or held by or for, a branch or agency in the State, e.g., deposit interest.

It should be noted that:

- The exclusion from tax for distributions received from companies resident in the State also applies to non-resident recipient companies; and

- Income received by a non-resident company which is not attributable to a branch or agency (such as rental income or deposit interest) is liable to Irish income tax. The specific provisions of any appropriate double taxation treaty should be considered.

s29(3)(c) TCA 97
Non-resident companies are liable to corporation tax on chargeable gains arising from disposals of assets used by the branch or agency and to capital gains tax on disposals of non-branch assets or any disposal of specified assets.

s29(3)(a)(b) TCA 97
Thus, non-resident companies are liable to capital gains tax on disposals of certain specified assets, including land in the State, minerals in the State or any rights, interest or other assets in relation to mining or minerals or the searching for minerals in the State.

Example 28.2

Rostock Ltd, a German resident company, has the following income and gains:

	Trading Income	*Jurisdiction*	*€*	*Extent of Corporation Tax Charge*
(a)	*Profits from trading*	*(Germany)*	*580,000*	*Not liable as trade not carried on in the State*
(b)	*Profits from trading*	*(Ireland)*	*180,000*	*Liable to Irish corporation tax, with credit or other relief for Irish tax paid under the terms of the appropriate treaty against its German tax liability*
	Capital Profits			
(c)	*Sale of trade premises*	*(Ireland)*	*48,000*	*Liable to corporation tax on chargeable gains*
(d)	*Sale of investments*	*(Ireland)*	*75,000*	*Liable to capital gains tax*
(e)	*Sale of development land*	*(Ireland)*	*120,000*	*Liable to capital gains tax*
(f)	*Sale of premises*	*(Germany)*	*92,000*	*Not liable – company not resident in the State, nor is the asset situated in the State*

Trading Income	Jurisdiction	€	Extent of Corporation Tax Charge
Investment Income			
(g) Deposit accounts	(Ireland)	10,000	Liable to corporation tax. Note: if the company had no trade in the State, it would be liable to income tax on its deposit income
(h) Deposit accounts	(Germany)	15,000	No liability – not an Irish source of income
(i) Dividends	(German subsidiaries)	148,000	Not liable to Irish tax
(j) Dividends	(Ireland)	134,000	Once the company has filed the necessary documentation with the Irish company, it will receive the dividends gross

28.5.3 Summary

The territorial scope of Irish corporation tax can be summarised diagrammatically as follows:

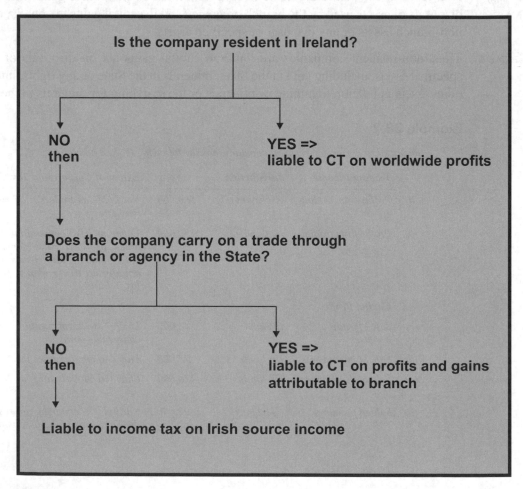

Is the company resident in Ireland?

NO then

YES => liable to CT on worldwide profits

Does the company carry on a trade through a branch or agency in the State?

NO then

YES => liable to CT on profits and gains attributable to branch

Liable to income tax on Irish source income

28.5.4   Company residence

Until 11 February 1999, the question of where a company resides was one of fact. The Courts by examining all of the evidence attempted to ascertain "where the central management and control actually abides". This dictum, taken from Lord Loreburns judgement in *De Beers Consolidated Mines v Howe* [1906] STC 198 was the guiding principle in deciding such cases. The place of incorporation, while a factor, was very much subsidiary to other considerations.

The site of management and control is still the most important factor in determining residence status in many instances. Accordingly, the meaning of the term merits further commentary. Control is concerned with where the directors hold their meetings and whether real decisions affecting the company are taken at those meetings.

This latter point is of importance where a foreign subsidiary is concerned. If the real control of the company and the guiding decisions are taken by the parent company, then the subsidiary may be resident where the parent company resides.

Factors which Determine Central Management and Control

In deciding where central management and control resides the following points should be considered:

List of factors

- Where are the directors' meetings held?

- Where do the majority of directors reside?

- Where are the shareholders' meetings, both general and extraordinary, held?

- Where is the negotiation of major contracts undertaken?

- Where are the questions of important policy determined?

- Where is the head office of the company?

- Where are:

    – the books of account kept?

    – the accounts prepared and examined?

    – the accounts audited?

    – minute book kept?

    – company seal kept?

    – share register kept?

■ From where are dividends, if any, declared?

■ Where are the profits realised?

■ Where are the company's bank accounts on which the secretary, etc., draws?

A combination of these factors will normally indicate the place of central management and control.

28.5.5 Irish registered non-resident companies

Under the system of case law precedent, if the central management and control of a company is located in Ireland, the company is treated as Irish tax resident and until 1999, no other criterion was relevant.

Many offshore activities were structured by companies or individuals who acquired an Irish registered company as the trading entity. Since these companies typically were not, until the publication of the Finance Bill 1999, resident in the State or carrying on a trade in Ireland, they were not liable to tax within the State.

Then a major legislative change was introduced which now treats an Irish incorporated company as resident for tax purposes.

s23A
TCA 97

As a result of this legislation, all companies incorporated after 11 February 1999 (date of publication of the Finance Bill 1999) will be regarded as Irish resident irrespective of the location of their central management and control. Companies incorporated prior to that date came within the provisions as and from 1 October 1999.

To ensure that these provisions do not clash with any treaty obligations and also to avoid creating difficulties for genuine trading companies, there are two areas of exemption.

The assumption of residence by reference to incorporation will **not** apply where:

The "trading exemption" applies

■ The company, or a related company, carries on a trade in the State and either the company is ultimately controlled by persons resident in an EU Member State or in a Treaty country;

or

■ The company or a related company is a quoted company; or

The "Treaty exemption" applies

■ The company is not regarded as resident in the State under the provision of a double taxation treaty between Ireland and another country.

Where either of these exemptions apply, the site of management and control remains the fundamental principle in determining residence status.

28.5.6 Summary

The various tax residence tests can be summarised as follows:

Overview of the tax residence tests

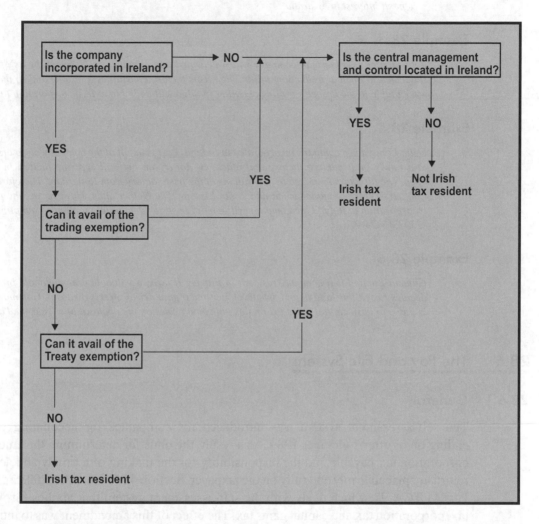

The following additional examples illustrate the residence rules and the territorial scope of Irish corporation tax.

Example 28.3

Alpha Limited is a UK incorporated company that manufactures clothes. It has several factories in England, France and Germany and a warehouse and offices in Ireland. All of the directors of Alpha Limited live in Ireland. Both directors' and shareholders' meetings take place in Ireland.

Therefore, as the controlling body of the company and its management are situated in Ireland, the place of residence is Ireland.

Alpha Limited has the following sources of profits, ALL of which will be liable to Irish corporation tax:

- *trading profits in Ireland;*
- *trading profits in France;*
- *rental income in USA;*
- *deposit interest in Australia.*

Example 28.4

Beta Limited is a German company which is owned and managed in Germany by its directors. It decided to open a production unit in Sligo. This factory constitutes a branch and so the profits attributable to the branch's trading activities in Sligo will be liable to Irish corporation tax.

Example 28.5

Delta Limited is a company incorporated in Ireland. Last year, all of the company directors moved to a newly built modern factory and offices in Rotterdam but still kept the factory in Ireland open. The directors managed the operations of the Irish factory from Rotterdam. Therefore, Delta Limited's centre of management and control is now The Netherlands. However, as the place of incorporation is Ireland the company will remain Irish resident unless it claims exemption under s23A(3) TCA 97.

Example 28.6

Gamma Limited is a company resident in France. It owns a valuable greenfield site in Naas. It decides to sell this land to an Irish developer and a gain arises on this disposal. Gamma Limited is liable to Irish capital gains tax on this gain as it arises on the disposal of a "specified asset".

28.6   The Pay and File System

28.6.1   General

The self-assessment system was introduced for companies for accounting periods ending on or after 1 October 1989. As a result, the onus for determining the amount of corporation tax payable and the responsibility for the making of a timely and accurate return are placed firmly and fully on the taxpayer. Section 42 Finance Act 2003 amended Part 41 TCA 97, which deals with the self-assessment system that applies for income tax, corporation tax and capital gains tax. The effect of this amendment was to introduce a pay and file system for corporation tax.

The obligations of a company with regard to paying corporation tax and filing its return are as follows. A company must:

- Compute and pay its preliminary tax liability;

- Lodge its return of income (including accounts and computations) with the Inspector within eight months and twenty-one days (twenty three days if filing and paying the return on ROS after 1 January 2009) days of the end of the accounting period; and

- Pay any balance of tax due by the return filing date.

A percentage of the returns made will be selected by the Revenue Commissioners for audit. The same Revenue audit procedures apply to both companies and individuals and students are referred to Chapter 10 for commentary on these procedures.

28.6.2   Payment of corporation tax

s958
TCA 97

For 2006 and subsequent years, all companies are required to pay their preliminary tax, i.e., 90% of their final tax liability, on the twenty-first day of the month before their accounting year-end.

Finance (No. 2) Act 2008 further amended the preliminary corporation tax filing dates and amounts.

The new rules apply for accounting periods commencing on or after 14th October 2008 and affect companies which are not deemed to be "small companies" (see 28.6.3) and the accounting period is longer than seven months.

The new rules introduce an extra preliminary date and amend the percentage paid on the existing preliminary date. The timetable and percentage payments are as follows:

Initial installment – this payment is due on the 21st day (23rd if paying via ROS) of the sixth month of the accounting period. The payment due is the lower of 50% of the previous periods corporation tax liability or 45% of the current years liability.

Final installment – this payment is due on the 21st day (23rd if paying via ROS) of the eleventh month of the accounting period. It must be equal to 90% of the current periods corporation tax liability including the tax due on any chargeable gains made between the initial installment date and the final installment due date less the initial installment paid.

Chargeable gains top-up – if the company makes a chargeable gain between the final installment date and the period end, it must pay 90% of the tax due on the chargeable gain within 31 days of the accounting period end.

The company must file its corporation tax return and pay the remaining 10% of the tax due by the 21st day (23rd if paying and filing on ROS) of the ninth month after the period end.

If the company underpays any of its preliminary tax installments it may be subjected to an interest charge, see section 28.6.5.

It is expected that these new requirements will give rise to considerable difficulties for tax practioners as they will be required to either base the initial installment on an accounting period that has over six months left to run or on the prior years tax which may not yet be fully calculated, as the return would not be due for a further three months.

Example 28.7

A Limited's accounting year end is 31 December. Its corporation tax liability for the year ended 31 December 2008 was €500,000. In June 2009 it is estimated that its corporation tax for the year ended 31 December 2009 will be €750,000. It makes two chargeable gains in the subsequent months giving rise to tax liabilities of €50,000 on a July 2009 gain and €80,000 on a December 2009 gain.

Therefore its total tax liability for the year ended 31 December 2009 is €880,000.

A Limited's pay and file requirements are as follows (assuming it does not use ROS)

21.06.09 Lower of €750,000 × 45% or 500,000 × 50%	*€250,000*
21.11.09 (€750,000 + €50,000) × 90% – €250,000	*€470,000*
31.01.10 (€750,000 + €50,000 + €80,000) × 90% – €250,000 – €470,000	*€72,000*

At this stage A Limited has now paid 90% (€792,000) of its overall liability

21.09.10 Lodge CT1 corporation tax return and pay €880,000 × 10%	*€88,000*

At this stage A Limited has now paid its total corporation tax liability of €880,000 in four installments.

28.6.3   Small companies

To ease the difficulties that "small companies" (i.e., companies where the tax liability for the preceding chargeable period does not exceed €200,000 since Finance Act 2008, previously €150,000) may have in assessing their preliminary tax obligations, special rules apply. From 2006 onwards, a small company can opt to base its preliminary tax payment on 100% of the prior year's corresponding corporation tax liability.

It should be noted that the status of a "small" company may change from time to time. A company that is regarded as a "small" company in one period may be treated as a "large" company for the next period and indeed revert to a "small" company again at a later point in the transitional period.

s958 TCA 97 In determining whether a company can base the first instalment of its preliminary corporation tax liability on its previous year's corresponding corporation tax liability the rules will be applied on the basis of a number of corresponding days in a company's accounting period. Readers are referred to Appendix I for further commentary on this matter.

A new company is entitled to make a nil preliminary payment if its final liability is not expected to exceed €200,000, provided its first payment is due after 5 December 2007, €150,000 if before this date.

28.6.4   Group preliminary tax

Prior to Finance Act 2007 each company's preliminary tax obligations were treated separately. If one company in a group underpaid its preliminary tax it would be liable to an interest charge on the underpayment at the rates noted in 28.6.5, notwithstanding that another group company may have overpaid its preliminary tax.

Finance Act 2007 amended s958 TCA 97 by introducing the concept of group preliminary corporation tax. If a group company (see 32.2.1) overpays its preliminary corporation tax it can elect to have the overpayment, known as the "relevant balance", treated as being part of a preliminary payment of a group company which has underpaid its preliminary tax.

To qualify for this relief the following conditions must be complied with:

(a) Both companies must be members of the same corporate group.

(b) Both companies must inform the Collector-General of the transfer.

(c) Both companies must not qualify for treatment as small companies.

(d) The company receiving the transfer must pay the balance of any tax owing on or before the due date.

(e) The surrendering company cannot claim the "relevant balance" as a deduction against its tax liability.

28.6.5   Failure to pay preliminary tax

s958(4B)
TCA 97

There are interest penalties for a corporate body which has failed to meet its preliminary tax obligations due to non-payment, insufficient payment or late payment of preliminary tax.

Interest charges will apply at the rate of 0.0219% (0.02731% to 30 June 2009) per day (8% p.a.) on late and insufficient payment of preliminary tax.

28.6.6   Filing of corporation tax return

s1084
TCA 97

A company must file a return of its income, i.e., a Corporation Tax Return Form (CT1) within eight months and twenty-one days (twenty-three days if paying and filing on ROS on or after 1 January 2009) of the accounting period end, see paragraph 28.6.3 above. Failure to do so will lead to surcharges and restrictions of reliefs which otherwise may be available to the company.

28.6.7   Failure to file a corporation tax return

s1084
TCA 97

A surcharge penalty (not to be confused with the surcharge payable by close companies in certain circumstances – see Chapter 33) applies when a company fails to deliver a return of income on or before the specified date in relation to the period for which the return is required. The surcharge is 10% of the company's corporation tax and the surcharge is to be treated in all respects as part of the company's corporation tax liability.

s1084
TCA 97
For accounting periods ending on or after 6 April 1995, the surcharge is graded as follows:

(a) Where the delay in filing is less than two months, the surcharge is reduced to 5% of the company's tax subject to a cap of €12,695.

(b) In other cases, the surcharge remains at 10% but is capped at €63,485.

The specified date is eight months and twenty-one days after the accounting period end.

The amount of corporation tax on which the surcharge is calculated is reduced by:

■ Any tax deducted by virtue of any of the provisions of the Tax Acts from any income, profits or chargeable gains, charged in the assessment to tax insofar as that tax has not been repaid or is not repayable to the chargeable person and insofar as the tax so deducted may be set off against the tax contained in the assessment to tax;

■ The amount of any tax credit to which the chargeable person is entitled in respect of any income, profits or chargeable gains charged in the assessment to tax; and

■ Any other amounts which are set off in the assessment to tax against the tax contained therein.

Note that preliminary corporation tax is not deducted in arriving at the amount surchargeable.

Example 28.8

A Ltd has a trading year-end of 31 December 2009. Its corporation tax liability is assessed at €21,000 and its CT1 return is sent to the Inspector of Taxes on 14 November 2010. The return should have been filed on or before 21 September 2010. As it is filed less than two months late, the surcharge is limited to 5%.

The surcharge is calculated as the corporation tax assessed €21,000 × 5%, i.e., €1,050. This surcharge is not deductible against future income.

Example 28.9

B Limited has a trading year-end of 31 July 2009. Its corporation tax liability is assessed at €311,000 and its CT1 return is sent to the Inspector of Taxes on 14 June 2010. The return should have been filed on or before 21 April 2010. As it is filed less than two months late, the surcharge is limited to 5%.

The surcharge is calculated as the corporation tax assessed of €311,000 × 5%, i.e., €15,550. As this surcharge exceeds €12,695 it is limited to the lower figure. This surcharge is not deductible against future income.

Example 28.10

C Limited has a trading year-end of 30 September 2009. Its corporation tax liability is assessed at €150,000. It has suffered Deposit Interest Retention Tax (DIRT) on its Schedule D Case IV income of €5,000 and received Professional Services Withholding Tax (PSWT) certificates (F45s) totalling €8,000. Its CT1 return is sent to the Inspector of Taxes on 14 September 2010. The return should have been filed on or before 21 June 2010. As it is filed more than two months late, the surcharge is at 10%.

	€
Corporation tax	*150,000*
Less DIRT	*(5,000)*
PSWT	*(8,000)*
Surchargeable amount	*137,000*
Surcharge at 10%	*13,700*

Even assuming that C Limited had paid the correct preliminary corporation tax on time (i.e. 90%), this is not taken into account when calculating the surcharge.

If a company makes a fraudulent or negligent return of income on or before the specified date, it is treated as having failed to make a timely return for the purposes of the surcharge unless the error in the return is remedied on or before the specified date. If the return is incorrect (but not fraudulently or neglectfully so) and it comes to the company's notice, the company will be regarded as having failed to make a timely return unless the error is corrected without unreasonable delay. These latter two points often arise in the context of a Revenue audit.

Claims to use certain losses are restricted where corporation tax returns for accounting periods ending on or after 1 April 1992 are submitted late. Full details of these restrictions are set out in Chapters 31 and 32.

28.7 Rates of Corporation Tax and Impact of European Union Policy

The rate of tax that applies to a company's profits is largely dependent on the type of income earned by the company. There have been fundamental changes to the rates structure for corporation tax over the past six years resulting in a myriad of rates that can apply depending on the type of income or gains of the company. The current standard rate of corporation tax is 12.5%, which applies for the financial years 2003 and onwards. The rate for the financial year 2002 was 16%.

28.7.1 Introduction of the 12.5% rate

With effect from 1 January 2003, Ireland boasts of having effected the smooth transition to a 12.5% rate of corporation tax, which was announced by the Minister for Finance in his Budget speech of 3 December 1997. The reduction in rate has been achieved by an annual 4% cut from 1998–2003. The table below indicates the dramatic reduction in the standard corporation tax rate since 1995.

Standard Corporation Tax Rates 1991–2003

Accounting Period	*Standard Rate**
1/4/1991 to 31/3/1995	*40%*
1/4/1995 to 31/3/1997	*38%*
1/4/1997 to 31/12/1997	*36%*
1/1/1998 to 31/12/1998	*32%*

1/1/1999 to 31/12/1999	*28%*
1/1/2000 to 31/12/2000	*24%*
1/1/2001 to 31/12/2001	*20%*
1/1/2002 to 31/12/2002	*16%*
1/1/2003 onwards	*12.5%*

* Lower rates have applied to certain companies with "small" profits from 1 April 1995.

Ireland has historically used corporation tax incentives to attract foreign direct investment. However, due to EU pressure, certain specific incentives could not be maintained in the long term. This has resulted in the withdrawal of earlier incentives aimed at encouraging inward investment. Some examples include:

■ Export sales relief (0%), which was considered incompatible with the Treaty of Rome;

■ Manufacturing relief, which will continue until 31 December 2010; and

■ The IFSC regime and the Shannon Free Airport Zone under which a 10% rate applied to 31 December 2005.

These reliefs had to be withdrawn prematurely as a result of action by the Commission in 1998 under the State Aid provisions of the Treaty. Ireland's response to this was to introduce a uniform low rate of corporation tax of 12.5%. As this rate applies to all trading companies and is not focused on a particular industry sector, it is not regarded as a State Aid from an EU perspective.

The move to a lower tax rate without specific incentives should continue to encourage long-term inward investment in Ireland.

Ireland has managed to achieve national fiscal autonomy with regard to corporation tax rates while adhering to the common framework recommended by the EU for its tax system generally. At the same time as introducing the 12.5% rate, Ireland has taken a number of steps to comply with the "code of conduct" signed up to by Finance Ministers of the Member States in December 1997. The code of conduct was drawn up as a result of a report produced in 1996 by Commissioner Monti entitled *Taxation in the European Union*, which was commissioned in order to examine tax-based incentives and to develop greater tax co-ordination across the EU.

28.7.2 Classification of profits by corporation tax rate

At present, and with effect from 1 January 2001, there are five rates of corporation tax on company profits as discussed below.

Rate		Application
(i)	*10%*	***Trading profits of manufacturing companies and certain activities grant-aided by the IDA***
		For qualifying operations established before 23 July 1998 or grant-assisted activities approved for grant assistance before 31 July 1998, the 10% rate applies until 31 December 2010.
		For those established on or after 23 July 1998 or where grant assistance was provided after 31 July 1998, the 10% rate applied until 31 December 2002. After this date the standard rate of 12.5% applies.

Rate		Application

International Financial Services Centre (IFSC) operations

The 10% rate for IFSC companies approved on or before 31 July 1998 applied to 31 December 2005. After this date the standard rate of 12.5% applies.

For those approved on or after 31 July 1998, the 10% rate applied until 31 December 2002. The 12.5% rate applies with effect from 1 January 2003.

Shannon Free Airport Zone companies

The 10% rate for Shannon Free Airport Zone companies approved on or before 31 May 1998 applied to 31 December 2005. After this date the standard rate of 12.5% applies.

For those approved on or after 31 May 1998, the 10% rate applied until 31 December 2002. After this date the 12.5% rate applies.

(ii) *12.5%* **Schedule D Case I and II income**

Profits taxable at 10% or 25% are excluded from qualifying under this rate.

The 12.5% rate applies to qualifying shipping activities with effect from 1 January 2001.

The 12.5% rate applies to all trading income after 1 January 2003, prior to this the applicable rate was 16%.

See 29.5.1 for a discussion regarding treatment of foreign dividends paid from trading profits.

(iii) *20%* **Profits arising from certain residential land deals to 31 December 2008.**

Chargeable gains (exception of foreign life assurance policies where the rate is 40%).

Chargeable gains are adjusted for the purposes of inclusion in the corporation tax computation such that effective tax at a rate of 25% (22% from 15th October 2008 to 7th April 2009 and 20% prior to that) is collected on the actual gain by applying the 12.5% rate to the adjusted amount.

(iv) *25%* **Passive non-trading income**

Applicable to Schedule D:

Case III (interest paid gross, dividends (unless included under s.21B TCA 97, see 29.5.1.), discounts, foreign income)
Case IV (interest paid net, royalties and other miscellaneous income) Case V (Irish rental income).

Income from "excepted trades", i.e., income from:

– land-dealing profits (including residential land from 1st January 2009, see (iii))) other than profits from construction operations,
   – working minerals, and
   – petroleum activities.

The lack of clarity regarding the distinction between trading and non-trading can in certain circumstances make the classification of profits very difficult. This arises largely due to the fact that there is no statutory definition of trading income.

28.7.3 Summary

If it is established that a source of income exists, further classification will be necessary as between different sources of income. The level of complexity in income classification is a relatively recent development in corporation tax. In the past, once a decision was made as between income and capital, the only further distinction that was necessary from an income perspective was between manufacturing and non-manufacturing activities. In addition the legislation is quite specific with regard to the type of activity it regards as manufacturing.

However, it is now also necessary to distinguish between trading income taxable at 12.5% and passive income taxable at 25%. The absence of a definition of trading income in legislation means that we are forced to rely on case law precedent and Revenue guidelines in making this distinction.

With regard to capital gains, there are two rates of tax applicable to chargeable gains, a 25% rate (22% for the period 15th October 2008 to 7th April 2009 and 20% prior to that) and a 40% rate, which applies to disposals of life assurance policies. While the same rate of tax applies to all disposals of land, a distinction must still be made between development land and non-development land. Students are referred to Chapter 26 for further discussion on this issue.

The chart below illustrates the inherent complexity in segregating income into its various classes.

Rates of tax

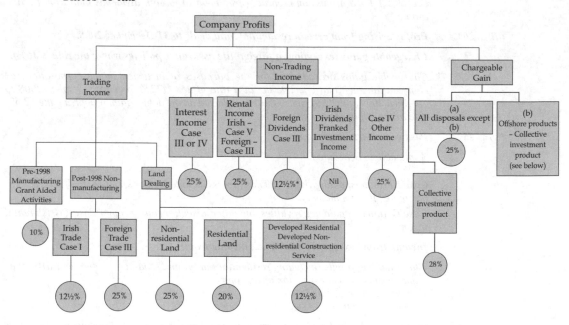

20% with effect from 1 January 2001 for offshore funds located in an EU/qualifying EEA State or a State which is a member of the OECD with which Ireland has a Double Tax Agreement.

The above chart illustrates the classification process which must be considered when deciding the appropriate rate of tax applicable to a company's profits.

The complexity arises largely due to the introduction of the 12.5% rate of corporation tax, which was introduced on a phased basis with effect from 1 January 2000. In addition, it is important to bear in mind that prior to the introduction of the current 12.5% rate, a 12.5% rate applied to the profits of certain small companies.

28.8   Other European Union Influences

While the political debate in terms of the proposed Common Consolidated Corporate Tax Base (CCCTB) has been gaining momentum recently, Ireland has effective sovereignty over the rate of tax that it applies. However, as regards other aspects of our corporation tax legislation, Ireland must comply with EU directives and EU case law.

28.8.1   EU Directives

To date, there have been four directives agreed by the EU which affect direct taxation of Irish corporations. These relate to:

1. *The taxation of parent and subsidiary companies – the Parent/Subsidiary Directive*

    This directive is concerned with a common system of taxation where parent companies and subsidiaries operate in different Member States.

    Section 31 Finance Act 1991, implemented this directive, i.e., Council Directive Number 90/435/EEC relating to parent and subsidiary companies. This legislation is now contained in s831 TCA 97 and provides credit for foreign tax against Irish tax on any distributions received from residents of other Member States.

2. *The taxation of mergers, divisions and contributions of assets – the Mergers and Exchange of Shares Directive*

    This directive concerns mergers, divisions, transfers of assets and exchanges of shares between companies located in different Member States.

    In Finance Act 1992, legislation was introduced to deal with this directive, i.e., Council Directive Number 90/434/EEC. This legislation, contained in s630 TCA 97, provides for the establishment of a common method of taxing mergers, divisions, transfer of assets and exchanges of shares, involving companies in different Member States.

    In Finance Act 2006, the EU directive introducing the European Company model, "SE", was given effect (Directive Number 2005/19/EC). This directive is designed to provide tax neutrality in relation to the activities covered by directive 90/434/EEC, for these new companies.

3. *Interest and royalty payments between associated companies – the Withholding Tax Exemption Directive*

Finance Act 2004 amended the withholding tax rules to incorporate EU Council Directive 2003/49/EC regarding interest and royalty payments within the EU to associated companies. An associated company is one in which one company can control 25% of the voting power of the other, or both companies are 25%-owned by a third, for a continuous period of two years. If these conditions are met, there is no obligation to withhold income tax on interest and royalty payments.

A condition of the regime is that any royalties paid in excess of an arm's length rate and any interest which is payable on loans in excess of 50 years will not qualify for exemption.

Not all EU countries are covered by the directive. For eight years from 1st July 2005 Greece and Portugal will continue to apply withholding tax on interest and royalties, while Spain will still withhold tax on royalty payments, for six years from 1st July 2005. The directive includes Switzerland. There are transitional arrangements in place for the newer member states.

4. *Exchange of information between EU Member States – The Savings Directive*

A directive on taxation of income and savings, which focuses on the exchange of information between European Member States, reached an agreement on 3 June 2003.

This directive was enacted into Irish legislation by Schedule 4 of Finance Act 2004. However, the various reporting/exchange of information provisions did not come into effect until July 2005. The directive applies only to interest payments to individuals. However, in many instances the paying agent, which carries the burden of compliance, will be a body corporate.

Notwithstanding the Mergers Directive referred to above, our corporation tax and capital gains tax codes already provided for certain relief on transactions such as an exchange of shares. However, the concept of division or merger does not exist in Irish company law and, consequently, no tax legislation has been introduced to cater for demergers.

In future years, it is expected that EU legislation and corresponding developments will be reflected in further tax changes, which will form an increasing part of our taxation code.

28.8.2   EU case law

From your study of Section II (Value-Added Tax) of the course, you should be aware that decisions of the European Court of Justice (ECJ) are becoming increasingly important for Irish legislation. The European Courts are prepared to overrule national Courts where there is a breach of fundamental freedoms. It is likely, going forward, that European case law will impact even more significantly on Irish legislation. The two cases which have impacted most significantly in the area of corporation tax are *ICI v Colmer* and the *St. Gobain* case. More recently, cases brought by Marks & Spencer and *FII Group Litigation v CIR* in the UK and referred to the ECJ are also significant. These cases have implications for Irish companies and are considered briefly in Chapters 29 and 31.

WHAT YOU SHOULD NOW KNOW

On completion of this chapter, you should be able to:

- ✓ Distinguish between a classical system of corporation tax and a system of imputation and describe the extent to which these systems have applied in Ireland since 1976.

- ✓ Describe the scope and territoriality of Irish corporation tax and identify sources of income which are subject to Irish corporation tax - Volume 2 Assigment 28.1.

- ✓ Explain the rules and factors to be taken into consideration in determining a company's residence status - Volume 2 Assignment 28.3, 28.4.

- ✓ State the due dates for filing of corporation tax returns and payment of corporation tax - Volume 2 Q28.1, Assignment 28.1, 28.5.

- ✓ Describe the requirements to pay preliminary tax and identify the amount payable - Volume 2 Q28.1, Assignment 28.1.

- ✓ Describe the consequences of late filing and late payment or underpayment of corporation tax.

- ✓ Discuss the factors that contributed to the introduction of the existing structure of corporation tax rates in Ireland.

- ✓ Identify the rate of corporation tax appropriate to different classes of taxable profit - Volume 2 Assignment 28.1.

- ✓ Discuss the impact of the EU on the Irish corporate tax regime historically and currently - Volume 2 Assignment 28.2.

- ✓ Comment on likely areas of EU influence on Irish corporation tax in the future.

- ✓ Complete Questions and the Assignments in Irish Taxation Law and Practice, Volume 2.

Appendix I

Preliminary Tax Payments for Small Companies

Similar to the facility afforded to individuals in paying preliminary income tax, small companies are entitled to base their corporation tax preliminary payments on the final tax liability for the previous year.

Where the company has a current 12-month period and a similar previous period of equal length, it is defined as small if its final corporation tax liability for the prior period is less than €200,000 if the current payment is due after 5 December 2007, €150,000 if before that date. If either period is less than 12 months, the following formulae must be used:

Current period less than 12 months – calculate relevant period limit:

$$€200,000 \times \frac{\textit{No. of days in current accounting period}}{365}$$

Prior period less than 12 months or of different length from current period – calculate corresponding corporation tax:

$$\textit{Prior period CT liability} \times \frac{\textit{No. of days in current accounting period}}{\textit{No. of days in prior accounting period}}$$

Example:

X Limited has a year end to 31 August 2009 (tax liability of €30,000) followed by a 10-month period to 30 June 2010 (tax liability of €300,000). To help with cash flow, X Limited wants to base its 2010 preliminary tax liability on its 2009 accounts. As one period is not of 12 months'duration, we must utilise the above formulae:

$$\textit{Relevant limit} \quad = \quad €200,000 \times \frac{304}{365} \quad = \quad €166,575$$

$$\textit{Corresponding CT} = €30,000 \times \frac{304}{365} = €24,986$$

As the relevant limit is higher than the corresponding corporation tax, the company qualifies as a small company. The company will base its preliminary payment on €24,986.

If a company qualifies for the small company relief, the payment amounts are based on the following rules:

Period ending in	First payment (% of previous final balance due)	Second payment (% of current final balance due)
2002	20%	90%
2003	40%	90%
2004	60%	90%
2005	80%	90%
2006 onwards	100%	N/A

The second payment must bring the total of the two preliminary payments to 90% of the current period liability.

29

CALCULATING THE CORPORATION TAX LIABILITY

In this chapter, you will deal with the following:

- Major differences between income tax and corporation tax

- Calculating taxable profits – methodology

- Accounting periods

- Application of corporation tax rates

29.1   Introduction

The purpose of this chapter is to provide a methodology for calculating total profits subject to corporation tax.

As you will be aware from your study of Section III, calculating the income tax liability of any individual taxpayer comprises two elements:

- calculating taxable income, i.e., the net income on which the taxpayer must pay tax; and

- applying the relevant income tax rates to that income in the hands of the taxpayer.

Broadly speaking, the same principle applies to companies. However, individuals are subject to income tax only on sources of income. Capital gains, which accrue to individuals, are subjected to a separate tax, i.e., capital gains tax. Companies pay corporation tax, not on "total income", but on "total profits", which comprises both income and gains. Aside from this major difference in the tax base for companies, there are also subtle differences in the rules for classifying and calculating the taxable income of a company. Unless otherwise stated, the Taxes Consolidation Act provides that income of a company is to be computed in accordance with income tax principles. The overall computation is broken down into the same classifications that apply for income tax purposes and calculations are in accordance with the laws applicable to those classifications. This chapter is concerned with revisiting those rules, which are common to both income tax and corporation tax and with developing a methodology for calculating the taxable profits of a company. Emphasis is placed on highlighting issues that are unique to corporation tax.

29.2   The Layout of a Corporation Tax Computation

The Taxes Consolidation Act specifies that different types of income must be taxed under specified "Schedules". Each schedule applies different rules for calculating the amount of income taxable under that Schedule. Income taxable under Schedule D is further classified under specified "Cases". Section 18(2) TCA 97 sets out the various cases under which income is to be assessed. This classification system has already been outlined in Chapter 8 but it is useful to revisit the subject as companies will typically earn income across a number of these cases. They are critical to the correct computation of a company's tax and it is essential that readers fully understand them.

The relevant categories affecting companies are as follows:

Schedule D Case I

Income from Irish trades, e.g., retail trades, manufacturing trades, etc.

Schedule D Case II

Income from the provision of professional services, e.g., accountancy services, legal services, etc.

Schedule D Case III

Interest received gross, foreign income.

Schedule D Case IV

Interest received net of deposit interest retention tax, any other miscellaneous sources of income not included under another Case or Schedule.

Schedule D Case V

Income from the letting of Irish property.

It should be clear from the above list that companies are only chargeable to tax on Schedule D income. As a company is not an individual, it cannot earn employment income and therefore it cannot be charged to tax under Schedule E.

The receipt of Irish dividends by a company (taxable in the hands of an individual under Schedule F) is treated as exempt income. As Irish dividends are simply an appropriation of profits already subjected to Irish corporation tax, there is no tax deduction for the paying company and therefore no charge to tax for the company receiving the dividend. This form of income is known as "franked investment income". Accordingly, a company cannot be charged to tax under Schedule F. Dividends received in respect of shareholdings in non-Irish resident companies are taxable under Schedule D, as in the case of individuals.

The sum of the amounts of income under each of the relevant categories or Cases is the **"total income"** of the company. Chargeable gains are added to this amount to calculate **"total profits"** subject to corporation tax. It is important to note that the terminology used for these total amounts is very relevant. The terms "income" and "profit" should not be confused. "Profit" includes chargeable gains; "income" does not include chargeable gains. The analysis can be summarised with the following equation:

INCOME + CHARGEABLE GAINS = TOTAL PROFITS SUBJECT TO
CORPORATION TAX

This terminology and the distinction between income and profits is very important, as certain reliefs are applied to income as opposed to profits, etc. In this regard, readers are referred to Chapter 30 and the formula for applying manufacturing relief.

Corporation tax is applied to the total profits figure at the rates identified in Chapter 28 and certain reliefs may be claimed against specific sources of income, total profits and the corporation tax liability. A pro forma corporation tax computation is set out in Appendix I.

29.3 Calculation of Tax-Adjusted Case I/II

As in the case of sole traders, calculating the trading or professional income of a company involves taking the "profit before tax" figure in the profit and loss account or income statement for a company using IFRS (see 29.3.4) and adjusting it to arrive at taxable profits. The figure used as a starting point is the profit before tax and before any appropriations of profit such as dividends, distributions, etc. Dividends and distributions are simply appropriations of the company's profit to the company's shareholders and accordingly, are not deductible in arriving at taxable profits.

In the vast majority of cases, the audited accounts of a company will not show the final figure to be taxed for the period. While the Revenue Commissioners require GAAP (generally accepted accounting practice) to be used in the computation of taxable profits, there are certain core tax principles and specific legislative sections, which give rise to differences between the accounting and taxable profit.

The object of the exercise is then to strip out this "profit before tax" figure:

- Case I/II income;

- Case III income;

- Case IV income;

- Case V income;

- Chargeable gains.

Always bear in mind that you will be stripping out income and expenses that are in the profit and loss account or IFRS income statement and recreating the taxable income figures. You can only strip out amounts that are already in the profit and loss account or IFRS income statement. If something is not booked to the profit and loss account or IFRS income statement you do not need to adjust profit before tax for that item.

In determining whether or not individual items in the profit and loss account or IFRS income statement need to be adjusted for, it is necessary to consider the four criteria identified in Chapter 15 for the purposes of calculating tax-adjusted Case I/II for income tax purposes. A brief synopsis of these criteria has been reproduced below as follows:

"1.   It is necessary to consider whether the item is capital in nature or income/ revenue related. In general, an adjustment is required for capital items. A number of Irish and UK decisions help to clarify the distinction between "capital" and "revenue". It is important to bear in mind that some capital expenses, which are disallowed for the purposes of calculating Case I, may be deductible in calculating chargeable gains.

2.   The item must be "trade" related. In general, items that do not relate to the trade are adjusted for in arriving at taxable Case I. The legislation specifically requires that for amounts to be deductible under Case I, the expenditure must be incurred "wholly and exclusively" for the purposes of carrying on the trade. This concept of "wholly and exclusively" is a complex area and has been the subject of much case law in Ireland and the UK over many years.

3. *In general, items of expenditure must have been incurred in the period. An adjustment will be required if an item relates to a movement on a general provision. Movements in provisions are only allowable where they relate to specific items, the amount of which can be determined with exactitude. Rough estimates of future expenditure are not allowable.*

4. *Certain specific items of expenditure are disallowed by statute notwithstanding that they are revenue in nature and may have been incurred wholly and exclusively for the purposes of the trade. The main provisions disallowing specific types of expenditure are addressed in 15.3.4 below."*

Taken from Chapter 15 – paragraph 15.3.

Broadly speaking, the methodology is the same for both individuals and companies and in general, the analysis and examples included in Chapter 15 also apply in calculating the Case I/II income of a company. However, there are certain exceptions to this rule and a number of issues unique to the calculation of the adjusted profits of a company merit further commentary.

The reader should also bear in mind the fundamental changes taking place for companies that have adopted IFRS accounts (see 29.3.4). This change affects plcs for periods beginning on or after 1 January 2005, while private companies are also entitled to adopt IFRS. From an accounting point of view, there are numerous differences between Irish GAAP, which is currently used, and IFRS. These differences are discussed in 29.3.4. The reader should note that the "profit and loss account" has been replaced by an "income statement" for IFRS-compliant companies. Therefore, for any examples that mention the profit and loss account, it is understood that the company has not yet adopted IFRS (because it is not a listed company and therefore is not obliged to or because, as a private company, it has made the decision not to do so).

29.3.1 Salaries and private expenses of owner-directors

Readers should understand the legal difference between a sole trader and the shareholders of a company. A sole trader is taxable under Case I/II on all his trading/ professional income in the taxable period. In calculating tax-adjusted Case I/II, he receives no deduction for his drawings or for his personal expenses during the period. To reclassify drawings as salary on the basis that it is referred to as such in the accounts would involve incorrectly classifying trading income as Schedule E income for tax purposes. The owner cannot employ himself and accordingly is taxed under Case I/II on all his earnings in the period irrespective of whether or not he spends or draws down these amounts. He must also add back the private element of any expenditure booked to the accounts, e.g., the private element of any motor expenses.

Companies are separate legal entities distinct from their owners and they are taxed on their income accordingly. The vast majority of companies in Ireland are family controlled; they will usually have two shareholders of which either one or both work in the company as full-time directors. The directors will draw a salary from the company, upon which they will pay tax under Schedule E and the company will get a deduction for this cost. The company is then taxed on the profits after the deduction for directors' salaries. Similarly, where the company funds personal or private expenses of the shareholder directors, such amounts are allowable in full on the basis that the expenditure is a cost of rewarding employees and the shareholder directors will be taxed on these amounts under the benefit in kind (BIK) rules (see Chapter 21). The following example illustrates the position where a company pays a salary to a shareholder director and funds personal expenses of that shareholder director. To facilitate an understanding of the distinction between Case I/II computations for sole traders and companies, readers should compare this example with Example 15.1 in Chapter 15.

Example 29.1

John is the majority shareholder in X Limited and works full-time for the company as managing director. The profit and loss account of X Limited for the year ended 31 December 2009 is as follows:

	€	€
Sales		*300,000*
Cost of sales		*(100,000)*
Gross profit		*200,000*
Less expenses:		
Depreciation	*20,000*	
Salaries and wages	*65,000*	
Light and heat	*1,000*	
Telephone	*1,500*	
Motor expenses	*3,000*	
Miscellaneous	*4,000*	*(94,500)*
Profit before tax		*105,500*

The salaries and wages include a salary of €25,000 paid to John.

X Limited operates from a room in John's home. The light and heat expense included in the accounts relates to the expenses for the house as a whole for the year. John pays the bill using the company cheque book. John has agreed with his Inspector of Taxes that one-fifth of this amount is business related.

The telephone expense relates to a separate line, which John has put in place exclusively for the purposes of the company's business.

The motor expenses relate to petrol and insurance expenses incurred by X Limited. The amount comprises an amount of €1,000 in respect of John's car, which is used 50% for business purposes (as agreed with the Inspector of Taxes), and €2,000 in respect of a salesman's car, which is used 60% for business purposes.

The miscellaneous expenses are all allowable.

The Case I computation of X Limited is as follows:

	€
Profit before tax	105,500
Add back:	
Depreciation	20,000
Tax-adjusted Case I	125,500

Note:

The salary of the managing director is a normal trading expense and is deductible in full in calculating Case I. Accordingly, no adjustment is necessary. John is taxable on the amount of this salary under Schedule E.

He is also taxed under Schedule E on other benefits accruing from his involvement in the company. Thus, the private elements of the light and heat and motor expenses are allowable for Case I purposes on the basis that they are costs of rewarding an employee. The benefits accruing to him would be taxable in his hands under Schedule E as a BIK. Thus, he would be taxable on a BIK of €800 in respect of the light and heat and €500 in respect of the motor expenses. In this regard, readers are referred to Chapter 21.

29.3.2 Dividends and distributions

It is a common misconception among shareholders of Irish companies that as they own the company, they can do what they wish with its assets and funds. However, any drawings by the shareholders may be classified as distributions and can give rise to onerous consequences under close company legislation (see Chapter 32). Incidentally, use of company assets and funds by shareholders may also impact upon company law and may lead to possible indictable offences, which would be reported to the Office of the Director of Corporate Enforcement by the company's auditor.

Any distributions or dividends made by a company are not allowed for tax purposes as they are not incurred "wholly and exclusively" for the purposes of the trade; they are paid to shareholders as a reward for taking the financial risk of investing in the company. Thus, they are treated as an appropriation of profits rather than as an expense incurred in earning the profit. The definition of distributions in the legislation is very wide and seeks to cover all possible payments made to a shareholder. The most common examples are:

■ Dividends;

■ Any amount received for the redemption of bonus shares (s130(2)(c) TCA 97);

■ Interest on securities convertible into shares (s130(2)(d)(ii) TCA 97);

- Transfer of assets to a shareholder for consideration less than the worth of the assets (s130(3)(a) TCA 97);

- Transactions within the provisions of close company legislation (see Chapter 32).

For accounting purposes, dividends are payable out of after-tax income. Accordingly, in starting with the profit-before-tax figure, there will generally be no need to make any adjustments in respect of dividends in arriving at tax-adjusted Case I. However, some distributions may be "buried" under expense headings in the profit and loss account and as such amounts will have been deducted in arriving at "profit before tax", they should be added back for tax purposes. For example, under close company legislation, expense payments to shareholders and certain "excess" interest payments to directors (on loans advanced to the company) may be regarded as distributions for tax purposes and accordingly must be added back if deducted in arriving at the profit before tax figure. In this regard, readers are referred to the commentary in Chapter 32.

Companies are not taxed on dividends received from Irish resident companies. These amounts are known as "franked investment income" and are deducted in calculating tax-adjusted Case I/II. Dividends received from foreign companies are also deducted for the purposes of calculating tax-adjusted Case I/II, and are taxable under Case I, II or III depending on the source of the profit, see 29.5.1.

29.3.3 Company capital allowance claims

The legislation governing the claim for capital allowances on capital expenditure incurred by individuals as discussed in Chapter 16 applies equally for companies. The main difference between a sole trader's capital allowance claim and a company's claim is that for income tax purposes, a capital allowance is treated as a relief, which is deducted from the taxable income, whereas for corporation tax purposes, the capital allowance is treated as a deduction in arriving at the taxable income. Therefore, in calculating the charge to corporation tax, it is included with deductions such as exempt income, profit on sale of fixed assets, non-taxable employment grants, etc., in arriving at tax-adjusted Case I.

If a company is making a claim for capital allowances it must calculate a separate claim for each accounting period. This important concept is particularly relevant in situations where a company has a period of more or less than 12 months in duration. In this regard, readers are referred to the analysis at 29.4 below.

29.3.3.1 Energy Efficient Equipment

To encourage "green" capital spending capital allowances at a rate of 100% under s285A TCA 97 are available for the acquisition of energy- efficient equipment as follows:

1. Motors and drives   - minimum spend – €1,000

2. Lighting   - minimum spend – €3,000

3. Building energy management systems - minimum spend – €5,000

The scheme commenced on 9 October 2008 and will run for three years. It is only available for companies.

Finance (No. 2) Act 2008 added four additional categories to the above list:

1. Information and communications
    technology   - minimum spend – €1,000

2. Heating and electricity provision   - minimum spend – €1,000

3. Ventilation and air conditioning controls   - minimum spend – €1,000

4. Electric and alternative fuels vehicles   - minimum spend – €1,000

The commencement date for the new categories is subject to ministerial order. In relation to vehicles at 4 above, this scheme will apply in priority to the CO2 capital allowances scheme in Part 11C TCA 97. Additional equipment types will be added to the list over time.

29.3.3.2 Intangible Assets

This section details the new intangible assets relief under section 291A TCA 1997, introduced by Finance Act 2009.

In recent years Ireland had been lagging behind in the provision of tax relief for the acquisition of intangible assets in relation to other European countries which was having an effect on the efficiency of Ireland as a holding company for companies with worldwide patents, brands etc.

Following on from recent changes in research and development discussed above, an intangible assets capital allowances scheme was introduced.

Specified Intangible Assets

The act introduces capital allowances for "specified intangible assets", as defined in section 291A TCA 1997.

These include costs incurred on intangible assets such as patents, registered designs, trademarks and names, brand names, domain names, copyrights, know-how (section 768 TCA 1997), licences etc and any goodwill related to these assets.

To be an intangible asset it must come within the definition under GAAP. Under IAS 38 an intangible asset is defined as "an identifiable non-monetary based asset without physical substance".

This would generally be an asset that has been created or purchased by the company and from which an income stream or reduced costs are proposed.

The scheme applies to any qualifying expenditure incurred on or after 7th May 2009.

The assets will be treated as qualifying for capital allowances under the normal rules, therefore they will be subject to balancing allowances/charges, etc.

Rates of Claim

The company will have two options in relation to relation to the wear and tear rate:

(1) 7% straight line for 14 years followed by 2% straight line in the 15th year

(2) An amount equivalent to the depreciation/amortisation charge in the income statement

The company can claim either option at its own discretion for each individual asset. It should be noted that under IAS 38, assets with an indefinite useful life are generally not depreciated/amortised and therefore the company will choose option (1) above, in order to obtain tax relief.

There will be no clawback if the asset is sold more than 15 years after the first accounting period in which it was capitalised, section 288 (3C) TCA 1997, provided it is not sold to a connected party, which claims wear and tear.

Restrictions on Claim – Relevant Trade

Unlike ordinary capital allowances, there is a restriction on the amounts of allowance that can be offset. The capital allowances can only be offset against income from relevant activities, section 291A (5) TCA 1997.

These activities include the managing, developing and exploiting of intangible assets.

These activities are treated as a separate trade for offset purposes, known as a relevant trade.

Section 291A (5) (b) TCA 1997 states that if the company has other trade income, the income from the relevant trade should be split on a just and reasonable basis.

The restriction also applies to interest borrowed to acquire or develop intangible assets.

Once the income of the relevant trade has been identified, a further restriction applies in that only 80% of the income can be sheltered by the capital allowances and interest, therefore a loss can never be created.

Any unutilised capital allowances or interest is carried forward. The capital allowances are restricted in priority to the interest in arriving at the overall 80% maximum limit

Calculation of IP Relief:

(1) Calculate relevant trading income

(2) Calculate capital allowances on specified intangible assets

(3) Calculate interest on relevant borrowings

(4) Set interest against 80% of the relevant trading income, carrying any excess forward

(5) Set capital allowances against any remaining income from (4), carrying any excess forward

Example 29.2

IP Limited incurred expenditure on specified intangible assets of €500,000 for the year ended 31ˢᵗ December 2009.

The company borrowed €400,000 to fund the expenditure and paid €40,000 in interest. The company has chosen the 7% over 14 years option.

Trade results before interest for the year ended 31ˢᵗ December 2009 are €140,000. This is €90,000 for IP management and €50,000 for other trading activities.

Calculate the usage of intangible assets relief under section 291A TCA 1997.

	€		€
Total Income	140,000	*Capital Allowances 500,000 × 7%*	35,000
Income from relevant trade	90,000	*Interest*	40,000
		Total Claim	75,000

Max Claimable, 80%	72,000	
Income from Relevant Trade	90,000	
Interest Allowable	(40,000)	*(Claimed first)*
Capital Allowances	(32,000)	*(after restriction)*
Taxable Relevant Trade	18,000	*(equals 20% of total relevant trade income)*
Add: Non Relevant Trade	50,000	
Total Income	68,000	
Corporation Tax @ 12.5%	8,500	

The restricted capital allowances of €3,000 (€35,000 - €32,000) are carried forward to be offset against future years relevant trading income.

When an intangible asset is included in the purchase of a trade, allowances can be claimed provided the company can show that its valuations are reasonable.

In all cases Revenue can engage experts (subject to not prejudicing the company's entitlement to trade secrecy) to assist in deciding whether the values or claims are just and reasonable.

In relation to the current relief for know-how under section 768 TCA 1997 and patents under section 755 TCA 1997, these types of expenditure are included in the new scheme but if the company wishes, it may continue to claim relief under these original sections on expenditure incurred to 7ᵗʰ May 2011.

The new section 291A TCA 1997 does not affect capital allowances for software under section 290 TCA 1997.

29.3.4 Accounting standards

29.3.4.1 Introduction

In Ireland, companies have traditionally followed UK guidelines promulgated by the Accounting Standards Board (ASB). The main bank of standards issued were Statements of Standard Accounting Practices (SSAPs) and these in turn are being slowly superseded by Financial Reporting Standards (FRSs). The standards used in Ireland (SSAPs and FRSs) are known as Irish and UK Generally Accepted Accounting Practice (GAAP) and their main objective is to ensure that accounts give a "true and fair view".

There has been a movement in recent years from shareholders, institutions and other interested parties calling for a convergence of the numerous and distinct standards being used in different parts of the world. To this end the International Accounting Standards Board (IASB) was formed in April 2001, from a previous body, the International Accounting Standards Committee (IASC), which had originally been charged with developing a worldwide set of accounting standards. The IASB after much consultation began to issue International Financial Reporting Standards (IFRSs). The objective of the harmonisation project is to ensure comparability of financial information across continents.

From an accounting perspective the main difference between Irish GAAP and IFRS GAAP is that Irish and UK GAAP promoted the "true and fair view", which involves basing the majority of balance sheet figures on historical cost (or lower, if current values were below cost), whereas IFRS calls for the use of "fair values". This entails restating assets at their year end market value and debiting/crediting the difference to the income statement, a concept not generally practiced under Irish and UK GAAP.

The IFRS guidelines only apply to listed companies registered in the EU for accounting periods commencing on or after 1 January 2005. However it is expected that over the coming years this will be extended. The ASB, which will continue for the time being to regulate non-listed companies in the UK and Ireland has stated that it intends to issue further FRSs which will be virtually identical to IFRSs. All companies are free to adopt IFRS from 1 January 2005, if they wish.

29.3.4.2 Amendments to TCA 1997

Section 48 Finance Act 2005 introduced IFRS legislation to the Taxes Consolidated Act. It inserted into s4 TCA 97 a definition of GAAP as follows:

"Generally accepted accounting practice means –

(a) in relation to the affairs of a company or other entity that prepares accounts (in this section referred to as 'IAS accounts') in accordance with international accounting standards, generally accepted accounting practice with respect to such accounts:

(b) in any other case, Irish generally accepted accounting practice"

The reference to IAS above derives from the definition provided by EC regulation number 1606/2002 which introduced IFRS into EU Member States. There is no mention of IFRS in the amendments to the TCA 1997, only to the EU term International Accounting Standard (IAS), which was superseded by IFRS.

Part (b) of the definition allows companies not using IFRS to carry on preparing accounts and taxation computations under Irish and UK GAAP.

Another definition is that of "Relevant Accounting Standards" (RAS). RAS is a set of accounts which have been prepared using IFRS or a form of Irish and UK GAAP which has been modified to give results similar to IFRS.

The four main sections in the TCA 97 are 76A, 76B and 76C and Schedule 17A. The sections only apply to Case I/II income.

Section 76A TCA 97 introduced the concept that taxable income (Case I and II) should be computed in accordance with generally accepted accounting principles subject "to any adjustment required or authorised by law".

Section 76B TCA deals with the taxing of financial instruments and is beyond the scope of this publication.

Section 76C is the first anti-avoidance section enacted to counter possible abuse during the introduction of IFRS. It is concerned with associated companies (see 32.2.6) and situations in which one adopts IFRS, while the other continues to use Irish and UK GAAP and they engage in intercompany transactions.

If as a result of these transactions the company preparing its accounts under IFRS gains a tax advantage (the section uses the same definition of tax advantage as S 811 TCA 97) then it is obliged to prepare its income liable to tax under Irish GAAP. A detailed discussion of this section is also outside the scope of this publication. Schedule 17A is dealt with below.

Section 76D TCA 1997 deals with leasing companies. It confirms the Revenue view that the accounting income of leasing companies must still be adjusted for taxation purposes, that is to say that it is subject "to any adjustment required or authorised by law", section 76A.

Therefore, in general, leasing companies will continue to be taxed on lease rentals less a capital allowance claim.

29.3.4.3 Differences between IFRS and Irish GAAP and their taxation implications

The purpose of the commentary here is to set out the major differences that companies will encounter if they have taken the decision to move from Irish GAAP to IFRS. It also sets out the taxation implications of such a move. It should be appreciated that the list below is that of the main sections which concern taxation matters. There are currently 49 IFRS standards in existence and it is beyond the scope of this publication to compare each one to the relevant SSAP or FRS and to analyse its taxation impact. However, a number of the changes in standards will necessitate a transitional arrangement during the move from Irish GAAP to IFRS and these are discussed below.

Once a company has moved to IFRS, it cannot reverse the decision (apart from in limited circumstances).

29.3.4.4 Bad Debts

Under Irish and UK GAAP (FRS 12) and IFRS (IAS 37), general provisions should not appear in accounts. However, the scope of FRS 12 does not extend to bad debts and the fair valuing of debtors in accordance with IAS 32 and 39 can result in certain differences between Irish/UK GAAP and IFRS.

Under Irish and UK GAAP companies may have two bad debt provisions – specific and general. The specific provision concerns debtors which have been identified as being unlikely to pay and are therefore provided for. The general provision normally involves taking a percentage of debtors and bases the provision on this amount. With both provisions, the resulting increase/decrease in the reserve is taken to the profit and loss account. For taxation purposes movements in the specific provision are allowed and no tax adjustment is required. The movement on the general provision is an adjusting item and is added back/deducted as appropriate.

Under IFRS (standard numbers IAS 32 and 39) a bad debt provision is only created when there is objective evidence that the amount concerned is not collectable. Thus, it is likely that general bad debt provisions will no longer feature in accounts following the transition to IFRS. For taxation purposes the provision will be fully allowable and no adjustment will be required. However, there are certain transitional measures which merit attention and these are addressed at 29.3.4.9 below.

29.3.4.5 Income Recognition

There is no specific FRS dealing with the issue of when to recognise revenue under Irish and UK GAAP. Historically the receipt of upfront fees would generally have been included in the profit and loss account in the period in which the income was received.

IAS 18 states that income should be recognised when it is probable that future economic benefits will flow to the company and they can be measured reliably. The introduction of IFRS to these companies will therefore give rise to the need to defer income received to future periods. For taxation purposes no adjustment need be made and the company will be taxed when the income is recognised in its income statement. However, adjustments may be required on account for the transition to IFRS and these are addressed below.

The Accounting Standards Board (ASB) issued UITF40 in relation to service income recognition. This is in response to concerns that FRS 5, Reporting the Substance of Transactions, did not properly account for work-in-progress on service income as it only provided for the cost incurred and for no element of profit.

It should be understood that work-in-progress (unbilled fees) can be very substantial in professional firms. The UITF calls for an uplift to include a profit element. Therefore the opening work-in-progress (based on the closing work-in-progress in the year prior to adoption of the UITF) will be restated to include a profit element, which will result in it being higher than the previous year's closing figure.

This adjustment (called the "counter balancing credit") would lead to an apparent one-off tax deduction during the changeover process.

This deduction is allowable, but it must be spread over five years. Readers are referred to 29.3.4.10 below.

29.3.4.6 Fixed Assets and Depreciation

There are no major differences between Irish and UK GAAP and IFRS in accounting for fixed assets and associated depreciation. Under both systems companies can choose between the cost model, in which the asset is stated at its historic cost less accumulated depreciation and the fair value model. If it utilises this latter option the asset is stated at its revalued amount (provided that this can be measured reliably) less accumulated depreciation. From a taxation point of view there has been a change in legislation on foot of the introduction of the Finance Act 2005 rules relating to the adoption of IFRS.

In previous years, if the costs associated with putting an asset into operation (for example use of the company's own labour) had been capitalised in the financial statements, the company would adjust its taxable income by deducting these capitalised costs. It did so on the basis that the expenditure was actually revenue in nature and in general, this was allowed by the Inspector of Taxes.

S 321(2A) TCA 97 has been inserted to provide that these capitalised costs will be included in the claim for capital allowances along with the actual asset. This will naturally give rise to higher upfront tax payments as it will take, for example eight years (in the case of plant and machinery) to receive a full deduction for labour costs, rather than a one year write-off pre-Finance Act 2005.

29.3.4.7 Other areas

Stocks and construction contracts

There are no major differences between Irish and UK GAAP (SSAP 9) and IFRS (IAS 2 and 11) and neither require a taxation adjustment.

Operating and finance leases

There are no major differences between Irish and UK GAAP (SSAP 21) and IFRS (IAS 17). The view of the Revenue is that the IFRS legislation introduced by Finance Act 2005 has not changed the tax treatment in practice as laid out in 16.2.8, 15.3.4.8,

15.3.4.9 and Appendix 3 of Chapter 15. (See 29.3.4.2 regarding the introduction of s76D TCA 97.)

Government grants

There are no major differences between Irish and UK GAAP (SSAP 4) and IFRS (IAS 20). Therefore there is no change in the accounting treatment or in the tax treatment applied (see 15.3.1.3).

Interest on borrowings

There are no major differences between Irish GAAP (FRS 15) and IFRS (IAS 23). IAS 23 requires interest on borrowings relating to capital assets to be capitalised until the asset is ready for use or sale. It had been practice, but was never enshrined in legislation, to allow interest on capital borrowings, including capitalised borrowings, to be deducted from taxable income. Section 81 (3) TCA 97 places this practice on a statutory footing.

The same section also ensures a continued deduction for research and development expenditure and confirms that the deduction for such expenditure is not affected by the expenditure being capitalised.

Goodwill

Irish and UK GAAP (FRS 10 and 11) differs from IFRS (IAS 36 and 38) in that whilst Irish and UK GAAP allows goodwill to be written off and impaired, IFRS allows impairment only.

Goodwill is not recognised under Irish corporation tax legislation and therefore, the write-off or impairment of goodwill is not deductible for tax purposes. Any amortisation or impairment costs are added back in the tax computation.

General provisions

Irish and UK GAAP (FRS 12) and IFRS GAAP (IAS 37) both allow the creation of specific provisions for expected actual costs. It was revenue policy to allow FRS 12 provisions and it is assumed that this will continue for IAS 37. Readers should bear in mind that this relates to provisions for liabilities and not provisions for impairment of assets, such as provisions for depreciation and bad debts, which are addressed at 29.3.4.4 and 29.3.4.6 above.

29.3.4.8 Transitional Arrangements – Schedule 17A TCA 97

Schedule 17A deals with the transitional measures to be adopted during the move from Irish and UK GAAP to IFRS. The schedule acts to ensure that no income or expense falls out of the tax net during the changeover periods.

There are two main parts to the schedule, one dealing with the effect of the transition on financial instruments (including bad debts) and the other with all other matters.

29.3.4.9 Transitional measures for bad debts – Schedule 17A para 3 TCA 97

As noted above financial instruments are beyond the scope of this publication but the following is an example of how bad debts are dealt with during the transitional period. Bad debts are included as a financial instrument under IFRS.

Example 29.3

New Co. PLC closed its books as at 31 December 2004 with the following bad debt provisions:

	Opening	*Movement*	*Closing*
	01.01.04		*31.12.04*
General Bad Debt Provision	*75,000*	*(25,000)*	*50,000*
Specific Bad Debt Provision	*125,000*	*50,000*	*175,000*
	200,000	*25,000*	*225,000*

For the year ended 31 December 2004 the company would deduct €25,000 from the accounting profit figure in arriving at tax adjusted Case I. There would have been no adjustment in respect of the movement in the specific reserve.

As New Co. is a plc it is obliged to commence implementing IFRS for the period beginning 1 January 2005. Under IFRS it reviews its bad debt provisions for trade accounts where there is objective evidence that certain amounts are not fully collectible. After the review its opening bad debt provision is €200,000, a decrease of €25,000 in the overall reserve.

For taxation purposes the general bad debt provision is ignored as the entire €50,000 has been disallowed since it was first created. The company will not however receive an allowance for the change in the specific provision from €175,000 to €200,000 (an amount of €25,000) until the annual IFRS reserve has fallen below the opening IFRS reserve by €25,000. This €25,000 increase is known as the "first time adoption adjustment".

For the next four years the closing provisions are as follows:

– 31 December 2005 bad debt provision of €230,000

– 31 December 2006 bad debt provision of €195,000

– 31 December 2007 bad debt provision of €185,000

– 31 December 2008 bad debt provision of €100,000

	Balance Sheet	*Income Statement*	*Tax Adjust*
	€	*€*	*€*
Opening provision as at 01.01.05	*200,000*		
Closing provision as at 31.12.05	*230,000*	*30,000 Note 1*	
Closing provision as at 31.12.06	*195,000*	*(35,000) Note 2*	*5,000*
Closing provision as at 31.12.07	*185,000*	*(10,000) Note 3*	*10,000*
Closing provision as at 31.12.08	*100,000*	*(85,000) Note 4*	*10,000*
Total transitional adjustment			*25,000*

Note 1 – As the reserve has increased, no allowance for the original €25,000 increase due to the IFRS changeover is allowed under the transitional arrangements.

Note 2 – As the reserve has fallen below the opening provision under IFRS by €5,000, this amount can be deducted from taxable income under the transitional arrangements. Note that there is a further €20,000 left to be adjusted for, providing the provision is reduced sufficiently.

Note 3 – The provision has fallen below the opening provision by a further €10,000, which is deducted from the taxable income, leaving a further €10,000 of a potential deduction.

Note 4 – The closing 2008 reserve has fallen €100,000 below the opening IFRS adjusted reserve of 1 January 2005, therefore the final €10,000 can now be claimed.

29.3.4.10 Transitional measures for other items – Schedule 17A para 2 TCA 97

If the change in accounts results in items other than bad debts and financial instruments falling out of the taxable accounts (either income or expenditure), then Sch 17A paragraph 2 spreads the item equally over five years.

There are two items which need to be dealt with for taxation purposes:

(a) – Deductible amount:

This is an expense which would ordinarily have been allowed against taxable income but because of the move from Irish GAAP to IFRS has not been included. Also any income which has been taxed twice, once under Irish GAAP and once under IFRS is a deductible amount.

(b) – Taxable amount:

This is a receipt which would ordinarily have been taxed as taxable income but because of the move from Irish GAAP to IFRS has not been included. Any expenditure which has been deducted twice, once under Irish GAAP and once under IFRS is also a taxable amount. The amount by which the taxable amount exceeds the deductible amount is taxed equally over five accounting periods and vice versa.

Example 29.4

New Co. PLC entered into a four-year contract on 1 January 2004. It received €180,000 as an upfront payment which it included in its profit and loss account for the year ended 31 December 2004 and was taxed accordingly,

As New Co. is a plc it is obliged to commence implementing IFRS for the period beginning 1 January 2005. Under IFRS it reviews its income recognition policies and notes that under IAS 18 it should release €45,000 of the upfront contract receipt each year to its income statement.

Without the transitional measures afforded by Schedule 17A TCA 97 the following scenario would arise:

	2004 €	2005 €	2006 €	2007 €	Total €
Revenue under Irish GAAP	180,000				180,000
Revenue under IFRS (Note 1)		45,000	45,000	45,000	135,000
Total amount taxable					315,000

Note 1 – *Under IFRS it would restate the 2004 accounts for comparison purposes by releasing the first €45,000 and remove the €180,000 from the income statement. The restatement however would not have any impact on the 2004 or 2005 corporation tax computations.*

New Co. would be left in a situation of being taxed twice on the same contract during the changeover in standards.

Under Schedule 17A paragraph 2 TCA 97 the "deductible amount" is €135,000 and the allowance is spread over five years at €27,000 per annum.

	2004	2005	2006	2007	2008	2009	Total
Irish GAAP	180,000						180,000
IFRS		45,000	45,000	45,000			135,000
Deductible amount		(27,000)	(27,000)	(27,000)	(27,000)	(27,000)	(135,000)
Total amount taxable							180,000

29.3.5 Research and Development Expenditure

Finance Act 2004 introduced new research and development (R&D) relief sections to replace the previous scheme, which had ceased in 1999. There had been growing calls for a new relief to be introduced over the last number of years due to the low rate of corporation tax in Ireland. Large multinationals, such as drug companies, were locating their R&D units in countries that had high corporation tax rates and generous R&D credits to maximise the tax relief. Ireland's corporation tax rate of 12.5% gave very little incentive to locate an R&D unit here.

The scheme has had minor amendments in each of the years since it was introduced in 2004. Over the years commentators had been calling for it to be widened considerably to make it into a refundable tax credit system, so as to appeal to a greater number of potential companies. The existing scheme did not appeal to a loss making start-up company, as the credit could only be set against taxation. If there was no tax the scheme was of little use. Finance (No. 2) Act 2008 has significantly amended the scheme to introduce a refundable element together with an increase in the credit percentage. The scheme operates as follows:

1. The base year for expenditure for each years claim is 2003. This means that any incremental expenditure in any year in excess of that incurred in 2003 qualifies for the relief. Prior to the Finance Act amendment the base year was set for years 2004 to 2013 as 2003 and would then move on one year subsequently.

2. The relief is calculated by allowing a tax credit of 25% of the qualifying expenditure against the corporation tax liability of the company. Expenditure incurred prior to

1 January 2009 is allowed at 20%. Qualifying expenditure incurred in 2009 of €100,000 would give a corporation tax credit of €25,000, which can be set directly against the corporation tax liability. For expenditure incurred prior to 1 January 2009 any unused credits can be carried forward to future periods. The relief is in addition to the normal deduction for expenditure incurred against Case I income.

For expenditure incurred on or after 1 January 2009 the credit operates as follows:

A. The credit is firstly set against the current periods corporation tax liability.

B. Any excess is then set back against the prior period. The excess is set against the tax liability of prior period(s) of corresponding length, s766 (4A) TCA 97.

C. Any remaining excess is then carried forward. Under s766 (4B) TCA 97 one third of the carry forward will be refunded after the due date of the filing of the corporation tax return for the period in which the R&D claim arose.

D. Any remaining excess is then set against the corporation tax liability of the next accounting period after the R&D claim, subject to allowing the subsequent R&D claim for that period take priority, s766 (4B) TCA 97.

E. Any remaining excess is then halved. The first half is refunded after the due date of the filing of the corporation tax return immediately after the filing of the corporation tax return that gave rise to the original claim. For example if a company made a claim in the year to 31 December 2009, the 50% in question would be refunded after the filing of the 31 December 2010 return, 21 September 2011, s766 (4B) TCA 97.

F. The remaining half is then set against the next periods corporation tax liability, s766 (4B) TCA 97.

Any final remaining excess is refunded after the filing of the second corporation tax return after the corporation tax return that gave rise to the original R&D credit, s766 (4B) TCA 97. In E. above this would be the return for the period ended 31 December 2011. The credit would be refunded after the return was filed on 21 September 2012.

A new section 766B TCA 97 has been introduced to limit any refund payable under s766 (4B) TCA 97

The maximum credit which may be refunded is the greater of:

(A) The total corporation tax paid in all accounting periods for the ten years prior to the period in which s766 (4A) TCA 97 relief is claimed or

(B) The total paye/prsi liability of the company in the period in which the R&D expenditure is incurred.

3. Qualifying expenditure is defined as expenditure incurred in a country of the European Economic Area (EEA) in the relevant year. The expenditure must qualify

for relief in the State and, in the case of an Irish resident company, must not qualify for tax relief outside the State. No relief is available for royalty payments which are exempt in the hands of the recipient.

4. The company claiming the relief must carry on a trade in the State, engage in R&D activities in the period and keep a record of all expenditure incurred.

5. The expenditure must be incurred in the areas of science and technology, and involve research and developmental activities. It must seek to achieve scientific or technological advancement or solutions to scientific or technological uncertainties. Expenditure on R&D buildings is excluded, as it has its own separate relief noted below.

6. The company is entitled to claim credit for any R&D undertaken by a university (in the EEA) on its behalf of up to 5% of the total R&D spend.

7. Relief can be claimed for expenditure incurred prior to the commencement of the company to trade (see paragraph 15.3.4.13 for commentary on pre-trading expenditure).

8. Relief is not available for any expenditure covered by grants.

9. Section 766A TCA 1997 which grants relief for expenditure incurred on an R&D building has also been amended by Finance (No. 2) Act 2008. Up to 31 December 2008 the relief was a 20% credit granted over four years on a straight line basis. To qualify, the company must be entitled to claim industrial buildings capital allowances on the building. The cost of the site is excluded, as is any expenditure covered by grants. The relief will be clawed back if the building is sold or ceases to be used within 10 years. Unlike section 766 TCA 1997, there is no base year or incremental expenditure concept. Therefore all expenditure qualifies.

The previous scheme was too rigid in that the building had to be used exclusively for R&D purposes. According to information released by the Department of Finance in 2008 there had never been a claim under the section.

The new widened conditions are as follows:

A. To be a qualifying building it must be used at least 35% of the time as an R&D building over a 4 year period (from the time it is first brought into use after being built or refurbished).

B. The credit will be 25% of the relevant expenditure. Relevant expenditure is the % of time it is used as an R&D building, which must be at least 35%. For example a building which costs €1,000,000 and is used for 40% of the time over the four year period would have an R&D credit as follows: €1,000,000 × 40% × 25% = €100,000.

C. If the building ceases to be used within 10 years of the commencement of the 4 year period noted in A, the relief is clawed back.

D. Similar claims to those noted in 2 above are available under this section and the refunds are also subject to the limits under s766B TCA 97.

10. EU approval has been granted for these reliefs with the exception of 9 above, which therefore has yet to come into force.

11. In situations were relief will be claimed on plant and machinery, the assets must be used "wholly and exclusively" for R&D. For practical reasons, this is not normally the case as the machinery is usually put to commercial use after the R&D process has finished. It is now open to the company's Inspector of Taxes to determine (presumably after representations from the company) the "just and reasonable" portion of plant and machinery to be allowed in the R&D claim.

"Just and reasonable" is not defined in the legislation.

12. There is also a provision to allow the revision of the R&D claim if the plant and machinery usage differs from that forecasted originally.

13. A further provision allows Revenue to consult external experts to assist in their determinations as to whether the R&D claim meets the legislative requirements. The company must be notified of the identity of the expert and of the information to be given to the expert.

If the company can prove that the disclosure of such information to the expert would be detrimental to its business, then Revenue will not engage the expert. It is then up to Revenue to decide on the claim internally.

14. The claim for the R&D expenditure must be made within 12 months of the end of the accounting period in which the expenditure was incurred. Ideally it would be made with the corporation tax return of the period.

Example 29.5

X Limited incurred qualifying R&D expenditure in 2003 of €250,000. This is the company's base year. The company incurs R&D expenditure of €900,000 in 2009, €1,000,000 in 2010, and €1,100,000 in 2011. Its corporation tax liabilities are as follows:

2008	€50,000
2009	€60,000
2010	€200,000
2011	€80,000
2012	€60,000
2013	€100,000
2014	€110,000

Tax Year	Tax Liability	R&D Credit Offset	
	€	€	
2008	50,000	(b) (50,000)	09
2009	60,000	(a) (60,000)	09
2010	200,000	(d) (187,500)	10
		(e) (12,500)	09
2011	80,000	(g) (80,000)	11
2012	60,000	(j) (60,000)	11
2013	100,000	(l) (14,167)	11
2014	110,000		

R&D Claims & Usage

Tax Year	2009	2010	2011
R&D Claim	650,000	750,000	850,000
Credit × 25%	162,500	187,500	212,500
2009 Offset	(a) (60,000)		
2008 Offset	(b) (50,000)		
2010 Offset	(e) (12,500)	(d) (187,500)	
2011 Offset			(g) (80,000)
2012 Offset			(j) (60,000)
2013 Offset			(l) (14,166) (see note 4)
Credit Refund	(c) (17,500) from 21/9/10 (see note 1)		
	(f) (11,250) from 21/9/11 (see note 2)		(i) (44,167) from 21/9/12 (see note 3)
	(h) (11,250) from 21/9/12 (see note 2)		(k) (14,167) from 21/9/13 (see note 4)

Notes:

Base year is 2003, €250,000

1. €162,500 – €50,000 – €60,000 × 33%

2. €162,500 – €50,000 – €60,000 – €17,500 – €12,500/2

3. €212,500 – €80,000 × 33%

4. €212,500 – €80,000 – €44,167 – €60,000/2

Example 29.6

A company incurred qualifying R&D expenditure in 2009 of €500,000 on an R&D building. The qualifying usage over the next four years is 60%. The relief will be €500,000 × 60% × 25% = €75,000 directly against the corporation tax liability. There is no base cost/year when dealing with R&D buildings.

29.4 Basis of Assessment and Accounting Periods

s27 TCA 97 The purpose of this section is to outline the importance of an accounting period in the context of the charge to corporation tax.

The income tax concept of tax years and the charge to tax of the profits of an accounting period ending in an income tax year does not apply for corporation tax purposes. Similarly, the complicated commencement and cessation rules addressed in Chapter 14 are not relevant. A company is chargeable to corporation tax in respect of its taxable profits for an accounting period irrespective of the income tax year. Thus, a company is chargeable on an "actual basis" in respect of accounting periods rather than in respect of tax years of assessment. The 31 December tax date is NOT relevant for corporation tax (unless it happens to be the company's accounting period end). A number of key features of corporation tax are fixed by reference to accounting periods, e.g., assessments to tax and filing of corporation tax returns (on form CT1), due dates for payment of tax, loss relief claims, etc.

29.4.1 Length of accounting periods

Usually an accounting period for corporation tax purposes corresponds to the company's period of account, i.e., the period for which the company prepares its annual accounts.

However, for tax purposes an accounting period cannot exceed 12 months. If a company's period of account extends beyond this maximum, it will then contain at least two accounting periods; the first will be of 12 months' duration and the second will relate to the remainder of the period. The Revenue Commissioners enforce the legislation strictly in this area and will reject returns that contain periods of longer than 12 months, even if the period is only a small number of days over a year.

The author has personal experience of a company which incorporated and commenced trading on 31 March. The client requested a 31 March annual accounting period end and therefore the first financial statements were prepared for the period 31 March 2000 to 31 March 2001 together with one corporation tax return. The return was rejected by the Inspector of Taxes on the basis that the period exceeded one year. The company was required to prepare returns for the period 31 March 2000 to 30 March 2001 and for the 31st March 2001, a one day period.

The company was loss making in the first period and therefore there was no loss to Revenue, however a strict interpretation of the legislation was applied.

Example 29.7

A company prepares accounts for an 18-month period to 30 June 2009. The corresponding accounting periods used to calculate the CT liability are:

1. *Twelve months to 31 December 2008.*

2. *Six months to 30 June 2009.*

29.4.2 Commencement and cessation of an accounting period

An accounting period commences on the occasion of any of the following:

1. the end of the preceding accounting period;

2. a company commences to carry on a trade;

3. a company becomes resident in the State;

4. a company acquires its first source of income (including interest on deposit);

5. a company commences to be wound up.

An accounting period ceases on the occasion of any of the following:

1. expiration of 12 months from beginning of an accounting period;

2. accounting date of the company;

3. a company beginning or ceasing to trade;

4. a company beginning or ceasing to be within charge to corporation tax in respect of its trade or (if more than one) of all the trades carried on by it;

5. a company beginning or ceasing to be resident in the State;

6. commencement or completion of a winding-up.

Example 29.8

AP Limited was incorporated in Ireland on 1 February 2008. The shareholders, who are also the company directors, subscribed for share capital on 1 April 2008 for cash of €100,000, which was put on deposit. The company commenced trading on 1 July 2008 and made its first set of accounts for a 15-month period to 30 September 2009.

Accounting Period	*Explanation*
1 April to 30 June 2008	*AP Limited acquires a source of income as the cash deposit creates interest income.*
1 July 2008 to 30 June 2009	*AP Limited commences trading. This accounting period extends to the maximum 12-month period allowed.*
1 July 2009 to 30 September 2009	*Accounting date of AP Limited.*

29.4.3 Allocation of profits between accounting periods

Where only one set of financial accounts covers more than one accounting period for tax purposes, profits will need to be allocated between two or more periods. For example, in Example 29.7 above, AP Limited has only one set of accounts for the period from 1 July 2008 to 30 September 2009, which comprises two accounting periods for tax purposes.

s4(6)
TCA 97

In these circumstances, the accounting profits of the "long" period are adjusted in the normal way and the resulting tax-adjusted trading profits of the company are apportioned to the different accounting periods on a time basis, according to the respective lengths of those periods.

Where the corporation tax rate changes during the accounting period identified for tax purposes, it may be necessary to again time apportion to the profits of that period to determine the income chargeable at each rate, or alternatively, to calculate a single effective rate for the period as a whole.

Example 29.9

Converse Limited commenced to trade on 1 December 2002 as a retail unit. The directors of the company decided on a December year-end for stock-taking purposes and made up accounts from the date of commencement to 31 December 2003, a period of 13 months.

Extracts from the accounts are as follows:

	€
Profit before tax	*50,000*
Included in the accounts are the following:	
General provision for obsolete stock	*5,000*
Pension accrual (paid in March 2004)	*4,000*

The provision for obsolete stock would not be allowable (as it is general in nature). The pension accrual is also not allowable as pension contributions are only allowed on a paid basis. Therefore for tax purposes, these amounts are added back and taxable Case I amounts to €59,000. As this income was earned in a period of more than 12 months in duration, it is necessary to make two tax returns.

The first return is for the first 12 months: 1 December 2002 to 30 November 2003. Case I for this period is €59,000 × 12/13 = €54,462.

The second return is for the period after the first 12 months and ending on the company's chosen period end: 1 December 2003 to 31 December 2003. Case I for this period is €59,000 × 1/13 = €4,538.

The rates of corporation tax chargeable on the company depend on the rates in force during the period. For the period 1 December 2001 to 30 November, the effective rate is as follows:

1 December 2002 to 31 December 2002 = 1 month 16% × 1/12 = 1.33%

1 January 2003 to 30 November 2003 = 11 months 12.5% × 11/12 = 14.46%

Therefore the company is taxed at 12.79% for this accounting period.

For the second period the company is taxed at 12.5%, as this was the rate in force during the period 1 December 2002 to 31 December 2003.

The legislation specifically provides that the tax-adjusted Case I income figure should be split on a time basis in the manner described above, notwithstanding that the company may have management accounting information at its disposal, which would allow the figure to be split on an actual basis.

Example 29.10

Rocky Road Limited normally prepares accounts to 30 June but, resulting from its decision to change this accounting period to 30 September, it prepares financial statements for the 15 months to 30 September 2008. Since the company is accustomed to a 30 June year-end, it may provide actual results both for the 12 months to 30 June 2008 and for the balance of the three months to 30 September 2008. This "actual" split should NOT be used as s4(6) TCA 97, tells us we must apportion on a time basis. We must therefore disregard the two distinct accounting periods and split the total 15-month adjusted Case I profits, etc., on a time basis, i.e., 12:3.

Not all items are allocated on a time-apportioned basis. While trading profits, as adjusted for tax purposes, are time apportioned, the legislation provides that other items, such as other sources of income, capital allowances, charges and chargeable gains, should be allocated to the specific period in which they actually arise. In this regard, readers are referred to the analyses in 29.4.4, 29.5 and 29.6 below.

29.4.4 Capital allowances in a corporation tax context

As already emphasised at 29.3.3 above, companies must calculate a separate capital allowance claim for each accounting period. Where an accounting period is shorter than 12 months in duration, the wear and tear allowance otherwise available is reduced proportionately.

Example 29.11

Converse Limited commenced to trade on 1 December 2008 as a retail unit. The directors of the company decided on a December year-end for stock-taking purposes and made up accounts from the date of commencement to 31 December 2009, a period of 13 months.

It purchased qualifying plant on 17 December 2008 for €10,000 and also purchased further plant in November 2009 for €5,000. In December 2009, it purchased qualifying plant for €6,000. All purchases were put in use immediately.

It is necessary to calculate two capital allowance claims as there are two accounting periods for tax purposes and it is necessary to time-apportion any claim relating to a period of less than 12 months in duration.

Income as calculated is €54,462 for the year ended 30 November 2009 and €4,538 for the month of December 2009.

	€
Tax Written Down Value 1 December 2008 – commencement date	*Nil*
Additions (1 December 2008 to 30 November 2009)	*15,000*
Wear and tear (1 December 2008 to 30 November 2009) (Note 1)	*(1,875)*
TWDV 30 November 2009	*13,125*
Additions (1 December 2009 to 31 December 2009)	*6,000*
Wear and tear (1 December 2009 to 31 December 2009) (Note 2)	*(219)*
TWDV 31 December 2009	*18,906*

Note 1:

€15,000 × 12.5% = €1,875

The company is entitled to deduct €1,875 from its income of €54,462 to arrive at taxable income of €52,587. It is important to note that even though the second purchase of plant was made in the last month of the period, a full year's allowance is granted as the asset was in use at the end of the period. No wear and tear is available in this period in respect of the plant purchased for €6,000 in the later period.

Note 2:

(€15,000 + €6,000) × 12.5% × 1/12 = €219.

The claim is time-apportioned as the period of account is of less than 12 months in duration.

29.5 Other Sources of Income

The purpose of this section is to explain how taxable income under Cases III, IV and V is calculated for corporation tax purposes. Unlike trading income, which is apportioned on a time basis, each of the cases listed below is computed on an actual basis. Therefore, in the case of an 18-month set of accounts which contains interest income, it will be necessary to ascertain the actual interest received in each period to arrive at the taxable income for each period.

In general, these other sources of income taxable under Cases III, IV and V will constitute some form of investment income and accordingly, will be classified as "passive income" and will be liable to tax at 25% in 2009.

29.5.1 Case III income

Included in this case is foreign income and gross interest received from banks, i.e., interest income received without deduction of deposit interest retention tax (DIRT).

Foreign income includes trading income, dividends and rents. Whether the trade should be taxed under Case I or Case III depends on the level of independence the foreign trade has from the Irish company. Case law precedent would suggest that if the foreign trade is managed or controlled from the State, it should be taxed under Case I, whereas if the trade is carried on entirely abroad, it should be taxed under Case III. Any income from the foreign trade included in the accounts of the main company should be deducted from the taxable income and taxed under Case III. Similarly any expenses should be added back in the main Case I computation and deducted against the Case III trade.

Up to Finance Act 2008, dividends from foreign companies received by an Irish company were automatically taxable under Case III, as opposed to dividends received from Irish companies, which were exempt. As a result of the FII Group Litigation Case (C-446/04) certain dividends received by Irish companies from EU/Tax Treaty resident companies will be taxed at trading rates (12.5%) rather than Case III (25%), the legislation is contained in s21B TCA 97. While a detailed discussion of the new legislation is beyond the scope of this publication, broadly speaking, when a foreign qualifying company, whose trading profits account for more than 75% of its total profits pays a dividend to an Irish company, that dividend is taxed at 12.5%.

For Irish companies whose ownership is less than 5%, the 12.5% rate will always apply regardless of the source of the foreign company's profits.

There are provisions for reviewing the 75% limit through an entire chain of companies.

The legislation is effective from 1 January 2007. (Dividends received on or after 31 January 2008)

The FII Group Litigation Case was originally a challenge to the UK system. Their system was very similar to Irish legislation and the case challenged the UK legislation on the basis that it was incompatible with EU freedom of establishment and free movement of capital.

The European Court of Justice found that if the ultimate tax on the foreign dividend after taking into account relief for the underlying taxes paid on the foreign company profits and withholding tax is no higher than the rate charged on the domestic dividend, the UK legislation would not breach EU law.

The Court did not clarify what they determined the rate on the domestic dividend to actually be, the actual domestic charge (0%) or inclusive of the underlying UK corporation tax charge (30%). It referred this matter back to the UK High Court, who found that the UK rules were incompatible with the freedom of establishment under the EU Treaty and were therefore invalid.

Foreign rents are taxed under Case III, unlike rent from property in the State, which is taxed under Case V.

Irish companies are entitled to receive interest on bank deposits and similar investments without deduction of DIRT. Section 256 TCA 97 grants an exemption from the DIRT requirements in the case of qualifying companies who make the necessary application. This ensures that deposit interest paid to such companies is not subject to DIRT. However, the interest is still fully liable to corporation tax under Case III, as no tax is deducted at source. To avail of the DIRT exemption, the investing company must file the necessary "DIRT-free declaration" and must furnish the relevant deposit-taker with its tax reference number.

Companies are only taxable on the actual interest received in the period, therefore any interest receivable accrued in the accounts should be deducted and taxed in the period in which it is actually received.

29.5.2 Case IV income

The main charge to tax under Case IV is interest received after deduction of DIRT. As noted above, companies who make the necessary declaration can have the interest paid to them without deduction of DIRT at source. However, even if a company suffers DIRT at source, the amount deducted will be credited against its overall corporation tax liability and any excess will be refunded. DIRT is non-refundable in the case of most individuals. As the interest under Case IV is paid net of DIRT (at a deduction rate of 25% from 8th April 2009, previously 23% from 1st January 2009 to 7th April 2009, and 20% prior to that) it will be necessary to re-gross the income for the Case IV computation.

Example 29.12

X Ltd receives €75 (net of DIRT) in August 2009 for the year ended 31 December 2009. In the corporation tax computation, the €75 will be deducted from the taxable Case I income and re-grossed (€75/75%) to €100 and charged to tax under Case IV. The DIRT suffered of €25 is credited against the company's total tax liability.

29.5.3 Case V income

A charge to corporation tax arises where a company receives rental income from Irish property and receipts from easements. Therefore, the following types of income are assessable under Case V of Schedule D:

- Rents in respect of any premises or lands in the Republic of Ireland, i.e., offices, shops, factories, land, etc.;

- Receipts in respect of an easement, i.e., any right, privilege or benefit in, over or derived from a premises, e.g., a right of way;

- Certain premiums received for the granting of a lease.

It is important to note that rental income derived from **foreign** property is assessable under Case III of Schedule D as foreign income.

Case V is assessed on the full amount of rental income receivable in an accounting period. Thus, if a company is entitled to receive rental income in the accounting period ended 31 December 2009, the income will be assessed on the company for that accounting period, even if the income was not received in the period.

The relevant date to create a commencement of a source of rental income for a company is the date on which income first **arises** from the Case V source and not when the Case V source is acquired. Income "arises" to the company when it becomes **entitled** to receive such rents, even though the income may not necessarily be received as yet.

The relevant date to trigger a cessation of a source of rental income for a company is the date on which the **source** is disposed of and not the date on which the income ceases. Thus, there is no cessation where a source continues to exist but does not produce income in a particular accounting period.

Capital allowances are available to companies who acquire and fit out certain properties. Depending on the tenants, allowances are available for the renting of industrial buildings or for the fit-out of residential properties. These are discussed in Chapter 18.

Each property should be dealt with separately and a computation done for each premises.

In the main computation any rental income received should be deducted from the taxable Case I income and any rental expenses should be added back and deducted from the gross rental income to arrive at the taxable Case V income. The main rental expenses allowable are covered in Chapter 18.

29.6   Chargeable Gains and Losses

As noted above, corporation tax is a tax on the PROFITS of a company which arise in a specific accounting period, while income tax taxes individuals on their INCOME in a year of assessment.

Profits in the context of a company mean income (trade, professional, interest, foreign, rental, etc.) plus chargeable gains. Therefore, any capital gains generated by a company in an accounting period will be subject to corporation tax and NOT capital gains tax as is the case for individuals. There are two exceptions to this principle:

(a) Development land gains are subject to capital gains tax (CGT).

(b) Disposals of non-trading assets by a foreign company in Ireland are subject to CGT.

A chargeable gain/loss arises for tax purposes when a company sells assets held for the purposes of its trade or held as investments.

The accounting profit or loss on the disposal of the asset is not included in the corporation tax computation as the profit/loss shown will be for accountancy purposes only. Therefore, it should be deducted/added back (depending on whether it is a profit or loss) for the purposes of calculating tax-adjusted Case I/II. A separate calculation of the capital gain/loss must be computed in accordance with CGT rules. Unutilised capital losses incurred in previous accounting periods can be carried forward and offset against current capital gains less current capital losses. The net gain is eventually taxed using the applicable CGT rate, currently 25% (22% from 15th October 2008 to 7th April 2009, prior to that it was 20%). However, as the gain is taken into the corporation tax computation and taxed at the standard corporation tax rate, it must be adjusted so as to give the correct CGT liability when taxed at 12.5% (standard corporation tax rate). This figure represents the "Adjusted Chargeable Gain" which must be included in the corporation tax computation to arrive at the company's total taxable profits for the accounting period.

It is important to reiterate that the only gains, which are not taken into the corporation tax computation, are development land gains and certain gains accruing to foreign companies. These gains are always calculated separately and the resultant liability is paid as capital gains tax and not as corporation tax.

Example 29.13

Company A acquired a premises in October 1990 for €100,000. This was subsequently sold in August 2009 for €273,000. The accounting profit on disposal shown in the profit and loss account is €173,000. A Ltd prepares accounts to 31 December 2009.

1. *Deduct the profit on disposal of €173,000 from "profit before tax" in the computation of tax-adjusted Case I income.*

2. *Calculate the capital gain on the disposal in the tax year to 31 December 2009.*

		€
Sales proceeds		*273,000*
Less cost of acquisition		
October 1990	*100,000*	
Indexed @ 1.442	=	*(144,200)*
		128,800
Less capital losses (current and brought forward)		*Nil*
		128,800

3. *The CGT on this capital gain is:*

   €128,800 × 25% = €32,200.

4. *The chargeable gain required to give a tax liability of €32,200, using the CT rate of 12.5% (applicable in 2009) is as follows:*

   $$€128,800 \times \frac{25\%}{12.5\%} = €257,600$$

5. *Therefore, the amount of €257,600 is included as a chargeable gain in the company's corporation tax computation. Taxed at the standard rate of 12.5% this will give tax payable of €32,200.*

Example 29.14

B Limited acquired the freehold interest in a factory in January 1984 for €75,000. It subsequently sold this factory on 20 December 2009 for €350,000. The accounting profit on the disposal of this fixed asset shown in the profit and loss account is €311,000. B Limited prepares its accounts to 31 December each year. Assess the tax implications of this transaction for B Limited.

1. *The profit of the disposal of the building of €311,000 must be deducted from the profit per the accounts in the Case I tax-adjusted profit computation.*

2. The capital gain on disposal in the tax year ended 31 December 2009 is as follows:

	€
Sales proceeds	350,000
Less cost of acquisition	
€75,000 × 2.003	(150,225)
Capital gain	199,775

3   The CGT on this capital gain is €199,775 × 25% = €49,944.

4   The chargeable gain required to give a tax liability of €49,944 using the CT rate ruling of 12.5% is as follows:

$$€199,775 \quad \times \quad \frac{25\%}{12.5\%} \quad = \quad €399,550$$

5. Therefore, €399,550 is included as a chargeable gain in B Limited's corporation tax computation for the accounting period ended 31 December 2009.

29.6.1   Restriction of chargeable losses by capital allowances

Losses on the disposal of trade assets are always restricted by capital allowances claimed during ownership. This ensures that the loss arising cannot be relieved twice, i.e., once under the capital allowances system and again under the CGT rules.

Example 29.15

A Limited sold plant in March 2009 for €10,000. It had purchased this in January 2006 for €30,000. For CGT purposes, there is an apparent loss as follows:

	€
Sales proceeds	10,000
Cost	(30,000)
Loss	20,000

The capital allowances claimed during the period of ownership are as follows:

	€
Cost in January 2006	30,000
W&T × 12.5% 2006	(3,750)
W&T × 12.5% 2007	(3,750)
W&T × 12.5% 2008	(3,750)
TWDV 1/1/2009	18,750
Sales proceeds	(10,000)
Balancing allowance	8,750

Total capital allowances and balancing allowance for the plant is €20,000. This is set against the loss of €20,000 thereby reducing it to nil.

Gains on the disposal of trade assets are not restricted by capital allowances previously granted. This is the case because in general, any such capital allowances previously granted are clawed back on disposal by way of a balancing charge.

29.7 Corporation Tax Exemption for Start-Up Companies

29.7.1 In an attempt to encourage economic activity in these recessionary times Finance (No. 2) Act 2008 introduced a relief from certain taxes for new start-up companies. Ireland has always had a very high proportion of small businesses and it is hoped that this new incentive can encourage more activity in this sector.

The intention of the relief is straight forward. If the corporation tax of the company in any one year is equal to or lower than €40,000 and the trade is a qualifying trade, the company is exempt from corporation tax in that year. The complications begin when the company has other income or more than one trade etc.

The legislation is contained in s486C TCA 97 and operates as follows:

1. The company must be incorporated within the EEA and can only have been in existence from 14 October 2008.

2. The trade can only have commenced on or after 1 January 2009, any relief will apply for the three years from the date of commencement.

3. The relief is available for income of a qualifying trade and gains on the sale of trade assets from that qualifying trade. A qualifying trade is a trade which is NOT one of the following:

   A. A trade that was carried on previously by another person (this rules out sole traders incorporating their trade into a limited company).

   B. An existing trade (this rules out forming a new company and acquiring a new trade).

   C. An excepted trade (see 28.7.2).

   D. A trade which would come within the s441 TCA 97 close company surcharge, a service company (see 33.4.3).

4. The company's Total Corporation Tax for the period must be equal to or lower than €40,000. Total Corporation Tax is defined as all corporation tax that is chargeable for the period but excluding income tax. Therefore it would include corporation tax on passive income and the close company surcharge but exclude income tax withheld, for example from a patent royalty payable under s239 TCA 97.

5. If the company transfers part of its qualifying trade to another connected company the relief will be unavailable to both companies. This is anti-avoidance legislation to prevent companies sharing income to avail of the €40,000 limit in group situations, where there has not been a genuine company incorporation to commence a new trade.

6. To quantify the relief available the company must calculate its Relevant Corporation Tax. Relevant Corporation Tax is Total Corporation Tax as calculated above less the following:

A. Tax on income at the 25% corporation tax rate

B. Close company surcharges

C. Tax on chargeable gains

7. The legislation requires that amounts which can be set against total profits (income and chargeable gains), typically expenses of management and non-relevant trading charges, must be set against income in priority to chargeable gains. Whilst this would be the most common approach in an ordinary situation, the taxpayer does have the option of offsetting against a chargeable asset in priority to income, however this option is now not available if a claim is being made under this legislation.

8. The Relevant Corporation Tax is then applied to the qualifying trade income over total income (defined as total income excluding income charged at the 25% corporation tax rate, essentially trade income). This will then give the amount to be deducted from the corporation tax charge.

9. The relief for the disposal of qualifying trade assets (assets used directly in the operation of the qualifying trade, including goodwill) is operated in the same method as Relevant Corporation Tax at 8 above. The corporation tax on chargeable gains is applied to net gains (profits less losses) on qualifying assets over net gains on all chargeable assets. This amount is then deducted from the corporation tax payable.

No relief is available for assets transferred under s617 TCA 97 (see 32.4.3).

29.7.2   Marginal Relief

As noted in 29.7.1 above the full exemption from corporation tax on the qualifying trade is only available if the Total Corporation Tax is equal to or lower than €40,000.

Marginal relief is available if the Total Corporation Tax is between €40,000 and €60,000. The corporation tax chargeable is reduced by an amount calculated by the following formula:

$3 \times (T{-}M) \times (A{+}B)/T$

The letters signify the following amounts:

T = Total Corporation Tax (see 29.7.1 above)

M = €40,000

A = Corporation Tax on the Qualifying Trade (see 29.7.1 above)

B = Corporation Tax on the disposal of Qualifying Assets of the Qualifying Trade (see 29.7.1 above)

29.7.3   Commencement of the relief

S. 486C TCA 97 will not commence until confirmation is received by the Minister for Finance that EU approval is not required.

Example 29.16

Newco Ltd commenced trading on 1st January 2009. Mr. A. incorporated his architectural practice which had been trading for many years and opened a new café.

Calculation of Corporation Tax Liability:

	€
Case I – Café	50,000
Trade Charges	(5,000)
Case II – Architect	40,000
Case V – Rent	10,000
Income:	95,000
Chargeable gain on shares	15,000
Non-Trade Charges	(7,000)
Profits	103,000
Case I: 50,000 – 5,000 × 12.5%	5,625
Case II: 40,000 × 12.5%	5,000
Gain 15,000 × 12.5%	1,875
Passive 10,000 – 7,000 × 25%	750
S.239 TCA 97 5,000 × 20%	1,000
Tax Payable	14,250
Relief (Note 1)	(5,625)
Relief (Note 2)	(0)
	8,625

Calculation of Relief:

Total Corporation Tax = €14,250 – €1,000 = €13,250. As total corporation tax is less than €40,000, relief is available.

Relevant Corporation Tax = €13,250 – €750 – (€15,000 × 12.5%) = €10,625, (this is €85,000 of net trading income × 12.5%).

Note 1

$$\text{Relevant Corporation Tax } €10,625 \times \frac{50,000 - 5,000}{50,000 + 40,000 - 5,000} = 5,625$$

Note 2

$$€15,000 \times 12.5\% = €1875 \quad \frac{0}{15,000} = 0$$

Example 29.17

NewCo Ltd commences trading on the 1 January 2009. Its Total Corporation liability for the year ended 31 December 2009 is €53,000. The charge can be analysed as follows:

Tax on qualifying trade - €25,000

Tax on rental income -   €20,000

Tax on qualifying assets sales €8,000

As the total corporation tax is in excess of €40,000 it cannot claim the full exemption. However, as the Total Corporation Tax is lower than €60,000 marginal relief applies as follows:

3 × (€53,000 - €40,000) × (€25,000 + €8,000)/€53,000 = €24,283.

This amount is deducted from the total tax payable of €53,000 leaving a net liability of €28,717.

29.8   Manufacturing Relief

29.8.1   Introduction

P+14 TCA 97 Manufacturing relief is relief from corporation tax in respect of income from the manufacture and deemed manufacture of goods in the State. The relief takes the form of reducing the rate of corporation tax to 10%. A general rate of 12.5% for trading profits applies since 1 January 2003 (see Chapter 28), a side-effect of which results in the phasing out of the 10% rate.

In general terms, it may be said that the relief applies to income from manufacturing or deemed manufacturing arising in the period 1 January 1981 to 31 December 2010, although for special trading houses, the relief expired on 31 December 2000 and for Shannon activities and Custom House Dock activities, the relief ceased on 31 December 2005. The 10% rate ceased to apply to shipping trades from 1 January 2001. New manufacturing projects established after 22 July 1998 were eligible for the 10% rate until 31 December 2002. From 1 January 2003, new projects are liable at the 12.5% rate.

As the relief only applies to companies who commenced to trade before 23 July 1998 and will cease on 31 December 2010 a detailed discussion of the availability of the relief and the mechanism for calculating it is outside the scope of this publication. The activities that qualified for the relief are listed in s443 TCA 97.

29.9   Method of Calculating the Relief

29.9.1   General

s448 TCA 97 There is no actual rate of 10%. The legislation provides that the normal corporation tax is reduced by the appropriate fraction to leave a 10% charge on the appropriate income. For example, with the standard corporation tax rate at 24% for the year 2000, the fraction to reduce to 10% is 7/12 (14/24). For the year 2001, with the standard corporation tax rate at 20% the fraction was ½. From the year 2003, with the standard rate of corporation tax at 12.5%, the fraction is 1/5 (2.5/12.5).

The Manufacturing Relief Formula

The formula sets out to:

(a) identify that portion of the company's corporation tax on income that is related to its manufacturing activity; and

(b) reduce that element of the corporation tax liability to an effective rate of 10%.

In other words, the figure for manufacturing relief is the difference between taxing the company's manufacturing income at 12.5%, the standard corporation tax rate, and taxing it at 10%.

The full formula is as follows:

$$\text{Corporation tax on trading income} \times \frac{\text{Case I Manufacturing income (1)} - \text{Manufacturing charges and losses (2)}}{\text{Total trading income less manufacturing charges and losses}} \times \frac{1}{5}$$

(1) If the company is involved in sales of own manufactured goods and sales of merchandise (goods purchased for direct resale), then the Case I Manufacturing is extracted as follows:

$$\text{Case I income} \times \frac{\text{Turnover (sales) of own manufactured goods}}{\text{Total turnover from own goods and purchased goods}}$$

(2) Where charges relate to both the manufacturing and non-manufacturing trade, the manufacturing charges are extracted as follows:

$$\text{Trading charges} \times \frac{\text{Turnover (sales) of own manufactured goods}}{\text{Total turnover from own goods and purchased goods}}$$

Example 29.18

A Limited is a manufacturing company which had the following results for the year ended 31 December 2009:

	€
Trading income (80% of turnover derives from manufacturing)	*250,000*
Charges on trade income paid	*15,000*

The company's manufacturing income and manufacturing trade charges are calculated as follows:

Manufacturing income:

$$\text{Trading income} \times \frac{\text{Turnover from manufactured goods}}{\text{Total turnover}}$$

$$= \text{€250,000} \times 80\% = \text{€200,000}$$

Manufacturing charges:

$$\text{Trading charges} \times \frac{\text{Manfacturing charges}}{\text{Trade charges}}$$

$$= \text{€15,000} \times 80\% = \text{€12,000}$$

The company's final Corporation Tax liability is calculated as follows:

Corporation Tax

		€
Case I		250,000
Less relevant trade charges		(15,000)
		235,000
Trading income	€235,000 @ 12.5%	29,375

Manufacturing relief:

$$\text{€ } 29,375 \times \frac{\text{€200,000} - \text{€12,000}}{\text{€250,000} - \text{€12,000}} \times \frac{1}{5} = \quad \frac{(\text{€4,641})}{\text{€24,734}}$$

WHAT YOU SHOULD NOW KNOW

On completion of this chapter, you should be able to:

- ✓ Describe the differences between the adjusted profits calculation for a sole trader and for a limited company - Volume 2 Assignment 29.1.

- ✓ Calculate the tax-adjusted Case I figure for a company - Volume 2 Q 29.1, Revision Q CT1, CT2.

- ✓ Identify a period of account for corporation tax purposes - Volume 2 Q 29.1, 29.4, Assignment 29.2.

- ✓ Calculate the capital allowance claim for a company - Volume 2 Q 29.1.

- ✓ Identify the period of account in which various sources of income are taxable. Volume 2 Q 29.1.

- ✓ Calculate the adjusted chargeable gain of a company - Volume 2 Q 29.3.

- ✓ Calculate the corporation tax liability of a company - Volume 2 Q 29.1, 29.2.

- ✓ Compute an R&D credit/refund claim – Volume 2 Assignment 29.3

- ✓ Claim exemption for a qualifying trade in a start-up company

- ✓ Calculate manufacturing relief and be aware of its expiry dates – Volume 2 Revision Q CT1

- ✓ Complete Questions and the Assignments in Irish Taxation Law and Practice, Volume 2.

Appendix I

Pro forma Corporation Tax Computation

Corporation tax computation for the twelve-month accounting period to 31/12/2009

	€	€
Case I		
Tax-adjusted trading profits y/e 31/12/2009 after capital allowances	X	
Less Allowable Case I losses forward	(X)	
Trade losses – current period and carried back	(X)	
Allowable trade charges	$\underline{(X)}$	X
Case III		
Foreign source income (trade/rental, etc.)	X	
Interest on Irish Government securities	X	
Foreign bond deposit interest	X	
Irish building society interest	X	
Irish commercial bank deposit interest	$\underline{X}$	X
Case IV		
Income subject to Irish tax at source	$\underline{X}$	X
Case V		
Income from the letting of property in the Republic of Ireland	X	
Less capital allowances	$\underline{(X)}$	X
Total income		X
Chargeable gains (as adjusted)		$\underline{X}$
"Total profits" = income + chargeable gains		X
Deduct Allowable non-trade charges paid during y/e 31/12/2009		(X)
Other losses, i.e., excess capital allowances		$\underline{(X)}$
Profits liable to corporation tax		$\underline{\underline{X}}$
Corporation tax liability		
Charge at appropriate rate (12.5%, 25%, etc.)		$\underline{X}$
		X
Deduct Trade charges and losses on a value basis		(X)
Add Close company surcharges from previous period		X
Income tax deducted by Company Limited on annual payments		X
Deduct Income tax suffered by deduction		(X)
Withholding tax for professional services		$\underline{(X)}$
R&D tax credit		
Net corporation tax liability payable		$\underline{\underline{X}}$

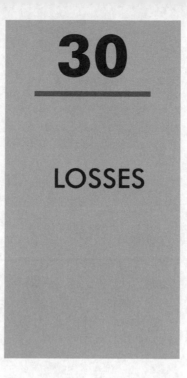

30

LOSSES

In this chapter, you will deal with the following:

- Changes introduced since Finance Act 2001 to date regarding the treatment of Case I/II losses

- The utilisation of Case I/II losses as allowances and as credits on a value basis

- The utilisation of manufacturing losses

- The utilisation of trade and non-trade charges

- The order of set-off under the various Case I/II loss provisions

- Treatment of non-trade losses

- Restriction of losses on late filing

30.1   Introduction

This chapter will consider how losses incurred by a company may be used by it against any other sources of income, either in its current accounting period, its previous accounting period or future accounting periods. Certain losses may also be surrendered to a fellow group or consortium member and this is discussed in greater detail in Chapter 31.

As with profits, obviously losses may arise under various Cases (see chart below which illustrates the various categories of losses that may arise). The manner in which losses are utilised depends on the Case from which they are derived.

Summary Chart

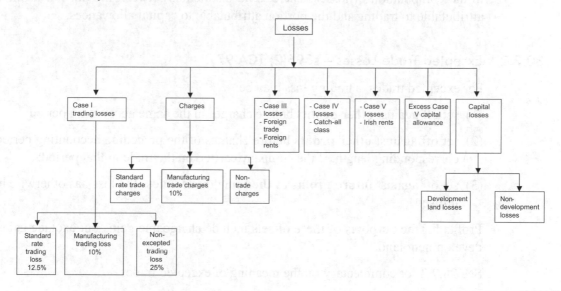

* You will note that the separation of Losses/Charges into different categories is a function of the rate at which the Losses/Charges are taxed, or the manner in which the Losses/Charges are calculated.

30.2   Categorisation of Losses

The main focus of this chapter is the current use of trading losses. Since the introduction of the standard 12.5% rate, and the 25% rate for "excepted" trades, a subsequent series of legislative amendments has made what used to be relatively straightforward loss relief provisions very complex. The 25% rate was introduced in 2000 with a phased introduction of a 12.5% rate for trading income. This disparity in the rates meant that losses could effectively be relieved at a rate which was 50% higher than the rate at which profits of the same trade would be taxed.

The first part of this chapter considers the use of trading losses. The "old rules" for claiming loss relief are first considered, and the new legislative amendments are then examined. The second part of the chapter focuses on non-trade losses. The final section discusses the impact of late filing on losses.

30.3 Trading Losses – Case I

30.3.1 Computation

Trading losses are computed using the same rules as for trading profits, i.e., under the rules of Schedule D Case I. Capital allowances of a company are treated as a trading expense deductible in arriving at Case I profit, and hence are automatically included in the computation of losses. There is no distinction between the portion of the loss attributable to trading and the portion attributable to capital allowances.

30.3.2 Excepted Trade Losses – s396(2) TCA 97

For excepted trades, a trading loss may be:

(1) set off against **other profits** before charges in the same accounting period;

(2) set off against **other profits** before charges of the preceding accounting period of corresponding length, if the company carried on the trade in that period;

(3) set off against **future profits of the same trade** unless the loss has otherwise been utilised.

Profits for the purposes of these offsets include chargeable gains but exclude gains on development land.

See 28.7.2 for commentary on the meaning of excepted trades.

30.3.3 Loss relief – Relevant Trades

There are three important terms concerning general trade losses:

1. relevant trading income;

2. relevant trading loss;

3. relevant trading charge.

Relevant trading income

This is a company's trading income (both 10% and standard rate income) other than income from "excepted trades" (see 30.3.2) and Case III income, i.e., income from foreign trades. The definition excludes passive income.

Income from excepted trades includes income from dealing in or developing land, (excluding construction activities), working minerals or operating mines, petroleum activities including exploration, extraction activities and exploitation of such rights.

Relevant trading loss

This is a loss incurred in a company apart from losses of excepted trades (see 30.3.2). It includes 10% and non-10% trade losses, effectively 12.5% losses from January 2003.

The only factor that readers need to bear in mind is that 10% trade losses are only available against 10% income up to 1 January 2003, after which date they may be offset against 12.5% income, see paragraph 30.5 below.

Relevant trading charge

These are charges on income paid by a company which are incurred wholly and exclusively for the purposes of a trade, again excluding charges paid for excepted trades. They include charges paid against 10% income, but s454 TCA 97 restricts the offset of 10% charges against 10% income up to 31 December 2002, after which they may be offset against standard rate income.

30.3.3.1 Set-off of trade losses against other income

s396A TCA 97 Under s396A TCA 97 losses incurred in a trade, the income from which is taxable at the standard corporation tax rate, may be set sideways in the current accounting period or back to the previous accounting period of the same length, but only against "relevant" trading income, i.e., trading income other than income taxable at the 25% rate, which includes income from "excepted trades" and investment income.

The following example illustrates how relief may be claimed under s396A TCA 97.

Example 30.1

Loss Limited's results for the last two accounting periods are as follows:

	Year ended 31/12/2008	Year ended 31/12/2009
	€	€
Case I (Trade 1)	50,000	(800,000)
Case I (Trade 2)	25,000	50,000
Case III	5,000	2,000
Case V	7,000	4,000

The s396A relief would operate as follows:

Corporation Tax computation for year ended 31/12/2009:

	€
Case I (Trade 1)	Nil
Case I (Trade 2)	50,000
s396A	(50,000)
Trading income	–
Case III	2,000
Case V	4,000
Total income	6,000

Corporation Tax computation for period ended 31/12/2008:

	€
Case I (Trade 1)	50,000
Case I (Trade 2)	25,000
s396A	(75,000)
Trading income	–
Case III	5,000
Case V	7,000
Taxable income	12,000

The company can carry the trade loss incurred in 2009 back against the corresponding previous period (12 months) and set €75,000 of its 2009 trade loss against its 2008 trade income. This leaves €675,000 of unutilised trade losses.

In the above example, after utilising s396A the company has €675,000 of losses available for relief under s396B (see 30.3.3.2) and s396(1) (see 30.3.3.3)

The length of the preceding period against which the loss may be set off is a period equal in length to the current accounting period in which the loss is incurred. For more complex examples involving accounting periods of less than 12 months in duration, readers are referred to paragraph 30.3.4 below.

30.3.3.2 Set-off of trade losses against non-trade profits

s396B TCA 97 Where a company has unutilised losses after claiming s396A TCA 97, these losses may be offset on a value basis, against income for the current accounting period and the previous accounting period of the same length. The value of the losses is computed by applying the tax rate in the year the loss **arises** and not the rate applicable in the year in which the losses are used. The losses are then given as a credit against corporation tax. For example, if a 2003 loss is being carried back to 2002, the credit given is at the rate of 12.5% and not 16%.

Loss relief under s396B, i.e., trading losses on a value basis, will only be granted to the extent that losses may not be relieved under other provisions. Accordingly, claims for loss relief under s396B may only be made when maximum loss relief has been claimed under s396A. The practical effect of this is that trading losses are first restricted for offset against trading income and if there is an excess unused amount of losses, they may be set against the corporation tax payable on other income by way of a credit on a value basis.

The legislation provides a formula to calculate the value of loss relief and also to calculate the amount of losses as a credit.

Formula for calculating value of loss available:

$$L \times \frac{R}{100}$$

where:

L = the amount of the relevant trading loss, and

R = the rate of corporation tax for the accounting period in which the loss arises.

Formula for calculating gross loss used as credit:

$$T \times \frac{100}{R}$$

where:

T is the tax saved, and

R is the rate of corporation tax for the accounting period in which the loss arises.

R may be a composite rate if the accounting period spans two periods. For example, for the accounting year ended 31 March 2003,

$$R = \left(16\% \times \frac{275}{365}\right) + \left(12.5\% \times \frac{90}{365}\right) = 15.13\%.$$

The position is best illustrated by examining the s396B claim that would apply in the case of Loss Limited in Example 30.1 above.

Example 30.2

Loss Limited's results for the last two accounting periods are as follows:

	Year ended 31/12/2008	*Year ended 31/12/2009*
	€	*€*
Case I	*50,000*	*(800,000)*
Case I (Trade 2)	*25,000*	*50,000*
Case III	*5,000*	*2,000*
Case V	*7,000*	*4,000*

The s396B relief would operate after the utilisation of the s396A relief as follows (numbers in bold signify order of use of losses):

Corporation Tax computation for year ended 31/12/2009

		€
Case I (Trade 1)		*Nil*
Case I (Trade 2)		*50,000*
s396A	*(1)*	*(50,000)*
		—
Case III		*2,000*
Case V		*4,000*
Total income		*6,000*
Corporation tax €6,000 × 25%		*1,500*
s396B credit €12,000* × 12.5%	*(3)*	*(1,500)*
Tax payable		

*€1,500 / 12.5% = €12,000.

Corporation tax computation for period ended 31/12/2008

		€
Case I (Trade 1)		50,000
Case I (Trade 2)		25,000
s396A	(2)	(75,000)
Trade income		–
Case III		5,000
Case V		7,000
Total income		12,000
Corporation tax €12,000 × 25%		3,000
s396B credit €24,000** × 12.5%	(4)	(3,000)
Tax payable		=

**€3,000 / 12.5% = €24,000.

Loss Table	€
Trading loss 31 December 2009	800,000
s396A claim 31 December 2009 (1)	(50,000)
s396A claim 31 December 2008 (2)	(75,000)
s396B claim 31 December 2009 (3)	(12,000)
s396B claim 31 December 2008 (4)	(24,000)
Loss available for carry forward	639,000

30.3.3.3 Carry forward of losses

S396(1)   Unrelieved trading losses may be carried forward for set-off against the trading income of the same trade in which the loss was incurred. A claim to carry forward a loss for set-off in succeeding accounting periods against income from the same trade may be made provided relief has not been claimed for an earlier year, i.e., under s396A or s396B. There is no time limit for making such a claim and the loss can be carried forward indefinitely provided the company continues to carry on the same trade. A loss forward must be set off against the first available income of the same trade for an earlier period in priority to a later period.

However, care needs to be exercised in calculating losses forward to ensure that the correct value of losses used has been taken into account.

30.3.3.4 Displacement of trading losses carried forward by non-trading charges claimed

S396B(5) TCA 97 requires an amount of unutilised trade loss that is to be carried forward under s396(1) TCA 97, to be reduced by the amount of trading losses which would have been utilised except that the company had non-trade charges available to set against profits. If the company made a s396B TCA 97 claim and also used non-trade charges such as protected interest, it would have to reduce the loss carried forward by the tax saved by using the charges.

Example 30.3

Charges Limited's results for the year ended 31 December 2009 are as follows:

	€
Case I	*(100,000)*
Case V	*10,000*
Non-trade charges	*5,000*
(qualifying interest on loan borrowed	
to invest in subsidiary)	

Corporation tax computation for the year ended 31 December 2009

	€
Case I	*0*
Case V	*10,000*
Non-trade charges	*(5,000)*
Profits	*5,000*
Corporation tax €5,000 × 25%	*1,250*
s396B credit €10,000 × 12.50%*	*(1,250)*
Tax payable	*0*
Loss table	
Trading loss 31 December 2009	*100,000*
s396B claim*	*(10,000)*
	90,000
s396B(5) deemed loss usage claim (Note)	*(10,000)*
Trade losses forward s396*	*80,000*

Note: as the company utilised both non-trade charges and s396B relief in the same period the trade losses carried forward must be reduced by the corporation tax saved in using the non-trade charges in preference to the trade losses.

The non-trade charges of €5,000 utilised saved tax at 25%, a saving of €1,250. The trade loss carried forward is deemed to be reduced by the extra s396B that would have been utilised but for the non-trade charges, that is €10,000 (€10,000 × 12.5% = €1,250).

The additional restriction does not amend the actual computation for the period, only the amount of losses carried forward.

Example 30.4

Loss Limited's results for the last three accounting periods are as follows:

	Year ended 31/12/2007	Year ended 31/12/2008	Year ended 31/12/2009
	€	€	€
Case I (Trade 1)	*50,000*	*(800,000)*	*100,000*
Case I (Trade 2)	*25,000*	*50,000*	*75,000*
Case III	*5,000*	*2,000*	*8,000*
Case V	*7,000*	*4,000*	*15,000*

In Example 30.2, we already calculated that the loss carried forward as at 31 December 2009 was €639,000. Part of this can be utilised under s396(1) as follows:

Corporation tax computation for year ended 31/12/2009:

	€
Case I (Trade 1)	*100,000*
s396(1)	*(100,000)*
Case I (Trade 2)	*75,000*
Case III	*8,000*
Case V	*15,000*
Income	*98,000*

Note that the loss carried forward can only be set against income of the same trade. The loss is not available for offset against the income of Trade 2. The remaining loss as at 31 December 2009 of €539,000 (€639,000 – €100,000 used in 2009) is carried forward for set-off against income from Trade 1 in future years.

30.3.4 Summary

In summary, the way in which a company can claim relief for trading losses is as follows:

1. Loss as an allowance, s396A TCA 97

Where a company has incurred a relevant trading loss which would have been taxable at the standard rate of corporation tax if a profit were made, then on making a claim, it may set that loss against other relevant trading income of the current accounting period, and if the claim so provides, against trading income of the preceding accounting period of corresponding length.

This applies to trading losses calculated by reference to Case I of Schedule D. It does not extend to trading losses calculated by reference to Case III of Schedule D, i.e., losses from a trade carried on abroad.

2. Excess loss as a credit, s396B TCA 97

Any excess losses are then available for offset on a credit and value basis against relevant corporation tax payable for either the current accounting period, or if the company was then carrying on a trade, the previous accounting period of corresponding length. Section 396B claims, i.e., those based on value and credit, are reduced by amounts already offset under s396 or s396A, i.e., those losses used as an allowance.

3. Loss as an allowance against trading income of future periods, s396(1) TCA 97

Trading losses may be carried forward against future Case I income from the same trade. Readers should be aware that loss relief under this section is not contingent on maximum claims having been made under s396A and s396B. A formal claim in writing must be made by the company in order to claim relief under either s396A or s396B (see paragraph 30.3.5). However, loss relief under s396(1) is automatic and no claim within a specified time frame is required. It is listed here as the third alternative for claiming relief for trading losses because in practice, most companies prefer to claim maximum relief in the earliest possible accounting period.

A series of practical examples best illustrate how these sections operate in practice.

Example 30.5

Izna Ltd had the following results for the accounting period ended 31/12/2009:

		€
Case I loss		(200,000)
Case V income		120,000

Ignoring other years and group relief, the corporation tax computation is as follows:

		€
Case V	€120,000 @ 25%	30,000
Loss as a credit on a value basis	€200,000 @ 12.5%	(25,000)
CT payable		5,000

Note that the trading loss may not be set against the Case V income, but can be used against corporation tax payable thereon as a credit on a value-only basis.

Example 30.6

Abacus Limited's results for the last three accounting periods are as follows:

	Year ended 31/12/2007	Year ended 31/12/2008	Year ended 31/12/2009
	€	€	€
Case I	(500,000)	200,000	400,000
Case III	5,000	10,000	20,000
Case V	10,000	20,000	40,000

Corporation tax computation for year ended 31/12/2007:

	€
Case I	Nil
Case III	5,000
Case V	10,000
Total income	15,000

Corporation tax computation for year ended 31/12/2008:

	€
Case I	200,000
s396(1)	(200,000)
	–
Case III	10,000
Case V	20,000
Total income	30,000

Corporation tax computation for year ended 31/12/2009:

	€
Case I	400,000
s396(1)	(300,000)
	100,000
Case III	20,000
Case V	40,000
Total income	160,000

Loss utilisation table

	€
Trade loss 31 December 2007	500,000
s396(1) claim 31 December 2008	(200,000)
s396(1) claim 31 December 2009	(300,000)
Loss available for carry forward	—

Note: The solution to this example is based on the assumption that Abacus Limited did not make a claim under s396B.

Example 30.7

Loss Leaders Limited had the following results:

	€
Accounting period – year ended 31/12/2008	
– Relevant Case I income	40,000
Accounting period – 6 months ended 30/6/2009	
– Relevant Case I loss	(60,000)

The company has no other income and wishes to claim immediate loss relief.

The loss can be carried back as follows:

	€
The profit for offset in the accounting period to 31/12/2008 is restricted to $€40,000 \times \dfrac{6}{12}$	20,000
Less available loss (S396A)	(20,000)
Balance of loss available for carry forward €60,000 – €20,000	(40,000)

Example 30.8

Loser Limited had the following results:

	€
Period of account 15 months ended 30/6/2008 – Case I profit	20,000
Accounting period year ended 30/6/2009 – Case I loss	(25,000)
	€

The 15-month period of account is divided into two accounting periods, one of 12 months and the other three months. Note the three-month period falls after the first 12-month period so that relief would be available as follows:

	€
Accounting period 3 months ended 30/6/2008 $\left(€20,000 \times \frac{3}{15}\right)$	4,000
Less loss for year ended 30/6/2009 restricted to	(4,000)
Period 12 months ended 31/3/2008 $\left(€20,000 \times \frac{12}{15}\right)$	16,000
Less loss year ended 30/6/2009 restricted to €16,000 $\times \frac{9}{12}$	(12,000)

The loss carried forward is therefore calculated as follows:	
Total loss	25,000
Less used in preceding 12 months:	
3 months	(4,000)
9 months	(12,000)
Loss available for carry forward	9,000

Example 30.9

The results of Loss Makers Limited for three accounting periods are as follows:

	€
12 months to 31 December 2009	
Loss in distribution trade	(600,000)
9 months to 31 December 2008	
Income from distribution trade	100,000
Case III interest income	60,000
12 months to 31 March 2008	
Income from distribution trade	20,000
Case III interest income	75,000

Loss Makers Limited corporation tax position would be as follows:

12 months to 31 December 2009

Nil corporation tax liability —

9 months to 31 December 2008

	€
Case I income	100,000
Less loss relief under s396A(3) TCA 97	(100,000)
	—
Case III income: €60,000 × 25%	15,000
Less loss relief under s396B(3) TCA 97:	
(€120,000* × 12.5%)	(15,000)
Nil corporation tax liability	—

* €15,000/12.5%

12 months to 31 March 2008   €

Case I income   20,000

Less loss relief under s396A(3) TCA 97: $\left(€20,000 \times \dfrac{3}{12}\right)$ (5,000)

Taxable Case I income   15,000
Case III   75,000
                                                                                         90,000

Corporation Tax:

Taxable Case I income: €15,000 × 12.5% (s22A TCA 97)   1,875

Case III income: €75,000 × 25%   18,750
                                                                                         20,625

Less loss relief under s396B(3) TCA 97 (Note 1): $\left(€18,750 \times \dfrac{3}{12}\right)$ (4,687)

Corporation tax liability   15,938

Note: The company must claim loss relief under s396A(3) TCA 97 prior to making a claim under s396B TCA 97. In addition, full relief is not available in respect of the 12 months to 31 March 2008 as only three of these months fall within the period which is equal in length to the accounting period in which the trading loss arose.

Trading losses available for carry forward by Loss Makers Limited under s396(1) TCA 97 are as follows:

                                                                                             €

Loss arising in 12 months to 31 December 2009   600,000

Loss relief claimed:
9 months to 31 December 2008
Under s396A TCA 97   (100,000)
Under s396B TCA 97   (120,000)

12 months to 31 March 2008   €
Under s396A TCA 97   (5,000)
Under s396B TCA 97: (€4,687/12.5%)   (37,496)
Unused trading loss carried forward against Case I income
of the same trade   337,504

Note 1: An alternative interpretation of the legislation may allow for a more generous s396B claim calculated on the basis of the total corporation tax charge for the period as opposed to corporation tax on passive income only. (In this instance, s396B would be calculated as €20,625 × 3/12.)

Example 30.10

Tough Times Limited's results for the last two accounting periods are as follows:

	Year ended 31/12/2008	Period ended 30/06/2009
	€	€
Case I	100,000	(300,000)
Case V	50,000	20,000

Corporation tax computation for period ended 30/06/2009

	€
Case I	Nil
Case V	20,000
Taxable income	20,000

		€
Corporation tax × 25%		5,000
s396B credit: €40,000* × 12.5%	*(2)*	(5,000)
Tax payable		–

*€5,000 / 12.5% = €40,000.

Corporation tax computation for year ended 31/12/2008

		€
Case I		100,000
s396A: $€100,000 \times \frac{6}{12}$	*(1)*	(50,000) Note 1
Total income		50,000
Case V		50,000
income		100,000

Corporation tax liability

		€
Trade income:	€50,000 × 12.5%	6,250
Case V:	€50,000 × 25%	12,500
		18,750
s396B:	€50,000** × 12.5% *(3)*	(6,250)
Corporation tax payable		12,500

**$€12,500 \times \frac{6}{12} /12.5\% = €50,000$ (Note 1).

Loss memo

	€	
Case I loss y/e 30/06/2009	300,000	
Utilised s396A 31/12/2008	(50,000)	*(1)*
Utilised s396B 30/06/2009	(40,000)	*(2)*
Utilised s396B 31/12/2008	(50,000)	*(3)*
Carry forward as s396(1)	160,000	

Note 1: The loss is only available for offset against 6/12 of the preceding year as the loss was incurred in a period of only six months' duration.

An alternative interpretation of the legislation may allow for a more generous s396B claim calculated on the basis of the total corporation tax charge for the period, as opposed to corporation tax on passive income only. (In this instance, s396B would be calculated as € 18,750 × 6/12).

30.3.5   Time limit for claims

The time limit for making claims for loss relief under s396A and s396B TCA 97 is two years from the end of the accounting period in which the loss was incurred. Relief under s396(1) is granted automatically, i.e., a formal claim for relief within a specified time frame is not required.

30.4 Relief for Trading Charges

30.4.1 Relief in current period

s243A and
s243B
TCA 97

Charges comprise interest, annuities and other annual payments, patent royalties, etc. These payments are treated as "pure income" receipts in the hands of the recipient. This effectively means that no expenses have been incurred in generating the income. Such payments, known as "charges on income" are set against the total profits of the company and not against the particular source of income with which the payment is actually connected.

Unlike losses, relief for charges is given on a paid basis. It should be noted that there is no relief for excess non-trade charges, i.e., non-trade charges, to the extent that they exceed total profits, will remain unrelieved. However, in the case of trading charges (i.e. charges incurred wholly and exclusively for the purposes of the trade) s243A TCA 97 and s243B TCA 97 operate in the same manner as s396A TCA 97 and s396B TCA 97 respectively, with the exception that there is no carry back to prior period(s).

Accordingly, where trading charges exceed the Case I income in respect of which they are paid, they may be offset against relevant trading income for the period in which they are paid under s243A TCA 97. Where trading charges exceed relevant trading income for the period in which they are paid, they may be used under s243B on a value or credit basis against the corporation tax liability for the period in which they are paid. It should also be noted that the following may not be reduced by the excess charges:

- Withholding tax; or

- Close company surcharge on undistributed income (see Chapter 32).

The following example best illustrates how charges can be relieved in the year in which they are paid.

Example 30.11

Z Limited's results for the year ended 31 December 2009 are as follows:

	Year ended 31/12/2009
	€
Case I	*50,000*
Case V	*100,000*
	€
Trade charges	*(100,000)*
Non-trade charges	*(30,000)*

Corporation tax computation for year ended 31/12/2009

	€
Case I	50,000
s243A	(100,000)
	–
Case V	100,000
Non-trade charges (s243)	(30,000)
Taxable profits	70,000

Corporation tax liability

		€	
Case V:	€70,000 × 25%	17,500	
s243B:	€50,000 × 12.5%	(6,250)	*[(€100,000 – €50,000) × 12.5%]*
Corporation tax payable		11,250	

Trade charges utilisation memo

	€
Trade charges paid	100,000
Utilised s243A	(50,000)
Utilised s243B	(50,000)
Unutilised	–

Example 30.12

Passive Limited's results for the year ended 31 December 2009 are as follows:

	€
Case I	25,000
Case V	10,000
Trade charges	(5,000)
Non-trade charges	50,000

Corporation tax computation for the year ended 31 December 2009

	€
Case I	25,000
Trade charges	(5,000)
	20,000
Case V	10,000
Non-trade charges	(30,000)
Profits	–

The non-trade charges not utilised €20,000 (€50,000 – €30,000), similar to trade charges, cannot be carried back to a previous period. However, whereas trade charges unutilised can be carried forward with s396(1) TCA 97, unutilised non-trade charges cannot and are effectively lost if not relieved in the period.

30.4.2 Carry forward of unused trade charges

s396(7) TCA 97

A company may add unused excess trade charges to trading losses for carry forward under s396(1) TCA 97. Excess charges are only available for use in the current accounting period or for carry forward as a trading loss. They may not be carried back.

The formulae for calculating the amount of charges that have been used on a value and credit basis and the amount available for carry forward are exactly the same as the formulae used for losses, see paragraph 30.3.3.2.

30.5 Order of Loss Relief Claims

The order in which losses may be utilised is as follows:

1. losses forward from a prior accounting period (s396(1));

2. current period losses to be used in the current accounting period (s396A);

3. carry back against preceding period of corresponding length (s396A);

4. carry forward to future accounting periods for offset against income from the same trade in which the loss was incurred (s396(1)).

Prior to the Finance Act 2003, there was no order of relief for claims under s396A and s396B. A company could choose the order in which it made the claims, but it must be borne in mind that losses available under s396B are reduced by s396 and s396A.

Section 59 Finance Act 2003 clarified that loss relief on a value basis (i.e., s396B) will only be given to the extent that losses cannot be relieved under other provisions.

The order of relief as a credit against relevant corporation tax is:

■ First for excess relevant trading charges (S243B);

■ Next for excess relevant trading losses (S396B);

■ Lastly for group relief available on a value and credit basis (S420B).

Thus, the order of loss relief claims can be summarised as follows:

Table 1

Section	Provision
396A* TCA 97	Trading losses against non-25% income
243A TCA 97	Relevant trade charges against non-25% income
243B TCA 97	Relief for charges on a value basis
396B TCA 97	Relief for losses on a value basis
420A TCA 97	Group relief for relevant losses and charges
456 TCA 97	Restrictions on group relief (restriction on the grouping of 10% losses against non-10% income)
420B TCA 97	Group relief on a value and credit basis

* The allowance under s396A TCA 97 must be claimed before claiming the following:

■ Non-trade charges; and

■ Management expenses; and

■ Other amounts claimable against profits,

with the exception of excess Case V allowances (see 30.10 below).

The Finance Act 2003 clarified the order of offset of relief by stating that relief could only be given for group relief on a value and credit basis where all other reliefs as outlined above have been claimed. The group relief provisions are considered in Chapter 30.

30.6   Trading Losses – Case III

s396(4),
s396(6)
TCA 97

Summary Chart

A trade is assessed under Case III if it is carried on wholly abroad. Profits from a trade carried on wholly abroad are taxable at 25%. Case III trading losses can only be used by way of carry forward for offset against future profits of the same trade. However, this includes interest or dividends on investments which would be taken into account as trading receipts, except for the fact that they were taxed under some other section. A claim for terminal loss relief may also be made. Case III losses may not be offset against other profits in the same accounting period or carried back to the preceding period in the same manner as losses calculated under Case I of Schedule D.

Finance Act 2007 legislated for the ECJ decision in the *Marks & Spencer v Halsey* case by giving limited relief for losses incurred in non-resident EU companies, see 31.2.

The basis for calculating a liability to tax for income assessable under Case III of Schedule D is to treat all income as arising from a single source s70 TCA 97. Therefore if foreign trading losses arise they will effectively be netted against other sources of

Case III income, which might include, for example, foreign rents, foreign securities and possessions, deposit interest etc. This netting will effectively give relief for the trading losses where there is another source of Case III income.

Example 30.13

Euro Limited has a trade carried on wholly abroad. It has incurred losses in this trade of €10,000 for the period ended 31 December 2009. For the same period it has earned deposit interest of €15,000, which is assessed to tax under Case III. The net amount assessable to tax under Case III Schedule D is €5,000.

30.7 Case IV Losses

s399(1)
TCA 97

Summary Chart

```
                        ┌──────────────┐
                        │   Case IV    │
                        │   Losses     │
                        └──────┬───────┘
              ┌────────────────┴────────────────┐
              ▼                                  ▼
      ┌──────────────┐                 ┌──────────────────┐
      │   Case IV    │                 │      Carry       │
      │ same period  │                 │  Forward Case    │
      │   S399(1)    │                 │       IV         │
      │   TCA 97     │                 │   indefinitely   │
      └──────────────┘                 │     S399(1)      │
                                       │     TCA 97       │
                                       └──────────────────┘
```

Case IV losses may only be set against other Case IV income of the same period and then carried forward indefinitely against future Case IV income. There is no time limit within which the claim to carry forward the losses may be made.

There is no facility to claim group relief for Case IV losses.

30.8 Case V Losses

s399(2),
(3),(4)
TCA 97

Summary Chart

Case V losses are those arising from Irish rents and are specifically described as "the aggregate of the deficiencies computed in accordance with section 97(1), which exceed the aggregate of the surpluses as so computed."

All Case V income is treated as arising from one source. Therefore, where there are a number of let properties, losses arising on one property may be netted against profits arising on another property. Where there is an overall loss arising, this loss may be carried back against Case V income of previous accounting periods of an equal length and any balance remaining may be carried forward indefinitely against future Case V income. Losses forward must bc uscd before losses carried back.

There is no facility for claiming group relief for Case V losses.

S399(4)
TCA 97

A claim for carry back of Case V losses must be made within two years from the end of the accounting period in which the losses were incurred.

Example 30.14

Rack Rent Ltd had the following results:

	€
Accounting period year ended 31/12/2008: Case V profit	*5,000*
Accounting period year ended 31/12/2009: Case V loss	*(7,000)*
There was a loss forward at 1/1/2008 of	*(2,000)*

Loss relief is given as follows:	
Case V: year to 31/12/2008	*€*
Profit	*5,000*
Less loss forward	*(2,000)*
	3,000
Loss carried back from year ended 31/12/2009	*(7,000)*
Loss available for carry forward	*(4,000)*

Example 30.15

Landlord Limited's results for three accounting periods are as follows:

	Year ended 31/12/2007	Year ended 31/12/2008	Year ended 30/06/2009
	€	*€*	*€*
Case I	*5,000*	*12,000*	*20,000*
Case III	*3,000*	*6,000*	*6,500*
Case V	*(2,000)*	*5,000*	*(4,000)*

Corporation tax computation for the year ended 31 December 2007

	€
Case I	*5,000*
Case III	*3,000*
Case V	*0*
Profits	*8,000*

Corporation tax €5,000 × 12.50%		625
Corporation tax €3,000 × 25%		750
Tax payable		1,375

The Case V loss of €2,000 is carried forward under s399 TCA 97.

Corporation tax computation for the year ended 31 December 2008

		€
Case I		12,000
Case III		6,000
Case V	5,000	
less s399 forward from 31/12/07	(2,000)	
	3,000	
less s399 back from 30/6/08 (1)	(1,500)	
		1,500
Profits		19,500

Corporation tax €12,000 × 12.50%		1,500
Corporation tax €7,500 × 25%		1,875
Tax payable		3,375

Corporation tax computation for the period ended 30 June 2009

	€
Case I	20,000
Case III	6,500
Case V	0
Profits	26,500

Corporation tax €20,000 × 12.50%	2,500
Corporation tax €6,500 × 25%	1,625
Tax payable	4,125

Loss table

Case V loss 30 June 2009	4,000	
s399 claim (1)	(1,500)	Note 1
s399 TCA 97 forward	2,500	

Note 1 – as the loss originated in a six-month period it is carried back against a corresponding prior period, 50% of the year ended 31 December 2008 and set against that period's taxable Case V income, €1,500 (€3,000 × 50%).

30.9 Excess Case V Capital Allowances

s308(3), (4) TCA 97

Summary Chart

The narrow treatment of "ordinary" Case V losses must be contrasted with the more favourable treatment available for excess Case V capital allowances. The excess may be:

■ Deducted from the profits of the accounting period (other income, plus non-development land capital gains); and/or

■ Deducted from profits of the immediately preceding accounting period (of equal length); and/or

■ Carried forward indefinitely against Case V income in future accounting periods.

A claim for group relief may be made for excess Case V capital allowances, see Chapter 31.

As excess Case V capital allowances are effectively relieved at 25%, none of the earlier value and credit restrictions, etc., apply to the offset of these allowances.

A claim for carry back of excess Case V capital allowances must be made within two years of the end of the accounting period in which the excess Case V capital allowances arise.

Example 30.16

Rent Excess Limited had the following results:

Year-end	Case I	Case III	Case V	Case V Capital Allowances
	€	€	€	€
31/12/2007	1,000	1,000	1,000	500
31/12/2008	500	500	1,000	6,000
31/12/2009	2,000	2,000	1,000	500

Accounting period year ended 31/12/2008

	€	€
Case I		500
Case III		500
		1,000

Less Case V excess capital allowances		
Case V	1,000	
Capital allowances	(6,000)	
Excess	5,000	(5,000)
Excess available for carry back or forward		(4,000)

Accounting period year ended 31/12/2007

Case I		1,000
Case III		1,000
Case V	1,000	
	(500)	500
		2,500
Less excess capital allowances carried back		(4,000)
Excess available for carry forward		(1,500)

Accounting period year ended 31/12/2009

Case I		2,000
Case III		2,000
	€	€
Case V	1,000	
Less capital allowances	(500)	
	500	
Excess brought forward	(1,500)	
Excess carried forward*	(1,000)	
Profits taxable		4,000

*The excess Case V capital allowances are available for carry forward against future Case V income under S399(1).

Example 30.17

Maria Limited's results for three accounting periods are as follows:

	Year ended 31/12/2007	Year ended 31/12/2008	Year ended 31/12/2009
	€	€	€
Case I	7,000	10,000	13,000
Case III	2,500	3,000	3,500
Case V	5,500	6,000	10,000
Case V capital allowances		(56,000)	
Chargeable gains	6,000		90,000

Corporation tax computation for the year ended 31 December 2007

	€
Case I	7,000
Case III	2,500
Case V	5,500

Income	15,000	
Chargeable gain	6,000	
Excess Case V capital allowances	(21,000)	(3)
Profits	0	

Corporation tax computation for the year ended 31 December 2008

		€
Case I		10,000
Case III		3,000
Case V	6,000	
Less Case V capital allowances	(6,000)	(1)
		0
Less excess capital allowances		(13,000)	(2)
Profits		0

Corporation tax computation for the year ended 31 December 2009

		€
Case I		13,000
Case III		3,500
Case V	10,000	
Less Case V loss forward	(10,000)	(4)
Case V		0
Income		16,500
Chargeable gain		90,000
Profits		106,500

	€
Corporation tax €13,000 × 12.50%	1,625
Corporation tax €90,000 × 12.50%	11,250
Corporation tax €3,500 × 25%	875
Tax payable	13,750

Loss table

	€	
Case V capital allowances 31/12/08	56,000	
set against Case V 31/12/08	(6,000)	(1)
Excess Case V capital allowances	50,000	
s308(4) claim	(13,000)	(2)
s308(4) claim	(21,000)	(3)
s399 Case V losses forward	16,000	
s399 claim	(10,000)	(4)
s399 TCA 97 forward		
s399 TCA 97 forward	6,000	

30.10 Capital Losses

s789(2)(4),
s31, s653
TCA 97

Summary Chart

Where a company makes a gain on a disposal of an asset, the gain is regarded as profit of the company for the purposes of corporation tax. Section 649 provides that where a company disposes of development land, the company is liable to capital gains tax on the disposal. The distinction between the two methods of taxing the gains have implications for how losses on disposal are relieved.

Section 31 allows the offset of current period losses against current period gains and allows for the offset of losses forward. Therefore capital losses on non-development land assets may be set against chargeable gains (other than capital gains on development land) in the current accounting period and any balance unused can be carried forward indefinitely with no time limit set for making a claim. Capital losses on development land can be set off against capital gains on any other kind of asset.

Section 653 restricts the offset of capital losses on ordinary disposals against development land disposals.

30.11 Restrictions on Loss Relief

30.11.1 Late filing

s1085 TCA 97 Claims over the utilisation of the following "loss" reliefs and certain other set-offs are restricted where corporation tax returns for accounting periods ending on or after 1 April 1992 are submitted late.

The claims affected are:

Section	Provision
308(4)	*Excess Case V capital allowances*
396(2)	*Current period and prior period losses*
396A(3)	*Ring-fenced trading losses*
399(2)	*Case IV and Case V losses*
396B	*Value and credit basis for claiming loss relief*
420	*Group relief*
420A	*Ring-fenced group relief*
420B	*Value and credit basis for claiming group relief*

Losses forward under s396(1) TCA 97 are not restricted

Where returns are submitted more than two months late, there is a 50% restriction on the amount of relief which would otherwise have been available. This restriction is limited to a total of €158,715.

Where the corporation tax return is submitted late but is filed within two months of its due date, a 25% restriction on the utilisation of losses arises. This is subject to a maximum restriction of €31,740.

Example 30.18

Disorganised Limited has the following results:

Year ended 31/12/2009	*€*
Case I loss	*(10,000)*
Case V profit	*20,000*

The company's liability to corporation tax for the accounting period ended 31/12/2009 is computed as follows:

		€
Case V	*€20,000 @ 25%*	*5,000*
s396B relief	*€10,000 × 12.5%*	*(1,250)*
CT payable		*3,750*

The amount of the loss of €10,000 available for set-off against the profits of accounting period ended 31/12/2009 on a value and credit basis is worth €1,250. However, Disorganised Limited fails to submit its return on time but plans to submit it within a month of its due date. They ask for advice on the revised amount of tax due.

The company's liability to corporation tax for accounting period ended 31/12/2009 is now computed as follows:

		€
Case V	€20,000 @ 25%	5,000
s396B relief	€10,000 × 12.5% × 75%	(938)
CT payable		4,062

Despite best intentions, the return is not filed until three months after its due date, Disorganised Limited asks for advice on the final amount due:

The company's liability to corporation tax for accounting period ended 31/12/2009 is revised as follows:

		€
Case V	€20,000 @ 25%	5,000
s396B relief	€10,000 × 50% × 12.5%	(625)
CT payable		4,375

The remaining Case I loss of €5,000 (€10,000 – €625/12.5%) is carried forward for offset against future income of the same trade.

WHAT YOU SHOULD NOW KNOW

On completion of this chapter, you should be able to:

- ✓ Understand the treatment of:
    - ♦ Case I/II trading losses – s396A, s396B, s396(1)
    - ♦ Volume 2 Q 31.1, 31.2, Revision Q CT3, CT5
    - ♦ Case III losses
    - ♦ Case IV losses
    - ♦ Case V losses – Volume 2 Q 31.4
    - ♦ Excess Case V capital allowances – Volume 2 Q 31.1
    - ♦ Trade charges – Volume 2 Q 31.3, Revision Q CT 5
    - ♦ Non-trade charges
    - ♦ Capital non-development land losses
    - ♦ Capital development land losses.

- ✓ Distinguish between the treatment of Case I/II excepted trade losses and relevant trade losses.

- ✓ Compute corporation tax computations while taking account of the following considerations:
    - ♦ losses arising where there are periods of differing length – Volume 2 Q 31.1, 31.2, 31.4;
    - ♦ losses arising in respect of various sources of income – Volume 2 Q 31.4, Assignment 31.1, 31.2.

- ✓ Claim loss relief in the correct order – Volume 2 Q 31.4.

- ✓ Calculate unutilised losses available for carry forward – Volume 2 Q 31.2.

- ✓ Restrict the reliefs available where returns are filed late.

- ✓ Complete Questions and the Assignments in Irish Taxation Law and Practice, Volume 2.

Corporation Tax

Summary Chart – Treatment of Losses

CASE I Relevant Trading Losses/Manufacturing Losses						
Case	III	IV	I	V	CG	DLG
2003						
2004						
2005						
2006						

s396(1)   Relevant Trading Losses as deduction
s396A(3)   do
s455   Manufacturing Loss
Time Limit: Carry back – two years from end of AP in which loss incurred
Time Limit: Carry forward: None

CASE I Excess Relevant Trading Losses on a Value Basis						
Case	III	IV	I	V	CG	DLG
2003						
2004						
2005						
2006						

TCA97 s396B. Time Limit: Current. Carry back: two years from end of AP. Set off: against relevant corporation tax of current preceding AP

CASE I Excepted Trading Losses						
Case	III	IV	I	V	CG	DLG
2003						
2004						
2005						
2006						

s399(1), (2)
Time Limit: Carry back – two years from end of AP in which loss incurred
Time Limit: Carry forward: None
Restrictions on use of 10% company losses

CASE IV Losses						
Case	I	III	IV	V	CG	DLG
2003						
2004						
2005						
2006						

s399(1)
Time Limit: None. Carry foward indefinitely

CASE V Excess Capital Allowance						
Case	I	III	V	IV	CG	DLG
2003						
2004						
2005						
2006						

s307
Time Limit: Carry back – two years from the end of the AP in which the excess arises
Time Limit: Carry forward – None

CASE III Trading Losses						
Case	I	IV	III	V	CG	DLG
2003						
2004						
2005						
2006						

s399(1), (4). Time Limit: none

CASE V Losses - Rents						
Case	I	III	V	IV	CG	DLG
2003						
2004						
2005						
2006						

s399(2), (3), (4). Time Limit: Carry back – two years.
Time Limit: Carry forward - none

CASE V Losses (i)						
Case	I	III	CG	DLG	IV	V
2003						
2004						
2005						
2006						

S78(4). Time Limit: None
See FA99 s57 (New Schedule 18A TCA97) which restricts the use "pre-entry losses" where a company joins a group

CASE V Losses (ii)						
Case	I	III	DLG	CG	IV	V
2003						
2004						
2005						
2006						

31

GROUPS: PAYMENTS, LOSSES AND TRANSFERS OF ASSETS

In this chapter, you will deal with the following:

- The meaning of a group for:

  - losses

  - capital gains

  - intra-group payments

- The utilisation of group loss relief

- The meaning of a consortium

- Relief from withholding tax on intra-group payments

- Relief for intra-group asset transfers

- Implications of leaving a capital gains group

31.1   Introduction

A company forms a separate legal entity for tax purposes. However, the relationships that exist between certain companies allow them to avail of reliefs that are not available to companies which operate on a stand-alone basis. This chapter examines the reliefs available and the conditions that are required to be satisfied in order to avail of those reliefs. A group relationship facilitates the offset of losses incurred by one company against profits of another, payments of interest and charges without the necessity to withhold tax and also the ability to transfer assets between group companies.

Unfortunately, the rules associated with group relief in its various formats as outlined are not straightforward. This is coupled with the fact that it is necessary to take account of other sections of the legislation (such as the loss relief provisions) in conjunction with group relief. In addition, there are different definitions of groups and consortia depending on the type of relief claimed, as well as different requirements for availing of relief. For this reason, the discussion is broken down into three sections: the first deals with losses in a group context; the second with relief for different payments made between groups; and the third with intra-group transfers of assets.

31.2   Group Relief for Losses

This section will consider the surrender of losses, excess capital allowances and charges between members of a group of companies.

31.2.1   Introduction

s411
TCA 97

Chapter 31 deals with losses incurred by a company and illustrates how these may be used within that same company. This chapter deals with losses, which have not otherwise been relieved, and how they may be transferred within a group of companies. The discussion deals with the relationship that is required in order to allow a claim for group relief (paragraph 31.2.2 below) and also with the type of reliefs that are available to a group of companies.

Where an Irish resident company, a subsidiary in another EU country with trapped losses (see 31.2.2.2) or an Irish branch of a company resident in a Member State of the European Union has trading losses, these losses may be offset against the profits of an Irish resident company or an Irish branch of a company resident in the European Union, or European Economic Area with which Ireland has a double taxation agreement (in reality these States are limited to Iceland, Norway and Lichtenstein). In order to claim such relief both companies must be within the same group during the period in which the losses were incurred.

The scheme of relief operates to permit one company in a group to surrender current year losses and certain other amounts including excess capital allowances and charges to another member of the group that has profits. The relief applies to current trading losses and excess charges only; trading losses forward cannot be surrendered.

The company transferring the loss is called the "surrendering company" and the company receiving the loss is called the "claimant company".

31.2.2   Definition of a group for the purposes of loss relief

In order to qualify for group relief, both the claimant company and the surrendering company must be members of the same group.

s412(1) TCA 97

Section 412(1) TCA 97 states that: *"Two companies shall be deemed to be members of a group of companies if one company is a 75% subsidiary of the other or both are 75% subsidiaries of a third company."*

31.2.2.1   Shareholding test and anti-avoidance legislation

For the purposes of group relief, the parent company, in addition to owning 75% (directly or indirectly) of the ordinary share capital of a subsidiary, must also be beneficially entitled to not less than:

- 75% of any profits available for distribution to the "equity-holders" of the subsidiary company; and

- 75% of any assets of the subsidiary company available for distribution to its "equity-holders" on a winding-up.

These anti-avoidance provisions (i.e., requirements regarding profit or asset distribution) are designed to defeat situations where ownership of ordinary share capital does not reflect one company's interest in its so-called subsidiary, and where a temporary group is established merely to avail of the relief.

Example of Shareholding Test

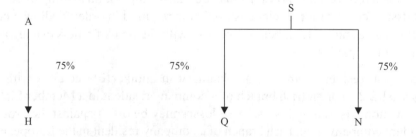

A Ltd and H Ltd form a group as do S Ltd, Q Ltd and N Ltd.

Shareholdings may also be held indirectly provided the 75% test is satisfied.

Group – Example indirect shareholding

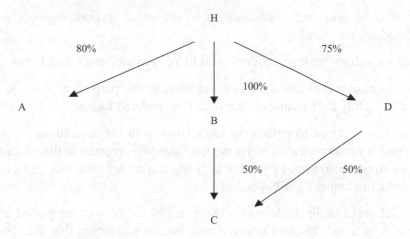

All the above companies are members of the same group because:

■ H Ltd owns 80% of A Ltd;

■ H Ltd owns 100% of B Ltd;

■ H Ltd owns 75% of D Ltd;

■ H Ltd owns 87.5% of C Ltd*

*100% of 50%	=	50%
and		
75% of 50%	=	37.5%
Total		87.5%

31.2.2.2 Residence

s411(1)(c)
TCA 97

In addition to the shareholding test and the stringent anti-avoidance provisions, there are requirements in relation to residence. In defining a group for the purposes of loss relief, one of the key areas that has been examined by the courts in recent years has been the residence of the claimant and surrendering companies.

Finance Act 2007 legislated for the ECJ decision in *Marks & Spencer v Halsey*, see Appendix I for a discussion on this case.

For accounting periods beginning on or after 1 January 2006 losses incurred in qualifying 75% non-resident EU subsidiaries will be available for set-off against the profits of the Irish resident parent.

To qualify for this relief the following conditions must be complied with:

(a) Both companies must be members of the same corporate group, with a 75% subsidiary relationship.

(b) The subsidiary must be resident in an EU/EEA state, other than Ireland.

(c) The company claiming the loss relief must be the parent and must be resident in Ireland. Only the parent can receive the surrendered losses.

(d) The loss is to be calculated in accordance with the legislation of the state the subsidiary is a resident of and is not available for surrender in that country, either in the current period, prior period or by being carried forward. Nor can it be allowable for use in another EU/EEA country.

(e) The claim must be made within two years of the accounting period in which the loss is incurred. In cases where it only becomes apparent that the loss cannot be carried forward, for example due to a cessation of the trade, the two-year period commences from date that the loss can no longer be carried forward.

(f) The loss transfer will not be allowable if arrangements have been entered into with a view to creating the loss in order to claim the relief and for no valid commercial reason.

(g) The Inspector of Taxes may request evidence of the claim prior to allowing the relief.

We have arrived at this position as a result of several key cases, which are outlined in detail in Appendix I. Up to 30 June 1998, group relief was restricted to Irish resident companies which were held by an Irish resident parent. However, resulting from the European Court of Justice decision in the ICI v Colmer case ([1996] STC 352; [1999] STC 874), the definition was extended to include other EU Member States. This extended the definition of a group to include a 75%-plus holding by an EU parent and extends further to include Irish branches of EU companies (EEA with effect from 1 January 2002). The *Marks & Spencer v Halsey* case (C–466/03) allows limited cross-border relief, while the recent Lidl Belgium Gmbh & Co.KG v Finanzant Heilbronn shows how far the European Court of Justice will permit utilisation of these losses.

31.2.3 Group relief for trading losses

s396A TCA 97 A claim for group relief may be made for a trading loss computed for the purposes of
s396B TCA 97 the TCA 97. By definition, this will include any capital allowances claimed for the period and consequently losses which may be surrendered by way of group relief will include capital allowances.

s420A TCA 97 The loss reliefs available under s396A TCA 97 and s396B TCA 97 operate for groups under s420A TCA 97 and s420B TCA 97, respectively.

s420B TCA 97 Accordingly, relevant trading losses of the "surrendering" company are first grouped against relevant trading income of the "claimant" company as an allowance under s420A. If there is an excess amount of unused losses after claiming such allowances, the excess may be grouped against the corporation tax payable on passive income/gains by way of a credit and value basis under s420B. (Readers are referred to Chapter 31 for a discussion on relevant trading losses and the value basis for claiming loss relief.) Where the excess after claiming losses against relevant trading income consists of relevant losses or charges, the credit under s420B is calculated by valuing those losses or charges at the standard rate of corporation tax for the accounting period in which they arise. Where the excess consists of 10% losses or charges (i.e., non-relevant losses or charges), the corporation tax of the claimant company is reduced by 10% of such losses or charges.

A straightforward example will illustrate the points involved.

Example 31.1

Two members of a qualifying group have results as follows for corresponding accounting periods:

	Sam Limited Accounting period ended 31/12/2009	Oisin Limited Accounting period ended 31/12/2009
	€	€
Case I (trade 1) profit (loss)	40,000	(250,000)
Case I (trade 2) profit (loss)	Nil	80,000
Case V income	100,000	20,000

This example ignores previous years.

After claiming all allowances due to it, Oisin Limited wishes to surrender and Sam Limited wishes to claim the optimum amount of losses available.

Oisin Limited – Corporation Tax Computation

	€
Case I income	80,000
Less loss relief under s396A(3) (relief as an allowance)	(80,000)
	Nil

	€
Case V income	20,000
CT @ 25%	5,000
Less loss relief under s396B(3) (value and credit)	(5,000)
Net CT payable	Nil

Loss used:	€
s396A(3) allowance	(80,000)
s396B(3) credit €5,000 × 100/12.5%	(40,000)
	(120,000)

Loss available for surrender: **€**

Case I loss   *(250,000)*
Loss used   *120,000*
Loss available for surrender   *(130,000)*

Sam Limited – Corporation Tax Computation

                                                                                 €

Case I   *40,000*
Less group relief s420A(3)   *(40,000)*
Net Case I   *Nil*

Case V   *100,000*
CT @ 25%   *25,000*
Less group relief s420B €90,000 @ 12.5%   *(11,250)*
CT payable   *13,750*

Comment on example

As the example shows, there are two ways of getting relief for group losses: one is as an allowance, and the other is as a credit.

Only relevant losses can be set against relevant income as an allowance under s420A(3). Losses not used as an allowance may be granted as a credit under s420B(3), thus giving relief on a value basis similar to the basis for granting personal tax credits. The credit is calculated by multiplying the loss remaining after any allowance claimed, by the standard rate of corporation tax for the accounting period. Where the credit exceeds the amount of corporation tax, it is restricted to the amount of such tax.

31.2.4   Restrictions and other relevant issues

A number of other relevant points in relation to claims for group relief merit further discussion. These are as follows:

1. Only current year losses may be surrendered, therefore losses carried forward or back may not be surrendered.

Example 31.2

Irish Losses Limited had the following results over two years:

	Year ended 31/12/2008	*Year ended 31/12/2009*
	€	*€*
Case I	*100,000*	*(250,000)*

The company had losses forward under s396(1) as at 31/12/2008 of €40,000.

The company's 100% subsidiary, Irish Profits Limited, had the following results over the same period:

	Year ended 31/12/2008	*Year ended 31/12/2009*
	€	*€*
Case I	*50,000*	*100,000*

Irish Losses Limited's computation for the year ended 31/12/2008 is as follows:

	31/12/2008
	€
Case I income	*100,000*
Less s396(1)	*(40,000)*
Less s396A(3)	*(60,000)*
	Nil

The balance of the 2009 loss, i.e., €250,000 less €60,000 (€190,000) is available to be surrendered to Irish Profits Limited. However, it can only set the loss against its income of €100,000, as this is the same year in which the loss was incurred in Irish Losses Limited. The loss cannot be set against the prior year's income of €50,000.

The balance of the loss is retained by Irish Losses Limited (€190,000 – €100,000) and carried forward against future income of the same trade.

2. Capital losses may not be surrendered. However, relief from corporation tax on chargeable gains arising on the inter-group transfers of assets is available and this is discussed in further detail at paragraph 31.4 below.

Example 31.3

In January 2009, Albion Limited makes a gain of €250,000 on the sale of a warehouse. In February 2009, Pendle Limited disposes of a warehouse, which results in a loss of €250,000. Both companies are 100% subsidiaries of Trent Limited and have a December 2009 year-end.

Pendle Ltd cannot transfer its loss to Albion Limited. Therefore Albion Limited will incur a chargeable gains tax liability and Pendle Limited must carry its capital loss forward to shelter future gains (excluding gains on development land which are ring-fenced).

3. A surrendering company can surrender all, or part only, of its losses in an accounting period. However, it cannot surrender more losses to a claimant company than that claimant company is capable of absorbing.

Example 31.4

In Example 31.2 concerning the position of Irish Losses Limited and Irish Profits Limited, the surrendering company, Irish Losses Limited, had a loss of €190,000 available to transfer. However, as Irish Profits Limited could only absorb €100,000, the amount that could be transferred was limited to this amount.

4. Losses can only be grouped against profits of a corresponding accounting period. Where the accounting periods of two companies claiming and surrendering losses are not co-terminous, the losses and profits of each company must be apportioned, usually on a time basis. This is calculated by:

   – time-apportioning the profit attributable to the corresponding accounting period; then

   – time-apportioning the loss attributable to the corresponding period; and

   – allowing group relief on the lower of the two.

Example 31.5

Company A with a year-end of 31 December 2009 has a trading loss of €100,000. Company B with a year-end of 30 June 2009 has a trading profit of €50,000.

The corresponding accounting period for A and B is 1 January 2009 to 30 June 2009 and is of six months' duration. Taking the lower figure of €50,000 × $^6/_{12}$, €25,000 of loss relief can be surrendered from A Limited to B Limited.

5. Group relief will only be given if the surrendering company and the claimant company are members of the same group throughout the whole of:

   – the surrendering company's accounting period in question; and

   – the claimant company's corresponding accounting period.

The impact of this is that where a company joins or leaves a group or consortium, the company joining or leaving is assumed to have an accounting period beginning or ending, respectively on the date on which they join or leave the group. Therefore in claiming group relief, the concept of notional accounting periods is introduced and profits and losses must be time-apportioned.

Example 31.6

Cain Limited has a trading profit of €90,000 for the year ended 31 December 2009. On 1 October 2009, it acquired the entire share capital of Able Limited. Able Limited incurred a loss of €60,000 in the year ended 30 November 2009.

The maximum relief that can be claimed or surrendered is the lower of each company's adjusted corresponding period profit or loss:

Cain Limited: €90,000 × $^2/_{12}$ = €15,000
Able Limited: €60,000 × $^2/_{12}$ = €10,000

Therefore Able Limited can surrender €10,000 of its loss to Cain Limited.

6. Both the claimant company and the surrendering company must consent to the group relief claim. While this is normally done with the submission of the CT1, a group relief claim may be made at any time within two years from the end of the accounting period of the surrendering company to which it relates. For example, if the surrendering company's accounting period was the year ended 31 December 2007, the claim must be made before 31 December 2009.

7. Losses incurred by a leasing company arising from excess capital allowances cannot be offset against non-leasing income. Finance Act 2005 amended TCA97 s403 to allow the leasing losses to be set against leasing profits of another group company for periods ending on or after 3 February 2005.

   With the cessation of the IFSC/Shannon manufacturing reliefs from 31 December 2005, Finance Act 2006 amended the definition of leasing to include ancillary services such as asset financing, services of leasing experts, profits on lease disposals etc.

   This extended definition ensures that where 90% of the activities are from leasing, the company will be able to offset its capital allowances against all leasing income (including items included under ancillary services).

8. A payment for group relief (to a maximum of the amount surrendered) is not taken into account in computing profits or losses of either company for corporation tax purposes. In practice, payment will most probably be made where there are minority interests and payments are generally valued at an amount equal to the tax saved by the claimant company.

9. Excess trading charges may be group-relieved in exactly the same manner as trading losses.

10. Any claim for group relief must be looked at in the context of a claim for other reliefs. Section 421 TCA 97 sets out how group relief interacts with other claims for losses and charges. Current year Case I losses and charges, and losses forward from a previous period must be used by the claimant company in priority to group relief. However, group relief may be claimed before claiming losses under s396A or s396B carry back of losses, or excess capital allowances s308(4) in subsequent periods. At a practical level this facilitates looking at the group position at a point in time without having to rely on having results for subsequent periods.

    The sections listed below should all be considered and claimed where appropriate in the order listed, prior to making a claim for group losses on a value and credit basis.

Section	Provision
396A	Trading losses against non-25% income
243A	Relevant trade charges against non-25% income
243B	Relief for charges on a value basis
396B	Relief for losses on a value basis
454	Restriction of certain charges on income (restriction on the offset of 10% charges against non-10% income to 31/12/02)
455	Restriction of certain losses (restriction on the offset of 10% losses against non-10% income to 31/12/02)
420A	Group relief for relevant losses and charges
456	Restrictions on group relief (restriction on the grouping of 10% losses against non-10% income to 31/12/02)
420B	Group relief on a value and credit basis

The following comprehensive example illustrates the operation of group relief in practice.

Example 31.7

Two members of a qualifying group have results as follows for corresponding accounting periods:

	John Limited Year-end 31/12/2008	Jack Limited Year-end 31/12/2008
	€	€
Case I	50,000	(60,000)
Case V	40,000	15,000

	Year-end 31/12/2009	Year-end 31/12/2009
Case I	(100,000)	180,000
Case V	20,000	25,000

Jack Limited – Computation for year ended 31/12/2008

	€
Case I	Nil
Case V	15,000
	15,000

	€
€15,000 × 12.5%	3,750
s396B: €30,000 × 12.5%	(3,750)
	Nil

Loss Memo – Jack Limited:

	€
Case I loss	60,000
s396B	(30,000)
s420A	(30,000)
	Nil

John Limited – Computation for year ended 31/12/08

	€
Case I	50,000
s420A (above)	(30,000)
s396A (from 31/12/2009)	(20,000)
	Nil
Case V	40,000
	€
€40,000 × 25%	10,000
€40,000 × 12.5% (from 31/12/2009)	(5,000)
	5,000

John Limited computation for 31/12/2009

	€
Case I	Nil
Case V	20,000
€20,000 × 25%	5,000
s396B: €40,000 × 12.5%	(5,000)
	Nil

Loss Memo – John Ltd:

	€
Case I loss	100,000
s396A (to 31/12/2008)	(20,000)
s396B (to 31/12/2009)	(40,000)
s396B (to 31/12/2008)	(40,000)
	Nil

Jack Ltd computation for 31/12/2009

	€
Case I	180,000
Case V	25,000
	205,000
€180,000 × 12.5%	22,500
€25,000 × 25%	6,250
	28,750

31.2.5 Excess capital allowances

S420(2)
TCA 97

Excess capital allowances may also be group-relieved. The excess capital allowances are those used in charging a company's income under Case V of Schedule D. The amount of allowances available for surrender is the excess of those allowances over the related income for the period in question. This does not include losses or capital allowances carried forward or back. As is the case with losses, the accounting period of the surrendering company and the claimant company must correspond with one another in order to make a claim for group relief.

The surrendering company does not have to utilise the excess capital allowances against its other income in priority to surrender group relief to an associated company.

The most usual example met in practice is excess Case V capital allowances in the case of let industrial buildings and capital allowances for plant or machinery leased otherwise than in the course of a trade.

Example 31.8

A Limited and B Limited are members of a group and have the following results:

	A Limited Year-end	B Limited Year-end
	31/12/2009	31/12/2009
	€	€
Case I	60,000	50,000
Case V	20,000	60,000
Case V capital allowances	(40,000)	(10,000)

A Ltd – Computation for year end 31/12/2009:

	€	€
Case I		60,000
Case V	20,000	
Case V capital allowances	(20,000)	
	Nil	–
		60,000
€60,000 × 12.5%		7,500

Loss Memo – A Limited:	€
Case V capital allowances	40,000
against Case V income	(20,000)
s420(2) B Limited 2009	(20,000)
	Nil

B Limited – Computation for year end 31/12/2009:

	€	€
Case I		50,000
Case V	60,000	
Capital allowances	(10,000)	

s420(2) (above)	*(20,000)*	
		30,000
		80,000
€50,000 × 12.5%		*6,250*
€30,000 × 25%		*7,500*
		13,750

31.2.6   Restriction of group relief

s1085(2)
TCA 97

Where a claimant company or a surrendering company fails to file a return of income on time, group relief is restricted. The restriction is calculated by reference to the length of delay in filing the return.

Where the filing delay is less than two months, the group relief claimable is reduced by 25% subject to a maximum restriction of €31,740.

Where the delay in filing exceeds two months then a restriction of 50% applies, subject to a maximum restriction of €158,715.

Similar restrictions apply to companies surrendering losses for group relief.

Example 31.9

Slug Ltd is a 75% subsidiary of Snail Ltd for the whole of the accounting period of 12 months ended 31 December 2009. The return of the company for the 12 months to 31 December 2009 shows the following:

	€
Snail Ltd	
Trading profits	*100,000*
Losses forward	*(20,000)*
Rental income	*10,000*
Capital allowances in rental property	*25,000*
Charges paid	*10,000*

Slug Ltd	
Trading loss	*(30,000)*

Snail Ltd claims relief in respect of excess capital allowances under s308(4) TCA 97, and also with the consent of Slug Ltd, the maximum amount of group relief which can be surrendered by Slug Ltd under s420A. The group companies failed to deliver their returns until 31 December 2010.

Corporation Tax Computation

Snail Ltd	*€*
Case I	*100,000*
Relief s396(1)	*(20,000)*
Case V	*Nil*

Charges	*(10,000)*
	70,000
Relief s308 excess capital allowances	
Restricted (€25,000 – €10,000) × 50%	*(7,500)*
	62,500
Group Relief s420A	
Restricted (€30,000 × 50%)	*(15,000)*
Amount chargeable to CT	*47,500*
CT due × 12.5%	*5,938*

Slug Ltd	**€**
Case I loss available for surrender (€30,000 × 50%)	*15,000*
Amount surrendered	*15,000*
Loss forward (€30,000 – €15,000)	*15,000*

31.2.7 Consortium loss relief

s411(3)
TCA 97

Consortium relief is very much an extension of group relief, if somewhat more restrictive, whereby losses can only be surrendered up from a trading company to the members of the consortium.

A qualifying consortium exists where the following conditions are met:

1. The company surrendering the relief is a trading company, and 75% (previously 100%) or more of the ordinary share capital of the company is owned by five or fewer companies. There is no minimum shareholding requirement. However, there is effectively a maximum shareholding as the consortium company must not be a 75% subsidiary of any one company.

2. All the companies making up the 75% ownership must be resident in a Member State of the EU, or in a Member State of the European Economic Area (EEA) with which Ireland has concluded a double tax treaty. Non-EU resident member companies or individuals will not be entitled to claim consortium loss relief.

A typical consortium structure is illustrated below.

The following points are relevant:

■ Loss relief may only be surrendered upwards from the consortium company to the member companies. There is no provision for the surrender of losses from a member company to a consortium company or any other member company.

■ The loss that can be surrendered to any member company is limited to that member company's percentage share in the consortium company.

■ Losses may also be surrendered by a holding company and by a 90% subsidiary of a holding company where the holding company is owned by a consortium.

Example 31.10

A Limited, B Limited, C Limited , D Limited and E Limited own 25%, 12%, 23%, 16% and 24% of F Limited respectively. F Limited incurred trading losses in the year-ended 31 December 2009 of €100,000.

Assuming all five consortium members have a December year-end, the following amounts can be surrendered from F Limited to each consortium member:

	€
A: €100,000 × 25%	25,000
B: €100,000 × 12%	12,000
C: €100,000 × 23%	23,000
D: €100,000 × 16%	16,000
E: €100,000 × 24%	24,000
Losses claimed	100,000

31.3   Intra-Group Payments

31.3.1   Introduction – obligation to deduct income tax

A company is obliged to deduct income tax at the standard rate (currently 20%) on certain payments. The income tax must be paid as part of the company's corporation tax liability. Details of the payments made under deduction of tax must be included in the company's corporation tax return. The payment is subject to corporation tax rules for preliminary tax payments and return filing deadlines.

s246 TCA 97 **The payments to which withholding tax applies are:**

■ Annual interest (subject to certain exceptions in the case of financial institutions),

■ Royalties, and

■ Annuities and other annual payments.

In certain instances, an exemption from withholding tax may apply where payments are made within the EU. Readers are referred to the commentary at 28.8.1 with regard to the provisions introduced by Finance Act 2004 in response to an EU Council Directive.

In all other instances, existing domestic legislation ensures that withholding tax will not apply where a 51% group relationship exists.

31.3.2 Group payments – relief from withholding tax

s410(4)(5)
TCA 97

The existence of a 51% group relationship or a consortium allows the aforementioned payments to be made without the necessity to deduct income tax.

31.3.3 Definition of a group

410(3)(4)
TCA 97

The group relationship and conditions that must be fulfilled in order to avoid withholding tax are as follows:

■ Both companies must be resident in an EU Member State or an EEA State with which Ireland has a double tax treaty. Where the recipient is not resident in the State the payment received must be taken into account for taxation purposes. Prior to 1 March 2005 the relief only applied if both companies were resident in the State;

■ The company making the payment must be a 51% subsidiary of the company receiving the payment; or

■ Both companies must be 51% subsidiaries of a company resident in a relevant EU Member State, or a relevant Member State of the European Economic Area, EEA (this basically adds Norway, Iceland and Lichtenstein to the EU States); or

■ A consortium relationship must exist.

A company is owned by a consortium if 75% or more of the ordinary share capital is beneficially owned by between five or fewer companies resident in the EU where the percentage shareholding by any of the companies can be as low as but not lower than 5%. The company paying the interest must be a trading or holding company owned by a consortium whose members include the company receiving the payment.

The 51% relationship may be either direct or indirect. The following examples illustrate some qualifying group relationships.

Example 30.11

A "51% Group"

(i) H Ltd can pay interest gross to A Ltd and vice versa.

(ii) H Ltd can pay interest gross to J Ltd and to A Ltd. A Ltd can pay interest gross to J Ltd and to H Ltd.

It is not necessary that a company be a direct 51% subsidiary of another for payments to be made gross.

Example 30.12

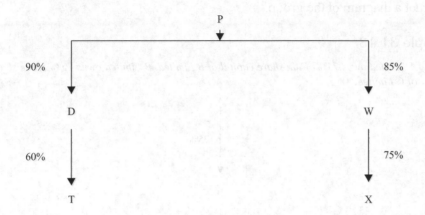

T Ltd is a 54% subsidiary of P Ltd, X Ltd is a 64% subsidiary of P Ltd. It follows that annual payments can be paid gross by all the members of the group.

31.4   Intra-Group Transfers of Assets

31.4.1   Introduction

Relief from corporation tax on chargeable gains arising on the intra-group transfer of assets is available where a qualifying "Capital Gains Group" relationship exists. The structure required for a capital gains group is somewhat different from that which is required for a corporation tax loss group and this is discussed in further detail in paragraph 31.4.2 below. The nature of the relief is considered in paragraph 31.4.3.

31.4.2   What constitutes a capital gains group?

s616 TCA 97 Section 616 states that a group shall consist of "a principal company and all its effective 75% subsidiaries". A principal company would be known in common parlance as "a parent company".

The anti-avoidance provisions found in the definition of a corporation tax loss group also apply. Hence, in addition to the shareholding requirement, it is also necessary that:

■ The parent should be entitled to not less than 75% of profits available for distribution to equity-holders; and

- The parent should be entitled to not less than 75% of the assets and available for distribution to equity-holders on a winding-up.

However, an additional consideration in the case of capital gains groups ensures that there is a clear distinction between the capital gains groups structure and the loss group structure. Where a member of a group has itself got an effective 75% subsidiary, that subsidiary is also a member of the group. The following examples best illustrate this point.

To fully understand the nature of a group structure, readers are advised in all cases to construct a diagram of the group.

Example 31.13

A Limited owns 75% of the share capital of B Limited. B Limited owns 75% of the share capital of C Limited.

For capital gains group purposes, A and B Limited are members of a group. B and C Limited are also members of a capital gains group. Therefore, C Limited is also a member of A and B's capital gains group as it is a 75% subsidiary of B Limited.

For losses, however, C Limited cannot be a member of A and B's group as A through B only holds 56.25% (75% × 75%) of C Limited. Therefore, A and B Limited and B and C Limited form separate loss groups.

Example 31.14

Fire Limited has the following holdings:

Wind Limited – 75% (Wind Limited in turn owns 80% of Sun Limited).

Water Limited – 75% (Water Limited in turn owns 60% of Earth Limited).

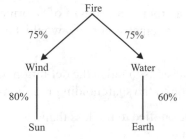

For capital gains group purposes, Fire Limited, Wind Limited and Water Limited are in a group as Wind Limited and Water Limited are both 75% subsidiaries of Fire Limited. Sun Limited is also part of this group as it is a qualifying subsidiary of Wind Limited. Earth Limited is not part of the group, however, as Water Limited owns less than 75% of it.

For losses, the group can only include Fire Limited, Wind Limited and Water Limited. Fire Limited's holding in Sun is only 60% (75% × 80%). It should be noted that Wind Limited and Sun Limited can form their own separate losses group as they have an 80% relationship.

Example 31.15

Pluto Limited owns 90% of the share capital of Mars Limited, which in turn owns 75% of the share capital of Mercury Limited. Both Pluto and Mercury own 55% and 40% of the share capital of Jupiter Limited respectively.

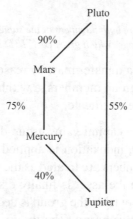

For capital gains purposes, all companies are in a group. Mars and Mercury are members through Pluto's 90% holding in Mars and the fact that Mercury is a 75% subsidiary of Mars. Pluto holds 55% of the shares in Jupiter directly and 27% through Mercury (90% × 75% × 40%). This gives it a holding in Jupiter of 82%.

For losses, all companies are part of the group except for Mercury Limited. Mars is a 90% subsidiary and Jupiter is an indirect subsidiary with 82%. However, Pluto's holding in Mercury (through Mars) is only 67.50% (90% × 75%) therefore it cannot be a member of the group. It is however in a loss group with Mars.

In order to be a principal company, or to be an effective 75% subsidiary, and therefore in order to be a member of a group, it is necessary that a company should be resident for tax purposes in an EEA State.

31.4.3 Transfers between group companies

s617
s648 TCA 97   Broadly speaking, the effect of the group relief is to ensure that no chargeable gain arises on a transfer of assets between group members. Where an asset is transferred from one group member to another, it is deemed to be transferred at a price which ensures that no gain and no loss arises to the company making the disposal.

The relieving provisions did not apply to transfers of development land on or after 28 January 1982 and before 24 April 1992.

s619
s589 TCA 97

For the purposes of the indexation provisions, all members of the group are regarded as one person so that the group member acquiring the asset takes over the same base acquisition date as the member from which the asset was acquired. Accordingly, when arriving at the deemed transfer price which would give rise to no gain/no loss for the company making the disposal, indexation is not applied.

Example 31.16

HEN LTD acquired an asset in 2001 for €40,000. In 2007, it incurred enhancement expenditure of €30,000 on the asset and then sold it to CHICKEN LTD in December 2009 for €80,000, which was its market value at that time.

If the two companies were not within the same group, HEN LTD would calculate its gain by deducting from the sale price, the cost and the enhancement expenditure, both figures uplifted by indexation.

However, if they are both members of the same group for CGT purposes, the asset is deemed to be transferred at a figure which gives HEN LTD no gain/no loss, i.e., €70,000.

Notwithstanding that a transfer may, by reason of s617, not give rise to a gain or a loss when made between group members, a withholding tax obligation may still exist in the absence of a clearance certificate.

Where a company in a capital gains group disposes of an asset acquired from another member of the group, indexation is applied as if all members of the group were one person. All group members are treated as the same person for the purpose of calculating the gain or loss when the asset is finally disposed of outside the group. The member disposing of the asset outside the group is deemed to be the one which initially acquired the asset when it first came into the group. Accordingly, the market value at 6 April 1974 (where applicable) and the indexation rules are preserved within a group.

Example 31.17

James Limited acquired an asset in June 1994 for €20,000. The asset was transferred to Flynn Limited, another company in the CGT group, in 1998 for €75,000. Flynn Limited sold the asset in June 2009 for €175,000. Flynn Ltd makes up accounts to 31 December in each year.

The amount to be included in the profits of Flynn Limited is calculated as follows:

	€
Consideration received by Flynn Limited	*175,000*
Cost to James Limited (indexed) €20,000 × 1.309	*(26,180)*
Gain	*148,820*
Notional CGT €148,820 at 25%	*37,205*
	€
Chargeable to corporation tax: €37,205 / 12.5%	*297,640*

The CT payable on the gain is €297,640 at 12.5% = €37,205

Example 31.18

Michaels Ltd owns all the issued share capital in Jones Ltd and 65% of the share capital in Flood Ltd.

In June 1996 Michaels Ltd bought a property for €100,000. In December 2001 the property was sold to Jones Ltd for €160,000. Jones Ltd extended the property in March 2009 at a cost of €40,000. Flood Ltd purchased the property from Jones Ltd for €350,000 in May 2009.

The corporation tax position for the year ended 31 December 2009 is as follows (assuming it is not development land):

In December 2001, Jones Ltd is deemed to have acquired the property for €100,000, i.e., an amount which results in no gain and no loss for Michaels Ltd. The sale of the property to Flood Ltd is a sale outside the group accordingly, a taxable gain arises to Jones Ltd calculated as follows:

Jones Ltd – taxable gain		*€*
Sales proceeds		*350,000*
Cost (to group) indexed		
	€100,000 indexed @ 1.251	*(125,100)*
Enhancement expenditure		
	€40,000 (not indexed)	*(40,000)*
Gain		*184,900*
Notional CGT	*€184,900 at 25%*	*46,225*
Chargeable to CT	*€46,225 × $\frac{100}{12.5}$*	*369,800*

Example 31.19

Head Ltd owns all the shares in Nose Ltd and Mouth Ltd. In 1990, Nose Ltd acquired an asset for €12,697. In 1995, it sold the asset to Mouth Ltd for €63,487. In March 2000, Mouth Ltd sold the asset to Head Ltd for €126,974. Head Ltd sold the asset to a non-group member on 2 May 2009 for €150,000.

No chargeable gain arises to Nose Ltd or Mouth Ltd under the group provisions. In calculating the gain of Head Ltd, it is treated as acquiring the asset in 1990 for €12,697; its gain will be calculated by deducting that cost (indexed from 1990) from the sales proceeds of €150,000.

		€
Consideration received by Head Ltd		*150,000*
Cost to Nose Ltd (indexed)	*€12,697 × 1.442*	*(18,309)*
Gain		*131,691*
Notional CGT	*€131,691 at 25%*	*32,923*
Chargeable to corporation tax:	*€32,923 / 12.5%*	*263,384*

The CT payable on the gain is €263,384 at 12.5% = €32,923.

Example 31.20

BLACK LTD acquired a building in May 1992 for IR£40,000 (€50,790). On 31 March 1994, BLACK LTD sold the building to its wholly owned subsidiary, SOOT LTD for IR£100,000 (€126,974). SOOT LTD sold the building outside the group on 12 April 2009 for €350,000.

Chargeable gains are calculated as follows:

BLACK's disposal		IR£
Cost		40,000
Deemed sale price		40,000
Gain/loss		Nil

SOOT'S disposal		€
Sale price		350,000
Cost as indexed	€50,790 × 1.356	(68,871)
Gain		281,129

Notional CGT	€281,129 at 25%	70,282
Chargeable to corporation tax: €70,282 / 12.5%		
		562,256

The CT payable on the gain is €562,256 @ 12.5% = €70,282.

31.4.4 Company leaving group

s623
TCA 97

In the case of most relieving provisions, there will normally be anti-avoidance provisions to prevent abuse of the relief and the CGT group relief provisions are no exception.

Provisions are made to effectively charge the tax foregone on a transfer within a group if the group company which acquires the asset leaves the group with that asset. The gain accrues to the company leaving the group, but in some cases, the parent of the group, or the group company from which the asset was acquired can also be held responsible for the tax involved.

Where a company ceases to be a member of a group, any asset which it acquired from other group members while it was a member of the group is deemed to be sold, and immediately reacquired by the company leaving the group at market value, at the date of acquisition from the other group company.

This has the effect of realising the gain, which was deferred on the original inter-company transfer within the group, and making it chargeable on the company leaving the group. It is a chargeable gain arising on the date of acquisition of the asset by that company and not the date the company leaves the group.

Only assets acquired intra-group within 10 years of the date of leaving the group are deemed disposed of in this fashion.

Example 31.21

The following is an Irish resident group of three companies:

HEAD LTD owns all shares in the subsidiaries LEG LTD and FOOT LTD. In January 2003, an asset was bought by LEG LTD for €20,000. In May 2003, it was transferred to FOOT LTD at its market value at that time (€40,000). In July 2003, the shares in FOOT LTD were sold to a non-group company, when the asset was still valued at €40,000. FOOT LTD subsequently sold the asset for €60,000 to HAND LTD (not a member of a group) in August 2009.

Under the group provisions, LEG LTD is treated as transferring the asset to FOOT LTD at no gain/no loss, i.e., the cost to FOOT LTD of acquiring the asset is deemed to be €20,000.

As soon as FOOT LTD leaves the group, it is deemed to have sold the asset in May 2003 for its market value at that date, i.e., €40,000. The gain therefore accrues to FOOT LTD in July 2003. The normal provisions for charging a gain on an asset acquired in January 2003 at a cost of €20,000 will apply.

For the sale to HAND LTD, the base cost is €40,000.

	€	
LEG LTD's disposal		
Cost	*20,000*	
Deemed sale price	*20,000*	
Gain/loss	*Nil*	

	€	
FOOT LTD's deemed disposal (on leaving the group)		
Sale price	*40,000*	
Cost €20,000	*(20,000)*	
Gain	*20,000*	
Notional CGT €20,000 at 20%	*4,000*	
Chargeable to corporation tax:		
€4,000 / 12.5%		*32,000*

The CT payable on the gain is €32,000 at 12.5% = €4,000

	€	
FOOT LTD's disposal (on sale to HAND LTD)		
Sale price	*60,000*	
Cost €40,000	*(40,000)*	
Gain	*20,000*	
Notional CGT €20,000 at 25%	*5,000*	
Chargeable to corporation tax:		
€5,000 / 12.5%		*40,000*

The CT payable on the gain is €40,000 at 12.5% = €5,000.

The legislation provides for any adjustment necessary to assess and collect the tax (i.e., additional assessments, etc.) to be within the time limit allowed for assessing and collecting the tax up to a period of 10 years after the date the company ceased to be a member of the group.

The gain will not crystallise in the following circumstances:

- transactions between associated companies that leave a group at the same time are ignored and accordingly, the gain on such transactions will not crystallise.

Example 31.22

A Limited, B Limited and C Limited are all members of a capital gains group. A Limited owns 100% of B Limited which in turn owns 100% of C Limited. In March 2000, C Limited sold an asset it had purchased for €30,000 in 1999 to B Limited for €50,000. No chargeable gain arose on this transaction due to group relief.

In June 2009, A Limited sold B Limited to D Limited. Despite the sale, the conditions for capital gains group relief are still in place and there is no chargeable gain on B Limited for the 2000 disposal by C Limited as both are still within their own group (and have now joined a group with D Limited).

■ A company that is wound up for *bona fide* commercial reasons, and not as part of a tax-avoidance scheme, is not to be treated as leaving a group.

■ If a company goes into liquidation, it is not deemed to have left a group for these purposes.

■ If the transfer under s617 took place more than 10 years previously, the gain will not crystallise.

Example 31.23

A Limited, B Limited and C Limited are all members of a capital gains group. A Limited owns 100% of B Limited which in turn owns 100% of C Limited. In March 1985, B Limited sold an asset it had purchased for €30,000 in 1983 to C Ltd for €50,000. No chargeable gain arose on this transaction due to group relief under s617.

In June 2009, B Limited sold C Limited to D Limited. As the original disposal took place over 10 years ago, there is no claw-back under s623.

■ If the company which originally disposed of the asset under s617 leaves the group, the gain will not crystallise.

■ *NB:* The gain only crystallises when the asset leaves the group.

Example 31.24

A Limited, B Limited and C Limited are all members of a capital gains group. A Limited owns 100% of both B Limited and C Limited. In March 2004, B Limited sold an asset it had purchased for €30,000 in 2003 to C Limited for €50,000. No chargeable gain arose on this transaction due to group relief.

In June 2009, A Limited sold B Limited to D Limited. Despite the sale, the conditions for capital gains group relief are still in place as the asset has not left the group (A and C are still in a capital gains group and C holds the asset).

31.4.5 Tax on company recoverable from other members of group

Assessed tax which has not been paid within six months of the due date by a group company may, within two years of the due date, be charged:

(a) to the principal company of the group at the time the gain accrued; and

(b) to any other company that was a group member in the two years ending on the date the gain accrued, that previously owned or had an interest in the asset, the disposal of which gave rise to the tax charge.

Such tax, if paid by the principal company or a previous owner of the asset, may be recovered from the company to which the gain accrued.

31.4.6   Group capital losses

There is no provision for transferring capital losses between group members. However, there is scope for tax planning so as to effectively benefit from capital losses in another group company.

Example 31.25

In January 2009, Florence Limited makes a gain of €250,000 on the sale of a warehouse. In February 2009, Rome Limited disposes of a warehouse which results in a loss of €250,000. Both companies are 100% subsidiaries of Bologna Limited and have a December 2009 year-end.

Rome Ltd cannot transfer its loss to Florence Ltd. Therefore, Florence Limited will incur a chargeable gains tax liability and Rome Ltd must carry its capital loss forward to shelter future gains (excluding gains on development land which are ring-fenced).

To avoid such a scenario, Rome Limited can transfer the asset to Florence Limited prior to its disposal (this will have no capital gains implications as both companies are in a group). Florence Limited will then dispose of both properties and set its chargeable loss against the chargeable gain, resulting in a nil liability.

31.4.7   Replacement of business assets by members of group – s620, TCA 97

For the purposes of rollover relief (see Chapter 27), all trades carried on by a capital gains tax group are treated as a single trade. Other group members may therefore be treated as having reinvested the disposal proceeds in new assets.

Consequently, if the company which purchased the replacement asset leaves the group, the gain which was rolled over will crystallise.

Example 31.26

A Limited and B Limited are members of a capital gains group. In July 2003, A Limited disposes of a trading asset for €100,000, which results in a gain of €20,000. B Limited purchased an asset for use in its trade in October 2002 for €120,000.

The investment by B Limited is deemed to have been made by A Limited. A Limited qualifies for rollover relief and can defer the gain arising on the sale of its asset until B's asset is sold and the proceeds not reinvested.

With the termination of rollover relief provided for by the 2003 Finance Act, this relief will be of much less significance in the future.

31.4.8   Provisions where companies cease to be resident in the State

s627 TCA 97 A company ceasing to be Irish resident on or after 21 April 1997 is treated as having disposed of, and immediately reacquired at market value on the departure date, all of its assets, apart from assets which, after the departure date, are situated in the State, or are used by a branch in the State. This exit charge effectively prevents companies from avoiding corporation tax on chargeable gains by disposing of assets during temporary periods of non-residence.

A company may also cease to be a member of a group on the occasion of going non-resident, in which case, the provisions of s623 will also apply. A simple example best illustrates the two deemed disposals that may arise.

Example 31.27

Clan Limited and Hugh Limited are members of a capital gains group. In July 2002, Clan Limited bought an asset for €50,000 which it sold to Hugh Limited in October 2004 for €60,000 (its market value at the time was €75,000). Hugh Limited operates two trades, one is a manufacturing trade in Bolivia which cost €200,000 in July 2000 and the other is a retail outlet in Leitrim which cost €185,000 in August 2001. In August 2009, Hugh Limited was sold to a group of Bolivian investors, which results in Hugh Limited becoming non-resident. At that time, the manufacturing trade was valued at €400,000 and the retail outlet at €375,000.

This has the effect of making the company liable on the inter-group disposal in 2004 under s617 and liable to a chargeable gain on the deemed disposal of the Bolivian manufacturing trade. As the Leitrim retail outlet is in the State, there is no chargeable gain until it is sold.

Hugh's deemed disposal of 2004 transfer (on leaving the group)	*€*	
Sale price	*75,000*	
Cost as indexed €50,000 × 1.049 (from 7/2002 to 10/2004)	*(52,450)*	
Gain	*22,550*	
Notional CGT €22,550 at 20% (rate in force at time of transfer)	*4,510*	
Chargeable to corporation tax:		
€4,510 / 12.5%		*36,080*

The CT payable on the gain is €342,400 @ 12.5% = €4,510

Hugh's disposal (on ceasing to be resident)	*€*	
Sale price	*400,000*	
Cost as indexed € 200,000 × 1.144 (from 7/2000 to 8/2009)	*(228,800)*	
Gain	*171,200*	
Notional CGT €171,200 at 25%	*42,800*	
Chargeable to corporation tax:		
€42,800 / 12.5%		*342,400*

The CT payable on the gain is €342,800 @ 12.5% = €42,800.

WHAT YOU SHOULD NOW KNOW

On completion of this chapter, you should be able to:

- ✓ Identify the members of a loss group - Volume 2 Q 32.2, Assignment 32.1, 32.2.

- ✓ Identify the members of a capital gains group - Volume 2 Q 32.1, Assignment 32.1.

- ✓ Calculate and utilise group loss relief - Volume 2 Q 32.2, 32.6, 32.7, Revision CT Q 3.

- ✓ Identify the correct order for set-off of group loss relief - Volume 2 Q 32.4, 32.6.

- ✓ Identify whether a consortium exists - Volume 2 Q 32.3, 32.1.

- ✓ Discuss the advantages of having a capital gains group in place and describe the implications of intra-group transfers of assets - Volume 2 Q 32.5, Revision CT Q3, Assignment 32.1.

- ✓ Describe the implications of a company leaving the group and calculate the resulting liabilities - Volume 2 Q 32.5, 32.8.

- ✓ Identify the implications of a group company going non-resident and calculate the resulting liabilities.

- ✓ Complete Questions and the Assignments in Irish Taxation Law and Practice, Volume 2.

Appendix I

ICI v Colmer – 30 June 1998

This case is hugely important in the context of the residence of group companies and merits a separate discussion.

ICI owned 49% of the share capital of a UK resident holding company with 23 subsidiaries, four of which were resident in the UK. One of the UK companies had losses and ICI wished to claim consortium relief. The Inland Revenue denied relief on the basis that such relief could only apply to companies resident in the UK.

All of the relevant companies were actually resident in the UK, i.e., ICI, the holding company and the loss-making subsidiary. However, Revenue argued that the holding company must "mainly" hold UK companies.

The Court of Appeal found that the definition of one section could not be applied to another, unless, of course, legislated for. However, the House of Lords upheld the Revenue appeal.

ICI won the case – the European Court of Justice ruled that the provision of the legislation which required a holding company's 90% trading subsidiaries to be resident in the UK was discriminatory against companies that had exercised their right to the freedom of establishment under Article 52 of the Treaty of Rome. Consequently national legislation was prevented from linking an accountable person's entitlement to a form of tax relief to its tax residency.

The case very much focused on the place of establishment and allowed relief on the basis that, if the majority of the subsidiaries were established in the UK, loss relief would have been allowed but as the majority of the subsidiaries were based outside the UK, loss relief had been denied.

This case resulted in an amendment to the legislation provided by s79 Finance Act 1999. This had the effect of allowing a parent company to include indirect holdings in any company for the purposes of determining 51% ownership, provided the shares were held through a company resident for tax purposes in any Member State of the EU.

The amending legislation allows an Irish company form a group with an Irish branch of a non-resident company under common control for the purposes of group relief. The practical impact for the purposes of this discussion is to allow:

■ Surrender of losses between two Irish resident subsidiaries of an EU parent;

■ Surrender of losses between an Irish resident subsidiary and Irish branch of an EU parent.

W (UK Resident)

75%   75%

S (IRISH RESIDENT)   T (IRISH RESIDENT)

Marks & Spencer case – 1 January 2002

The other case worthy of note with regard to new developments in the area of group loss relief is the UK Special Commissioners' decision in the *Marks & Spencer* case. Marks & Spencer claimed relief for losses incurred by French, German and Belgian subsidiaries against its UK profits.

The foreign subsidiaries were not resident in the UK in the relevant years and no part of the subsidiary activities were carried on in the UK. Consequently the losses at issue were outside the scope of UK tax. The Inspector of Taxes refused the claim for group relief on the basis that the foreign subsidiaries were not resident in the UK as required under domestic UK legislation. Marks & Spencer appealed the case on the basis that the denial of loss relief constituted an infringement of Article 43 of the Treaty of Rome, which concerns freedom of establishment. In this respect, in all its recent case law the European Court of Justice has noted that although direct taxation is a matter for the Member States, they must nevertheless exercise their direct powers consistently with Community Law.

The Special Commissioner, Dr. John Jones, ruled that Marks & Spencer was not entitled to the relief. He stated that the relevant principles established by the case law of the ECJ are clear on the matter and found it unnecessary to refer the case to the ECJ for guidance. The Appeal Commissioner distinguished this case from *ICI v Colmer* stating that the discriminatory rule did not relate to the identity of the subsidiaries but rather concerned ICI's right to establish subsidiaries in other Member States. If ICI exercised its right to do so it would no longer be among the category of eligible claimants for the losses in question. In this case, by contrast, the domestic legislation prevents the foreign subsidiaries from surrendering their losses. The inability to claim loss relief is as a consequence of UK restrictions on losses.

The case was appealed to the European Court of Justice to overturn the Special Commissioner's decision. The Advocate-General issued a preliminary ruling on 7 April 2005 stating that Marks & Spencer's claim was justified. He stated that the "principle of territoriality cannot justify the current restriction". The European Commission supported Marks & Spencer, while seven states (including Ireland) supported the UK Inland Revenue.

The European Court of Justice gave its ruling on 13 December 2005, Case C-446/03.

While recognising the right of the UK Revenue to formulate its own internal tax legislation in this area, especially to prevent tax avoidance, the ECJ felt that the legislation went too far in its aims and breached the rights to freedom of establishment.

The ruling stated that where the "non-resident subsidiary has exhausted the possibilities available in its State of residence of having the losses taken into account," it can then seek to have the losses transferred to the UK company.

Therefore, the ruling does not facilitate a straightforward surrender of loss relief from a non-resident subsidiary to a UK parent, as would be the case if the subsidiary was UK resident. Such relief for losses of a non-resident subsidiary may only be claimed as a last resort.

Finance Act 2007 legislated for the ECJ decision, see 31.2.2.2 for a detailed review of the legislation.

The legislation puts a very strict interpretation on the ECJ ruling as regards the actual claiming of the relief, the main point being that the subsidiary would apparently have to cease trading in order to surrender any relief to the Irish parent, as the relief is only available if the subsidiary can **never** claim relief for its own loss.

Leading tax commentators have heavily criticised the legislation, stating that it does not fully implement the ruling and would probably not survive either a case taken by an aggrieved Irish parent company to the ECJ or an EU challenge itself.

Due to Ireland's low corporation tax rates it is unlikely that any major multinational would be interested in having the relief surrendered to a parent based in the state.

The legislation does not sit easily with our stated notion of being an open, low-tax, flexible economy.

In the recent Lidl Belgium Gmbh & Co. KG v Finanzamt Heilbronn case the European Court of Justice set out how far they believe cross border loss relief can be taken.

In this ruling, losses in a Luxembourg branch of Lidl were prohibited from being transferred to the parent company in Germany on the basis that they would be allowable against future years Luxembourg profits. They stated that to allow the company's claim may give rise to a double allowance, once in Germany and once in Luxembourg against future income.

The European Court of Justice recognised that the treatment was not in keeping with the principle of freedom of establishment (as losses in a German branch could be set against the German parent company's profit) but that the prohibition was important to preserve the tax system in both countries.

32

CLOSE COMPANIES

In this chapter, you will deal with the following:

- Introduction
- Close company definitions

- Impact of close company legislation on individuals and companies
- Calculation of close company surcharges

32.1   Introduction

The purpose of this chapter is to explain the reasoning behind the close company legislation and to define the numerous terms in the legislation. The chapter also sets out in detail the disadvantages to a company and its shareholders/directors when it is deemed to be a close company.

The legislation was enacted to ensure that shareholders (mainly in owner-managed companies) could not use their dominant position in the company to withdraw funds or have expenses paid by the company in a manner which eroded the tax base. The vast majority of companies in Ireland are owned and managed by families. An analysis of a section of accounts filed with the Companies Office shows that in a large percentage of cases, a company may have an issued share capital of between €1 and €2,000 and that these shares would usually be held between husband or wife, brothers, etc.

The following example shows just how the tax base could be eroded without close company legislation.

Example 32.1:

John Murphy is a self-employed practising architect with an annual tax-adjusted net profit of €100,000. John is single and apart from the annual single tax credit has no other tax credits or reliefs.

John's income tax liability is as follows:

		€
Profit from profession		*100,000*
Taxed at 20%	*€36,400 × 20%*	*72,080*
Taxed at 41%	*€63,600 × 41%*	*26,076*
PRSI & levies	*€75,036 × 7%*	*5,525*
PRSI & levies	*€24,964 × 8%*	*1,997*
Income levy	*€75,036 × 1.67%*	*1,253*
	€24,964 × 33%	*749*
Single tax credit		*(1,830)*
Total income tax liability		*40,777*

Therefore from gross income of €100,000, John has after tax cash of €59,223 (€100,000 – €40,777).

John expects to have a similar income in the following year and decides to set up John Murphy Ltd. The company's annual tax liability would be as follows:

	€
Profit from company	*100,000*
Taxed at 12.5%	*100,000 × 12.5% = €12,500*

The company would have after tax cash reserves of €87,500. John then decides to take this from the company as an interest-free loan. This leaves him better off in cash terms by €28,277 (€87,500 – €59,223). (Note 1)

It is the above type of scenario that the close company legislation seeks to prevent. Now that the gap between income tax and corporation is as wide as it has been for the last 20 years, a greater focus can be expected on the anti-avoidance aspects of the legislation. The particular scenario above is prevented by s438 TCA 97, which is covered later in the chapter.

Note 1: This example ignores the possible Company Law implications regarding loans.

32.2 Close Company Definitions

32.2.1 Close company

s430
TCA 97

A close company is defined as an **Irish resident company,** which is CONTROLLED by:

(a) five or fewer participators and their associates; or

(b) participators who are directors, without any limitation on the number.

32.2.2 Participator

s433
TCA 97

A participator is any person having an interest in the capital or income of a company. The term includes:

(a) a shareholder (the most common example you will come across);

(b) any person who possesses or is entitled to acquire share capital or voting rights in the company, e.g., an option-holder;

(c) any loan creditor of a company (defined below);

(d) any person entitled to receive or participate in distributions from the company or any amounts payable by the company to loan creditors by way of premium on redemption; or

(e) any person who can secure income or assets (whether present or future) of the company, which will be applied either directly or indirectly for his/her benefit, i.e., position of power.

32.2.3 Associate of a participator

s433
TCA 97

An associate means, in relation to a participator:

(a) any relative or business partner of the participator

(Relative includes husband, wife, ancestor, lineal descendant, brother or sister. Therefore all "in-laws" are excluded as are nieces and nephews);

(b) the trustees of any settlement of which a participator or any relative of his/hers (living or dead) is the settlor.

Where the participator is interested in shares of the company which are subject to any trust or are part of the estate of a deceased person, an associate would be any other person interested therein, e.g., trustees, executors and beneficiaries. In this definition trusts for employees, directors and their dependents and approved pension funds are specifically excluded.

An associate of an associate cannot be linked to a participator, e.g., a person's wife's/husband's sister's shareholding cannot be added to his/her shareholding if he/she is taken as the participator. However, if it is the wife/husband who is treated as the participator, then the shareholdings of her husband/his wife and her/his sister would be added to her/him shareholding as her husband/his wife and her/his sister are two different associates in their own right.

32.2.4 Director

s433(4)
TCA 97

This term includes:

- Any person occupying the position of directors by whatever name called;

- Any person in accordance with whose directions or instructions the directors are accustomed to act;

- Any person who is a manager of the company and is either on his own or with one or more associates the beneficial owner of or able to control (directly or indirectly) 20% or more of the ordinary share capital of the company.

Remember that the definition specifically refers to directors. Once a company is controlled by directors, it is a close company regardless of the number of directors included in the "control".

32.2.5 Loan creditor

s433(6)
TCA 97

A detailed discussion of the term loan creditor is outside the scope of this publication, suffice to say that the term generally means a creditor in respect of any debt incurred by the company apart from ordinary trade debts or bank borrowings.

32.2.6 Associated company

s432(1)
TCA 97

A company is to be treated as another's associated company at any given time if, at that time or any time within the previous year, one of the two has control of the other or both are under the control of the same person or persons.

32.2.7 Control

s432(2)
TCA 97

A person is regarded as having CONTROL of a company if he/she exercises OR if he/she is able to exercise OR if he/she is entitled to acquire control whether direct or indirect over the company's affairs and in particular, if he/she possesses or is entitled to acquire the GREATER PART of:

(a) the ordinary (voting) share capital of the company; or

(b) the total share capital of the company (including preference shares); or

(c) the income of the company on a full distribution among participators (ignoring the rights of loan creditors); or

(d) the assets of the company on a full distribution to shareholders in the event of a winding-up.

"Control" in the above situation means more than 50% (this could be 50.001%, however). Therefore, five participators or fewer who own 50.001% or more of the voting share capital of a company have control of the company and the company would thus be deemed to be a close company. If eight directors control the company, it is deemed to be a close company as the second part of the close company definition does not place a maximum number on the amount of directors needed to ensure close company status.

32.2.8 Exceptions

Certain companies are specifically excluded from close company status:

(1) companies not resident in Ireland;

(2) companies controlled by or on behalf of the State, which would NOT be close if the State's interest were ignored. FA2003 extended this exemption to include companies controlled by EU Member States or States with which Ireland has a tax treaty;

(3) some public/quoted companies which satisfy certain conditions. A detailed discussion on this point is beyond the scope of this publication and exemptions under this section are relatively uncommon in practice;

(4) companies controlled by one or more other companies, which are "open companies" provided they cannot be treated as "close" EXCEPT by including as one of the "five" or fewer participators a company which is not close. A non-resident company which holds shares in the company in question is deemed to be a close company for the purpose of this exception if it would be a close company if it were Irish resident.

32.2.9 Chart to determine whether a company is a close company

The following chart is useful in determining whether or not a company is a close company.

Example 32.2:

A Ltd has an issued share capital of €100,000 held as follows:

	€
Mr. Kennedy (Manager)	*45,000*
Mrs. Kennedy	*6,000*
Ten other unrelated shareholders	*49,000*
	100,000

Mr. Kennedy and Mrs. Kennedy are associates. Therefore, they are treated as one participator. As five or fewer participators control 51% of the company's share capital, the company is regarded as close. It should also be noted that Mr. Kennedy is deemed to be a director of the company as he owns 20% or more of the company's ordinary share capital (even though his title is Manager).

Example 32.3:

B Ltd is an unquoted company and has an issued share capital of 50,000 €1 ordinary shares and €100,000 in €1 preference shares. The preference shares are non-participating and non-voting. None of the directors is a participator in the company.

The capital is held as follows:

	SHARES			CONTROL VIA	CONTROL VIA
	Ordinary	Preference	Equates to	Votes (Top 5)	Issued share capital (Top 5)
	€	€		€	€
Paul	4,000	–		4,000	–
Noel	7,500	10,000		7,500	17,500
Fiona	2,000	25,000		2,000	27,000
Emma	2,500	9,000		2,500	11,500
Francis	800	12,000		–	12,800
Margaret	1,000	6,000		1,000	7,000
Others (owning <500)	32,200	38,000		–	–
	50,000	100,000		17,000	75,800

CONTROL TESTS

1. Using the first of the four control tests, voting power, only 34% (17,000/50,000) of the voting power is controlled by five or fewer participators, therefore the company is not a close company using this test.

2. However, under the second control test, total share capital, more than half of the total issued share capital (ordinary and preference) is held by five or fewer participators, i.e., 50.53% (75,800/(100,000 + 50,000)). Therefore, the company is close.

Example 32.4:

C Limited has an issued share capital of €100,000 held by the following directors:

		€
Paul	Director	12,000
Martin	Director	10,000
Colleen	Director	4,000
Bríd	Director	5,000
Aidan	Director	6,000
Justin	Director	12,000
Kenneth	Director	9,000
Others (each owning <5,000)		42,000
		100,000

The company is not under the control of five or fewer participators as the top five participators only control 49% of the company (Paul, Martin, Aidan, Justin and Kenneth). However, it is under the control of its directors (58%) and is therefore a close company irrespective of the number of directors.

If we revise the facts of the above example, such that Justin is a manager and not a director, the position is as follows:

- As Justin does not hold 20% or more of the ordinary share capital he does not rank as a director;

- The company's directors then hold 46% of the issued share capital which means that it is not director-controlled and is therefore an "open" company.

Example 32.5:

D Limited has an issued share capital held as follows:

	%
Paul	*6*
Joanne (Paul's wife)	*5*
Noel (Paul's brother)	*6*
Marie (Paul's daughter)	*3*
Fiona (Paul's sister)	*5*
George (son of Noel, i.e., Paul's nephew)	*9*
Emma (Paul's sister)	*15*
Rogan Limited (Company controlled by Paul)	*6*
Margaret (Paul's mother)	*5*
5 others, unconnected to Paul or each other, each holding 8%	*40*
	100

Paul's own interests are aggregated with those of his associates, i.e., Joanne, Noel, Marie, Fiona, Emma, Rogan Limited and Margaret. All these shareholders are treated as one participator. Note that George, who is Paul's nephew, is not an associate as he is not within the scope of the definition of relative. He would, however, be treated as the second participator in the company. Between both participators they control 60% and adding three more from the 8% each shareholders leaves five participators holding 84% of the company. Therefore, D Limited is treated as a close company.

32.3 Impact of Close Company Status on Individuals and Companies

The purpose of this unit is to summarise the disadvantages, which flow from a company having a "close company" status and also to explain what the anti-avoidance measures aim to prevent.

32.3.1 Benefits to participators and associates

s436
TCA 97

Any expenses incurred by a close company in providing benefits or facilities of any kind for a participator or an associate will be treated as a distribution made by the company. This means that the amount of the expense is "added back" in the tax-adjusted profits of the Case I computation and the recipient is treated as if the value of the benefit is income received under Schedule F. The company is obliged to account for dividend withholding tax (DWT) and pay this over to the Collector-General based on the **actual value of the benefit.** The company has a right to demand repayment of this withholding tax at 20% from the participator, although in practice this may prove difficult. The individual is liable to income tax on the gross value of the benefit actually received.

The company has a DWT liability equal to the tax credit attaching to the distribution. Expenses incurred on such items as living accommodation, entertainment, domestic and other services would all be classed as benefits to the participator.

The following expense payments are not treated as distributions:

(1) any expense made good, i.e., reimbursed, to the company by the participator;

(2) any expense incurred in providing benefits or facilities to directors or employees, which are already assessable as benefit in kind under Schedule E (s118 TCA 97); (From 1 January 2004 these benefits are taxed at source through the company's payroll.)

(3) any expense incurred in connection with the provision for the spouse, children or dependants of any director or employee of any pension, annuity, lump sum or gratuity to be given on his/her death or retirement.

Example 32.6:

In March 2009, Gormally Limited incurred an expense of €1,500 in providing a luxurious Caribbean cruise for a shareholder, who is neither an employee nor a director. The shareholder is an associate of a participator in Gormally Limited, which is a close company. Accounts are prepared to 31/12/2009.

IMPLICATIONS:

A) Corporation Tax

1. *The expense of €1,500 is disallowed and is added back in the adjusted Case I profit computation as it is treated as a distribution.*

2. *The company must account for DWT as it is deemed to have made a distribution. The expense paid is treated as the distributed amount.*

   DWT of €300 (€1,500 × 20%) is payable. This amount is payable to the Collector-General on or before the fourteenth day after the month the benefit was paid, in this case 14 April 2009.

3. *The net effect of 1. and 2. above is that the company has paid €1,500 for the holiday and also €300 withholding tax. In this situation, it could seek recovery of €300 from the shareholder as it only intended to give a benefit of €1,500.*

B) Income Tax

The shareholder is not assessed under Schedule E as he is not an employee or Director but is treated as having received a distribution liable under Schedule F. The amount is €1,500 and the related dividend withholding tax is €300.

If the shareholder pays income tax at the marginal rate, then the additional income tax payable (ignoring the impact of PRSI and levies) would be as follows:

	€
Schedule F	*1,500*
Income tax payable at 41%	*615*
Less DWT	*(300)*
Additional income tax payable by shareholder	*315*

The company is entitled to demand repayment from the shareholder of the tax credit.

32.3.2   Interest paid to directors and their associates

This piece of legislation is concerned with any interest on loans paid by a close company to, or to an associate of, a person who:

(a) is a director of the close company or of any company which controls or is controlled by the close company; AND

(b) has a material interest in the company. A person has a material interest in a close company if he/she is able to control more than 5% of the ordinary share capital of the close company, or of any other company that controls it.

Such interest payments in excess of a prescribed limit will be treated as a distribution. The practical effect of this treatment is as follows:

(1) For the company, excess interest is added back in the tax-adjusted Case I profit computation. The company must also account for dividend withholding tax (DWT) at the standard rate of income tax, i.e., 20% on the excess amount treated as a distribution. The company is also obliged to withhold tax at the standard rate on the interest allowed under s239 TCA 97. This tax is payable with the company's corporation tax liability.

(2) For the recipient, excess interest is treated as a distribution received and is taxable under Schedule F. The recipient director is also taxed on the interest allowed, but in this case, under Schedule D Case IV. He or she will get credit for the DWT withheld on the excess interest and also for the tax withheld on the allowable interest.

A director has a material interest if he/she, either on his/her own or with any one or more of his/her associates, is the beneficial owner of, or is able to control, directly or indirectly MORE THAN 5% of the ordinary share capital.

The prescribed limit is calculated firstly as an "overall" limit. The overall limit is then apportioned between the various directors affected (those with a material interest) on the basis of the amounts of interest paid to each of them.

The overall limit is 13% per annum on the LOWER of:

(a) the total of ALL loans on which interest to directors (or their associates) with a "material interest" was paid by the company in the accounting period; OR

(b) the nominal amount of the issued share capital of the close company PLUS the amount of any share premium account, taken at the BEGINNING of the accounting period.

For the purposes of (a) above, where the total of all loans varies during the accounting period, the average total over the period is to be taken.

In practice a company is usually in financial difficulty when its directors are required to invest in the company and therefore a return on the investment is not generally an issue.

If a return is required it is recommended that a directors fee or increased salary be processed through payroll in preference to the complicated calculation of allowable interest and the implications of overpaying interest.

Example 32.7:

Rogan Limited is a close company whose issued share capital is €10,000 (10,000 €1 ordinary shares). The company has no share premium account. In the accounting period ended 31/12/2009, it received the following loans:

	Shareholding	Loans	Interest Paid
	€	€	€
1/1/2009 Philip (Director)	3,333	30,000	4,500
1/1/2009 George (Director)	300	20,000	3,000
1/1/2009 Elizabeth (wife of George)	300	–	
1/1/2009 Joanne (Director)	500	10,000	1,500

The corporation tax and income tax consequences for Rogan Limited are as follows:

The following Directors are affected by the provisions of s437 TCA 97:

1. Philip is a Director and holds 33% of the ordinary share capital.

2. George is a Director and together with his associates, i.e., his wife Elizabeth, he holds over 5% of the ordinary share capital.

3. Joanne does not come within this provision as she holds EXACTLY 5% of the ordinary share capital and does not therefore have the necessary "material interest".

The overall limit is the lower of:

		€	€
(a)	13% of (€30,000 + €20,000)	6,500	
(b)	13% of €10,000	1,300	1,300

Interest paid to Directors with a material interest is:

Philip		4,500
George		3,000
		7,500
Overall limit		(1,300)
Excess (treated as a distribution)		6,200

This excess of €6,200 is added back in Rogan Limited's tax-adjusted Case I profit computation.

The overall limit is apportioned among the relevant Directors according to the interest paid to each:

	INTEREST PAID	LIMIT		EXCESS TREATED AS DISTRIBUTION
	€		€	€
Philip	4,500	$\frac{4,500 \times 1,300}{7,500}$ =	780	3,720
George	3,000	$\frac{3,000 \times 1,300}{7,500}$ =	520	2,480
	7,500		1,300	6,200

The dividend withholding tax liability of Rogan Limited for the accounting period ended 31/12/2009 is as follows:

€6,200 × 20% = €1,240.

The company is also obliged, under s239 TCA 97 to deduct tax at the standard rate from the allowable interest paid:

Philip   €780 × 20% = €156

George   €520 × 20% = €104

The income tax implications (ignoring PRSI and levies) for Philip are as follows (assuming he is taxed at 41%):

	€
Schedule F	*3,720*
Schedule D Case IV	*780*
Income	*4,500*
Income tax at 41%	*1,845*
Less DWT credit (€3,720 × 20%)	*(744)*
Less interest tax credit	*(156)*
Net income tax payable	*945*

32.3.3   Loans to participators

s438 & s439 TCA 97 Where a close company makes a loan to an individual who is a participator or an associate of a participator, the company will be required to pay income tax in respect of the amount of the loan grossed up at the standard rate (i.e., 20%) as if this grossed up amount were an annual payment under s239 TCA 97 (and not Schedule F, which applies to expenses or excess loan interest paid by the company).

The income tax due cannot be set off against the company's corporation tax liability. When the loan, or part of the loan, is repaid by the participator (or associate), the tax paid or a proportionate part of it will be refunded to the company (without interest), provided a claim is made within 10 years of the year of assessment in which the loan is repaid.

There are three exceptions to the above treatment of loans to participators:

(a) Where the business of the company is or included the lending of money and the loan is made in the ordinary course of that business, the provisions do not apply.

(b) Loans made to directors or employees of the company (or an associated company) are outside of the scope of the provisions if:

1. the amount of the loan together with all other loans outstanding made by the company (or an associated company) to the borrower (or his/her spouse) does not exceed €19,050; AND

2. the borrower works FULL-TIME for the company; AND

3. the borrower does NOT have a material interest (as defined previously – more than 5% of ordinary share capital) in the company or an associated company. If the borrower subsequently acquires a material interest, the company will be requested to pay income tax in respect of ALL loans outstanding to the borrower at that time.

(c) The provisions do not apply where the debt is incurred for the supply of goods or services in the ordinary course of business, UNLESS the period of credit given exceeds six months or is longer than credit terms normally given to customers.

It is important to note that the loan is NOT regarded as income in the individual's hand unless and until the loan is forgiven by the company. In this case, the income tax is not recoverable by the company and the "grossed-up" loan is assessed on the participator for income tax purposes. The loan is "grossed-up" at the standard income tax rate applicable in the year of forgiveness and not at the rate for the year it was advanced. Also, the write-off is NOT deductible against the company's Case I profits.

Example 32.8:

Griffiths Limited makes an interest-free loan of €40,000 to a full-time working Director, Chris Griffiths, in the accounting period ended 31/12/2009. Mr. Griffiths holds 10% of the close company's ordinary share capital. The loan is subsequently forgiven in the accounting period ended 31/12/2010.

What are the corporation tax and income tax consequences?

NOTE: This loan to a participator does NOT qualify for the exception at (b) above because Mr. Griffiths has a material interest in the company and the amount of the loan exceeds €19,050.

*1. **Corporation tax implications for Griffiths Limited:***

    (a) Accounting period ended 31/12/2009: income tax of €40,000 × 20/80, i.e., €10,000 is payable by the company with its corporation tax under s239 TCA 97. No deduction is allowed in the company's accounts for the loan or the tax paid.

    (b) Accounting period ended 31/12/2010: the income tax paid is now irrecoverable and the write-off is not a tax-deductible expense in the adjusted Case I profit computation.

*2. **Income tax implications for Mr. Griffiths:***

    (a) Year of assessment 2009: Mr. Griffiths is charged to income tax on the notional benefit in kind on an interest-free loan, currently at 12.50%.

    (b) Year of assessment 2010: the loan write-off is treated as Schedule D Case IV income in the amount of €40,000 100/80 , i.e., €50,000. Credit is given for the €10,000 suffered by the company so that only a higher rate liability arises (i.e., the marginal rate in force in 2010.). It is important to bear in mind that if Mr. Griffiths has insufficient income tax payable to fully utilise this credit, the balance is not repayable.

32.4   Calculation of Close Company Surcharges

32.4.1   Introduction

The disadvantages discussed above mainly affect participators and directors of close companies personally. Legislation was also enacted to narrow the gap between income tax rates for individuals (approx 50% – income tax, income levy and PRSI/levies for the self-employed) and corporation tax rates for companies (12.5% on trading income and 25% on passive income). The legislation levies a surcharge on undistributed income at either 20% or 15% depending on the type of company (see below). This surcharge is in addition to the corporation tax charge that the company would have paid on its income and therefore has the result of bringing the effective rate of corporation tax closer to income tax levels.

As the surcharge is only charged on undistributed income, the chief method of avoiding a surcharge is to distribute the income in the form of a dividend. However, by declaring a dividend, the shareholders will be charged to tax under Schedule F normally at the marginal rate of income tax.

The two surcharge types affect passive income and professional income and both are discussed below. It can be seen therefore that the surcharge legislation is an effective tool for ensuring that certain types of income cannot be sheltered in a company to avail of Ireland's low corporation tax rates. Despite much media speculation in recent years regarding the extension of the surcharge to all undistributed income (i.e., to include Case I trading income), no major changes have been made in this respect.

32.4.2 Close company surcharge on undistributed income

s440 TCA 97

The purpose of this commentary is to set out the provisions relating to an additional surcharge of 20%, which is levied on the undistributed rental and investment income of a close company.

An additional 20% corporation tax surcharge is levied on a close company, which does not distribute income, derived from investments or rental property (termed "investment" and "estate" income respectively).

Companies which would be entitled to avail of the participation exemption, s626B TCA 97 scheme) (which allows holding companies resident in Ireland to sell shares in 5% subsidiaries free of capital gains tax) are not required to include in its surchargeable income dividends received from its non-resident qualifying subsidiaries. However, as dividends received from Irish subsidiaries are Franked Investment income and are therefore surchargeable, this placed them at a tax disadvantage compared to non-Irish EU/DTA dividends. Finance Act 2008 introduced an election mechanism for distributions payable after 31 January 2008. Where both the payee and recipient jointly elect, the recipient is not surcharged on the dividend and the payee does not receive a deduction against its own surchargeable income.

As noted above a company may declare a dividend in order to reduce its undistributed income and therefore its exposure to the surcharge. Any dividend declared by the company must be paid within 18 months of the period end. Therefore, to reduce the surcharge for year ended 31 December 2008 the dividend must be declared and paid on or before 30 June 2010. The surcharge is paid with the following year's corporation tax. Thus, for a company with a year-end of 31 December 2008, the surcharge is paid with the corporation tax for the year ended 31 December 2009 (unless the company has paid dividends for 2008).

In addition to ordinary dividends declared and paid, deemed distributions such as participators' expenses (s436 TCA 97), excess interest to directors (s437 TCA 97) and distributions under s130 TCA 97 are also included in reducing a company's undistributed earnings for surcharge purposes.

Step-by-step surcharge calculation for trading company, s440

The following step-by-step procedure facilitates calculation of the close company surcharge in accordance with s440 TCA 1997.

		€
(i)	**Calculate "Income"**	X
	Income from Case I, III, IV and V	(X)
	Deduct current losses, i.e., s396A, s399 TCA 97	(X)
	Deduct relevant trade charges, i.e., s243A TCA 97	(X)
		X
(ii)	**Calculate "Estate and Investment Income"**	
	Answer from (i) × (Passive Income/Total Income)	X
	Add Franked Investment Income (FII)	X
	Deduct relevant charges (charges deductible against all profits, i.e., s243 TCA 97).	(X)
		X
(iii)	**Calculate "Distributable Estate and Investment Income"**	
	Answer from (ii)	X
	Less corporation tax on passive income as reduced by relevant charges	(X)
	Less 7.5% trading deduction on above sum	(X)
		X
(iv)	**Calculate surcharges – deduct distributions from (iii) and multiply by 20%.**	

Example 32.9:

Troy Ltd, a close company, has the following income, chargeable gains and charges on income for its 12-month accounting period ended 31 December 2009.

	€
Trading income (non-professional)	*40,000*
Rental income	*10,000*
Bank interest (Gross)	*6,000*
FII (Gross)	*4,000*

The company paid charges of €5,000 in respect of its trading activities and claimed €10,000 of loss relief in respect of loss relief under s396(1) for a loss that arose in the accounting period ended 31/12/2008.

The company incurred expenses on behalf of a participator of €400 under s436 TCA 97 (the participator was neither a director nor an employee of the company) and the final dividend of €2,000 for the year ended 31/12/2009 was declared and paid on 1 February 2010.

1.	*Calculate the "income" of the company*		€
	Schedule D	*Case I*	*40,000*
		Case III	*6,000*
		Case V	*10,000*
			56,000
	Less relevant trading charges		*(5,000)*
			51,000

Note that no allowance is given for the loss carried forward. The surcharge calculation is on current year activity only.

2. **Calculate the "Estate and Investment Income"**

		€	€
First calculation			
FII			4,000
$€51,000 \times \dfrac{€16,000}{€56,000}$			14,571
			18,571
Deduct:			
Relevant charges (against all profits)			Nil
"Estate and Investment Income"			18,571

3. **"Distributable Estate and Investment Income"**

Estate and Investment Income		18,571
Less corporation tax (€14,571 × 25%)		(3,643)
		14,928
Less trading discount at 7.5%		(1,120)
		13,808

4. **Surchargeable amount**

	€	€
Distributable Estate and Investment Income		13,808
Less distributions for the period		
Expenses of participator	(400)	
Final dividend declared and paid	(2,000)	
		(2,400)
Surchargeable amount		11,408
Surcharge at 20%		2,282

This surcharge is treated as part of the corporation tax liability for the accounting year ended 31/12/2010. As the company has 18 months to declare and pay dividends, it has until the following year to actually pay the surcharge. If no further distributions are made by the company, by 30/06/2011, the surcharge will be payable with the corporation tax for 31/12/10. The first payment will be due on 21/11/09 (90%) with the second payment (10%) being due when the return is filed, at the latest by 21/9/11. If the company pays the first preliminary payment on 21/11/09 and subsequently pays a dividend in March 2011 in respect of the year ended 31/12/2009, it will receive a refund or a set-off against its other CT liabilities.

De minimus relief

Section 440(1)(b) TCA 97 provides that no surcharge is imposed in any case where the excess of the "distributable estate and investment income" for an accounting period over the distributions made for that accounting period is €635 or less.

There is also an element of marginal relief where the "excess" to which the 20% surcharge is applied exceeds €635 by a small amount. This limits the amount of the surcharge so as not to be higher than 80% of the amount by which the "excess" is greater than €635. Thus, the marginal relief applies if the "excess" is between €636 and €846.

Thus, if the "excess" or the surchargeable amount is €746, the surcharge is calculated as €746 × 20%, i.e., €149.

In these circumstances, marginal relief limits the amount of the surcharge to: (€746 – €635) × 80%, i.e., €89 (€111 × 80%).

Reduction if accumulated undistributed income is less than excess

Section 440(2) TCA 97 provides for a reduction in the amount (the "excess") on which the surcharge is levied for an accounting period if the "excess" is more than the "accumulated undistributed income" of the company at the end of that accounting period. If this occurs, the 20% surcharge is calculated on the amount of that accumulated undistributed income (subject to the same €635 *de minimis* exclusion mentioned above).

The accumulated undistributed income at the end of the accounting period is taken as per the accounts of the company plus any transfer to capital reserves, bonus issues or other transactions which would reduce the accumulated income available for distribution.

Example 32.10:

Take the case of Troy Ltd, the close company dealt with in Example 32.9. If the financial accounts at period end December 2009 show reserves available for distribution of €7,000, this figure would be surchargeable instead of the €11,408 as previously calculated.

Surcharge: €7,000 × 20% = €1,400.

32.4.3   Surcharge on service companies, s441 TCA 97

32.4.3.1 Meaning of service company

Section 440 TCA 97 is concerned with surcharging undistributed passive income. Given, however, the wide variance between marginal income tax for professionals (47%) and the lower rate of corporation tax for incorporated professional companies (12.5%), the s441 TCA 97 surcharge on service company income seeks to narrow that gap. The surcharge applies to "active" income where professional persons incorporate in an effort to avoid paying the top rate of personal tax on their fee income. This surcharge is known as the professional services surcharge and is levied on 50% of the annual professional income at a rate of 15%. Passive income is still subject to a surcharge at 20%.

A service company is defined as a close company:

(a) whose business consists of or includes the carrying on of a profession or the provision of professional services;

(b) which holds or exercises an office or employment;

(c) whose business consists of or includes the provision of services or facilities of whatever nature to or for:

  (i)   a company within the categories (a) and (b) described above,

  (ii) an individual or partnership which carries on a profession,

  (iii) a person who holds or exercises an employment,

  (iv) a person or partnership connected with any of the above.

The term "service company" applies only where the principal part of the company's income which is chargeable under Schedule D Case II is derived from the profession, the provision of professional services, an employment, the provision of certain services or facilities or a combination of these activities. Examples of such companies would include companies established by professionals such as auctioneers, journalists, opticians, etc.

As the legislation provides no definition of a profession, it has fallen upon the Courts to interpret its meaning. In the Irish case of *Mac Giolla Mhaith (Inspector of Taxes) v Cronin & Associates Ltd* ((1984) 3 ITR 211), the Inspector of Taxes imposed a surcharge under s441 TCA 97 on the basis that the company's advertising business was a profession. The company appealed this decision and after losing the appeal before the Appeal Commissioners and winning before the Circuit Court, the case appeared before the High Court in July 1984.

The High Court found in favour of the company. The following extract from the judgement is relevant:

> *"Having read these meanings, I am left in the position that the statute has provided a conundrum which I cannot solve. If the addition of the word 'vocation' does include all occupations, callings, businesses, habitual employments and professions, it seems unnecessary to have the word 'profession' at all. The word 'profession' even as extended by the word 'vocation' must have some limitations. Similarly, it must have been intended to effect some extension but, as I cannot guess what this extension was intended to be I am not in a position to state that the inference drawn by the President of the Circuit Court was not correct."*

See Tax Briefing 48 for a list of activities described by Revenue as being chargeable services.

"Professionals" are taken to include architects, auctioneers, surveyors. In the following tax cases, the listed activities were also held to constitute a profession:

■ an optician – *CIR v North and Ingram* ([1918] 2 KB 705);

■ a journalist – *CIR v Maxse* ((1919) 12 TC 41);

■ an actress – *Davies v Braithwaite* ((1931) 18 TC 198);

In the case of *Barker and Sons v CIR* ([1919] 2 KB 222), a stock-broker was held not to be a professional.

One guiding principle regarding whether a company is carrying on a professional service can be taken from how the income of the company is earned. Are the employees who earn fees for the company members of professional organisations? Have they sat exams for their profession? Are they employed by the company on the basis of their qualifications and membership of these bodies? A company who earns the majority of its income from its professional staff would generally be considered to be a professional service company and therefore within the scope of the s441 TCA 97 surcharge.

The key point to remember is that a surcharge applies to both passive and active income in the case of service companies. The passive income surcharge is calculated in a manner identical to that provided for by s440 TCA 97 (see the four-step process outlined above). The addition of a surcharge on 50% of the active income of service companies is provided for by s441 TCA 97.

Step-by-step surcharge calculation for service company, s441

1. Calculate the **"distributable trading income"** (trading income less relevant trade charges and after standard rate corporation tax).

2. Calculate half of the **"distributable trading income"**.

3. Add to amounts at 2. above the **"distributable estate and investment income"** (net of the 7.5% trading discount). This is the same calculation as used for the s440 surcharge and is calculated as follows:

    (i) Calculate "Income":

    Income from Case I, III, IV and V

    Deduct current losses, i.e., s396A, s399 TCA 97

    Deduct relevant trade charges, s243A TCA 97

    (ii) Calculate "Estate and Investment Income":

    Answer from (i) $\times$ $\dfrac{\text{Passive Income}}{\text{Total Income}}$

    Add Franked Investment Income (FII)

    Deduct relevant charges (charges deductible against all profits, s243 TCA 97

    (iii) Calculate "Distributable Estate and Investment Income":

    Answer from (ii)

    Less corporation tax on passive income as reduced by relevant charges

    Less 7.5% trading deduction on above sum

Steps (i)–(iii) are the same steps as (i)–(iii) for s440 TCA 97, as both surcharges calculate the net undistributed passive income in the same manner.

4. From the figure at 3. above, deduct all distributions declared for the accounting period and paid during or within 18 months of the end of the accounting period to give the total surchargeable amount. This figure is required for the purposes of step 7. (see below).

5. Deduct the distributions made from the total of "distributable estate and investment income" (the figure calculated at 3. (i)–(iii) above).

6. Apply a 20% surcharge to the resulting figure at 6. which represents the excess of the total of distributable estate and investment income over the distributions made.

7. Apply a 15% surcharge to the total surchargeable amount at 4., minus the excess figure calculated at 5. above.

Example 32.11:

This example uses amounts identical to those in Example 32.9 above (for s440 TCA 97 surcharge) except that the company is now a professional company.

Troy Ltd, a close company, has the following income, chargeable gains and charges on income for its 12-month accounting period ended 31 December 2009.

	€
Trading income (professional)	40,000
Rental income	10,000
Bank interest (Gross)	6,000
FII (Gross)	4,000

The company paid charges of €5,000 in respect of its trading activities and claimed €10,000 of loss relief under s396(1) for a loss, which arose in the accounting period, ended 31/12/2008.

The company incurred expenses on behalf of a participator of €400 under s436 TCA 97 (the participator was neither a Director nor an employee of the company) and the final dividend of €2,000 for the year ended 31/12/2009 was declared and paid on 1 February 2010.

1. **The distributable trading income of the company is calculated as follows:**

	€
Case II	40,000
Less relevant trade charges	(5,000)
	35,000
CT at 12.5%	(4,375)
Distributable trading income	30,625

2. Calculate half of the distributable trading income, €30,625/2, i.e., €15,312.

3. Add to amount at point 2., the distributable investment and estate income (net of trading discounts).

Distributable Estate and Investment Income: €

Schedule D	Case II	40,000
	Case III	10,000
	Case V	6,000
		56,000
Less relevant trading charges		(5,000)
		51,000

	€
$€51,000 \times \dfrac{€16,000}{€56,000}$	14,571
Franked Investment Income	4,000
Estate and Investment Income	18,571
Less corporation tax (€14,571 × 25%)	(3,643)
	14,928
Less trading discount at 7.5%	(1,120)
	13,808

"Distributable Estate and Investment Income"	13,808
Half of distributable trading income	15,312
Total	29,120

4. Less distributions made (2,400)

Total surchargeable amount 26,720

5. Excess of Distributable Estate and Investment Income over distributions made.

	€
Distributable Estate and Investment Income	13,808
Less distributions made	(2,400)
	11,408

6. Surcharge at 20% on €11,408 = €2,282

7. Surcharge at 15%

	€
Total surchargeable amount	26,720
Less excess levied at 20%	(11,408)
Total	15,312

Surcharge at 15% = €2,297

Therefore, the total surcharge assessed on the company is €2,282 + €2,297 = €4,579.

WHAT YOU SHOULD NOW KNOW

On completion of this chapter, you should be able to:

- ✓ Explain the rationale for close company legislation and discuss its increasing significance in the context of modern tax rates.

- ✓ Define a "close company" and identify "close companies" when given key information relating to shareholdings. – Volume 2 Q 33.3, Assignment 33.2.

- ✓ Describe the tax implications for participators/directors and close companies of engaging in certain transactions. – Volume 2 Q 33.2, 33.4 Revision CT Q6, Assignment 33.1.

- ✓ Calculate the surcharges on undistributed profits for close companies in receipt of both trading income and professional service income. – Volume 2 Q 33.1,33.4,33.5,33.6, Revision CT Q4, Revision CT Q 6.

- ✓ Complete Questions and the Assignments in Irish Taxation Law and Practice, Volume 2.

Section VI

Capital Acquisitions Tax

33

BASIC PRINCIPLES OF CAPITAL ACQUISITIONS TAX

In this chapter, you will deal with the following:

- The territorial scope of CAT
- The calculation of CAT liabilities
- The calculation of the taxable value of benefits

- Exemptions from CAT
- Advanced reliefs
- Administration and payment of CAT

33.1 Introduction

Capital Acquisitions Tax (CAT) provides for both gift and inheritance tax on assets passing from one individual to another. As the name suggests, it is a tax on acquisitions and accordingly, liability for payment generally rests with the recipient of the gift or inheritance.

CAT was first legislated for in the CAT Act 1976 and its introduction coincided with the abolition of estate duties, arising on legacies and under succession law. It was originally intended to complement an annual wealth tax; in the absence of a tax on gifts, wealth tax could be avoided or reduced where a donor made sufficient gifts to reach a lower wealth tax bracket. However, the annual wealth tax was short-lived and was, in fact, abolished with effect from 5 April 1978, i.e., within three years of its original introduction. The provisions of the CAT Act 1976 and subsequent Finance Acts were consolidated in 2003 and can now be found in the CAT Consolidation Act 2003 (CATCA 2003).

33.2 Terminology

Before considering the provisions of CAT legislation in detail, a number of terms merit definition. In many instances, the definitions provided for by legislation differ from the common sense meaning anticipated by non-professionals. For example, it is possible to acquire an 'inheritance' from an individual who is still living, and, in fact, a 'gift' may be taken from someone who is deceased.

s4 CATCA 2003

s9 CATCA 2003

A "**gift**" or "**inheritance**" is deemed to be taken whenever there is a "**disposition**" by a "**disponer**" whereby a "**donee**" or "**successor**" becomes "**beneficially entitled in possession**" to a "**benefit**", otherwise than for full consideration.

s3 CATCA 2003

An "**inheritance**" is taken "**on a death**" whereas a "**gift**" is taken otherwise than "**on a death**". The legislation outlines the circumstances which constitute '**on a death**'. In addition to covering the situation where property passes directly from the deceased to a beneficiary under the terms of a will or under intestacy, the term also includes the death of a "**disponer**" within two years of the "**date of disposition**". Accordingly, where an individual dies within two years of making a gift, the property transferred constitutes an inheritance.

An inheritance is also taken where a life interest is terminated on the death of a life tenant.

Example 33.1

If John settles property on his brother Mike for life with the remainder to his niece Helen absolutely then Helen takes an inheritance from John on the death of Mike. This is the case albeit that John may still be living when Helen becomes entitled to her remainder interest.

Conversely, a "gift" arises otherwise than "on a death" and accordingly, it is possible to envisage a situation whereby a "donee" takes a gift from someone who is deceased.

Example 33.2

If John grants a limited interest of 10 years duration to his brother Mike with the remaining interest in the property to his niece Helen absolutely, then Helen takes a gift from John on the expiry of the intervening limited interest. This is the case albeit that John may have died in the interim period.

s2 CATCA
2003

The "disponer" may be defined as the individual who is the source of the benefit, while the "donee" or "successor" is the person who ultimately receives the benefit. A "disposition" may be defined as any act or omission or failure by an individual, as a result of which, the value of the individual's estate is reduced. Thus, it would include not only the transfer of property otherwise than for full consideration, but also the provision of any benefit or the waiver of any debt. In addition, a 'disposition' can include any reciprocal arrangement whereby the disponer binds a third party to the provision of a benefit to a donee or successor. Correctly identifying the disponer and the donee or successor is imperative as the relationship between the two is a key determinant in the level of CAT payable.

Example 33.3

If Tom owes Eileen €50,000 and Eileen agrees to waive this debt provided Tom pays Sean €10,000, then in these circumstances, two separate benefits are taken. Tom takes a benefit of €40,000 being the amount of the debt that is waived less the consideration that he is required to pay Sean. Sean takes a benefit of €10,000, being the cash received from Tom. Eileen is the ultimate source of both benefits and accordingly, is the disponer. This is the case notwithstanding that the benefit to Sean is indirectly provided through Tom. Tom and Sean are the donees.

s2 CATCA
2003

"Beneficially entitled in possession" may be defined as having a current (as opposed to a future) right to enjoy the property comprising a gift or inheritance.

Example 33.4

By deed of conveyance, Emma gifts her son Emmet a limited interest in a particular property for a period of 5 years with absolute ownership transferring to her granddaughter Dervla, thereafter. In these circumstances, Emmet becomes beneficially entitled in possession to his benefit immediately, i.e., when the deed is executed. However, when the deed is executed, Dervla merely has a future interest in the property. CAT does not arise until she becomes beneficially entitled in possession to her remainder interest, i.e., until 5 years have elapsed.

s2 CATCA
2003

The "**date of disposition**" may be defined as the date on which the disponer binds himself to provide the benefit in question. In the case of a benefit taken by a will or intestacy, this will generally be the date of death. Normally, the "**date of disposition**" will be the date on which the value of the disponer's estate is reduced and this frequently coincides with the "**date of the gift**" or the "**date of the inheritance**". However, the "**date of the gift**" is defined as the date on which the beneficiary becomes beneficially entitled in possession. Accordingly, in Dervla's case in Example 33.4 above, the date of the gift is 5 years after the original date of disposition.

Similarly, the "**date of the inheritance**" is generally the date of death of the disponer, i.e., the "**date of disposition**". However, on the cessation of a life interest, the date of the inheritance is the date of death of the life tenant or "**middleman**". This would obviously differ from the original date of disposition.

Where a gift becomes an inheritance by virtue of the disponer's death within two years of disposition, the date of the inheritance is the original date of the gift.

s2 CATCA
2003

"Benefit" includes any "estate, interest, income or right". Thus, it would include any interest in a property, either absolute or limited, and it would also include any annuity or other periodic payment. The valuation of benefits for CAT purposes is considered at section 33.6 below. Certain benefits and certain dispositions are exempt from CAT and these are considered at Section 33.5 below.

33.3   Territorial Scope

s6 CATCA
2003
s11 CATCA
2003

Prior to 1 December, 1999, the scope of CAT depended on the domicile of the disponer. Where the disponer was Irish domiciled on a date of disposition prior to 1 December 1999, the property comprising the disposition was taxable in full irrespective of where it was situated. Where the disponer was non-Irish domiciled, only so much of the gift or inheritance as was situated in the State was subject to CAT.

Finance Act 2000 introduced changes such that the scope of CAT is now based on residence or ordinary residence. Thus, for dispositions on or after 1 December 1999, the entire property comprising a gift or inheritance is taxable where:

■ the disponer is resident or ordinary resident in the State, or

■ the donee or successor is resident or ordinarily resident in the State, or

■ the property is situated in the State.

Thus, Irish property (property situated in the Republic of Ireland) is always taxable. With effect from 2 February 2006, this would include shares in a private company incorporated outside of the State to the extent that these shares derive their value from property situated in the State. Foreign property is only taxable if the disponer is resident or ordinarily resident in the State or if the donee or successor is resident or ordinarily resident in the State. Where a gift or inheritance passes between individuals who are neither resident or ordinarily resident in the State, then to the extent that the gift or inheritance comprises only a portion of property situated in the State, then only a similar proportion of the gift or inheritance will be taxable.

In general, the Income Tax rules for determining residence and ordinary residence apply (see Chapter 9, section 9.3). However, in order to ensure that foreign domiciled individuals, who are only in Ireland for a short period of time, will not trigger an Irish CAT liability, additional rules apply. A non-domiciled individual will not be considered resident or ordinarily resident in the State for CAT purposes until 1 December 2004 and then only when he or she has been resident in the state for 5 consecutive tax years prior to the date of disposition (in the case of the disponer) or the date of the gift or inheritance (in the case of the beneficiary).

It should be borne in mind that the above rules apply in general and not necessarily in the case of discretionary trusts, which are beyond the scope of this analysis. In addition, the rules regarding the territorial scope of CAT determine whether or not a particular disposition is 'taxable'. This does not necessarily infer that a CAT liability will arise. The particular gift or inheritance may be exempt from CAT (see Section 33.5 below) or may be less than the relevant group threshold (see Section 33.4 below).

33.4   Method of Calculation

Schedule 2
CATCA
2003

Broadly speaking, CAT is calculated by applying tax at a rate of 20% to the excess over a tax-free threshold amount. The Finance (No. 2) Act 2008, amended the rate to 22% for gifts and inheritances taken on or after 20 November, 2008. Finance Act 2009 amended the rate further to 25% for gifts and inheritances taken on or after 8 April, 2009. All gifts and inheritances taken by a donee or successor on or after 5 December, 1991, which come within the same group threshold, are aggregated, to determine the amount of tax payable on the current gift.

Group thresholds

There are three tax-free group thresholds and these are determined by the relationship between the disponer and the beneficiary. These group thresholds were introduced on 1 December, 1999 (to replace an existing system of class thresholds) and are as follows:

Group A: €381,000	Broadly speaking, this applies to dispositions from a parent to a child.
Group B: €38,100	This applies to dispositions to lineal ancestors and descendants (other than those included in Group A above), brothers, sisters, nephews and nieces.
Group C: €19,050	This applies to dispositions not covered under Group A or B above.

Finance Act 2009 amended the above group thresholds in respect of gifts or inheritances taken on or after 8 April 2009. The new thresholds are as follows:

Group A: €304,775

Group B: €30,478

Group C: €15,239

The group thresholds are indexed in line with inflation and the indexation factor for 2009 is 1.424.

The indexed group thresholds for 2007, 2008 and 2009 are set out in the table below.

Group	Relationship to Disponer	Group Threshold			
		2007 (after indexation)	2008 (after indexation)	01/01/09–07/04/09 (after indexation)	on or after 08/04/09 (after indexation)
A	Son/Daughter	€496,824	€521,208	€542,544	€434,000
B	Lineal Ancestor / Descendant/Brother/Sister/ Niece/Nephew	€49,682	€52,121	€54,254	€43,400
C	Relationship other than Group A or B	€24,841	€26,060	€27,127	€21,700

Source: www.revenue.ie

In determining which group threshold applies to particular dispositions, preferential treatment is given to some relationships in certain circumstances.

Group A applies not only to dispositions to a natural child, but also to a step child, an adopted child and a foster child, subject to certain conditions. This threshold also applies to certain grandchildren of the disponer who take a benefit under a marriage settlement, and also, to dispositions to a minor child of a deceased child, i.e., dispositions from a grandparent to a grandchild under the age of 18, whose parent is deceased (see example 33.6 below). Furthermore, a parent taking an inheritance (but not a gift) from a child can qualify for the Group A threshold.

Certain nephews/nieces will be treated as 'favoured' nephews/nieces and accordingly, will be treated, in certain circumstances, as sons/daughters qualifying for the Group A tax-free threshold. This preferential treatment applies only to gifts/inheritances of trading or business assets to a niece or nephew who has worked substantially on a full-time basis in the business, trade or profession for a period of five years. The 'full-time' requirement is satisfied where the niece or nephew works more than 24 hours a week in the business. Where the business is exclusively carried on by the disponer, his spouse and the favoured niece or nephew, then this requirement is relaxed to 15 hours a week. Where the disponer carries on his business through the medium of a limited company, the Group A threshold is extended to gifts and inheritances consisting of shares in that company.

Example 33.5

On 1 May 2009, Michael White dies and leaves his farm worth €900,000 and publicly quoted shares worth €150,000 to his nephew John who has worked full-time on the farm for the last 10 years.

As the farm is a trading asset and as John has worked full-time on the farm for the requisite period of 5 years, the group threshold applicable to the inheritance of the farm is €434,000. The normal group threshold applicable to dispositions to a nephew (i.e., €43,400) applies in respect of the shares as these do not constitute a business asset. (Note: agricultural relief may apply to farm – see Section 34.7 below.)

The legislation also provides for a relaxation of the normal group threshold rules in respect of dispositions to the surviving spouse of a deceased person. In these circumstances the surviving spouse is deemed to 'stand in the shoes' of the deceased spouse and vis-à-vis the deceased spouse's relationship with the disponer, the surviving spouse may qualify for a more favorable tax threshold in computing any CAT liability due.

Example 33.6

John and Mary are married and have one child, Grace. Michael is Mary's father.

In 2004, Michael gave John €50,000 and Grace (aged 8) €80,000.

In 2005, Mary died.

In 2009, Michael gave John 100,000 and Grace (aged 11) €150,000.

John qualifies for the Group C threshold in respect of the gift from Michael in 2004. He is effectively treated as stranger as he is not a blood relative of the disponer.

Grace qualifies for the Group B threshold in respect of the gift from Michael in 2004. She is a lineal descendant of the disponer.

John qualifies for the Group A threshold in respect of the gift from Michael in 2009, given that his deceased spouse was a daughter of the disponer.

Grace qualifies for the Group A threshold in respect of the gift from Michael in 2009, as she is the minor child of a deceased child of the disponer.

Aggregation and computation

All benefits from disponers in the same category taken on or after 5 December 1991 are aggregated for the purposes of ascertaining whether or not the tax-free group threshold has been exceeded. Thus, if benefits have been received from an aunt, an uncle and a sister, all three benefits are aggregated and where the aggregate amount exceeds €43,400 (for benefits received on or after 8 April, 2009), CAT applies. A beneficiary may not benefit from €43,400 tax free from each person within the same group threshold.

Calculating the CAT liability in respect of the first benefit taken since 5 December 1991 is very straightforward. If the taxable value is less than the group threshold, no CAT arises. Where the taxable value exceeds the group threshold, the excess is taxed at 25% (for benefits received on or after 8 April, 2009).

Example 33.7

On 1 July 2009, Helen's uncle dies and leaves her a cash sum of €40,000. She has received no other benefits since 5 December 1991.

As the taxable value is less than the group threshold of €43,400, no CAT arises.

Example 33.8

On 1 July 2009, Anne's nephew dies and leaves her a cash sum of €40,000. She has received no other benefits since 5 December 1991.

Taxable value		€40,000
Group threshold:	€21,700 @ Nil	
Balance:	€18,300 @ 25%	€4,575
CAT liability		€4,575

Example 33.9

On 1 July 2009, June's son dies and leaves her a cash sum of €600,000. She has received no other benefits since 5 December 1991 and had not previously gifted her son any benefits.

Taxable value		€600,000
Group threshold:	€434,000 @ Nil	
Balance:	€166,000 @ 25%	€41,500
CAT liability		€41,500

Example 33.10

On 1 July 2009, Sophie's son gave her a cash sum of €500,000. She has received no other benefits since 5 December 1991.

Taxable value net of annual gift exemption		€497,000	*(See 33.5 below for commentary on annual gift exemption)*
Group threshold:	€43,400 @ Nil		
Balance:	€453,600 @ 25%	€113,400	
CAT liability		€113,400	

Where other benefits have been received since 5 December 1991, calculating the CAT liability involves a three step process.

'Step 1' involves calculating the CAT on the current aggregate – Aggregate A, i.e., the aggregate of the current benefit and all previous benefits from within the same group threshold taken on or after 5 December 1991.

'Step 2' involves calculating the CAT on the previous aggregate – Aggregate B, i.e., the aggregate of all previous benefits from within the same group threshold taken on or after 5 December 1991, excluding the taxable value of the current benefit.

'Step 3' involves calculating CAT on the current benefit as the excess of the CAT on Aggregate A over the CAT calculated in respect of Aggregate B.

Example 33.11

On 1 August 2009, Bernadette received an inheritance of €400,000 from her father. She had previously received the following benefits:

January 1990, a gift of €30,000 from her mother

25 December 1991, a gift of €6,000 from her brother

March 1993, an inheritance of €140,000 from her mother

February 2004, an inheritance of €20,000 from her aunt

Step 1: Calculation of Tax on Current Aggregate – Aggregate A

Note: *The gift from her mother in January 1990 is not aggregated as it was received prior to 5 December 1991.*

The gift from her brother and the inheritance from her aunt are not aggregated as these are not covered by the Group A threshold applicable to the current benefit.

Thus, the only prior benefit to be aggregated is the inheritance from her mother on 1 March 1993.

Aggregate A:	Current inheritance from father	€400,000
	Inheritance from mother 1/3/'93	€140,000
		€540,000

Group threshold:	€434,000 @ Nil	
Balance:	€106,000 @ 25%	€26,500

| CAT liability on Aggregate A | | €26,500 |

Step 2: Calculation of Tax on Aggregate B

| **Aggregate B:** | Inheritance from mother 1/3/'93 | €140,000 |

As this is less than the Group A threshold of €434,000, the CAT on Aggregate B is nil.

Step 3: Calculation of Tax on Current Benefit

CAT on Aggregate A	€26,500
CAT on Aggregate B	(Nil)
CAT on current benefit	€26,500

Example 33.12

Philip received the following benefits in 2009:

1 May 2009, a cash gift of €10,000 from his friend John

7 August 2009, a cash gift of €50,000 from his uncle

13 October 2009, a gift of shares from his father worth €200,000

Philip had previously received the following benefits:

25 December 1990, a gift from his mother of €100,000,

10 March 1991, a gift from his father of €200,000,

6 April 2000, an inheritance of publicly quoted shares worth €60,000 from his cousin,

6 May 2003, an inheritance of €20,000 from his aunt.

Cash gift from John:

Aggregate A:	*Current gift net of exemption*	€7,000
	Inheritance from cousin 6/4/'00	€60,000
		€67,000

| *Group threshold:* | €21,700 @ Nil | |
| *Balance:* | €45,300 @ 25% | *€11,325* |

| *CAT liability on Aggregate A* | | *€11,325* |

| *Aggregate B:* | *Inheritance from cousin 6/4/'00* | €60,000 |

| *Group threshold:* | €21,700 @ Nil | |
| *Balance:* | €38,300 @ 25% | *€9,575* |

| *CAT liability on Aggregate B* | | *€9,575* |

| *Tax on current benefit* | *(€11,325 – €9,575)* | *€1,750* |

Cash gift from uncle:

Aggregate A:	*Current gift net of exemption*	€47,000
	Inheritance from aunt 6/5/'03	€20,000
		€67,000

| *Group threshold:* | €43,400 @ Nil | |
| *Balance:* | €23,600 @ 25% | *€5,900* |

| *CAT liability on Aggregate A* | | *€5,900* |

| *Aggregate B:* | *Inheritance from aunt 6/5/'03* | €20,000 |

*As this is less than the Group B threshold
of €43,400, no CAT arises.*

| *CAT liability on Aggregate B* | | *Nil* |

| *Tax on current benefit* | | *€5,900* |

Gift of shares from father:

There were only two previous benefits covered by the Group A threshold and as both of these were taken prior to 5 December 1991, they are ignored. As the taxable value of the current benefit (€197,000) is less than the Group A threshold of €434,000, no CAT is payable on the gift from the father.

The CAT liabilities in respect of the gifts from John and the uncle are payable on separate dates, i.e., 4 months after the valuation dates (the dates of the gifts) – see Section 33.8.

33.5   Exemptions

s69 CATCA
2003

With effect from 1 January 2003, an annual exemption of €3,000 applies in respect of gifts taken by any one donee from any one disponer. Thus, in computing the amount of a gift to be aggregated, the first €3,000 of the total value taken from the same disponer in any calendar year is disregarded. For gifts taken before 1 January 1999, the annual small gift exemption was €635 and for gifts taken between 1 January 1999 and 1 January 2003, the annual small gift exemption was €1,270. This exemption does not apply to inheritances. However, there is no claw-back of the exemption where a gift becomes an inheritance by virtue of the disponer's death within 2 years.

Example 33.13

On 2 June 2009, John's father died leaving him the residue of his estate valued at €390,000.

John had previously received the following benefits:

On 1 June 1995, an inheritance from his mother of €280,000

On 1 August 1998, a gift from his stepmother of €5,000

On 25 December 1998, a gift from his stepmother of €3,000

On 1 June 2000, a gift from his sister of €50,000

On 25 December 2000, a gift from his stepmother of €3,000

Aggregate A:	*Current inheritance*	*€390,000*
	Gift from stepmother in 2000 (Note 1)	*€1,730*
	Gift from stepmother December 1998 (Note 2)	*€3,000*
	Gift from stepmother August 1998 (Note 3)	*€4,365*
	Inheritance from mother in 1995	*€280,000*
		€679,095

Group threshold:	*€434,000 @ Nil*	
Balance:	*€245,095 @ 25%*	*€61,273.75*

CAT liability on Aggregate A	*€61,273.75*

Aggregate B:	*Gift from stepmother in 2000*	*€1,730*
	Gift from stepmother December 1998	*€3,000*
	Gift from stepmother August 1998	*€4,365*
	Inheritance from mother in 1995	*€280,000*
		€289,095

As this is less than the Group A threshold of €434,000, no CAT arises.

CAT liability on Aggregate B	*Nil*

Tax on current benefit	*€61,273.75*

Note 1: As this gift was received in 2000, the relevant annual exemption is €1,270. The fact that John has already qualified for an annual exemption of this amount in respect of a gift taken from his sister in 2000 does not preclude him from getting the annual exemption in respect of a gift from a separate disponer.

Note 2: The annual small gift exemption is not available as it has already been claimed against an earlier gift from this disponer in this calendar year.

Note 3: As this gift was received in 1998, the relevant annual exemption is €635.

A number of other exemptions exist for specific benefits / dispositions. These are summarised as follows:

s70 - 71
CATCA 2003
■ Gifts and inheritances taken by spouses / surviving spouses are exempt from CAT and are not aggregated for the purposes of calculating CAT on other benefits.

s79 CATCA
2003
■ Inheritances taken by a parent from a child, where the child had taken a non-exempt benefit from either parent in the preceding five years, are exempt from CAT.

s81 CATCA
2003
■ In order to encourage non-nationals to invest in Irish Government stock, certain Government securities are exempt from CAT where the donee or successor is neither domiciled or ordinarily resident in the State at the date of the gift or inheritance, and;

– the disponer is neither domiciled or ordinarily resident in the State at the date of disposition, or;

– the disponer was the beneficial owner of the securities for fifteen years previously (six years where the disponer acquired the securities prior to 24 February 2003).

s72 CATCA
2003
■ The proceeds of qualifying insurance policies are exempt from CAT where the policy is taken out for the purposes of paying CAT. Thus, the proceeds of such policies must be used to pay any CAT arising on the death of the insured. In the absence of this relief, the proceeds of a life assurance policy taken out for the purposes of paying CAT would be aggregated with other benefits and would thus result in an increased tax liability. These policies are historically known as Section 60 (s60) policies. The relief has been extended to also cover policies effected for the purposes of paying CAT arising on gifts in certain circumstances.

s77 CATCA
2003
■ Certain objects of national interest are exempt from CAT provided they are not disposed of by the beneficiary within six years of the valuation date. This relief applies to works of art, scientific collections, libraries, stately houses and gardens, etc. and also to shares in companies holding such heritage property. The relief only applies where the property is kept permanently in the State and where there are facilities for public viewing.

s86 CATCA
2003
■ A gift or inheritance of a dwelling house (and grounds of up to one acre) is exempt from CAT where the following conditions are met:

– In general, the beneficiary must have occupied the dwelling house continuously, as his only or main residence, for a period of three years prior to the date of the gift or inheritance, provided the disponer was compelled by reason of age or infirmity to depend on the services of the recipient for that period.

 – For gifts taken on or after 20 February 2007, the dwelling house must be owned by the disponer for the three-year period prior to the gift.

 – For gifts taken on or after 20 February 2007, where replacement property is the subject of a gift, the period of occupancy of the replaced property by the recipient will only be taken into account where either the replaced property or the dwelling house, which is the subject of the gift, was also owned by the disponer prior to the date of the gift.

 – At the date of the gift or inheritance, the beneficiary must not have an interest in, and must not be beneficially entitled to, any other dwelling house.

 – In general, where the beneficiary is under the age of 55, he or she must continue to occupy the dwelling house for a period of six years commencing on the date of the gift or inheritance.

A clawback of the exemption applies in certain circumstances.

s76 CATCA 2003 ■ Gifts or inheritances taken for public or charitable purposes are generally exempt from CAT.

In addition, superannuation payments to employees, certain retirement benefits, compensation, redundancy, gambling winnings, prizes, certain support and maintenance payments and certain benefits taken by permanently incapacitated individuals are exempt from CAT. For further commentary on these exemptions, readers are referred to the Irish Taxation Institute publication "Capital Acquisitions Tax" by Condon, J.

33.6   Taxable Value

s28 CATCA 2003   In general, the taxable value of a gift or inheritance is calculated by deducting the market value of any consideration payable by the donee or successor from the 'incumbrance-free' value. The 'incumbrance-free' value is calculated by deducting any liabilities and expenses payable out of the gift or inheritance from the market value of the property comprising the gift or inheritance. Thus, a pro-forma computation of taxable value can be presented as follows:

	€
Market value	X
Less: liabilities, cost and expenses	(X)
Incumbrance-free value	X
Less: consideration payable by beneficiary	(X)
Taxable value	X

The approach is somewhat different in the case of agricultural property and business property (see Section 33.7) and further refinements are also necessary in valuing limited interests (see below).

Market value

s26 CATCA 2003 — Market value may be defined as the price which the property would secure if sold on the open market on the 'valuation date'. Certain provisions, which apply in valuing shares in a private company, are beyond the scope of this analysis.

In the case of a gift, the valuation date is normally the date of the gift. In the case of inheritance, the valuation date is normally the earlier of:

- the earliest date on which any person becomes entitled to retain the subject matter of the inheritance on behalf of the successor; or

- the actual date of retainer; or

- the actual date of delivery or payment to the beneficiary.

The valuation date is an important concept, not only because it is the date on which the property is valued for CAT purposes, but also because it is the date on which certain tests are applied for the purposes of ascertaining entitlement to agricultural relief and business property relief (see section 33.7) and it is the date on which CAT becomes payable (see section 33.8).

Deductible liabilities, costs and expenses

s28 CATCA 2003 — Most costs associated with the transfer of property, e.g., legal costs and stamp duties, are fully deductible in arriving at the incumbrance-free value of a gift or inheritance. In the case of inheritances, any debts of the deceased, funeral expenses and costs of administering the estate are fully deductible. In general, expenses and liabilities of the deceased are deductible from the residue of the estate. However, in some instances, specific property may be charged with the payment of a liability and such liabilities must be deducted in arriving at the incumbrance-free value of the particular property.

Liabilities that are contingent on the happening of some future event, and liabilities that may be reimbursed from some source, are not deductible. In addition, liabilities associated with exempt assets may not be deducted for the purposes of ascertaining the taxable value of non-exempt property.

Furthermore, the amount of any CAT liability or interest or penalty payable under the legislation is not deductible.

Consideration paid by the donee/successor

s28 CATCA 2003 — To arrive at the taxable value, the incumbrance-free value is reduced by any consideration payable by the beneficiary. The payment of consideration can take the form of the donee or successor undertaking to discharge a liability of the disponer, or indeed an undertaking to pay an amount to, or discharge a liability of, some third party.

Example 33.14

Mr X owes Mr Y €20,000 and Mr. Y agrees to waive this debt provided Mr X pays Mr Z €5,000. In these circumstances, the incumbrance-free value of the benefit taken by Mr X is €20,000. The taxable value is calculated as €15,000, i.e. €20,000 less the consideration of €5,000 payable to the third party Mr. Z. Incidentally, Mr. Z also takes a benefit from Mr X, in this case valued at €5,000 – see commentary on Example 33.3 above.

Where consideration is payable in respect of a gift or inheritance which comprises both taxable and non-taxable property, then the amount of the consideration deductible needs to be apportioned on a pro-rata basis.

Valuation of annuities

s5(5) CATCA
2003

Where a gift or inheritance involves the provision of an amount to a beneficiary on an annual basis, special rules are applied in determining the market value of such dispositions. The method of valuation depends on whether or not the annuity is charged on a specific property. Where an annuity is charged or secured on a particular property, it is valued using the following formula:

$$\text{Market value of property} \times \frac{\text{annual value of benefit}}{\text{annual value of property}}$$

Example 33.15

Tom gives an annuity of €10,000 to his daughter Kate. The annuity is secured on a rental property which Tom owns in Dublin. The rental property is valued at €420,000 and it produces annual rental income in the amount of €30,000.

The annuity is valued as: €420,000 × $\frac{€10,000}{€30,000}$ = €140,000

s5(2)(b)
CATCA
2003

Where an annuity is not secured on any particular asset, the value of the benefit is taken to be the market value of the capital sum which must be invested in Government stock to acquire an amount of income equivalent to the annuity. The relevant Government stock is the latest issue prior to the date of disposition, which is not redeemable within 10 years. A list of appropriate Government securities may be obtained from the Department of Finance or from the Capital Taxes Division of the Revenue Commissioners.

Example 33.16

Michael covenants to pay an annuity in the amount of €15,000 to his mother Mary, aged 60, for the remainder of her life. The latest Government stock issue, which was not redeemable within 10 years was a 6% government bond. The price per stock unit (valued at €1.00) on the valuation date was €0.95.

*In order to produce an annual income of €15,000 by investing in Government stock, it would be necessary to purchase €250,000 worth of Government bonds, i.e., €15,000 / 6%. At a discount of €.095 on the valuation date, it would cost €237,500 (€250,000 * 0.95) to purchase the appropriate amount of Government stock. Thus, the market value of Mary's benefit is calculated as €237,500.*

Where an annuity or any other benefit is taken for a period certain, which is of less than 50 years in duration, or alternatively, where an annuity is granted for the duration of the life of an individual or where property is granted to an individual for life, further adjustment is necessary to reflect the fact that the beneficiary does not have a permanent or absolute interest in the subject matter of the disposition.

Valuation of limited interests

s2 CATCA 2003

A limited interest may be defined as an interest which is not an absolute interest. It may be an interest for a period certain or it may be an interest for the duration of a life or for the lives of specified individuals.

s28(4) CATCA 2003

As a limited interest is less than a full or absolute interest, CAT legislation provides for the application of a limiting factor to the incumbrance-free value so as to ensure that the taxable value is reduced accordingly. The shorter the duration or the expected duration of the limited interest, the smaller the taxable value.

Thus, the pro-forma computation of taxable value can now be refined as follows:

	€
Market value	X
Less: liabilities, cost and expenses	(X)
Incumbrance-free value	X
Adjustment for limited interest	
(Multiplication by limited interest factor)	X
Less: consideration payable by beneficiary	(X)
Taxable value	X

The appropriate limited interest factor is taken from Table A or Table B as set out in Parts II and III of the First Schedule to the CAT Consolidation Act 2003 and as reproduced in Appendix I to this chapter.

Table A is concerned with the factors to be applied in valuing a life interest.

Example 33.17

Tom transfers a farm for life to his son Pat on 1 July 2009, with the remainder on Pat's death transferring to Pat's son Martin. The farm is valued at €500,000 on 1 July 2009 and Pat was 58 years old at this time. Legal fees on the transfer of the limited interest amounted to €8,000. The taxable value of Pat's benefit is calculated as follows:

	€
Market value	*500,000*
Less: liabilities, cost and expenses	*(8,000)*
Incumbrance-free value	*492,000*
Adjustment for limited interest	
(Multiplication by .6129 – Table A)	*301,547*
Less: consideration payable by beneficiary	*(Nil)*
Taxable value	*301,547*

Martin will take an inheritance from Tom on the date of Pat's death (irrespective of whether or not Tom is still living). This will be valued as an absolute interest on the basis of the open market value of the farm on the date of Pat's death.

Example 33.18

Michael covenants to pay an annuity in the amount of €15,000 to his mother Mary, aged 60, for the remainder of her life. In consideration, Mary agrees to transfer publicly quoted shares to Michael. These are valued at €10,000 on the grant of the annuity.

The latest government stock issue, which was not redeemable within 10 years was a 6% government bond. The price per stock unit (valued at €1.00) on the valuation date was €0.95.

*In order to produce an annual income of €15,000 by investing in Government stock, it would be necessary to purchase €250,000 worth of Government bonds, i.e., €15,000 / 6%. At a discount of €.095 on the valuation date, it would cost €237,500 (€250,000 * 0.95) to purchase the appropriate amount of Government stock. Thus, the market value of Mary's benefit is calculated as €237,500.*

The taxable value of Mary's benefit is calculated as follows:

	€
Market value	*237,500*
Less: liabilities, cost and expenses	*(Nil)*
Incumbrance-free value	*237,500*
Adjustment for limited interest	
(Multiplication by .6475 – Table A)	*153,781*
Less: consideration payable by beneficiary	*(10,000)*
Taxable value	*143,781*

Special rules for valuing interests for the lives of more than one person are beyond the scope of this analysis.

Table B deals with the valuation of interests for a period certain of less than 50 years in duration. (It is reproduced in Appendix I to this chapter.) Where an interest is for a period of 50 years or more in duration, no adjustment is necessary. Thus, in Example 33.15 above, no further adjustment is necessary if Tom grants the annuity to Kate for a period of 50 years or more. Where an amount is provided for a period of less than 50 years, the relevant factor from Table B must be applied to the incumbrance-free value.

Example 33.19

Tom gives an annuity of €10,000 to his daughter Kate for a period of 5 years. In consideration, Kate agrees to waive a debt in the amount of €2,500 owed to her by her brother Jack.

The annuity is secured on a rental property which Tom owns in Dublin. The rental property is valued at €420,000 and it produces annual rental income in the amount of €30,000.

The annuity is valued as: $€420,000 \times \dfrac{€10,000}{€30,000} = €140,000$

The taxable value of Kate's benefit is calculated as follows:

	€
Market value	*140,000*
Less: liabilities, cost and expenses	*(Nil)*
Incumbrance-free value	*140,000*
Adjustment for limited interest	
(Multiplication by .2869 – Table B)	*40,166*
Less: consideration payable by beneficiary	*(2,500)*
Taxable value	*37,666*

If this is Kate's first gift from a disponer to which the Group A threshold applies, no CAT will arise on this benefit.

Jack receives a benefit from Tom in the amount of €2,500. On the assumption that this is Jack's first benefit from Tom in the current calendar year, the benefit will be exempt on the basis that it is less than €3,000, the annual gift exemption.

33.7   Advanced Reliefs

33.7.1   Agricultural relief

s89 CATCA
2003

Agricultural relief has existed since the introduction of Capital Acquisitions Tax in 1976. The relief operates by reducing the market value of specified "agricultural property" in calculating the taxable value of a gift or inheritance taken by a qualifying "farmer".

"**Agricultural property**" includes the following:

agricultural land, pasture and woodlands situated in the State;

crops, trees and underwood growing thereon;

houses and other farm buildings situated on the property;

livestock, bloodstock and farm machinery thereon; and

the EU single farm payment entitlement.

The Finance (No. 2) Act 2008 amended the definition of "agricultural property" to agricultural land, pasture and woodlands situated in a member state. The amendment ensures that the relief will apply to agricultural property situated in any Member State of the European Union and not just in the Republic of Ireland. The amendment applies to gifts and inheritances taken on or after 20 November 2008.

Shares deriving their value from agricultural property do not qualify for agricultural relief. However, such shares and certain other assets may qualify for business relief – see section 33.7.2 below.

A "farmer" is defined as any individual whose assets are represented mainly by agricultural property. For the purposes of this condition, an 80% test applies. Thus, at least 80% of the gross market value of all property to which the individual is beneficially entitled (after taking the gift or inheritance) must consist of agricultural property as defined above. No deduction is made for mortgages, etc. Following an amendment introduced by Finance Act 2006, there is no requirement that the individual be domiciled in the State. It is not necessary for the beneficiary to actually farm the agricultural property. Thus, agricultural relief commonly applies in the case of let property.

With effect from 1 February 2007, for the purposes of the 80% test, the value of an "off-farm" principal private residence, which is a non-qualifying asset, is to be determined, after deducting any borrowings on that residence.

Example 33.20

John owns a house in Dublin valued at €360,000 and he has a mortgage of €280,000. His only other assets are as follows:

■ *a bank deposit of €3,500; and*

■ *publicly quoted shares worth €10,500.*

In June 2009, he inherits farmland worth €720,000 plus an old farmhouse and buildings situated on the farm worth €310,000. His inheritance also includes livestock and farm machinery worth €60,000.

The gross market value of all property owned by John, after taking the inheritance, is €1,184,000 (after deducting the mortgage of €280,000). The gross value of agricultural property is €1,090,000. Thus, the percentage of John's assets represented by agricultural property is 92% (1,090 / 1,184). Thus, John is a "farmer".

Example 33.21

In December 2009, Mary's uncle gave her a small farm worth €165,000. At this time, her only other assets were a bank deposit account of €10,000 and a car worth €25,000.

The percentage of Mary's assets represented by agricultural property is 82.5% (165 / 200). Thus, she is a "farmer" for the purposes of claiming agricultural relief.

s89 (6)
CATCA 2003
The "80%" test does not apply in the case of agricultural property which consists of trees and underwood.

Calculation of relief

For gifts and inheritances of agricultural property, the relief is calculated by reducing the market value of the property by a flat rate of 90%.

Example 33.22

On 1 August, 2009, Michael transfers agricultural property with a market value of €400,000 to his daughter Ann. Ann qualifies as a farmer. The agricultural value of the property is calculated as follows:

	€
Market value of agricultural property	*400,000*
Relief – 90% reduction of market value	*(360,000)*
Agricultural value of property	*40,000*

Given that the full market value of the agricultural property is reduced by 90% in order to arrive at the agricultural value, any liabilities, costs and expenses payable out of the property and any consideration paid for the property must be proportionately reduced before being deducted from the agricultural value.

Thus, the pro-forma computation of taxable value can be refined as follows:

	€
Agricultural value	X
Less: proportion of liabilities, cost and expenses	(X)
Incumbrance-free value	X
Less: proportion of consideration payable by beneficiary	(X)
Taxable value	X

Example 33.23

On 1 August 2009, Michael transfers agricultural property with a market value of €400,000 to his daughter Ann. Ann qualifies as a farmer. The lands are charged with a mortgage of €200,000 and Ann by way of consideration is obliged to pay her brother Conor an amount of €100,000.

The taxable value of the gift is calculated as follows:

	€
Market value of agricultural property	400,000
Relief – 90% reduction of market value	(360,000)
Agricultural value of property	40,000
Less: proportion of mortgage charged on land	(20,000)
Incumbrance-free value	20,000
Less: proportion of consideration payable by beneficiary	(10,000)
Taxable value	10,000

Where a gift or inheritance comprises both agricultural and non-agricultural property, any expenses etc relating to both component parts will need to be apportioned. 10% of expenses etc relating to agricultural property will be allowable and expenses relating to the non-agricultural property will be allowable in full. Thus, it is necessary to calculate the taxable value of each component separately.

Example 33.24

Tom transfers the following assets to his grandson Liam on 25 December, 2009:

	Market Value
	€
Farmland in Tipperary	350,000
Woodland in Kerry	100,000
Farm buildings situated on above farmland	140,000
Holiday cottage in Donegal	100,000
Farm machinery	30,000
Bloodstock	420,000
	1,140,000

The farmland is mortgaged for €80,000. In consideration for the transfer, Liam has agreed to pay his grandfather an amount of €250,000.

Legal and other costs associated with the transfer amount to €25,000 and these are payable out of the gift.

Liam's only other assets are his principal private residence worth €140,000 (with a mortgage outstanding of €40,000) and a bank deposit account of €5,000.

Calculate the taxable value of benefits taken.

Liam is a farmer. After taking the gift from his grandfather, more than 80% of his gross assets comprise agricultural property, calculated as follows:

$\frac{€1,040,000*}{€1,245,000**}$ = 83.5%

* (€350,000 + €100,000 + €140,000 + €30,000 + €420,000)

The holiday cottage in Donegal does not constitute agricultural property.

** (€1,140,000 + €140,000 − 40,000 + €5,000)

Debts charged on the property comprising the gift or inheritance are taken into consideration in apportioning expenses and consideration between agricultural and non-agricultural property.

Step 1: Computation of Taxable Value of Agricultural Property

	€
Market value of agricultural property	1,040,000
Relief – 90% reduction of market value	(936,000)
Agricultural value of property	104,000

Less: Proportion of mortgage charged on land (10%)
  (relates exclusively to agricultural property) (8,000)

Legal expenses applicable to agricultural property

$$€25,000 \times \frac{€1,040,000 - €80,000}{€1,140,000 - €80,000} = €22,642$$

Restrict to 10%	(2,264)	(10,264)
Incumbrance-free value		93,736

Less: Consideration applicable to agricultural property

$$€250,000 \times \frac{€1,040,000 - €80,000}{€1,140,000 - €80,000} = €226,415$$

Restrict to 10%	(22,642)
Taxable value of agricultural property	71,094

Step 2: Computation of Taxable Value of Non-Agricultural Property

	€
Market value of holiday cottage	100,000

Less: Legal expenses applicable to non-agricultural property

$$€25,000 \times \frac{€100,000}{€1,140,000 - €80,000} = 2,358$$

Incumbrance-free value	97,642

Less: Consideration applicable to non-agricultural property

$$€250,000 \times \frac{€100,000}{€1,140,000 - €80,000} = (23,585)$$

Taxable value of non-agricultural property	74,057

Step 3: Calculation of Total Taxable Value of Property

	€
Taxable value of agricultural property	71,094
Taxable value of non-agricultural property	74,057
Total	145,151

Clawback of relief in certain circumstances

Agricultural relief will be withdrawn or partially clawed back in the following circumstances:

s89(4)(a)
CATCA
2003

s102A CATCA
2003

- Where the agricultural property is sold (or compulsorily acquired) within six years of the date of the gift or inheritance and is not replaced within four years by other agricultural property, agricultural relief is withdrawn or clawed back. Where only a portion of the sales is reinvested in replacement agricultural property, a partial clawback arises. The clawback does not apply in relation to the sale of crops or timber, or where the beneficiary dies before the sale or compulsory acquisition. The retention period is extended by four years to 10 years in respect of development land, i.e., a clawback applies to agricultural relief granted in respect of the development value of the land where development land is disposed of in the period commencing six years after the date of the gift or inheritance and ending 10 years after that date. For commentary on the meaning of "development land," readers are referred to Chapter 26, section 26.2.1.

s89(4)(c)
CATCA
2003

- Agricultural relief is also withdrawn in circumstances where the beneficiary is not resident in the State for all of the three tax years immediately following the tax year in which the valuation date falls.

33.7.2 Business property relief

A relief, very similar to agricultural property relief, applies to relevant business property. Agricultural property which fails to qualify for agricultural relief may qualify for business property relief provided the relevant criteria for business property relief are met. Thus, an individual who fails the "farmer" test as described at section 33.7.1, may qualify for business property relief. It should also be noted that certain benefits will qualify as "agricultural property" but will not constitute "business property" as defined below. For example, farmland that has been left will qualify for agricultural relief but may not qualify for business property relief.

s94 CATCA
2003

Relief will only apply to property that was held for a minimum period of five years to the date of a gift. If an inheritance is taken, the relevant holding period is two years prior to the date of the inheritance. Ownership by the disponer's spouse is aggregated for the purposes of establishing the duration of the holding period.

"**Business property**" is defined as:

- The business or an interest in the business, in the case of a business carried on by a sole trader or by a partnership. "Business" includes the exercise of a profession, vocation or trade. An interest may include a life interest or an annuity charged on business property.

- Unquoted shares or securities of a company carrying on a business provided that the beneficiary will (after taking the gift or inheritance), either:

    – own more than 25% of the voting rights of the company, or

- control the company within the meaning of s16 CATCA 2003, or

- own at least 10% or more of the aggregate nominal value of all the issued shares and securities of the company and have worked fulltime in the company (or in the case of a group, for any company or companies in the group) throughout the period of 5 years ending on the date of the gift or inheritance.

■ Individual items of land, buildings, and plant and machinery owned by the disponer or by a partnership but used wholly or mainly for the purposes of a business carried on by a company controlled by the disponer or by a partnership of which the disponer was a partner. The item of property and the partnership interest or shares in the company must be taken as a gift or inheritance by the same beneficiary from the same disponer. Furthermore, the partnership interest or the shares or securities must qualify as relevant business property and the item of property must have been used by the company or by the partnership throughout the minimum ownership period.

Businesses which are involved wholly or mainly in property or share dealing, or in managing investments are specifically excluded from the relief. Individual assets used in the business, will not qualify for the relief if transferred to the beneficiary without the business.

Calculation of relief

s92 CATCA 2003   The relief takes the form of a reduction of 90% in respect of the net market value of the business. This is calculated by reducing the market value of the assets used in the business (including goodwill) by the market value of any business liabilities. The value of any asset not being used for the purposes of the business is ignored. Readers are referred to the example at 33.25 below.

Clawback of relief

s101 CATCA 2003   Where the business ceases to trade within a period of six years after the valuation date, the relief will be clawed back unless the business is replaced within one year by other relevant business property. There will be no clawback of the relief where the business ceases as a result of bankruptcy or insolvency. The relief will also be clawed back if, within a six year period after the valuation date, business property is sold or compulsorily acquired and not replaced within one year by other relevant business property.

s102A CATCA 2003   The retention period is extended by four years to 10 years in respect of development land, i.e., a clawback applies to business property relief granted in respect of the development value of property where the property is disposed of in the period commencing six years after the date of the gift or inheritance and ending 10 years after that date. For commentary on the meaning of 'development land', readers are referred to Chapter 26.

33.8 Administration and Payment of CAT

33.8.1 Filing of returns

s46 CATCA 2003   A return showing details of any gift or inheritance received must be filed within four months of the valuation date. Obligation to file a return is imposed on both the donee/successor and on the donor of gifts. A return must be filed by the donee/successor when the aggregate value of all taxable benefits taken from disponers within the same group threshold (since 5 December 1991) exceeds 80% of the group threshold amount. In relation to gifts, a return must also be filed by the donor where gifts amounting to more that 80% of the group threshold have been made to a particular beneficiary.

The return must show details of the property comprising all benefits to be aggregated. An estimate of the market value of all such property must also be provided.

s53 CATCA 2003   A surcharge of up to 30% may be imposed on accountable persons who underestimate the market value of any property included in a return for CAT purposes.

33.8.2 Payment of CAT

s51 CATCA 2003   In general, CAT becomes due for payment on the valuation date. However, no interest is charged if the CAT due is paid by the return filing date, i.e., within four months of the valuation date. If the tax is not paid within that period, simple interest accrues at a rate of 0.0273% per day for the period from the valuation date to the date of actual payment.

Interest on overdue tax is not deductible for income tax purposes.

s54 CATCA 2003   An accountable person may elect to pay tax on real property and on limited interests means of five equal yearly instalments, subject to the payment of interest at the normal daily rate on unpaid tax. Such interest must be added to each instalment and paid at the same time as the instalment.

s55 CATCA 2003   In the case of agricultural or business property, the daily interest rate is reduced to 0.0204% i.e., 75% of the normal rate.

s56 CATCA 2003   In certain circumstances, inheritance tax may be settled in whole or in part by the surrender of certain government securities at face or par value, albeit that their market value may be less. This effectively facilitates a discount on the payment of inheritance tax. This option is only available where the securities have been part of the estate of the deceased for at least 3 months.

33.8.3 Credit for capital gains tax

s104 CATCA 2003   In the case of a gift, a CGT liability and a CAT liability will normally arise on the same event, i.e., there will be a CGT liability for the donor and a CAT liability for the donee. CGT paid by the disponer may be credited against the CAT liability of the donee. The credit is limited to the lower of the CAT and CGT arising on the gift. Where the CGT liability and CAT liability do not arise on the same event, there is no credit for CGT arising. Thus, where an individual disposes of an asset to a third party and subsequently gifts the sales proceeds to a family member, there is no relief for the CGT arising on the disposal as the CGT and CAT arise separately, as a consequence of two separate transactions. However, in the case of a direct transfer of the asset to a family member, CGT and CAT may arise as a consequence of one single event and in such instances the credit relief may be available.

With effect from 2 February 2006, the credit relief for CGT against the CAT liability, will no longer apply where the beneficiary disposes of the property within two years of having acquired it.

Example 33.25

John gifted 100% of the shares in Staples Limited to his daughter Anne on 1 June 2009. The company had been incorporated in March 1994 by John with original share capital valued at €100. John is 60 years old and has worked full-time for the company since incorporation. The shares in Staples Limited were valued at €960,000. The company's net assets (at market value) on this date were as follows:

	€
Factory premises	*150,000*
Investment property	*550,000*
Goodwill	*100,000*
Plant and machinery	*50,000*
Stock	*90,000*
Trade debtors	*80,000*
Trade creditors	*(60,000)*
	960,000

Anne had received no benefits from any disponer previously.

John's CGT liability June 2009:

	€
Deemed sales proceeds / market value	*960,000*
Cost: €100	
Indexed @ 1.356	*(136)*
Gain	*959,864*
Retirement relief (Note 1)	*(338,776)*
	621,088
CGT @ 25%	*155,272*

Note 1: Relief rate = Chargeable business assets

$$\qquad\qquad\qquad\qquad \text{Total chargeable assets}$$

$$= \frac{150,000 + 100,000 + 50,000}{150,000 + 550,000 + 100,000 + 50,000}$$

$$= 35.29\%$$

*Exempt portion of gain = €959,864 * 35.29%*

$$= €338,776$$

Anne's CAT liability:

	€
Market value of shares	960,000
Value attributable to investment property	(550,000)
Value excluding investment property	410,000
Business property relief	(369,000)
	41,000
Value attributable to investment property	550,000
	591,000
Small gift exemption	(3,000)
	588,000

Group threshold:	€434,000 @ Nil	
balance:	€154,000 @ 25%	38,500

Deduct: CGT attributable to gift of shares (Above)	(155,272)	
CAT payable	Nil	*(no refund of CGT due)*

Tax Facts

Did you know that taxes similar to capital acquisitions tax are not a new phenomenon, death or estate taxes were in fact used by the ancient Egyptians, Greeks and Romans?

Did you know that while most countries operate some form of inheritance tax, not all countries tax the beneficiary? In some countries, for example in the UK, it is the estate that is taxed and not the beneficiaries.

WHAT YOU SHOULD NOW KNOW

On completion of this chapter, you should be able to:

- ✓ Define a number of legal terms that feature prominently in CAT legislation.

- ✓ Describe the territorial scope of CAT and identify the circumstances in which benefits will be taxable.

- ✓ Identify the appropriate group threshold for various relationships and circumstances.

- ✓ Calculate the CAT liability where a number of benefits have been received since 5 December 1991.

- ✓ Describe the main exemptions and reliefs from CAT provided for by legislation.

- ✓ Calculate the taxable value of various benefits, including annuities and limited interests.

- ✓ Define 'agricultural property' and 'business property.'

- ✓ Describe and identify the circumstances in which agricultural relief and business property relief will apply.

- ✓ Apply agricultural relief and business property relief in calculating CAT liabilities.

- ✓ Describe the system of administration and payment of CAT.

- ✓ Complete Questions and the Assignments in Irish Taxation Law and Practice, Volume 2.

References and Recommended Further Reading

CONDON, J. (2007), *Capital Acquisitions Tax,* Irish Taxation Institute.

FITZPATRICK, T. (ed.) (2008), *Law of Capital Acquisitions Tax,* Irish Taxation Institute.

MARTYN, J. and P. RECK (2008), *Taxation Summary,* Irish Taxation Institute.

Appendix I

TABLE A

Factors to be Applied in Valuing a Life Interest

Years of age	Joint Factor	Value of an interest in a capital of €1 for a male life aged as in column 1	Value of an interest in a capital of €1 for a female life aged as in column 1
(1)	(2)	(3)	(4)
0	.99	.9519	.9624
1	.99	.9767	.9817
2	.99	.9767	.9819
3	.99	.9762	.9817
4	.99	.9753	.9811
5	.99	.9742	.9805
6	.99	.9730	.9797
7	.99	.9717	.9787
8	.99	.9703	.9777
9	.99	.9688	.9765
10	.99	.9671	.9753
11	.98	.9653	.9740
12	.98	.9634	.9726
13	.98	.9614	.9710
14	.98	.9592	.9693
15	.98	.9569	.9676
16	.98	.9546	.9657
17	.98	.9522	.9638
18	.98	.9497	.9617
19	.98	.9471	.9596
20	.97	.9444	.9572
21	.97	.9416	.9547
22	.97	.9387	.9521
23	.97	.9356	.9493
24	.97	.9323	.9464
25	.97	.9288	.9432

Years of age (1)	Joint Factor (2)	Value of an interest in a capital of €1 for a male life aged as in column 1 (3)	Value of an interest in a capital of €1 for a female life aged as in column 1 (4)
26	.97	.9250	.9399
27	.97	.9209	.9364
28	.97	.9165	.9328
29	.97	.9119	.9289
30	.96	.9068	.9248
31	.96	.9015	.9205
32	.96	.8958	.9159
33	.96	.8899	.9111
34	.96	.8836	.9059
35	.96	.8770	.9005
36	.96	.8699	.8947
37	.96	.8626	.8886
38	.95	.8549	.8821
39	.95	.8469	.8753
40	.95	.8384	.8683
41	.95	.8296	.8610
42	.95	.8204	.8534
43	.95	.8107	.8454
44	.94	.8005	.8370
45	.94	.7897	.8283
46	.94	.7783	.8192
47	.94	.7663	.8096
48	.93	.7541	.7997
49	.93	.7415	.7896
50	.92	.7287	.7791
51	.91	.7156	.7683
52	.90	.7024	.7572
53	.89	.6887	.7456
54	.89	.6745	.7335
55	.88	.6598	.7206
56	.88	.6445	.7069
57	.88	.6288	.6926

Years of age (1)	Joint Factor (2)	Value of an interest in a capital of €1 for a male life aged as in column 1 (3)	Value of an interest in a capital of €1 for a female life aged as in column 1 (4)
58	.87	.6129	.6778
59	.86	.5969	.6628
60	.86	.5809	.6475
61	.85	.5650	.6320
62	.85	.5492	.6162
63	.85	.5332	.6000
64	.85	.5171	.5830
65	.85	.5007	.5650
66	.85	.4841	.5462
67	.84	.4673	.5266
68	.84	.4506	.5070
69	.84	.4339	.4873
70	.83	.4173	.4679
71	.83	.4009	.4488
72	.82	.3846	.4301
73	.82	.3683	.4114
74	.81	.3519	.3928
75	.80	.3352	.3743
76	.79	.3181	.3559
77	.78	.3009	.3377
78	.76	.2838	.3198
79	.74	.2671	.3023
80	.72	.2509	.2855
81	.71	.2353	.2693
82	.70	.2203	.2538
83	.69	.2057	.2387
84	.68	.1916	.2242
85	.67	.1783	.2104
86	.66	.1657	.1973
87	.65	.1537	.1849
88	.64	.1423	.1730
89	.62	.1315	.1616

Years of age	Joint Factor	Value of an interest in a capital of €1 for a male life aged as in column 1	Value of an interest in a capital of €1 for a female life aged as in column 1
(1)	(2)	(3)	(4)
90	.60	.1212	.1509
91	.58	.1116	.1407
92	.56	.1025	.1310
93	.54	.0939	.1218
94	.52	.0858	.1132
95	.50	.0781	.1050
96	.49	.0710	.0972
97	.48	.0642	.0898
98	.47	.0578	.0828
99	.45	.0517	.0762
100 or over	.43	.0458	.0698

TABLE B
Valuation of Interests:
Less than 50 Years

Number of years (1)	Value (2)	Number of years (1)	Value (2)
1	.0654	26	.8263
2	.1265	27	.8375
3	.1836	28	.8480
4	.2370	29	.8578
5	.2869	30	.8669
6	.3335	31	.8754
7	.3770	32	.8834
8	.4177	33	.8908
9	.4557	34	.8978
10	.4913	35	.9043
11	.5245	36	.9100
12	.5555	37	.9165
13	.5845	38	.9230
14	.6116	39	.9295
15	.6369	40	.9360
16	.6605	41	.9425
17	.6826	42	.9490
18	.7032	43	.9555
19	.7225	44	.9620
20	.7405	45	.9685
21	.7574	46	.9750
22	.7731	47	.9815
23	.7878	48	.9880
24	.8015	49	.9945
25	.8144	50 and over	1.0000

Note:
Column (2) shows the value of an interest in a capital of €1 for the number of years shown in column (1).

Charts

LIST OF CHARTS

Income Tax

Corporation Tax

Capital Gains Tax

Capital Acquisitions Tax

Stamp Duties

Value-Added Tax

Capital Allowances

* Note: These charts were first published in the Irish Taxation Institutes publication: Taxation Summary 2008 and are reproduced with permission.

CHART 1
Income Tax Allowances

	90/91	91/92	92/93	93/94	94/95	95/96
	IR£	IR£	IR£	IR£	IR£	IR£
Single Person	2,050	2,100	2,100	2,175	2,350	2,500
Married Couple	4,100	4,200	4,200	4,350	4,700	5,000
Widowed person (in year of bereavement)	4,100	4,200	4,200	4,350	4,700	5,000
Widowed person (subsequent years)	2,550	2,600	2,600	2,675	2,850	3,000
Widowed person with dependent child (additional)	1,550	1,600	1,600	1,675	1,850	2,000
First year after bereavement	-	1,500	1,500	1,500	1,500	1,500
Second year after bereavement	-	1,000	1,000	1,000	1,000	1,000
Third year after bereavement	-	500	500	500	500	500
Single Parent - additional	2,050	2,100	2,100	2,175	2,350	2,500
Income Limit of Child	720	720	720	720	720	720
Incapacitated Child	600	600	600	600	600	600
Income Limit of Child	720	2,100	2,100	2,100	2,100	2,100
Dependent Relative allowance	110	110	110	110	110	110
Income Limit	3,566	3,777	3,877	4,133	4,149	4,270
Blind Person	600	600	600	600	600	600
Both Spouses Blind	1,400	1,400	1,400	1,400	1,400	1,400
Age allowance: Single/Widowed Person	200	200	200	200	200	200
Married	400	400	400	400	400	400
Employed person taking care of incapacitated person	5,000	5,000	5,000	5,000	5,000	5,000
Employee allowance	800	800	800	800	800	800
PRSI allowance	286	286	286	286	286	140

CHART 1 (*continued*)

	96/97	97/98	98/99	99/00		00/01
				@ Standard Rate 24%	@ Marginal Rate 46%	@ Standard Rate 22%
Single Person	2,650	2,900	3,150	4,200	-	4,700
Married Couple	5,300	5,800	6,300	8,400	-	9,400
Widowed person (in year of bereavement)	5,300	5,800	6,300	8,400	-	9,400
Widowed person (subsequent years – without dependent child)	3,150	3,400	3,650	4,200	500	5,700
Widowed person with dependent child (additional)	2,150	2,400	2,650	1,050	2,650	4,700
First year after bereavement	1,500	1,500	5,000	-	5,000	10,000
Second year after bereavement	1,000	1,000	4,000	-	4,000	8,000
Third year after bereavement	500	500	3,000	-	3,000	6,000
Fourth year after bereavement	-	-	2,000	-	2,000	4,000
Fifth year after bereavement	-	-	1,000	-	1,000	2,000
Single Parent - additional	2,650	2,900	3,150	1,050	3,150	4,700
Income Limit of Child	720	720	720	-	720	720
Incapacitated Child	700	700	800	-	800	1,600
Income Limit of Child	2,100	2,100	2,100	-	2,100	2,100
Dependent Relative allowance	110	110	110	-	110	220
Income Limit	4,440	4,601	4,848	-	5,152	5,536
Blind Person	700	700	1,000	-	1,500	3,000
Both Spouses Blind	1,600	1,600	2,000	-	3,000	6,000
Age allowance: Single/Widowed Person	200	400	400	-	400	800
Married	400	800	800	-	800	1,600
Incapacitated Person - employment of carer	7,500	7,500	8,500	-	8,500	8,500*
Home Carers' allowance (Max)	-	-	-	-	-	3,000
Employee allowance	800	800	800	1,000	-	-
PRSI allowance	-	-	-	-	-	-

*Relief available at marginal rate.

CHART 2
Income Tax Credits

	Tax Year 2001	Tax Year 2002	Tax Year 2003	Tax Year 2004	Tax Year 2005	Tax Year 2006	Tax Year 2007	Tax Year 2008	Tax Year 2009
	IR£	€	€	€	€	€	€	€	€
Single Person	814	1,520	1,520	1,520	1,580	1,630	1,760	1,830	1,830
Married Couple	1,628	3,040	3,040	3,040	3,160	3,260	3,520	3,660	3,660
Widowed Person									
– in year of bereavement	1,628	3,040	3,040	3,040	3,160	3,260	3,520	3,660	3,660
– without dependent children	962	1,820	1,820	1,820	1,980	2,130	2,310	2,430	2,430
– with dependent children	814	1,520	1,520	1,520	1,580	1,630	1,760	1,830	1,830
Widowed Parent									
– first year after bereavement	2,000	2,600	2,600	2,600	2,800	3,100	3,750	4,000	4,000
– second year after bereavement	1,600	2,100	2,100	2,100	2,300	2,600	3,250	3,500	3,500
– third year after bereavement	1,200	1,600	1,600	1,600	1,800	2,100	2,750	3,000	3,000
– fourth year after bereavement	800	1,100	1,100	1,100	1,300	1,600	2,250	2,500	2,500
– fifth year after bereavement	400	600	600	600	800	1,100	1,750	2,000	2,000
One-Parent Family									
– widowed person	814	1,520	1,520	1,520	1,580	1,630	1,760	1,830	1,830
– other person	814	1,520	1,520	1,520	1,580	1,630	1,760	1,830	1,830
Incapacitated Child Max.	238	500	500	500	1,000	1,500	3,000	3,660	3,660
Dependent Relative Max.	33	60	60	60	60	80	80	80	80
Income Limit	4,989	9,352	9,852	10,373	10,997	11,912	12,745	13,473	13,837
Blind Person	444	800	800	800	1,000	1,500	1,760	1,830	1,830
Both Spouses Blind	888	1,600	1,600	1,600	2,000	3,000	3,520	3,660	3,660
Age Credit:									
– Single/Widowed Person	119	205	205	205	205	250	275	325	325
– Married	238	410	410	410	410	500	550	650	650
PAYE Max.	296	660	800	1,040	1,270	1,490	1,760	1,830	1,830
Home Carer Max.	444	770	770	770	770	770	770	900	900
Trade Union Subscriptions		45	26	40	40	60	60	70	70
Employment of Carer for Incapacitated Person Max.	7,400 @ Marginal Rate	30,000 @ Marginal Rate	30,000 @ Marginal Rate	30,000 @ Marginal Rate	30,000 @ Marginal Rate	30,000 @ Marginal Rate	50,000 @ Marginal Rate	50,000 @ Marginal Rate	50,000 @ Marginal Rate

CHART 3
Income Tax Rates

Tax Year	Single/ Widowed	Married Couple	Rate
1990/91	6,500 3,100 Balance	13,000 6,200 Balance	30% 48% 53%
1991/92	6,700 3,100 Balance	13,400 6,200 Balance	29% 48% 52%
1992/93	7,475 Balance	14,950 Balance	27% 48%
1993/94	7,675 Balance	15,350 Balance	27% 48%
1994/95	8,200 Balance	16,400 Balance	27% 48%
1995/96	8,900 Balance	17,800 Balance	27% 48%
1996/97	9,400 Balance	18,800 Balance	27% 48%
1997/98	9,900 Balance	19,800 Balance	26% 48%
1998/99	10,000 Balance	20,000 Balance	24% 46%
1999/00	14,000 Balance	28,000 Balance	24% 46%

CHART 3 (continued)

Tax Year	Single/ Widowed	Married Couples, One Income	Married Couples, Two Incomes	One-Parent Family	Rate
	£	£	£	£	
2000/01	1–17,000 Balance	1–28,000 Balance	1–34,000* Balance	1–20,150 Balance	22% 44%
Note: Transferable between spouses up to a maximum of £28,000 for any one spouse.					
	£	£	£	£	
2001	1–14,800 Balance	1–21,460 Balance	1–29,600* Balance	1–17,131 Balance	20% 42%
Note: Transferable between spouses up to a maximum of £21,460 for any one spouse.					
	€	€	€	€	
2002	1-28,000 Balance	1-37,000 Balance	1-56,000* Balance	1-32,000 Balance	20% 42%
Note: Transferable between spouses up to a maximum of €37,000 for any one spouse.					
	€	€	€	€	
2003	1-28,000 Balance	1-37,000 Balance	1-56,000* Balance	1-32,000 Balance	20% 42%
Note: Transferable between spouses up to a maximum of €37,000 for any one spouse.					
	€	€	€	€	
2004	1-28,000 Balance	1-37,000 Balance	1-56,000* Balance	1-32,000 Balance	20% 42%
Note: Transferable between spouses up to a maximum of €37,000 for any one spouse.					
	€	€	€	€	
2005	1-29,400 Balance	1-38,400 Balance	1-58,800* Balance	1-33,400 Balance	20% 42%
Note: Transferable between spouses up to a maximum of €38,400 for any one spouse.					
	€	€	€	€	
2006	32,000 Balance	41,000 Balance	64,000* Balance	36,000 Balance	20% 42%
Note: Transferable between spouses up to a maximum of €41,000 for any one spouse.					
	€	€	€	€	
2007	34,000 Balance	43,000 Balance	68,000* Balance	38,000 Balance	20% 41%
Note: Transferable between spouses up to a maximum of €43,000 for any one spouse.					
	€	€	€	€	
2008	35,400 Balance	44,400 Balance	*70,800 Balance	39,400 Balance	20% 41%
Note: Transferable between spouses up to a maximum of €44,400 for any one spouse.					
	€	€	€	€	
2009	36,400 Balance	45,400 Balance	*72,800 Balance	40,400 Balance	20% 41%
Note: Transferable between spouses up to a maximum of €45,400 for any one spouse.					

CHART 4

Exemption Limits

Single & Widowed	99/00 £	00/01 £	2001 £	2002 €	2003 €	2004 €	2005 €	2006 €	2007 €	2008 €	2009 €
Under 65 Years	4,100	4,100	3,034	5,210	5,210	5,210	5,210	5,210	5,210		
Over 65 and under 75	6,500										
75 and over	6,500										
65 and over		7,500	6,290	13,000	15,000	15,500	16,500	17,000	19,000	20,000	20,000

Married Couples	99/00 £	00/01 £	2001 £	2002 €	2003 €	2004 €	2005 €	2006 €	2007 €	2008 €	2009 €
Under 65 Years	8,200	8,200	6,068	10,420	10,420	10,420	10,420	10,420	10,420		
Over 65 and under 75	13,000										
75 and over	13,000										
65 and over		15,000	12,580	26,000	30,000	31,000	33,000	34,000	38,000	40,000	40,000

Note: The income limits are increased for each dependent child as follows:

	99/00 £	00/01 £	2001 £	2002 €	2003 €	2004 €	2005 €	2006 €	2007 €	2008 €	2009 €
First and Second Child	450	450	333	575	575	575	575	575	575	575	575
Third and Subsequent Child	650	650	481	830	830	830	830	830	830	830	830

*Marginal Relief rates	40%	40%	40%	40%	40%	40%	40%	40%	40%	40%	40%

*Marginal relief restricts the amount of tax payable to the amount by which total income exceeds the exemption limit, at the above marginal relief rate.

CHART 5

PRSI Rates and Levies

EMPLOYEE – CLASS A1				HEALTH CONTRIBUTION
	Employer Rate*	Employee		Employee Rate
		Income €	Rate	
2008	10.75%	0–50,700	4%	2%
	10.75%	50,701–100,100	NIL	2%
	10.75%	100,101 onwards	NIL	2.5%
2009 – From 01/01/09 to 30/04/09	10.75%	0–52,000	4%	2%
	10.75%	52,001–100,100	NIL	2%
	10.75%	100,100 onwards	NIL	2.5%
2009 – From 01/05/09 to 31/12/09	10.75%	0–75,036	4%	4%
	10.75%	75,037 onwards	NIL	5%

Notes:

*Employers' PRSI is 8.5% on earnings of €365 pw or less in 2008 and 2009.

Employees are exempt from PRSI on the first €127 per week or €26 per week for employees on a modified PRSI rate. Employees earning €352 or less per week in 2008 and 2009 are exempt from PRSI and Health Contribution. However, where earnings exceed €352 per week in 2008 and 2009, the employee's PRSI-Free Allowance remains at €127 per week or €26 per week for employees on a modified PRSI rate. Employees earning €500 or less per week in 2008 and 2009 are exempt from the Health Contribution.

Recipients of a Social Welfare Widow's or Widower's Pension, Deserted Wife's Benefit/Allowance or One-Parent Family Payment are exempt from paying the Health Contribution. All Medical Card holders (including people aged 70 or over) are also exempt from this contribution.

SELF-EMPLOYED	INCOME	PRSI (Min.)	HEALTH CONTRIBUTION
2008	If income < €26,000	3% (€253)	NIL
	€26,000 – €101,000*	3%	2%
	Over €101,000	3%	2.5%
2009	If income < €75,036	3% (€253)	3.333%
	€75,036 – €100,100	3%	4%
	Over €100,100	3%	4.167%

Notes:

Self employed persons are exempt from the Health Contributions where the annual income is €26,000 or less in 2008 & 2009. The minimum annual PRSI contribution is €253.

In the case of Schedule E, income on which PRSI is calculated is net income after superannuation. In the case of Schedule D, income is after capital allowances but before pension contributions. There is no liability to PRSI where reckonable income is below €3,174. This test is applied separately to the income of husband and wife.

CHART 6

Mortgage Interest Relief

(a) Maximum Allowable

	Maximum Allowable	
Tax Year 2008	**First-Time Buyers*** €	**Other** €
Single Person	10,000	3,000
Married / Widowed	20,000	6,000
Tax Year 2009	**First-Time Buyers*** €	**Other**** €
Single Person	10,000	1,000
Married / Widowed	20,000	2,000

(b) Rate of Tax Relief

Year of Mortgage	First-Time Buyers*		Others	
	2008	**2009**	**2008**	**2009**
Years 1 + 2	20%	25%	20%	15%
Years 3, 4 + 5	20%	22.5%	20%	15%
Years 6 + 7	20%	20%	20%	15%

* First-time buyers who claimed mortgage interest relief for the first time in the tax year 2003 or later. The increased limit applies for a period of seven years beginning with the tax year in which mortgage interest was claimed for the first time.

** With effect from 1 May 2009 the number of tax years in respect of which mortgage interest relief may be claimed is 7 years for both first time and non-first time buyers.

CHART 7

Specified Amounts for the Restriction of Capital Allowances and Leasing Charges for Passenger Motor Vehicles

Chargeable Periods Ending	SPECIFIED AMOUNT
	€
Between 1/1/2002 - 31/12/2005 inclusive	22,000
Between 1/1/2006 - 31/12/2006 inclusive	23,000
On or after 1/1/2007	24,000

CHART 8

Civil Service Motor Travel Rates

(For individuals who are obliged to use their cars in the normal course of their duties).
RATES PER KILOMETRE (1 mile = 1.609 kilometres)

MOTOR CARS			
Effective from 1 July 2007 to 30 June 2008			
Official Motor Travel in a Calendar Year	**Engine Capacity**		
	Up to 1,200cc	1,201cc to 1,500cc	1,501cc and over
Up to 6,437km	52.16 cent	61.66 cent	78.32 cent
6,438km and over	27.08 cent	30.96 cent	36.65 cent
Effective from 1 July 2008 to 4 March 2009			
Official Motor Travel in a Calendar Year	**Engine Capacity**		
	Up to 1,200cc	1,201cc to 1,500cc	1,501cc and over
Up to 6,437km	52.16 cent	61.67 cent	78.76 cent
6,438km and over	28.29 cent	31.49 cent	37.94 cent
Effective from 5 March 2009			
Official Motor Travel in a Calendar Year	**Engine Capacity**		
	Up to 1,200cc	1,201cc to 1,500cc	1,501cc and over
Up to 6,437km	39.12 cent	46.25 cent	59.07 cent
6,438km and over	21.22 cent	23.62 cent	28.46 cent

CHART 8 (continued)

MOTORCYCLES				
Effective from 1 July 2007 to 30 June 2008				
Official Motor Travel in a Calendar Year	**Engine Capacity**			
	150cc or less	**151cc to 250cc**	**251cc to 600cc**	**601cc and over**
Up to 6,437km	18.92 cent	26.35 cent	31.13 cent	37.96 cent
6,438km and over	11.89 cent	16.94 cent	19.48 cent	22.59 cent
Effective from 1 July 2008 to 4 March 2009				
Official Motor Travel in a Calendar Year	**Engine Capacity**			
	150cc or less	**151cc to 250cc**	**251cc to 600cc**	**601cc and over**
Up to 6,437km	19.30 cent	26.80 cent	31.62 cent	38.12 cent
6,438km and over	12.49 cent	17.75 cent	20.93 cent	23.46 cent
Effective from 5 March 2009				
Official Motor Travel in a Calendar Year	**Engine Capacity**			
	150cc or less	**151cc to 250cc**	**251cc to 600cc**	**601cc and over**
Up to 6,437km	14.48 cent	20.10 cent	23.72 cent	28.59 cent
6,438km and over	9.37 cent	13.31 cent	15.29 cent	17.60 cent

Reduced Motor Travel Rates

(For individuals who are not obliged to travel in the normal course of their duties but who occasionally use their car for business purposes).

Effective from 1 January 2003		
Engine Capacity up to 1200cc [cent]	**Engine Capacity 1201cc to 1500cc [cent]**	**Engine Capacity 1501cc and over [cent]**
19.52	21.88	23.87
Effective from 1 July 2008		
19.52	22.18	25.99

CHART 9

Civil Service Subsistence Rates

(a) Domestic Subsistence Rates

• Effective from 1 July 2007 to 30 June 2008

Class of Allowances	Night Allowances			Day Allowances	
	Normal Rate	Reduced Rate	Detention Rate	10 hours or more	5 hours but less than 10 hours
A Rate	€144.45	€133.17	€72.21	€43.13	€17.60
B Rate	€141.60	€121.11	€70.83	€43.13	€17.60

• Effective from 1 July 2008 to 4 March 2009

Class of Allowances	Night Allowances			Day Allowances	
	Normal Rate	Reduced Rate	Detention Rate	10 hours or more	5 hours but less than 10 hours
A Rate	€145.32	€133.97	€72.64	€44.81	€18.28
B Rate	€143.58	€122.81	€71.82	€44.81	€18.28

Salary levels corresponding to above classes:

A – Salary exceeds €66,302 per annum
B – Salary is below €66,302 per annum

• Effective from 5 March 2009

Class of Allowances	Night Allowances			Day Allowances	
	Normal Rate	Reduced Rate	Detention Rate	10 hours or more	5 hours but less than 10 hours
A Rate	€108.99	€100.48	€54.48	€33.61	€13.71
B Rate	€107.69	€92.11	€53.87	€33.61	€13.71

Salary levels corresponding to above classes:

A – Salary exceeds €69,695
B – Salary is below €69,695

Normal Rate - up to 14 nights
Reduced Rate - next 14 nights
Detention Rate - next 28 nights
Special Rules apply to absences over 56 nights

(b) Foreign Subsistence Rates

Details of quantum of Civil Service subsistence rates for certain foreign countries are available from any regional Revenue office.

CHART 10

(a) Interest on Overdue Tax

In the case of income tax, corporation tax, capital gains tax, gift tax and inheritance tax remaining unpaid on or after 1 April 2005, the basis for the calculation of interest is by reference to a daily rate for all periods of delay, whether before or after 1 April 2005, instead of a monthly basis for periods up to 31 August 2002 and a daily basis thereafter. In the case of stamp duties, due to the variation in the rates which applied for various purposes in the past, the new rate will only apply for periods of delay arising on or after 1 April 2005. The duty rates applying in the case of income tax, corporation tax capital gains tax and capital acquisitions tax are as follows:

Period	Percentage
From 6 April 1963 to 31 July 1971	0.0164%
From 1 August 1971 to 30 April 1975	0.0246%
From 1 May 1975 to 31 July 1978	0.0492%
From 1 August 1978 to 31 March 1998	0.0410%
From 1 April 1998 to 31 March 2005	0.0322%
From 1 April 2005 to 30 June 2009	0.0273%
From 1 July 2009 to the date of payment	0.0219%

The reduced rates from 1 April 2005 to 30 June 2009 and the measures outlined above do not apply to indirect taxes, such as excise duties and VAT, and taxes such as PAYE, relevant contracts tax, professional fees withholding tax, DIRT and other withholding and exit taxes which are collected by employers and others on a fiduciary basis. The rates applicable from 1 April 2005 are as follows:

Period	Percentage
From 1 April 2005 – 30 June 2009	0.0322%
From 1 July 2009 to date of payment	0.0274%

(b) Interest on Tax Overpaid

Rates of Interest		
1.50% per month or part of a month	From 6.4.76	To 5.7.78
1.25% per month or part of a month	From 6.7.78	To 26.5.86
1.00% per month or part of a month	From 27.5.86	To 31.7.90
0.60% per month or part of a month	From 1.8.90	To 31.3.98
0.50% per month or part of a month	From 1.4.98	To 31.8.02
0.0161% per day or part of a day	From 1.9.02	To 31.10.03*
0.011% per day or part of a day	From 1.11.03*	

* See 1.1.13 for details in relation to the period for which interest will be paid.

CHART 11

Average Rates of Exchange IR£/£Stg.

Year ended	Rate	Year ended	Rate
5.4.1980	.94995	5.4.1991	.9318
5.4.1981	.84582	5.4.1992	.9288
5.4.1982	.81138	5.4.1993	1.0095
5.4.1983	.83307	5.4.1994	.9737
5.4.1984	.80780	5.4.1995	.9981
5.4.1985	.84080	5.4.1996	1.033
5.4.1986	.8441	5.4.1997	1.023
5.4.1987	.9374	5.4.1998	.9016
5.4.1988	.9055	5.4.1999	.8695
5.4.1989	.8527	5.4.2000	.8128
5.4.1990	.9101	5.4.2001	.7801
		P/E 31.12.2001	.785

Divide £Stg by these factors to obtain IR£ equivalent

Average Rates of Exchange versus Irish Pound

	1999/00	2000/01	2001
US dollar	1.3093	1.1511	1.1252
Sterling	0.8128	0.7801	0.7850
Danish krone	9.4444	9.4706	9.4571
Japanese yen	145.73	127.638	137.75
Swiss franc	2.0342	1.9534	1.9087
Swedish krona	11.0248	10.9017	11.8583
Norwegian krone	10.3975	10.3306	10.1508
Canadian dollar	1.9262	1.7327	1.7481
Australian dollar	2.0323	2.0790	2.1916

Average Rates of Exchange versus Euro*

	2002	2003	2004	2005	2006	2007	2008
US dollar	0.946	1.1312	1.2439	1.2441	1.2556	1.3705	1.4708
Sterling	0.629	0.6919	0.6786	0.6838	0.6817	0.6843	0.7962
Danish krone	7.43	7.4307	7.4399	7.4518	7.4591	7.4506	7.4560
Japanese yen	118.10	130.97	134.44	136.85	146.02	161.25	152.46
Swiss franc	1.467	1.5212	1.5438	1.5483	1.5729	1.6427	1.5874
Swedish krona	9.16	9.1242	9.1243	9.2822	9.2544	9.2501	9.6152
Norwegian krone	7.51	8.0033	8.3697	8.0092	8.0472	8.0165	8.2237
Canadian dollar	1.484	1.5817	1.6167	1.5087	1.4237	1.4678	1.5594
Australian dollar	1.738	1.7379	1.6905	1.6320	1.6668	1.6348	1.7416

* €1 = IR£0.787564 – Changeover date 1/1/2002

CHART 12

Specified Amounts (Preliminary Income Tax)

Year of Assessment	Paying Direct	Paying by Direct Debit
2004 et seq.	90% or 100% of p.y.	105% of p.p.y.
2003	90% or 100% of p.y.	142% of p.p.y.
2002	90% or 135% of p.y.	105% of p.p.y.
2001	90% or 74% of p.y.	78% of p.p.y.
1990/01 - 2000/01	90% or 100% of p.y.	105% of p.p.y.

CHART 13

Preferential Loans (Specified Interest Rates)

Tax Year	1998 /99	1999 /00	2000 /01	2001	2002	2003	2004	2005	2006	2007	2008	2009
Residential Home Loan	7%	6%	4%	6%	5%	4.5%	3.5%	3.5%	3.5%	4.5%	5.5%	5%
Other Loan	11%	10%	10%	12%	12%	11%	11%	11%	11%	12%	13%	12.5%

CHART 14

Retention Tax on Payments for Professional Services

The persons who are required to deduct tax from payments for professional services are as follows and include, where any person is a body corporate, any subsidiary resident in the State are listed in Schedule 13 TCA 1997 as follows:

A Minister of the Government

A local authority within the meaning of Section 2(2) of the Local Government Act, 1941

A body established under the Local Government Services (Corporate Bodies) Act, 1971

Primary Care Reimbursement Service

The Attorney General

The Comptroller and Auditor-General

The Director of Public Prosecutions

The Commissioner of Valuation

The Chief Boundary Surveyor

The Director of Ordnance Survey

The Revenue Commissioners

The Public Appointments Service

The Commissioners of Public Works in Ireland

The Clerk of Dáil Éireann

The Legal Aid Board

A vocational education committee or a technical college established under the Vocational Education Act, 1930

Teagasc

A harbour authority

An Foras Áiseanna Saothair

Údarás na Gaeltacha

The Industrial Development Agency (Ireland)

An Bord Tráchtála - The Irish Trade Board

Shannon Free Airport Development Company Limited

The National Tourism Development Authority

An institution of higher education within the meaning of the Higher Education Authority Act, 1971

The Radiological Protection Institute of Ireland

A voluntary public or joint board hospital to which grants are paid by the Minister for Health in the year 1988/89 or any subsequent year of assessment

An authorised insurer within the meaning of Section 145 of the Income Tax Act, 1967

(continued on following page)

CHART 14 (continued)

An Bord Glas

An Bord Pleanála

Dublin Airport Authority public limited company

Arramara Teoranta

Blood Transfusion Service Board

Bord na gCon

Bord Gáis Éireann

Bord Iascaigh Mhara

Bord na Móna plc

Coillte Teoranta

Córas Iompair Éireann

Custom House Docks Development Authority

Electricity Supply Board

Housing Finance Agency public limited company

Irish National Petroleum Corporation Limited

Irish National Stud Company Limited

National Building Agency Limited

National Concert Hall Company Limited

An Post National Lottery Company

Nítrigin Éireann Teoranta

An Post

Radio Telefís Éireann

Royal Hospital Kilmainham Company

The Environmental Protection Agency

Forbairt

Forfás

The Irish Aviation Authority

The National Economic and Social Council

The National Economic and Social Forum

The National Roads Authority

Temple Bar Properties Limited

The Irish Film Board

An educational institution established by or under Section 3 of the Regional Technical Colleges Act 1992 as an Institute of Technology

The Dublin Institute of Technology

An Bord Bia

Area Development Management Limited

The Combat Poverty Agency

(continued on following page)

CHART 14 (continued)

The Commissioners of Irish Lights
Dublin Transportation Office

The Higher Education Authority

The Independent Radio and Television Commission

Horse Racing Ireland

The Labour Relations Commission

The Marine Institute

The Pensions Board

The Commission for Communications Regulation

The Law Reform Commission

National Standards Authority of Ireland

Enterprise Ireland

Dublin Docklands Development Authority

A Referendum Commission established by Order made under Section 2(1) of the Referendum Act 1998

Office of the Ombudsman

The Standards in Public Office Commission

The Office of the Information Commissioner

The Central Fisheries Board

A regional fisheries board established by virtue of an Order made under Section 10, Fisheries Act, 1980

A County Enterprise Board

Western Development Commission

The Equality Authority

Commissioners of Charitable Donations and Bequests for Ireland

Commission for Electricity Regulation

Any regional authority established by an Order made under Section 43 (1), Local Government Act, 1991

The Eastern Regional Health Authority, the Health Boards Executive or an area health board established under the Health (Eastern Regional Health Authority) Act, 1999

Irish Sports Council

An Bord Uchtála

National Disability Authority

Aquaculture Licences Appeals Board

Office of the President

Director of the Equality Tribunal

Data Protection Commissioner

(continued on following page)

CHART 14 (continued)

Competition Authority

Chief State Solicitor

Central Statistics Office

Commission to Inquire into Child Abuse

National Sports Campus Development Authority

Digital Media Development Limited

Citizens Information Board

Human Rights Commission

Pensions Ombudsman

The Dublin Institute for Advanced Studies

Pre-Hospital Emergency Care Council

Refugee Appeals Tribunal

Sustainable Energy Ireland – The Sustainable
Energy Authority of Ireland

The Health Insurance Authority

Commission for Aviation Regulation

Railway Procurement Agency

The National Council on Ageing and Older People

National Qualifications Authority of Ireland

BreastCheck, The National Breast Screening Programme

The National Council for the Professional Development of Nursing and
Midwifery

Mater and Children's Hospital Development Ltd

The National Consultative Commission on Racism and Interculturalism

Office of Tobacco Control

The Marine Casualty Investigation Board

National Treasury Management Agency as regards the performance of
functions by it conferred on, or delegated to, it by or under Part 2 of the
National Treasury Management Agency (Amendment) Act 2000 (State
Claims Agency)

National Development Finance Agency

The National Council for Curriculum and Assessment

The State Examinations Commission

Children Acts Advisory Board

National Treatment Purchase Fund Board

The Mental Health Commission

Crisis Pregnancy Agency

Irish Medicines Board

(continued on following page)

CHART 14 (continued)

National Educational Welfare Board

Oifig Choimisinéir na dTeangacha Oifigiúla

The Health Service Executive

Commission for Public Service Appointments

Commission for Taxi Regulation

National Council for Special Education

National Library of Ireland

An Education Support Centre established under Section 37 of the Education Act 1998

The Road Safety Authority

Grangegorman Development Agency

The Railway Safety Commission

The Teaching Council

EirGrid

The Further Education and Training Awards Council

The Irish Auditing and Accounting Supervisory Authority

Limerick Northside Regeneration Agency

Limerick Southside Regeneration Agency

The Health Information and Quality Authority

Telifís na Gaeilge

Food Safety Authority of Ireland

National Social Work Qualification Board

Sea-Fisheries Protection Authority

National Centre for Partnership Performance

National Economic and Social Development Office

CHART 15

Tax and Interest as Preferential Debt

(In winding-up of insolvent companies and on appointment, under floating charge, of a receiver)

Type of tax	Preferential Debt	Legislation
Income Tax	Tax for any twelve months assessed up to 5 April/31 December next before "the relevant date" and all interest thereon	Sections 98 and 285 Companies Act 1963
Corporation Tax	Do	S974 TCA 1997
Capital Gains Tax	Do	S982 TCA 1997
VAT	Tax for the last twelve months ending before "the relevant date"	S62 FA 1976
Interest on VAT	All	Do
PAYE & PRSI	Tax for the last twelve months ending before the "relevant date"	S994 TCA 1997 S995 TCA 1997
Interest on PAYE & PRSI	Do	Do
Deductions on Construction Contracts	Do	S1000 TCA 1997

NOTES:

(a) "the relevant date" means

  (i) where the company is ordered to be wound up compulsorily, the date of the appointment (or first appointment) of a provisional liquidator or, if no such appointment was made, the date of the winding-up order, unless in either case the company had commenced to be wound up voluntarily before that date; and

  (ii) Where sub-paragraph (i) does not apply, the date of the passing of the resolution for the winding-up of the company.

(b) No preferential debt exists as to (a) Capital Acquisitions Tax, (b) Wealth Tax and (c) interest on these taxes.

(c) Where a person holds a fixed charge on the book debts of a company and the company fails to pay PAYE and VAT, the holder of the fixed charge will, on notification from the Revenue Commissioners, become liable to pay the PAYE and VAT.

The amount payable is subject to an overall limit of the amount collected under the fixed charge after the date of notification from the Revenue Commissioners.

(d) PAYE and PRSI includes:

  (i) amounts deducted for the income tax month in which the "relevant date" occurs.

  (ii) amounts which, apart from the provisions of Regulation 31A of the Income Tax (Employments) Regulations 1960, would otherwise have been due to be remitted at the "relevant date".

CHART 16

Income Tax Time Limits

(References are to Taxes Consolidation Act 1997 unless otherwise stated)

Section	Topic	Claim etc.	Claim to be made within
S930	Error or Mistake	All	Four years of end of year of assessment
S787	Retirement annuity premiums	Against income of previous year	31 October of following year
S298	Capital allowances on plant and machinery	Lessor	Two years of end of year of assessment
S305	Excess of capital allowances over income from leasing plant or industrial buildings	Set-off of excess against other income of the year of assessment	Two years of end of year of assessment
S381	Trading/ professional losses	Set-off against other income of year of assessment	Two years of end of year of assessment
S865	Irish repayment claims	All	Four years of end of year of assessment
S195	Artists, writers etc.	Exemption from income tax	Year of assessment
S1023	Husbands and wives	Separate assessment	1 April in year of assessment (continues until withdrawn)
S1016	Husbands and wives	Single assessment	Year of assessment (continues until withdrawn)
S503	Investment in corporate trades	Set-off against income of year of assessment	Two years of end of year of assessment
S66	Trading etc. profits	Second and third year adjustment	On submission of third year return

CHART 17
Rates of Corporation Tax – General

(See Chart 44 for Rates from 01/01/1977)

ACCOUNTING PERIOD	STANDARD RATE	HIGHER* RATE	LOWER** RATE
1/4/1991 to 31/3/1995	40%	n/a	n/a
1/4/1995 to 31/3/1997	38% (First £50,000 @ 30%)	n/a	n/a
1/4/1997 to 31/12/1997	36% (First £50,000 @ 28%)	n/a	n/a
Y/E 31/12/1998	32% (First £50,000 @ 25%)	n/a	n/a
Y/E 31/12/1999	28% (First £100,000 @ 25%)	n/a	n/a
Y/E 31/12/2000	24%	25%	12.5%
Y/E 31/12/2001	20%	25%	12.5%
Y/E 31/12/2002	16%	25%	12.5%
Y/E 31/12/2003 & onwards	12.5%	25%	n/a

Note:

* Higher rate applies to Case III, Case IV, Case V and Income from mining and petroleum activities and dealing in non-residential land.

**Lower rate applies to trading profits less than £50,000 for the year 2000. Marginal relief applies where trading profits are between £50,000 and £75,000 for the year 2000.

Lower rate applies to trading profits less than £200,000/€254,000 from 1 January 2001. Marginal relief applies where trading profits are between £200,000/€254,000 and £250,000/€317,500.

A special rate of 20% applies to profits arising from dealing in or developing residential land (See Chart 18)

See 2.2 with regard to the 10% "manufacturing rate".
See 2.1.11 with regard to "new companies".

CHART 18

Rates of Corporation Tax – Property Dealing & Development

Year	Non-Residential Land	Residential Land	Developed Residential	Developed Non-Residential	Construction Services
2000	25%	20%	20%*	24%	24%*
2001	25%	20%	20%	20%	20%
2002	25%	20%	16%	16%	16%
2003 to 2008	25%	20%	12½%	12½%	12½%
2009	25%	25%	12½%	12½%	12½%

* *For the year 2000, in the case of the sale of a completed residential unit, an apportionment will be required on a 'just and reasonable basis' to establish the percentage of profit attributable to the sale of serviced land (to include all works on the land prior to laying of foundations) which will be taxable at the 20% rate, and to establish the percentage attributable to construction work which is taxable at the 24% rate.*

CHART 19
Corporation Tax - Preliminary Tax

The payment date for preliminary corporation tax was brought forward from six months after the end of the accounting period to the 21st of the month before the end of the accounting period, over a transitional period of five years. During the transitional period the preliminary tax may be paid in two instalments, ensuring that the total of the two instalments is atleast 90% of the final liability for the period in question.

A summary of the minimum first instalments payable is as follows:

A/C Period Ending In	Standard Company Minimum % of Final Liability	"Small" Company* Option Minimum % of Prior Period Liability
2002	18%	20%
2003	36%	40%
2004	54%	60%
2005	72%	80%
2006 et seq.	90%	100%

* A company is regarded as a "small" company if its corresponding corporation tax liability for the preceding chargeable period does not exceed:

(i)   €50,000 in respect of preliminary tax payable on or before 6 December 2006.

(ii)   €150,000 in respect of preliminary tax payable between 7 December 2006 and 5 December 2007.

(iii) €200,000 in respect of preliminary tax payable on or after 6 December 2007.

New companies that do not expect their corporation tax liability for the first year to exceed the following limits are not obliged to pay preliminary tax in that first year:

(i)   €150,000 in respect of accounting periods in respect of which preliminary tax is payble between 7 December 2006 and 5 December 2007.

(ii)   €200,000 in respect of accounting periods in respect of which preliminary tax is payble on or after 6 December 2007.

Large Companies

In the case of "large companies"(i.e. companies with a tax liability of more than €200,000 in their previous accounting period), for accounting periods commencing on or after 14 October 2008, preliminary corporation tax is payable in two instalments as follows:

1st instalment   – in the sixth month of the accounting period but not later than the 21st of the relevant month and the amount payable is the lower of:

– 50% of the corporation tax liability in the preceding accounting period or

– 45% of the corporation tax liability in the current accounting period.

2nd instalment – in the eleventh month of the accounting period but not later than the 21st of the relevant month and the amount payable must bring the total preliminary tax paid up to 90% of the corporation tax liability for the current accounting period.

CHART 20
Corporation Tax Payment Dates and Form CT1 Filing Dates

Accounting Periods Ended	1st Instalment	2nd Instalment	Balance of Tax (if any) and CT1 Filing Date
1 January 2002 - 31 July 2002	28 June 2002	On a date 6 months after the accounting period ends but not later than 28th day of the month in which that day falls	On a date 1 month from the notice of assessment. (Form CT1 is due on a date 9 months after the end of the accounting period)
1 August 2002 - 31 December 2002	On a date 31 days before the end of the accounting period but not later than 28th day of the month in which that day falls	On a date 6 months after the accounting period ends but not later than 28th day of the month in which that day falls	On a date 1 month from the notice of assessment. (Form CT1 is due on a date 9 months after the end of the accounting period)
1 January 2003 - 1 July 2003	On a date 31 days before the end of the accounting period but not later than 28th day of the month in which that day falls	On a date 6 months after the accounting period ends but not later than 28th day of the month in which that day falls	Together with the Form CT1 on a date 9 months after an accounting period ends but no later than 21st day of that month
2 July 2003 - 31 December 2005	On a date 31 days before the end of the accounting period but not later than 21st day of the month in which that day falls	On a date 6 months after the accounting period ends but not later than 21st day of the month in which that day falls	As above
1 January 2006 onwards	As above	No second instalment (export for "large companies", see Chart 19)	As above

<u>Notes</u>

Special rules apply for accounting periods of less than one month and one day. In this situation the payment of the first instalment is due on the last day of the accounting period but not later than 28th day of the month or 21st day of the month as appropriate.

The rules above relate to the payment of corporation tax including corporation tax on chargeable gains. If capital gains tax is due as in the case of development land the payment dates for capital gains tax apply.

CHART 21
Manufacturing Relief and Investment in Corporate Trades (Section 443 TCA 1997)

Type of Company	10%	RICT
Manufacturing	Yes	Yes
Manufacturing Services	Yes	Yes
90% Related Sales Company	Yes	No
"New" Shannon Company	Yes	Yes
Fish, Engineering	Yes	Yes
Services, Ship Building	Yes	Yes
Data Processing and Computer Software Development Services	Yes	Yes
Services qualifying for IDA Employment Grants	No	Yes
Designated Funds	No	Yes
R & D Company	Yes	No
Financial Services in Custom House Dock Area	Yes	No
Shipping Activities	Yes	Yes
Tourist Activities	No	Yes
Export Sales of Trading Houses	Yes	Yes
Plant Cultivation by "Micro Propagation and Plant Cloning"	Yes	Yes
Factory Ships	Yes	No
Services Re Data Processing	Yes	Yes
Construction and Leasing of Advance Factories	No	Yes
Internationally Traded Service	No	Yes
Film Production for Cinema or TV	Yes	No
Meat Processing in EC-approved Factory	Yes	Yes
Fish Processing	Yes	Yes
Remanufacture or Repair of computer equipment or sub-assemblies	Yes	Yes
Repair or maintenance of Aircraft, Aircraft Engines or Components	Yes	Yes
Service Activities to Ships and OffShore Platforms etc.	Yes	No
Certain Agricultural or Fishery Society Activities	Yes	No
Newspaper Advertising	Yes	No
Recycling Activities	No	Yes

Note: With effect from 1 January 2003, the requirement that a company engaged in manufacturing must be entitled to claim manufacturing relief in order to qualify for the purposes of the BES no longer applies.

CHART 22
Corporation Tax Time Limits

(References are to Taxes Consolidation Act 1997 unless otherwise stated)

Section	Topic	Claim etc.	Claim to be made within
S307	Plant and Machinery Industrial Buildings	Disclaimer of Initial Allowances	Two years of the end of the accounting period for which the claim arises
S308	Excess Case V Capital Allowances	Against other profits of same accounting period or preceding accounting period	Two years of the end of the accounting period in which the excess arises
S83	Excess management expenses of investment companies	Against franked investment income of same accounting period	Two years of the end of the accounting period in which the excess arises
S396	Trading losses	Against other profits of same accounting period or preceding accounting period	Two years of the end of the accounting period in which the loss is incurred
S399	Case V losses	Against other Case V income of preceding accounting period	Two years of the end of the accounting period in which the loss is incurred
S157	Trading losses	Against franked investment income of same accounting period or preceding accounting period	Two years of the end of the accounting period in which the loss is incurred
S429	Group Relief and Consortium Relief	For surrender of trading losses and other amounts eligible for relief	Two years from the end of the accounting period of the surrendering company
S882	New Companies	Advise Inspector of commencement etc.	Within thirty days of commencement
S883	Liability to Corporation Tax	Notification to Inspector	Twelve months from end of accounting period

CHART 23
Indexation Factors for Capital Gains Tax

Tax Year Expenditure Incurred	Indexation Factor for Disposals in Tax Year																	
	1987/88	1988/89	1989/90	1990/91	1991/92	1992/93	1993/94	1994/95	1995/96	1996/97	1997/98	1998/99	1999/00	2000/01	2001	2002	2003	2004 et seq.
1974/75	4.756	4.848	5.009	5.221	5.355	5.552	5.656	5.754	5.899	6.017	6.112	6.215	6.313	6.582	6.930	7.180	7.528	7.528
1975/76	3.842	3.916	4.046	4.217	4.326	4.484	4.568	4.647	4.764	4.860	4.936	5.020	5.099	5.316	5.597	5.799	6.080	6.080
1976/77	3.309	3.373	3.485	3.633	3.726	3.863	3.935	4.003	4.104	4.187	4.253	4.325	4.393	4.580	4.822	4.996	5.238	5.238
1977/78	2.837	2.892	2.988	3.114	3.194	3.312	3.373	3.432	3.518	3.589	3.646	3.707	3.766	3.926	4.133	4.283	4.490	4.490
1978/79	2.621	2.672	2.760	2.877	2.951	3.059	3.117	3.171	3.250	3.316	3.368	3.425	3.479	3.627	3.819	3.956	4.148	4.148
1979/80	2.365	2.410	2.490	2.596	2.663	2.760	2.812	2.861	2.933	2.992	3.039	3.090	3.139	3.272	3.445	3.570	3.742	3.742
1980/81	2.047	2.087	2.156	2.247	2.305	2.390	2.434	2.477	2.539	2.590	2.631	2.675	2.718	2.833	2.983	3.091	3.240	3.240
1981/82	1.692	1.725	1.782	1.857	1.905	1.975	2.012	2.047	2.099	2.141	2.174	2.211	2.246	2.342	2.465	2.554	2.678	2.678
1982/83	1.424	1.451	1.499	1.563	1.603	1.662	1.693	1.722	1.765	1.801	1.829	1.860	1.890	1.970	2.074	2.149	2.253	2.253
1983/84	1.266	1.290	1.333	1.390	1.425	1.478	1.505	1.531	1.570	1.601	1.627	1.654	1.680	1.752	1.844	1.911	2.003	2.003
1984/85	1.149	1.171	1.210	1.261	1.294	1.341	1.366	1.390	1.425	1.454	1.477	1.502	1.525	1.590	1.674	1.735	1.819	1.819
1985/86	1.082	1.103	1.140	1.188	1.218	1.263	1.287	1.309	1.342	1.369	1.390	1.414	1.436	1.497	1.577	1.633	1.713	1.713
1986/87	1.035	1.055	1.090	1.136	1.165	1.208	1.230	1.252	1.283	1.309	1.330	1.352	1.373	1.432	1.507	1.562	1.637	1.637
1987/88	–	1.020	1.054	1.098	1.126	1.168	1.190	1.210	1.241	1.266	1.285	1.307	1.328	1.384	1.457	1.510	1.583	1.583
1988/89	–	–	1.034	1.077	1.105	1.146	1.167	1.187	1.217	1.242	1.261	1.282	1.303	1.358	1.430	1.481	1.553	1.553
1989/90	–	–	–	1.043	1.070	1.109	1.130	1.149	1.178	1.202	1.221	1.241	1.261	1.314	1.384	1.434	1.503	1.503
1990/91	–	–	–	–	1.026	1.064	1.084	1.102	1.130	1.153	1.171	1.191	1.210	1.261	1.328	1.376	1.442	1.442
1991/92	–	–	–	–	–	1.037	1.056	1.075	1.102	1.124	1.142	1.161	1.179	1.229	1.294	1.341	1.406	1.406
1992/93	–	–	–	–	–	–	1.019	1.037	1.063	1.084	1.101	1.120	1.138	1.186	1.249	1.294	1.356	1.356
1993/94	–	–	–	–	–	–	–	1.018	1.043	1.064	1.081	1.099	1.117	1.164	1.226	1.270	1.331	1.331
1994/95	–	–	–	–	–	–	–	–	1.026	1.046	1.063	1.081	1.098	1.144	1.205	1.248	1.309	1.309
1995/96	–	–	–	–	–	–	–	–	–	1.021	1.037	1.054	1.071	1.116	1.175	1.218	1.277	1.277
1996/97	–	–	–	–	–	–	–	–	–	–	1.016	1.033	1.050	1.094	1.152	1.194	1.251	1.251
1997/98	–	–	–	–	–	–	–	–	–	–	–	1.017	1.033	1.077	1.134	1.175	1.232	1.232
1998/99	–	–	–	–	–	–	–	–	–	–	–	–	1.016	1.059	1.115	1.156	1.212	1.212
1999/00	–	–	–	–	–	–	–	–	–	–	–	–	–	1.043	1.098	1.138	1.193	1.193
2000/01	–	–	–	–	–	–	–	–	–	–	–	–	–	–	1.053	1.091	1.144	1.144
2001	–	–	–	–	–	–	–	–	–	–	–	–	–	–	–	1.037	1.087	1.087
2002	–	–	–	–	–	–	–	–	–	–	–	–	–	–	–	–	1.049	1.049
2003 et seq.	–	–	–	–	–	–	–	–	–	–	–	–	–	–	–	–	–	1.00

NOTE: No indexation is available for expenditure made within 12 months prior to the date of disposal.

CHART 24

Capital Gains Tax Rates

Date of Disposal	Development Land Sold for Residential Development	Development Land (other than for Residential Development)	Foreign Life Assurance Policies and Offshore Funds[1]	All Other Assets (Normal Rate)[2]
08/04/2009 onwards	25%	25%	40%	25%
15/10/2008 to 07/04/2009	22%	22%	40%	22%
1/12/1999 to 14/10/2008	20%	20%	40%	20%
23/4/1998 to 30/11/1999	20%	40%	40%	20%
12/2/1998 to 22/4/1998	40%	40%	40%	20%
3/12/1997 to 11/2/1998	40%	40%	20%	20%

Notes:

1. The rates quoted for offshore funds are for the chargeable gains on disposals of interests in offshore funds which are "distributing funds" (funds which are not non-qualifying funds), since gains on disposals of interests in non-qualifying offshore funds are taxed as income (and not capital gains). See page 126 in relation to tax other than capital gains tax.

2. The "All Other Assets" do not include the assets of certain special investment products (special portfolio investment accounts, special investment schemes and special investment policies) where gains on disposals are charged to capital gains tax at 20% from 6 April 1999 within the fund (and not on the beneficiary). The rate was 10% before 6 April 1999.

CHART 25

Capital Acquisitions Tax Rates

(see Chart 52 for earlier years)

Rates from 30 January 1991 to 10 April 1994

Slice	Cumulative Slice	Rate of Tax %	Tax Thereon	Cumulative Tax
Threshold	Threshold			
Amount	Amount +	nil	nil	nil
10,000	10,000	20	2,000	2,000
40,000	50,000	30	12,000	14,000
50,000	100,000	35	17,500	31,500
Balance		40		

Rates from 11 April 1994 to 30 November 1999

Slice	Cumulative Slice	Rate of Tax %	Tax Thereon	Cumulative Tax
Threshold	Threshold			
Amount	Amount +	nil	nil	nil
10,000	10,000	20	2,000	2,000
30,000	40,000	30	9,000	11,000
Balance		40		

Rates from 1 December 1999 to 19 November 2008

Slice	Rate of Tax %
Threshold	
Amount	Nil
Balance	20%

Rates from 20 November 2008 to 7 April 2009

Slice	Rate of Tax %
Threshold	
Amount	Nil
Balance	22%

Rates from 8 April 2009

Slice	Rate of Tax %
Threshold	
Amount	Nil
Balance	25%

CHART 26

Capital Acquisitions Tax Class Thresholds

Relationship to donor/testator	From 1/12/1999 to 31/12/2000 £	2001 £	2002 €	2003 €	2004 €	2005 €	2006 €	2007 €	2008 €	2009 01/01/09 – 07/04/09 €	2009 08/04/09 – 31/12/09 €
Child or minor child of deceased child or parent where s116 FA 1991 applies	300,000	316,800	422,148	441,198	456,438	466,725	478,155	496,824	521,208	542,544	434,000
Lineal ancestor (other than a parent where s116 FA 1991 applies), lineal descendant (other than a child or minor child of a deceased child), brother, sister, child of brother or sister	30,000	31,680	42,215	44,120	45,644	46,673	47,815	49,682	52,121	54,254	43,400
Any other person	15,000	15,840	21,108	22,060	22,822	23,336	23,908	24,841	26,060	27,127	21,700

CHART 27

Rates of Stamp Duty

(1) Residential Property (effective from 5 November 2007)

Consideration (or Aggregate Consideration) exceeds €127,000	Rate
First €125,000	NIL
Next €875,000	7%
Excess over €1,000,000	9%

Note: To fully preserve the exemption that applied prior to the introduction of the above rates, transactions where the consideration (or aggregate consideration) does not exceed €127,000 continue to be exempt from stamp duty.

Section 91 SDCA 1999 provides for an exemption from stamp duty for purchasers of certain smaller new residential properties where the purchaser is an owner-occupier but not a first-time buyer, and Section 92 provides for a reduction in stamp duty for similar purchasers of certain larger new residential properties.

First-Time Buyers – Instruments executed on or after 31 March 2007

Finance (No. 2) Bill 2007 provides for the abolition of stamp duty for all owner-occupying first-time buyers of houses and apartments, whether new or second-hand. The change applies to instruments executed on or after 31 March 2007. It also provides for a refund procedure for persons who, by virtue of this change, became entitled retrospectively to relief or additional relief. Such persons will be entitled to claim a repayment of duty paid from the Revenue Commissioners.

(2) (a) Non-residential Property (effective from 4 December 2002 to 14 October 2008)

Value	Rate
Up to €10,000	0%
€10,001 – €20,000	1%
€20,001 – €30,000	2%
€30,001 – €40,000	3%
€40,001 – €70,000	4%
€70,001 – €80,000	5%
€80,001 – €100,000	6%
€100,001 – €120,000	7%
€120,001 – €150,000	8%
Over €150,000	9%

CHART 27 (continued)

(2) (b) Non-residential Property (effective from 15 October 2008)

Aggregate Consideration	Rate of Duty
Up to €10,000	Exempt
€10,001 to €20,000	1%
€20,001 to €30,000	2%
€30,001 to €40,000	3%
€40,001 to €70,000	4%
€70,001 to €80,000	5%
Over €80,000	6%

CHART 28
VAT Fourth Schedule Services

If Supplier is	and Recipient is	The Place of Supply is	The Person liable for Irish VAT is
Foreign	Irish Business	Ireland	Irish Business Recipient
Foreign	Irish Private	Abroad	No Irish Liability
Irish	Irish Business or Private	Ireland	Irish Supplier
Irish	Business outside Ireland	Abroad	No Irish Liability
Irish	Private in EU	Ireland	Irish Supplier
Irish	Private outside EU	Abroad	No Irish Liability

The above rules are modified where the supplier has an establishment in the country of the recipient.

NOTE: VAT FOURTH SCHEDULE SERVICES include:

Services that are taxed where received viz.:

(i)   Transfers and assignments of copyrights, patents, licences, trade marks and similar rights;

(ia) Hiring out of movable goods other than means of transport;

(ii) Advertising services;

(iii) Services of consultants, engineers, consultancy bureaux, lawyers, accountants and other similar services, data processing and provision of information (but excluding services connected with immovable goods);

(iiia) Telecommunications services in certain circumstances. The definition of telecommunications services was modified in the Finance Act 2000;

(iiib) Radio and television broadcasting service;

(iiic) Electronically supplied services;

(iiid) The provision of access to, and of transport or transmission through, natural gas and electricity distribution systems and the provision of other directly linked services.

(iv) Acceptance of any obligation to refrain from pursuing or exercising in whole or in part, any business activity or any such rights as are referred to in paragraph (1);

(v)   Banking, financial and insurance services (including reinsurance, and financial fund management functions but not including the provision of safe deposit facilities) in certain circumstances;

(vi) The provision of staff;

(vii) The services of intermediaries who act in the name and for the account of a principal when procuring for him any services specified in paragraphs (i) to (vi).

CHART 29
VAT-Exempted Activities

The main exempted activities are:

Admission to sporting events.
Circus admissions.
Certain lettings of immovable goods.
Medical, dental and optical services.
Certain agency services.
Insurance services.
Certain banking and stock exchange activities.
Transport of passengers and their baggage.
Betting.
Funeral undertaking.
Certain theatrical and musical performances.
Certain welfare and non-profit-making activities.
Management of collective investment undertakings, including the functions of collective portfolio management, as listed in Annex II to Directive 2001/107/EC, where those functions are supplied by the person with responsibility for the provision of those functions for the undertaking.
Chiropody.
Educational services including pre-school education facilities.
Certain child-care and homecare services.

Note: With effect from 1 January 2010, the exemption for agency services in relation to the arrangement of passenger transport or accommodation will no longer apply. VAT will therefore be chargeable on travel agency services with effect from this date.

CHART 30

VAT Zero Rate

> **The main zero-rated goods and services are:**
>
> Most food and drink of a kind used for human consumption, most exports of goods and services relating to exports of goods, oral medicine, fertilizers, most articles of personal clothing and footwear suitable for children under 11 years of age, certain services relating to marine safety, certain books and booklets including atlases, certain medical equipment and appliances, certain navigation services and supplies to certain international bodies.

Note: Finance (No. 2) Act 2008 amended the VAT rate applicable to the sale of tea and coffee. According to Revenue, the amendment clarified that the zero rate applies to non–drinkable tea and coffee. The sale of tea and coffee in drinkable form is subject to VAT at 13.5%.

CHART 31
VAT 10% Rate

The goods and services liable at this rate are:

Domestic dwellings for which a contract with a private individual has
been entered into before 25 February 1993, short-term hire of cars under
an agreement made before 25 February 1993 and at charges fixed at the
time of the agreement, lettings of hotel and holiday accommodation
under an agreement made before 25 February 1993 and at charges fixed
at the time of the agreement.

CHART 32
VAT 13.5% Rate

The main goods and services liable at this rate are:

Immovable goods, services consisting of the development of immovable goods, concrete and concrete blocks, hotel and holiday accommodation, short term hiring of cars, boats, tents, caravans, mobile homes, tour guide services, fuel for power and heating, coal, peat, timber, electricity, gas, heating oil, hotel and restaurant meals, admissions to cinemas, cabaret, certain live theatrical and musical performances and to certain exhibitions, waste disposal, general agricultural and veterinary services, use of commercial sporting facilities, car driving instruction, care of the human body, general repair and maintenance services, certain imports and supplies of works of art, antiques and collectors' items, certain green fees, brochures, periodicals and newspapers, live poultry and live ostriches, animal insemination services, livestock semen, cooked food purchased at takeaway, supermarket, garage or other outlet, children's car safety seats, micanthus, rhizomes, seeds, bulbs, roots and similar goods used for the agricultural production of biofuels, and non-oral contraceptive products.

Note: Finance (No. 2) Act 2008 amended the VAT rate applicable to the sale of tea and coffee. According to Revenue, the amendment clarified that the zero rate applies to non-drinkable tea and coffee. The sale of tea and coffee in drinkable form is subject to VAT at 13.5%.

CHART 33
VAT 21.5% Rate

The main goods and services liable at this rate are:

Adult clothing and footwear including materials for their manufacture, household durable and non-durable goods, drink and certain foods, goods for personal use, sport and recreational goods, educational goods, agricultural goods, non-oral medicines, most building materials, office equipment and stationery, most services such as telecommunication services, accountancy services (including farm accountancy services), legal services, advertising services, other goods and services not liable at another rate.

CHART 34

VAT Thresholds

Persons supplying services	€25,500 - 1/7/1994 - 30/4/2006 €27,500 - 1/5/2006 - 28/2/2007 €35,000 - 1/3/2007 - 30/4/2008 €37,500 from 1/5/2008
Persons supplying goods	€51,000 - 1/7/1994 - 30/4/2006 €55,000 - 1/5/2006 - 28/2/2007 €70,000 - 1/3/2007 - 30/4/2008 €75,000 from 1/5/2008
Persons making intra-Community acquisitions	€41,000
Persons making mail order or distance sales into the State	€35,000

In the case of supplies in the State and intra-Community acquisitions, registration is obligatory where the appropriate turnover threshold is exceeded or is likely to be exceeded in any 12-month period.

The distance sales threshold is based on a calendar year.

There is no VAT registration threshold in respect of the cross-border receipt of Fourth Schedule services by a person for business purposes.

CHART 35
VAT Multiplier

VAT multiplier to be used when valuing an interest in immovable goods from 1990 to date.

DATE ISSUE	REDEMPTION YIELD	MULTIPLIER
21 May 1991	9.30 per cent	10.75
24 January 1992	9.11 per cent	10.98
14 June 1993	7.37 per cent	13.57
15 October 1993	6.87 per cent	14.56
17 August 1994	8.56 per cent	11.68
15 May 1995	8.52 per cent	11.74
19 April 1996	6.93 per cent	14.43 (Note 1)
17 September 1997	6.26 per cent	15.97
11 May 1999	4.26 per cent	23.47 (Note 2)
29 January 2002	5.14 per cent	19.45
1 March 2003	3.377 per cent	29.61
1 February 2004	4.702 per cent	21.27

1. The operative date for the multiplier of 14.43 is 26 March 1997.
2. The operative date for the multiplier of 23.47 is 30 June 1999.

CHART 36
Capital Allowances

Initial Allowances

Expenditure Incurred	Plant and Machinery	Industrial Buildings	Hotels	Farm Buildings
1.4.71 - 5.4.74	100%	20%	10%	-
6.4.74 -15.1.75	100%	20%	10%	20%
16.1.75 - 5.4.80	100%	50%	10%	20%
6.4.80 - 31.3.88	100%	50%	10%	Nil
1.4.88 - 31.3.89	*75%	*50%	10%	Nil
1.4.89 - 31.3.91	*50%	*50%	10%	Nil
1.4.91 - 31.3.92	*25%	*25%	10%	Nil
1.4.92 onwards	Nil	Nil	Nil	Nil

* A rate of up to 100% applies to qualifying services companies in the Customs House Docks Area or in the Shannon Customs-Free Area, subject to varying time limits.

Writing Down and Wear-and-Tear Allowances

Expenditure Incurred	Plant and Machinery	Industrial Buildings	Hotels	Farm Buildings
1.4.71 - 5.4.74	Up to 100%	2%	10%	10%
6.4.74 -15.1.75	Up to 100%	2%	10%	10%
16.1.75 - 1.2.78	Up to 100%	4%	10%	10%
2.2.78 - 5.4.80	Up to 100%	Up to 100%	Up to 100%	10%
6.4.80 - 31.3.88	Up to 100%	Up to 100%	Up to 100%	Up to 30%
1.4.88 - 31.3.89	*Up to 75%	*Up to 75%	Up to 75%	Up to 30%
1.4.89 - 31.3.91	*Up to 50%	*Up to 50%	Up to 50%	Up to 50%
1.4.91 - 31.3.92	*Up to 25%	*Up to 25%	Up to 25%	Up to 25%
1.4.92 - 26.1.94	15%	4%	10%	10%
27.1.94 - 31.12.00	15%	4%	15%	15%
1.1.01 - 3.12.02	20%	4%	15%	15%
4.12.02 onwards	12.5%	4%	4%**	15%

* A rate of up to 100% applies to qualifying services companies in the Customs House Docks Area or in the Shannon Customs-Free Area, subject to varying time limits.

INDEX

R